JOB
A Commentary in the Wesleyan Tradition

*New Beacon Bible Commentary

JOB
A Commentary in the Wesleyan Tradition

A. Wendell Bowes

BEACON HILL PRESS
OF KANSAS CITY

Copyright 2018 by Beacon Hill Press of Kansas City

Beacon Hill Press of Kansas City
PO Box 419527
Kansas City, MO 64141
www.BeaconHillBooks.com

ISBN 978-0-8341-3562-8

All rights reserved. No part of this publication may be reproduced, stored in a retrieval system, or transmitted in any form or by any means—for example, electronic, photocopy, recording—without the prior written permission of the publisher. The only exception is brief quotations in printed reviews.

Cover Design: J.R. Caines
Interior Design: Sharon Page

Unless otherwise indicated, all Scripture quotations are from the Holy Bible, New International Version® (NIV®). Copyright © 1973, 1978, 1984, 2011 by Biblica, Inc.™ Used by permission of Zondervan. All rights reserved worldwide. www.zondervan.com.

The following version of Scripture is in the public domain:

The King James Version (KJV)

The following copyrighted versions of Scripture are used by permission:

Good News Translation® (Today's English Version, Second Edition) (GNT). Copyright © 1992 American Bible Society. All rights reserved.

The New American Standard Bible® (NASB®), copyright © 1960, 1962, 1963, 1968, 1971, 1972, 1973, 1975, 1977, 1995 by The Lockman Foundation. www.Lockman.org.

The New English Bible (NEB), © the Delegates of the Oxford University Press and the Syndics of the Cambridge University Press 1961, 1970.

The New JPS Hebrew-English Tanakh (NJPS), © 2000 by The Jewish Publication Society. All rights reserved.

The New King James Version® (NKJV). Copyright © 1982 by Thomas Nelson, Inc. All rights reserved.

The Holy Bible, New Living Translation (NLT), copyright © 1996, 2004, 2015 by Tyndale House Foundation. Used by permission of Tyndale House Publishers, Inc., Carol Stream, IL 60188. All rights reserved.

The New Revised Standard Version Bible (NRSV), copyright © 1989 National Council of the Churches of Christ in the United States of America. All rights reserved.

The Revised Standard Version (RSV) of the Bible, copyright 1946, 1952, 1971 by the Division of Christian Education of the National Council of the Churches of Christ in the USA. All rights reserved.

Library of Congress Cataloging-in-Publication Data
Names: Bowes, A. Wendell, author.
Title: Job / A. Wendell Bowes.
Description: Kansas City, MO : Beacon Hill Press of Kansas City, 2018. |
    Series: New Beacon Bible commentary | Includes bibliographical references.
Identifiers: LCCN 2018024991 | ISBN 9780834135628 (pbk.)
Subjects: LCSH: Bible. Job—Commentaries.
Classification: LCC BS1415.53 .B69 2018 | DDC 223/.107—dc23 LC record available at https://lccn.loc.gov/2018024991

The Internet addresses, email addresses, and phone numbers in this book are accurate at the time of publication. They are provided as a resource. Beacon Hill Press of Kansas City does not endorse them or vouch for their content or permanence.

DEDICATION

In Memory of

Alpin and Betty Bowes
Ray and Hazel Miller

With many thanks to
my students at
Northwest Nazarene University
and
the Nampa College Church Old Testament
Sunday school class
for their insights and thoughtful questions
as we wrestled with the book of Job

COMMENTARY EDITORS

General Editors

Alex Varughese
    Ph.D., Drew University
    Professor Emeritus of Biblical
        Literature
    Mount Vernon Nazarene University
    Mount Vernon, Ohio

George Lyons
    Ph.D., Emory University
    Professor Emeritus of New Testament
    Northwest Nazarene University
    Nampa, Idaho

Section Editors

Robert Branson
    Ph.D., Boston University
    Professor Emeritus of Biblical
        Literature
    Olivet Nazarene University
    Bourbonnais, Illinois

Alex Varughese
    Ph.D., Drew University
    Professor Emeritus of Biblical
        Literature
    Mount Vernon Nazarene University
    Mount Vernon, Ohio

Kent Brower
    Ph.D., The University of Manchester
    Vice Principal
    Senior Lecturer in Biblical Studies
    Nazarene Theological College
    Manchester, England

George Lyons
    Ph.D., Emory University
    Professor Emeritus of New Testament
    Northwest Nazarene University
    Nampa, Idaho

CONTENTS

General Editors' Preface	13
Abbreviations	15
Bibliography	19
Table of Sidebars	25
INTRODUCTION	27
A. Author	28
B. Date	29
C. Text	33
D. Unity	34
E. Theological Topics	34
F. Historicity	35
COMMENTARY	37
I. PROLOGUE: JOB 1—2	37
A. Introduction of Job (1:1-5)	38
B. The Examiner Questions Job's Righteousness and Integrity (1:6-12)	47
C. Job's First Test: He Loses His Wealth and His Children (1:13-22)	53
D. The Examiner Again Questions Job's Righteousness and Integrity (2:1-6)	61
E. Job's Second Test: He Loses His Health (2:7-10)	64
F. The Friends Arrive (2:11-13)	71
II. JOB'S ANGUISH: JOB 3	77
A. I Wish I Had Never Been Conceived or Born (3:1-10)	78
B. I Wish I Had Died at Birth (3:11-19)	83
C. I Wish My Life Would End Now (3:20-26)	87
III. FIRST CYCLE OF SPEECHES: JOB 4—14	95
A. Eliphaz's First Speech (4:1—5:27)	96
1. May We Speak with You? (4:1-6)	97
2. People Reap What They Sow (4:7-11)	99
3. Listen to What God Has Revealed to Me (4:12-21)	103
4. Trouble Is Inevitable (5:1-7)	110
5. God Is the Only Genuine Source of Help (5:8-16)	114
6. Sometimes God Disciplines Us (5:17-27)	118

B. Job's Response to Eliphaz (6:1—7:21)	127
1. I Am in Anguish (6:1-13)	128
2. You, My Friends, Are Worthless (6:14-30)	132
3. All Human Beings Have a Hard Lot in Life (7:1-6)	138
4. My Death Is Imminent (7:7-10)	141
5. God, Leave Me Alone (7:11-21)	143
C. Bildad's First Speech (8:1-22)	150
1. Seek God and Live an Upright Life (8:1-7)	150
2. Previous Generations Confirm What I Am Saying (8:8-10)	154
3. There Is No Hope for the Godless (8:11-19)	155
4. God's Ways Are Always Just (8:20-22)	157
D. Job's Response to Bildad (9:1—10:22)	160
1. God's Wisdom and Power Are Overwhelming (9:1-13)	160
2. It Is Futile to Argue with God (9:14-21)	164
3. God Is Not Just (9:22-24)	166
4. Oh, for a Mediator! (9:25-35)	168
5. God, Why Have You Turned against Me? (10:1-17)	172
6. God, Leave Me Alone (10:18-22)	178
E. Zophar's First Speech (11:1-20)	180
1. I Wish That God Would Speak to You (11:1-6)	180
2. God's Wisdom and Power Are Much Greater than Ours (11:7-12)	182
3. Turn to God and He Will Restore You (11:13-20)	184
F. Job's Response to Zophar (12:1—14:22)	187
1. I Am as Wise as You Are (12:1-6)	188
2. Nature Teaches Us That God Controls Everything (12:7-10)	189
3. God's Power Is Overwhelming (12:11-25)	190
4. You Friends Are Worthless Counselors (13:1-12)	195
5. I Have Prepared My Case (13:13-19)	197
6. God, What Have I Done Wrong? (13:20-28)	199
7. Human Beings Are Destined for Trouble (14:1-22)	202
IV. SECOND CYCLE OF SPEECHES: JOB 15—21	**209**
A. Eliphaz's Second Speech (15:1-35)	210
1. Do You Know More than We Do? (15:1-13)	210
2. All Human Beings Are Sinful (15:14-16)	213
3. The Wicked Suffer Terribly (15:17-35)	213
B. Job's Response to Eliphaz (16:1—17:16)	218
1. My Friends, You Are Miserable Comforters (16:1-6)	218
2. God Has Made Me His Target (16:7-17)	220
3. I Have a Witness (16:18-22)	223
4. I Have No Hope for a Better Life (17:1-16)	226
C. Bildad's Second Speech (18:1-21)	231
1. Why Do You Treat Us as Stupid? (18:1-4)	232
2. The Wicked Die Suddenly and Are Not Remembered (18:5-21)	233
D. Job's Response to Bildad (19:1-29)	238
1. My Friends, Why Do You Persist in Tormenting Me? (19:1-6)	239

	2. God Is the One Who Has Caused My Misery (19:7-12)	240
	3. My Social Relationships Have Disintegrated (19:13-22)	242
	4. I Will Be Vindicated Someday (19:23-29)	245
E.	Zophar's Second Speech (20:1-29)	251
	1. I Have to Speak Again (20:1-3)	252
	2. The Wicked Suffer a Sudden Divine Reversal (20:4-29)	253
F.	Job's Response to Zophar (21:1-34)	258
	1. My Friends, Please Listen to Me (21:1-5)	259
	2. The Wicked Do Well in Life (21:6-16)	259
	3. God Does Not Judge Correctly (21:17-26)	262
	4. My Friends, You Are Wrong (21:27-34)	264

V. THIRD CYCLE OF SPEECHES: JOB 22—27 — 267

- A. Eliphaz's Third Speech (22:1-30) — 269
  1. Job, You Are a Sinner (22:1-11) — 269
  2. God's Transcendence Is Not a Hindrance to His Ability to Judge (22:12-20) — 272
  3. Repent, and You Will Be Restored (22:21-30) — 274
- B. Job's Response to Eliphaz (23:1—24:17, 25) — 277
  1. I Wish I Could Talk to God (23:1-7) — 279
  2. I Am Confident but Terrified (23:8-17) — 280
  3. Why Does God Not Punish the Wicked? (24:1-17, 25) — 282
- C. Bildad's Third Speech (25:1-6; 24:18-24) — 287
  1. God's Power and Purity Far Surpass That of Humanity (25:1-6) — 288
  2. The Wicked Are Destroyed Because of Their Evil Deeds (24:18-24) — 289
- D. Job's Response to Bildad (26:1-14; 27:1-12) — 290
  1. You, Bildad, Have Not Helped Me a Bit (26:1-4) — 291
  2. God's Power Is Evident in All Areas of the Cosmos (26:5-14) — 292
  3. I Swear That I Am Innocent (27:1-6) — 294
  4. May God Punish My Enemy (27:7-12) — 295
- E. Zophar's Third Speech (27:13-23) — 297
  1. God Will Surely Punish the Wicked (27:13-23) — 297

Excursus 1: Progress in the Narrative — **299**

VI. INTERLUDE: THE SOURCE OF WISDOM: JOB 28 — 303

- A. Humans Are Skilled in Finding Hidden Minerals and Gems (28:1-11) — 305
- B. Where Can One Find Wisdom? (28:12-19) — 306
- C. Only God Knows How to Find Wisdom (28:20-28) — 307

VII. JOB'S MANIFESTO: JOB 29—31 — 311

- A. My Former Life (29:1-25) — 312
  1. God Was Blessing Me (29:1-6) — 312
  2. My Community Respected Me (29:7-17) — 313
  3. I Was Enjoying the Good Life (29:18-20) — 315
  4. People Sought My Advice (29:21-25) — 316

B.	My Present Humiliation and Suffering (30:1-31)	316
	1. I Am Mocked by My Community (30:1-15)	317
	2. God Continues to Make Me Suffer (30:16-23)	319
	3. My Condition Worsens Even Though I Plead for Help (30:24-31)	320
C.	My Innocence and Personal Integrity (31:1-40)	321
	1. I Have Not Looked Lustfully at Young Women (31:1-4)	322
	2. I Have Not Been Dishonest or Strayed from God's Way (31:5-8)	324
	3. I Have Not Committed Adultery (31:9-12)	324
	4. I Have Not Mistreated My Servants (31:13-15)	325
	5. I Have Not Withheld Compassion from the Needy (31:16-23)	326
	6. I Have Not Substituted Wealth or Pagan Worship for My Worship of God (31:24-28)	327
	7. I Have Not Been Vindictive against My Enemy (31:29-30)	328
	8. I Have Not Withheld Hospitality from the Passing Traveler (31:31-32)	328
	9. I Have Not Hidden My Transgressions from Public View (31:33-34)	328
	10. I Am Prepared to Defend Myself, if God Will Just Tell Me What I Have Done Wrong (31:35-37)	329
	11. I Have Not Exploited My Land or Laborers (31:38-40)	330

VIII.	**ELIHU'S SPEECHES: JOB 32—37**	**335**
A.	Introduction of Elihu (32:1-5)	338
B.	Elihu's First Speech (32:6—33:33)	340
	1. True Wisdom Comes from God and May Be Acquired at Any Age (32:6-10)	340
	2. I Will Succeed Where the Friends Have Failed (32:11-14)	340
	3. I Will Hold Nothing Back (32:15-22)	341
	4. Job, You Can Trust Me to Tell You the Truth (33:1-7)	342
	5. Job, You Are Wrong to Claim You Are Pure and God Treats You like an Enemy (33:8-12)	343
	6. Job, You Are Wrong to Complain That God Will Not Speak to You (33:13-30)	344
	7. Job, Listen to Me! (33:31-33)	347
C.	Elihu's Second Speech (34:1-37)	348
	1. You Friends, Listen to Me! (34:1-4)	348
	2. Job Is Making Preposterous Claims (34:5-9)	348
	3. It Is Unthinkable to Accuse God of Being Unjust (34:10-15)	349
	4. Job, if God Is All-Powerful, He Is Also Just (34:16-30)	350
	5. Job, You Are a Rebel against God (34:31-37)	352
D.	Elihu's Third Speech (35:1-16)	353
	1. Job, You Are Wrong to Claim That God Is Unjust and There Is No Benefit in Serving Him (35:1-8)	353
	2. God Does Not Answer the Prayers of the Wicked (35:9-13)	354
	3. Neither Will He Answer Your Complaints, Job, Because They Are Meaningless (35:14-16)	355

E.	Elihu's Fourth Speech (36:1—37:24)	355
	1. I Will Speak on God's Behalf (36:1-4)	356
	2. God Corrects the Righteous and Punishes the Wicked (36:5-15)	356
	3. Job, Quit Pursuing Your Own Worthless Solutions to Your Problems (36:16-21)	358
	4. God Is Awesome in Power and Beyond Our Understanding (36:22—37:13)	359
	5. Job, Can You Do What God Can Do? (37:14-24)	362
IX.	**GOD'S SPEECHES AND JOB'S RESPONSE: JOB 38:1—42:6**	**367**
	A. God's First Speech (38:1—40:2)	369
	1. I Will Question You (38:1-3)	369
	2. Could You Have Created the World the Way I Did? (38:4-11)	371
	3. Can You Operate the World the Way I Do? (38:12-38)	372
	4. Can You Control the Animal Kingdom the Way I Do? (38:39—39:30)	375
	5. Would You Care to Respond? (40:1-2)	378
	B. Job's First Response to God (40:3-5)	381
	C. God's Second Speech (40:6—41:34 [40:6—41:26 HB])	381
	1. Can You Administer Justice Better than I Can? (40:6-14)	382
	2. Can You Control the Hippopotamus? (40:15-24)	384
	3. Can You Control the Crocodile? (41:1-34 [40:25—41:26 HB])	387
	D. Job's Second Response to God (42:1-6)	393
X.	**EPILOGUE: JOB 42:7-17**	**399**
	A. God Rebukes the Three Friends (42:7-9)	401
	B. God Restores Job's Fortunes (42:10-17)	403
	Excursus 2: Interpreting the Book of Job	***407***

GENERAL EDITORS' PREFACE

The purpose of the New Beacon Bible Commentary is to make available to pastors and students in the twenty-first century a biblical commentary that reflects the best scholarship in the Wesleyan theological tradition. The commentary project aims to make this scholarship accessible to a wider audience to assist them in their understanding and proclamation of Scripture as God's Word.

Writers of the volumes in this series not only are scholars within the Wesleyan theological tradition and experts in their field but also have special interest in the books assigned to them. Their task is to communicate clearly the critical consensus and the full range of other credible voices who have commented on the Scriptures. Though scholarship and scholarly contribution to the understanding of the Scriptures are key concerns of this series, it is not intended as an academic dialogue within the scholarly community. Commentators of this series constantly aim to demonstrate in their work the significance of the Bible as the church's book and the contemporary relevance and application of the biblical message. The project's overall goal is to make available to the church and for her service the fruits of the labors of scholars who are committed to their Christian faith.

The *New International Version* (NIV) is the reference version of the Bible used in this series; however, the focus of exegetical study and comments is the biblical text in its original language. When the commentary uses the NIV, it is printed in bold. The text printed in bold italics is the translation of the author. Commentators also refer to other translations where the text may be difficult or ambiguous.

The structure and organization of the commentaries in this series seeks to facilitate the study of the biblical text in a systematic and methodical way. Study of each biblical book begins with an **Introduction** section that gives an overview of authorship, date, provenance, audience, occasion, purpose, sociological/cultural issues, textual history, literary features, hermeneutical issues, and theological themes necessary to understand the book. This section also includes a brief outline of the book and a list of general works and standard commentaries.

The commentary section for each biblical book follows the outline of the book presented in the introduction. In some volumes, readers will find section ***overviews*** of large portions of scripture with general comments on their overall literary structure and other literary features. A consistent feature of the commentary is the paragraph-by-paragraph study of biblical texts. This section has three parts: **Behind the Text**, **In the Text**, and **From the Text**.

The goal of the **Behind the Text** section is to provide the reader with all the relevant information necessary to understand the text. This includes specific historical situations reflected in the text, the literary context of the text, sociological and cultural issues, and literary features of the text.

In the Text explores what the text says, following its verse-by-verse structure. This section includes a discussion of grammatical details, word studies, and the connectedness of the text to other biblical books/passages or other parts of the book being studied (the canonical relationship). This section provides transliterations of key words in Hebrew and Greek and their literal meanings. The goal here is to explain what the author would have meant and/or what the audience would have understood as the meaning of the text. This is the largest section of the commentary.

The *From the Text* section examines the text in relation to the following areas: theological significance, intertextuality, the history of interpretation, use of the Old Testament scriptures in the New Testament, interpretation in later church history, actualization, and application.

The commentary provides **sidebars** on topics of interest that are important but not necessarily part of an explanation of the biblical text. These topics are informational items and may cover archaeological, historical, literary, cultural, and theological matters that have relevance to the biblical text. Occasionally, longer detailed discussions of special topics are included as *excursuses.*

We offer this series with our hope and prayer that readers will find it a valuable resource for their understanding of God's Word and an indispensable tool for their critical engagement with the biblical texts.

Roger Hahn, Centennial Initiative General Editor
Alex Varughese, General Editor (Old Testament)
George Lyons, General Editor (New Testament)

ABBREVIATIONS

With a few exceptions, these abbreviations follow those in *The SBL Handbook of Style* (Alexander 1999).

General
→	see the commentary at
AD	anno Domini (precedes date)
ANE	ancient Near East(ern)
b.	born
BC	before Christ (follows date)
ca.	*circa*, around
ch(s)	chapter(s)
col.	column
diss.	dissertation
ed(s).	editor(s); edition
e.g.	*exempli gratia*, for example
Eng.	English
et al.	*et alii*, and others
etc.	*et cetera*, and the rest
HB	Hebrew Bible
Heb.	Hebrew
ibid.	*ibidem*, in the same place
i.e.	*id est*, in other words, that is
lit.	literally
LXX	Septuagint
mg.	marginal
MT	Masoretic Text
n.	note
NT	New Testament
OT	Old Testament
pl.	plural
repr.	reprinted
rev.	revised
sg.	singular
sic	error in the original
v(v)	verse(s)
vol(s).	volume(s)
x	number of times a form occurs

Modern English Versions
GNT	Good News Translation (Today's English Version)
KJV	King James Version
NASB	New American Standard Bible
NEB	New English Bible
NIV	New International Version
NJPS	Tanakh: The Holy Scriptures: The New Jewish Publication Society Translation
NKJV	New King James Version
NLT	New Living Translation
NRSV	New Revised Standard Version
RSV	Revised Standard Version

Print Conventions for Translations

Bold font	NIV (bold without quotation marks in the text under study; elsewhere in the regular font, with quotation marks and no further identification)
Bold italic font	Author's translation (without quotation marks)
Behind the Text:	Literary or historical background information average readers might not know from reading the biblical text alone
In the Text:	Comments on the biblical text, words, phrases, grammar, and so forth
From the Text:	The use of the text by later interpreters, contemporary relevance, theological and ethical implications of the text, with particular emphasis on Wesleyan concerns

Ancient Sources

Old Testament

Gen	Genesis	Dan	Daniel		
Exod	Exodus	Hos	Hosea		
Lev	Leviticus	Joel	Joel		
Num	Numbers	Amos	Amos		
Deut	Deuteronomy	Obad	Obadiah		
Josh	Joshua	Jonah	Jonah		
Judg	Judges	Mic	Micah		
Ruth	Ruth	Nah	Nahum		
1—2 Sam	1—2 Samuel	Hab	Habakkuk		
1—2 Kgs	1—2 Kings	Zeph	Zephaniah		
1—2 Chr	1—2 Chronicles	Hag	Haggai		
Ezra	Ezra	Zech	Zechariah		
Neh	Nehemiah	Mal	Malachi		
Esth	Esther				
Job	Job				
Ps/Pss	Psalm/Psalms				
Prov	Proverbs				
Eccl	Ecclesiastes				
Song	Song of Songs/Song of Solomon				
Isa	Isaiah				
Jer	Jeremiah				
Lam	Lamentations				
Ezek	Ezekiel				

(Note: Chapter and verse numbering in the MT and LXX often differ compared to those in English Bibles. To avoid confusion, all biblical references follow the chapter and verse numbering in English translations, even when the text in the MT and LXX is under discussion.)

New Testament

Matt	Matthew
Mark	Mark
Luke	Luke
John	John
Acts	Acts
Rom	Romans
1—2 Cor	1—2 Corinthians
Gal	Galatians
Eph	Ephesians
Phil	Philippians
Col	Colossians
1—2 Thess	1—2 Thessalonians
1—2 Tim	1—2 Timothy
Titus	Titus
Phlm	Philemon
Heb	Hebrews
Jas	James
1—2 Pet	1—2 Peter
1—2—3 John	1—2—3 John
Jude	Jude
Rev	Revelation

Apocrypha

Bar	Baruch
Add Dan	Additions to Daniel
Pr Azar	Prayer of Azariah
Bel	Bel and the Dragon
Sg Three	Song of the Three Young Men
Sus	Susanna
1—2 Esd	1—2 Esdras
Add Esth	Additions to Esther
Ep Jer	Epistle of Jeremiah
Jdt	Judith
1—2 Macc	1—2 Maccabees
3—4 Macc	3—4 Maccabees
Pr Man	Prayer of Manasseh
Ps 151	Psalm 151
Sir	Sirach/Ecclesiasticus
Tob	Tobit
Wis	Wisdom of Solomon

Old Testament Pseudepigrapha

1 En.	*1 Enoch*

Modern Journals and Reference Works

ABD	*Anchor Bible Dictionary* (see Freedman)
ACCS	Ancient Christian Commentary on Scripture (see Simonetti)
ANET	*Ancient Near Eastern Texts Relating to the Old Testament* (see Pritchard)
BDB	*A Hebrew and English Lexicon of the Old Testament* (see Brown)
BETL	Bibliotheca ephemeridum theologicarum lovaniensium
CDCH	*The Concise Dictionary of Classical Hebrew* (see Clines 2009)
DCH	*Dictionary of Classical Hebrew* (see Clines 1993-2011)
GKC	*Gesenius' Hebrew Grammar* (see Gesenius)
HALOT	*The Hebrew and Aramaic Lexicon of the Old Testament* (see Koehler)
IBHS	*An Introduction to Biblical Hebrew Syntax* (see Waltke)
ISBE	*The International Standard Bible Encyclopedia*
JSOT	*Journal for the Study of the Old Testament*
JSOTSup	Journal for the Study of the Old Testament: Supplement Series
NIDOTTE	*New International Dictionary of Old Testament Theology and Exegesis* (see VanGemeren)
TDOT	*Theological Dictionary of the Old Testament* (see Botterweck)
TOTC	Tyndale Old Testament Commentaries
TWOT	*Theological Wordbook of the Old Testament* (see Harris)

Greek Transliteration

Greek	Letter	English
α	alpha	a
β	bēta	b
γ	gamma	g
γ	gamma nasal	n (before γ, κ, ξ, χ)
δ	delta	d
ε	epsilon	e
ζ	zēta	z
η	ēta	ē
θ	thēta	th
ι	iōta	i
κ	kappa	k
λ	lambda	l
μ	mu	m
ν	nu	n
ξ	xi	x
ο	omicron	o
π	pi	p
ρ	rhō	r
ρ	initial *rhō*	rh
σ/ς	sigma	s
τ	tau	t
υ	upsilon	y
υ	upsilon	u (in diphthongs: au, eu, ēu, ou, ui)
φ	phi	ph
χ	chi	ch
ψ	psi	ps
ω	ōmega	ō
ʼ	rough breathing	h (before initial vowels or diphthongs)

Hebrew Consonant Transliteration

Hebrew/Aramaic	Letter	English
א	alef	ʼ
ב	bet	b
ג	gimel	g
ד	dalet	d
ה	he	h
ו	vav	v or w
ז	zayin	z
ח	khet	ḥ
ט	tet	ṭ
י	yod	y
כ/ך	kaf	k
ל	lamed	l
מ/ם	mem	m
נ/ן	nun	n
ס	samek	s̱
ע	ayin	ʻ
פ/ף	pe	p; f (spirant)
צ/ץ	tsade	ṣ
ק	qof	q
ר	resh	r
שׂ	sin	ś
שׁ	shin	š
ת	tav	t; th (spirant)

BIBLIOGRAPHY

Alden, Robert L. 1993. *Job*. The New American Commentary. Vol. 11. Nashville: Broadman & Holman.
Alexander, Patrick H., et al. 1999. *The SBL Handbook of Style*. Peabody, MA: Hendrickson Publishers.
Andersen, Francis I. 1976. *Job: An Introduction and Commentary*. Tyndale Old Testament Commentary. Downers Grove, IL: InterVarsity.
Atkinson, David. 1991. *The Message of Job: Suffering and Grace*. The Bible Speaks Today. Downers Grove, IL: InterVarsity.
Balentine, Samuel E. 2006. *Job*. Smyth and Helwys Bible Commentary. Macon, GA: Smyth & Helwys.
Begg, Christopher T. 1994. Comparing Characters: The Book of Job and the *Testament of Job*. Pages 435-45 in *The Book of Job*. Edited by W. A. M. Beuken. BETL. Vol. 114. Leuven: Leuven University Press.
Bergant, Dianne. 1982. *Job, Ecclesiastes*. Old Testament Message. Vol. 18. Wilmington, DE: Michael Glazier.
Borowski, Oded. 1998. *Every Living Thing: Daily Use of Animals in Ancient Israel*. Walnut Creek, CA: AltaMira.
Boss, Jeffrey. 2010. *Human Consciousness of God in the Book of Job: A Theological and Psychological Commentary*. London: T&T Clark/Continuum.
Botterweck, G. Johannes. 1975. bĕhēmāh; bĕhēmôth. Pages 6-20 in vol. 2 of *Theological Dictionary of the Old Testament*. Translated by John T. Willis, Geoffrey W. Bromiley, David E. Green, and Douglas W. Stott. 15 vols. Grand Rapids: Eerdmans.
Botterweck, G. Johannes, Helmer Ringgren, and Heinz-Josef Fabry, eds. 1974-2006. *Theological Dictionary of the Old Testament*. Translated by John T. Willis, Geoffrey W. Bromiley, David E. Green, and Douglas W. Stott. 15 vols. Grand Rapids: Eerdmans.
Bowes, Alpin Wendell. 1988. A Theological Study of Old-Babylonian Personal Names. 2 vols. PhD diss., Dropsie College (Merion, PA).
Brown, Francis, S. R. Driver, and Charles A. Briggs. 1907. *A Hebrew and English Lexicon of the Old Testament*. Oxford: Clarendon.
Brueggemann, Walter. 1997. *Theology of the Old Testament: Testimony, Dispute, Advocacy*. Minneapolis: Fortress.
Burrell, David B., with A. H. Johns. 2008. *Deconstructing Theodicy: Why Job Has Nothing to Say to the Puzzled Suffering*. Grand Rapids: Brazos.
Chapman, Milo L. 1967. Job. Pages 17-123 in vol. 3 of *Beacon Bible Commentary*. 10 vols. Kansas City: Beacon Hill Press of Kansas City.
Chase, Steven. 2013. *Job*. Belief: A Theological Commentary on the Bible. Louisville, KY: Westminster John Knox.
Childs, Brevard S. 1979. *Introduction to the Old Testament as Scripture*. Philadelphia: Fortress.
Clemons, James T. 1988. Suicide. Pages 652-53 in vol. 4 of *The International Standard Bible Encyclopedia*. Edited by Geoffrey W. Bromiley. 4 vols. Grand Rapids: Eerdmans.
Clines, David J. A. 1989. *Job 1-20*. Word Biblical Commentary. Vol. 17. Dallas: Word Books.
———. ed. 1993-2011. *The Dictionary of Classical Hebrew*. 8 vols. Sheffield: Sheffield Academic/Phoenix.
———. 1994. Why Is There a Book of Job and What Does It Do to You if You Read It? Pages 1-20 in *The Book of Job*. Edited by W. A. M. Beuken. BETL. Vol. 114. Leuven: Leuven University Press.
———. 2003. The Fear of the Lord Is Wisdom (Job 28:28): A Semantic and Contextual Study. Pages 57-92 in *Job 28: Cognition in Context*. Edited by Ellen van Wolde. Biblical Interpretation Series. Vol. 64. Leiden: Brill.
———. 2006. *Job 21-37*. Word Biblical Commentary. Vol. 18A. Nashville: Thomas Nelson.
———. ed. 2009. *The Concise Dictionary of Classical Hebrew*. Sheffield: Sheffield Phoenix.
———. 2011. *Job 38-42*. Word Biblical Commentary. Vol. 18B. Nashville: Thomas Nelson.
Crenshaw, James L. 2005. *Defending God: Biblical Responses to the Problem of Evil*. Oxford: Oxford University Press.

———. 2011. *Reading Job: A Literary and Theological Commentary*. Macon, GA: Smyth & Helwys.

Davidson, A. B. 1884. *The Book of Job, with Notes, Introduction and Appendix*. The Cambridge Bible for Schools and Colleges. Cambridge: Cambridge University Press.

Day, John. 1994. How Could Job Be an Edomite? Pages 392-99 in *The Book of Job*. Edited by W. A. M. Beuken. BETL. Vol. 114. Leuven: Leuven University Press.

Delitzsch, F. 1949. *Biblical Commentary on the Book of Job*. Vol. I. Translated by Francis Bolton. Grand Rapids: Eerdmans.

Dell, Katharine J. 1991. *The Book of Job as Sceptical Literature*. Beihefte zur Zeitschrift für die alttestamentliche Wissenschaft. Vol. 197. Berlin: Walter de Gruyter.

Dell, Katharine, and Will Kynes, eds. 2013. *Reading Job Intertextually*. Library of Hebrew Bible / Old Testament Studies, 574. New York: Bloomsbury.

Dhorme, Édouard. 1984. *A Commentary on the Book of Job*. Translated by Harold Knight. Nashville: Thomas Nelson.

Dow, Thomas Edward. 2010. *When Storms Come: A Christian Look at Job*. McMaster Divinity College Press Ministry Studies Series, 1. Eugene, OR: Pickwick.

Driver, Samuel Rolles, and George Buchanan Gray. 1921. *A Critical and Exegetical Commentary on the Book of Job*. International Critical Commentary. Edinburgh: T&T Clark.

Eaton, J. H. 1985. *Job*. Old Testament Guides. Sheffield: JSOT Press.

Eisen, Robert. 2004. *The Book of Job in Medieval Jewish Philosophy*. New York: Oxford University Press.

Estes, Daniel J. 2013. *Job*. Teach the Text Commentary Series. Grand Rapids: Baker Books.

Ewald, Georg Heinrich. 2004. *Commentary on the Book of Job*. Theological Translation Fund Library, 28. Translated by J. Frederick Smith. Williams and Norgate, 1882. Repr. Eugene, OR: Wipf & Stock.

Fokkelman, Jan P. 2012. *The Book of Job in Form: A Literary Translation with Commentary*. Studia Semitica Neerlandica. Vol. 58. Leiden: Brill.

Freedman, David Noel, ed. 1992. *The Anchor Bible Dictionary*. 6 vols. New York: Doubleday.

Fyall, Robert S. 2002. *Now My Eyes Have Seen You: Images of Creation and Evil in the Book of Job*. New Studies in Biblical Theology, 12. Downers Grove, IL: InterVarsity.

Gammie, John G. 1989. *Holiness in Israel*. Overtures to Biblical Theology. Minneapolis: Fortress.

Gesenius, W. 1910. *Gesenius' Hebrew Grammar*. Edited and revised by E. Kautzsch and A. E. Cowley. Second ed. Oxford: Clarendon.

Gibson, John C. L. 1985. *Job*. Daily Study Bible. Philadelphia: Westminster.

Girard, René. 1987. *Job: The Victim of His People*. Translated by Yvonne Freccero. Stanford: Stanford University Press.

Glatzer, Nahum N. 2002. *The Dimensions of Job: A Study and Selected Readings*. Schocken Books, 1969. Repr. Eugene, OR: Wipf & Stock.

Goldingay, John. 2013. *Job for Everyone*. Old Testament for Everyone. Louisville, KY: Westminster John Knox.

Good, Edwin M. 1990. *In Turns of Tempest: A Reading of Job with a Translation*. Stanford: Stanford University Press.

Gordis, Robert. 1965. *The Book of God and Man: A Study of Job*. Chicago: University of Chicago.

———. 1978. *The Book of Job: Commentary, New Translation, and Special Studies*. Studies in Jewish History, Literature and Thought, Moreshet Series, 2. New York: Jewish Theological Seminary of America.

Gray, John. 2010. *The Book of Job*. The Text of the Hebrew Bible, 1. Edited by David J. A. Clines. Sheffield: Sheffield Phoenix.

Greenspahn, Frederick E. 1984. *Hapax Legomena in Biblical Hebrew: A Study of the Phenomenon and Its Treatment Since Antiquity with Special Reference to Verbal Forms*. Society of Biblical Literature Dissertation Series, 74. Chico, CA: Scholars Press.

Greenstein, Edward L. 2003. The Poem on Wisdom in Job 28 in Its Conceptual and Literary Contexts. Pages 253-80 in *Job 28: Cognition in Context*. Edited by Ellen van Wolde. Biblical Interpretation Series. Vol. 64. Leiden: Brill.

———. 2006. Truth or Theodicy? Speaking Truth to Power in the Book of Job. *Princeton Seminary Bulletin* 22/3, New Series: 238-58.

Gutiérrez, Gustavo. 1987. *On Job: God-Talk and the Suffering of the Innocent*. Translated by Matthew J. O'Connell. Maryknoll, NY: Orbis Books.

Haar, Murray J. 1999. Job After Auschwitz. *Interpretation* 53/3:265-75.

Habel, Norman C. 1985. *The Book of Job: A Commentary*. Old Testament Library. Philadelphia: Westminster.
Harris, R. Laird, Gleason L. Archer, Jr., and Bruce K. Waltke, eds. 1980. *Theological Wordbook of the Old Testament*. 2 vols. Chicago: Moody.
Hartley, John E. 1988. *The Book of Job*. New International Commentary on the Old Testament. Grand Rapids: Eerdmans.
Hoffman, Yair. 1996. *Blemished Perfection: The Book of Job in Context*. JSOTSup, 213. Sheffield: Sheffield Academic.
Hyland, Ann. 2003. *The Horse in the Ancient World*. Stroud, Gloucestershire, UK: Sutton.
Jacobsen, Thorkild. 1970. *Toward the Image of Tammuz and Other Essays on Mesopotamian History and Culture*. Harvard Semitic Series. Vol. 21. Edited by William L. Moran. Cambridge: Harvard University Press.
———. 1987. *The Harps That Once . . . : Sumerian Poetry in Translation*. New Haven, CT: Yale University Press.
Janzen, J. Gerald. 1985. *Job*. Interpretation: A Bible Commentary for Teaching and Preaching. Atlanta: John Knox.
———. 2009. *At the Scent of Water: The Ground of Hope in the Book of Job*. Grand Rapids: Eerdmans.
Jastrow, Morris, Jr. 2007. *The Book of Job: Its Origin, Growth, and Interpretation*. J. B. Lippincott, 1920. Repr. Eugene, OR: Wipf & Stock.
Job, John. 1977. *Job Speaks to Us Today*. Atlanta: John Knox.
Johnson, Timothy Jay. 2009. *Now My Eye Sees You: Unveiling an Apocalyptic Job*. Hebrew Bible Monographs, 24. Sheffield: Sheffield Phoenix.
Jones, Ivor H. 1992. Musical Instruments. Pages 934-39 in vol. 4 of *Anchor Bible Dictionary*. Edited by David Noel Freedman. 6 vols. New York: Doubleday.
Kaufmann, Yehezkel. 1960. *The Religion of Israel: From Its Beginnings to the Babylonian Exile*. Translated and abridged by Moshe Greenberg. New York: Schocken.
Kelly, B. H. 1962. *Ezra, Nehemiah, Esther, Job*. Layman's Bible Commentaries. London: SCM Press.
Kelly, Joseph F. 2002. *The Problem of Evil in the Western Tradition: From the Book of Job to Modern Genetics*. Collegeville, MN: Liturgical.
Kidner, Derek. 1964. *The Proverbs: An Introduction and Commentary*. Tyndale Old Testament Commentaries. London: Tyndale.
Kissane, Edward J. 1946. *The Book of Job: Translated from a Critically Revised Hebrew Text with Commentary*. New York: Sheed & Ward.
Knauf, Ernst Axel. 1992. Tema. Pages 346-47 in vol. 6 of *Anchor Bible Dictionary*. Edited by David Noel Freedman. 6 vols. New York: Doubleday.
Koehler, Ludwig, and Walter Baumgartner. 2001. *The Hebrew and Aramaic Lexicon of the Old Testament*. Translated and edited by M. E. J. Richardson. 2 vols. Leiden: Brill.
Konkel, August H. 2006. Job. Pages 1-249 in vol. 6 of *Cornerstone Biblical Commentary*. Carol Stream, IL: Tyndale House.
Kushner, Harold S. 2012. *The Book of Job: When Bad Things Happened to a Good Person*. New York: Schocken.
Larrimore, Mark. 2013. *The Book of Job: A Biography*. Lives of Great Religious Books. Princeton: Princeton University Press.
Lo, Alison. 2003. *Job 28 as Rhetoric: An Analysis of Job 28 in the Context of Job 22-31*. Supplements to Vetus Testamentum. Vol. 97. Leiden: Brill.
Longman, Tremper, III. 2012. *Job*. Baker Commentary on the Old Testament: Wisdom and Psalms. Grand Rapids: Baker Academic.
Magdalene, F. Rachel. 2007. *On the Scales of Righteousness: Neo-Babylonian Trial Law and the Book of Job*. Brown Judaic Studies, 348. Providence, RI: Brown University.
Mangan, Céline. 1991. The Targum of Job. Pages ix-98 in *The Aramaic Bible*. Vol. 15. Edited by Kevin Cathcart, Michael Maher, and Martin McNamara. Collegeville, MN: Liturgical.
McGinnis, Claire Mathews. 2001. Playing the Devil's Advocate in Job: On Job's Wife. Pages 121-41 in *The Whirlwind: Essays on Job, Hermeneutics and Theology in Memory of Jane Morse*. Edited by Stephen L. Cook, Corrine L. Patton, and James W. Watts. JSOTSup, 336. London: Sheffield Academic.
McKeating, Henry. 1971. The Central Issue of the Book of Job. *Expository Times* 82:244-47.
McKenna, David L. 1986. *Job*. Communicator's Commentary. Waco, TX: Word Books.
Miller, Patrick D. 1994. *They Cried to the Lord: The Form and Theology of Biblical Prayer*. Minneapolis: Fortress.

Nam, Duck-Woo. 2003. *Talking About God: Job 42:7-9 and the Nature of God in the Book of Job*. Studies in Biblical Literature. Vol. 49. New York: Peter Lang.

Newsom, Carol A. 1996. The Book of Job: Introduction, Commentary, and Reflections. Pages 317-637 in vol. 4 of *The New Interpreter's Bible*. Edited by Leander E. Keck. 12 vols. Nashville: Abingdon.

———. 1999. Job and His Friends: A Conflict of Moral Imaginations. *Interpretation* 53/3:239-53.

———. 2003. *The Book of Job: A Contest of Moral Imaginations*. Oxford: Oxford University Press.

O'Connor, Kathleen M. 2012. *Job*. New Collegeville Bible Commentary. Vol. 19. Collegeville, MN: Liturgical.

Oswalt, John N. 1980a. *bārak*. Pages 132-33 in vol. 1 of *Theological Wordbook of the Old Testament*. Chicago: Moody.

———. 1980b. *kā'ab*. Page 425 in vol. 1 of *Theological Wordbook of the Old Testament*. Chicago: Moody.

Patrick, Dale. 1977. *Arguing with God: The Angry Prayers of Job*. St. Louis: Bethany.

Perdue, Leo G. 1991. *Wisdom in Revolt: Metaphorical Theology in the Book of Job*. JSOTSup, 112. Sheffield: Sheffield Academic.

Perdue, Leo G., and W. Clark Gilpin, eds. 1992. *The Voice from the Whirlwind: Interpreting the Book of Job*. Nashville: Abingdon.

Pfeffer, Jeremy I. 2005. *Providence in the Book of Job: The Search for God's Mind*. Brighton, UK: Sussex Academic.

Pope, Marvin H. 1973. *Job: Introduction, Translation, and Notes*. Anchor Bible. Vol. 15. Third ed. Garden City, NY: Doubleday.

Pritchard, James B., ed. 1969. *Ancient Near Eastern Texts Relating to the Old Testament*. Third ed. with supplement. Princeton: Princeton University Press.

Pyeon, Yohan. 2003. *You Have Not Spoken What Is Right About Me: Intertextuality and the Book of Job*. Studies in Biblical Literature. Vol. 45. New York: Peter Lang.

Reichert, Victor E. 1985. *Job: Hebrew Text and English Translation with an Introduction and Commentary*. Soncino Books of the Bible. Rev. ed. by A. J. Rosenberg. London: Soncino.

Reimer, David J. 1997. *ṣdq*. Pages 754-57 in vol. 3 of *New International Dictionary of Old Testament Theology and Exegesis*. Grand Rapids: Zondervan.

Reyburn, William D. 1992. *A Handbook on the Book of Job*. New York: United Bible Societies.

Robinson, H. Wheeler. 1955. *The Cross in the Old Testament*. London: SCM Press.

Rodd, C. S. 1990. *The Book of Job*. Epworth Commentaries. London: Epworth.

Rose, Martin. 1992. Names of God in the OT. Pages 1001-11 in vol. 4 of *Anchor Bible Dictionary*. New York: Doubleday.

Rowley, H. H. 1976. *Job*. New Century Bible Commentary. Rev. ed. Grand Rapids: Eerdmans.

Scherer, Paul. 1954. The Book of Job: Exposition. Pages 905-1198 in vol. 3 of *The Interpreter's Bible*. 12 vols. New York: Abingdon.

Schifferdecker, Kathryn. 2008. *Out of the Whirlwind: Creation Theology in the Book of Job*. Harvard Theological Studies, 61. Cambridge, MA: Harvard University Press.

Seitz, Christopher R. 1989. Job: Full-Structure, Movement, and Interpretation. *Interpretation* 43/1:5-17.

Seow, C. L. 2013. *Job 1-21: Interpretation and Commentary*. Illuminations. Grand Rapids: Eerdmans.

Simonetti, Manlio, and Marco Conti, eds. 2006. *Job*. Vol. 6 of Ancient Christian Commentary on Scripture. Downers Grove, IL: InterVarsity.

Smick, Elmer B. 1988. Job. Pages 841-1060 in vol. 4 of *The Expositor's Bible Commentary with the New International Version*. 12 vols. Grand Rapids: Zondervan.

Snaith, Norman H. 1968. *The Book of Job: Its Origin and Purpose*. Studies in Biblical Theology, Second Series, 11. Naperville, IL: Allenson.

Spittler, R. P. 1983. Testament of Job: A New Translation and Introduction. Pages 829-68 in vol. 1 of *The Old Testament Pseudepigrapha*. Edited by James H. Charlesworth. Garden City, NY: Doubleday.

Swart, Ignatius, and Robin Wakely. 1997. *ṣrr*. Pages 853-59 in vol. 3 of *New International Dictionary of Old Testament Theology and Exegesis*. Grand Rapids: Zondervan.

Terrien, Samuel. 1954. The Book of Job: Introduction and Exegesis. Pages 875-1198 in vol. 3 of *The Interpreter's Bible*. 12 vols. New York: Abingdon.

———. 2004. *Job: Poet of Existence*. Bobbs-Merrill, 1957. Repr. Eugene, OR: Wipf & Stock.

Ticciati, Susannah. 2005. *Job and the Disruption of Identity: Reading Beyond Barth*. London: T&T Clark.

Tsevat, Matitiahu. 1992. The Meaning of the Book of Job. *Hebrew Union College Annual* 37 (1966): 73-106. Repr. Roy B. Zuck, ed. *Sitting with Job: Selected Studies on the Book of Job*. Pages 189-218. Eugene, OR: Wipf and Stock.
Tur-Sinai, N. H. 1967. *The Book of Job: A New Commentary*. Jerusalem: Kiryat Sefer.
Van der Lugt, Pieter. 1995. *Rhetorical Criticism and the Poetry of the Book of Job*. Oudtestamentische Studiën. Vol. 32. Leiden: Brill.
VanGemeren, Willem A., ed. 1997. *New International Dictionary of Old Testament Theology and Exegesis*. 5 vols. Grand Rapids: Zondervan.
Van Selms, A. 1985. *Job: A Practical Commentary*. Text and Interpretation. Translated by John Vriend. Grand Rapids: Eerdmans.
Van Wolde, Ellen. 1997. *Mr and Mrs Job*. Translated by John Bowden. London: SCM Press.
———. 2003. Wisdom, Who Can Find It? A Non-Cognitive and Cognitive Study of Job 28:1-11. Pages 1-35 in *Job 28: Cognition in Context*. Edited by Ellen van Wolde. Biblical Interpretation Series. Vol. 64. Leiden: Brill.
Vicchio, Stephen J. 2006a. *Job in the Ancient World*. Vol. 1 of *The Image of the Biblical Job: A History*. Eugene, OR: Wipf & Stock.
———. 2006b. *Job in the Medieval World*. Vol. 2 of *The Image of the Biblical Job: A History*. Eugene, OR: Wipf & Stock.
———. 2006c. *Job in the Modern World*. Vol. 3 of *The Image of the Biblical Job: A History*. Eugene, OR: Wipf & Stock.
Von Rad, Gerhard. 1972. *Wisdom in Israel*. Translated by James D. Martin. Nashville: Abingdon.
Wakely, Robin. 1997. kelaḥ. Pages 652-54 in vol. 2 of *New International Dictionary of Old Testament Theology and Exegesis*. Grand Rapids: Zondervan.
Waltke, Bruce K., and M. O'Connor. 1990. *An Introduction to Biblical Hebrew Syntax*. Winona Lake, IN: Eisenbrauns.
Walton, John H., with Kelly Lemon Vizcaino. 2012. *Job*. The NIV Application Commentary. Grand Rapids: Zondervan.
Weiss, Meir. 1983. *The Story of Job's Beginning: Job 1-2: A Literary Analysis*. Jerusalem: Magnes.
Wesley, John. 1765. *Explanatory Notes upon the Old Testament*. Vol. 2. Bristol: William Pine.
Westermann, Claus. 1981. *The Structure of the Book of Job, A Form-Critical Analysis*. Translated by Charles A. Muenchow. Philadelphia: Fortress.
Wharton, James A. 1999. *Job*. Westminster Bible Companion. Louisville, KY: Westminster John Knox.
Whybray, Norman. 1998. *Job*. Readings: A New Biblical Commentary. Sheffield: Sheffield Academic.
Wilson, Gerald H. 2007. *Job*. New International Biblical Commentary. Peabody, MA: Hendrickson.
Witherington, Ben, III. 1994. *Jesus the Sage: The Pilgrimage of Wisdom*. Minneapolis: Fortress.
Youngblood, Ronald F. 1980. tāpal. Page 978 in vol. 2 of *Theological Wordbook of the Old Testament*. Chicago: Moody.
Zuck, Roy B., ed. 1992. *Sitting with Job: Selected Studies on the Book of Job*. Eugene, OR: Wipf and Stock.
Zuckerman, Bruce. 1991. *Job the Silent: A Study in Historical Counterpoint*. New York: Oxford University Press.

TABLE OF SIDEBARS

Sidebars	Location
Camels	1:3
The Examiner	1:6
Sabeans and Chaldeans	1:17
The Disasters as Great Literature	1:18-19
Disease in the Ancient World	2:7-8
Sheol	3:17-19
Cause-and-Effect Reasoning	4:10-11
Universal Sinfulness	5:7
God's Chastenings	5:17
Number Patterns	5:19
Suicide in the Bible	6:8-9
Mythological Characters in Job	7:12
Words for "Sin" in the Book of Job	7:21
The Wisdom Traditions	8:10
Is Jesus the Answer to Job's Request for a Mediator?	9:33
Light and Darkness in Job	11:17
God's Paradoxical Nature	16:19
Mockers	30:2-8
Lust	31:1-4
Social Activism	31:16-23
The Interior Dimension of Holiness	31:33-34
Job and Jeremiah	Behind the Text for 38:1—42:6
Theophanies	38:1

INTRODUCTION

The book of Job is one of the most profound literary, theological, and philosophical works ever written. It is a book without equal that has challenged the world's best thinkers ever since it first appeared.

The story concerns a man named Job who experienced a series of calamities that tested his faith in God. Outside the book of Job, this character is mentioned only in Jas 5:11 where he is praised for his "perseverance" and in Ezek 14:14, 20 where he is commended for his "righteousness." In both passages he is viewed as an ancient example of a person who was extremely devoted to God—a hero of the faith, so to speak.

The book takes up a topic that was well-known in the ancient world—the innocent sufferer. Other works on this topic include: the Sumerian "Man and His God" (*ANET*, 589-91); the Akkadian "I Will Praise the Lord of Wisdom" (*ANET*, 434-37, 596-600) and "The Babylonian Theodicy" (*ANET*, 601-4); and the Egyptian "A Dispute over Suicide" (*ANET*, 405-7) and "The Protests of the Eloquent Peasant" (*ANET*, 407-10). All of these were written many centuries before Job, so the topic was known to the Israelites (on the relationship between these texts and Job, see Hartley 1988, 6-11; Seow 2013, 51-56; or Vicchio 2006a, 1:15-21). The author of Job tackles this topic from a monotheistic viewpoint that separates it from the other works.

Job falls into a genre of literature known as the wisdom literature. In recent years some scholars have argued strongly for other classifications, such as "parody" (Dell 1991, 109-57) or "apocalyptic" (Johnson 2009, 15-77), but there is no widespread agreement on removing Job from the wisdom literature genre. Four books in the OT are usually placed in this genre: Proverbs, Ecclesiastes, Song of Songs, and Job (plus two in the Apocrypha: Wisdom of Solomon and Ecclesiasticus/Sirach). In addition, there are wisdom sayings and forms scattered throughout the Psalms and Prophets. There are also countless wisdom forms in the NT Gospels. Jesus used them frequently in his teaching (e.g., aphorisms, proverbs, beatitudes, and parables). Witherington estimates that at least 70 percent of Jesus' teaching was in the form of wisdom sayings (1994, 155-56).

Some of the wisdom literature is very positive about the ability of people to achieve *the good life* through righteous living. The book of Proverbs contains hundreds of rules for right living that promise definite, personal rewards. Other wisdom writings are more skeptical about discovering any order to life. According to Ecclesiastes, life is only vanity—without substance, without value, and fleeting. The book of Job falls somewhere in between. The prologue, epilogue, and ch 29 provide happy scenes at both ends of Job's life when he was blessed by God. But the dialogues describe a middle time period when he was wracked by physical pain, social ostracism, mental anguish, and spiritual doubts about God. As a result, some scholars place this book closer to Proverbs and others closer to Ecclesiastes.

Generally speaking, the wisdom literature focuses on universal issues that transcend any one culture. It commonly addresses questions such as: What is the meaning of human existence? What is God's relationship to human beings? Is there any order in this world? Why do good people sometimes suffer awful tragedies and diseases? The writers who first addressed these issues in written form appeared sometime in the first half of the third millennium BC. Down through the centuries there has been no lack of writers on these subjects, even to the present day.

A. Author

The author of the book is unknown. Jewish speculation in the Talmud pointed to Moses as the author, but hardly anyone accepts this theory today. What we do know about the author is mainly of a general nature.

- The author was obviously an Israelite. His theology and view of life are centered in a monotheistic faith. And he uses the divine name Yahweh throughout the prologue and epilogue.
- The author was a sage who knew of the wisdom tradition in the ancient Near East (ANE) and appreciated its viewpoint on life. He was probably familiar with some of the wisdom literature from other nations. It is well-known that the sages of the ancient world came primarily from the upper classes. Their social position was sometimes reflected in their writings (e.g., Prov 10:22; 14:24; 18:11; 22:4). Thus, it is not surprising that the hero of the book is a fabulously wealthy individual. And the intended au-

dience probably consisted of people like Job—wealthy, upper class, highly literate, intellectual, and leisured (Clines 1994, 4).
- The author was a very learned, intelligent writer. How he gained his education is unknown, but his use of the Hebrew language is impressive. He uses proverbs, laments, beatitudes, rhetorical questions, hymns, riddles, curses, and legal disputations, to name a few of his literary skills. The book displays an excellent knowledge of the star constellations, mining practices, precious metals and gems, hunting terminology, the characteristics of many wild animals, the travels of caravaners, and legal procedures. It also contains a large technical vocabulary illustrated by five words for a "lion," six terms for an "animal trap," and five synonyms for "darkness." Somehow, the author gained an extensive knowledge of names and customs that existed hundreds of years before his time. In addition, he writes as someone who had traveled to other countries, particularly Egypt. In short, this book has "a richer vocabulary than any other biblical book" (Gordis 1965, 160). It is a literary gold mine.
- This book was probably written by a person who had experienced severe suffering and could identify with the character of Job. And just like Job, this writer had found relief through a personal encounter with God. The book of Job is the author's attempt to share with the world what he had learned.

B. Date

For a number of reasons, the composition of the book is sometimes placed in the patriarchal period (archaeologically known as the Middle Bronze period, 2000-1550 BC).
- The book never speaks of the nation of Israel or its historical traditions. Neither is there mention of the Jerusalem temple or the priesthood. Rather, Job offers his own sacrifices (1:5), just like the patriarchs did (Gen 12:7-8; 13:18; 22:9; 26:25; 33:20; 35:7). This would have been unthinkable after the nation was established and the temple was built.
- Job's wealth is measured in terms of animals and servants (Job 1:3), much like the description of the patriarchs (Gen 12:5; 13:2; 14:14; 24:35; 32:5 [6 HB]). Also, the one term that the author uses for a unit of money (qĕśîṭâ; actually a weight of silver; Job 42:11) appears only in the patriarchal stories (Gen 33:19; Josh 24:32).
- Job's long life span of 140 years (Job 42:16) seems to fit the patriarchal period the best. Abraham lived to 175 (Gen 25:7), Ishmael to 137 (Gen 25:17), Isaac to 180 (Gen 35:28), Jacob to 147 (Gen 47:28), and Joseph to 110 (Gen 50:22, 26).
- The epic nature of the book is similar to the stories of the patriarchs in Genesis. Some scholars have also compared it to earlier Ugaritic epics such as "The Legend of King Keret" and "The Tale of Aqhat" (ANET, 142-55).

- Ezekiel places Job in company with Noah and Dan'el (probably the Ugaritic hero Dan'el) as one of three great non-Israelite heroes who lived in the distant past before Israel existed (Ezek 14:14, 20).
- The poetic part of the book repeatedly uses names for God that were common in the patriarchal stories, for example, *El* (Gen 14:18-20; 35:1), *Elohim* (Gen 17:3, 9), and *Shaddai* (Gen 17:1; 35:11). The covenantal name Yahweh that was revealed to Moses at the burning bush appears almost exclusively in the prose sections of the book (Job 1:1—2:13; 42:7-17).
- Many of the personal and place names in the book have indirect connections with names known in the patriarchal period (→ 2:11).
- The story of Job is similar to a number of other ancient stories that speak of a wealthy man who came on hard times and tried to figure out how to get out of them (see beginning of Introduction). These stories were circulating in the ancient world centuries before the nation of Israel. So Israelites would have connected Job with much earlier times.

However, none of the reasons above *requires* a patriarchal date for the *writing* of the book. All of them can be explained as the author's attempt to provide an ancient setting for Job's story, much like a historical novelist today would create a setting in the Middle Ages or the eighteenth century utilizing ancient names and customs. The average Israelite reader would probably have regarded Job as a contemporary of Abraham because of the author's use of these archaic elements.

Other factors strongly support a date for the writing of the book sometime during the first millennium BC.
- Iron is repeatedly mentioned as a useful metal (19:24; 20:24; 28:2; 40:18; 41:27 [19 HB]). Although the technology for smelting iron was developed around 1200 BC, it took a couple more centuries before this technology became commonplace in the Mediterranean world. The author of Job writes at a time when iron was well-known, that is, the first millennium.
- The description of the horse as a warhorse (39:19-25) fits an Israelite audience best in the first millennium. Horses and chariots became an important part of military engagements about the middle of the second millennium BC. But they were used principally by the major powers such as the Egyptians and the Hittites. An Israelite author would probably not mention their usefulness in warfare until after they became a part of Israel's army during the reign of Solomon (960-922 BC).
- Job's possessions included large numbers of domesticated camels (→ "Camels" sidebar at 1:3). Camels may have become domesticated in some desert regions as early as 1500 BC, but they were used only on a very limited basis. They were much more common during the first millennium when they became the principal means of transportation along the desert trade routes that originated in southern Arabia. Tema (6:19), one of the centers of the camel caravan trade, did not rise to prominence until the middle of the eighth century BC (Knauf 1992, 6:346).

- The Sabeans and Chaldeans who raided Job's animals (1:15, 17) probably did not exist as ethnic groups prior to the first millennium. Certainly, Israelite readers of the book would not have understood these terms before the first millennium.
- The use of the divine name Yahweh in the prologue, epilogue, and divine speeches calls for a date after the time of Moses (Exod 3:14-16; 6:2-3). The author of Job is writing to an Israelite audience who understood the name of their deity as Yahweh. The appearance of other names for God in the poetic section is mainly a literary technique intended to provide an archaic setting for the story.

Is it possible to narrow the date of writing within the first millennium?

- Many scholars have tried to relate the book to Israel's greatest national disaster—the destruction of Jerusalem in 587 BC and their forced exile to Babylonia. They suggest that this would be the most likely time for someone to write about suffering. However, this argument is rather flimsy. The book is about personal suffering, not national suffering, and personal suffering occurs in all eras. Further, unlike Job who had no knowledge of the reason for his troubles, the cause of the destruction and exile was well-known. For over 150 years Israel's prophets had predicted that God would judge the people for their sins. So there really is no connection between Job's suffering and the exile.
- Much more relevant to the date of the book is the rise to prominence in the middle of the first millennium of the Chaldeans, forming an empire known as the Neo-Babylonian Empire. King Nebuchadnezzar of biblical fame was the most well-known of their kings. A later king, Nabonidus (556-539 BC), moved to the oasis at Tema in the Arabian desert for the last ten years of his reign. Because the Chaldeans became hated by Israel after they destroyed Jerusalem in 587 BC, it is unlikely that an Israelite author would include them in his story immediately after that event, that is, during the exile. Thus, the mention of the Chaldeans in the book suggests a date prior to 600 or after 500 BC (when the Neo-Babylonian Empire was only a distant memory; → 1:17 and "Sabeans and Chaldeans" sidebar at 1:17).
- In a similar vein, the nation of Edom was regarded as a traitor immediately after the destruction because these people had helped the Babylonian army (Ps 137:7). Also, they profited off of Judah's exile by taking over towns and land to the south of Jerusalem. It would have taken some time for the wounds from Babylonia and Edom to heal. In contrast, in the book of Job, there is no hint of any animosity toward Edom. In fact, it is probably the setting for the story.
- Another relevant point is the character of "the Satan/Examiner" in Job. His role is much different from that found in a later book of the OT, such as 1 Chr 21:1 (450-300 BC) or in the intertestamental literature. This

might suggest a date in the first half of the first millennium when this name was not yet regarded as an evil character.
- Ezekiel's reference to Job (14:14, 20) indicates that the Israelites were quite familiar with an ancient righteous man named Job by at least the beginning of the sixth century BC. However, it is unclear whether Ezekiel knew of the book of Job or only of an oral tradition about him.
- There are a number of passages in Job that are similar to passages in other OT books. The most relevant, according to Seow, are: Jeremiah, Lamentations, and Deutero-Isaiah, all from the sixth century BC (2013, 41-42). The whole concept of innocent suffering is strongly reminiscent of the Suffering Servant passages in Isaiah. Hartley lists a total of fifty-four passages in Job that find parallels in other books (1988, 11-12; see also Dell and Kynes 2013). While this list is quite helpful in showing the interrelationship between various writings in the OT, it does not prove that Job was written later. It is often very difficult to determine who was influenced by whom or whether both were influenced by a third source.

All of the above evidence suggests two possible dates for the writing of Job. One is the seventh century (700-600 BC). There was a revival of interest in wisdom literature at the beginning of the century under Hezekiah's leadership (Prov 25:1). Israel's hatred of the Chaldeans and Edomites had not yet materialized. And the development of the Satan's character into an evil person had not yet occurred. Further, there was significant suffering in Judah during this century.

At the beginning of the century, Sennacherib made the Judeans pay a heavy price for their resistance to his demands. In the middle of the century, the Assyrians continued to impose their will throughout the reign of Manasseh, who himself brought persecution against the faithful. At the end of the century, Judah experienced the death of Josiah, followed by more harsh treatment from Egypt and Babylonia. This period also included the unjust suffering of Jeremiah. All of this together may have influenced the author to consider writing on the topic of the innocent sufferer.

A second possibility is the first half of the fifth century (500-450 BC). This would have allowed enough time for the hatred of the Chaldeans and Edomites to subside. The fall of the Neo-Babylonian Empire to the Persians was sufficient evidence that God had judged them for their cruelty to Judah. Of significant importance, the captives were exposed to many new ideas while in Babylonia, and then under the control of the Persians (beginning in 539 BC). The more intellectual members of the captivity may have had the opportunity to study the wisdom literature of Mesopotamia, and this may have led to a revival of interest in this genre. This time period could easily have expanded their intellectual horizons to some of the universal human issues that transcended the nationalistic interests of the returning exiles.

Some have suggested that there was also an increased emphasis on the individual, rather than the community, during this century (Gordis 1965, 149-50;

Tsevat 1992, 213-14; see Jer 31:29-34; Ezek 18:1-32). However, this is a circular argument that cannot be upheld. The book of Proverbs and Gen 2—3 indicate that individual responsibility for sin was found throughout Israel's history (Kaufmann 1960, 329-32). And further, the wisdom literature of Mesopotamia and Egypt provides evidence of a long tradition on this theme throughout the ANE. In the fifth century, the Israelites would not yet have changed their views on the nature of the Satan or the nature of the afterlife, but they were becoming more aware of what the Persian religion Zoroastrianism taught on these topics. In addition, Darius' (522-486 BC) Behistun Inscription may have inspired Job's words in Job 19:23-24, and Deutero-Isaiah's discussion of the Suffering Servant may also have influenced the author.

The latest possible date for the writing of Job is probably around 450 BC, before the influences of Ezra who turned the people's attention inward and onto the Law. This date also precedes the writing of Chronicles, where the character of "the Satan" has changed (1 Chr 21:1). The main problem with the fifth century is the disastrous condition of Judah at this time. Would there even have been any wealthy, intellectual, upper-class people living in Judah before 450 BC?

The book of Job will probably never be dated precisely, but these two dates seem the most likely, based on the evidence at hand. Fortunately, the date is not significant for understanding the message of the book, for this is timeless literature.

C. Text

The Hebrew text of Job is very difficult. Every scholar who has worked on this book has had to wrestle with its translation as well as its interpretation. The large vocabulary (mentioned earlier) is enhanced by a sizable number of words that scholars call *hapax legomena*—words that appear only once in the OT (from the Greek, meaning "once said" [Greenspahn 1984, 1, n. 1]). Greenspahn notes 39 absolute *hapax* (exceeded only by Isaiah at 43) and another 110 nonabsolute (1984, 199). *Hapax* are usually very difficult to translate because of a lack of comparative texts. Further, hundreds of words appear with an archaic spelling. Seow believes this was done on purpose to add to the ancient setting of the story (2013, 20). These features, along with a number of other difficult grammatical constructions, have challenged the best Hebrew scholars for centuries. Repeatedly, one finds passages where all commentators agree (something very unusual in the scholarly world) that the exact meaning is uncertain. Here one must fall back on good speculation as the only option.

The text of the LXX (Greek translation made about two centuries before Christ, called the Septuagint) is about four hundred lines shorter than the MT (the standard Hebrew text, called the Masoretic Text, from ca. AD 500-1000). These omissions are scattered throughout the book. Not all of them are explainable, but many are due to abridgments or difficulties in trying to read the Hebrew text. Seow suggests that the translator was trying to make the text more "reader-friendly" (2013, 6-7).

D. Unity

There are three characteristics of the book that have led some scholars to question its unity. First, the division of the book into prose (Job 1—2, 42) and poetic sections (chs 3—41) suggests that two writers were involved in the composition of the book at two different periods of time. Second, the scrambled nature of the text in chs 24—27 is very confusing. There has obviously been some damage to the text at this point, but there is no unanimity on how to put the text back together (→ Behind the Text for ch 22). Third, the speech by Elihu (chs 32—37) seems to interrupt the flow of the book. Elihu gives his long monologue and then disappears. He is not mentioned in the prologue or epilogue, and his speech does not add a great deal to the story (according to some scholars). Some see Elihu as a later intrusion.

However, it is very hard to trace the history of the book's composition. This writer's personal viewpoint is that Job was written by one author. A very gifted and creative person enlarged upon an original kernel of a story about an innocent sufferer that had been circulating in oral (and maybe written) form for centuries. The remnants of the original kernel influenced the writing of the prologue and epilogue. But with great skill, the author added the poetic parts of the book, creating drama, tension, climax, and resolution. In doing so, he crafted a timeless literary masterpiece. Thus, this book should not be treated as a historical narrative like the life of David or Solomon in Samuel and Kings. This is great literature at its finest.

Most likely, the writing of a book of this length and depth took a long time, maybe an entire lifetime (Gordis 1978, 548). The author could have made many additions and eliminated parts at numerous times during the course of its composition. This would help explain the appearance of the Elihu speech, a speech that provides the viewpoint of a younger person from a Hebrew background. Without the aid of a computer to cut and paste new material, the author added a lengthy introduction to Elihu (32:1-5) rather than try to write him into earlier or later sections (for more comment, → Behind the Text for ch 32).

At some point after the book was completed, it became damaged in chs 24—27. The confusion that resulted will probably never be fully resolved. But the message of the book in this section is understandable and should be retained, even if we do not know the exact speaker for each part. Gordis sums up the unity in these words: The book is "a superbly structured unity, the work of a single author of transcendental genius, both as a literary artist and as a religious thinker, with few peers, if any, in the history of mankind" (1978, 581).

E. Theological Topics

In popular thinking, the book of Job is usually associated with suffering. The main character is a good man who is obviously blessed in many ways. But he loses everything of value to him in life. Why did this happen, and what could he have done to prevent it? How can he now extricate himself from this predicament? The author forces readers to see themselves in the character of Job and ask the same questions he asked. This topic is still popular today as seen in Harold Kushner's best seller *When Bad Things Happen to Good People* (Random House, 1978).

From there our minds wander to the mysterious problem of evil. Where does evil come from? Why does it exist? Should the devastation caused by lightning (1:16), wind (1:19), floods, and earthquakes be considered evil, or just a natural disaster? And is this adversarial character called "the Satan/Examiner" still active in our world today?

As we dig a little deeper, we soon discover that this is also a book about the nature of God. What kind of God is this who allows the most righteous person in the world to suffer unjustly and then speaks to him of the animal kingdom instead of consoling him? Does he know when I suffer today? Does he cause my suffering? Does he do anything to help me when I call upon him to relieve my distress? We find in this book that God is a very mysterious being. He cannot be put in a box. He has freedom to act or not to act as he chooses.

This thought then raises questions about the cosmos. What is the nature of our world? Did God create an ordered world, as the book of Proverbs suggests? Or is this a world of chaos where evil and pain can break in at unexpected moments and lead to a sense of meaninglessness?

Clearly, Job is more than a book about suffering. Suffering is simply the framework that guides us into thinking about deeper issues. This is the reason why this book is so timeless. It deals with universal questions that have intrigued and perplexed humanity since the beginning of time. Each generation of philosophers, theologians, writers, and artists has had to wrestle with the questions that face Job. We will come back to these questions as they relate to the overall message of the book after examining the content of the narrative in more detail.

For many readers, the book of Job will leave them unsatisfied. They will find by the end that they have more questions than answers about God and the world and their place in the world. But whatever failings the book may have in resolving the great questions of life, it does force us to wrestle with some of the most significant issues humans must face. And it also points us in the proper direction—toward God—to find answers that are meaningful. As the author says in his eloquent interlude, "The fear of the Lord—that is wisdom" (28:28).

F. Historicity

Did a person named Job really live? The answer to this question is inevitably going to be speculative, for there is very little evidence to go on. The story as we now have it seems to be epic in nature, and it begins much like a "once upon a time" folktale: "There was once a man . . ." (1:1a NRSV). It is also similar to a number of other ANE tales about an innocent sufferer. In most of these, the relationship to a historical individual is questionable. Further evidence of the literary character of the book is the fact that the dialogues are all in poetry. Real people do not speak to one another in poetic verse.

Some have suggested that the book is a lengthy parable, much like the parables that Jesus told. This is certainly possible. None of the value of the book's message would be lost if it were just a parable, like the Good Samaritan.

On the other hand, this writer's personal, subjective opinion, after having worked with the book for a number of years, is that a man named Job could have lived at some point prior to Israel's existence as a nation. This person could very well have lived in the area of Edom/northwestern Arabia. As described in the book, this man was very wealthy and had an outstanding reputation. But he suddenly lost it all. After a lengthy period of time, his fortunes turned and he regained his wealth and status in life. The story of his life and his search for answers became part of an oral tale that was passed down through many generations. By the time the story reached the author of Job, its parameters were well established. But the author saw it as an ideal framework upon which to build a much larger story dealing with some of the great issues of life. Once the book of Job was written, its majestic quality was quickly recognized. It easily supplanted the much shorter original tale that soon disappeared entirely.

This story has many parallels with other ANE tales about innocent sufferers. But some major differences exist. For example, the author of Job takes the reader into the courts of heaven and reveals at the beginning of the story the exact cause of Job's suffering. The reader does not have to wonder about this cause until the very end. Another significant difference is the monotheistic background to the story. Whether the original tale was monotheistic is unknown.

The scenario above is obviously subjective, but not out of the question. Through the discoveries of archaeology, a number of ancient tales that were once thought to be purely fiction are now known to be embellishments on a historical person or event (Gordis 1965, 66). It is doubtful whether Job's historicity will ever be proven, but at least that possibility does exist.

COMMENTARY

I. PROLOGUE: JOB 1—2

BEHIND THE TEXT

The book of Job begins with a prologue—a skillfully constructed, prose narrative that is divided into six scenes. The first five scenes alternate back and forth between earth and heaven. The sixth is a short transition into the next major section—the dialogues. The scenes are as follows:

    A. Introduction of Job (1:1-5)
    B. The Examiner Questions Job's Righteousness and Integrity (1:6-12)
    C. Job's First Test: He Loses His Wealth and His Children (1:13-22)
    D. The Examiner Again Questions Job's Righteousness and Integrity (2:1-6)
    E. Job's Second Test: He Loses His Health (2:7-10)
    F. The Friends Arrive (2:11-13)

The prologue sets the stage by introducing us to the main human character (Job) and two divine characters (God and his Examiner [the Satan]). In scene one, we learn the basic facts about Job and his family. In scenes two and four, we are privy to a conversation between God and his Examiner over the reason for Job's piety. The Examiner believes Job is only righteous for what he can get out of it. God believes differently but permits the Examiner to test Job to see if his theory is correct. In scenes three and five, Job goes about his normal activities until he experiences four dreadful disasters and then a serious illness. Immediately his status changes from a righteous, wealthy, well-respected individual to a pauper in poor health. He never receives a single clue as to why he is the recipient of these calamities.

The method of Job's testing is similar to experiments in many science labs today. Scientists who are developing new drugs will add or remove single agents in order to test the reaction of each agent in combination with the others. The experiment proceeds, focusing on one agent at a time, until the correct combination is achieved. The Examiner is also conducting something of a scientific experiment. He is determined to prove that a person will only pursue a godly life when there is a connection with a reward system. His first experiment is a failure. No change is observed in Job's behavior. So he requests that God allow a second experiment involving Job's health. He is confident this is the key that will finally unmask Job as a spiritual fraud, but he fails again.

Once the stage is set, the Examiner disappears and is not heard from again. God also disappears until ch 38 where he delivers a magnificent oration. However, new characters make their appearance at the end of ch 2, and the action moves on into the main part of the book.

IN THE TEXT

A. Introduction of Job (1:1-5)

The first section of the prologue introduces us to the main character, whose name is the title of the book. We learn that he is a non-Israelite by the name of Job living somewhere to the east of Israel. He is very wealthy, he has a large family, and he possesses a sterling reputation as a follower of Israel's God. Job also regularly offers sacrifices of intercession as a precaution for his children's sanctity.

■ 1 Job's name (*'iyyôb*) is Semitic but non-Hebrew. It appears as early as the nineteenth century BC in the Egyptian Execration texts, and later in a list of Egyptian slaves (eighteenth century BC), the Alalakh tablets (eighteenth century BC), the Mari tablets (sixteenth century BC), the Amarna letters (fourteenth century BC), and the Ugaritic tablets (thirteenth century BC). The meaning of the original Semitic name is probably something like: "where is my father?" (Clines 1989, 10-11). This could be interpreted as a compensation name, indicating that the child's father had died before the child was born (Bowes 1988, 1:98-99). Or more likely, it could be an "implicit cry for divine help" meaning: "where is my (divine) father?" (Clines 1989, 11). This question was certainly much on Job's mind throughout the book.

Some have suggested that the name became associated in popular thinking with the Hebrew verb *'yb*, meaning "to hate." One of Job's complaints was that God hated him. He was God's "enemy," **the hated one** (*'ōyēb*; 13:24) (Gordis 1978, 10). But there is no evidence in the book of Job that God ever hated Job (Weiss 1983, 20). More likely, the name simply reflects the archaic origin of the story.

Job's home was located in the land of Uz (*'ûṣ*; rhymes with "boots"). The exact location of Uz is unknown, for there were multiple locations with this name in biblical times. One possibility is southern Edom/northwestern Arabia (Gen 36:28; 1 Chr 1:42; Lam 4:21). Edom had a strong reputation as a center of wisdom teachings (Jer 49:7-8; Obad 8-9). Two of the animals Job owned (camels and sheep) were common in this region. Also, the area is connected with Tema and Sheba (Job 6:19). The reference in Jer 25:20 is sometimes used in support of this region, but Jeremiah's Uz seems to be somewhere in the Sinai desert, between Egypt and the Philistines. Another possibility is northern Syria/northern Mesopotamia (Gen 10:23; 22:21; 1 Chr 1:17). The other two animals Job owned (oxen and donkeys) were better suited to this region. The area of Edom/northwestern Arabia seems to best fit all the facts of the story and is the location preferred by this writer. In any case, the name is non-Hebrew, thus contributing to the universal character of the story.

Job's character is described with four attributes, all of them of a religious nature. The first two (**blameless and upright**) are difficult to put into English, but they basically mean that Job's character was **complete** and **straight**. **Blameless** (*tām*) is an adjective from the verb *tmm*. It means that something is finished, completed. The adjective is sometimes defined in relation to its twin adjective *tāmîm*, which is used in connection with the sacrificial ritual. The sacrificial animal was to be *tāmîm*, that is, "without defect" (Lev 22:19). Hence, the KJV translates *tām* in v 1 as "perfect." But innocence in regard to sin, rather than perfection, is the meaning of Job's characteristic. He was "whole, free from sin, completely right with God, and at peace with his world" (Habel 1985, 86). He had reached a level of spiritual maturity/completeness that was pleasing to God and noticeable to everyone who knew him.

Upright (*yāšār*) refers to the behavior of those who are following the straight path of righteousness, turning neither to the right nor to the left (Prov 4:25-27). This behavior is not forced or hypocritical, but it proceeds from a heart that is devoted to God. The two adjectives *tām* and *yāšār* are linked together in other places in the OT, such as Ps 37:37 and Prov 2:7.

The third attribute, **he feared God** (*Elohim*), is a common description of those who acknowledge God's lordship through reverence and worship. Clines suggests that this attribute emphasizes "the emotion of fear felt by humans in the presence of God" (2003, 72). But it is really more than that. Fearing God means to submit one's life to the lordship of God, and then from that moment on, to conduct one's behavior in all the ways that God directs. This statement appears frequently in the Psalms with Yahweh as the object instead of God (e.g., Ps 15:4).

There it usually refers to Israel as *a community* that feared Yahweh. Here it describes one man who is extremely devoted to the God of Israel.

The use of **feared God** in Job 1:1 has another purpose in addition to identifying Job as a worshipper of Yahweh. This attribute is at the heart of the wisdom literature. The theme verse in Proverbs (1:7) emphasizes this point, and the concept is expressed again and again throughout the wisdom literature and some of the Psalms. Characterizing Job as a person who **feared God** is, in essence, placing him within the parameters of what it means to be a *wise* person. He was living up to the standard that the wisdom theology held up as the ideal.

The word for **God** (*Elohim*) is a very common Hebrew word appearing approximately 2,570 times in the OT. In the prologue the author uses it alternately with Yahweh—the covenantal name revealed to Moses at the burning bush (Exod 3:14-16; 6:2-3). The total number of names applied to God in the book is six: *El* (56x), *Eloah* (41x), *Yahweh* (32x), *Shaddai* (31x), *Elohim* (17x), and *Adonai* (1x) (Seow 2013, 271). Each name is indicated in the commentary when it appears (for further discussion on the meaning of each name, see Rose 1992, 4:1001-9).

Whereas the first two of Job's attributes are in parallel, the third and fourth are opposites. **Shunned** [*swr*] **evil** signifies the avoidance of or turning away from activities and attitudes that are displeasing to God. In the narrative literature of the OT, the word is used to describe the negative behavior of people who "turn away" from God (1 Sam 12:20). But in the wisdom literature and some psalms, the word describes the positive behavior of those who turn away from evil in order to serve God (Ps 37:27; Prov 3:7). The same thought is emphasized in Paul's admonition to the Thessalonians (1 Thess 5:22). The third and fourth attributes are linked together again and placed in a wisdom context in Job 28:28.

Thus, in a nutshell, Job was a man with whom God was extremely pleased. His inner spiritual life and his outward behavior embodied all that God desires for every human being—"clean hands and a pure heart" (Ps 24:4*a*). And he was also an example to those seeking to follow the way of wisdom. McKenna notes, "Every great civilization, nation, or institution is developed and sustained by the image of the person who exemplifies the values and aspirations of the culture" (1986, 29). Though not an Israelite, Job was that person who best exemplified the heart of Israelite culture.

■ **2** While large families are a thing of the past in most modern societies, Job's family was as ideal as a person could hope for in ancient times. A large family was seen as a blessing from God (Ps 127:3-5). The greater proportion of sons is an indication that sons were more highly prized than daughters in Israelite society. **Seven sons and three daughters** are numbers that add up to ten. All of these numbers signify completeness. This was an ideal family.

The sons are now grown and living in their own houses (Job 1:4). There is no mention of any daughters-in-law or grandchildren in Job's family. Such an omission would be highly unusual in the real world, but not unexpected in a story.

The author presents only the information that is necessary to tell the story of the central character Job. He does not get sidetracked with lesser characters.

■ **3** Job was also blessed with great wealth, as measured in the patriarchal terms of animals and servants. He owned **seven thousand sheep** (goats would certainly be included) and **three thousand camels, five hundred yoke of oxen**, and **five hundred** female **donkeys**. Again, the symbolism of the numbers is evident. Both groups of animals add up to ten—ten thousand or ten hundred. The **servants** to take care of them were numerous.

Modern readers pass hurriedly over this verse, assuming it is just an inventory of Job's animals; but the verse reveals far more than that. In fact, it raises an interesting question about Job's primary occupation. **Oxen** were farm animals used for plowing by sedentary persons who lived in houses and owned land. Farming could only take place in locations where there was sufficient rainfall, usually ten inches per year or more. The large number of oxen would indicate that Job had large land holdings. **Sheep** and goats were generally tended by people who lived in tents and moved from place to place with their flocks. The raising of these animals occurred in areas of lesser rainfall, and hence their owners usually lived in the dryer areas between the farmland and the desert. Sheepherders are usually classified as seminomads.

Camels were ideally suited for desert regions. They were the primary pack animals along the Arabian trade routes that brought spices and incense from Arabia to Egypt, Palestine, and Syria. Their owners were merchants and traders who were on the trail for weeks at a time, and they are classified as nomads. **Donkeys** were also pack animals that were used for carrying products, but they could not operate in very arid regions where camels could. In addition, donkeys were used on farms for plowing and hauling goods.

So what was Job—a farmer, a seminomad, or a nomad? In the ancient world a person usually had only one occupation. No doubt, the ancient reader of this story was puzzled at first by the variety of animals that Job owned. But then the light would have dawned. The mention of all of these animals in large numbers is a way of magnifying Job's wealth. He was occupied in several types of business activities. He had a central location that he called home and where he farmed. In addition to fields of grain, he also owned large olive orchards (29:6). He may have lived in a city (29:7) or on a large estate outside the city. But he was wealthy enough to hire servants to carry on other moneymaking activities for him far from his home. Because he conducted business in multiple places, a series of calamities was needed to destroy all of his livelihood (1:13-17).

Camels

According to the archaeological evidence, camels were probably not domesticated until the early Late Bronze period (1550-1200 BC). Even then, the evidence is very sparse. At first, camels seem to be limited to nomadic peoples in Arabia and southern Transjordan. Their value at that time was primarily for milk.

Sometime during the Late Bronze period they were first used as pack animals. They were especially effective along the Arabian incense route. The OT connects them mainly with people who lived along this route during the first millennium BC: Midianites (Judg 6:5), Amalekites (1 Sam 15:3), Ishmaelites (1 Chr 27:30), and the queen of Sheba (1 Kgs 10:2).

The mention of camels in the story of the patriarchs (Gen 12:16; 24:10-67; 30:43; 31:34; 32:15 [16 HB]; 37:25) has been much debated by scholars, because there is no archaeological evidence at present that camels were used in large caravans in the Middle Bronze period (2000-1550 BC). Thus, the mention of camels in Genesis may be an anachronism. This has relevance for the dating of the book of Job (→ Introduction: Date). In any case, three thousand camels would have been considered extreme wealth in any period of time.

He was the greatest man among all the people of the East concludes the description of Job's character (for a similar superlative statement with regard to a biblical character, see the description of Solomon in 1 Kgs 4:29-30 [5:9-10 HB]). The question this statement raises is: Greatest in what? Some regard this phrase as a reference to Job's wealth, that is, he was the wealthiest person in the East. However, there is abundant evidence of kings and others in ancient times who possessed more wealth than Job. A more likely interpretation is that it sums up all of Job's characteristics that have just been enumerated. His piety, his character, his family, and his wealth were all ideal. In essence, Job was a *superman*; better yet, a *supersaint*. He had it all. Of course, the author is embellishing Job's description here to make his point that Job was the greatest human being alive at the time. He was the ideal individual. We are being set up for the horrendous tragedy that will take place very shortly.

The East (*qedem*) usually refers to one of two different localities: southern Transjordan/northwestern Arabia (Judg 6:3), or northern Syria/northern Mesopotamia (Gen 2:8; 29:1; Num 23:7). In this context, the term could mean one or both of these geographic areas. This is probably the location of Uz, as well (→ Job 1:1). **The East** was also known for its wisdom, so this enhances Job's character as a wise person.

■ **4** Job's seven **sons** hosted regular family gatherings that rotated among their homes. There is every indication that these were joyous times of feasting. They were kind enough to invite their **three sisters**, who apparently still lived at home, to join them. For some unknown reason, Job and his wife did not attend these times of feasting. The passage does not clearly indicate the purpose of their gatherings. Some suggest that they celebrated an annual festival of seven days where each son took his turn as host (Pope 1973, 8). But the literal Hebrew "(in) the house of each (on) his day" points to each son's birthday as the occasion for their happy celebrations (→ 3:1 where the same phrase "his day" [*yômô*] refers to Job's "birthday").

We are given very few details about Job's family. We would expect some type of description about how the sons were involved with their father in the family business and farming operations. Instead, the only comment we have about the sons is that they liked to party. Thus, Whybray characterizes them as "irresponsible" (1998, 30). That may be true, but we have little evidence to go on. Perhaps their main purpose in the story is simply to set the stage for the future disaster when all the children will be together in one place at one time. Thus Job's grief is increased by a multiple of ten.

■ **5** Job cared deeply about his children. His concern for them even extended to offering sacrifices on their behalf in case they might have slipped during the time of feasting and said or done something offensive to God. So **early in the morning**, after the celebration had concluded the night before, Job was up interceding for his children. As the head of his household, he acted as their priest/mediator. This type of activity was certainly foreign to Israelite thinking after the inauguration of the Israelite priesthood and tabernacle under Moses. Only the priests offered the sacrifices, and then only at the official places of worship. However, this activity fits very well within the context of the patriarchal stories.

The exact details of Job's actions are unclear. What does "send and sanctify them" (NRSV) mean? According to Gordis, this double verbal form can be used to show the initiation of an action, meaning that Job "would begin purifying his children" after each feast (1978, 12). Others see the verb "send" as a separate action indicating that Job "would send servants to summon his children" to join him for a ritual that would "decontaminate them from any stain they might have incurred" (Clines 1989, 16). Still others suggest that the message Job "sent" to his children was a word of instruction to prepare themselves ritually through washings and change of garments before they participated in the burnt offering the next day (Rowley 1976, 29). There is not enough evidence in the text to settle the matter. And it is not even clear whether the children were present when Job offered the sacrifices. He may have offered the sacrifices alone.

"Sanctify them" (*qdš*; NRSV) means "he took all the necessary measures to ensure that they were acceptable to God as holy (see Exod 19:10, 14; 1 Sam 16:5)" (Seow 2013, 270). It is "an anticipatory statement that is immediately thereafter amplified" by the information about the particular sacrifice Job used to purify them (Clines 1989, 16-17).

The ritual for the **burnt offering** (*'ōlâ*) is described in Lev 1:1-17. The sacrificial animal (a bull, sheep, goat, turtledove, or pigeon) was completely consumed in the fire on the altar. That Job was able to do this after each feast for every one of his children is another indication of his great wealth. Normally, the purpose of a **burnt offering** was for atonement (Lev 1:4). But some passages indicate other purposes (e.g., for determining God's will [Num 23:1-3, 14-15, 29-30], or for requesting God's intervention [1 Kgs 18:37-38]). Of course, we do not know whether the non-Israelite Job was following Israelite practices exactly.

Some have tried to describe these feasts as drunken, rowdy orgies that needed forgiveness, but there is no indication in the text that they are condemned. Job's sacrifices were offered because **perhaps** his children had sinned. If Job had known that orgies were going on, he would not have used the word **perhaps**.

One can almost sense a generational issue here. Job's children were not bad kids. They just had not yet matured to the level of Job's spirituality. He was probably concerned that they were sometimes careless about religious matters or failed to recognize the subtleties of temptation.

So the purpose of his sacrifices was a precautionary activity to protect the purity of his children. Since he did not attend the feasts personally, he had no direct knowledge concerning whether his children had sinned, only that there was a possibility that they may have said or done something to grieve God.

Cursing is a vocal activity, so we would assume that Job was especially concerned about what they said. A later verse (Job 1:13) mentions that they were "drinking wine" at these celebrations. Perhaps he feared that one of his children had said something that was offensive to God while under the influence of alcohol. On the other hand, whatever sinning or cursing may have taken place was apparently done in secret (**in their hearts**), or at least privately among themselves. For the types of activities that constitute cursing God in the OT, see Deut 8:17; 9:4; 29:19 [18 HB]; Pss 14:1; 53:1 [2 HB]; Isa 14:13-14; 47:8, 10; Zeph 1:12 (Walton 2012, 60).

Job's actions typify those of caring parents in all cultures who worry excessively about their children. Often *doing something* provides a measure of relief to anxious parents. Wesley's comments on this verse emphasize the importance of praying regularly and specifically for each of our children (1765, 1518).

The verb **have sinned** (*ḥṭ'*) means "to miss or fall short of a mark." In biblical terminology, that mark is God's will or plan. Cursing God certainly falls under the category of sin. In fact, it is the most extreme form of sin, punishable by death (1 Kgs 21:10). Throughout the prologue, the phrase **cursed God** (*Elohim*) refers to uttering derogatory or evil words against God. It does not mean to request that another deity bring harm to God.

Cursed God is used as a literary catchword to link the scenes in the prologue together. In the first scene, Job's children may have cursed God (Job 1:5). In the second and fourth scenes, the Examiner predicts that Job "will surely curse you [God]" (v 11; 2:5). In the fifth scene, Job's wife encourages him to curse God (2:9). As we move out of the prologue and into Job's lament (ch 3), the author continues the theme of cursing, except he adds an element of surprise. Job is now cursing, as the Examiner predicted, but the object is his birthday rather than God (3:1).

The word for **cursed** (*qll*) does not appear in the Hebrew text of 1:5. Instead, the word "blessed" (*brk*) is used. Almost unanimously translators believe that "blessed" does not make sense in this context. The best explanation is that "blessed" has been substituted for **cursed** as a euphemism to avoid writing the blasphemous phrase **cursed God**. The substitution of an extremely opposite word would alert the reader that a change was made for religious reasons. The same change is made in v 11, 2:5, and 2:9. Similar substitutions are made in 1 Kgs 21:10 and Ps 10:3. Whether these changes were made by the original author or a later scribe is unknown.

Balentine is one of the few commentators who suggests that "blessed" may be the correct reading after all. He proposes that Job's fear is that his children have blessed God without first asking God for forgiveness (2006, 49), but the evidence is not strong enough to outweigh the traditional translation.

This verse contributes further evidence of Job's piety. Not only was his own spiritual condition impeccable and exemplary, but he also interceded for others on a regular basis. He went "beyond what might be considered as required for a righteous person" (Boss 2010, 17). He was truly a remarkable example of godliness, a "supersaint" in all aspects of his life.

FROM THE TEXT

1. **Job as a Non-Israelite.** The use of a non-Israelite as the main character in the story is one example of the author's genius. Could a genuine Israelite have asked the harsh questions that Job asks and accused God of the things that Job does and still be seen as righteous? Probably not, in the minds of many. But the author does not have to face this issue. He can let Job be completely honest and say anything he wants, since he is a non-Israelite.

Further, the whole non-Israelite setting for the story (e.g., names of places and characters, names for God) tells us that the author was not writing about an Israelite problem. He was writing about a universal problem that all human beings experience—unjust suffering. Thus, the book has had universal appeal ever since it was written.

2. **Sinless Job.** The description of Job given in 1:1 is crucial to understanding the story. Job was not just a nice guy, not just a person of honesty and integrity, not just a good father and outstanding citizen in his community. He was *the ideal* human being. He was completely devoted to God's will. He was an exemplary person of faith. He was fair, honest, compassionate, and righteous in his dealings with other people. And he avoided every kind of evil. Throughout the prologue the author emphasizes this description of Job again and again until there is no possibility of misconception on our part.

In v 3 Job is described as "the greatest man among all the people of the East." In v 8 God himself repeats the four characteristics of Job mentioned in v 1, and then he adds the superlative statement: "There is no one on earth like him." God repeats the same words exactly in 2:3. The author wants us to believe that Job was even better than Abraham, Moses, and David. He certainly succeeded, for no other OT character is described with such exalted characteristics.

Of course, this raised major concerns for many Jewish scholars who had trouble accepting Job, a non-Israelite, as greater than Israel's greatest heroes. "While some rabbis did not deny the possibility of a righteous Gentile, few would accept the idea that a Gentile could be more righteous than a Jew" (Balentine 2006, 45). The fact that Job was non-Israelite made him something of a patron saint to early Christian writers.

The Fathers of the Church, for example Jerome, Augustine, and Gregory the Great, regarded Job, the righteous Gentile, as a saint who was part of the true Christian community . . . even though he lived before the time of Christ. Further, as one who endured his sufferings patiently, Job not only exemplified Christian virtue; he also prefigured Christ. (Balentine 2006, 45)

For theological reasons primarily, commentators shy away from crediting Job with sinlessness. They are more comfortable with terms like: "a man of integrity," "a man of great piety," and "a man of untarnished character and devout faith." It is true; Job was all of these. But the combination of the four attributes in v 1 (which are repeated two more times in the prologue), plus the two superlative comments in vv 3, 8, and 2:3 ("the greatest man among all the people of the East" and "There is no one on earth like him"), plus the comment in 1:22 and again in 2:10 that he was *without sin* certainly present Job's spiritual condition as ideal. The whole point of the prologue is to reveal that Job was *without acts of sin in his life*, and therefore his suffering was unjustified.

He was accused of sinning by the three friends and by Elihu. He was encouraged to sin by his wife. And the Examiner predicted that he would turn against God and sin. But nowhere in the book is there any evidence that Job sinned during the events and conversations that ensued. This is not a pronouncement that he was perfect in character or that he had never sinned. Rather, it simply means that at the time of the events in the story he was in a proper relationship to God. Whatever sins he may have committed in the past were now forgiven. His heart was right with God and this was evident in his behavior. From the perspective of the OT, Job was a holy person who had no need to confess to God because he had no sin in his heart to confess. Clines rightly warns us:

> The often-repeated comment that the term [*tām*] does not mean that Job is sinless . . . is questionable; for the contrast in the book is almost invariably between the "righteous" and the "wicked" and there is no doubt that from the viewpoint of the author and the hero himself, Job is "righteous." That the righteous are imperfect is sometimes suggested . . . , but in Job's case the issue is never whether his sins are serious or slight but simply whether he is a sinner or not. (1989, 12)

In our contemporary world, we argue and wrestle over the fine points of theology, for example, the difference between sins and mistakes, the difference between acts of sin and the state of sin, and the origin of inherited depravity and its effects on every human being. We state our positions and come armed with proof texts and carefully reasoned arguments. The author of Job will have none of that. For him, simply stated, a sinner Job was not. He was an ideal, exemplary servant of God.

IN THE TEXT

B. The Examiner Questions Job's Righteousness and Integrity (1:6-12)

■ **6** The scene shifts to heaven in vv 6-12. The divine assembly has gathered to hear a word from **the Lord** (*Yahweh*). Throughout the prologue (and the epilogue) the author uses the Israelite covenantal name *Yahweh* to refer to God (→ v 1). This is a clear indication that the author is Israelite in both nationality and theology, and he is writing to an Israelite audience.

The nature of the divine realm has always been something of a mystery to humanity. We do learn in this passage that in heaven there are other beings besides God himself. The literal Hebrew phrase for **angels** is "sons of God" (*běnê hā'ĕlōhîm*), but they are not "sons" in a father-son relationship. The word "sons" here simply means the members of a certain group or classification—in this case, "all the beings of a divine nature who reside in the heavens." They are the servants or messengers of God who do his will/bidding. The NIV, following the LXX, uses the word **angels** for these beings, but in popular thinking people tend to think of angels as brilliant winged creatures in human form. The book of Job gives us no description of what these "sons of God" look like, so a better translation is probably "heavenly beings" (NRSV) or "members of the heavenly court" (NLT).

Other OT passages that support the concept of a heavenly court with multiple divine beings in obedience to God include: 1 Kgs 22:19-22 ("all the multitudes of heaven"); Pss 29:1 ("heavenly beings"); 82:1 ("great assembly"); 89:5 [6 HB] ("the assembly of the holy ones"); and 89:7 [8 HB] ("the council of the holy ones"). Further evidence is found in passages that use the plural "us" and "our" in statements made by God, such as Gen 1:26; 3:22; 11:7; and Isa 6:8. There is no hint of polytheism in any of these passages, although the idea may have been borrowed from other religions. The passage in 1 Kgs 22:19-22 seems to imply that on occasion God calls his heavenly court into session to hear their reports, ask for advice, and give them instructions. Such a meeting is described in Job 1:6.

Of all the divine beings gathered before God on this occasion, he is only interested in conversation with one of them called the **Satan** (*haśśāṭān*). By mentioning the **Satan** separately from the other divine beings, the author focuses our attention on him and creates the opportunity for the conversation that follows. In Hebrew *śāṭān* means: "adversary, enemy, accuser, one who challenges or tests another party." In Job the term always appears with the definite article attached (*haś-śāṭān*, meaning "the adversary"). Thus, it is a title, describing the role of this character in the narrative, not a personal name.

In the prologue of Job, and also in Zech 3:1-2, the **Satan** plays a unique role as the divine being who raises questions about people's piety and challenges their claims of righteousness. He is the heavenly skeptic who considers Job's reputation as given in Job 1:1-3 as questionable. He is the investigative detective who cuts through the surface perceptions of spirituality and demands proof of one's motivation. He is the Examiner who tests and probes and challenges people's faith. As Reyburn says, "Testing people is his job" (1992, 39). And he is given the power by God to bring disasters into people's lives as a means of confirming or disproving their claims. Disasters have a way of bringing out the true spiritual stature of a person. This divine being is the proverbial person from Missouri who says to each of us: "Show me your faith. Prove it!" In order to distinguish this divine being in Job from the evil person by the name of Satan in NT theology, we will use the title the Examiner when this character is mentioned in the commentary.

In the book of Job the Examiner appears only in the prologue (chs 1—2) and then disappears. So he is really a minor character in the book. His appearance is intended only to set the stage and frame the issues that will be the focus of the remainder of the book. None of the human characters in the book ever suggest that the Examiner is the actual or possible cause of Job's misfortunes. In fact, none of them are even aware that he exists. However, his appearance does raise an interesting question about his continued relationship with evil today. When people experience misfortune in their lives, should they assume that the Examiner is connected with it in some way? We will come back to this issue later in the commentary, but at the very least, we can say that the book of Job does not support the concept that the Examiner is the ultimate cause of trouble in our world.

The Examiner

Many concepts and words in the Bible have gone through a process of development. This should not be surprising, considering that the OT was written over a period of eight hundred to a thousand years and the NT was added after that. God's revelation did not stand still during that long period of time. It progressed in stages, climaxing finally in the revelation of Jesus Christ. Such concepts as: (1) the nature of the afterlife, (2) the final judgment, (3) the Messiah, and (4) the Satan have all experienced these stages of development. The evidence is found in the Bible itself.

Who is this character called "the Examiner" (the Satan)? Most Christians read the book of Job after they have already familiarized themselves with the character of Satan in the NT. They assume that Satan has the same characteristics in both Testaments, but that is not the case. In the NT, Satan is the archenemy of God who tempted Jesus three times (Matt 4:1-11), who enticed Judas to betray Jesus (Luke 22:3), and who opposed Paul's ministry (1 Thess 2:18).

In the book of Revelation he is kicked out of heaven after losing a war against Michael and the other angels (Rev 12:7-9). Later, at the end of time, he is imprisoned for a thousand years and then released for a brief period. Upon his release, he gathers all his demonic forces and makes one last charge against the heavenly hosts. But his final defeat is predicted, and he will be forced to endure eternal punishment in the lake of fire and sulfur (Rev 20:1-10). Satan in the NT is a demonic, personal source of evil who does everything he can to destroy God's kingdom.

The OT conception of the Satan is much different. The word *śāṭān* appears twenty-seven times, fourteen of which are in the prologue of the book of Job. The word is applied to both human (1 Sam 29:4; 2 Sam 19:22 [23 HB]; 1 Kgs 5:4 [18 HB]; 11:14, 23, 25; Ps 109:6) and supernatural characters (Num 22:22, 32; 1 Chr 21:1; Zech 3:1, 2 [2x]). In most of these passages, the best translation is "enemy" or "adversary." For example, in 1 Sam 29:4 the Philistine kings were afraid that David would turn against them and become their *śāṭān* ("enemy"). In Num 22:22, 32 the angel of the Lord who stood in the road and blocked Balaam's donkey is called a *śāṭān* ("adversary") of Balaam. Only in one passage in the OT (1 Chr 21:1) is the word used as the personal name of a demonic figure. In that passage it is the name of the being who incited David to take a census (but see 2 Sam 24:1). The book of Chronicles is one of the last books written in the OT (probably 450 to 300 BC), and it reflects a later development of the character of the Satan.

We do not know exactly when and how this development took place, but many scholars believe it happened under the influence of the Persian religion Zoroastrianism during the period when the Jews were under the control of the Persian Empire. Other writings that portray the Satan in a similar demonic fashion are found in the intertestamental literature called the Apocrypha and the Pseudepigrapha, which come from late Judaism and early Christianity. Some scholars suggest that the Satan's character in Job is a response to Persian dualism (Seow 2013, 273-74). The author was trying to show that the Satan was subordinate to God, not equal. More likely, the conception of the Satan in Job existed before Israel came in contact with the Persians.

With that background in mind, the best way to view the OT description of the Satan is as a figure in the process of development. In the book of Job the Satan is not a demonic figure at all. Rather, he is a part of the heavenly court along with other "sons of God," and he has a specific role to play of testing and challenging people's faith, "probing human behavior according to God's directives in search of truth and faithfulness" (Balentine 2006, 52). Later, in the postexilic period his character begins to change under the influence of Jewish interaction with other cultures.

By the time of the NT period he is known as the demonic archenemy of God. He is called the devil and is equated with the serpent (Gen 3) who tempted Adam and Eve. And his role at the end of time is described in the book of Revelation. All of this is to say that it is best to put aside one's NT view of Satan when reading the book of Job. The closest that the author comes to mentioning a character like the NT Satan is the reference to "death's firstborn" and "the king of terrors" (18:13-14).

The history of Christianity is loaded with commentaries on Job that seek to equate the OT Satan with the NT character by the same name (see ACCS, 6:4-6, 11 for some examples). Today there is more of an honest attempt to describe the character of the Satan in the context of the OT. Thus, we will use the term "the Examiner" in this commentary. A summary of his description as given in the book of Job is as follows: (1) he is one of the divine beings in the heavenly court; (2) he has a specific mission from God to test and examine the validity of people's claims of piety; (3) he is given the power to bring disasters into people's lives to aid in his investigation; (4) he is under the control of God. He cannot bring disaster without asking permission. For certain, he is not the demonic figure of NT theology, and he is not the serpent in the Garden of Eden who tempted Adam and Eve.

■ 7 A dialogue begins between Yahweh and the Examiner. It seems very innocent at first. **Where have you come from?** Yahweh asks. This inquiry is not an admission of ignorance concerning the Examiner's activities. It is simply a way for Yahweh to draw the Examiner into conversation. The Examiner's response is: **From roaming throughout the earth, going back and forth on it.** The Examiner is not trying to be evasive or naive. His intent is to inform Yahweh that he has carried out his assignment as the chief Examiner of humanity, investigating the entire earth (see Zech 4:10).

The implication gathered from the ensuing conversation is that the Examiner is responsible for observing the activities of all human beings. Hartley's observation that he is "like an emperor's spy looking for any secret disloyalty to the crown" (1988, 73) is a little too harsh. He is neither a spy nor the head of God's secret police. Rather, his task is to observe people and accumulate evidence concerning individuals who need divine attention for one reason or another. Part of his assignment is to bring accusations against those whom he believes are hypocrites or spiritual frauds.

The word **roaming** (šwṭ) is a little too casual. The same verb is used by David in his instructions to his officials concerning the census. He tells them to investigate thoroughly the entire land so that he will have an accurate report on the size of the population (2 Sam 24:2; see also Num 11:8; Jer 5:1; Amos 8:12). In a similar way, the Examiner travels widely and purposely to conduct a careful investigation of the entire human population.

■ 8 Yahweh's next question is: **Have you considered my servant Job?** Obviously, he is proud of Job, for Job is the most outstanding example of piety in the world (**There is no one on earth like him**). Certainly the Examiner would have noticed Job if he had traveled over the entire earth; and he would have thought deeply about whether Job's superb reputation as a righteous man was true. No doubt, Yahweh suspected already that the Examiner would challenge the legitimacy of Job's righteousness. So he repeats the author's description of Job as given in Job 1:1, confirming that this is an accurate account of the chief character in the story.

If you were the owner of a factory and visitors had just made a tour, you would probably ask them at the end of the tour if they had seen the most outstanding machine or product in your factory. That is exactly what Yahweh wants to press home to the Examiner here. In effect, he is saying, "Did you see my servant Job? He is everything I want human beings to be—a supersaint. You certainly will not find any evidence that he is a spiritual fraud. Don't you agree?"

The description of Job as **my servant** is further evidence of God's extreme pleasure with Job. He ranks up there with Israel's greatest heroes. This phrase is usually reserved for people with outstanding religious credentials, for example,

Abraham, Isaac, and Jacob (Exod 32:13), Moses (Num 12:7), and the prophets (Isa 20:3). The Babylonian king Nebuchadnezzar is the only other non-Israelite in the OT called "God's servant" (Jer 25:9; 43:10). This has nothing to do with piety or obedience, but only with the fact that Nebuchadnezzar was used by God to destroy Judah in the sixth century BC.

■ **9-11** The Examiner's attitude immediately changes to skepticism. **Does Job fear God** [*Elohim*] **for nothing?** is a rhetorical question (v 9). The implication of this skeptical remark is: "Job may be a supersaint outwardly, but he is only righteous because of how greatly you have blessed him. Look at all his possessions and his ideal family. No wonder he is righteous. Anyone will serve you, Yahweh, if you bribe them with enough blessings." The Examiner believes that God has gained Job's obedience by showering him with one blessing after another. He points out how Job's wealth has increased substantially, **so that his flocks and herds are spread throughout the land** (v 10). In addition, God has put a barrier (**hedge**) around Job to protect him from danger and evil. Thus, the motivation for Job's piety is based solely on his secure life and abundant rewards.

The only way to prove that this connection between piety and rewards is false is to remove the rewards. The Examiner believes that if Job's rewards are taken away, he will turn against God and will do so openly (**to your face** [v 11]), not inwardly, as Job's sons may have done (v 5). So he challenges God to prove him wrong by removing all of Job's rewards. Only then will God know whether Job is truly committed to him.

In v 11 the Examiner uses two imperative verbs (**stretch out** and **strike**, or lit. "touch") to indicate his determination to get to the bottom of this issue. In Jer 1:9 these verbs are linked in a positive context in the account of Jeremiah's calling ("Then the LORD reached out his hand and touched my mouth"). But more frequently they are used in contexts that speak of touching someone with the intent of bringing harm (Exod 3:20; 2 Sam 14:10). Here the Examiner calls for God to break down the hedge of protection and bring harm to everything that belongs to Job—his family and possessions. Job needs to experience the troubles of life in order to see whether his faith will continue or crumble.

For a second time, the word for **curse** is not in the Hebrew text. It is implied by the use of its opposite—"bless" (→ v 5).

■ **12** Interestingly, Yahweh never attempts to refute the Examiner's charges concerning the hedge and the blessing in v 10. His silence probably should be interpreted as his concurrence that the Examiner is partially correct: "It is true. I have blessed Job abundantly and provided a hedge of protection around him. And furthermore, I am pleased to do so for one who is so obedient to me."

Yahweh knows that the accusations against Job are false. And he is willing to allow pain into Job's life in order to prove that the Examiner is wrong. So he accepts the Examiner's challenge and allows him to harm Job's family and possessions: **everything he has is in your power**. The next section describes how devastating the Examiner can be. However, Yahweh places one limitation on the

Examiner's assault: **on the man himself do not lay a finger**. He cannot touch Job's person, only the things belonging to him. Yahweh does not want Job killed, because that would end the test. No doubt, the Examiner is confident the test will come out the way he predicted, but there is no description of what he is thinking as he leaves.

FROM THE TEXT

1. God Is Responsible. Who is responsible for the harm that will come to Job in the next section? We wish we could place the blame on the Examiner as the direct cause. This would certainly make our understanding of God a lot easier. But in 1:12 the Examiner is plainly under the control of God. He cannot do anything without permission. Therefore, the one who grants him this permission is ultimately responsible. In 2:3 God even admits that he is responsible, and the author confirms this in 42:11.

Why would God lower the hedge of protection and allow such devastation into the life of his favorite righteous person? Does this not cast God in a rather dismal light? How can he be a good God and allow such events to happen? This is the age-old question of God's power versus his goodness. The reason why God approves Job's awful tragedy is not explained, other than in its relationship to the test. It is foolish and speculative to try to push beyond that and analyze the mind of God. But in a similar vein, God's participation in the test of Abraham (Gen 22:1-14) is not explained either. The interpretation of both tests needs to focus on the reason for the test and the response of the person being tested, not the character of God. Some issues have no good explanation and remain unresolved.

If God is omniscient, why does he allow the test to proceed? He could just tell the Examiner the answer and be done with it, and in doing so he would save Job a lot of pain and anguish. This question challenges God's knowledge. How much does God know about the future? Theologians have argued this question for a long time. Some describe God as totally omniscient about every human activity—past, present, and in the future. Others limit his knowledge to the range of possibilities. God has to wait like everyone else to see how events actually turn out. The answer to this question will have to wait until we have more evidence from the book about the nature of God's knowledge.

What we can say for sure is this: The description of God to this point is of one who believes that Job will triumph in the test. God has complete confidence that Job's faith is genuine because he knows Job thoroughly. But the test needs to take place so that all heaven and earth will know that while piety may be rewarded, truly righteous people do not serve God for what they can get out of it. There is a higher motivation. Job's response is needed to prove this.

2. Challenges to Israel's Faith. By this point in the narrative, one senses that the stakes are higher than simply whether Job is righteous. The Examiner is using his skepticism of Job's character to challenge two basic concepts in Israelite belief. The main attack is against the traditional Hebrew wisdom theology as expressed in numerous passages, such as Lev 26, Ps 1, and the book of Proverbs. The wisdom theology believed that righteousness and rewards/success were related. If people serve God, they will be blessed. If they do not serve God, they will experience bad consequences. Therefore, everyone should desire to serve God because they will be rewarded in some way. In modern terminology, this is closely related to *the gospel of success*. The focus of the Examiner's challenge is on the motivation for righteousness. If people live righteous lives only because it improves their well-being, then they are not really righteous. They are only self-interested success seekers. Such so-called righteousness is only a means to an end.

The second challenge is subtler, but even more devastating. It concerns the nature of God himself. Is God truly good and worthy of reverence, or is he only a *rich uncle* who passes out rewards to gain respect? The Examiner's challenge implies that God is not such a good person after all. He only receives humanity's obedience and worship because he can grant them favors.

Thus, in just a few verses of ch 1, we are presented with a tremendous challenge to the integrity of God and the Hebrew faith. Much is at risk here if Job turns against God as the Examiner predicted. At this point, the issue has to do with the nature of God and why people serve him. We have not yet gotten to the problem of suffering.

IN THE TEXT

C. Job's First Test: He Loses His Wealth and His Children (1:13-22)

The third section of the prologue describes events that occur on earth again, some unknown length of time after the end of scene two. This scene takes us back to the family celebrations mentioned in v 4. The children are gathered at the home of the eldest brother enjoying one of their regular feasts. Job remains at his own home, while the care of his animals continues in separate places under the direction of the servants. The stage is set for a series of four sudden disasters that leave Job and the reader breathless. It is clear that the characters of scene three are completely unaware of the heavenly conversations that have taken place in scene two. In order to appreciate the full emotional impact of these events on Job, one should read scenes one (vv 1-5) and three (vv 13-22) in sequence and skip scene two momentarily. Nowhere in scene three does the author mention the cause of the disasters. However, the assumption is that all of them were caused by the Examiner because of the evidence from scene two.

■ **13-15** Our attention is now focused on one of the celebrations enjoyed by Job's children. This one happens to be **at the oldest brother's house** (v 13). One new addition to the description given earlier in v 4 is the mention of **wine**, perhaps an indication of lavishness.

The four catastrophes that descend upon Job all happen in rapid succession. Good compares them to a fireworks display "where one shower of stars explodes into another and that into a third" (1990, 196). The author uses a familiar storytelling technique of placing each disaster in a common format that describes how Job received the message. In each case only one person survives the disaster and brings the awful news to Job in poetic form. While the first messenger is telling his sad tale, the second arrives. And as the second is finishing his report, the third arrives. This continues until all four reports are given. So the four disasters are linked together in close relationship, heightening the impact of their announcement and the severity of the blow against Job. We must wait until the very end of the fourth report to discover Job's reaction to all of this. Usually one disaster is enough to flatten most of us for days at a time, but sometimes life is especially cruel, bringing problems in bunches. Such was Job's situation. We have to admire the Examiner for knowing how to really *hurt a guy*.

The first messenger begins his report by noting the farm activities with which he was associated. It was a normal day. **The oxen were plowing and the donkeys were grazing nearby.** The mention of **plowing** is our only clue as to the time of year when this took place. In Near Eastern countries the dry summer months leave the ground as hard as a rock. Plowing usually takes place in the late fall and winter months, after the fall rains have softened the soil enough to work a plow.

Suddenly a group of marauding bandits from the area of Sheba fell on the servants, killing all except one and taking the **oxen** and **donkeys** away. The messenger stresses the fact that he is the only one to escape this disaster. His literal comment is: ***And only I escaped, I alone, to report to you.***

Although **Sabeans** (šĕbā' = Sheba) are mentioned in Isa 45:14 as a tall race of people in Nubia, Africa, it is unlikely that people from south of Egypt would be raiding Job's animals. More likely, Job's raiders were from the southern Arabian Peninsula, particularly the country of Yemen today. The queen of Sheba who visited Solomon (1 Kgs 10:1-13) was from this area. The Sabean territory was the originating point of the spice and incense trade. In the first millennium these people used camel caravans to transport their goods all across the ANE. If these were the people intended by the author of Job, one wonders why they would be interested in Job's oxen and donkeys rather than his camels.

The principal objection to this location is its great distance from Palestine (approximately 1,200 miles). But it is probable that the author purposely intended to name people who lived a great distance away (→ "Sabeans and Chaldeans" sidebar at Job 1:17). There may also be a closer connection with northern and central Arabia. Over time, the Sabeans of southern Arabia established caravansaries (way stations) along the major trade routes for the benefit of their caravaners. A small group of Sabeans from the south may have resettled in northern Arabia to help facilitate these way stations. This may be the background for the association of Sheba with Tema in 6:19 and with Dedan in Gen 10:7 and 25:3.

■ 16 The second messenger arrives as the first is still finishing his story. His message also conveys the news of a great disaster, this time on the sheep. No one profited from this disaster as both **the sheep and the servants** were killed. This disaster was caused by an act of nature—probably lightning. **The fire of God** (*Elohim*) only occurs in this passage in the OT, but similar phrases are found elsewhere: fire of/from Yahweh (Num 11:1; 16:35; 26:10; 1 Kgs 18:38), fire from heaven (2 Kgs 1:10, 12, 14), fire from Yahweh from heaven (Gen 19:24), and unfanned fire (Job 20:26). In each passage the fire is seen as a divine instrument of destruction, thus implicating God in its occurrence.

■ 17 The third messenger delivers a report that is similar to the first, only it is the **Chaldeans** who are the bandits this time. Their attack is directed against the camels, the last group of Job's animals. Here a further detail about the plan of attack is revealed: **the Chaldeans formed three raiding parties** in order to accomplish their raid. The reason for this is not given, but perhaps the information is intended to show the futility of escape when attacked from three directions. Such a military strategy is well-known in the OT (Judg 7:16; 9:43; 1 Sam 11:11; 13:17).

The Chaldeans (*kaśdîm*) were an ethnic group in southern Mesopotamia who first appeared in the ninth century BC. They were dominated at the time by the Assyrians. During the latter part of the seventh century, they seized control of Babylonia and formed the Neo-Babylonian Empire. With the help of the Medes, they eliminated the Assyrians. The Neo-Babylonian Empire lasted until 539 BC when it was conquered by the Persian king Cyrus. One of the Chaldean rulers was Nebuchadnezzar, who destroyed Jerusalem in 587 BC.

As with the Sabeans (Job 1:15), the same problem of identification with the traditional homeland of the Chaldeans applies here. The Chaldeans lived approximately five hundred miles east of Palestine, as the crow flies. But no one followed the crow across the Arabian desert. The normal route was to follow the Fertile Crescent northward through northern Mesopotamia and around the northern end of the desert and then head southwest through Syria. This distance was about three hundred miles farther than the direct route. Again, it is unlikely that people from so far away would have conducted a raid on Job.

However, some Chaldeans lived closer. Genesis 22:21-22 connects the Chaldeans ("Kesed") with Aram and northern Mesopotamia. It could be that groups of Chaldeans had migrated to parts of northern Mesopotamia. This would place them in closer proximity to Palestine.

A third possibility connects these Chaldeans with those who moved to Tema in the Arabian desert with Nabonidus in the sixth century BC. This would be a more likely point of origin for raiders on Edom. This possibility has implications for the dating of the book (→ Introduction: Date). In any case, the Israelites would have known little about the Chaldeans until the rise of the Neo-Babylonian Empire. And then, their knowledge would not have identified them as a raiding party. The Chaldeans at that time were one of the major powers in the Near East.

Sabeans and Chaldeans

There is a strong likelihood that the names of these ethnic groups were chosen for two specific reasons—their direction (→ "The Disasters as Great Literature" sidebar at 1:18-19) and their great distance from Israel. Many Israelites in the middle of the first millennium would have recognized the names "Sabeans" and "Chaldeans," but they would have known little about them. Both of these groups lived too far from Israel for any meaningful contact. Today, it would be like saying people from Nepal and Mongolia attacked the United States.

When the author of Job named the bandits who attacked Job from the south, he could have chosen the most likely suspects—the Midianities, the Edomites, or the Amalekites. But this would only have aroused nationalistic sentiments in the mind of the reader and left the impression that this was just another border conflict perpetrated by known marauders. These groups had a long history of harassing Israel and other nations. Likewise, when he named the bandits from the north, he could have chosen the Syrians. But because all these groups were closer to Israel and better known, they did not suit his purpose. He wanted to add an additional element of mystery by forcing Job and his readers to consider how people from so far away could have caused these disasters. We can well imagine that when Job heard the names of these people (the Sabeans and the Chaldeans) he immediately sensed that this was more than just a small border raid by local marauders. This series of disasters was so unlikely that it pointed to a Higher Being. Somehow God was connected to these dreadful events.

■ **18-19** The fourth disaster is the most devastating. The loss of Job's **sons and daughters** meant the end of his family lineage (v 18). Animals and servants could be replaced over a period of time with lots of hard work, but the loss of children was especially cruel. This disaster was caused by another act of nature. **A mighty wind swept in** from the east off the Arabian **desert** (v 19). Again, this was unexpected, as the normal weather patterns move from west to east in the Near East. One imagines something like a tornado here, but no description of the wind is given other than that it was **mighty**. Some commentators connect this wind with the sirocco winds that blow in from the desert, but these are known more for their intense heat than their strength to blow down a house.

Job's ten children **were feasting and drinking wine at the oldest brother's house**. Whatever the building materials were in his house, they were not strong enough to withstand the wind. No doubt, the children were huddled inside for protection, but the house fell in on them and killed them all. **Four corners** indicates the totality of the house's destruction. The Hebrew word for **them** (*hannĕ'ārîm*) is the same word translated as "servants" in vv 15-17. Here the context clearly calls for an identification with Job's children who were in the house. Again, only one servant escaped to bring Job the report.

The Disasters as Great Literature

As commentators repeatedly point out, the author has woven into this section a number of skillful literary techniques. First, there are four disasters. The number four "symbolizes the completeness of the ruin" (Clines 1989, 30). Other passages where disasters occur in groups of four are: Ezek 14:12-23; Zech 1:18-21 [2:1-4 HB]; and Rev 9:13-15. Second, the four disasters come from the four points of the compass. The Sabeans are from the south, the lightning is a part of storms that normally come in from the west, the Chaldeans are from the north, and the mighty wind sweeps in from the desert on the east. Third, there is an alternation back and forth in the nature of the disasters. Disasters one and three are human caused. Disasters two and four are acts of nature.

Fourth, there is always only one person who survives the disaster and brings a report to Job. And each messenger arrives just as the preceding messenger is finishing his report. So there is an accumulative buildup of tension in the story for maximum emotional effect.

Fifth, all four disasters are unexpected and unlikely. Like a bolt of lightning out of a cloudless sky, they suddenly transform Job's peaceful world into chaos.

There is something mysterious about how all this could have happened in such a short period of time. The author skillfully uses the mystery of the disasters to challenge the typical human way of thinking about tragedy. When things go extremely wrong, people tend to look for a cause and to assign blame in order to relieve the emotional impact that always comes with such events. But Job has no one to blame. He has no one to sue. He has no one on whom to project his anger and grief. The reason for these disasters is unknown to Job. Therefore, he has to endure the whole burden of these tragic events in his own soul. These types of details cause us to marvel at the literary skill of the author.

■ **20-21** Job's first response to the four disasters is the traditional one of grief. He tears his robe, shaves his head, and enters into a time of mourning. There are five active verbs in v 20, indicating an immediate physical response to the report from the messengers. First, Job **got up** implying that he was sitting throughout the report from the messengers. Then he **tore his robe**, which refers to ripping a tear in one's outer garment (→ 29:14 on the nature of Job's clothing). There are numerous examples of this practice in the OT. They usually occur after a person has received dreadful news (e.g., Jacob [Gen 37:34], Joshua [Josh 7:6], David [2 Sam 1:11], Ezra [Ezra 9:3], and Mordecai [Esth 4:1]; also Caiaphas [Matt 26:65]).

He **shaved his head** is another long-standing expression of grief (Isa 15:2; Jer 16:6; 41:5; Ezek 7:18; Amos 8:10; Mic 1:16). The fourth verb, he **fell to the ground**, indicates that Job prostrated himself on the ground before the Lord. He was probably kneeling with his face on the ground, for the fifth verb is: he **bowed down**. Some versions translate the fifth verb as "worshiped" (NJPS, NRSV). The fourth and fifth verbs are indications of Job's submission to a higher authority. He does not yet know why these disasters happened to him in such a brief period of time, but already he senses a supernatural involvement. Later he will plead with

God to give him a full explanation, but for now he can only bow in agony before his Creator.

Every culture has its own unique customs for expressing grief. These are usually customs of long standing that have become deeply ingrained in the society. Probably the majority of the population cannot even explain why they do them. They just know this is the way one is supposed to express grief. Pope notes that the customs of "tearing one's robe" and "shaving one's head" as a sign of grief existed in other Semitic cultures of the ANE, such as Assyria and Ugarit (1973, 15). This would indicate that the Israelites adopted these long-standing practices from other cultures. Interestingly, the Mosaic law actually forbids the "shaving of one's head" (Lev 19:27-28; 21:5; Deut 14:1), probably because of connections with pagan rites of lacerating the skin. But the Law was not successful in rooting out this practice among the Israelites, for it continued throughout their history. Apparently, the practice was already a part of Israelite culture before the Law was written, and so the Law was ineffective in preventing it. Since Job was a non-Israelite, there was no restriction for him with this practice.

Job's second response is vocal and poetic: "**Naked I came from my mother's womb, and naked I will depart. The Lord gave and the Lord has taken away; may the name of the Lord be praised**" (Job 1:21). The meaning of the first sentence is clear: "I was born with nothing, and I will die with nothing" (GNT). The dead cannot take any of this world's goods with them into the afterlife. But scholars have noted the strange way it is worded. The Hebrew actually reads: "Naked I came forth from the womb of my mother, and naked I will return thither." The second clause sounds like he thinks he will return to his mother's womb when he dies. But that is hardly likely. Probably the simplest and most likely explanation is that the author has created a mixed metaphor whose parts should be kept separate. The first metaphor describes birth as the coming forth from a mother's womb. The second metaphor likens death to a return to the dust of the ground (Gen 3:19). "Nakedness" is the connection that binds the two metaphors together. We come forth and we return "naked" of this world's goods (see Eccl 5:15 [14 HB]; 1 Tim 6:7).

Job, then, moves quickly to expand on his first statement. Even though we enter and depart this world with nothing, we do accumulate some quantity of goods in the interval in between. From the biblical standpoint these goods are all gifts from God that illustrate his grace toward his creatures and demand our accountability and stewardship (**The Lord gave**). Some may also be God's rewards for our obedience. But now God has taken away all the goods Job has accumulated over his entire life (**the Lord has taken away**). Job is going to have to go on living without them.

What is extremely interesting here is that Job does not point the finger of blame at the Sabeans or the Chaldeans or even the forces of nature. The severity, the totality, and the suddenness of his losses are so great that he disregards all secondary causes and attributes the entire group of disasters to God. In his mind, his losses cannot be just a coincidence; this has all the earmarks of the hand of God. By saying this, Job is acknowledging that God has the right to do as he wishes. However, we need to avoid all attempts to generalize Job's situation to all the problems in life. Clines rightly observes that this passage does not support the view that God is "the author of everything that occurs in the world. Job is making no global statement of divine causality, but a pious utterance of his sense of how entirely his fate lies in the hands of God" (1989, 38).

Job concludes his brief comments by directing our attention away from his own grief and focusing it on Yahweh (**may the name of the L**ORD **be praised**). The meaning of this statement is that God is truly worthy of receiving our praise and we should honor him by doing so. **Be praised** (*brk*) can also be translated ***be blessed***. Frequently the OT uses *brk* to describe the activity of God in blessing his people. It means "to endue with power for success, prosperity, fecundity, longevity, etc." (Oswalt 1980a, 1:132). However, it can also be used to express human praise back to God for his goodness. This latter usage is what Job intends. The same wording is found in Ps 113:2. **The name of the L**ORD is a synonym in the OT for "the Lord."

Christian scholars have sometimes connected Job's comments here with Jesus' statement in the Sermon on the Mount concerning the importance of laying up treasures in heaven rather than on earth (Matt 6:19-21) (e.g., see Augustine [ACCS, 6:9]). However, Jesus' statement connects the loss of our treasures with moths, rust, and thieves, rather than God. Job focuses on the fact that earthly treasures are only temporary gifts from God that he can take back at any time.

Job 1:21 and 12:9 are the only places in the book where Job himself, a non-Israelite, uses the Hebrew word *Yahweh* (**the L**ORD) for God's name. Is it likely that he would use the Israelite covenantal name for God? Probably not. What we have here is "a Hebrew ritual formula" (Gordis 1978, 18) that is so well-known that the author feels compelled to depart briefly from the non-Israelite setting of the story, even though this reveals his true identity as an Israelite. The formula also serves the author's purpose in identifying "Job's God as the very same God whom Israel worshiped" (Smick 1988, 4:883, n. 21).

What exactly does Job's pronouncement in 1:21 indicate about his state of mind? Is it really possible to be this cool, calm, and collected following the loss of ten children and all one's wealth? And is this the way God wants each of us to respond when faced with great losses? Or does Job live on a different spiritual plain than the rest of us?

Some have tried to psychoanalyze Job and compare his reaction to the stages of grief that people go through following the death of a family member. They have suggested that at this point in the story Job is demonstrating signs of denial and repression. The impact of his losses has not sunk in. He has not yet faced reality. It is impossible to pinpoint what the author intended here, but denial is certainly one possibility, especially so since Job's emotions change dramatically in ch 3 and following. There seems to be some development in his emotional stability between the prologue and the later chapters.

Others take more of a philosophical approach. Clines thinks that Job's statement is an example of "pessimistic wisdom," similar to what we find in the book of Ecclesiastes (1989, 36). It reflects a soul that has experienced the face of death and recognized that all this world's goods and rewards are nothing but "vanity." "His words simply verbalize the psychological identification with the dead that he has already made by his ritual acts of mourning" (ibid.).

A third interpretation is that Job's reaction reveals "resignation to the divine will" (Hartley 1988, 78). Job recognizes that God is sovereign over all of life, and he has the right "to give" and "to take" whatever and whenever he chooses. The only good option we have as human beings is to resign ourselves to God's will and give praise to his name.

Janzen suggests that Job is simply mouthing words without personal meaning, formal and conventional words taught to him by his culture and religion that mask his true feelings of grief (1985, 31). Van Wolde concludes that Job "speaks in the standard formula of faith, but hasn't yet worked through his own suffering" (1997, 16).

Other scholars take a more positive fifth approach. Job is an example of outstanding faith and trust in God. He is "a model of submissive piety and obedient surrender to a God whose ways are not our ways and whose thoughts are not our thoughts (Isa 55:8)" (Alden 1993, 62). Job is still the supersaint of 1:1-5. He has not turned against God in spite of huge losses beyond human comprehension. Whether we can follow his example or not is not the issue.

There certainly will not be unanimous agreement on the interpretation of v 21, but one important piece of evidence is v 22, which is probably the best commentary on v 21. There the author plainly reveals his hand. It is not Job's emotional state of mind that is the key issue. Rather, it is Job's victory over the Examiner that the author wants to emphasize. Job has passed the test the Examiner designed. He **did not sin**. He did not curse God as the Examiner had predicted. Instead, he bowed in submission to God and worshipped. He thus confirmed his own reputation as stated in v 1 and vindicated God's trust in him ("There is no one on earth like him" [v 8]). We are left with the strong conviction that Job is a truly remarkable person indeed.

However, lest we think that no other human's conduct could be the same as Job's, consider the life of Horatio Spafford. Alden notes that Spafford, too, lost his children—four of them—on a boat crossing the Atlantic. Somehow, he was able to gain control of his emotions and compose the words to the hymn "It Is Well with My Soul" in 1873 (1993, 61).

■ **22 In all this** is interpreted by some as a reference to Job's *words* in v 21, meaning he did not say anything sinful in his initial remarks. This is supported by the parallel passage in 2:10, which definitely refers to Job's speech. But more likely, the phrase is meant to summarize Job's *entire behavior* so far in reaction to all his calamities (1:14-19). "In spite of everything" (GNT) he has maintained his faith in

God and his sterling reputation. He has done nothing to diminish God's pleasure with his life.

Job certainly did not turn against God and **sin** (*ḥṭ'*). He may have believed that God caused these disasters, but he was not willing to curse God or accuse him of any evil motive. Neither did he charge **God with wrongdoing**. The Hebrew for **wrongdoing** (*tiplâ*) has been translated many ways: "anything unseemly" (Gordis 1978, 6), "something that was unworthy" (Reyburn 1992, 55), "contempt" (Habel 1985, 94), "blame" (Pope 1973, 17), "sinful folly" (Youngblood 1980, 2:978), something "contrary to his holy nature" (Hartley 1988, 78, n. 23). Perhaps something like the following is what is intended here: "He found in God no inappropriate, reproachable, or blameworthy action" (Chapman 1967, 32). He may have been justified in charging God with wrongdoing (Whybray 1998, 32), especially if he had known about the conversation between God and the Examiner in vv 6-12. But he refused to be disrespectful or question God's motives in bringing so much grief into his life.

No doubt, by the end of v 22, the reader is curious about the reaction to the disasters from other members of Job's family, such as his wife (2:9) and his brothers and sisters (42:11). They, too, must have felt his pain. But the narrative quickly moves on to the next scene and leaves us wondering. The story is totally about Job, so only the most essential information that is relevant to him is presented by the author.

D. The Examiner Again Questions Job's Righteousness and Integrity (2:1-6)

The fourth section of the prologue takes us back to heaven where the heavenly court is in session again. After the formalities of the initial conversation between Yahweh and the Examiner, Yahweh gets down to business. He is still extremely proud of Job, and he makes a point of this by noting how Job has continued to maintain his sterling reputation and righteousness. However, Yahweh is somewhat annoyed that the Examiner talked him into testing Job. He is unhappy that his prime example of piety on earth is suffering. For his part, the Examiner is also unhappy that the results did not turn out as predicted, but he is not yet ready to concede defeat. He requests permission to test Job again at a deeper level of suffering. Yahweh agrees to the second test, and so the Examiner leaves to carry it out.

■ **1-2** In scene four the heavenly court (lit. "the sons of God") is assembled again before Yahweh as in scene two. Since the wording in vv 1-2 is almost identical to 1:6-7, see the comments there. Repetition of the earlier dialogue is a common storytelling technique. Again the Examiner (the **Satan**) is singled out for special attention. Yahweh wants to know where he has been. The Examiner responds with the same answer (except for a slight variation in the Hebrew). This time the Examiner is not totally honest, for he has been involved in many more activities than simply observing human behavior. He never mentions the four disasters (1:14-19) he had inflicted on Job, probably because his testing failed to achieve the outcome he had predicted.

The phrase **to present himself before him** (v 1) is added to the Examiner's appearance this time. It is missing in the LXX. Gordis suggests that **before him** (which does not appear in 1:6) should be translated "against him," indicating the Examiner's "rebelliousness" (1978, 19). But that suggestion may be reading too much between the lines. It is probably either an addition for variety's sake or a lead-in to the Examiner's presence being recognized before his report begins. Rowley says the additional phrase adds nothing to the meaning (1976, 34).

■ **3** Even though the Examiner fails to mention the test, Yahweh is not willing to let the results of the test go unnoticed. He directs the conversation toward Job. And he repeats his evaluation of Job given the last time he and the Examiner met (1:8). Yahweh is still delighted with Job. The results of the Examiner's test have only increased his admiration for this faithful servant. Truly, **there is no one on earth like him.**

According to Yahweh, Job **still maintains his integrity**. The word for **integrity** (*tummâ*) is one of the noun forms of the adjective **blameless** (*tām*) that appeared first in 1:1, 8. Following the discussion in 1:1, we might translate *tummâ* as "completeness or wholeness with God." Job still believes he is right with God in every area of his life, and according to God he is correct.

However, there seems to be an element of regret on God's part that he accepted the Examiner's challenge. He now knows how devastating the Examiner's attacks have been and the emotional pain Job is experiencing. So he criticizes the Examiner for leading him to permit these disasters. Pope is one of the few commentators who interprets **you incited me** (*swt*) with a positive tone: "Yahweh here gives the Satan credit for instigating the experiment" (1973, 19). Most others believe this passage reflects God's displeasure with the Examiner for proposing the experiment in the first place.

Of course, the traditional interpretation raises questions about the nature of God. Is God so weak that he can be talked into bringing harm against his choicest servant Job? Whybray addresses this issue by stating that the author probably did not intend for the characterization of either God or the Examiner to be taken as a wholly true and complete representation of their natures. Rather, he created the dialogues in heaven to provide "a dramatic irony that would persist throughout the book—that the reader knows what Job does not: that his misfortunes are due to a decision made in heaven to test him" (1998, 29). Thus, the conversation in heaven provides a reason for misfortune that Job and his friends never consider, namely that some misfortunes may be caused by God through the agency of his Examiner.

The Examiner seemed to be intent on destroying Job (lit. "swallow him up"), but his attacks proved to be worthless. There is a subtle play on words between Yahweh's statement **without any reason** and the Examiner's statement in 1:9 "for nothing." Both come from the same Hebrew term (*ḥinnām*), but their application is quite different. The Examiner's statement (1:9) implied that Job required a reason to serve Yahweh—a reward. Job would not do it "for nothing." In contrast, Yahweh's statement (2:3) means that the Examiner did not prove the need to conduct the test. Therefore, Yahweh allowed it "for nothing." He harmed Job without a good reason to do so.

Balentine draws a fascinating comparison between the story of Job's misfortunes and humanity's fall in the Garden of Eden, using their similar locations "in the East" as a starting point (2006, 41-43). Whereas Adam's punishment was the result of his sin, Job's was the result of his righteousness. Therefore, Adam was driven from the garden for a good reason, but Job's suffering occurred for no good reason at all.

Hartley rightly notes the major significance of this verse in the overall scheme of the book. It places the ultimate responsibility for Job's disasters on God's shoulders. "With these words [**you incited me against him**] Yahweh accepted full responsibility for Job's plight. He would not concede any of his authority to the Satan" (1988, 80). And Clines presses this insight further. By admitting his responsibility for Job's suffering, God has definitively shown that all suffering is not the result of sin. It is indeed possible for humans, even righteous humans, to suffer for other reasons, including "gratuitously." Thus, "the law of retribution has been broken!" (1989, 42-43).

■ **4-5** The Examiner's first test did not go very well for him. "Job's faith had proved tougher than he expected" (Andersen 1976, 91). Job still remained the greatest example of piety in the world according to Yahweh's evaluation (v 3). But the Examiner is not ready to admit defeat. He boldly challenges Yahweh to remove one more reward from Job's life—his health. His intent is to make Job so ill that he will fear death and turn against Yahweh to save his life.

His first words—**Skin for skin!** (v 4*a*)—have been discussed extensively, but there is no unanimity on their meaning (see Gordis 1978, 20; Driver-Gray 1921, 21-22; or Clines 1989, 43-45 for comments on many interpretations). The only agreement is that this is a very old proverb whose original meaning is unknown. Gordis calls it "a folk-saying which has been stripped down to its essentials by dint of repetition" (1978, 20). Its origin was probably in the ancient marketplaces where buyers and sellers bartered over the purchase of commodities (Seow 2013, 302).

In the present context, the meaning of the proverb is dependent on v 4*b*: **A man will give all he has for his own life**. It symbolizes the exchange the Examiner believes Job will make to protect his life. If God will remove Job's health, Job will give up everything that is his, including his faith in God, in order to safeguard his existence. In fact, if Job suspects that God is attempting to destroy him through disease, he will turn on God and **curse** (v 5; lit. "bless" as in 1:5, 11) him.

Skin for skin, then, is a proverb that is purposely ambiguous. The author inserted it here for dramatic effect. But it also functions as a literary catchword that introduces the topic of Job's health and connects it with the Examiner's challenge concerning **flesh and bones** and with the skin disease that Job will soon experience (2:7).

In the Hebrew, **flesh and bones** is actually reversed ("his bone and his flesh"). Alden calls this a literary merismus, that is, totality expressed by opposites. "The body consists of hard parts (bones) and soft parts (flesh)" (1993, 64). Other passages that connect **flesh and bones** include Gen 2:23; Prov 14:30; and Ezek 37:5-8.

■ **6** The fourth scene ends with permission being granted for a second test. The major difference between the tests is this. The first one gave the Examiner control only over Job's possessions ("everything he has is in your *hands*" [Job 1:12]). In the second test God gives the Examiner control even over Job himself (**he is in your hands** [2:6]). However, he cannot harm Job so extensively that he dies, because that would bring the test to an end. Thus, whatever disease the Examiner chooses must be nonfatal.

Why does Yahweh agree to a second test? After all, Job survived the first test and proved that the Examiner's theory was wrong. And furthermore, Yahweh already admitted in v 3 that he was annoyed in allowing the first test. Perhaps, as Clines notes, "the trial had not been severe enough" (1989, 42), and Yahweh recognized the logic of the Examiner's argument. As noted in the earlier illustration concerning experiments in the science lab (beginning of ch 1), an experiment is only valid if all possible agents are taken into account. If even one element is left out, the experiment does not have proof. Thus, one additional element—Job's health—still needs to be considered. So in the second test, God allows the Examiner to raise the stakes and intensify Job's level of suffering. Everything that could possibly be considered a reward from God will now be removed. Only Job's life will be spared.

E. Job's Second Test: He Loses His Health (2:7-10)

Back on earth, the Examiner quickly afflicts Job with a painful skin disease. Job finds himself in agony, sitting on a pile of ashes, scratching his sores for relief. Suddenly Job's wife appears for the first time. Her advice to her husband is to curse/bless God and die. However, Job will not yield to the temptation to give up his relationship with God, even if the advice comes from his own wife. His answer to her classifies her as foolish, that is, lacking in wisdom.

■ **7-8** The first words of v 7 are a hurried transition into scene five. The Examiner is eager to begin the second test. Job is suddenly stricken with a severe skin disease over his entire body—**from the soles of his feet to the crown of his head**. The Hebrew term for Job's **sores** is *šĕḥîn*. The root of this word is found in other Semitic languages with the meaning "be hot or inflamed" (Clines 1989, 49). The word appears multiple times in the OT and is usually translated as "skin boils."

This skin disease is the one that God inflicted on the Egyptians as the sixth plague (Exod 9:9-11). Moses warned the Israelites that this same Egyptian skin disease would befall them if they turned away from Yahweh and the covenant (Deut 28:27, 35). Hezekiah nearly lost his life with this disease (2 Kgs 20:7; Isa 38:21). Leviticus 13:18-23 speaks of the examination procedure necessary to be declared healed of this disease. And in the NT, the first bowl of God's wrath at the end of time will be a skin disease (Rev 16:2).

Scholars have attempted to identify Job's affliction based on the evidence from Job 2:7 as well as other passages scattered throughout the book. Hartley summarizes the symptoms as follows:

Painful pruritus (2:8), disfiguration (2:12), purulent sores that scab over, crack, and ooze (7:5), sores infected with worms (7:5), fever with chills (21:6; 30:30), darkening and shriveling of the skin (30:30), eyes red and swollen from weeping (16:16), diarrhea (30:27), sleeplessness and delirium (7:4, 13-14), choking (7:15), bad breath (19:17), emaciation (19:20), and excruciating pain throughout his body (30:17). (1988, 82)

Based on the symptoms above, biblical scholars and medical experts have suggested some of the following diseases as possibilities: "elephantiasis, biskra button, eczema, erythema, smallpox, leprosy, malignant ulcers, and many others" (Reyburn 1992, 60). Some commentaries have extensive discussions on the merits of these diseases (Clines 1989, 48-49; Driver-Gray 1921, 22-24; Hartley 1988, 82; Rowley 1976, 35-36). However, it is difficult to determine which of the symptoms are primary medical diagnoses and which are secondary complications or simply the author's poetic description. The fact that there are so many possibilities is good evidence that we cannot give a precise name to Job's illness. All we can say is that he had a severe, painful skin disease over his entire body.

A piece of broken pottery is called a potsherd or simply a sherd (Job 2:8). Pottery breaks very easily when dropped, so there was a constant demand for new vessels from the potter's shop in every community. Broken pieces were thrown out in the street in front of the house or gathered up and taken to the town dump. There are literally tens of thousands of these potsherds at the site of every city in the ANE. Over time they became mixed up in the soil, but they do not disintegrate if the pot was fired in a kiln. They can survive for thousands of years in the ground. One can walk across any tell in the Near East today and still see thousands of sherds on the surface. This writer had the assignment of digging out a city dump while on three archaeological excavations in Jordan. There were over 25,000 animal bones and 5,000 pieces of broken pottery in this one dump.

The Hebrew term for **scraped himself** (*grd*) is what scholars call a *hapax legomenon*, that is, a word appearing only once in the OT (→ Introduction: Text). These words are often difficult to translate. Scholars generally use clues found in the context and comparisons with cognate words in postbiblical Hebrew and other Semitic languages. In this context, the word means "scrape" (Greenspahn 1984, 107).

Some think the purpose of Job's scraping was to lacerate his skin as a sign of grief over the death of his children (Pope 1973, 21). Other ancient religions practiced this ritual, but it was strictly forbidden in Israelite law (Lev 19:28; Deut 14:1). Most scholars reject this view and accept the traditional meaning that Job was scraping himself to relieve the intense itching caused by his disease. The LXX clarifies the meaning with this further explanation: "He was scraping away the pus from his sores."

Among the ashes refers to the location where Job was sitting at this point in the story. The LXX adds a further word of clarification: "on the dunghill outside the city." Over time, the trash at a garbage dump would form a mound that gradually increased in height. Periodically the dump would be burned and covered with dirt to keep down the stench and keep scavengers away. Hence, ashes would be plentiful at such a site.

Various suggestions have been made as to Job's purpose in going to the ash heap. One is that he was there "because of the contagious character of his disease and his loathsome appearance" (Gordis 1978, 21). Another is that he wanted to give "public prominence to his plight" (Habel 1985, 96). Job was mourning for his children like David for his stricken son (2 Sam 12:16). Or perhaps he was retreating to the place of outcasts (Rowley 1976, 36). Since we do not know the exact nature of Job's disease, we cannot confirm that his disease was contagious. Neither do we know whether his decision to go to the ash heap was his own or was forced on him by others out of fear. We do know that his appearance had changed for the worse (Job 2:12).

Perhaps Job quarantined himself as a precaution against contagion. Or perhaps he felt isolated, rejected, and alone and needed a place to get away from the stares of curious and gossipy family and neighbors. The ash heap provided a place of solitude where he could mourn over significant losses and talk to God. The context seems to support this last possibility, for Job complains later about his estrangement from family and friends (19:13-22). Whether Job remained at the ash heap for the rest of his illness or went back and forth to his home is unknown. A couple of passages hint at the possibility of his leaving at times (19:15-18; 30:28).

There is some dispute over the time when Job began his stay at the ash heap. The governing verbal form in the clause **as he sat among the ashes** is a participle (*yōšēb* = "sitting"). Participles generally provide no indication of the beginning point of an action. Most scholars believe Job's "sitting" began after he was afflicted with the skin disease. The reason is because the clause is located at the end of v 8 and seems to describe the circumstances for the main verb (**took**) at the beginning of the sentence. However, a few take the view that the participle can be stretched all the way back to v 7. In that case, Job went to the ash heap to mourn the loss of his children and possessions after the first test and was afflicted while sitting there (Clines 1989, 49). Such an interpretation is possible, but the traditional interpretation seems better.

Disease in the Ancient World

The introduction of Job's disease into the story adds a new element that is often difficult for modern readers to understand because of our more advanced medical knowledge about illness and its causes. As is well-known, ancient people had no knowledge of bacteria and viruses. The origin of a specific disease was usually a mystery, and so it was normal for them to suspect a supernatural cause—either from heaven or the underworld (in a polytheistic culture; → 5:7, "sparks [Heb. ***the sons of Resheph***] fly upward"). Ironically, the book of Job with its emphasis on the Examiner's role in causing disease probably strengthened the view in ancient people's minds that all disease had a supernatural origin.

In addition to ignorance about the cause of disease, the ancients' knowledge of the severity of each disease was limited also. One never knew whether a disease was terminal or not. In Job's case, he was not privy to the heavenly conversation in scene four where God told the Examiner to spare Job's life. For all he knew, he had a terminal disease with only a few days or weeks left to live. His wife also believed he would never recover (2:9). Therefore, all of Job's reactions must be viewed against the background of a person expecting to die.

Because diseases were connected with the supernatural, people naturally turned to their god(s) for healing. Seeking divine help was commonplace among all peoples of the ancient world. The book of Psalms contains numerous examples of Israelite laments requesting healing from an illness (e.g., Pss 6, 22, 38, 39, 41, etc.).

■ **9** The appearance of Job's wife at this juncture in the narrative adds to the drama of the story. Where has she been all this time? How is she coping with the loss of her ten children? And why does she say so little and then disappear? Unfortunately, many of our questions about her will remain unanswered because her appearance is so brief that it is difficult to make any meaningful evaluation of her character. She is mentioned only here in a two-verse conversation with Job, and then in two other passages (19:17; 31:10), but just in passing. She had to appear sometime in the book, or we would surmise that Job was a widower. On the other hand, she is not a central character, so the author feels no obligation to continue her role beyond this brief appearance.

Because we know so little about Job's wife, various attempts have been made over the centuries to fill in her character with additional information. For example, the Aramaic Targum gave her the name of Dinah because she acted foolishly like the Dinah of Gen 34:1-10. The pseudepigraphic *Testament of Job* called her Sitis, "a name derived from Ausitis, the LXX translation of Uz" (Clines 1989, 53), and added six chapters on their family life. And the LXX added about a dozen lines to her speech (→ other additions at Job 42:17). All of these later additions present her in a much more compassionate light. They reveal her agony over the calamities that struck her husband and family. While interesting, these are what Clines calls "the midrashic tendency to provide details about minor characters and to elaborate brief speeches" (1989, 53).

What we actually know about Job's wife is limited to two comments in 2:9. Her first words are a question to Job: **Are you still *holding on to* your integrity?** The Hebrew participle here means that Job's action is ongoing. In fact, it never stops. From the beginning of the book to the end, Job continues to hold on to his blamelessness and righteousness before God. She uses the same word for **integrity** that God used in v 3 (*tummâ*; "completeness or wholeness with God"). There is no doubt in her mind that Job is whole in his relationship with God. After all, she is married to him, so she knows him better than anyone else. She has been observing him through all of his trials and enduring them along with him. And in her mind, he is still the same old Job. So this is not a question seeking information. It is a question about *why?* "Why are you still holding on to your relationship with God? What good has it gotten you?" Her question focuses on the appropriateness of continuing on the same course of action, when it has brought only sorrow and suffering.

Her second comment is a double command: **Curse God** [*Elohim*] **and die!** There are multiple interpretations of how these two imperatives are related to one another and whether *brk* should be translated as **curse** or "bless" (→ 1:5).

(1) "Curse God, so that you will die!" GKC interprets the second imperative as a result clause (§110, *f*[*a*]). The emphasis is on "cursing God" as a way to end one's misery, because everyone knows that such foolish behavior will bring a quick death (Exod 22:28 [27 HB]; Lev 24:10-16). Terrien describes this as "a theological method of committing suicide" (1954, 3:921).

(2) "Curse God before you die!" The emphasis here is on revenge. Job's wife believes her husband has a terminal illness and will die very shortly. She is angry at this turn of events and would like to see God cursed while Job is still alive as a way of getting back at God for what he has done to her husband. "She wants God cursed more than she wants (even if it means) her husband's death" (Andersen 1976, 93, n. 1).

(3) "Curse God and then die!" This interpretation treats the two imperatives as independent clauses. The focus is on accountability: "Lay the blame on God where it rightly belongs. Let everyone know that he is at fault and that you have maintained your integrity to the end. And then you can die in peace and be rid of your misery."

(4) "Bless God and die!" Terrien suggests that we may regard both the question and the commands from Job's wife as sarcastic criticism: "Do you still pretend to be a perfect man? Do you not see that such a horrible succession of calamities proves beyond doubt that you are a sinner? Bid God farewell and die!" (1954, 3:921). If this interpretation is correct, then Job's wife is basically of the same mind as Job's three friends. They all believe that Job is a sinner.

(5) "Continue blessing God (like you have been doing in the past), even though you may die!" Balentine proposes this interpretation as a possible alternative to the traditional negative portrayal of Job's wife. He regards her as "an agent of comfort and compassion" to her stricken husband who needs to be viewed sympathetically rather than negatively (2006, 63).

(6) "Bless God, if that is what you want to do, but you will die as a fool!" Here Job's wife is focused on the *foolishness* of Job's actions rather than their sinfulness. In fact, she believes that Job is a righteous person, but he is foolish to continue blessing God and holding on to his integrity. He would be better off to abandon his integrity and seek a better way of life. If correct, this interpretation ties v 9 to the wisdom theology and to v 10 where Job reacts by calling his wife's statements "foolish." Wesley supports this view (1765, 1522).

Before settling on one interpretation, the purpose of Job's wife in the narrative needs some clarification. The vast majority of commentators, beginning with the church fathers and extending up to modern times, treat her as a negative character. Many believe she is the human face of the Examiner, used to tempt Job much like Eve tempted Adam in the Garden of Eden. She has been called the "devil's assistant" (Augustine) and "Satan's tool" (Calvin), and "Thomas Aquinas thought that the Satan spared her, in the calamities of chapter 1, precisely in order to use her against Job" (Clines 1989, 51). Wesley also believes she had been spared "to be a troubler and tempter" of Job (1765, 1522). One quickly senses that Job's wife is not well liked by Christian commentators. She is treated with much more sympathy in Jewish and Muslim writings (Andersen 1976, 92).

However, there are other, more positive ways of evaluating the role of Job's wife in the narrative. One way is to regard her as a real marital partner to her husband, a loving wife without a name but with a deep concern for her husband's well-being. "She spoke out of the strong emotional, marital bond between them" (Hartley 1988, 84). And she offered an alternative, pragmatic course of action that would relieve the suffering of the one she loved. Her heart's cry is still echoed today in the minds of many who wrestle with the issue of euthanasia and knowing when to "pull the plug": "I can't stand to see you suffer like this anymore."

Another interpretation is that she is a literary device that the author uses to evoke a response from Job with regard to the loss of his health. Up to this point, Job has not uttered a word about his disease. It is important for the reader to know his reaction before the three friends arrive and the long dialogues begin. So the author gives us a two-sentence reaction from Job and then a comment that "Job did not sin" (v 10). Thus, we know that the Examiner has still not been able to shake Job's faith, and the description of Job in 1:1 has survived intact. A number of scholars support this evaluation of Job's wife (Clines 1989, 50; Driver-Gray 1921, 25; Hartley 1988, 83).

A third interpretation is that of van Wolde, who sees the wife's role as very significant (1997, 26). Up to now, the author has alternated the meaning of the verb *brk* between "curse" (1:5, 11; 2:5) and "bless" (1:10, 21). The reader must now make a decision about how to translate this sixth appearance of the word. Is Job's wife telling her husband to curse or bless God? Van Wolde believes the author purposely intended the word *brk* to be ambiguous, thus creating two choices for Job. He can either "curse" God, thus abandoning his relationship with God and expressing his anger at how God has treated him unjustly. Or he can "bless" God, continuing as he has in the past to accept automatically everything that God sends his way with words of blessing on his lips (1:21). Either way, he is going to die very shortly.

By offering Job this choice, his wife moves the plot toward the dialogue section of the book. She very subtly but strategically plants a seed in Job's mind to consider another way of responding to calamity than that supported by the wisdom theology. Job's response to her suggestion is negative, as seen in the next verse. But the seed has been planted, and it will burst forth and blossom in the next chapter. According to van Wolde, Job will change from a "believer" to a "questioner" (1997, 26).

Job's wife leaves us with many unanswered questions, but she does play an important role in the narrative. The one temptation we need to avoid is to read too much between the lines. The brevity of her appearance should make us cautious. The author may have purposely described Job's wife with ambiguous terms. As Andersen notes, "It must be admitted that we cannot tell just what she is proposing, and even less what her motive was" (1976, 93, n. 1).

■ **10** There are no clues concerning the emotional intensity of Job's response, but at face value it seems to be calm and detached from the crisis at hand, just like his response to the first four disasters (1:20-22). He brushes aside his wife's emotional outburst in 2:9 by connecting her remarks with the words of someone who is **foolish**. Clines suggests three possible meanings for the word **foolish** (*nĕbālâ*) based on its usage in other OT passages.

(1) It may refer to an "intellectual-moral" state of mind that is the opposite of wise (Deut 32:6) (1989, 53). The wisdom literature typically describes the foolish person as one who is "lacking in discernment" (Andersen 1976, 92).

(2) It may indicate an "ethical-religious" condition of the heart that is synonymous with "wicked" (*rāšā'*) (Ps 14:1) (Clines 1989, 53-54). A number of scholars support this interpretation (Hartley 1988, 84; Reyburn 1992, 61; Smick 1988, 886).

(3) A third usage is in reference to a "social" condition that is "low-class" or "common" as opposed to "noble" (Prov 17:7; Isa 32:5) (Clines 1989, 54). Clines supports this position, interpreting Job's comment as follows: "You talk like a low-class, irreligious woman; such words are beneath you" (ibid.).

The word **foolish** is used again at the end of the book to describe God's evaluation of the three friends (Job 42:8). It is not likely that God is referring to the friends as either "low-class" or "wicked." Rather, they are primarily guilty of misunderstanding Job's situation and making false claims about God's character. Therefore, the most likely interpretation of Job's reference to **foolish** is an "intellectual-moral" state of mind. Gordis calls it "blindness to religious truth" (1978, 22).

When 2:9 and 10 are joined in context, the passage clearly supports this meaning. In v 9 Job's wife accuses him of foolishly holding on to his integrity in the face of overwhelming calamity. Job tosses these accusations back at her in v 10: "You are the one who is talking foolishly, not me!" (paraphrased). His statement plainly accuses her of acting in a manner that is contrary to the way of wisdom. It is unclear whether Job is comparing her to a particular group of foolish women or whether this was a common put-down for someone who lacked understanding. Perhaps he is reflecting Qoheleth's comment about the overall lack of wisdom in the world (Eccl 7:27-28).

Job then asks his wife a rhetorical question: **Shall we accept good from God** [*Elohim*]**, and not trouble?** The implication is that both good and bad will come our way eventually, and we should not be surprised when they do. The question is directly parallel with Job's earlier comment in 1:21: "The LORD gave and the LORD has taken away." There (1:21) the form was more of a general wisdom saying. Here (2:10) the application is directly to Job and his wife (**we**). Job wants her to accept this attitude, too, that he has already affirmed. By implication, Job is describing an attitude that is appropriate for all humanity.

In both of Job's comments (1:21 and 2:10) the good and the bad are described as coming from God. This should not be interpreted in support of the view that God is the cause of all things in life, both good and bad. It does, however, suggest that God sometimes causes bad things to happen to good people, and we should be prepared to accept them when they occur.

Trouble (*ra'*) has a wide variety of meanings, including "moral evil," but here it likely refers to "the calamities and disasters of life" as in Amos 3:6 (Habel 1985, 96). The word is placed in conjunction with **good** (*tôb*) to describe the opposite poles of events in any person's life. Hebrew will sometimes use extremes to describe totality. Job is suggesting that we need to learn how to accept both the good and the bad and everything in between.

The word **accept** should not be associated with an attitude of resignation, as if one had no other choice. Neither is it the attitude of the stoic who suffers without feeling or complaint. Andersen notes that it is "a good active word, implying cooperation with Providence, not mere submission" (1976, 93). As Job demonstrates, he has developed a deep and faithful trust in God that is willing to accept whatever comes his way in life. For him, as for Joseph, God knows best (Gen 45:5, 7-8).

In all this refers to all the events since the previous summary statement in Job 1:22. Some of the Jewish rabbis interpreted the statement **Job did not sin in what he said** as referring to Job's *speech* only; in his heart he really was angry. But the author's comment is not intended to contrast oral sins with sins of the heart. Rather, this is the author's judgment that the Examiner failed in his attempt to show that righteousness was dependent on rewards. Job had survived the worst attacks the Examiner could inflict, and he had done so without cursing. He was truly a supersaint who served God "for nothing" (1:9).

Since the Examiner is now a proven failure, his presence in the narrative is no longer needed; so he vanishes completely in the remainder of the book (→ Behind the Text for 42:7-17). But the results of his devastating attacks will remain for some time. The narrative will now move on to deal with further reactions from Job and speculation about the reasons for Job's suffering. From Job's perspective, what is the meaning of these attacks from the Examiner? Do they have a purpose? If so, what is it? Readers will also be asked to consider the application to their own lives. How are human beings supposed to continue their faith in God in the aftermath of horrendous personal disasters?

F. The Friends Arrive (2:11-13)

Verses 11-13 form a transition between the five scenes of the prologue (ch 1—2) and the dialogue between Job and his three friends (chs 3—27). The stage has now been set. God and the Examiner are now out of the picture. However, Job must still endure the effects of his skin disease and the losses of his children and wealth. In this short section, three of Job's friends come from distant locations to comfort him. They are so overwhelmed by Job's suffering that they cannot muster up the courage to say a word for seven days. However, their extensive speeches will become the framework for the main part of the book in chs 4—27.

Why are there *three* friends in the story? The Sumerian, Akkadian, and Egyptian works that are similar to Job (→ Introduction) all use only one character to dialogue with the protagonist. Perhaps the author intended to indicate that the view in opposition to Job was widespread. Or maybe the author wanted to add to Job's woes by sending a larger delegation. No one has satisfactorily answered this question.

■ 11 The author identifies Job's friends by their names and home locations. Numerous suggestions have been made as to the origin of these names using biblical references. The first friend is **Eliphaz the Temanite** (*ĕlîpaz hattêmānî*). This name appears in Gen 36:4, 10-12, 15-16, and 1 Chr 1:35-36 as the firstborn son of Esau and Adah. He and his descendants settled in the land of Edom, to the southeast of the Dead Sea (Gen 36:6-9, 19, 43). Teman was one of the sons of Eliphaz (Gen 36:11, 15, 40-42; 1 Chr 1:36, 53). His name became associated with one of the regions of Edom called "the land of the Temanites" (Gen 36:34; 1 Chr 1:45). Teman may have been the name of a town in Edom as well (Jer 49:7, 20; Ezek 25:13; Amos 1:12; Obad 8-9; Hab 3:3). It is unlikely that the author of Job intended for the Eliphaz of his story to be identified as the son of Esau. But the connection with the land of Edom is certainly in mind.

The second friend is **Bildad the Shuhite** (*bildad haššûḥî*). His name is not found outside the book of Job. Clines conjectures that Bildad may mean "son of Hadad" (1989, 58), a Mesopotamian storm god. Seow relates it to an Old South Arabic name *brdd* meaning "The Pious One of Dād ('the Paternal Uncle')" (2013, 526). The evidence is not conclusive for either one. Shuah is the name of one of Abraham's sons by Keturah (Gen 25:1-2; 1 Chr 1:32). All of Keturah's sons settled somewhere to the east of the land of Canaan (Gen 25:6).

Job's third friend is **Zophar the Naamathite** (*ṣôpar hanna'ămātî*). The name is similar to Zippor (*ṣippôr*), the father of Balak, king of Moab (Num 22:2, 4, 10, 16), but an exact equivalent to Zophar is not found in the OT. Naamah is the name of the daughter of Lamech (Gen 4:22), the name of an Ammonite woman whom Solomon married (1 Kgs 14:21; 2 Chr 12:13), and also the name of a town near Lachish during the conquest period (Josh 15:41). None of these occurrences seem to be related to the Naamah of the book of Job.

Most of the personal and place names discussed above have connections with the book of Genesis. Based on this evidence, it is probable that the average Israelite reading the book of Job would have associated all three friends with the archaic period described in Genesis, and their locations with regions to the east and south of the land of Canaan. Such connections, although imprecise, may have been intended by the author to give an archaic flavor to the narrative and to continue the non-Israelite setting as already introduced through the previous non-Israelite names (Job, Uz, Sabeans, Chaldeans).

The author labels Eliphaz, Bildad, and Zophar as **friends** (*rēaʿ*). According to the biblical usage of *rēaʿ*, a friend can be anyone from a good neighbor who "loves at all times" (Prov 17:17), to an adviser to the king (1 Chr 27:33), to an opponent in a legal case (Prov 18:17). The word can also refer to other people in general. For example, one of the commands of the Law (which Jesus declared as the second great commandment [Matt 22:39]) was to "love your *rēaʿ* as yourself" (Lev 19:18).

Hartley suggests that Job and the three friends may have previously developed an intimate relationship by means of a covenant, such as the covenant between David and Jonathan (1 Sam 20:16-17). He cites Job 6:14-15, 21-23, 27 as evidence for this covenant (1988, 85). Others are not convinced by this evidence and hold that the nature and length of any previous relationship between Job and the friends are unknown. About all we can say for sure is that Job had some previous contacts with these three individuals, and because of these contacts the friends felt obligated to visit him and provide comfort and encouragement. Their appearance is commendable, considering the fact that no one knew the exact nature of Job's illness and whether it was contagious.

The book of Proverbs is an excellent source for defining the characteristics of a good friend. Kidner summarizes these characteristics as four in number: "constancy," "candour," "counsel," and "tact" (1964, 45). Job truly needed that kind of support from his friends, as does every person when faced with misfortune. We will see in the dialogue section (chs 4—27) whether Job's friends live up to these characteristics and deserve to be called "good friends."

The word for **troubles** (*rāʿ/rāʿâ*) has already appeared three times in the book with its normal meaning of "moral evil" (1:1, 8; 2:3). On occasion, however, the word may refer to general troubles and disasters in life without any moral connotation (Isa 45:7; Jer 39:12). This latter meaning is intended in Job 2:11 and 42:11.

The three friends, upon hearing of Job's misfortunes, apparently communicated with each other and **met together by agreement** at a common place so as to arrive at Uz in a group rather than singly. The length of time for all this to take place is unknown, mainly because the distances between Uz, Teman, Shuah, and Naamah are not stated. However, we can assume that Job's illness lasted for a considerable length of time before the friends arrived, based on his comments in several places (7:3; 19:13-20; 30:16-17, 27). Also, one has to allow enough time for Job's disease to ravage his body and change his appearance significantly (2:12).

The author clearly spells out the purpose of the visit using three infinitives at the end of the verse: **go** (*bwʾ*), **sympathize** (*nwd*), and **comfort** (*nḥm*). *Nwd* is associated with bodily movement and means to express sympathy by shaking the head or rocking the body back and forth (Jer 15:5). *Nḥm* means to provide comfort in times of great distress (2 Sam 12:24; Isa 40:1-2; 66:13). The same two words are used again at the end of the book (Job 42:11) to describe the comfort Job's relatives and friends bring to him after God restores his fortunes.

■ **12-13** The first two clauses in v 12 are quite awkward in Hebrew, and the various English translations do not clear up the matter. Most likely, some additional words are needed to separate the friends' first view of Job at some distance away, from the actual recognition of him and emotional outburst at the dump itself. The NIV implies that the three friends **could hardly recognize** Job **from a distance**, but surely one would not expect them to recognize him from far away. The meaning of v 12 is probably something like this: "As they came in sight of Uz, they could see a figure sitting outside the gate on the city dump. They did not recognize who it was. When they arrived at the dump and realized that the figure was Job whom they were seeking, they were overwhelmed with emotion."

There are a number of terms in the OT used to describe customary, ritual practices that express feelings of extreme anguish or mourning for the dead. They include: weeping, mourning, lamenting, fasting, tearing one's clothes, putting dust or ashes or dirt on one's head, pulling out one's hair or shaving one's head, sitting on the ground, and wearing sackcloth. Four of these terms are used in vv 12-13 to describe the reaction of Job's friends to his outward appearance.

"Weeping" refers to a type of ritual wailing accompanied by tears. "Tearing one's robe" usually means to make a rip in one's outer garment, although the under garments could also be torn (→ 29:14). "Putting dust or dirt or ashes on one's head" is also a common ritual activity, but this is the only passage that speaks of throwing the dust "in the air" (NRSV; lit. "toward heaven"), and letting it fall on one's head (implied). The awkwardness of the phrase "toward heaven" is resolved by the LXX and the NIV by omitting the phrase.

Some have tried to connect this passage with the account of the sixth plague (Exod 9:8-10) where Moses threw ashes into the air bringing a plague of boils on the Egyptians (Habel 1985, 97). But it is not likely that the friends are trying to imitate Moses and bring a plague on themselves. Gordis proposes a different purpose, calling this ritual an "apotropaic rite, in order to ward off the evil from themselves" (1978, 24). Hartley suggests a "symbolic connection between dust and the nature of Job's malady" (1988, 86, n. 9). More likely, "throwing dust into the air" is simply another one of the customary rituals that expresses extreme anguish. Sitting **on the ground** is the final ritual that enables them to identify with Job's misery.

The ritual practices that express feelings of extreme anguish or mourning for the dead sometimes appear singly in the OT, but more often, as in this passage, they are connected in groups of two, three, or four. The following list illustrates some of these connections: Gen 23:2; 37:34-35; Josh 7:6; 1 Sam 4:12; 2 Sam 1:11-12; 13:19; Ezra 9:3-5; Neh 1:4; Esth 4:1; Lam 2:10; Ezek 27:30-31; Joel 2:12-13.

Seven days and seven nights seems like a rather long period to go without speaking, but it probably symbolizes an ideal period of time to show one's respect and sympathy for their friend Job. Actually, the length of time was dependent on Job's silence. No doubt, the friends were stunned by the severity of Job's physical condition and confused about how to start the conversation. They needed to hear his reaction to his circumstances before attempting their own words of comfort.

Thus they were willing to wait for Job to speak first. Habel notes that the period of silence may also have been used for a literary purpose. It "is important in the plot of the narrative, for it allows time for bitterness and rage to build up within Job before they explode in the curses of Job's next speech (ch. 3)" (1985, 98).

The term **seven days** appears in other places as a proper amount of time to mourn over the dead. Joseph mourned for his father for seven days (Gen 50:10), the people of Jabesh Gilead fasted for seven days in honor of Saul (1 Sam 31:13), and David mourned for seven days prior to his baby's death (2 Sam 12:15-18). In a similar vein, Ezekiel sat for seven days among the exiles after receiving his prophetic calling (Ezek 3:15). The addition of **and seven nights** is probably just a poetic flourish intended to emphasize the length of the silence.

The Hebrew term for **suffering** (*kĕ'ēb*) can refer to either physical pain or mental anguish (Oswalt 1980*b*, 1:425). The three friends probably sensed that Job was experiencing both.

By Job 2:13, we have reached a turning point in the story. God has won his contest with the Examiner, and the Examiner has disappeared. Job has maintained his faith in God even though he is suffering terribly. Why not end the story here with a statement about Job's faithfulness and God's victory over the Examiner? Or why not add a brief scene back in heaven that includes an acknowledgment of defeat by the Examiner? Why do we need another forty chapters in this book?

It is in the remaining chapters that the true literary and theological skills of the author are revealed. Along with a change from prose to poetry, the focus of the book shifts from examining Job's continued piety in the face of loss to discussing the possible reasons for Job's distress and what he needs to do to restore his health, family, and possessions. The author skillfully takes us through one reason after another as presented by the three friends and an additional person named Elihu who appears well along into the book. Each friend argues passionately and logically for his position, and Job responds with arguments just as forceful. Here we see that the friends are much more than personal acquaintances. They are actually sages come to provide wise counsel—the wisdom of the ages, the best understanding of suffering that humans have discovered since the beginning of time. This next section is the essential core of the book of Job.

FROM THE TEXT

Job's Predicament. Job had two strikes against him. First, he had experienced four major disasters on the same day that cost him his family and his wealth. All these disasters had some element of mystery about them. Two came from the heavens and two were caused by unlikely distant peoples. Anyone in the ancient world would have suspected that this chain of disasters was more than a coincidence. It had all the earmarks of a supernatural origin. As we know from the prologue, Job was correct to suspect that God was behind these disasters. His only ignorance concerned the reason why God had brought this trouble into his life.

Second, Job had a disease that was connected with the wrath of God. Every Israelite who read or heard the book of Job would have made an immediate mental connection with the sixth plague and with Moses' warnings in Deuteronomy (→ Job 2:7). Job was a non-Israelite, but certainly he would have puzzled over the sudden onset of his disease. All signs pointed to a divine causation of some type. The logical conclusion in the ancient world was that Job had grieved God in some way and this was his punishment.

In presenting the story this way, the author has created a paradox. On the one hand, Job has been declared a model of piety, an ideal saint of God without sin. But on the other hand, Job has all the appearance of a sinner who is experiencing the wrath of God. How can this be? Of course, Job and his friends have not read the prologue, so they are unaware of the ultimate reason for these calamities. But even for the Israelites who had read the prologue, there was still a mystery about disease and disaster. Were they random occurrences or divinely caused? If they were divinely caused, were they signs of God's wrath or a test of one's faith? Even with all our advanced knowledge today about the natural world and about disease, these questions still remain relevant and problematic.

II. JOB'S ANGUISH: JOB 3

BEHIND THE TEXT

Chapter 3 begins a long section of poetry that extends to 42:6. This is the heart of the book, and it is truly great literature by a skilled wordsmith. Before engaging this part of the book, readers should familiarize themselves with the characteristics of Hebrew poetry, such as parallelism, meter, stanzas, figurative language, and so forth (see Andersen 1976, 37-41; Hartley 1988, 33-35; or Seow 2013, 74-85). Otherwise, serious errors of exegesis and interpretation will occur.

In this section there is a major change in the author's presentation of the story. As Balentine notes, throughout the prologue the author makes clear, interpretive statements that describe how he wants us to understand Job's character. But from ch 3 through 42:6 the characters are allowed to speak for themselves. Readers will have to make interpretive judgments about each of them based solely on the content of their speeches and the reaction expressed by other characters (2006, 79-80).

Most scholars regard ch 3 as a self-contained literary unit more closely akin to a monologue than a dialogue. Job is not addressing anyone in particular, although certainly the three friends (2:11-13) and God are listening. A few treat this chapter as the first speech in the dialogues and rearrange the divisions so that Job always speaks first and the friends respond; for example: first cycle, chs 3—11; second cycle, chs 12—20; third cycle, chs 21—31 (Clines 1989, xxxvi-xxxvii). However, while chs 3, 28, and 29—31 are indirectly a part of the dialogues, they are different enough from the other chapters to require separate sections in the outline. Thus, we will treat each as a separate unit. Much like the well-known announcement at the Indianapolis 500 Mile Race ("Ladies and gentlemen, please start your engines"), ch 3 sets the dialogues in motion but quickly yields to the main action.

Job's attitude in this chapter is significantly different from the prologue (1:20-22; 2:10). He is no longer the steady person of faith who hides his feelings deep within. He is now on fire emotionally over the turn of events in his life. He is so distressed that he wishes to die on the spot and go to Sheol (→ From the Text for ch 3). In dramatic fashion Job's words explode out of his mouth. Like a bottled-up geyser, he suddenly erupts with great emotional intensity revealing his fear, anger, and pain. His speech includes words of both cursing and lament.

Most scholars call ch 3 a lament, but the content and form are unlike the more familiar laments in the Psalter. There the plea is always for God to change the speaker's *present* situation and create a new and hopeful *future*. In Job 3 the focus is on the *past* and Job's desire that his life had never had a beginning. Further, Job never directly asks God to relieve his present distress through healing or the restoration of his fortunes. Rather, he wishes he had never existed. Then he would have avoided all his troubles. Job's speech also differs from the Psalms in that it lacks a concluding word of assurance that God will hear his prayers and meet his needs. Instead, Job ends by bewailing his fear and inner turmoil.

Job speaks of three wishes in this chapter. The granting of any one of them would remove him from his present suffering.

A. I Wish I Had Never Been Conceived or Born (3:1-10)
B. I Wish I Had Died at Birth (3:11-19)
C. I Wish My Life Would End Now (3:20-26)

IN THE TEXT

A. I Wish I Had Never Been Conceived or Born (3:1-10)

The city dump at Uz has been quiet for seven days. The three friends, respectful of Job's privacy and great suffering, have not uttered a word. Job's speech in this chapter breaks the tension created by the silence and provides the opportunity for the friends to begin speaking, once Job has finished. Job begins with a curse against his birth date. He wishes that the two main events that gave him life—his conception and his birth—could be removed from the calendar. Then he would never have experienced this world and its calamities.

■ 1 Verses 1-2 are the author's prose introduction to Job's first speech. **After this** refers to the seven days of silence in 2:13. It provides the literary transition from the prologue to the new scene in ch 3. **Job opened his mouth** is the same type of literary formula used to introduce Jesus' speech known as the Sermon on the Mount: "And he opened his mouth and taught them, saying . . ." (Matt 5:2 RSV). **The day of his birth** is simply "his day" (*yômô*) in Hebrew. The verses that follow provide enough context to indicate that his birth date is the day he has in mind.

This is the first appearance of a Hebrew word for **cursed** in the book, even though the English translations have already used the word four times (1:5, 11; 2:5, 9). In these earlier passages the word *brk* ("bless") was used as a euphemism to substitute for the blasphemous expression "curse God." Here in 3:1 the actual Hebrew word *qll* ("curse") appears (also in 24:18). Other words for "curse" are found in 3:8.

The word **cursed** seems very out of character when used to describe a person of Job's outstanding piety (chs 1—2). However, Job is not the only righteous person in the Bible to have uttered terrible curses. Scholars have noted the similarities between this passage and Jer 20:14-18. Balentine points out "four basic motifs" that are common to both passages: "a curse of the day of birth," "the announcement of a male child's birth," "the blocking of the womb," and "being born to see 'trouble'" (2006, 83). Some have tried to use this as evidence for dating the book of Job. But as mentioned in the Introduction, there is no consensus on which passage came first.

Cursing one's birth date is pointless since that day is long past and cannot be changed, no matter how intense the imprecation. But both Job and Jeremiah were at the point of extreme despair over personal circumstances. To express their anguish by cursing God would be blasphemous, so the object of their cursing is their birth date—a bygone event that cannot be undone. Therefore, these curses are without power. Their principal purpose is to provide an outlet for these individuals' intense emotional pain without jeopardizing their relationship with God. They reveal troubled souls crying out for help (→ "Job and Jeremiah" sidebar at Behind the Text for Job 38:1—42:6).

■ 2 **He said** in Hebrew is literally: ***Then Job answered and said***. This seems strange since no conversation has taken place for seven days. But Rowley notes, "The Hebrew verb ['*nh*, 'answered'] is often used where no previous speech has been mentioned, when it means speaking in response to a situation or occasion" (1976, 38). In the book of Job, the phrase "then 'so-and-so' answered and said" is quite common. The statement is a catchphrase that the author uses twenty-seven times to organize the dialogue section. It appears at the beginning of each speech by the three friends (4:1; 8:1; 11:1; 15:1; 18:1; 20:1; 22:1; 25:1) and at the beginning of Job's responses (6:1; 9:1; 12:1; 16:1; 19:1; 21:1; 23:1; 26:1; 27:1 and 29:1 with slight modification). In the latter part of the book the statement appears four times in Elihu's speech (32:6; 34:1; 35:1; 36:1 with slight modification), three times in Yahweh's speech (38:1; 40:1; 40:6 with slight modification), and twice in Job's speech (40:3; 42:1).

■ **3** Job's first words are a curse against the beginning of his life as a human being. Both the **day** of his **birth** and the **night** of his conception are mentioned. Although human conception and birth are normally separated by a period of nine months, the poetic parallelism of the verse draws them together as if they were one event. Job wishes that his life had never begun, so he could have avoided the suffering he has had to endure. Cursing his birth date is his way of relieving the intense emotions bottled up inside him.

The Hebrew for **boy** (*geber*) normally refers to "a strong, young man," but in this context it means simply "a male." **Day** and **night** are frequently connected in the OT (e.g., Gen 1:5; Ps 1:2) and are occasionally personified (e.g., Job 32:7 [**Age** for "days"]; Ps 19:2-4 [3-5 HB]), as they are here. In the verses that follow, Job will expand his comments on **day** in 3:4-5 and on **night** in vv 6-10.

■ **4** That day—*would that it had been* **darkness**, *would that* **God** [*Eloah*] **above had not cared** about it, *and would that the* **light** *had not shined* on it. The Hebrew verb forms in vv 4-9 are imperfects. Following the normal pattern of curse language, these are usually translated as jussives (GKC, §109*a*; e.g., **may it turn to darkness**, etc.). However, the context of the passage requires a different rendering. The activities wished for in vv 4-9 would have prevented Job's birth and thus spared him much suffering. But Job's birth had already taken place. Therefore, in this section Job is expressing not a curse, but an intense wish—a deep longing for what might have been. If God had not brought this day into existence by shining light on it, it would have disappeared into oblivion and Job's present troubles would never have happened. Thus, after the initial curse in v 3, vv 4-9 are better rendered with the optative phrase "would that" followed by the English past perfect tense, for example, *would that it had been darkness* (v 4*a*). As Clines notes, "The form is the form of a curse, but the function is to bewail his unhappy lot" (1989, 79).

Seow notes several examples of Mesopotamian laments containing similar types of curses/wishes against bygone days (2013, 314; see texts in Jacobsen 1987, 65 and 473). As in Job 3, these laments wish that an earlier day had been removed from the calendar so as to prevent tragedy from happening.

That day—a reference to Job's birth date—appears first in the sentence to emphasize its importance and to pick up the theme of "day and night" from v 3. If Job's birthday had always remained in **darkness**, life would not have begun for him.

The Hebrew word for **God** (*Eloah*) is usually taken as the singular form of *Elohim* (→ 1:1). *Elohim* is a very common word for God, appearing approximately 2,570 times in the OT. In contrast, the singular *Eloah* appears only 57 times in the OT, 41 of them in the poetic parts of Job. It is probable that the author used this rare word for God's name to further support the archaic, non-Israelite setting for the book.

The Hebrew form of the first clause—***would that it had been darkness*** (*yĕhî ḥōšek*)—is clearly connected by way of contrast with God's first words of creation (Gen 1:3), "Let there be light" (*yĕhî 'ôr*). Job regrets that God did not speak words of darkness to his birth date instead of light.

■ 5 ***Would that darkness and deepest darkness had claimed it, would that a thick cloud had settled upon it, would that darkenings of day had terrified it.*** Here Job uses four synonyms for the darkness he wishes had encompassed his birth date. The first is **darkness** (*ḥōšek*), which appears 23 times in Job. The second is ***deepest darkness*** (*ṣalmāwet*), which is used 10 times in Job. Driver-Gray describe this word as "the strongest word which Hebrew possesses to express the idea of *darkness*" (1921, 32). Its exact origin is disputed. Many understand it as a compound noun meaning "darkness of death" (from *ṣēl māwet*) or "shadow of death" (Ps 23:4 NIV mg.). In other words, this is the kind of deep darkness found in Sheol (Job 10:21-22; 38:17). The word is used later in 28:3 to describe the total darkness found in an underground mine. Amos 5:8 connects it with the chaotic power of darkness that encompassed the great deep before the first act of creation (Gen 1:2).

The third synonym for darkness is ***a thick cloud*** (*'ănānâ*). If a thick cloud had enveloped Job's birthday, then all light would have vanished from that day. The fourth synonym is **blackness** (lit. ***darkenings of day*** [*kimrîrê yôm*]). This may refer to the darkenings caused by severe storms, clouds of locusts, or even eclipses of the sun. Such occasions frequently ***terrified*** ancient people because they hinted at mysterious divine or demonic forces at work in the world.

If an intense darkness (as described by these four synonyms) had claimed possession of the day of Job's birth and never allowed God's command ("Let there be light") to penetrate its blackness, then Job would never have existed.

■ 6 ***That night***—***would that*** thick darkness ***had seized it, would that it had not joined with*** the ***days of the year, would that it had not*** entered ***the number of*** the ***months.*** Job now turns his attention from "that day" (v 4) to ***that night***—the night when he was conceived. Since night is already dark, Job wishes that **thick darkness** had taken hold of it and never let go. He uses an additional synonym for "darkness" here (*'ōpel*) that appears five other times in the book (10:22 [2x]; 23:17; 28:3; 30:26). The word is similar in meaning to the other words for "darkness" in 3:4-5 and is often used in parallel with them.

Job regrets that the night of his conception was included in the master calendar of time. How much better it would have been if a gap of darkness had filled that space instead. In v 6*b*, the MT reads *yiḥad*, meaning "rejoice" (NRSV). "Rejoice" does not fit the context, so most versions emend the text to *yēḥad*, meaning "join with," "be united with," **be included among.**

■ 7 ***Behold*** that night, ***would that it had been*** barren, ***would that a*** shout of joy ***had not entered it.*** If the night of Job's conception had not produced a child, there would have been no reason to rejoice. The adjective **barren** (*galmûd*) occurs three times in Job (here; 15:34; 30:3), always referring to something that is lacking or nonproductive.

■ **8** *Would that* **those who curse** *a day had cursed (that night),* **those who are ready to rouse Leviathan.** In the ancient world, skilled sorcerers were sometimes employed to cast a curse against someone (Num 22—24). Job wishes that such a person had cast a spell over the night of his conception. He particularly calls on those who are able to rouse up **Leviathan**, the mythological, multiheaded sea dragon (→ "Mythological Characters in Job" sidebar at Job 7:12). **Leviathan** will appear later in the book as the name of the crocodile (41:1-34). In 3:8 he is simply the name for the personified forces of chaos. Job believed that if the most skilled sorcerers in the world—those who are able to upset the order of life and cause chaos to break out on any given day—had cast their spells and recited their incantations against the night of his conception, then surely his conception would not have taken place. But, alas, they did not.

Because **Leviathan** is a sea monster, it is very tempting to emend the word for **day** (*yôm*) to "sea" (*yām*). This would contribute to the parallelism of the verse. Many scholars accept this emendation, but the harder reading is **day**, and thus more likely the original. Perhaps the author used *yôm* on purpose, knowing that it would immediately bring to mind *yām* for most readers and thus convey both meanings.

There are two different words for **curse** in v 8*a*. Both are synonyms of *qll* in 3:1. The first (**those who curse**) is from *'rr*, which occurs around sixty times in the OT but only here in Job. The word is used repeatedly in Deut 27—28 as a word of judgment against anyone who violates the covenant: "Cursed is anyone who . . ." Jeremiah uses this word twice to curse his birthday (Jer 20:14-15). In Job 3:8 it refers to the activities of skilled sorcerers such as Balaam (Num 22:6) who cast spells for a profit. The second word for **curse** (*nqb*; **had cursed [that night]**) occurs again in Job 5:3, as well as multiple times in the story of Balaam (Num 22—24).

■ **9** *Would that the stars of its [night's] twilight had* **become dark.** Job continues to add metaphors to emphasize again his wish that the night of his conception had remained an empty darkness. **Stars of its twilight** can refer to the stars of either dawn or dusk, and it is used both ways in the book of Job ("dawn" in 7:4; "dusk" in 24:15). Here the reference is clearly to the **morning stars** just before dawn, possibly the planets Mercury and Venus. Their continual brightness, even as the night sky begins to lighten, heralds the rising sun and the creation of a new day. Job wishes these celestial lights would have become dark on the night of his conception, thus depriving the sun of its forerunners and preventing it from rising. Then the night of his conception would have continued in its darkness.

Would that it had hoped for light but there was none (v 9*b*) describes the eager expectation one has for the light of each new day. Job wishes that this expectation had never been satisfied on the night of his conception. Then even the first rays of the sun would not have appeared. **The first rays of dawn** has been translated by various commentators as "eyelashes of dawn," "eyelids of dawn," or "eyeballs of dawn." The evidence is not conclusive for any one translation. Nevertheless, the meaning is plain. This is a beautiful poetic metaphor for the first rays of sunlight each morning.

■ 10 Here we finally arrive at Job's reason for cursing his birth date and wishing his life had not begun. Because "that night" (v 7) did not prevent his conception, Job has had to endure innumerable troubles. In this verse "night" is personified again (→ v 3) as a creature able to prevent conception.

Human conception was something of a mystery to ancient people. They certainly did not have knowledge of the microscopic nature of sperm and eggs, but they did know that sexual intercourse was necessary to produce a baby. The woman's womb provided a repository for the man's semen that solidified into an embryo (→ 10:10-11). They also believed that God was somehow involved in conception. Witness the stories of Abraham and Sarah (Gen 18:9-14; 21:1-2), Jacob and Rachel (Gen 30:22-23), Elkanah and Hannah (1 Sam 1:19-20), and so forth.

In Hannah's case the passage specifically states that God had "closed Hannah's womb" (1 Sam 1:6). In other words, in spite of intercourse between husband and wife, God had so affected Hannah's reproductive organs that she was incapable of producing children. The doors of her womb were shut, so to speak, preventing Elkanah's semen from entering her womb. In a figurative way, Job gives night the same power to close a woman's **womb**. Night failed to prevent his father's semen from entering his mother's **womb** and creating a new child.

The word for **trouble** (*'āmāl*) has a variety of meanings depending on its context. In Ecclesiastes it is used repeatedly to mean human "toil, hard work, labor" (see Eccl 1:3; 2:10-11; etc.). In the book of Job, however, it refers to all Job's distressful experiences in chs 1 and 2—disaster, death, disease, suffering, and alienation. Thus, the translation **trouble** is a good one. "It is Job's term for the sum of the afflictions that have come upon him" (Clines 1989, 89). The word occurs eight times in the book (3:10; 4:8; 5:6-7; 7:3; 11:16; 15:35; 16:2).

B. I Wish I Had Died at Birth (3:11-19)

Beginning with v 11, Job shifts his focus from events prior to his birth to those immediately following. Even if the day of his birth and the night of his conception (vv 3-10) had been unable to prevent his birth, why had he not been stillborn or died quickly afterward from neglect or lack of nourishment? Job begins this section with a series of questions that are sometimes described as rhetorical, but they point to no expected answer. The essence of the questions is to raise again the issue of why Job had come into existence in the first place. If he had not lived, he would never have experienced his terrible troubles.

■ 11 Verses 11-12 are both *why* questions followed by a three-line description of Sheol. This format is repeated in vv 16-19, indicating the beautiful poetic symmetry of the passage (Clines 1989, 95). The synonymous questions in these verses reveal Job's deep longing to have died in childbirth, either as a stillborn child or immediately after exiting his mother's womb. The two parallel verbs **perish** (*mwt*) and **die** (*gw'*) can indicate death from natural causes or from violence. In most usages in Job, they refer to natural death. **At birth** is literally "from the womb."

■ **12** Job repeats his desire to have died during childbirth with a question about his reception into the world. "Why were there people present at my birth to welcome me into the world and begin providing for my needs? If no one had shown up to care for me, I would have died."

The basic meaning of this verse is plain, but scholars have wrestled with the details of its interpretation. Whose **knees** and whose **breasts** are inferred? Naturally we think of Job's mother—the child exiting the womb between the mother's knees. But other suggestions have been proposed. (1) Following Gen 50:23 where Joseph lived long enough to see his great-grandchildren born "on his knees," Driver-Gray have proposed that the knees belong to Job's father, indicating he was able to hold Job on his lap and accept him into the family (1921, 36; Gordis 1978, 36-37). (2) Clines accepts the word **knees** as a metaphor for the mother's lap, connecting the parallel words **knees** and **breasts** to describe the child's position as lying on his mother's lap while nursing (1989, 90). Second Kings 4:20 describes a son lying on his mother's knees, and Isa 66:12 likens Jerusalem to a mother who plays with her children on her knees. (3) Wesley believes the **knees** were those of the midwife who assisted in Job's birth (1765, 1525). In Gen 30:3 Rachel gives her maidservant to Jacob so that the girl will become pregnant and give birth "on my [Rachel's] knees" (NKJV). Clines notes the suggestion by B. Stade of "a custom among Bedouin women of being seated upon the knees of a midwife while giving birth." The knees of the midwife served as "a kind of birthing chair" (1989, 90). All the above suggestions are possible, leading to the conclusion that the passage will probably remain ambiguous. Job simply wished that no **knees** or **breasts** had been present to **receive** him when he was born, so he would have died quickly.

■ **13-15** These verses are one long sentence describing Job's belief that his death at birth would have ushered him into a much more preferable existence. Had that happened (*IBHS*, 668), he would now be in a state of **peace** and **rest** in Sheol (v 13). Although Job's conception of the afterlife is far different from that of Christians, he did believe that life continues on beyond the grave. It is just not a *meaningful* life.

As the sentence continues in vv 14-15, Job imagined that if he had died in childbirth and gone to Sheol he would now be in company with royalty and people of wealth and power. These people, while living, **built** impressive cities and monuments and accumulated **gold** and **silver** for themselves. "Counselors of the earth" (NRSV) probably refers to high government officials and/or advisers to the king. None of these important people were now enjoying their building projects, honor, and wealth, for they were all **at rest**.

There has been much scholarly discussion about the meaning of v 14*b*. The verb *bnh* can mean either "build" or "rebuild" depending on the context. The question is whether the context speaks of earlier building projects that have now become ruins or of earlier ruins that have now been rebuilt into cities and monuments. Some follow the NIV reading: **who built for themselves places now lying in ruins** (Rowley 1976, 42; Habel 1985, 102). Others support the NRSV: "who rebuild ruins for themselves" (Gordis 1978, 37; Clines 1989, 72-73). Such rebuilding projects were very common in ancient times.

Archaeologists have shown that most ancient cities were actually a series of cities, one on top of the other, built, destroyed, and rebuilt many times over hundreds of years. Either reading can be derived from the Hebrew text, and it is difficult to make a choice when both types of building projects were well-known in ancient times. At this point, Clines has probably gathered the most evidence to support the NRSV reading as the correct one (1989, 72-73).

■ **16** Job repeats his intense longing that his life had never begun (→ v 11). The Hebrew for **stillborn child** (*nēpel*) appears only two other times in the OT (Ps 58:8 [9 HB]; Eccl 6:3). It pertains to a fetus that *falls* out of its mother's womb before it is capable of life on its own. It **never saw the light of day** because it was buried immediately after exiting its mother's womb. In another occurrence of *nēpel* (Eccl 6:3-5), Qoheleth echoes Job's thought here. It is better to be a stillborn child than live a life of unhappiness and misery, for a stillborn child is at rest.

■ **17-19** In Job 3:18-19 Job lays out three sets of social relationships where one party clearly has the advantage over the other: **taskmasters** over **captives** (v 18), **the great** (v 19) over **the small**, and "masters" (NRSV) over **slaves**. The context, therefore, supports the notion that v 17 is to be interpreted similarly. **The wicked** are the oppressors and **the weary** are the oppressed. Job states that in Sheol all turmoil and social conflict between these groups will come to an end. The Hebrew for **the weary** (*yĕgî'ê kōaḥ*; lit. "the exhausted ones of strength") is a unique phrase that appears only here in the OT.

In Sheol, **captives** (probably prisoners of war) need not fear the oppression from their **taskmasters** any longer, for both are at rest together. **Captives** were often pressed into hard labor by a local king to construct royal building projects. Their labor was organized and directed by **taskmasters**. The word for "taskmaster" (*nōgēś*; NRSV) also appears in Exod 3:7; 5:6, 10, 13-14 for the Egyptian taskmasters who directed the Israelite forced labor.

The small and **the great**, and everyone in between, are all in Sheol. No one can avoid death and the afterlife. But in Job's Sheol there is none of the turmoil, social tensions, and even hostility that all too often characterize relationships on earth between social classes. In death, all people—from **kings**, "counselors" (NRSV), and **rulers**/"princes" (vv 13-15) to **the weary**, **captives**, and **slaves** (vv 17-19)—are equally at rest. This was the main attraction of Sheol for Job. Intriguingly, Job's description of Sheol does not touch at all on some of the principal causes of his own turmoil—disease and natural disasters. One would think that he would describe Sheol as a place devoid of these problems as well. Instead, his focus is on human relationships, as if he were presenting a sociologist's view of the afterlife.

Both **small** and **great** are rungs on the ladder of success with which Job could identify. In the early years of his life (1:1-5 and ch 29), Job found himself in company with those of high standing. But the Examiner's attacks reduced him to the status of the lowly. His fame, fortune, and good health were long gone. He now knows what it is like to live in poverty, in misery, and in isolation. So by this point in the book he probably identifies more with **the small** than with **the great**.

Sheol

The Israelite conception of Sheol (the afterlife) is not clearly defined in any one place in the OT. We have to draw from a number of passages, and even then the description is not complete. One of the most helpful passages is Ps 88, where Sheol is described as a deep, dark pit under the ground where people descend after death (vv 4, 6 [5, 7 HB]). The inhabitants live a shadowy existence as shades/ghosts (v 10 [11 HB]). There is no evidence of God's steadfast love, faithfulness, or miraculous acts in Sheol (vv 11-12 [12-13 HB]). Neither is there communion with God. People feel forsaken, cut off from God. They cannot even praise him in Sheol because they do not remember him (vv 5, 10, 12 [6, 11, 13 HB]).

Other passages in the OT speak of a "place of silence" (Ps 115:17), a place from which no one can escape (Ps 89:48 [49 HB]), and a place where everyone goes—both the righteous and the wicked. In 1 Sam 28:19 we read that Samuel, God's holy prophet, as well as sinful King Saul and his sons all went to Sheol. And righteous Jacob also was headed toward Sheol (Gen 37:35).

The book of Job adds further descriptive terms. In the passage under discussion (Job 3:13-19), Sheol is seen as a place where all social classes are found, from kings to slaves and small to great (vv 14-15, 19), a place where there is no conflict between people of different social status (vv 17-18), and a place of quiet and peaceful rest (vv 13, 17). Other passages speak of a place of gloom, deep darkness, and chaos (10:21-22), and a place of dust that people enter through bars or gates (17:16). It is also a place where people lose contact with the living (14:21).

None of the descriptors above sound very attractive, either to us or the ancient Israelites. In fact, Israelites did not want to go to Sheol. They were terrified by the thought and sometimes pleaded with God to heal them from a terminal illness (Ps 6:2 [3 HB]) or spare them from descending to the pit (Ps 28:1-2). The laments in the Psalter are filled with mournful pleas for God to deliver the psalmist from death. There is no passage anywhere in the OT that portrays the positive confidence in life after death that is found in the NT, such as Jesus' words in John 14:1-3 and Paul's in Phil 1:21.

If Sheol was such an unpleasant place, why did Job want to go there? Granted, Job was not an Israelite, but his belief system about the afterlife was totally Israelite in nature. Therefore, he had nothing positive to look forward to in Sheol—no mansion over the hilltop, no streets of gold, no city that needs no sun. So why did he want to die? Simply stated, Job wanted to die in order to rid himself of his awful existence. Even as bad as Sheol might be, from Job's perspective it sounded a lot better than continuing in this life. And if his birth had never occurred or he had experienced death shortly after birth, so much the better. Ecclesiastes 4:2-3 expresses the same thought.

In Job 3 we see for the first time how deeply Job has been hurt by the troubles of chs 1 and 2. Job has lost his way in life. He believed that God had created a hedge around him (3:23) that prevented him from living a meaningful life. Life now had no purpose for him. He was living in mental and emotional chaos and at the same time experiencing intense physical pain.

Most people of religious faith have great difficulty in understanding Job's desperate longing to die. They are uncomfortable with the notion that someone could be so devoid of hope that they desire death more than life. Wesley even calls it a sin to harbor such thoughts. It is "ungrateful to the giver of life, and shews a sinful indulgence of our own passion" (1765, 1526).

However, just like Job, there are people today who feel such a deep sense of frustration and anger at life that they want to die. For them, life has no hope or future. They are living in chaos. With Job, they see death as an escape route, a way out, a more attractive option than rebuilding their lives around something solid, such as a family member, a friend, a cause, or an experience with God.

The topic of euthanasia (lit. "easy death"), especially as it relates to terminal illnesses, is an issue of great relevance and importance in the field of medical ethics today. Job's experiences do not provide an answer to this complex problem, but they do help us identify with people like him who are experiencing intense physical and emotional pain. They help us begin to understand why a few desire death over life.

C. I Wish My Life Would End Now (3:20-26)

Having failed to prevent his conception and birth, Job now directs his attention to the present moment. He wishes he would die right now (also 6:8-9). The format of this section is a little different. The questions in 3:20-23 are asked in the third-person plural, leading some to believe that Job was expanding his horizons to include other sufferers besides himself and speaking of life in general. This may be true, but one can easily see that Job's own personal suffering was at the heart of his mournful questions.

■ 20-22 Throughout ch 3 Job has skillfully woven together the dual themes of light and darkness. **Light** (v 20) for him represents life, and darkness means death. He has already expressed his anger at being born and receiving the light of life (vv 4, 16). He wishes he had remained in darkness. Verses 20-22, which are one long sentence, simply rephrase that anger in a more general way. Job asks, "Why does the light of life come to people who are **in misery**, who are **bitter of soul**, who **long for death**, and who **rejoice when they reach the grave**?" This is a generic question that is intended to include everyone who has ever experienced any of these four conditions, but the description fits Job perfectly. The question is addressed to no one in particular, but God is implied as the one who gives the light (→ also vv 11, 12, 16, 23).

In misery (v 20) indicates people who are suffering. **Bitter of soul** refers to persons who are deeply distressed by life situations (e.g., Hannah at the time she was childless [1 Sam 1:10]). **Long for death** (Job 3:21) is a phrase that expresses a yearning to die. This longing is even greater than that of people who "dig" (NRSV) for **hidden treasure**. Job's metaphor could be a reference to grave robbers who search for valuables buried with a corpse in a tomb, or to prospectors who dig in the earth for precious metals and gems (28:1-11). Since Sheol and hidden treasure are both under the ground, the metaphor is appropriate. Revelation 9:6 alludes to Job 3:21 when it describes people as longing to die to escape the great tribulation in the last days.

In v 22 Job speaks of the joy experienced by suffering people when they finally **reach the grave**. The reason for their joyfulness is the end of their misery. Job earnestly wanted to know why God allows life to continue for those who long to end it.

■ 23 Here Job reveals his confusion in trying to understand God's pathway for his life. His calamities have turned his former peaceful existence into chaos. His mind is now disoriented. He does not know which way to go because the way forward **is hidden**. He is like a blind person without any bearings. So **why is life given** to people such as this (this question is not found in the MT, but it is inferred from v 20, which it parallels)? They would be better off dead. Throughout ch 3 Job has repeatedly mentioned that the path to Sheol is the only viable option available to him—whether before birth, after birth, or at the present moment.

People can lose their way in life for a variety of reasons: their own foolish choices, the actions of other people, circumstances beyond their control, and so forth. In this verse Job deals with the obstructions caused by **God** (*Eloah*). God **has hedged** him **in**. This verb has already appeared in 1:10 in the mouth of the Examiner who accused God of placing a hedge of blessing around Job that kept him from experiencing life's troubles. Ironically, now Job speaks of a different kind of hedge—a hedge of obstruction that keeps people from finding their way in life. Hedges, just like walls around cities or fences around yards, can be used to keep people and things in or out. They can be protective (1:10) or restrictive (3:23), depending on one's perspective (Rowley 1976, 44).

The Hebrew word for **way** (*derek*) has three usages in Job. (1) It may refer to a road or pathway that leads from one location to another (6:18). (2) It may be used as a metaphor for the pathway in life that one is taking. This is the meaning in 3:23. Job believed God had obstructed the pathway of his life with the result that he was confused and disoriented. (3) The most frequent usage is in reference to the two main spiritual pathways of life—"the way of the righteous" and "the way of the wicked" (Ps 1:6). An example of the former is found in Job 4:6. This meaning is featured prominently in the wisdom literature, the Psalms, and the Prophets.

■ 24 The imagery in 3:24 is somewhat confusing since **food** and **water** are both sources of nourishment that are normally ingested rather than poured out. Wesley (supported by the NASB) believes that Job is referring to the sight of his food, which reminded him of his wretched life and brought forth more groaning (1765, 1526). Every time he ate, he knew he was nourishing his body to live another day in pain. He would have rather quit eating and die.

Gordis (supported by the NRSV) holds that the imagery relates to the regularity of food and water (1978, 39). Job's groans gush forth from him on a regular basis just like bread and water are served daily. Clines (supported by the NIV) goes a step further by suggesting that Job's moans and groans are not just *like* food; they *are* his food: "For my sighs are my daily bread" (1989, 68). The issue is unresolved, but the message is clear. Job is very vocal about his suffering. He bellows forth moans and groans that would make most people uncomfortable in his presence.

■ **25-26** These verses are the explanation for Job's audible groanings (v 24). Fear has such a grip on him that he literally trembles. His life lacks **peace, quietness,** and **rest**. He used the Hebrew words for **quietness** and **rest** in v 13 to wish for himself a better life in Sheol. But alas, his wishes were not realized. Now he must live with raging, inner **turmoil** (see v 17).

What exactly is the fear that Job was experiencing? Gordis suggests "the natural sense of insecurity felt by any sensitive human being with regard both to his actions and to his fate" (1978, 39). Normal people sometimes have anxieties and nightmares about possibilities—a brain tumor, a horrible accident, a confrontation with a burglar in one's home, a terribly embarrassing social situation, the welfare of one's children, or the death of one's parents, to name a few.

Perhaps Job had always possessed a lingering fear that something bad would disrupt his peaceful life. If so, he was right, for his anxieties turned out to be more than possibilities. They were a present reality. In support of Gordis' suggestion, one could add the depiction of Job in the prologue. There we learn that he was a cautious individual who took no risks in guarding the integrity of himself and his family. He even went overboard to protect his children by offering sacrifices for them just in case one of them had sinned (1:5).

However, other scholars argue that by the time we reach ch 3 Job's fears are no longer just natural anxieties. After the attacks by the Examiner, he became possessed with a "debilitating fear" that controlled his entire life (Habel 1985, 112). The verbs used in v 25 carry an intensified meaning that speaks of one who is even trembling with fear. Indeed, the words that form his testimony in the third section of his speech (vv 20-26) are all forceful words of pain and torment. He is a person in such misery that he longs for death. In this section we start to see the terrible burden that Job carried within. Clines describes his emotions as "deep, raw, and terrifying" (1989, 104), while Hartley depicts him as "filled with deep agitation, which encompasses physical torment, agony of mind, and social discomfort" (1988, 100).

The time when Job's intense fears first began is impossible to pinpoint. Perhaps they started with the announcement by the first messenger (1:14). Or perhaps they settled in after all the damage had been done by the Examiner and Job had time to reflect on its meaning and impact on his life. In any case, 3:25 implies that Job had known prior to his afflictions that trouble can strike at any time, for he had lived long enough to see others affected. But evidently, he had always believed, as do most of us, that tragedy only happens to *someone else*. We delude ourselves into believing we are immune from the tragedies of life. No one is ever prepared for disaster, much less five of them at one time. Job had to learn the hard way that life is full of zigs and zags.

FROM THE TEXT

1. Reasons for Job's Fears. Job certainly had a number of obvious reasons to be fearful. The loss of all his animals left him in financial ruin. His reputation was in shambles. His days on earth were probably numbered due to a disease that could be terminal. And his pride and investment in his family had now come to an end, for his children were all dead. These were serious problems to reckon with, and they should not be trivialized. But we all have known people who have experienced one or more of them and still been able to create a meaningful life for themselves. So what drove Job to consider Sheol as his only viable option? Was it a combination of these losses or something else? There were probably at least three contributing elements to Job's terrifying fears.

First, the order in his world was gone. As a whole, the wisdom literature supports the belief that order is embedded in our universe. God not only created the world but also ordered it in ways that provide stability and regularity. One of our tasks as human beings is to discover this order and live in harmony with it. By following the patterns of life that God has established, we not only learn more about God and his handiwork but also can enjoy life as God intended from the beginning. The book of Proverbs emphasizes this concept of order over and over again using hundreds of short sayings. Job also believed in this concept completely. His life as described in Job 1:1 was a model of righteous living. Every aspect of his conduct had God's approval (v 8).

However, sometimes in spite of our best efforts, life goes topsy-turvy. The foundations on which we have built our faith are shaken. The lighthouses on the shore that always provided guidance go dark. Because of the Examiner's assaults, Job had become disconnected from the order of life. All he had trusted in for years was shattered. He describes in 3:23 how he had lost his way. He was confused and disoriented by events that seemed random and meaningless. This was at the heart of Job's desire to go to Sheol, for in Sheol he knew there was still order in the form of rest (v 13).

Second, the future was uncertain. Job was not paranoid, but he did have good reason to fear the future. The reader knows that the prologue reveals *all* the calamities that Job was going to experience. The Examiner did his dirty work with the permission of God and then disappeared completely at the end of ch 2. But Job did not read the prologue and was not privy to the conversations that took place in heaven. All he knew was that four disasters and a painful disease had struck him one after the other in very short order. He retreated to the city dump to try to sort things out, but he had no assurance his ordeal was over. For all he knew, there could still be further assaults against him or his wife or his extended family. The future looked bleak indeed. So much trouble in so little time had left Job terrified there was still more to come.

Third, God's relationship to all of Job's troubles was unknown. Job certainly sensed from the very beginning that God was connected in some way with his suffering (1:21). A number of factors seemed to confirm that these disasters were no mere coincidence. But beyond that, Job was completely in the dark. Nothing he had experienced previously had prepared him for the onslaught by the Examiner. No doubt, while sitting alone on the city dump for many days, he had pondered over some of the following questions: "God, how are you related to my troubles? Did you cause them? If so, why? Are you aware of what has happened to me? If I pray for relief, will you answer me?"

A strong relationship with God is a crucial contributing factor to our overall well-being. Wholeness in body, mind, and spirit is necessary for complete health. Life is uncertain, bringing serious diseases to our body and fearful anxieties to our mind from time to time. But a belief in God provides a rock of stability outside of this world to which we can anchor our soul through the storms of life. Job needed to hear directly from God about his relationship to the calamities in the prologue. And this is why later in the book he repeatedly pleads with God for an explanation of his troubles. Without some kind of assurance from God, he will remain terrified.

The key to understanding Job's state of mind in ch 3 is v 23. Job believed that his pathway was hidden, obstructed by a hedge he could not see over or around. He could not move forward because he could not see the way, and he could not go back because the Examiner had taken away all the meaningful things in his past. Job would remain in this sad plight for many more chapters until God chose to meet with him in ch 38. In the meantime, his only hope was that God would put him out of his misery and send him to the depths of Sheol.

2. Why the Change in Job's Character? Every reader of the book is immediately struck by the sharp difference in Job's character between the prologue and ch 3. How could a person change so drastically from the calm, cool, collected Job of 1:21 to the agitated, angry, cursing Job of 3:11? The following questions are inevitable.

- Is there really a change in Job, or do we just get to know more about him? We certainly know more about Job in ch 3, but there also seems to be a definite change that expresses itself in very forceful language. So the correct answer is probably some of both.
- Is Job going through a series of emotional stages, like the normal stages of grief? Perhaps. This is a possibility, but not provable without more information.

- Is Job's reaction in the prologue (1:21) an example of a public statement given by someone in complete shock? And now (ch 3) that he has had some time to live with his problems and reflect on them, the reality of what he has lost has sunk in? We have all witnessed on TV the sad confessions of people in high places who have been caught in wrongdoing. Their prepared statements are usually short and delivered without emotion. They are for public presentation only and reveal nothing of the person's true feelings. Again, this is a possibility with Job, but we would need more information.
- Is Job's response in the prologue simply a literary device to prove the Examiner wrong? The statement does prove the Examiner wrong, but it also reveals a side of Job that we need to see before we are introduced to the raw emotions of ch 3. We need to know the heights from which he has fallen and how deeply he has been hurt.
- Or is the author simply letting the nature of his material dictate the level of emotion that belongs in each section? Most likely, the author intended for the narrative in the prologue to present a straightforward story with the necessary characters and plot, and he reserved the high-intensity emotional language for the poetic dialogues. In reality, perhaps the author has blended some percentage of all these possibilities in creating his literary masterpiece.

3. What Do We Learn about Job in Ch 3 That We Did Not Know in the Prologue? We learn that Job is a normal human being like the rest of us. He had all the typical emotions that any human being possesses, and he used an earthy language to express it. Clines believes ch 3 was written to reveal Job's inner feelings, and he calls this chapter "the drama of a human soul" (1989, 104). By sharing with us his deepest feelings and darkest fears, Job draws us into his world of trouble. Although his loud cursings and groanings make us very uncomfortable, we cannot turn away from him, for his humanity and vulnerability are so much like ours. But in return we gain a friend who will serve us well by asking God the very questions we would like to ask. And perhaps, if we continue to share his journey until the end of the book, we will receive an answer we can live with.

We also learn that Job's God accepts his ranting and raving. Job is never condemned for his emotional language, even when he curses his birthday (v 3). That is not to say that his emotional outbursts are appropriate in a social setting. It is simply to point out that God accepts our personal prayers to him that are laced with emotional overload. Emotions are a part of our humanity. God does not force us to put aside our human nature in order to communicate with him. This lesson is taught in other books of the OT as well, such as in the confessions of Jeremiah and the imprecatory psalms.

Christianity has sometimes been led astray into a false understanding of human emotion—a Puritan, stoical self-control that allows for no outward expression of feeling at all. But such a belief is totally contrary to Scripture (see Andersen 1976, 100-101, for an excellent discussion of this topic in relation to Job). People who have been deeply hurt in life are not likely to utter shallow clichés. They are more likely to use a language like Job's that is earthy and coarse. God accepts it all without rebuke, for which we all are thankful.

3:1-26

III. FIRST CYCLE OF SPEECHES: JOB 4—14

BEHIND THE TEXT

4:1—
14:22

The dialogue between Job and his three friends is a series of short speeches that form the nucleus of the book (chs 4—27). Eliphaz is the first to speak, followed by Bildad and Zophar. In between each of the friends' presentations, Job responds. This entire series of speeches is called one cycle, which then repeats two more times. The length of time for the three cycles is unknown, but it is not important to the story. "The reader forgets the passage of time" (Good 1990, 298).

Scholars usually call this section "The Dialogues," but it is not a typical human conversation. In real life, people talk back and forth in short statements, jumping from topic to topic and sometimes interrupting each other in mid-sentence. In contrast, the book of Job contains a carefully crafted set of speeches. Each person presents his argument and then the next follows. The speakers do not always address the issues raised by the previous speaker. Sometimes they return to earlier topics, and other times they go off in a completely different direction. Although some of the speeches get pretty heated, there is always a proper decorum. No one is ever interrupted, and the speakers always appear in the same order. This section is more like a staged production than an actual dialogue.

In these speeches the author uses the characters to present popular explanations for Job's suffering and recommendations for its cure. These interpretations are part of what is called the wisdom theology or wisdom tradition. This theology appears in other sections of the OT, especially the book of Proverbs. In Job, the author forces us to test some of the ideas of the wisdom theology against the reality of Job's troubles. How do they measure up when examined against the hardships of real life? Many parts of the wisdom theology appear in the NT and are still ingrained in popular thinking today (e.g., "You reap what you sow"). Thus, the majority of the friends' arguments will sound very familiar and convincing to modern readers. For this reason, the book of Job is just as relevant today as it was to the ancient Israelites.

There is a great temptation to categorize the characters in the book as either good guys or bad guys, but these classifications are greatly oversimplified. The hero of the story is supposedly Job, but he is severely criticized by God for some of the things he says. Likewise, the three friends are usually seen as the villains because they are denounced by God in the epilogue, but many of the things they say are true. So, one must be cautious and critical in analyzing the dialogues. A reader cannot just pick up isolated statements and assume they are true or false depending on who spoke them. The entire context of the book is needed in order to make an accurate evaluation. Therefore, we will wait until the speeches are finished before passing judgment on each character. For now, we will simply exegete the basic content of each speech and examine the reaction given by the other speakers.

The author of the book does not give us a description of the character of each friend, as he did with Job in the prologue. Nevertheless, we do gain some insight into their personalities. Generally speaking, Eliphaz is classified as the mystic of the group because of his supernatural vision in ch 4. Bildad is called the traditionalist because he repeatedly looks to the past to find support for his arguments. And Zophar is the dogmatist who emphasizes the same point over and over. But these are only generalizations. We will learn much more about them as we listen to their presentations.

The age of the three friends has been a matter of much speculation. Two verses (12:12; 15:10) imply that they were all older than Job, perhaps even as old as his father, but the relative age between the friends is not known. Eliphaz is sometimes called the oldest because he is the first to speak. Also, his speeches are a little longer than the others, and he is the only friend addressed directly by God at the end of the book (42:7-8). However, this evidence may only point to his preeminence among the three and not his age.

IN THE TEXT

A. Eliphaz's First Speech (4:1—5:27)

Now that Job has spoken and broken the long silence, the three friends feel free to address Job directly with their thoughts. Job did not speak specifically to them in ch 3, but they had listened and no doubt were shocked and dismayed by what they heard. Job's words did not fit the old Job they had known before. They were eager to express their views and help Job understand his situation.

Eliphaz's first speech is rather mild in tone, considering that Job had just delivered an emotional death wish. But the wise old sage chose to bypass any criticism of Job's outburst and focused instead on universal principles by which the universe operates. This first speech is the gentlest in the entire book. It divides into the following sections:

1. May We Speak with You? (4:1-6)
2. People Reap What They Sow (4:7-11)
3. Listen to What God Has Revealed to Me (4:12-21)
4. Trouble Is Inevitable (5:1-7)
5. God Is the Only Genuine Source of Help (5:8-16)
6. Sometimes God Disciplines Us (5:17-27)

1. May We Speak with You? (4:1-6)

Eliphaz the Temanite (→ 2:11) begins by complimenting Job on past examples of his righteousness. Then he chides Job a little for not following his own advice and urges him to return to the tried and true basis for his faith in the past.

■ 1 Eliphaz's words are introduced with an introductory formula that follows the pattern of all the speeches in Job (→ 3:2).

■ 2 Some of the words used to describe Eliphaz's opening remarks are: "polite," "diplomatic," "respectful," and "cautious." He wants to speak, but he is worried that Job may take offense, so he gently eases into the conversation. His first words are a question: **If someone ventures a word with you, will you be *upset*?** Eliphaz fears that Job may be "offended" (NRSV) if someone mentions his suffering. But Eliphaz cannot keep quiet: **Who can keep from speaking?** (lit. "who can hold back with words?"). The Hebrew for "words" is not the more common *dābār* as in the first clause, but the much rarer Aramaic loanword *millâ*, which appears thirty-four times in Job. Thirteen times it has the Aramaic plural ending *-în*, which is used in poetic passages and later books of the OT (*IBHS*, 118).

After hearing Job's outbursts in ch 3, some people would likely back off from any meaningful conversation and engage only in small talk, lest Job be further offended. But Eliphaz plunges right into the conversation as soon as he is given an opening. He says he feels compelled to talk. He does not give reasons for this urgency, but some scholars suggest his main concern is to defend God and correct Job's attitude before God brings more suffering (Driver-Gray 1921, 40). More likely, Eliphaz sensed that Job was troubled and in need of counsel (4:5). He wanted to share a vision he had received from God (vv 12-21), and he believed he had some wise advice to offer that had proven true in the past (5:27).

■ 3-4 Job's conduct in earlier days was exemplary. Eliphaz points out four activities that Job engaged in before disaster struck. All of them are examples of the type of deeds performed by a righteous person. The imperfect verb forms in three of the verbs suggest that Job performed these acts of righteousness continually (GKC, §107*e*). Even though he was wealthy beyond description, he did not turn to a life of luxurious excesses. He took a particular interest in those who were less fortunate than himself.

First, Job **instructed many** people (4:3). The verb here (*ysr*) "refers particularly to moral and religious instruction, both by word and by discipline" (Hartley 1988, 105). The word is often connected with "rebuke" and "chastening" as a method of teaching. This verse is the only place where the word appears in Job, but it occurs fourteen times in Proverbs and Psalms, most of them with the meaning "correct" or "chasten."

Second, Job **strengthened feeble hands**—the hands of those who were too weak to do necessary things for themselves. Third, Job ***raised up*** those who stumbled (Job 4:4). These were people who were staggering or actually falling from weariness, heavy burdens, or attack from enemies (Ps 27:2; Isa 40:30; Lam 5:13). Fourth, Job **strengthened faltering knees**. He offered his help to people who had collapsed from the trials of life. The same concept of **feeble hands** and **faltering knees** appears in Isa 35:3 and Heb 12:12. Eliphaz does not give any evidence for these four activities in Job's life, but apparently, he had had enough contact with Job in the past to have knowledge of his compassion for others. Job himself will provide the evidence for his kindheartedness in Job 29:7-25.

Eliphaz's words of praise in these two verses are some of the most complimentary remarks directed at Job anywhere in the dialogues. His purpose is to get Job's mind off his present troubles and force him to think about the advice he has given to other people in the past who have experienced terrible suffering.

■ **5** Eliphaz takes up Job's present predicament in 4:5. At one time Job had been a helper and counselor to others in distress, **but now** he himself is in need of assistance. There has been a reversal of roles. Eliphaz's point is that Job should not turn away from the very advice he had handed out to others. His argument is well taken. Sometimes people in the helping professions (e.g., ministers, physicians, nurses, counselors, social workers) are unable to deal with problems in their own lives. Even though they have helped hundreds of others, they find it extremely difficult to examine themselves objectively. They may need outside support and advice.

The **trouble** that has now come to Job is the result of the calamities in the prologue. It has left him ***upset*** (v 5*a*; the same word was used in v 2*a*) and ***extremely troubled*** (v 5*b*; Gen 45:3; 2 Sam 4:1). There is actually no Hebrew word for **trouble** in this verse, but a word like it is implied from the context (GKC, §144*b*). **It strikes you**. The Hebrew for **strikes** (*ng'*) in this context means "to touch" with negative results. The same word was used by the messenger in Job 1:19 to report how the wind "struck the four corners of the house."

■ **6** Next Eliphaz points out the resources available to Job to help him through his difficulties. In particular, he directs his attention back to his faith in God (lit. "fear"; probably a shortened form for "fear of God") and his character (**blameless**

ways) before the disasters struck. The author clearly intended to connect Eliphaz's comment here with the description of Job in the prologue ("blameless" [*tōm*] is the noun form of the adjective *tām* used in 1:1). There his character was beyond reproach. He was a supersaint who feared God and lived out a life of moral wholeness. But now, Job's mournful cries and curses in ch 3 have alarmed Eliphaz. He fears that Job has abandoned his former faith and religious practices. He encourages Job to reestablish his **confidence** (*kislâ*) and **hope** (*tiqwâ*) for the future in the resources that worked for him in the past.

This verse is worded in the form of a rhetorical question intended to reconnect Job with a time in his life when things were going well for him. When people have lost their way in life, it helps to return to prior days when the pathway was clear, and to review in one's mind the reasons why life was successful at that time. In essence, Eliphaz is asking, "At one time you trusted in God and your righteous ways. Why did you stop? Do not turn back from your former ways!" In the NT Paul encouraged the Philippians with similar words: "Keep on doing the things that you have learned and received and heard and seen in me, and the God of peace will be with you" (Phil 4:9 NRSV).

Commentators are divided over the tone of voice used by Eliphaz in Job 4:5-6. Are his words "a warning" (Smick 1988, 895), "a mild reproof" (Hartley 1988, 107), "sarcasm" (McKenna 1986, 59), or "a sympathetic encouragement" (Clines 1989, 121)? In later speeches, Eliphaz will turn more antagonistic, but here he seems to be very respectful of Job. Andersen suggests that this early in Eliphaz's speeches we should give him "the benefit of the doubt, and find his words, not a taunt, but a kindly reminder that Job's past life of godliness has given him resources for the present crisis" (1976, 111).

On the surface Eliphaz's advice seems reasonable. Job certainly needed to maintain his trust in God and practice a morally wholesome lifestyle whether he was doing well or experiencing trouble. However, Eliphaz was operating from the assumption of the wisdom theology that God *always* rewards the righteous. Therefore, Job's condition would improve if he regained his confidence and hope in God. The problem with that line of reasoning is that it fails to take into account the real cause of Job's difficulties. Eliphaz and the other friends will continue to misdiagnose Job's condition because they are oblivious to the conversation between God and the Examiner in the prologue.

2. People Reap What They Sow (4:7-11)

Eliphaz now takes up the issue of divine retribution. He asks Job to consider a general truism of the wisdom theology that has universal application: we reap what we sow. All people receive the exact consequences that correspond to the choices they make in life. God does not play favorites. He abides by the orderly principles he has established in the moral universe. Eliphaz presents his own observations of life as proof that this is true and then uses a proverbial illustration concerning lions to conclude his argument.

Verses 7-11 are significant in the overall scheme of the book as they touch on the topic of theodicy (the justice of God). How does one explain human suffering while at the same time defending God's omnipotence, justice, and goodness? Balentine notes how the entire OT generally supports the doctrine of rewards and retribution. God does punish the wicked. "However, as the dialogues unfold, Eliphaz and the friends exemplify how this truth may be overstated or misapplied. Theirs is the approach of those who maintain a safe distance from the suffering of others in order to defend doctrine at the expense of compassion" (2006, 109). But he also states that the OT allows for exceptions and protests against the doctrine of rewards and retribution. And the book of Job is one of the chief protestors. It "preserves the most sustained challenge to the validity of divine retribution in Hebrew scripture" (ibid.).

■ **7 Consider now** is Eliphaz's way of introducing a universal principle he believes Job already accepts. The principle is presented in the form of two parallel rhetorical questions about the fate of people who are righteous. Does Job know of any persons considered **innocent** or **upright** who have ever **perished** or been **destroyed**? The expected answer is no. God never punishes the righteous. **Innocent** (*nāqî*), a word used six times in Job, refers to persons free of blame or guilt. The word is used in parallel with **upright** (*yāšār*; 1:1), meaning "morally straight."

At first reading, Eliphaz's question appears patently false, for righteous people grow old and die, just like everyone else. However, he is more likely speaking of the avoidance of premature death (Clines 1989, 124). Likewise, Eliphaz is not advocating that righteous people never experience trouble. Later in this speech (5:17-26) he admits that trouble does come to all. But any trouble that befalls righteous persons is used by God to discipline his people for their own good. In Eliphaz's mind, righteousness always, without exception, leads to a long, full life with very little trouble. This is a universal principle of the wisdom theology, but by implication, Eliphaz is referring to Job. Job has already been described as **upright** in 1:1, and he is still living. Therefore, he should be hopeful about his restoration.

■ **8** The universal principle in 4:7 has a corresponding negative side. While the righteous may avoid bad consequences, the wicked are doomed to trouble and failure. Again, there are no exceptions. Eliphaz describes this principle as one he has **observed** throughout his life. He presents it in the form of an agricultural illustration: **those who plow** and **sow** will **reap**. Just as the farmer's harvest follows logically from the prior steps of plowing and sowing, so by implication, **evil** and **trouble** are harvested by those who plant their seeds. The verbs **plow** and **sow** are active verbs, indicating purposeful intent on the part of the sower. These are people "who [do] not merely fall into sin, but deliberately cultivate sin, or sin of set purpose" (Rowley 1976, 46). The word for **evil** (*'āwen*) is a common term in the OT, generally rendered "wickedness," "evil," or "iniquity." In this verse it is paired with **trouble** (*'āmāl*), which is one of Job's key terms to describe his suffering (3:10). In 11:14 it is paired with ***injustice*** (*'awlâ*), and in 15:35 with "deceit" (*mirmâ*).

■ **9** Here Eliphaz uses the sensory image of **God's** [*Eloah*] **breath** (*nĕšāmâ*) as a metaphor for the divine destructive power that brings the wicked to an untimely death. Paul used the same imagery to describe the destruction of "the man of lawlessness" by Jesus at the time of his second coming ("with the breath of his mouth" [2 Thess 2:8]). The parallel term in Job 4:9*b* is **blast** (*rûaḥ*), a very common word in the OT for "breath," "wind," or "spirit." **God's breath** can be viewed in a positive sense in passages such as the creation story (Gen 1:2; 2:7). But here (as also in Exod 15:8; 2 Sam 22:16; Isa 40:7; Hos 13:15) the wind is a powerful blast from God's nostrils (*'appô*; lit. "his nose," metaphorically **his anger**) that causes death. Eliphaz makes it clear that the destruction of the wicked is not dependent on fate or natural causes. Rather, God is the one who causes them to **perish**.

■ **10-11** Habel calls Job 4:10-11 a proverb (1985, 126). Using a cause-and-effect method of reasoning, Eliphaz likens the demise of a den of lions to the destruction of the wicked (vv 8-9). When the teeth of the adult lions are broken (presumably by God), their ability to hunt is gone. The effect on the entire den is the scattering of the animals and their inevitable death. Eliphaz's point is that even the mightiest of the wicked are inevitably punished by God. The use of a lion as a metaphor for the wicked appears also in Pss 10:9; 17:12; 22:13 [14 HB], 21 [22 HB].

Very uniquely and skillfully, the author employs five words for "lion," indicating the richness of his vocabulary. The words are: *'aryēh* (**lions**), *šaḥal* ("fierce lion" [NRSV]; the translation is missing in the NIV), and *kĕpîrîm* (**great lions**) in Job 4:10, and *layiš* (**lion**) and *lābî'* (**lioness**) in v 11. Altogether, the five synonyms probably have slight differences of meaning referring to the age, gender, and ferocity of the lions, but these details are lost (see Seow on the meaning of each word [2013, 397-98]). We have already seen that this author likes to parade a series of synonyms one after the other for maximum poetic and emotional effect. He does this with the words for "darkness" (3:5-7; 10:21-22) and for "miscarriage" (NASB)/"stillborn" (3:16).

The structure of 4:10*a* is difficult because there is no verb in the Hebrew. Clines attempts to rectify the difficulty by inserting the verb "cut off" as a parallel to **broken** ("The roar of the lion, the growl of the young lion, are cut off" [1989, 107]). Some such verb may be implied. **Roar** is the same word used of Job's "groans" in 3:24. The word for **broken** (*ntʿ*) is another *hapax legomenon* (→ 2:8). Scholars differ over its origin and meaning, but many interpret it as a by-form of Hebrew *ntṣ* influenced by Aramaic (ibid., 110). Greenspahn proposes "crushed" as the meaning (1984, 138-39).

Cause-and-Effect Reasoning

In 4:7-11 Eliphaz states his belief in a world that is rigidly ordered by God. For him, there are direct, moral, cause-and-effect relationships embedded in the very fabric of life. Righteousness always produces blessing, and wickedness brings judgment and destruction. Nothing can violate this principle of rewards and retribution. Eliphaz does not yet apply this teaching directly to Job. He is trying to be kind and respectful, and so he is primarily focused on the judgment of the wicked. But he will soon hear the arguments of the other friends and Job's responses. This will prompt him to make an application to Job's situation.

There are several problems with Eliphaz's argument. First, he refused to allow for exceptions to the overall principle. "You reap what you sow" is a basic tenet of the wisdom theology that is supported throughout the OT (Prov 22:8; Isa 3:10-11; Hos 8:7; 10:13) and the NT (Mark 4:24; Rom 2:9-11; Gal 6:7). It even has much older roots in the literature of the ANE (e.g., this Akkadian proverb: "Last year I ate garlic and this year my belly became inflamed" [ANET, 594]). The principle is obvious to any human being with enough common sense to observe examples of human suffering over a period of time. One has only to read the newspaper each morning to see this principle illustrated in everyday life.

However, this principle, like most of the teachings in the wisdom theology, is only as good as its supporting evidence. And when one starts gathering evidence, exceptions to the rule always rear their unwelcome heads. Job was one such exception. But there are many other examples in both Testaments of righteous people who suffered severely through no fault of their own: Moses (Num 14:1-12), David (I Sam 24:1-2 [2-3 HB]), Elijah (I Kgs 19:1-2), the innocent blood shed by the evil king Manasseh (2 Kgs 21:16), Jeremiah (Jer 20:7-10), the man born blind (John 9:1-3), Paul (2 Cor 11:21-29), and of course Jesus. Add to that the long list of examples in Heb 11.

Eliphaz would not allow Job to be an exception to his principle. Thus, he had "no place in his theology to put Job except among the guilty and the godless" (Alden 1993, 85). Job must be either righteous or wicked. Since he did not look like a righteous person anymore, he must be wicked. In spite of Eliphaz's insistence that he had investigated all of life and had an airtight case, he was a very poor scientist. He had not proven his case and never would be able to prove it because he refused to admit there are exceptions to the rule. One of these exceptions was standing directly in front of him. Eliphaz had allowed himself to be trapped in a deductive style of reasoning that protects the sought-after conclusion by disallowing any evidence that is contradictory or paradoxical.

Second, Eliphaz refused to consider other factors that might affect the application of the principle. If he had stopped and thought about the agricultural illustration he gave, he would have immediately recognized that it was not foolproof.

It is true that a harvest generally follows plowing and planting. But not every harvest is guaranteed or of the same quality. Other factors such as the amount and timing of the rain, the temperature of the ground, the amount of sunshine, the quality of the seeds, the nutrients in the soil, and the diligence of the farmer also enter into the equation. One can put the same kind of seeds into the ground in Alaska and in Florida and get vastly different results. Experiences in life—such as genetic abnormalities, disease, poor family environment, little educational training, few opportunities for work, and natural disasters—do impact the overall success or failure of people. Eliphaz refused to make allowance for these other factors and thus blindly categorized all sufferers as wicked.

Many of the sayings in the book of Proverbs must be interpreted in this same way; for example, the well-known proverb, "Train children in the right way, and when old, they will not stray" (Prov 22:6 NRSV). On the surface, this seems to be a hard-and-fast guarantee that all children raised in good moral families will turn out all right. Generally speaking, the principle is one that all parents should take to heart and use to guide their moral teachings to their children. However, the proverb does not take into account other factors, such as human free will and the influence of other people outside the family.

Third, Eliphaz's process of reasoning was flawed. Job had the reputation of being righteous, but his physical appearance and life events appeared to show the effects of God's judgment. Therefore, working backward from the effect to the cause, Eliphaz assumed that Job was guilty of sinning (→ From the Text for Job 37). He did not know what the sin could be, but the effect it had produced on Job's life was obvious. Further, since Job obviously looked like a sinner, if he continued to deny it, he was also a hypocrite. Such a method of reasoning is dangerous. It is true that sin produces suffering, but one cannot reverse the equation and hold that every person who is suffering has sinned. Suffering can occur for numerous reasons, and we will explore some of these reasons in the following chapters (→ Excursus 2: Interpreting the Book of Job following the commentary on Job 42:17).

3. Listen to What God Has Revealed to Me (4:12-21)

In the third section of his speech Eliphaz tells of a divine visitation he received that applies to Job's situation. He saw a supernatural being that scared him out of his wits and heard a muffled voice speak of the tremendous moral gulf between God and humanity. This passage is subdivided into two sections: (1) Eliphaz's description of what he actually experienced the night of his vision (vv 12-16), and (2) the content of the divine message he heard (vv 17-21).

Some scholars liken Eliphaz's experience to that of the OT prophets who also received visions. According to Jewish tradition, Eliphaz is "one of the seven Gentile prophets" in the Bible (Gordis 1978, 48). But the differences are too many to classify him as such. Eliphaz's vision was from a divine being, but he does not state that it was directly from God. The circumstances were frightening and "spooky" (Andersen 1976, 113) rather than strong and reassuring. And the message was hushed and partially inaudible rather than clear and exhortatory. Generally speaking, the OT prophets did not talk much about *how* they received their messages, but they did strongly insist that they received a clear vision or a deep inner impression from God himself. Their testimony was usually something like this: "I saw visions of God" (Ezek 1:1), "I saw the Lord, high and exalted, seated on a throne" (Isa 6:1), "The word of the LORD came to me" (Jer 1:4), and "This is what the Sovereign LORD showed me" (Amos 7:1).

■ 12 Eliphaz's divine visitation came to him in the middle of the night. He does not state exactly when this event took place, but apparently it was recent enough for him to remember vividly all the details. The experience was terrifying to him, involving three of his senses: his hearing (Job 4:12), his sight (v 16), and his sensations of touch (vv 14-15).

Just as thieves go about their business at night in a secretive manner, so a "spirit" (v 15) stole silently into Eliphaz's presence to deliver a message. In the Hebrew sentence, the prepositional phrase **to me** (v 12) is placed at the very beginning to emphasize Eliphaz's insistence that he is the only one who received this revelation. **My ears caught a whisper of it.** Scholars have suggested two possible meanings for *šēmeṣ* (**whisper**). One is the NIV translation, and the other is "little": "my ears caught only a fragment of it" (Clines 1989, 107). Either translation conveys the sense that the message Eliphaz received was somewhat muffled, probably due both to the manner of its deliverance and Eliphaz's state of terror.

■ **13-14** *With disturbed thoughts from visions of the night.* The Hebrew for **disturbed thoughts** (*śĕ'ippîm*) is a rare word appearing only in Job (here and 20:2). It probably refers to the disrupted and confused thoughts of one who is jolted awake in the middle of the night. *Visions of the night* could refer to a dream while sleeping or a vision after one has awakened. Eliphaz does not use the more normal Hebrew word for "dream" (*ḥălôm*), so perhaps he is describing a vision he received after awakening in the night. On the other hand, he may have been too groggy to distinguish whether he was awake or asleep. The two words for "vision" (*ḥizzāyôn*) and "dream" (*ḥălôm*) are paired in 7:14, 20:8, and 33:15, so the distinction may be minute or nonexistent. The **deep sleep** (*tardēmâ*) of 4:13*b* appears in the stories of Adam (Gen 2:21), Abraham (Gen 15:12), and Saul (1 Sam 26:12) as a divine-induced trance. But here the phrase **on people** indicates that Eliphaz is not claiming a trance for himself, but rather is referring to that period in the night when most people are fast asleep.

Eliphaz completes the sentence begun in Job 4:13 with words that describe his fear as so intense he was literally shaking all over. **Fear** (v 14; from *pḥd*) is the same word used by Job in 3:25 to describe his (lit.) "shaking fear." His choice of vocabulary signals his empathy for Job by saying that he, too, knows what it is like to be seized with an overwhelming fear. Eliphaz was so afraid that even his **bones** (his bodily framework) were shuddering. Old Testament poets typically mention a person's bones when referring to an intense emotion or severe illness that affects the entire body (Pss 6:2 [3 HB]; 51:8 [10 HB]).

■ **15** All of a sudden Eliphaz felt a movement across his face. Being in the dark, he was not sure whether it was just a breeze or the presence of a spirit, but it so frightened him that his **hair . . . stood on end**. Wesley interprets the word for **spirit** (*rûaḥ*) as "an angel in visible shape" (1765, 1528). But *rûaḥ* has already been used twice in Job to mean "wind" (1:19) or "blast" of wind (4:9). From a translation standpoint, **wind** is probably the better rendering for two reasons: (1) *rûaḥ* is never used in the OT to refer to "disembodied spirits" (Rowley 1976, 48); and (2) when *rûaḥ* appears as a masculine noun, as in v 15, it "always refers to a wind or breath" (Clines 1989, 111). Nevertheless, the breeze that Eliphaz felt on his face seemed to suggest the entrance of someone else into his room, for v 16 denotes that he saw a form and heard a voice. Thus, Eliphaz recognized he was not alone; he was in the presence of a supernatural being.

■ **16** In the darkness Eliphaz saw a visible shape of someone in front of him. He did not recognize who it was, but he clearly believed it was a supernatural messenger. And the message had great relevance to Job's situation. "It stood still" (NRSV) contains no subject in Hebrew, but most translations supply an indefinite subject such as "it," with the word **form** (v 16*b*) as its antecedent. **I could not tell** (*nkr*; v 16*a*) is the same verb used by the three friends when they first saw Job and could not recognize him (2:12). What Eliphaz saw was the outward shape or features of someone. The Hebrew for **form** (*těmûnâ*) is used for the form or likeness of God (Ps 17:15) or the image of an idol. In the Ten Commandments (Exod 20:4), God forbids the Israelites to make idols in the "form" or likeness of things in heaven or on the earth or in the water. In Num 12:8 Moses was privileged to see the "form" of Yahweh when they communicated face to face.

The **hushed voice** that Eliphaz heard has several possible interpretations. The same two words appear in the Hebrew of 1 Kgs 19:12 with the translation "gentle whisper" (the adjective modifying the noun). A second interpretation treats the conjunction *wā* as separating the two words; thus the rendering: "there was silence, then I heard a voice" (NRSV). A third interpretation is to take *děmāmâ* (**hushed**) from an alternative root of *dmm*, meaning "to wail" (BDB, 199). Clines follows this reading: "I heard a roaring voice" (1989, 112).

The evidence is not conclusive, but the context of the entire section reflects a mysterious, eerie quietness with whispering sounds (Job 4:12) and rustling breezes (v 15), rather than a loud, booming voice. Thus, the first or second interpretations are better. Hartley, following the second interpretation, may be correct that the Elijah story may have influenced the author of Job. Thus, there is emphasis on the silence that preceded the hushed voice (1988, 113 n. 20).

■ **17** Up to this point, Eliphaz has focused on his own physical and emotional reaction to the divine visitation, but in vv 17-21 he recounts the actual words he heard. Scholars are divided over the length of the divine message. Some extend the quotation marks from v 17 to v 21. Others regard only v 17 as the actual message, with vv 18-21 as Eliphaz's interpretation, what Clines calls "wisdom's extensions of it" (1989, 134). In any case, this is what Eliphaz believed Job needed to hear.

With two parallel, rhetorical questions, the divine visitor raises the issue of humanity's relationship to God: ***Can any human being [claim to] be righteous in the presence of God [Eloah]? Can any man [claim to] be pure in the presence of his Creator?*** The Hebrew for **human being** is *'ĕnôš*, a word used eighteen times in Job (more than any other OT book). The parallel term in v 17*b* is **strong man** (*geber*), which refers to the male gender and implies a man's man, a *real* man (Reyburn 1992, 101). In v 17*b* the translation **man** is adequate. Job has already used *geber* in his statement about the night "a male child" was conceived (3:3) and in his complaint that God had placed a hedge around him—a strong man (3:23).

This is the first appearance of an important family of words in the book of Job—***be righteous***. The verb *ṣdq* (***be righteous, just***) occurs seventeen times, the noun *ṣedeq* (***righteousness***) six times, the noun *ṣĕdāqâ* (***righteousness***) four times, and the adjective *ṣaddîq* (**righteous**) seven times. These words refer to "living in conformity to the will of God" (see Reimer 1997, 3:754-57, on the usage of this word in Job). The parallel term **be pure** (*ṭhr*) occurs frequently in passages related to ritual cleanness (e.g., the purity laws in Lev 11—15). But it also can refer to moral cleanness, as it does here.

The words **God** and **Creator** are both preceded by the Hebrew *min* of comparison. Some translations, such as the NIV, treat this particle as a comparative term yielding **more righteous than** and **more pure than**. However, the intent of the question is not to determine who is *more* righteous—humans or God? Both Eliphaz and Job would have considered this an improper treatment of God. Rather, the divine questioner is asking if *anyone* can claim to be righteous in the presence of God (as in the NRSV). Job 4:18-19 make it clear that no creature, whether in heaven or on earth, can measure up to God's absolute moral perfection.

These rhetorical questions imply another universal principle (→ 4:7) in Eliphaz's mind: Because every human being falls far short of God's moral perfection, everyone should expect some disciplinary action from God (5:17-26) to improve their level of righteousness. Job is no exception. He may be considered innocent and upright from a human perspective (4:7) and thus not suffer an early death, but his life still contains areas that need improvement. God will continue to correct and educate him for as long as he lives. Job will try to answer these questions that Eliphaz poses, but he will need to think about them for some time before making an attempt (9:2-35). He will eventually deny that Eliphaz is correct in his assumptions about human sinfulness (27:5-6; ch 31).

■ **18-19** Eliphaz continues to support his principle that humans are significantly inferior to God by comparing them to angels. **His servants** and **his angels** are in parallel and refer to the same category of divine beings (4:18). Eliphaz will use another synonym for them very shortly ("holy ones" [5:1]). Not a lot is known about the characteristics of angels in the OT, but they are always seen as possessing a higher level of intimacy with God. Eliphaz's point is that even these divine beings are separated from God by an enormous gulf. God does not **trust** them with his divine plans, and they are not morally perfect as is God himself. Therefore, if God regards angels, which are on a higher spiritual level than humans, as inferior to him and capable of error, **how much more** inferior are human beings (4:19)? Eliphaz does not mean "to discredit the angels; he merely wishes to exalt the perfection of God" (Terrien 1954, 3:940).

In v 18*b* the Hebrew for **error** (*tohŏlâ*) is a *hapax legomenon* (→ 2:8) whose origin and meaning are uncertain. Scholars have made a number of proposals to arrive at a reasonable translation. Some alternative suggestions are: "folly," "madness," "contrariness." The evidence for any of these is speculative, so the issue remains problematic (see Seow 2013, 404-5).

The main criticism of Eliphaz has to do with his premise. How does he know that **God . . . charges his angels with error**? The OT is silent on this point, so where did this idea come from? Wesley applies this verse to fallen angels (1765,

1529), but that belief is more appropriate to the intertestamental period. Further, Eliphaz seems to indict all of God's heavenly creatures, not just fallen ones.

Eliphaz now moves logically from angels to human beings with three phrases (**those who live in houses of clay, whose foundations are in the dust**, and **who are crushed more readily than a moth** [v 19]) as metaphors for the frailty of our physical bodies. In the NT Paul uses a similar image when he describes our human body as an "earthly tent" (2 Cor 5:1). The reference to **houses of clay** is "the first reference in Hebrew literature to the idea of the body as the residence of the human being" (Clines 1989, 134). The thought is repeated in Job 10:9 and 33:6. **Dust** is the material out of which God created human beings (Gen 2:7; 3:19; 1 Cor 15:47-49), so there is a connection here with the creation story.

The reference to **moths** (Job 4:19c) is somewhat confusing. Throughout both Testaments, moths are consistently spoken of as insects that cause destruction, especially of clothing (13:28; Ps 39:11 [12 HB]; Isa 50:9; 51:8; Hos 5:12; Matt 6:19-20; Jas 5:2). Hartley applies this imagery to Job 4:19 as well: "Those who dwell in houses of clay . . . are crushed by a moth" (1988, 110). The meaning is that "the moth is the instrument that hastens the destruction of houses composed of mud bricks" (ibid., n. 10).

However, others see little damage that a moth can do to a house and suggest that in this verse the moth should be seen as the victim rather than the aggressor. By translating *lipnê* (**more readily than**) as "like, as, in the manner of" (as in Job 3:24), a different meaning emerges: "who are crushed like a moth" (NRSV). Our human bodies are composed of fragile material (**clay** and **dust**) that can be crushed very readily—as easily as one crushes a moth.

■ **20** Total destruction may unexpectedly befall any human being. **Between dawn and dusk** (lit. "from morning to evening") life can suddenly end. People can arise in the morning with vigor and plans but be gone before the sun sets—their bodies **broken to pieces** (lit. "smashed into smithereens"). The verb here (*ktt*) is used for the destruction of the golden calf (Deut 9:21) and the bronze serpent of Moses (2 Kgs 18:4). But it also appears in contexts where an object is beaten into something more useful, for example, "They will beat their swords into plowshares" (Isa 2:4).

In Job 4:20b, **unnoticed**, "unobserved" (NASB), or "without any regarding it" (NRSV) are typical renderings for *mibbĕlî mēśîm*. But it is an awkward phrase that has produced many emendations and interpretations (see Clines 1989, 113-14). The most accepted emendation is to add the word *lēb* (lit. "heart") after the causative (Hiphil) participle *mēśîm*, thus producing the more reasonable translation: ***without taking it to heart***, or ***without considering*** (→ 1:8). The antecedent of the phrase is the indefinite "they" in the main verb of the clause (**they perish**). The translation, then, would be: *Without taking it to heart, they perish forever*. Without preparing for death and without considering the vulnerable position they are in (living in "houses of clay" [4:19]), human beings are "caught unaware" (Hartley 1988, 115) by the suddenness of death. This interpretation provides a much better parallel to the thought of v 20*a*. **Forever** (*lāneṣaḥ*) appears four other times in Job (14:20; 20:7; 23:7; 36:7) and is quite common in the Psalms.

■ **21** This verse has received much comment, but its basic meaning is understandable. It continues the imagery from v 20 of a premature and sudden death. Without **wisdom**, a person's life will collapse swiftly like a **tent** whose **cords** are removed.

Habel defines **wisdom** (*ḥokmâ*) as "that mature level of insight, skill, perception, and understanding which is consistent with the underlying principles of order that inform the cosmos" (1985, 257). Generally, it refers to the ability to understand life through God's eyes and to live accordingly (Ps 111:10). As expected in a wisdom literature book, the family of words related to "wisdom" appears quite frequently. The noun *ḥokmâ* ("wisdom") occurs eighteen times, the adjective *ḥākām* ("wise") eight times, and the verb *ḥākam* ("be wise") twice. Job 4:21 is the first appearance of any of these words in the book of Job. Eliphaz mentions **wisdom** here as a quality that is lacking in the lives of many people. They die without having acquired it. This comment is directed toward humanity in general, but it is probably a subtle suggestion that Job needs some instruction in the ways of wisdom.

FROM THE TEXT

1. **The Relevance and Validity of Eliphaz's Vision**. In the ancient world there were all kinds of prophets, seers, diviners, magicians, astrologers, and soothsayers who claimed to have a divine message from their god. There is clear evidence for this in Mesopotamian, Egyptian, Hittite, and Ugaritic literature. Some of these individuals were regarded as true spokespersons for their deity, and their advice was eagerly sought by kings. Others were just plain quacks who were seeking to gain influence or wealth. Only the prophets and seers received their revelations through visions and dreams. The others used various physical objects, such as the stars or sheep livers, to determine the divine will. In the Bible, both Testaments mention revelations that came from God via visions and dreams. For example, Solomon in the OT (1 Kgs 3:5) and Joseph in the NT (Matt 1:20). The difference between visions (*ḥezyōnôt*) and dreams (*ḥălōmôt*) is not clearly stated. In fact, the two words are paired and used interchangeably in three passages in Job (7:14; 20:8; 33:15).

The nature of the reception of divine messages is such that it could be easily manipulated. Thus, there were many false prophets, seers, diviners, and so forth, in Israel and other ancient countries. The true prophets had to contend with these charlatans continually (Deut 13:1-5 [2-6 HB]; Jer 23:25-32; 27:9-10; 29:8-9; Zech 10:2). The validity of Eliphaz's vision is an issue with which Job is confronted. And we as readers also must make an evaluation. Eliphaz claimed that his revelation was from God, whether directly or through a divine messenger. But is this the kind of message that God would want delivered to a very sick person who wants to die? The message certainly does not provide the help that Job is looking for, and therefore its relevance is questionable.

The importance of the vision in Eliphaz's speech cannot be overstated. It is his trump card, so to speak. It cannot be disproved by Job, so it gives him an advantage in the debate. As Alden notes, "It is hard to argue with people who claim to have special revelation" (1993, 86). What is intriguing about Eliphaz's vision is that it is introduced so early in the dialogues. One would have expected him to produce his trump card later when the dialogues started heating up. Instead, this is one of the first things he mentions. It is also intriguing from the standpoint that the sages usually placed greater emphasis on the oral and written wisdom traditions handed down from bygone eras, rather than direct divine revelation.

People of faith who desire to share their religious experience with others often relate what is called in Christian circles "a testimony." They will use statements such as: "God saved me" or "God said to me." These are important personal experiences that cannot be denied by the listener because they reveal privileged information that is not available to anyone else. The listener will only be prone to accept them as valid if the quality and reliability of the messenger is such as to encourage belief. Further confirmation may come if the listener compares the experience of one testimony with that of thousands of others across the centuries who have had the same experience.

2. Transcendence. Transcendence is a theological term that refers to the great distance between God and humanity. It means that God is far removed. There is a Grand Canyon between us, if you will. The concept is expressed in a number of ways in the OT, some of which are discussed in the book of Job. In this brief section of his first speech (4:17-21), Eliphaz mentions several of them.

- Humans are inferior to God in terms of morality. Who can claim to be righteous in the presence of one who is morally perfect (v 17)? Even the angels are inferior to God. How much more are human beings (v 19)?
- Humans are inferior to God in terms of the security of their dwelling place. God dwells in the heavens, but humans live in flimsy houses of clay and are as vulnerable to death as a lowly moth (v 19).
- Humans are inferior to God in terms of time. He is eternal, but humans are cut off suddenly in the middle of the day (v 20). They perish from this life forever and go to a dismal place called Sheol.
- Humans are inferior to God in terms of wisdom. He is all-wise, but humans live without wisdom, without considering God's plan for their life, unaware of their quickly approaching death (v 21).

The sum of it is: we are made of *lesser stuff*.

The problem with Eliphaz's overemphasis on transcendence is that he sets up an impossible barrier for humanity to cross. This gulf is so great that human beings cannot even communicate with God, much less enjoy his love and fellowship. In the area of morality, Eliphaz has in effect shut the door on the possibility of being completely righteous in this life. If the standard is to reach God's level of moral perfection, and even the angels cannot do that, then certainly humanity is doomed to failure as well.

Who can bridge this great gulf between God and humanity? Eliphaz believes that no one can. As his speech continues in 5:1, he anticipates that question by answering that even the angels are ineffective as intermediaries. Job is also aware of this great gulf. A little later in the book he will confirm Eliphaz's doctrine of transcendence and bemoan the fact that there is no one to bring God and him together to arbitrate their dispute (9:33).

Is Eliphaz correct in his evaluation of the human predicament? Yes and no. Yes, in the sense that there really is a great gulf between God and humanity, and humanity is inferior to God in many, many ways. Both Testaments support this doctrine. But no, to the belief that there is no intermediary. As the NT writers correctly point out, because humans are incapable of crossing the great divide by themselves, God provided the means to bring himself and humanity together by sending his Son, the God-human, as the necessary and effective intermediary. Thus, God's immanence comes into play in the NT in ways that OT characters could not have imagined.

IN THE TEXT

4. Trouble Is Inevitable (5:1-7)

Eliphaz begins the fourth section of his speech by asking Job where he plans to seek help. He then lays out the consequences of not going to the right source. Verses 2-5, which focus on "the fool," seem to be a digression, but in actuality Eliphaz is laying the groundwork for his next main point. The fool illustrates how not to react to trouble. In vv 6-7 he reemphasizes that everyone will experience some trouble in their lifetime, and then in v 8 he presents his main point, which is the proper way to deal with trouble. If he were in Job's situation, he would commit his case to God because God is able to help the needy (vv 9-16).

So here Eliphaz lays out for Job two pathways for the future. He can either pursue the way of the fool that leads to his own death and trouble for his children (vv 2-5), or he can turn to God and trust the one who "performs wonders that cannot be fathomed, miracles that cannot be counted" (v 9).

■ **I** After listening to Job's mournful questions in ch 3, Eliphaz knows that Job needs help. So he presses Job on where he thinks he can find some counsel. "Do you believe **the holy ones** can help you?" The rhetorical nature of the question assumes that they will be of no help. **Holy ones** (*qĕdōšîm*) is usually thought to refer to angels, although some believe it refers to God (Gordis 1978, 51-52). But the word appears five other times in the OT with the meaning of angels (15:15; Ps 89:5, 7 [6, 8 HB]; Dan 8:13; Zech 14:5). This is the fourth synonym the author has used for angels (→ "sons of God" [*bĕnê hā'ĕlōhîm*; Job 1:6; 2:1], "his servants" [*'ăbādāyw*; 4:18], and "his angels" [*mal'ākāyw*; 4:18]).

In Mesopotamian religion of the Old Babylonian period (ca. 2000-1600 BC), the concept of a personal god became very common (Jacobsen 1970, 5, 13, 19, 37-38, 45, 395 n. 108). These personal gods were usually minor deities who were called upon to intercede with the great gods of the pantheon on behalf of an individual. Prayers could be offered to and through one's personal god for such things as guidance, protection, the birth of a healthy child, relief from suffering, and so forth (see "Man and His God," *ANET*, 589-91).

Some commentators believe Eliphaz is speaking of a similar type of religious practice here, only calling on angels instead of minor deities to intercede with God (Pope 1973, 41-42). However, the first clause of the verse is the key question: "Where are you going to find help for the problems in your life?" The second clause simply rules out the possibility of securing help from the angels, probably for two reasons: (1) Eliphaz has already denied the angels any effectiveness in influencing God (4:18); and (2) Job's problems are not the kind that can be solved by help from anyone other than God. As he goes on to mention in 5:6-8, human sinfulness and its consequences are a fundamental human problem that can only be addressed by God.

This verse is confusing from the standpoint that Eliphaz, who has just described a revelation he received from a divine messenger (4:12-21), is now denying the ability of angels to provide help for Job. Eliphaz seems hypocritical here, but perhaps he thought of his own situation as unique. Another possibility is that he surmised that Job was harboring a secret sin and thus would not merit a divine visitation. There has also been much discussion on the tone of voice that Eliphaz used in this verse. Some regard his words to Job as "a taunt" (Pope 1973, 41), "a challenge" (Alden 1993, 90), or "a warning" (Rowley 1976, 51). More likely, he is simply pointing out to Job the futility of seeking help from heavenly beings other than God (Hartley 1988, 117; Clines 1989, 138).

This is the first time that someone has spoken of an intermediary to bridge the gap between God and humanity (→ From the Text for ch 4). While Eliphaz's comments are very brief, the issue will appear again from the mouth of Job after he has had more time to ponder the implications of this intriguing concept (9:33; 16:19; 19:25). In 5:1 Eliphaz is mainly interested in someone to provide answers to Job's questions and perhaps to intercede for him. But Job's primary interest will be for a mediator who will be able to arbitrate the dispute between himself and God.

■ 2 This verse is usually regarded as a proverb. The direct objects (**a fool** and **the simple**) are placed first in their respective clauses for emphasis. The **fool** (*ĕwîl*) is the person who stubbornly refuses to accept advice but continually babbles on about nothing (Prov 1:7; 10:14; 12:15; 15:5). The word is common in Proverbs but is used only here and in 5:3 in Job. The **simple** one (*pōteh*) is the person who is naive, undisciplined, and easily led. This individual will believe anything. The more common noun form for "simple" (*petî*) does not appear in Job but is found fifteen times in Proverbs. Both the **fool** and the **simple** do stupid things. The difference is that the **fool** does them arrogantly on purpose while the **simple** falls into them by accident because of an undisciplined lifestyle.

The **fool** and the **simple** not only cause pain to themselves but actually bring about their own early demise as the result of their self-centered, emotional excesses. **Resentment** or "vexation" (*ka'aś*; NRSV) is **anguish** one feels when wronged unjustly. It manifests itself in anger. In the next chapter Job admits to Eliphaz that he possesses this emotion (6:2). ***Anger*** (rather than **envy**) comes from a word (*qin'â*) that basically means "zeal." It can be used in both positive (Ps 69:9 [10 HB]; Isa 9:7) and negative (Ps 79:5) contexts. In Job 5:2*b* it refers to a ***furious anger*** felt by someone such as a jealous husband (Prov 6:34) or an angry God (Deut 29:20 [19 HB]).

Eliphaz is not calling Job a fool here, but he is suggesting that Job change his attitude before he finds himself in company with other fools. Job sounded very strange in Job 3, much like a fool. He was emotionally upset and wanted to die. In Eliphaz's mind, a righteous person should act much differently.

■ **3** Verses 3-5 of ch 5 are Eliphaz's personal observations (**I myself have seen**) of people he regards as fools. Just like trees form a root system, so fools establish a lifestyle and attitudes that contribute to their downfall. The dreadful consequences of their choices affect both themselves and their families.

The word for **house** (*nāweh*) in v 3*b* refers to more than a building. Its most frequent usage is in reference to the seasonal pasturelands where shepherds journeyed with their flocks (e.g., Isa 65:10; Jer 33:12; Amos 1:2). Sometimes these pastures were located at a great distance from the home of the sheep owner. The land was probably not legally owned by the shepherds. It was mainly open range land available for their usage. It was considered a part of their livelihood because of years of annual migrations. Thus, the word needs to be understood in a broader sense as both the dwelling (whether a building or a tent) and the land used by the fool. A phrase such as ***his lands and dwelling*** is probably more appropriate here.

The first-person active verb in Job 5:3*b* has created much discussion. The literal translation is something like: "but I cursed his lands and dwelling suddenly." This sounds like Eliphaz pronounced a curse against the fool and caused the disastrous consequences in vv 4-5. Most scholars reject this translation for two reasons: (1) no one is comfortable with attributing curses to Eliphaz; and (2) in the context of Eliphaz's entire speech (chs 4—5), he seems more interested in describing the consequences that people bring on themselves through their bad choices, than causing those consequences himself.

Some translations follow the LXX, which emends the verb to the third person, yielding: "his [their] dwelling place was quickly consumed." But the first-person verb is preferable as a parallel to the verb in v 3*a*. The best translation is possibly something like: ***I immediately expressed contempt for his lands and dwelling***.

■ **4** Fools not only destroy themselves (v 2) and their habitation (v 3) but also bring trouble on the rest of their family. Their children are vulnerable to harm because they are orphans **without a defender**. "They are crushed in the gate" (NRSV). The NIV renders "gate" into **court** because the gate was where business and legal matters were normally conducted (Ruth 4:1-12). **Crushed** is the same word used in reference to the ease of crushing moths (Job 4:19). The intent of this verse is to describe the vulnerability of the children of fools, once their father has perished. Some have suggested that Eliphaz is cruelly connecting Job's calamities in the prologue with the disasters that befall fools, but there really is no connection. Here it is the foolish father who perishes, not the children.

■ **5** The problems faced by the children of the fool continue in v 5. Even **the hungry** and **the thirsty** (i.e., the poor of the land) take advantage of the fool's death and haul off his produce and possessions. Apparently, the remaining family members are defenseless to protect their property (v 4). This verse is very difficult to translate and interpret, especially the second clause. There is no general consensus on its exact meaning, and many believe the MT has been corrupted (Gordis 1978, 53-54; Clines 1989, 115-16).

■ **6** *Evil* (*'āwen*) and **trouble** (*'āmāl*) (these are also paired in 4:8) afflict every human being. But what is their source? They are certainly not caused by God, for he is righteous and pure (4:17). Neither do they originate out of nature or our environment—like weeds **sprout from the ground**. In Eliphaz's thinking, they are caused by human beings who are morally inferior to God (4:17). Thus, humanity has no one to blame except itself for all the troubles it experiences in life. Even supersaint Job should expect some suffering.

■ **7** The verb in 5:7a is a passive form of *yld*: "human beings are born to trouble" (NRSV). In other words, trouble is inevitable because of human sinfulness. To some scholars, this sounds too close to fatalism—"that humans are destined for trouble by decisions that are fixed and permanent" (Balentine 2006, 115). They prefer a revocalization to the causative (Hiphil) stem, yielding: "human beings give birth to ('generate' [Seow 2013, 436-37]) trouble." This rendering focuses on trouble's origin rather than its inevitability. Either interpretation is possible as they are supported by other statements made by Eliphaz (e.g., 4:8, 17; 5:6, 7b).

As surely as **the sons of Resheph** [*běnê rešep*] **fly upward** has caused much comment. *Rešep* appears only six times in the OT, each with a slightly different meaning: a "plague" (Deut 32:24; Hab 3:5), "bolts of lightning" (Ps 78:48), "arrows" (Ps 76:3 [4 HB]), and "flashes of fire" (Song 8:6 NRSV). Here in Job 5:7 the LXX and the church fathers (ACCS, 6:27-28) interpreted this word as referring to "birds." Many modern versions prefer the translation **sparks** (from "sons of the flame" [lit.]).

Today scholars are more inclined to connect this word with a Canaanite god named Resheph, who was equated with the Mesopotamian god Nergal—"the god of pestilence and the netherworld" (Pope 1973, 42). ***The sons of Resheph***, then, are the mythological demons of plague and pestilence that arise from the underworld to afflict humanity from time to time. Most likely, ***the sons of Resheph*** is an idiomatic phrase and thus beyond precise definition. Whatever the exact meaning of *rešep*, Eliphaz's intention is to use a well-known expression as a metaphor for the inevitability of trouble. No one can avoid it.

Universal Sinfulness

The basic sinfulness of humanity was hinted at earlier in 4:17-19. In 5:6-7 the topic is more clearly stated. All human beings are sinful from birth, the result of the fall in Gen 3. Humanity is not morally flawed because of a natural predisposition at the time of creation or because God chose to infect the human race with evil at some point in time. God made humans in his own image (Gen 1:27; 5:1) and intended them to be morally perfect. On the contrary, every human being is morally flawed because of a momentous decision by Adam and Eve in the Garden of Eden, and we have suffered the consequences ever since. Just as surely as **the sons of Resheph** fly upward, so will all humanity have to contend with the trouble that results from sinfulness. For that reason alone, trouble is inevitable. It is a part of the human condition—"the common lot of mankind" (Wesley 1765, 1530).

Both Christians and Jews accept this fundamental doctrine, although differences of interpretation exist relative to how this condition originated. In simple terms, Christianity believes that all humanity is sinful *because of* Adam. Judaism holds that all humanity is sinful *like* Adam. Other scriptures that support this doctrine are: Pss 14:2-3; 53:2-3 [3-4 HB]; Rom 3:10-11, 23. Habel points out that this belief in the universal sinfulness of humanity is much older than this reference in Job (1985, 130). In the Sumerian wisdom text "Man and His God" we find these words: "They say—the sages—a word righteous (and) straightforward: 'Never has a sinless child been born to its mother, . . . a sinless *workman* has not existed from of old'" (*ANET*, 590).

5. God Is the Only Genuine Source of Help (5:8-16)

In the fifth section of his speech Eliphaz counsels Job to follow a different course of action. He should turn to God for help because only God can help him. This section enumerates some of the many ways God governs his world.

■ 8 In a verse filled with alliteration in Hebrew, Eliphaz is convinced he knows the correct thing to do in this situation, and he would do it if he were in Job's shoes. "I would seek God" (NRSV), he says. At one level, "seeking God" can refer to something as simple as inquiring for information or approval from God (Gen 25:22; 1 Kgs 22:5). At a much higher level, "seeking God with a whole heart" is equivalent to the crux of Israelite religion as spelled out in the *Shema* (Deut 6:4-5; Ps 119:2). "Seeking God" is also a way of describing one's petition to God for deliverance from fear (Ps 34:4 [5 HB]), from trouble (Ps 77:2 [3 HB]), from oppression (Ps 69:32 [33 HB]), or from sin (Ps 78:34). In these passages the phrase is a synonym for praying to God, for petition is an integral component of prayer (Miller 1994, 86-114).

Eliphaz has already eliminated the angels as useful helpers (4:18; 5:1). How much better to go to the source of all help and place one's case directly in God's hands. There are two words for **God** in this verse—*El* (v 8*a*) and *Elohim* (v 8*b*; the NIV translates as **him**). This is only for poetic variation. In the second clause the Hebrew for **my cause** (*dibrātî*) is a rare word in the OT, derived from *dbr* ("speak").

Some connect it with legal terminology, as if Job had a legal case to present to God (Andersen 1976, 119). But more likely the word refers to Job's overall situation: "If I were in your shoes, I would tell God all my troubles and listen for his answer."

Almost universally, Eliphaz's comment is treated as his *hypothetical* response, as **if** he were experiencing Job's suffering. But a few suggest that Eliphaz is here testifying to an ongoing personal practice: "I myself pray to God and leave my case in his hands" (Clines 1989, 143). Clines' proposal credits Eliphaz with a great deal more personal piety than most scholars are willing to give him. On the other hand, "seeking God" was the common practice of the sages, so both interpretations may apply here.

Eliphaz's attitude in v 8 is not spelled out, but scholars have attributed a wide range of possibilities. Some of the early church fathers believed Eliphaz was rebuking Job for not seeking God in the past (ACCS, 6:28-29). Others have suggested he was issuing a call to repentance (Gordis 1978, 55; Rowley 1976, 54; Wesley 1765, 1530). On the other hand, he may simply be offering Job "careful counsel that will not offend or show disrespect" (Balentine 2006, 116; Clines 1989, 143).

Balentine and Clines are probably closer to the truth here. Eliphaz may have had some private concerns about Job's status with God, but he does not express them outwardly in his first public speech. The entire message is one that a typical sage could deliver. It raises important universal principles for Job to think about and encourages him to "hang in there. God is only disciplining you for a brief time; things will change very shortly for the better." "Seeking God" would be the normal advice a sage would give to anyone, regardless of circumstances (Prov 1:7).

Thus, one should view Job 5:8 as a word of helpfulness and encouragement that points Job toward the only genuine source of help that is available. Of course, Job already knew this, as we are aware from the prologue. But Eliphaz wanted to make sure that the conversation was framed in terms that are relevant to life as seen through the eyes of the sages. A reminder of the important issues in life is always helpful in times of crisis.

■ **9** Verses 9-16 are a literary unit that is usually called a doxology or a hymn of praise. The poem uses the typical praise language found in the hymns of the Psalter, exalting God's power over both the natural world and human activities.

The purpose of the hymn is twofold. (1) This is Eliphaz's rationale to support his statement in v 8 about why he would seek God for help. God is omnipotent, a doer of great and marvelous deeds. (2) Eliphaz wished to emphasize God's ability to reverse the course of events in people's lives and point them in a new direction with a new future. His hope was that Job would put aside the calamities of the past and refocus his attention on the God who does great things. In effect, Eliphaz is saying, "If God can reverse the fortunes of others, then surely he can do the same for you too."

This is a tremendous word of hope for Job that points to a much different future than the alternative—the way of the fool (vv 2-5). The imagery of a divine reversal in the life of an individual is well supported in both Testaments (e.g., 1 Sam

2:8; Pss 18:27 [28 HB]; 75:7 [8 HB]; 113:7-9; 147:6; Matt 21:40-44; Luke 1:52; Jas 4:10). In Job 20:4-29 Zophar borrows the language of a divine reversal, but he applies it to the wicked who suddenly experience God's judgment for their sins.

Verse 9 of ch 5 functions much like a title for God, describing his attribute of omnipotence. The verse begins with a participle (lit. "the one who does") that refers back to its antecedent ("God") in v 8. There are a series of these participles in the following verses (vv 10*a*, 10*b*, 12*a*, 13*a*), all denoting attributes of God that are continually operative. The same usage of participles appears later in a speech by Job (9:5-10). **Wonders** (*gĕdōlôt*; lit. "great deeds"; Pss 71:19; 106:21; 145:6) and **miracles** (*niplāʾôt*; lit. "miraculous deeds"; Pss 78:4; 105:5; 106:7, 22) are the two activities that God performs. They are paired here and used synonymously in the OT (especially in Psalms) in reference to "God's deeds in creation" or "his deeds of salvation in history" (Hartley 1988, 121).

God's activities are further enhanced by descriptive phrases referring to the quality of his wonders (**that cannot be fathomed** [lit. "without searching"]) and their quantity (**that cannot be counted** [lit. "without number"]). Both the quality and quantity are beyond human comprehension and description. Ironically, in building up God's unsearchable ways, Eliphaz has undercut his own claim to have knowledge about Job's situation (v 27; 4:7-8).

■ **10** The first of God's great and marvelous deeds is the sending of **rain** to water **the earth** (lit. "the face of the earth"). From a biblical perspective, Yahweh is not a weather god, but he does control the weather (Gen 7:4; Ps 104:13; Jer 10:12-13). God himself will confirm this concept later in the book (Job 38:25-28). And it will also appear in the interlude (28:26) and in Elihu's speech (36:27-33). One of the classic examples of God's control of the weather is the story of Elijah's confrontation with the 450 prophets of Baal and the 400 prophets of Asherah on Mount Carmel (1 Kgs 17:1; 18:1-46).

Rain is a vital necessity in any land for the growing of crops and the raising of animals. The Israelites did not have a modern meteorological explanation for the cause or lack of rain. They simply believed that God provided rain on a regular basis, mainly in the fall and winter months, as one of his "wonders."

■ **11** The second of God's great and marvelous deeds is the raising of the lowly to an elevated position. **The lowly** (*šĕpālîm*) refers to people of low social and economic standing. Synonyms are found in Job 5:15 ("the needy") and v 16 ("the poor"). God **sets** them **on high**, that is, he reverses their fortunes. This does not mean he makes them kings or presidents, although he is certainly able to do so. It means that their well-being is remarkably and miraculously improved. In the NT Mary's Song emphasizes this concept of God's power to "lift up" the lowly ("He . . . has lifted up the humble" [Luke 1:52]). In similar fashion James exhorts his readers to "humble [themselves] before the Lord, and he will lift [them] up" (4:10).

Those who mourn (Job 5:11*b*) is a participle from *qdr*, which means "be dark and dirty." The word is used in other passages to refer to people in mourning (e.g., Pss 35:14; 38:6 [7 HB]; 42:9 [10 HB]; 43:2). This meaning may derive from the dark clothing and dirty ashes sprinkled on the heads of the bereaved or from the dark, gloomy spirit that accompanies grief. Gordis suggests an alternative meaning more in parallel with "the lowly"—"the afflicted" (1978, 56). This is a possibility.

■ 12-14 The third of God's great and marvelous deeds is to humble those who are clever and cunning in their own eyes. The high and mighty seem secure in their craftiness, but God is able to undermine their **plans** and successes (v 12). **He thwarts** is from the Hebrew *prr*, which is usually translated "break," as in "breaking my covenant" (Deut 31:20). It appears in Job 16:12 with that meaning. Here, however, and in 15:4 and 40:8 the word carries the meaning of "breaking up," "disrupting," or "foiling the plans of others." The adjective **crafty** (*'ărûmîm*) is used eight times in Proverbs with the positive meaning of "prudent" (e.g., Prov 12:16). But it appears twice in Job (here and 15:5, plus the infinitive construct in 5:13) and once in Genesis with the negative meaning of "cunning" or **crafty** ("Now the serpent was more crafty" [Gen 3:1]). The word for **success** (*tûšiyyâ*) is usually rendered one of two ways in Job: either as **wisdom/insight** (11:6; 12:16; 26:3) or as "the results of wisdom," that is, **success** (here and 6:13).

Not only does God prevent the crafty from achieving their plans, but he even turns their plans against them so they are caught in their own schemes (5:13). Other passages in the OT reflect this same imagery of God's enemies falling into their own pit or being ensnared in their own trap (e.g., 18:7-10; Pss 7:14-16 [15-17 HB]; 35:7-8; 57:6 [7 HB]; Prov 1:18; 26:27; 28:10). The Hebrew for **wise** is normally applied in the wisdom literature to people who are living according to God's plans (Job 4:21), but in 5:13 it refers to people who are wise in their own eyes. The parallel terms **the crafty** (v 12) and **the wily** (v 13) make this clear.

The wily refers to "one who is morally twisted, contorted" (2 Sam 22:27; Prov 8:8). The Hebrew for **are swept away** (*mhr*) carries the idea of hastiness. So the meaning is something like this: **the schemes of the wily are *hastily ended*.** In 1 Cor 3:19 Paul quotes Job 5:13 as an illustration of God's overpowering wisdom compared to "the [human] wisdom of this world." There is no comparison in Paul's mind.

Verse 14 continues to emphasize the difficult straits in which **the crafty** and **the wily** find themselves after God has reversed their fortunes. They stumble around like those who encounter a solar eclipse in the middle of the day. The sudden **darkness** forces them to **grope** blindly with their hands for something secure to hang onto.

■ 15 This verse returns to the theme of God's care for "the lowly" (v 11) using a different term—**the needy** (*'ebyôn*). This word refers generally to anyone of low social or financial status. The emphasis is on their neediness. God protects these people from those who try to harm them. A number of scholars are uncomfortable with the muddled syntax of this verse and have proposed many emendations (Clines 1989, 117). They expect to find two neatly arranged clauses of synonymous parallelism. Instead, this verse in Hebrew contains only one verb located at the beginning (**he saves**) and one direct object located at the very end (**the needy**).

However, the MT as reflected in the NIV makes sense and may just be a poetic variation in style.

The phrase **from the sword in their mouth** is awkward but understandable, provided the antecedent of **their** is understood to be **the powerful** in the latter part of the verse. Clines has captured the meaning with the literal translation "from the sword [that proceeds] from their mouth" (1989, 117), while Gordis proposes a freer translation "from their sharp tongue" (1978, 57). Either is acceptable. In the OT the tongue, teeth, lips, or mouth of the wicked are often likened to a sharp sword that is able to pierce a person's soul (Pss 52:2 [4 HB]; 55:21 [22 HB]; 57:4 [5 HB]; 59:7 [8 HB]; 64:3 [4 HB]; Prov 5:3-4; 12:18; 25:18; 30:14; Isa 49:2). Verbal abuse and harassment are just as harmful as physical assault. Thus **the needy** are in need of a protector **from the clutches of the powerful**.

■ 16 **So the poor have hope** is the climax toward which Eliphaz has been proceeding in section five of his speech. **Hope** (*tiqwâ*) is the key word (→ Job 4:6). **The poor** (*dal*) refers to people of low social status who are weak and helpless. The emphasis is on their helplessness, although they may also be financially destitute because of their social status. Eliphaz has already pointed Job toward hope for a better future based on the spiritual quality of his past life. Here he espouses a further reason for hope. God always takes care of "the lowly" (v 11), "those who mourn" (v 11), "the needy" (v 15), and **the poor** (v 16). He is their Redeemer. He reverses their fortunes and raises them to a better life (v 11). Therefore, Job has every right to expect God to reverse his fortunes, for he now identifies himself with this same group of people.

Injustice shuts its mouth describes the overall impact of God's reversals on "the crafty" (v 12), "the wily" (v 13), and "the powerful" (v 15). They are forced to shut their mouths (1) because of astonishment at God's activities in raising the lowly (vv 11, 15-16), (2) from embarrassment over their own failures and entrapments (vv 12-14), or (3) because of the sheer power of God's great and marvelous deeds (vv 9-10). Perhaps some combination of the three is intended. Human craftiness, wisdom, and strength (vv 12, 13, 15) are no match for the omnipotence of God (v 9). Therefore, one should always turn to God, as Eliphaz has already instructed in v 8. God will not allow injustice to triumph over his people. **Injustice** (*'ōlātâ*, from *'awlâ*) refers to the conduct of "the crafty," "the wily," and "the powerful" who attempt to destroy the lowly (vv 12-15). Their conduct "is personified here as having a mouth, either to devour the poor or to boast" (Reyburn 1992, 114). Such conduct is usually considered wickedness (the same thought is repeated in Ps 107:42).

6. Sometimes God Disciplines Us (5:17-27)

Eliphaz concludes his first speech with comments about God's discipline. Since all people are guilty of sin and experience the consequences of their bad choices, God takes the initiative to correct their sinfulness. And he does so by disciplining them, just as parents discipline their children when they misbehave.

Persons who are experiencing God's discipline should be grateful that God cares enough about them to correct their errors. If they will turn from their errant ways and heed God's instructions, God will reward them with a blessed life.

■ 17 **Behold, blessed is the one whom God** [*Eloah*] **corrects**. The interjection **behold** (*hinnēh*; not translated in the NIV) brings attention to Eliphaz's sixth and final topic. It is an example of poetic anacrusis (a word at the beginning of a line that is not part of the meter pattern). The second word is *'ašrê* (**blessed**), which is the normal Hebrew introduction to a beatitude. Beatitudes appear in the OT forty-three times. They are especially prominent in the Psalms (e.g., Ps 1:1). The word **blessed** is not a well-understood term in the English language, so translators have suggested numerous alternatives such as: "truly happy is," "how fortunate is," "how rewarding is the life of," "to be envied is," "oh the bliss of," and so forth. The word is never spoken to or by God (in contrast to *brk*, also meaning "bless"). It is always used by people to describe or pronounce a state of well-being on another person or nation. Eliphaz uses the word to pronounce well-being on the person whom God disciplines. The intended recipient of this blessing is, of course, Job whom Eliphaz believes is in need of instruction from God. Thus, Job should count himself fortunate that God has chosen to correct his errors.

The verb **corrects** (*ykḥ*) means "set someone right." It usually implies chastening and reproval and is sometimes used in legal contexts. For example, someone has strayed from God's will, and the only way to bring the person back is through some type of corrective treatment (2 Sam 7:14). Elihu echoes this same thought in Job 33:19.

From a human perspective, God's corrections are usually regarded as negative and hurtful, but God regards them as necessary and good. A D or an F on a student's exam is not intended as punishment but as a wake-up call to study harder. Clines (following W. B. Stevenson) likens God's correction to a "Celestial Surgeon" who cuts away the diseased flesh for our good (1989, 148). In John 15:1-2, Jesus uses a similar analogy—the gardener who cuts off the dead branches from the vine and prunes the good branches to improve the quality of the harvest.

Do not *reject* **the discipline of the Almighty** is an exhortation to Job to accept the troubles he has received and learn from them. **Discipline** (*mûsār*) is usually associated with instruction in the wisdom theology. The imagery is drawn from the family setting where parents discipline their children in order to direct them toward maturity. An undisciplined child is a child headed for disaster (Prov 22:15; 23:13-14). God is like a parent who disciplines his children (Deut 8:5). His corrective measures are a sign that he cares enough about his children's well-being to invest himself in their lives. Thus, "suffering may be seen not as something that puts a gulf between a human being and God but as something that binds them together" (Clines 1989, 148).

Shaddai as a name for God (→ 1:1 for other names for God) appears numerous times in Job and is usually rendered **the Almighty** based on the connection with Akkadian *šadû* ("mountain"). But, the etymology is uncertain and the exact meaning is unknown (for a full discussion see Seow 2013, 443-44). The word appears primarily in Genesis and Exodus (e.g., Gen 17:1; 28:3; 35:11; Exod 6:3). Its usage in Job provides a sense of antiquity to the book. Any Israelite reading this book would immediately think of the patriarchal period.

Some scholars describe this verse as a word of "congratulations" (Clines 1989, 149). Others see it as a word of "warning" (Hartley 1988, 125). The truth probably lies somewhere in between. This is a typical wisdom response to help Job understand his suffering. Eliphaz wants Job to know that suffering is a valuable teaching tool that God puts to good use in educating his people. Thus, even though Job's pain and heartache are severe, he should consider himself fortunate that God is actively pursuing his plan for Job's life through the disasters that have befallen him. God's discipline is a sign of his love and grace (Prov 3:11-12). The exact same thought is found in Ps 94:12.

God's **discipline** is a basic tenet of the wisdom theology that helps to explain some of the mysteries of life. We would expect Eliphaz to get around to this topic sooner or later since he represents the wisdom tradition. Many troubles can be explained by the law of retribution ("you reap what you sow"), but some remain mysterious. Why do they happen? The doctrine of God's discipline is a catchall category into which the sages inserted all the unexplained troubles of life. These mysterious times of trouble are opportunities to reflect on what God might be saying to us to correct us. "Troubles are tests; the person who realizes this responds creatively. The rebellious only make more trouble for themselves by resentment (see 5:2)" (Andersen 1976, 121). In the next five verses Eliphaz will describe some of the tests God sends upon his people to discipline them: sickness and injury (Job 5:18), calamity (v 19), famine and war (v 20), verbal abuse and violent attacks (v 21), and encounters with wild animals (v 22).

God's Chastenings

Does God really discipline those whom he loves? The answer is yes according to both Testaments. In addition to the previously mentioned passages (vv 17-26; Ps 94:12; Prov 3:11-12), there are numerous passages in the Prophets that speak of God's disciplinary actions (e.g., Isa 5:5-6; Hos 11:5-7; Amos 4:6-12). These could be interpreted as examples of God's wrath and judgment against sin. But when God brings times of suffering upon his own covenantal people, he intends it for their rehabilitation, redemption, and restoration, not their destruction. Passages such as Pss 66:10-12; 118:18; Jer 31:18-20; and Hos 11:8-9 make this clear. In Heb 12:5-13 the author quotes Prov 3:11-12 and then explains how God brings trials and misfortunes into people's lives to strengthen them and make them better people.

God's discipline should be expected as a normal part of the Christian life, just as the parental discipline of children is a normal practice in the home. Without discipline, a parent-child relationship does not really exist (Heb 12:8). God as disciplinarian is an important concept in understanding the nature of God. He is truly a God of love who cares deeply about each human being, but his love is not the emotional expressions of an overly sentimental, doting grandfather who can see no wrong. His love always has our best interests at heart and thus is sometimes expressed as the tough love of discipline that is needed to correct our bad behavior and attitudes.

■ 18 Eliphaz now begins a list of calamities that God uses to discipline his people. These are possible tests that God may find necessary to use, not that each calamity is inflicted on every person. Clines' translation is very helpful here: "For he *may* wound . . . , he *may* smite" (1989, 108; emphasis added). Each test is coupled with God's positive efforts to rescue and restore the afflicted person. "The same God who inflicts the pain will heal the wound as soon as his instructional purpose is accomplished" (Hartley 1988, 125). Thus, the author emphasizes acts of healing and restoration as well as those that bring harm. This is the reason why persons enduring distress should count themselves "blessed" (v 17). God will eventually heal and restore them. With regard to the severity of the test, Wesley makes the observation that even though God brings trouble into our life, "he never makes a wound too great, too deep for his own cure" (1765, 1532).

Both physical pain and mental anguish are included in the words **For he wounds**. Thus, it may not be obvious from outward appearance that someone has been wounded by God. The hurts may be internal. **But he also binds up**. This verb (*ḥbš*) refers to the ministry of healing through the binding up of wounds (v 18) or broken hearts (Isa 61:1).

The Hebrew for **he injures** (*mḥṣ*) usually appears in passages describing God as "smiting" or "smashing" his enemies (e.g., Ps 110:5-6). Thus, a translation emphasizing the severity of some of God's disciplinary actions would fit the context of Job 5:18 better (such as "he strikes" [NRSV]). But God also **heals** those he has struck; he makes them whole again.

Eliphaz's words here are not unique. Both Isa 30:26 and Hos 6:1 attribute the exact same actions to God, in disciplining and then restoring his people. Further, in Deut 32:39 these words appear from the mouth of God as a self-description of his treatment of Israel: "I have wounded and I will heal."

■ 19 The number pattern (**six . . . seven**) in v 19 introduces a list of **calamities** (*ṣārôt*) from which God will **rescue** (*nṣl*) his people. Scholars have wrestled with the items in this list, trying to make them correspond with the number seven. The problem is that two of the disasters are mentioned twice. And it is not clear whether the pain and injuries of v 18 or the calamities of v 19 are intended to be included in the list.

Gordis combines and reinterprets some of the items, producing a list of exactly seven "mass disasters": "famine, war, fire, flood, drought, rocks, and wild beasts" (1978, 59). However, not all scholars agree with his analysis. The best solution is not to hold too rigidly to an exact equivalence of **seven**. The author may have intended here "to express merely an indefinite total" (GKC, §134*s*).

Eliphaz's point in the entire sixth section of his speech is that God may bring trouble into the lives of his people for disciplinary purposes, but **he will rescue** them before they are destroyed. Thus, Job should expect to be delivered soon from the troubles he is enduring.

Number Patterns

Number patterns are what scholars call ascending numeration. One number is stated and then followed in the second clause by the next higher number. The first clause "cites a number that would be sufficient by itself and then increases this number by one as a way of emphasizing the comprehensiveness of the statement" (Balentine 2006, 117). Number patterns are mostly found in the wisdom literature, but four of the prophets make use of them as well: "one/two" (33:14; 40:5; Ps 62:11 [12 HB]); "two/three" (Job 33:29; Isa 17:6; Hos 6:2; Amos 4:8); "three/four" (Prov 30:15-16, 18-19, 21-23, 29-31; Amos 1:3—2:8); "four/five" (Isa 17:6); "five/six" (2 Kgs 13:19); "six/seven" (Job 5:19; Prov 6:16-19); "seven/eight" (Eccl 11:2; Mic 5:5 [4 HB]).

Number patterns are a poetic device mainly used for rhetorical effect, but sometimes they help to organize the poet's thoughts. In this case, the higher number is the organizing principle. For example, in Prov 6:16-19 the "six/seven" pattern is used, followed by seven items that God hates. The same is true in Prov 30:15-16, 18-19, 21-23, and 29-31, using the "three/four" pattern. However, in Eccl 11:2 the only purpose of the "seven/eight" pattern is for poetic effect, since no disasters are listed.

■ **20** The two calamities in v 20 are **famine** (*rāʿāb*) and **battle** (lit. "war"; *milḥāmâ*). Both may be directly caused by human beings, but the OT prophets make it clear that God sometimes brings these events on humanity for the purpose of discipline or judgment (Isa 14:30; 51:19; Jer 18:21; Ezek 14:13-14, 17-18). **Death** (*māwet*) is the end result of **famine**, but God's people will be spared. How and when this is accomplished is not spelled out. Certainly Eliphaz is aware that all human beings will eventually succumb to **death**, but one of the principles of the wisdom theology is that God watches over the righteous, to **deliver** (*pdh*) them out of the midst of life's storms.

The verb *pdh* is used prominently in the book of Deuteronomy to refer to God's act of redemption in freeing the Israelites from Egypt. God "ransomed" Israel from the bondage of slavery (Deut 7:8; 9:26; 13:5 [6 HB]; 15:15; 21:8; 24:18) by taking the lives of the firstborn sons of all the Egyptians. The verb refers to more than simply liberation. It implies that a price has been paid to secure one's deliverance. Hence, the translation ***ransom*** or "redeem" (NRSV) is preferable.

The word appears in the perfect stem, which normally is translated in past time, but the context calls for future time: "he ***will redeem you*** whenever you face these troubles in the future." Gordis calls this "the perfect of prophetic certitude" (1978, 59).

■ **21** The next two calamities are verbal abuse and violent physical attacks. The word for **lash** (*šôṭ*) refers to a whip used to prod people (1 Kgs 12:11; Isa 10:26) or horses (Prov 26:3). This is the only passage in the OT that likens the tongue to a whip. **The lash of the tongue** is probably a general phrase for all types of verbal abuse, such as slander, harassment, malicious verbal confrontations, and so forth. The righteous person **will be protected** (lit. "hidden"; *ḥbʾ*) when these verbal onslaughts occur. **Destruction** (*šōd*) refers to violent physical attacks that bring devastation. The noun is used primarily by the prophets and often in parallel with other Hebrew words for "violence" (*ḥāmās*; Jer 6:7) and "destruction" (*šeber*; Isa 51:19). Again, God's people **need not fear** when these attacks occur, for God will rescue them.

■ **22** This verse has some interpretation problems. First, the word for **destruction** (*šōd*) is the same word used in Job 5:21. It is not clear whether the author intended a different type of calamity or a repetition of the same one. Second, the word for **famine** (*kāpān*) is not the same as the one in v 20. *Kāpān* is a rare word borrowed from Aramaic that appears only here and in 30:3 in the entire OT, so there is not a lot of context to use in defining the word. Gordis attempts to solve the difficulties by connecting **destruction** and **famine** in a hendiadys as one calamity, hence "the ravage of famine" (1978, 44). However, some attempts to combine the words in a hendiadys are driven partly by the desire to end up with seven total calamities (→ 5:19). Most scholars leave the two words as two separate disasters and suggest that *kāpān* and *rāʿāb* (v 20) may refer to famines caused by different agents, such as disease, drought, insects, or enemy destruction. The righteous person **will laugh** (*śḥq*) at these additional calamities because of the assurance of divine deliverance (v 19). The tone of this laughter is that of scorn and mockery.

The word for **wild animals** (*ḥayyôt*; lit. "living creatures") is used for either wild or domestic animals. In the story of creation (Gen 1:24-30; 2:19-20) it refers to all the animals that God created. But Eliphaz clearly has wild animals in mind in this verse. While Palestine and surrounding areas did not have an abundance of predatory animals in ancient times, the Bible does mention some: lions and bears (1 Sam 17:34), wolves and leopards (Jer 5:6), boars (Ps 80:13 [14 HB]), wild dogs (1 Kgs 14:11), and so forth. (For a full listing see Borowski 1998, 196-207.) God's people **need not fear** such animals, for when they appear God will intervene (Job 5:19).

■ **23** In vv 23-27 Eliphaz turns from a depiction of God as the one who disciplines his people (v 18) to a description of the future blessings that await the person who accepts God's discipline as a necessary corrective and a beneficial learning experience (v 17). Eliphaz uses second singular verbs and pronouns throughout this section to make it clear that Job is the intended recipient of these blessings. But Job must first accept Eliphaz's words as true (v 27) and not reject the corrective calamities that God has brought on him. The picture of the future that Eliphaz paints for Job in v 23 is a utopia where humanity lives in harmony with the world of nature, both animate and inanimate. Such a peaceful world did not exist after the fall (Gen 3), but the vision resurfaced occasionally in the words of the prophets in connection with the coming messianic age (e.g., Isa 11:6-9; Hos 2:18 [20 HB]).

Scholars have struggled with the meaning of Job 5:23a. How can a person make **a covenant** with inanimate objects such as **the stones of the field**? A metaphorical interpretation is needed here. In Eliphaz's vision of the future, Job will be at peace with his environment. Objects that were once obstructions or dangers will be in harmony with him.

Parts of Palestine are abundantly rocky and hilly, making agriculture almost impossible. One of the first tasks of a farmer in preparing new land for cultivation is to remove the thousands of rocks so the soil can be plowed and planted (Isa 5:2). If they are not removed, the seeds will not grow (see Matt 13:5-6 where Jesus incorporates this image in his parable of the four soils). Farmers usually move the rocks from the center of their field to the edges and stack them to form a protective wall. Perhaps Eliphaz envisioned for Job a future in which the stones of the field work to his advantage as a protective wall, rather than to his disadvantage in preventing the land from being planted.

The wild animals in Job 5:23b are the same animals mentioned in v 22. In the future these animals **will be at peace** (*šlm*) with Job. Gordis suggests that the causative passive (Hophal) stem indicates that the wild animals "are caused, i.e., persuaded, to make peace with you" (1978, 60). Here again, as in vv 18-22, God allows obstructions and dangers to exist. But he turns bad situations into good as part of his disciplinary actions and blesses those who turn to him.

■ **24** Eliphaz now builds on the divine blessings mentioned in the previous verse by assuring Job of the well-being of his household. In the future it will be in good order and prospering. Eliphaz does not mean that Job necessarily lived in a **tent**, for the word can be used in the broader sense of one's dwelling or house (Pss 78:51; 132:3). This is the meaning here. As already noted (Job 1:3), Job probably lived in a permanent house where he farmed. But he was extremely wealthy and able to hire many servants to carry on other business activities for him at a distance.

For the word for **property** (*nāweh*), → 5:3. **Find nothing missing** (*ḥṭ'*) is one of the principal verbs for "sin" in the OT. Its basic meaning is "miss the mark." In the context of v 24, the "mark" is the security and well-being of Job's house and property. The verb is part of a conditional sentence that stresses God's protection for his people: "Should you inspect your property, you will find nothing missing" (GKC, §159g).

■ **25** Another blessing Job can expect in the future is a large family with many **children** (*zeraʿ*) and **descendants** (*ṣeʾěṣāʾîm*). In spite of his previous losses, Job will eventually gain a new family that will be too numerous to count. The great number of his descendants is compared to **the grass of the earth**. The word for **grass** (*ʿēśeb*) can refer either to the specific type of vegetation that oxen eat (Ps 106:20) or, as a broader term, to all the plants and vegetation that God created on the third day (Gen 1:11). In either case, the meaning of the passage is similar to God's promise to Abraham that his descendants would be as numerous as "the dust of the earth" (Gen 13:16) and the stars in the heavens (Gen 15:5).

■ **26** The final blessing Job can expect from God is a full, vigorous life to the very end. **In full vigor** is the NIV rendering for *běkelaḥ*, but no one knows precisely what the phrase means. Some follow the NIV translation, emphasizing the strength of the person up until death (as with Moses [Deut 34:7]). Others, like the NRSV, prefer a meaning related to maturity or completeness of life ("in ripe old age"). The word *kelaḥ* appears only twice in the OT (here and Job 30:2). The context of the latter passage supports the meaning **vigor**, but a number of scholars favor the NRSV translation for 5:26 (for a discussion of the arguments on each side see Clines 1989, 118-19, or Wakely 1997, 2:652-54). Eliphaz likens a full life to grain that has been cut and stacked but not yet threshed. It is brought up to the threshing floor in full maturity at the right time.

■ **27** Eliphaz attempts to grab Job's attention for one final thought by introducing v 27 with the word **behold** (*hinnēh*; not translated in the NIV). **We have examined** [*ḥqr*] **this** means "we have looked into the matter thoroughly and are convinced that we are correct." The use of the first-person pronoun **we** is Eliphaz's way of including his two friends in support of his beliefs. It also enables him to claim the backing of hundreds of sages in the wisdom tradition back through centuries of time. Job has just heard from Eliphaz's lips the wisdom of the ages—principles that have been studied thoroughly and proven correct. In Eliphaz's mind, they are just as true as the fact that an apple falls downward from the tree. **It is true** is literally "thus it is" (*ken hî'*). The word **this** refers to more than just the last few verses. It includes all of his speech—every point.

So hear it (*šěmā'ennâ*) is a good translation of the MT. But some scholars prefer emending the verb to the first-person plural *šěmā'nuhâ* (***we have heard it***) in order to make the second clause parallel with the first (Gordis 1978, 60). This suggestion is possible and is supported by the LXX, but the MT also fits the context and is preferred by most versions and commentators.

Apply it is the NIV rendering for *da'* (***know it***). If one follows the MT, the last line of Eliphaz's speech includes two imperative verbs and the emphatic pronoun **you** (*'attâ*). Clearly, he wishes to press home his views to Job in one final challenge. He softens his commands by connecting his beliefs with the wisdom of the sages before him, but his overall purpose cannot be disguised: ***You! Hear it and know it for yourself!***

FROM THE TEXT

1. **Summary of Eliphaz's First Speech.** In his first speech, Eliphaz very cautiously begins to raise issues that will become more developed as the dialogues continue. He tries to build some rapport with Job by picking up some of Job's words and giving them a new interpretation through his own eyes. For example, Job said that he encountered trouble after he was born (3:10). Eliphaz equates all trouble with evil and declares that all the wicked experience trouble by bringing it

on themselves (4:8; 5:6-7). Job said he was so distressed that his groans poured out of him like springs of water (3:24). Eliphaz uses the same Hebrew word to describe the roar of lions (4:10), a symbol for the wicked whom God causes to perish with a blast of his anger. Job spoke of his fear and dread (3:25) and how the personified night of his conception brought him trouble (3:10). Eliphaz says that he, too, has had a nighttime experience that evoked the same emotions (4:14).

So far Job has not yet accused God of anything or claimed his own righteousness. He has only stated his anguish and his wish he had never been born. So Eliphaz focused on some new ways for Job to look at his problems. He attempted to create a logical framework of universal principles by which to view all of life. He would like to engage Job in conversation on these grounds, but he has no idea as yet of the direction Job will go in his response.

Eliphaz was particularly concerned to share insights from the wisdom traditions that applied to Job's situation. These principles had proven true over centuries of time. Job could count on them to explain his troubles and help him recover. The main points of his speech are as follows:

- Job, you are well-known for helping others, and you have had a long relationship with God that will stand you in good stead now.
- God created the world with a built-in system of morality. The righteous are rewarded and the wicked are punished. "There are no exceptions and no loopholes, because God guarantees both the system's design and its performance" (Balentine 2006, 120). All people reap what they have sown.
- No one is completely pure in comparison to God (Rom 3:23). Therefore, all should expect to receive some suffering in this life as punishment for their sins. Suffering is part of the human experience.
- Turn to God for help and answers. He is able to work miracles and reverse the fortunes of those who are suffering because he is sovereign over all creation.
- Sometimes God disciplines his creatures for their own good. Know that if God is disciplining you now, it will only be for a short time, and then he will deliver you from trouble and bless you abundantly. Think about the long-term rewards, not the short-term pain. And learn from what God is trying to teach you.
- There is hope for you, Job, if you will only accept the basic principles of the wisdom theology and call on God to help you.

2. Eliphaz's Counseling Ability. All the blessings Eliphaz offered to Job in 5:23-26—harmony with nature, security of his household, a large family, and a long, vigorous life—were valid because they are supported by other OT passages. But they seem very uncompassionate and perhaps even cruel when presented to a man who has just lost his livelihood, his children, his health, and his dignity. Eliphaz had good intentions in describing a better future for Job that he hoped would attract Job's attention and get his mind off the past. And most of what he said is true or at least partially true.

However, he seemed more interested in laying out the principles of the wisdom theology than in actually comforting a man with a broken spirit. He was locked into a rigid, black-and-white world of rewards and punishments. Such a world only exists in theory, not in actuality. What Eliphaz needed was a basic course in Counseling 101 if he truly wanted to help Job. As Balentine notes, "Before we take up the ministry of comforting others, it is wise to ask ourselves if our intent is to help them find their place in God's world or in ours" (2006, 121).

Eliphaz also needed some help with his theology. He was too confident that his views on God and the world were correct. But God's character and actions cannot be confined to a few wisdom principles.

B. Job's Response to Eliphaz (6:1—7:21)

BEHIND THE TEXT

In his first speech Eliphaz the sage eloquently made point after point drawing from his vast knowledge of the wisdom theology. One would expect Job to react to some of these points, either agreeing with them or debating their relevance to his situation. Instead, Job returns immediately to the major theme of his complaints in ch 3: his pain is unbearable and he longs for death. As mentioned earlier, each speaker addresses the issues that are on his mind. Sometimes the response engages directly with the previous speech, and other times, as in this speech, the speaker goes a different direction.

Job does connect his thoughts with several key words from Eliphaz's first speech to show that he was listening; for example, the words: "anguish"/"resentment" (5:2; 6:2); "hope" (4:6; 6:8); "crush" (4:19; 5:4; 6:9); "success" (5:12; 6:13); and "fear" (4:14; 6:14) (Habel 1985, 141). However, he fails to see how Eliphaz's advice can relieve his suffering. Eliphaz spoke of God's ability to undo his misery and restore his well-being (5:11, 15-16), but Job's desire is to die, not live (6:8-9). Eliphaz encouraged Job to seek God and submit to his will (5:8), but Job believes God has already sought him out to destroy him (6:4). Eliphaz viewed Job's problems "'from above,' as if he were God" and as if Job were impure and needed discipline (4:17; 5:4, 17), whereas Job views his problems "'from below,' as a sufferer" (Balentine 2006, 124). He questions why God would be interested in pursuing any human being (7:17-18). Like the American proverb, "Men are from Mars, women are from Venus," Job and Eliphaz seem to be from different planets. They talk past each other rather than to each other.

The divisions of Job's speech are as follows:
1. I Am in Anguish (6:1-13)
2. You, My Friends, Are Worthless (6:14-30)
3. All Human Beings Have a Hard Lot in Life (7:1-6)
4. My Death Is Imminent (7:7-10)
5. God, Leave Me Alone (7:11-21)

IN THE TEXT

1. I Am in Anguish (6:1-13)

Job begins by defending his emotional outburst in ch 3. He was simply reacting to the calamities that had befallen him in the prologue. And he still wishes God would take away his life, for he sees no hope for the future.

■ **1** For comments on the introductory formula → 3:2.

■ **2** Job could tell from Eliphaz's reaction in chs 4—5 that his words in ch 3 were quite alarming. So as soon as Eliphaz finishes speaking, he responds with a rationale for his earlier comments. He had spoken out of the emotional pain caused by the heavy burden he carried inside. He begins with a hopeless wish—**If only my anguish could be weighed**. Eliphaz already pointed out in his first speech that **anguish** (*ka'aś*; "vexation" [NRSV]) was an improper way to respond to life's troubles (5:2). It is the response of a fool, rather than a righteous person. Whether improper or not, Job confesses here that **anguish** is exactly the emotional state in which he finds himself. He does not concede that he is a fool, but he does admit to possessing severe mental and emotional pain.

The parallel word to **anguish** in v 2*b* is "calamity" (NSRV; *hawwâ*; **misery**). The term refers to physical disasters that *fall* on a person (Pss 38:12 [13 HB]; 91:3), such as Job experienced in the prologue. Thus, in Job 6:2 Job is speaking of both his troubles and the emotions these troubles have produced in him. He wishes both of them could be **weighed** on the **scales** of life.

■ **3** Job envisions placing his troubles and emotional anguish on one side of the balance scales and the world's sand on the other. If such a weigh-in could be arranged, then it would be clearly evident that even all the **sand** along all the seashores in the whole world would not equal the weight of his burden.

This explains why his words in ch 3 were "rash" (NSRV; **impetuous**). They were literally "squeezed out of him" (Clines 1989, 170). The only other place in the OT where the word "rash" appears is Prov 20:25 where it refers to speaking hastily before considering the consequences. A similar meaning is intended here. In essence Job is saying to Eliphaz: "You do not really understand my pain. It is heavier than you can imagine. This is the reason why my earlier words [in ch 3] were so emotional and unrestrained."

■ **4** The Almighty (*Shaddai*) is now likened to a divine archer who uses Job as his target (→ also 16:12-14). Multiple **arrows** laced with **poison** have found their mark, and now Job's **spirit** (*rûaḥ*) is slowly dying as the **poison** spreads throughout his body. "God's arrows" are a metaphor in the OT for the famines, plagues, wars, animal attacks, and even lightning that God sends in judgment against his enemies and those who disobey him (Deut 32:23-25; Pss 7:12-13 [13-14 HB]; 38:1-3 [2-4 HB]; 144:6; Lam 3:12-13; Ezek 5:15-17). The word for **poison** refers occasionally to the venom of a snake (Deut 32:24, 33; Ps 58:4 [5 HB]), but it appears about eighty times as a metaphor for the wrath of God (e.g., Isa 51:20). In Job 6:4*b* Job describes these attacks as **God's** [*Eloah*] **terrors** that **are marshaled against** (*'rk*) him. This verb means "to arrange something in proper order as a preparation for an activity." It can refer to preparing a legal case (13:18) as well as drawing up the battle lines in preparation for war (Judg 20:20, 22). Thus, God is like an army commander marshaling his weapons of terror against an enemy.

We know from earlier passages (Job 1:21; 2:10; 3:23) that Job attributed all his troubles to God from the very beginning. But here the intensity and motivation of God's actions are increased immeasurably. God did not just take away (1:21) Job's possessions, family, and health, or hedge him in (3:23). He actually attacked him with poisoned arrows and marshaled the forces of terror against him. From this point on, Job's description of God will be intensely negative. Job now believes that God regards him as an enemy and is trying to punish him for some unknown reason.

Eliphaz has already described God as a deity who "wounds" and "injures" in order to discipline his people, but he always "binds up" and "heals" when the test is over (5:17-18). Therefore, Eliphaz encouraged Job to submit to God and endure his afflictions, for healing would eventually come. Conversely, Job believed his wounds were far more severe than any normal divine discipline. His wounds were the attack of a God who wanted to destroy him. This produced a major dilemma in Job's mind. How can the God who rewarded him so bountifully in the past now turn on him and cruelly attack him? Job has no explanation for this turn of events. He will struggle to understand this issue until the very end of the book.

■ **5** Here Job employs what is probably an old proverb to justify further his emotional outburst in ch 3. A self-evident negative response is implied by the two rhetorical questions. The verbs **bray** and **bellow** depict the sounds that animals make when in distress. Animals that have plenty to eat do not **bray** or **bellow** for help. Similarly, humans who are experiencing the good life do not cry out and complain. Job believed he had a right to complain because he had lost so much. "Excessive suffering demands excessive speech" (Balentine 2006, 124).

The **wild donkey** is a symbol for all wild animals that must search for their food—the wild grass that thrives in uncultivated areas. The word for **grass** (*deše'*) appears in Gen 1:11-12 in reference to all vegetation that God created, but in the familiar Ps 23:2 it refers only to the wild grasses that sheep and goats eat. The same meaning applies here. The parallel **ox**, on the other hand, represents the domestic animal kingdom. These animals receive some of their food from farmers as **fodder**—a mixed mash of grains (Isa 30:24).

■ **6** Like Job 6:5, this double rhetorical question is probably a well-known proverb. It seems awkward in this context because it must maintain its original form, but there is likely a connection with v 5 in the sense that **tasteless food** would elicit a loud complaint if **salt** were not available. Most people want their food to be savory.

The translation of v 6*b* is complicated by the uncertainty of the meaning of the phrase *rîr ḥallāmût*. The Hebrew *rîr* appears only one other time in the OT, in reference to the mucus discharge from David's nose and mouth when he acted as a madman before the Philistine king Achish (1 Sam 21:13 [14 HB]). There the NIV has "saliva" and the NRSV "spittle." The second Hebrew word in the phrase (*hallāmût*) occurs only here, so scholars typically look for a cognate in Aramaic, Arabic, or Akkadian. At present, there is no consensus on the meaning, but the majority seems to favor an unidentifiable plant that produced a tasteless sap (see Hartley 1988, 131, n. 4 for a discussion of the possible translations). The context of the question in Job 6:6*b* implies that people will not eat the sap of this plant because it is tasteless.

What is this tasteless food about which Job is complaining? Some scholars equate it with Eliphaz's speech (Habel 1985, 146; Andersen 1976, 128). Job was looking for comfort from a friend, but instead he received only tasteless drivel that did not apply to his situation. More likely, it refers to Job's troubles. God has metaphorically given him food that is worthless—a life of suffering. Therefore, he has brayed like a **wild donkey** and bellowed like an **ox** (v 5). As Wesley notes, "Men commonly complain of their meat when it is but unsavoury, how much more when it is so bitter as mine is?" (1765, 1534).

■ **7** In a further thought about his food, Job notes that he will not even **touch** the food that God has brought him because **such food makes me ill**. It has the potential to bring harm. In v 7*b* ***the sickness of my food*** is probably an idiomatic expression for "my rotten food." To eat such food would be like feeding on **sickness**. Thus, the sense of the passage moves progressively downward from good food (v 5) to "tasteless food" (v 6) to rotten food (v 7). Eliphaz had suggested that Job accept the food of God's discipline (5:17) because it would strengthen him and eventually lead to a good life. But Job wished to reject God's food as being harmful to his well-being. His loud complaints (6:3) were his reaction to receiving such rotten food.

■ **8-9** Job now returns to the main topic of his first speech—his longing to die (3:20-23). Death is the only solution for those who are "in misery" and "bitter of soul" (3:20). Here Job states directly for the first time that he wishes for God to end his life now. His request is: I wish "that it would please God [*Eloah*] to crush me" (6:8 NRSV). **Crush** (v 9*a*) is the same verb used by Eliphaz to describe the ease with which a moth may be snuffed out (4:19). Human life is just as frail as the moth's.

In 6:9*b* Job pictures God's **hand** as being restrained from taking further action. He wishes that God would remove whatever is holding him back and let the full power of his wrath **cut off** Job from this life of anguish. The Hebrew for **cut off** (*bṣ'*) is used here, as in Isa 38:12, as a metaphor for death. Just as the weaver cuts off the threads from the loom when the cloth is finished, so Job wishes God would cut him off from this life.

Job's **request** and **hope** (Job 6:8) may seem morbid, but his pain and anguish have led him to this frame of mind. Interestingly, Job never considers suicide as an option. Even though his wife may have wanted him to do that (2:9), Job recognizes that the beginning and ending points of life are in God's hands. Like Moses (Num 11:15) and Elijah (1 Kgs 19:4), Job requests an immediate death. He probably felt like his sickness had already brought him very close to death, so it would not take much for God to finish him off. Like a great racehorse with a broken leg that is put down to spare it any more suffering, Job asks God to destroy the little that is left of his life as a final act of compassion. Surely a God who cares about him would see the value of this.

Suicide in the Bible

Suicide is: "The taking of one's own life, or causing it to be taken by another, regardless of motive, circumstances, or method used" (Clemons 1988, 4:652). There are several biblical examples of suicide or attempted suicide that fit this definition: Abimelech (Judg 9:53-54), Samson (Judg 16:28-30), Saul and his armor-bearer (1 Sam 31:3-5), Ahithophel (2 Sam 17:23), Zimri (1 Kgs 16:18), Jonah (Jonah 1:11-15), Judas (Matt 27:3-5), and the Philippian jailer (Acts 16:27-28). Christianity has never regarded Jesus' death as a suicide, but rather as a voluntary surrender to the will of his heavenly Father (Mark 14:35-36; Luke 23:46; John 7:33-34; 8:22; 13:1).

In spite of these numerous examples, there is no clear teaching on the morality of suicide in either Testament. Nevertheless, both Judaism and Christianity have looked disfavorably on suicide for three reasons. (1) In most of the examples above, the individuals behaved in dishonorable or sinful ways prior to their deaths. Thus their deaths, even at their own hands, could be viewed as a judgment against their bad choices in life. (2) God is regarded as the giver of life (Gen 1:26-27), the one who breathed his own breath into the first human creature (Gen 2:7) and pronounced his creation as good (Gen 1:31). Since life comes from God, any attempt to terminate life prematurely, even one's own, is an affront against God as the Creator. (3) God's sovereignty over human life is extended to his power over death as well (Job 1:21; Ps 116:15). God forbids the taking of human life (Exod 20:13), because humans are made "in his own image" (Gen 9:6 NRSV). The God who brought human life into existence will also determine when it is time to be concluded. Human beings are not to tamper with God's plans for each person. At the same time, some Israelites did ask God for an early death. Both Moses (Num 11:15) and Elijah (1 Kgs 19:4) pleaded with God to take their lives, just as Job does. In each case, God rejected their pleas and encouraged them to continue their ministries.

■ **10** If God would grant Job's request to die quickly (Job 6:8-9), then at least he could die peacefully with a clear conscience knowing he had never dishonored God or disregarded his commands. His reputation as blameless and upright was more important to him than his continued existence. The singular noun **the Holy One** (*qādôš*) may be a shortened form of the phrase "the Holy One of Israel." This is one of Isaiah's favorite expressions for God (e.g., Isa 1:4; 5:19), which the author may have adapted for a non-Israelite speaker. The plural of the word has already appeared in Job 5:1 where it is rendered "angels" (NLT) or "holy ones."

The second clause is usually regarded as parenthetical. Its meaning is obscure because it contains another *hapax legomenon* (*sld*; → Job 2:8). Some follow the LXX and the Aramaic Targum with the meaning "I would even exult in unrelenting pain" (NRSV). Others support a rabbinic Hebrew interpretation: "even while I recoiled in unrelenting pain" (Clines 1989, 156). The latter is preferable in this context. The **unrelenting pain** Job speaks of is the kind associated with childbirth (Jer 22:23; Mic 4:9).

■ **11-13** Eliphaz had tried to encourage Job with promises of a long life, peace and security in his old age, and many descendants (Job 5:24-26). But Job is not willing to wait for his circumstances to change. He is ready to die now (6:8-9). In vv 11-13 he utters a series of rhetorical questions that describe his anguish. He looks and feels like a person about ready to die. He simply does not have the **strength** to go on any further (v 11). Why should he still **be patient**? Is there something he can do to pull himself up by his own bootstraps (v 13*a*)? Job is certain the answer is no. Even though he possesses all the qualities of a wise person (1:1), his wisdom has failed him now. **Success** (6:13), meaning "the ability to handle life's troubles using the inner resources that wisdom provides" (→ 5:12), **has been driven** from him.

In 6:12 Job compares his anguish to the hardness and enduring quality of **stone** and **bronze**. Someone with that kind of strength could continue to hold on to life until things improved. But Job is not made of that kind of stuff. Jeremiah received a promise from God that he would be strengthened and made "a fortified city, an iron pillar and a bronze wall" in order to withstand the attacks from his enemies (Jer 1:18). But so far, all that Job has received from God is silence.

2. You, My Friends, Are Worthless (6:14-30)

In the second section of his speech, Job addresses his relationship with his three friends. He wants them to stand by him in his time of need. That is what friends are supposed to do. Instead, they have turned against him. So he asks them to teach him if he is wrong in his thinking. But so far, they have been of no help. Granted, he has only heard from Eliphaz. But he assumes that all three support Eliphaz's view.

■ **14** All commentators agree that v 14 is an introduction to the topic of disloyalty, but there are multiple ways to translate and interpret it. Here are three different approaches. (1) In the NIV and NRSV, Job is criticizing the three friends for withdrawing their loyalty from him. In doing so, they are turning away from God: **Anyone who withholds kindness from a friend forsakes the fear of the Almighty.** See Hartley (1988, 137-38), Whybray (1998, 52), Crenshaw (2011, 67), and Driver-Gray (1921, 62-63). (2) In the NJPS, Job is emphasizing the obligation of friends to show each other loyalty even if one of them turns away from God: "A friend owes loyalty to one who fails, though he forsakes the fear of the Almighty." See Seow (2013, 451), Habel (1985, 148), Balentine (2006, 127), and Pope (1973, 49). (3) In the NASB (1977 edition), Job is speaking of the need to be loyal to a friend "lest" it destroy the friend's trust in God: "For the despairing man there should be kindness from his friend; lest he forsake the fear of the Almighty." See Terrien (1954, 3:956).

In spite of a lack of consensus, it is apparent that Job is distressed over Eliphaz's lack of compassion in his first speech (chs 4—5). He was expecting loyalty/steadfast love/**kindness** (*ḥesed*) from his friends. Instead, he received a lecture on the principle of retribution and a subtle hint that God was probably disciplining him. The word *ḥesed* (also 10:12; 37:13) is the covenantal term for God's steadfast love. The word can also be used of human love (1 Sam 20:8, 14, 15). In the context of Job 6:14, the term implies both "loyalty to Job" and "sympathy for his plight" (Pope 1973, 52).

■ **15-17** The lack of loyalty displayed by Job's friends is illustrated by a comparison to the well-known **wadis** (*naḥal;* v 15) of the Near East. These streambeds contain water in the rainy season, sometimes even overflowing, but they dry up as soon as the rains stop. Job's friends act similarly. They have offered friendship in the past and they profess it now, but so far, they have failed to provide the emotional support he desperately wants and needs. He addresses them as **my brothers**, not because they are kinsmen, but as a general term to express his association with them in years gone by. He thought he could depend on them to provide answers and encouragement. Instead, they have proved to be "treacherous" (*bgd;* NRSV). The verb here means "act deceitfully, treacherously" (Isa 24:16; Lam 1:2; Mal 2:10-11, 14-16). It is used in situations where a relationship such as a marriage or covenant has been established and then broken by one of the parties in a deceitful way. In Job's mind, the friends have deceitfully broken whatever friendship relationship they had before.

The Hebrew for **overflow** (*'br*) refers to movement from one place to another as in "passing over" the Jordan River (see Josh 1:2) or "passing through" the land of the Amorites (see Num 21:22-23). A number of versions, including the NIV, support the meaning of **overflow**, in the sense that the water passes over its channel in the rainy season (Isa 8:7-8). An alternative translation is "pass away" (NKJV, NRSV), meaning that the water drains out of the streambed in the dry season leaving the channel bare. Job 30:15 supports this reading, referring to clouds that have "passed away" (NASB, NRSV). The context of 6:15 can support either meaning, as v 16 speaks of the rainy season when the wadis are full of ice and snow, and v 17 refers to the **dry season** when no water is found. Thus, the original intent of the passage is unclear.

Verse 16 elaborates on the appearance of wadis in the winter months. The exact translation is problematic (Clines 1989, 160), but the RSV is closest to the MT: "which are dark with ice and where the snow hides itself." This suggests a wadi that is frozen over with dark ice and has caught blowing snow in its channel. The NIV translation follows a different interpretation that is based on an emendation in the second clause. Here the picture is one of a channel that is filled with rapidly moving dirty water and chunks of ice from the melting snow. Either interpretation is possible, although the NIV is less preferable due to the need for an emendation.

Verse 17 comments on the nature of wadis in the dry season. Once the ice and snow melt and the rains cease, it is only a short time until the water disappears and the channel is completely dry.

■ **18-20** The imagery now changes from wadis to **caravans** (in both vv 18 and 19, most scholars emend *'orḥôt* ["paths"] to *'ōrĕḥôt* [**caravans**]). Perhaps the three friends came by caravan to visit Job and can identify with his comments.

Water is a critical necessity for caravaners traveling through the desert. In order to find it, they may need to **turn aside** from the main road (v 18). Failure to find a water source will result in their death. Job describes the desert as a **wasteland** (*tōhû*). This is the same Hebrew word used of the formless nothingness that existed before God began his creative activity (Gen 1:2). It appears again in Deut 32:10 in reference to the roadless desert areas that the Israelites traversed during the wilderness wandering period.

Job connects **the caravans** he is aware of with **Tema** and **Sheba** (Job 6:19). **Tema** was an oasis town in northwest Arabia that served as a caravansary (way station) for caravan trade from southern Arabia (→ Introduction: Date). **Sheba** refers to an area in the southern Arabian Peninsula (specifically Yemen) where the lucrative trade in incense and spices originated (→ 1:15 for a more hostile description of the people of Sheba). These caravaners have traveled these roads before. They know where all the oases and wadis are located. They are **confident** that the water will be there (v 20). But this time the results are different. **They are distressed** when they fail to find water in the wadi because they know this could mean their death.

■ **21** Here Job addresses his friends in the second person for the first time. Unfortunately, the Hebrew is defective, and scholars are unsure of the exact translation. The general consensus is that Job is expressing unhappiness with his friends' attitude toward him. At the first sign of trouble their loyalty dries up, and they fear getting too close, lest Job's troubles rub off on them. They retreat to their standard wisdom theology. Job, on the other hand, is looking for their help and sympathy. But like the caravaners from Tema and Sheba, his expectations are dashed.

In v 21*b* Job refers to himself as **something dreadful** (*ḥătat*). This is a general term that probably includes his appearance, his losses, and his words. Job's situation is just too much for the friends to comprehend, and so they **are afraid**.

■ **22-23** Next Job asks the friends if there is something he has said to cause them to back away from their loyalty to him. His first two questions deal with monetary demands. "Have I said, 'Make me a gift'? Or, 'From your wealth offer a bribe for me'?" (NRSV). The wisdom traditions warn against borrowing and lending. One who engages in such practices is taking the risk that wrong expectations by either party or unforeseen circumstances may destroy a friendship (Prov 22:7: "the borrower is the slave of the lender" [NRSV]). Even promising surety for a friend's debt can lead to a strained relationship (Prov 6:1-5; 11:15; 17:18; 20:16; 22:26; 27:13). One is better advised simply to give a gift to those in need (Prov 3:27-28) than to make a loan that may not be paid back. Job is testifying that he is aware of the wisdom traditions and has never engaged in risky or questionable borrowing practices. He has never requested money from anyone. Whether Job ever needed such help from his friends in the past is unknown and irrelevant. The point is simply that he has never made monetary demands on them that might have clouded their friendship. So why are they acting so cautiously now?

Job's questions in Job 6:23 concern hypothetical social demands. "[Have I said,] 'Save me from an opponent's hand'? Or, 'Ransom me from the hand of oppressors'?" (NRSV). Job is confident that he has never requested their help in ridding himself of an enemy or an evil person intent on terrifying him. Thus, the strained relationship that is developing between Job and his friends cannot be attributed to social demands Job may have forced on them. As far as he knows, he has done nothing to destroy their friendship. **Ransom** (*pdh*) implies that a price has been paid to secure one's release (5:20). The Hebrew for **oppressors** (**ruthless**) denotes evil people or nations that cause terrifying fear in others (Ps 86:14; Isa 29:20; Ezek 28:7).

■ 24 Job senses that his friends are thinking differently than he is, so he asks them to instruct him. The verb **teach** (*yrh*) occurs seven times in Job with a variety of teachers as the subject, including God (34:32; 36:22), Job (27:11), the wisdom of the ages (8:10), and even the animals and plants (12:7-8). The well-known noun Torah (*tôrâ*; "instruction, law") is derived from this verb. Job offers to **be quiet** while they instruct him.

The question of who needs to speak up and who should remain silent is bandied about throughout the book. Job and his friends and a younger person named Elihu (chs 32—37) each accuse the other of being unwilling to be quiet and listen (11:3; 13:5, 13; 33:31, 33). As the dialogue continues, the reader soon realizes that God is the only one who has remained silent. But finally even God can hold back no longer (chs 38—41). His powerful and penetrating speeches leave everyone else speechless.

In his first speech, Eliphaz stated that all human beings are imperfect in comparison to God, and thus they should expect some amount of trouble in their life (4:17-19; 5:6-7, 17). Job now asks his friends for a full explanation of how this principle applies to him. **Show me where I have been wrong**, he says. The verb **I have been wrong** (*šgh*) most frequently refers to going astray morally. It is used along with its cognates *šgg* and *šĕgāgâ* in contexts that refer to the committing of unintentional errors (Lev 4:2, 13, 22, 27; 5:15, 18; Num 15:24-29). Job is convinced that the troubles in his life are not due to any willful sin he has committed. And the prologue makes it clear he is correct. But since Eliphaz suggested that God might be disciplining him (5:17), Job wants to know what wrongs Eliphaz has in mind. He is willing to admit that he may have committed an unintentional error of which he is unaware. This is only in the realm of possibility, though. He demands hard evidence from his friends that he is guilty of such an error. Up to this point, Eliphaz has talked only in generalities. Now Job asks for the specifics:

"If you think I have strayed from God's will, then show me. I will shut up so that you may set me right."

Job's request is like the psalmist who pleads for God to show him any "hidden faults" (Ps 19:12-14 [13-15 HB]). Here we see the heart of a person who is extremely serious about his spiritual relationship with God, even to the extent of being willing to expose unintentional errors committed in ignorance or by accident, negligence, or inadvertent oversight. These acts are not willful and thus not intended to cause harm, but they inevitably do. Because they are violations of the OT law, they grieve God, thus requiring atonement through a specific sacrifice called the sin offering (*ḥaṭṭā'ṭ*). This sacrifice is discussed in Lev 4—5 and Num 15:22-29.

■ **25** At first glance, Job's comments in Job 6:25a seem very straightforward: **honest words** (lit. "words of straightness/uprightness") can be **painful** to other people. However, scholars disagree significantly over the interpretation. Who is doing the speaking and who is experiencing the pain? Since **uprightness** has already been established as a characteristic of Job (1:1), it seems logical he is referring to his own past words in ch 3. These words were spoken honestly. Yet they were received by the friends as painful and even shocking. This interpretation also finds connections with Job's words in 6:28 and 30 where he testifies he has not spoken lies or "wickedness."

The meaning, then, of v 25 is expressed in two rhetorical questions: "How can my honest words about my agony be painful and upsetting to you? What can you possibly find in my words to reprove?" The answer is: "There is nothing for you to reprove because I have spoken the truth." Habel (1985, 139) and Balentine (2006, 129) support this interpretation.

On the other hand, the **honest words** of v 25 may find their context in the previous verse (v 24), where Job invites his friends to teach him where he is wrong. He wants them to speak honestly with him, even if it causes him pain. The sense of the first clause, then, is an exclamatory statement followed by a rhetorical question: "If you are able to show me where I have been wrong, how painful your honest words will be to me! Nevertheless, I am willing to listen to your criticisms, even if they hurt. But so far you have failed to point out anything that is wrong with my life. What have you reproved?" Clines (1989, 181) and Seow (2013, 465) accept this interpretation. This writer prefers the first interpretation, but it is impossible to settle on a definitive meaning since the verse is highly ambiguous.

■ **26** The interpretation of v 26 is also difficult. The literal translation is: **Do you mean to correct** *words* [*millîm*], **and treat** the words ['*imrê*] *of a despairing man* **as wind?** The NIV, NRSV, and NASB regard the first term for *words* (*millîm*) as a reference to Job's words in ch 3, yielding: "Do you think you can succeed in correcting 'my' words?" This makes the second clause a synonymous parallel to the first. An alternative interpretation (NJPS; Hartley 1988, 139; Pope 1973, 49; Clines 1989, 181) connects *words* with the speech of Eliphaz in chs 4—5. This yields: "Do you think you can succeed in correcting [me with 'your'] words?" Eliphaz's words in clause one are contrasted with Job's in clause two.

While either interpretation is possible, the point Job is trying to make is found in the second clause. He is frustrated that his friends regard his own words as nothing more than wind. He has failed to secure their sympathy and support. This is just another illustration to add to his earlier comparison of his friends to a wadi (6:15-17). There is no significance to the appearance of two different synonyms for **words** (*millîm* and *'imrê*) other than for poetic variety.

■ **27** Job's frustration slips into sarcasm in v 27. He likens the friends to cruel, callous creditors who would do anything to recover a bad debt. They would see nothing wrong with dividing up a dead man's estate, including selling his children into slavery or treating a former friend as just a piece of merchandise to be bought and sold. Job is not accusing his friends of engaging in these ruthless activities, but he sarcastically upbraids them for treating him with the same merciless disdain. They are acting like harsh traders at a typical Near Eastern market haggling over the price of merchandise.

■ **28** Here Job demands his friends' attention. He has just criticized them for being as worthless as waterless wadis (vv 15-17) and accused them of callous disregard for his plight (v 27). He now asks them to look directly at him. He wants their undivided attention. Perhaps their gaze has drifted downward or to the side as his criticisms of them have intensified. Job calls them back to attention and utters an oath that he is telling "the truth, the whole truth, and nothing but the truth." Verse 28*b* reads literally "If I would lie to your face," which the NIV renders into a rhetorical question: **Would I lie to your face?** However, the *'im* is probably best regarded as an oath particle converting the verb to its opposite meaning and yielding the emphatic denial: *I swear I will not lie to your face!* (see Num 14:30; 1 Sam 17:55; and Ps 89:35 [36 HB] for identical usages of *'im*; Clines 1989, 156; Rowley 1976, 65).

■ **29** Now that he has their attention, Job requests that the friends reconsider and reject the ideas expressed in the speech of Eliphaz. This needs to happen in order to make a right evaluation of Job's situation. Habel suggests that this may be "equivalent to a call to repentance" (1985, 150). Twice Job asks them to "turn" from their inaccurate beliefs about him and accept his testimony as truthful (the NIV uses two different translations here [**relent** and **reconsider**], but they are from the same verb, *šwb* ["turn"]).

May there be no injustice (*'awlâ*; v 29*a*) may be interpreted as applying to Job ("there is no injustice in me" [Clines 1989, 156; Gordis 1978, 66]) or to the friends ("may there be no injustice in you" [Pope 1973, 49; Hartley 1988, 140]). The NIV follows the second interpretation, which seems reasonable considering that the imperative ahead of it is directed at the friends. Job is arguing for their conversation to be based on solid, truthful evidence and not on misinformed speculation.

The meaning of v 29*b* is uncertain because the literal translation ("my righteousness is still in it") is confusing. Is the antecedent of the word "it," "righteousness" (yielding "my righteousness is still in itself," meaning "it still exists")? Or does "it" refer to Job's "words" (v 26) as being righteous (yielding "my righteousness is still in my words")? The NIV follows a third possibility connecting "it" with the whole topic they have been discussing (yielding "the issue of my righteousness is still in question in your minds, and therefore **my integrity is at stake**"). The correct interpretation is uncertain.

■ **30** Here Job uses a rhetorical question to make the point that his own mouth has spoken nothing but the truth: *Is there injustice* [v 29] *on my tongue?* Earlier in his speech, he spoke of his ability to discern differences in the taste of food (vv 6-7). He could readily identify food that was tasteless or made him sick. He now returns to this same imagery in the second clause: **Can my *palate* not discern *[my] troubles?*** What Job means is that he is able to distinguish between correct and incorrect interpretations of his troubles. He knows they are not self-inflicted wounds, but rather come from an outside source. The correct answer to the question in v 30*b* is: "Yes, you are unable, for you have not read the prologue and are not aware of the conversation between God and the Examiner." However, within the limitations of his knowledge, Job is able to discern much more about his troubles than the friends can, for he knows his heart and they do not.

3. All Human Beings Have a Hard Lot in Life (7:1-6)

The third section of Job's speech is basically a soliloquy addressed to no one in particular. He turns from criticizing his friends to commenting on the difficulties that all humans experience. Most likely, calamity had never darkened his door until the Examiner paid him a visit. But now that he knows what it is like to suffer, he has come to realize that his experiences are no different from those about him. His own personal troubles are only an illustration of the common lot of humanity. His words are similar to those of the psalmist: "Our days may come to seventy years, or eighty, if our strength endures; yet the best of them are but trouble and sorrow, for they quickly pass, and we fly away" (Ps 90:10).

■ **1** Job knows that his suffering has been extreme, but he refuses to call himself unique. No human being can avoid what Job calls **hard service** (*ṣābā'*). This Hebrew word and its verbal root (*ṣb'*) usually refer to military forces and activities. The noun can be used with either human armies or divine hosts. One especially common usage (279x) is in the divine title "The Lord of hosts" (*yhwh ṣĕbā'ôt*; e.g., Ps 24:10). However, in Job 7:1 and two other passages (14:14; Isa 40:2) the word simply means **hard labor**, which is the lot of every human being. No doubt, Job's readers would automatically connect the cause of this **hard labor** with the story of the fall in Gen 3.

Job compares the exhausting, toilsome labor of human existence to that of **hired laborers**. These are persons who are hired to perform a task, in contrast to slaves who are forced to do it. In ANE cities, as in many modern ones, day laborers typically gathered at a designated place each morning waiting to be hired out for work by whoever needed them. Their status in life was generally poor.

■ 2 As mentioned in v 1, the **slave** and the **hired laborer** work for different reasons. Yet both long for the end of the day when their work will cease. Then the slave will find some relief in the shade, and the hired man will receive his wages. **Shadows** (*ṣēl*) refers to any shade from the sun cast by objects such as clouds (Isa 25:5), rocks (Isa 32:2), plants (Jonah 4:6), and so forth. These shadows tend to lengthen in the late afternoon and evening. Thus, the word **evening** is added in the NIV, although it does not appear in the Hebrew. The word for "wages" (*pōʻal*; NRSV) usually refers to a person's "deeds" (lit.; either God's or a human being's); but here and in Jer 22:13, the word means *the pay* they receive for their work.

Versions differ over whether Job 7:2 expands on v 1 or introduces v 3. Many follow the latter, connecting vv 2 and 3 together with only a comma between them. However, the NJPS and GNT (following Gordis [1978, 78-79] and Dhorme [1984, 98]), connect v 2 with v 1. This interpretation seems more likely, because v 2 provides the reason why the life of every person can be compared to that of **a hired laborer**. Just as slaves and day laborers long for the work day to end, so human beings have an intense desire for their lives of "hard service" (v 1) and suffering to end. This is one of Job's justifications for his earlier requests to die (3:20-22; 6:8-9).

■ 3 Job now likens his own suffering to that of humanity in general. Like others, he has experienced **months of futility** and **nights of misery**. Futility (*šāwʼ*) generally refers to "worthlessness," although some passages imply that deception (31:5) or iniquity (11:11) may have led to this sense of worthlessness. Perhaps Job is hinting here that God has deceived him in bringing about his suffering. The word for **misery** (*ʻāmāl*) is one of Job's favorite expressions for his troubles (→ 3:10).

Months indicates an extended period of time. Scholars have proposed various estimates of the duration of Job's suffering based on this verse and others throughout the book. The pseudepigraphic *Testament of Job* (5:19; 6:19; 7:9) suggests a period of seven years, but nowhere does the book of Job give a specific number of months or years.

Job notes that his experiences **have been allotted** and **assigned** to him. By this he means that someone caused him to inherit his troubles (Dan 1:5; Jonah 1:17 [2:1 HB]). He does not mention who may have done the assigning, but he has already implicated God in Job 6:4. At the very end of this speech he will clearly accuse God of causing his suffering (7:11-21).

■ 4 Job's nights are no better than his days. Instead of restful sleep, his mind is wide awake and his body tosses to and fro. No doubt, his restlessness is driven by his anguish over the troubles that have befallen him (6:2) and the pain his body is forced to endure (7:5). **How long before I get up?** expresses his dread of the many hours of sleeplessness that haunt him every night. Time seems to move very slowly in the darkness.

The final clause reads literally, "I am full of restlessness until dawn." "Restlessness" (*nědudîm*) is another *hapax legomenon*. It is thought to be derived from *ndd*, which is used in connection with the fluttering of birds' wings in Isa 10:14; 16:2. Here it refers to the **tossing and turn**ing that Job experiences while trying to sleep.

Dawn (*nešep*) is the twilight period before the sun comes up in the morning (3:9). However, other contexts require the meaning "dusk" or **evening twilight** (24:15).

■ **5** Job's physical appearance is disgusting. His skin is covered with maggots and dirt, and numerous scabs are oozing blood and pus where they have been scraped away. Job feels as if he is wearing a garment of filth. The word for **worms** (*rimmâ*) appears five times in Job. At least three of them (17:14; 21:26; 24:20) refer to the maggots that appear on decaying flesh after death. Job probably has patches of his skin that are rotting away and already infested with maggots. Other sections of his skin have scabbed over. The Hebrew phrase for **scabs** is *gîš* [Kethib]/*gûš* [Qere] *'āpār* (lit. "clods of dirt"). This is the only verse in the OT that contains the word *gûš*, and the phrase is difficult to understand. Possibly Job sees his scabs as dark, raised bumps against his skin that look like lumps of dirt. It is also possible that Job could have applied a poultice of mud over his sores to ease the itching, and these looked like clods of dirt when dry.

Verse 5*b* describes a skin disease with boils that break open and ooze pus, scab over and harden, and then break open again as Job scrapes them with a potsherd (2:7-8). However, there is a slight difference of interpretation. The Hebrew verb for **broken** (*rg'*) comes from one of two roots—one meaning "to become still" and the other "to stir up" (*CDCH*). The NRSV follows the first ("my skin hardens") and the NIV the second (**my skin is broken**). According to Isa 1:5-6, the ancient treatment for skin diseases and wounds was threefold: cleansing, bandaging, and soothing with oil. Apparently, Job was not following this practice.

■ **6** In vv 2-4 Job bemoaned the long duration of each day and night that moved so slowly. Here in v 6 he compares his total life span to the swiftness of the weaver's shuttle that darts quickly back and forth from one side of the loom to the other. He continues with this thought in vv 7-8 as well. He clearly believes his life will end very shortly. The word for **weaver's shuttle** (*'ereg*) means "loom" in Judg 16:14, but here the translation **weaver's shuttle** is generally accepted as correct (although Seow opts for "weaver's web" [2013, 503-4]).

Job 7:6*b* presents two problems of interpretation. First, the Hebrew word for **hope** (*tiqwâ*) can be translated in two ways. The usual translation is **hope** (4:6; 5:16; 6:8), yielding this rendering: **My days . . . come to an end *with the ceasing of* hope**. The sense of the passage is that the end of Job's life is quickly approaching amidst a thick cloud of gloom and hopelessness from which he cannot rid himself. However, a number of scholars prefer the meaning "thread" because of the weaving metaphor in the first clause and the use of the word in Josh 2:18, 21 in reference to Rahab's "scarlet cord." Further, Hezekiah uses the same imagery of being cut off from the loom of life when describing his own approaching death (Isa 38:11-12; Hartley 1988, 146, n. 12). Such an interpretation yields the following: "My days . . . come to an end as the thread runs out" (Andersen 1976, 135). Both readings are attractive and supported by good evidence, so the interpretation remains problematic. The author may have intended to be ambiguous so as to hint at both meanings.

The second problem concerns whether Job is speaking of the **end** (→ 4:9) of "all his days" (i.e., his life) or the end of "each individual day" (Clines 1989, 163). The former is preferable in light of the two verses that follow.

4. My Death Is Imminent (7:7-10)

In this short fourth section and continuing to the end of the chapter Job finally addresses God directly using second singular verbs and pronouns. The theme of this section is his approaching death and its consequences both to himself and to God.

■ **7** The singular imperative verb **remember** indicates that Job is now addressing God rather than the three friends. This is the first time he has done so. The NIV inserts the phrase **O God** to make it clear to whom he is speaking, though the words are not in the Hebrew text. In many other passages in the OT (especially the laments like Pss 25:6-7; 79:8 NRSV), the word **remember** appears as a plea to God from someone in great distress. The word is "a fundamental petition for deliverance" (Hartley 1988, 146-47, n. 6). However, in Job 7:7 Job is not pleading for deliverance. He is pleading that God will take into consideration the limitations of his humanity. The usage is similar to Ps 103:14: "he remembers that we are dust."

The word for **breath** (*rûaḥ*) is used with a variety of meanings in its thirty-one appearances in Job: the "mighty wind" that took the life of Job's ten children (1:19); the "blast" of God's anger that destroys the wicked (4:9); the **breeze** that brushed Eliphaz's face during his night vision (4:15); Job's own life ("my spirit" [6:4]); and ***speech that is worthless***, that is, hot air without meaning (6:26). Here in 7:7 Job reminds God that his life is like an exhaled ***puff of air***—weak, unsubstantial, and fleeting (Ps 78:39). In addition to the word **breath**, the OT uses a number of other similes to refer to the fleeting nature of human life. For example, in Hos 13:3 the length of life is compared to a "cloud [KJV, NASB]/mist," "dew," "chaff," and "smoke," and in Ps 103:15 to "grass" and the "flower of the field."

In Job 7:7*b* Job expresses his view that the good life for him is now gone forever. The days of enormous wealth, outstanding reputation, ideal family, and good health (as described in chs 1—2) are behind him, and he anxiously awaits his approaching death. **Happiness** is the translation used by a number of versions for the Hebrew word *ṭôb*, but the context of 7:7 calls for more than just a joyous emotional experience. Job is here referring to his earlier state of well-being as a recipient of God's blessings. In other words, he will never see good times or the good life again.

The good life is an important topic in all the wisdom literature, especially the book of Proverbs. The sages sought repeatedly to define it and to encourage all to seek it diligently. Of course, the good life is always connected in the OT with "the fear of the LORD" (Prov 1:7), and this is the crux of the problem Job is wrestling with throughout the book. He knows what the good life is, and he knows he has done everything the wisdom theology has taught him about achieving it. His life was a model of faithfulness to God, and yet it had taken a sudden turn for the worse and no one could explain to him *why*. The only remaining course of action that seemed reasonable to his confused mind was death.

■ **8** Just as Job has been deprived of ever seeing the good life again, so God will soon experience the deprivation of ever seeing his servant Job again. God may look for him but he will not find him, for Job is headed to Sheol—a place of separation from God (Pss 6:5 [6 HB]; 88:5 [6 HB], 10-12 [11-13 HB]; → "Sheol" sidebar at Job 3:17-19). **The eye that now sees me** could refer to anyone who sees Job **now**, whether human or divine. But 7:8*b* makes it clear that Job is addressing his remarks primarily to God, whom he calls in v 20 the "watcher of humanity" (NRSV).

Job describes his approaching death with the word *'ênennî* (**I will be no more**). This is called by grammarians "the particle of nonexistence." But Job is not speaking of his nonexistence in a metaphysical sense. He is referring to his absence from the world of human activity, for he proceeds in vv 9-10 to describe his future existence in Sheol. The word *'ênennî* is repeated in v 21 with the same meaning, and also in the account of Enoch's passing to the afterlife in Gen 5:24 ("he was no more").

It is interesting in this passage that Job never pleads with God to give him more years of life. Rather, his words are more of a simple, straightforward statement of what will happen after he dies. But perhaps Job had a subtler purpose in mind. By emphasizing his absence, Job might have been trying to draw attention to the cause and consequences of his death. Perhaps he wished to prick God's conscience a little by pointing out that God's attacks were about to result in the loss of his most faithful servant. Once Job departed for Sheol, then no one—not even God—would be able to see him. "In place of a victim there will be a vacuum" (Habel 1985, 160).

■ **9** Using the simile of a **cloud** that appears briefly and then **vanishes** into thin air, Job expands further on his imminent death. Once a cloud is **gone**, it is gone forever. Human life can be viewed in a similar vein. Our brief human journey quickly leads to **Sheol**, from which there is no return. In the ancient world, Sheol was thought to be under the ground. Job's words in v 9*b* reflect this concept: *so the one who "goes down" to Sheol will not "come up."*

The concept of Sheol as "the land of no return" is well-known in ancient Mesopotamian literature. It appears once in the Sumerian work from the early second millennium BC titled "Inanna's Descent to the Nether World" (*ANET*, 53-57, line 82), five times in the later Akkadian version "Descent of Ishtar to the Nether World" (*ANET*, 106-9, obverse lines 1, 12, 41; reverse lines 6, 14), and possibly three times in "Nergal and Ereshkigal" from the even later Neo-Assyrian period (*ANET*, 507-12, lines i, 7; ii, 13; vi, 46).

Even though the netherworld bears the title "the land of no return," the myths do mention a few individuals who escaped the underworld. The goddesses Inanna and Ishtar certainly did, as well as other gods and divine helpers. But for human beings, there was no escape from the clutches of Sheol once a person had died (→ further comments on Sheol at 3:19). The author of Job was familiar with the concept of "the land of no return," for he used it here and again in 10:21; 14:12; and 16:22.

■ **10** **A house** is the place where a person lives, but Job is referring to the broader and more personal concept of his ***home***. All the activities and relationships that take place in his home will end when Job dies. Thus, not only will his relationship with God be broken (v 8), but so will his relationship with his family. **His place will know him no more** refers to the void in his family that cannot be filled. The exact wording of this clause appears also in Ps 103:16 where the brevity of human life is contrasted with the eternal nature of God's love.

5. God, Leave Me Alone (7:11-21)

The final section of Job's speech is pointedly directed at God. God had become his oppressor, bringing suffering to both his body and soul. If God will not destroy him as he requested in 6:8-9, thus releasing him from his agony, then he desires that God will at least leave him alone so he can die in peace. Job is almost paranoid in his belief that God still has him in his sights. He feels like there is a target painted on his back and God is watching his every move.

■ **11** Job makes it very clear that he will not go to Sheol quietly. He will not sit in a corner sulking and mulling over his thoughts to himself. Rather, he believes he has a right to **speak out** and **complain** about God's treatment of him. His justification for this course of action is the awful inner agony he is experiencing, in addition to the physical pain. He describes it as **the anguish of my spirit** and **the bitterness of my soul**. **Anguish** (*ṣar*) refers to a sense of "physical and/or mental claustrophobia, being hemmed in by enemies or by circumstances" (Swart and Wakely 1997, 3:855). **Bitterness** describes people in great inner turmoil (3:20). Job repeats this thought at the beginning of his next speech (10:1).

■ **12** The ANE produced numerous stories of conflicts between the gods. The behavior of these gods was not ideal, but it helped ancient people understand the forces of nature in a prescientific world. One well-known Mesopotamian myth was the story of creation known as *Enuma Elish*. In this myth the national Babylonian god Marduk fought a tremendous battle against the chaotic sea monster Tiamat (*ANET*, "The Creation Epic," 60-72, 501-3). After he triumphed over her, he split her body in two like a shellfish (IV, line 137) creating the dome of the firmament and the earth beneath. He then posted guards (IV, line 139) to keep the heavenly waters above her carcass from overwhelming the earth beneath.

Another significant myth in Canaanite culture was the conflict between Baal, god of the rain and the storms, and Yamm, god of the sea (*ANET*, "Poems About Baal and Anath," 130-31). Baal defeated Yamm and then placed boundaries around him to prevent him from intruding onto the land. In both of these myths there is a sea-god or sea monster (dragon) who threatens the peace of the divine realm and provokes a conflict that must be dealt with by the gods. Once this monster is defeated, a guard is posted to prevent further trouble.

Job draws on this ancient imagery in v 12 in his complaint against God. He accuses God of treating him like one of these ancient monsters who needed to be caged, defeated, or slain. His blunt question to God is: "Why are you so overly hostile to me? Am I a threat to you like the great sea monsters of the ancient myths who battled with the gods of the pantheon?" The words for **sea** (*yām*) and **monster of the deep** (*tannîn*) lack the definite article in Hebrew, so they are probably proper names referring to the ancient mythological gods (monsters) by those names. Hence, "Sea" and "Dragon" (NRSV) are appropriate English renderings.

The reader cannot help but see the irony in this verse—a pitiful human being asking Almighty God if he is a threat, like the mythological sea monsters, to the divine order in the world (Habel 1985, 162). However, as Balentine notes, Job may have more power than he realizes. His line of questioning may be even more threatening to God than the ancient monsters (2006, 138). He may look pitiful, but his questions to God are some of the most profound that have ever been asked. They go to the heart of God's character, questioning his goodness, power, justice, and compassion. This may be part of the reason that God responds with such forcefulness later on (chs 38—41).

Mythological Characters in Job

The book of Job contains a number of allusions to mythological sea monsters. This indicates the author's familiarity with a number of myths that were well-known in the ANE. The following list includes all the mythological sea characters in the book: **Sea** (*yām*)—7:12; 9:8; 26:12 (perhaps 3:8); **Sea-dragon** (*tannîn*)—7:12; **Leviathan** (*liwyātān*)—3:8; 41:1 [40:25 HB]; **Rahab** (*rahab*)—9:13; 26:12; and **the fleeing serpent** (*nāḥāš bārîaḥ*)—26:13.

These characters are mentioned by other biblical writers as well: **Sea** in Ps 74:13; **Sea-dragon** in Pss 74:13; 148:7; Isa 27:1; 51:9; Jer 51:34; **Leviathan** in Pss 74:14; 104:26; Isa 27:1; and **Rahab** in Pss 87:4; 89:10 [11 HB]; Isa 51:9. This suggests a widespread knowledge of the ancient myths by some of the Israelite writers. The author of Job did not regard these characters as real, but he was not opposed to using them as illustrations. In the same way, an author today might use a Paul Bunyan story or one of the Grimm brothers' fairy tales to illustrate a point without accepting the reality of the characters' existence.

■ **13-14** Job's first desire in this speech was to die (6:8-9), but instead he has had to endure "hard service," "months of futility," and long "nights of misery" (7:1-4). Verses 13-14 are a further comment on the nature of his nocturnal suffering. For normal people the nighttime is a time to rest and forget the problems of the day. A good night's sleep usually provides new energy and insight. Job's hope is that sleep will do the same for him. He looks to his **bed** and his **couch** for **comfort**, hoping that his **complaint** will go away by morning.

Instead of rest, Job's nights are filled with nightmares. His **dreams** and **visions frighten** and **terrify** him as they would anyone, leaving him exhausted and on edge both day and night (the stem of both verbs [Piel] indicates an intensified meaning). He is sometimes scared out of his wits at night. Restful sleep is a rare occurrence.

Job makes it clear by the use of second singular verb forms that God is the cause of these nightmares, just as he was the cause of the calamities in chs 1—2. These nocturnal experiences are another piece of evidence to support his contention that God has gone out of his way to be hostile to him. The comparison of his situation to the sea monsters in 7:12 is not an exaggeration at all. By mentioning his nighttime visions, Job is able to connect his experiences with Eliphaz's vision in 4:12-21. However, the purpose of Eliphaz's vision was to reveal a divine message while the visions Job received were intended to terrify.

■ **15** The conclusion of this long sentence that began in v 13 is a request to die. The literal translation is: "so that my soul chooses strangling, (and) death, rather than my bones." The noun **strangling** (*maḥănāq*) appears only here in the OT, but its meaning is clear from the two appearances of its verb root (*ḥnq*) in 2 Sam 17:23 and Nah 2:12 [13 HB]. "Rather than my bones" (*mē'aṣmôtāy*) is awkward, resulting in numerous emendations and translations (see Clines 1989, 165). However, BDB notes that the plural form of "bone" (*'eṣem*) is used frequently in Psalms and Proverbs to refer to the "entire person," that is, "one's whole being" (782, 1*d*) (Pss 6:2 [3 HB]; 31:10 [11 HB]; 32:3; 35:10; 38:3 [4 HB]; 51:8 [10 HB]; Prov 3:8; 14:30; 15:30; 16:24). This interpretation fits best with Job 7:15 as well, yielding: **I prefer strangling and death, rather than *my present existence***. Job may also be making a subtle comment about his appearance—nothing left but skin and bones.

A few scholars translate ***soul*** (*nepeš*) as "throat" and treat ***my bones*** as the subject of v 15*b* (see parallels in Pss 6:2-3 [3-4 HB]; 35:9-10; Prov 16:24). This yields: "So my throat prefers strangling, my bones desire death" (Habel 1985, 152; Hartley 1988, 148; Seow 2013, 489). However, the traditional translation makes sense and the meaning is similar.

■ **16** The desire to die continues in Job 7:16 (→ 10:20; 14:6). The verb for **I despise** (*m's*) appears frequently in the OT in reference to people rejecting God's will or God rejecting disobedient people (see 1 Sam 15:23 for both usages). The word has already appeared with this meaning in Job 5:17. In 7:16 the verb lacks an object and reads literally "I reject." Many versions, including the NIV and NRSV, believe the context calls for a direct object such as **my life** and treat Job's comment as a loathing or hatred of his present condition. This translation makes good sense. Job has just stated in the previous verse that he would rather die than live, and his desire in v 16 is that he **would not live forever**.

In v 16*b* Job pleads with God to leave him alone so that he can die in peace. According to the progression of the story, God has not allowed any more trouble into Job's life since he permitted the Examiner to take away Job's health (2:7). Nevertheless, Job is possessed with a terrifying fear that God still has more trouble stored up for him. He points to his persistent nightmares (7:14) as evidence of God's intentions. Job's perceptions may not coincide with the reality of God's actions, but his nightmares were certainly real to him.

Job's words continue in v 16*b* with a comment on the shortness of his life. He uses the word *hebel*—the much-used term for "vanity" in the book of Ecclesiastes (1:2, 14; etc.). The word has several nuances of meaning depending on its context. It can refer to an object's "lack of substance" (empty, shallow, unsubstantial), its "short life span" (fleeting, transitory, short-lived), or its "lack of value" (worthless, futile). The NIV accepts the third nuance (**my days have no meaning**), probably based on the usage of this word in its other occurrences in Job (9:29; 21:34; 27:12; 35:16). However, other versions such as the NRSV follow the second nuance with the rendering: "my days are a breath." This translation is closer to the context, which requires a parallel term for the temporal word **forever** in the first clause. Also, Job has just commented that his life is quickly coming to an end (7:7-10).

■ **17-18** Most scholars regard vv 17-18 as a satirical parody on Ps 8:3-5 [4-6 HB]. Both passages use rhetorical questions that address the issue of human insignificance in comparison to God's greatness. But whereas Ps 8 stresses the paradox of humanity's importance and draws attention to our closeness to God, the passage in Job expresses a desire that God would move farther away. ***Leave me alone***, Job cries out in bitterness (Job 7:11, 16, 19), believing that God's intentions are hostile rather than helpful. **That you make so much of them** (v 17) is from *gdl*, meaning "exalt, make great." The usage of this verb here satirizes the psalmist's description of humanity as being "made . . . a little lower than God," being "crowned . . . with glory and honor," and being "given . . . dominion over the works of [God's] hands" (Ps 8:5-6 [6-7 HB] NRSV). Certainly, Job did not feel exalted while living at the city dump in great pain.

Job uses three parallel clauses to describe God's actions against humanity. God focuses his **attention** (lit. "heart") on them, makes a careful inspection of them **every morning** (Job 7:18), and **tests** them again and again throughout each day. In Job's thinking, this is "unrelenting surveillance" (Pope 1973, 62). It is true that Job is speaking here about God's treatment of all human beings in general. But his observations are colored by his own experiences. In this chapter he has testified that God terrifies him every night (vv 13-14) and hounds him every day (vv 17-18). No wonder he prefers "strangling and death" over life (v 15).

■ **19** Job continues the emphasis on God's laser-like attention toward him. Bitterly, he asks, "How long will this surveillance go on? Will you never leave me alone?" In the book of Psalms there are frequent requests for God to turn his attention *toward* the needs of his people. Petitions for God to "turn" (Ps 6:4 [5 HB]), "remember" (Ps 74:2; → Job 7:7), "look" (Ps 25:18-19), and "hear" (Ps 5:1-2 [2-3 HB]) are common ways of expressing the desire of an individual or community for God to come to their rescue. In a few cases the psalmist wants God to turn his attention *away*, but this is usually because of guilt over sin (Pss 25:7; 51:9 [11 HB]).

Job's request for God to **look away** from him is not due to guilt, however. It is due to his sense of being singled out for significant punishment. He desires that this treatment would stop. **Or let me alone even for an instant?** is a paraphrased translation that reads literally, "Will you not let me loose until I swallow my spit?"

Scholars are unanimous that this is an idiomatic expression similar to one in Arabic that refers to a brief moment in time. The sense of the clause is something like this: "Will you not even allow me to catch my breath for a moment?"

■ **20** The literal translation of v 20a is: "(If) I have sinned [*ḥṭ'*], so what do I do to you?" The protasis is a rare form of a conditional clause with a perfect verb stem indicating "a condition already fulfilled in the past" (GKC, §159h). Thus, the word **if** is added in the English translation as in 4:2, which uses the same grammatical construction. Job's purpose in speaking this way is not to admit that he is a sinner. Nor is it to trivialize any sin he may have committed in the past (13:26). Neither is he arrogantly claiming some level of sinlessness not attainable by other human beings. Rather, he is suggesting a hypothetical possibility that might impact God in some way. The emphasis is on the apodosis: **what have I done to you** that would cause you to attack me with such force? This thought is repeated almost exactly in 35:6 from the mouth of Elihu.

Most Christian theologies contain extensive treatments on the nature of sin and its effect on humanity, but little is mentioned about how sin affects God. However, the OT contains a number of passages on the impact of human sin on God. Here are some examples from the Psalms: (1) God is grieved (Ps 78:40). (2) God's anger is aroused (Pss 6:1 [2 HB]; 38:1 [2 HB]; 78:21, 31, 49-50, 58-59; 102:10 [11 HB]). (3) God turns his face away from sinners and withdraws his presence (Pss 51:9 [11 HB]; 78:60; 143:7). (4) God's judgment is brought to bear against all sinful acts (Pss 51:4 [6 HB]; 143:2). In addition, there are multiple passages in the Prophets that confirm these same divine reactions when the community of Israel turned away from God. Thus, the issue for Job was not a denial that sin affects God. If he had sinned, he knew that God was grieved. Rather, Job's belief was that God had attacked him far more severely than any sin of his might merit (Job 7:12, 14, 17-19). Even if he had sinned, God was guilty of overkill. The punishment did not fit the crime. Why use a sledgehammer to kill a fly when a fly swatter will do?

The phrase "You watcher of humanity" (*nōṣēr hā'ādām*; NRSV) is certainly ironic. But it is also a bitter word of sarcasm. When used of God, *nṣr* usually means "to watch over in a protective way" (Deut 32:10; Pss 12:7 [8 HB]; 31:23 [24 HB]; 32:7; 40:11 [12 HB]; 61:7 [8 HB]; 64:1 [2 HB]; 140:1, 4 [2, 5 HB]; Isa 26:3; 27:3; 42:6; 49:8). But Job did not wish to characterize God as one who cares about humanity. Rather, his experience of God was even worse than the author of Prov 24:12 who knew that nothing can be hidden from God. For Job, God is the all-seeing eye who secretly watches his every move seeking every opportunity to bring more harm on his poor, helpless soul.

Why have you made me your target? Target (*mipgā'*) appears only here in the OT. The root (*pg'*) has several meanings, one of which is: "to fall upon or attack someone with the intent to kill them" (1 Kgs 2:25, 29, 31, 32, 34, 46). Job has already portrayed himself as the object of God's attacks (Job 6:4; 7:12, 14, 17-19), but here he puts a specific name on his role—a **target**. He believed the Divine

Archer had purposely singled him out for special punishment. The divine arrows had already found their mark and infected his body with the poison that would soon end his life (6:4).

Have I become a burden to you? is mentioned in a small Jewish collection of verses known as the *Tiqqune Sopherim* ("corrections of the scribes"). These passages all contain modifications in the MT that were made early on by the scribes to avoid casting God in a bad light (Gordis 1978, 82-83). As it stands, the MT reads: "Why have I become a burden to myself" (*'ālay*)? However, the original text probably attributed this burden to God and read: "Why have I become a burden to you" (*'āleykā*)? The latter reading is supported by the LXX and is followed by most versions.

The Hebrew for **burden** (*maśśā'*) is used in some passages to refer to the load of goods that animals such as donkeys carried on their backs (Exod 23:5). It may also be applied to "someone who gets in the way" or "hinders progress" (2 Sam 15:33; 19:35 [36 HB]). Job is here asking God why he treats him like a hindrance that needs to be eliminated so God can proceed with his activities.

■ **21** This verse contains another in the series of questions to God that began in Job 7:12 and continues in vv 17-21. This question finds its meaning in the conditional clause in v 20: "If I have sinned." Again, Job is not admitting that he is a sinner, but is only raising a hypothetical question. "Assuming I have sinned, God, what would you do about it? Would you not want to forgive me instead of making me your target [v 20], especially since I am about to die and disappear from your sight?" The question presupposes that if Job sinned, God would speak up and say something to him about it. He would then forgive Job when he repented. But God has remained silent to this point, and Job's conscience is clear. Therefore, the issue of sin in Job's life can only be discussed from the standpoint of a hypothetical possibility.

Job knew that God was able to **pardon** (*nś'*) and **forgive** (*'br*) human sin. The verb *nś'* in this context means "lift up" or "take away" a person's sin. The parallel verb *'br* carries much the same meaning—"cause to pass away" or "take away" (BDB, 719). The reason God was not able to forgive Job's sin was because there was no sin to forgive. Job knew this, as well as God; and the reader is also aware of this. Job is still a person who fears God and turns away from evil (1:1). Job raises the issue of forgiveness here, hoping that God can be prodded into either confirming or denying his need of forgiveness before death snatches him away.

Job believed his death was imminent. One day **soon**, God will find that Job is missing. He will probably mount a careful search, but it will be too late. Job will have passed out of this world into Sheol. **Dust** (*'āpār*) is a reference to death/Sheol (→ 17:16), for "dust" is what humans are made of (Gen 2:7), and to "dust" they will return (Gen 3:19). **But I will be no more** (*'ênennî*) is the particle of nonexistence (→ Job 7:8).

Words for "Sin" in the Book of Job

In vv 20-21 Job brings together the three primary words for "sin" in the OT. They appear as a group again in 13:23 and twelve other passages in the OT. First, the verb *ḥṭ'* and its noun form *ḥaṭṭā't* (155x in the OT) refer to "the failure to follow God's way" (lit. "miss the mark"; → 1:5). The verbal form appears in 7:20 ("If I have sinned"). Second, the noun *pešaʿ* (93x in the OT) is usually translated "transgression," although the NIV has **offenses** in v 21. This word signifies "a willful disobedience against God, a rebellion against his authority." Third, the noun *ʿāwōn* (231x in the OT) is usually rendered "iniquity," although the NIV has **sins** in v 21. This word refers to "an act that is crooked, bent, out of line." These three synonyms are used interchangeably throughout the OT. They are not three kinds of sin, but rather the totality of sin seen from three different perspectives.

FROM THE TEXT

Summary of Job's Response to Eliphaz. Job makes it clear that his friends have let him down. They are more interested in defending the wisdom theology than comforting his anguish. He really needed someone to listen to his side of the story, someone to bounce ideas off of and empathize with his plight. He quickly recognized that Eliphaz was not that kind of a friend, and he assumed that Bildad and Zophar were of similar mind.

Therefore, after a brief scolding of the friends, Job turned his attention to God, hoping that something he said would prod God into conversation. He wanted God to know two things about him. First, he is in such physical and emotional agony that he wishes to die quickly. Second, he is completely baffled over why God has caused him so much suffering. Is he such a threat that God must repeatedly attack him with all his might? This is not the kind of God that Job knew before the calamities. Since God is not talking, Job will have to wait for an answer to that question. But at least he now knows where he needs to go to find answers.

The main points of Job's speech are as follows:
- I admit I spoke rashly in my earlier speech, but it was because of my intense anguish and pain.
- My friends who came to console me are a big disappointment. I was expecting compassion. Instead, Eliphaz gave me a wisdom lecture.
- Why is God tormenting me? He treats me like a target, arrow after arrow finding its mark. What have I done to deserve such awful treatment? God, please leave me alone so I can die by myself in peace.
- Let's assume I have sinned. What difference does that make in the grand scheme of the cosmos? Have I harmed God or disrupted his divine order? Shouldn't he tell me if I have sinned and then forgive me when I repent?
- I wish God would end my life right now.
- I am still willing to listen if someone can tell me where I am wrong.

- A difficult, miserable life is the common lot of all humanity. Not a single person is exempt.

C. Bildad's First Speech (8:1-22)

BEHIND THE TEXT

Like the other two friends, Bildad was shocked at the change in Job's appearance when he first arrived. His distress was deeply visible (2:12-13). However, his first reaction had long since disappeared by this point in the story. Job's mournful wishes that he had never been born (3:1-26; 6:8-9), his criticism of Eliphaz's first speech (6:14-30), his sense of imminent death (7:7-10), and his requests for God to leave him alone (7:11-21) did not sit well with Bildad. As he saw it, Job needed to be confronted with the wisdom of the ages and forced to acknowledge its truth. Thus, as soon as Bildad saw an opening, he wasted no time in getting to the heart of the issue: "The wisdom tradition has much to teach us. If you will accept it for yourself, you will be restored."

Bildad's speech contains four sections:
1. Seek God and Live an Upright Life (8:1-7)
2. Previous Generations Confirm What I Am Saying (8:8-10)
3. There Is No Hope for the Godless (8:11-19)
4. God's Ways Are Always Just (8:20-22)

IN THE TEXT

1. Seek God and Live an Upright Life (8:1-7)

After a pointed jab at Job's blustery words, Bildad, the traditionalist, gets to the topic that is burning within him. God can always be counted on to govern the world in a just manner. If Job will accept this wisdom principle for his own life and seek to live righteously, God will restore him to his former greatness. His future years will be even greater than before the calamities struck.

■ **1** The author introduces Bildad's first speech with the standard introductory formula used throughout the book (→ 3:2). Bildad's name and home (Shuah) have been loosely connected with Abraham's clan in Genesis (→ 2:11), but the evidence is not conclusive.

■ **2** In contrast to Eliphaz's gentle approach, Bildad prefers a blunt, in-your-face method of attack. He begins his first speech by criticizing Job for his continual whining about his sufferings. **How long** expresses his frustration with Job's wordiness and distorted theological concepts. In the Psalms the phrase "how long" appears in laments pleading with God for relief from a major distress. In Job, by contrast, it is used to criticize another person for excessive wordiness and/or major errors of understanding (18:2; 19:2). Ironically, Bildad's frustration has no effect on the length of Job's future remarks, for the conversation will continue for many more chapters.

Bildad calls Job's speeches thus far **a blustering wind** (*rûaḥ kabbîr*). This is interpreted by some as a "windbag," that is, a very talkative person whose words are full of hot air but lack substance. However, the word *kabbîr* when used to modify **wind** suggests ***a mighty wind*** that stirs things up, even to the extent of causing damage. This criticism from Bildad is not unexpected, for Job has already accused the friends of regarding his words as nothing more than wind (6:26).

■ 3 Bildad is frustrated with Job because he believes Job has distorted God's character by accusing God of unjust and unrighteous behavior. He quickly jumps to God's defense using two rhetorical questions: **Does God pervert justice? Does the Almighty pervert what is right?** The anticipated answer is: "No, that is impossible." **God** (*El*) and **the Almighty** (*Shaddai*) are used in parallel here as well as 8:5 (→ 1:1; 5:17 on the names for God in Job). Both names are emphasized by being placed at the beginning of their clause directly after the interrogatives. **Justice** (*mišpāṭ*) is a legal term referring to God's standards by which he governs the world. **What is right** (*ṣedeq*; usually translated "righteousness") refers to "behavior that conforms to the will of God" (→ 4:17). Both terms are similar in meaning and are often paired together in the same verse (e.g., Pss 9:8 [9 HB]; 33:5; 72:1-2; 99:4; Amos 5:24).

The verb **pervert** (*'wt*) means "bend, make crooked, distort something from its normal state" (see Eccl 7:13). Since justice and righteousness are inherent attributes of the nature of God (Deut 32:4), any deviation from these characteristics would upset the whole concept of God according to the wisdom theology. This issue is critical for Bildad and must not go unchallenged. In reality, Job has not specifically accused God of either injustice or unrighteousness. But when he complained that God had attacked him much more severely than he deserved (7:20) and that God had not offered him forgiveness for any hypothetical sins (7:21), Bildad regarded Job's words as a challenge to the integrity of God.

■ 4 As proof of God's justice, Bildad raises the issue of the death of Job's children. In the prologue (1:18-19), the only explanation given for this calamity was a great wind caused by the Examiner to test Job's faith. But neither Job nor Bildad were aware of the Examiner's involvement. They both believed that God was the ultimate cause. Bildad was certain that the children had brought this misfortune on themselves. God, being a just God, had simply delivered them over to the consequences of their sin (lit. "the power of their transgression" [NRSV]). Job, on the other hand, was totally confused about the reason for their death because God had remained silent.

The key to interpreting this verse is the translation of the Hebrew particle *'im* at the beginning. Normally *'im* is used to introduce a conditional clause and is translated as "if." The NRSV and the NJPS follow this interpretation. Others such as the NIV believe *'im* cannot refer to a hypothetical condition because Job's children were already dead. The NIV uses **when** to express this second possibility, and the NEB even converts the clause to a statement of fact: "Your sons sinned against him." However, Hebrew grammar does allow for a conditional relationship that has already been fulfilled in the past to be expressed with *'im* and the perfect stem of the verb (GKC, §159*l, n*). That is exactly what appears in this verse, and thus "if" is the preferable translation: "If your children sinned against him" (NRSV). By using this conditional particle, Bildad is able to get his point across without directly accusing Job's children of sin. Of course, Job is completely aware of what Bildad is implying, for this was the reason why he had earlier offered sacrifices for his children (1:4-5). In a later speech (18:19) Bildad will again bring up this topic, but there he will not be so ambiguous. He will blame the death of Job's children on Job's own sin rather than theirs.

The connection between sin and suffering is a cause-and-effect argument that lies at the heart of Bildad's theology (→ "Cause-and-Effect Reasoning" sidebar at 4:10-11). This logical relationship provides an adequate explanation for all the suffering in life, including the death of Job's children. Sin always produces suffering, and therefore if one sees suffering, its cause can be traced back to sin. This law of retribution is a steadfast, universal principle embedded by God in the order of life that proves his justice. Nothing can change it, in Bildad's thinking, without denying the very nature of God. No doubt, Bildad felt justified in mentioning the children because their deaths were a perfect example of God's justice. But he offers no proof that the children sinned, other than their death.

Whether or not the children sinned, one has to wonder why a person would be so insensitive even to mention this awful tragedy to a man who has just lost ten children. Bildad's comments seem very callous, and perhaps even cruel (→ From the Text for ch 18). He seems more interested in defending God and the principles of the wisdom theology than in helping a weary traveler along the way of life. Job was correct in his earlier evaluation that his friends were deceitful and undependable (6:15).

■ **5-6** These two verses are one long sentence introduced by two conditional clauses with *'im*. Here the conditions are clearly in the future (as opposed to the past in 8:4). Bildad encourages Job to seek God and live an upright life. If he will do so, God will certainly respond and restore him to his previous standing. Again as in v 3, Bildad uses two names for God—*El* and *Shaddai*. He also inserts the singular pronoun **you** (*'attâ*) in both conditional clauses to emphasize that his advice is directed specifically at Job and is not just a general principle.

The two verbs in v 5 draw Job's attention away from his problems and point him toward a solution focused on God. The first verb **seek . . . earnestly** (*šḥr*; → 7:21) occurs mostly in the wisdom literature and Psalms, in contexts that refer to seeking after God. The second verb **plead with** (*ḥnn*) is an important part of the prayer language in the Psalms, usually spoken by a person in great need of God's help. It appears frequently in the laments as an appeal for God to have mercy on the speaker(s) (e.g., Pss 6:2 [3 HB]; 51:1 [3 HB]; 123:3). The specific verb stem that appears in Job 8:5 is used in other passages to describe pleas for mercy from various individuals such as Joseph (Gen 42:21), Moses (Deut 3:23), Solomon (1 Kgs 8:59), and Esther (Esth 8:3).

The entire verse, then, is an encouragement to pray earnestly to God for relief from distress. It echoes Eliphaz's recommendation in Job 5:8 to submit his cause to God. Certainly no one would find fault with this advice by both Bildad and Eliphaz.

In 8:6a Bildad adds a further condition to solving Job's problems. Not only must he actively pray for God's mercy, but he must also live a life that is morally straight. The implication is that God will definitely not help him if there is still sin in his life. **Pure** (*zak*) is an adjective that can be used to describe the finest quality of olive oil (Exod 27:20 NRSV) or incense (Exod 30:34). The word may also refer to "right moral behavior" that is "untainted or flawless" (Walton 2012, 165; Prov 16:2; 20:11; 21:8). The four occurrences in Job all carry the latter meaning (8:6; 11:4; 16:17; 33:9).

Upright (*yāšār*) is the same word that described Job's character in 1:1. It means "be morally straight." Ironically, Bildad adds this to the list of conditions even though Job has been characterized as upright since the beginning of the book.

If Job meets the conditions of 8:5-6, God **will rouse himself**. The verb '*wr* has already appeared in 3:8 in reference to those who "rouse [up] Leviathan." The word does not imply "waking from sleep," as if God has been asleep all this time and is not mindful of Job's sufferings. Rather, in this context it suggests a stirring into action from a state of inactivity.

God will also "grant well-being [*šlm*] to your righteous home" (NJPS). In other words, he will make Job's life whole or complete again. "Your righteous home" is literally "the estate of your righteousness" (*něwat ṣidqekā*; → 5:3 for the meaning of *nāweh*, as "the place of one's habitation and all of one's lands and possessions"). The phrase is somewhat ambiguous, referring either to "the abode which is rightfully his . . . , or the dwelling characterized by his righteousness" (Habel 1985, 175). The NIV adopts the first meaning, but the second seems preferable based on Jer 31:23 ("abode of righteousness" [NRSV]). "The righteousness of Job is regarded poetically as inhabiting his 'estate'" (Clines 1989, 198-99). Thus, the full meaning of Job 8:5-6 is something like this: *If you will diligently seek God and plead for mercy from the Almighty, and if you are pure and upright, surely then he will stir into action for you and make whole the place where your righteousness dwells.*

■ **7** *Though your beginning was small, your end will become very great.* Here Bildad reinforces the idea of restoration by promising even greater blessings in the future for the person who seeks God and lives an upright life. Hartley calls this "the positive side of retribution: righteous behavior is rewarded with prosperity" (1988, 157). Based on the description of Job's life in 1:1-3, it is hard to imagine how his future could be any greater. Yet when the story concludes, we see that Bildad was correct in his advice, for Job's rewards are doubled (42:12, 16). The author even uses the same Hebrew words—*beginning* (*rē'šît*) and *end* (*'aḥărît*)—to make the connection between Bildad's prediction and its fulfillment. This supports the unity of the book by tying the epilogue into the dialogue section. ***Beginning*** designates Job's prior life before the calamities struck. It is the same word used at the beginning of the creation story in Gen 1:1. ***End*** refers to Job's future life in general (Gen 49:1; Prov 23:18; Isa 46:10).

2. Previous Generations Confirm What I Am Saying (8:8-10)

In vv 8-10 Bildad moves from words of advice to the reason why his advice is valid and worthy of Job's consideration. He believes his views are ancient and time-proven by generations of sages before him.

■ **8-9** If Job was serious when he asked his friends to teach him (6:24), then Bildad has just the lesson for him to learn. **The former generation** (lit. "the first generation" [*dōr rîšôn*]) has much to teach the present generation. Scholars have discussed how far back Bildad may have had in mind, but it is impossible to determine any specific time period based on his brief comments. Most likely, he is simply alluding to the generations prior to his own.

Job 8:8*b* is literally "And ascertain the searching of their fathers." The word "searching" (*ḥēqer*) refers to earlier investigations by the sages into a variety of topics such as the meaning of human existence and the nature of the good life. The results of these investigations are what are called the wisdom theology or the wisdom tradition. This tradition is what Bildad wants Job to consider carefully.

The antecedent of "their fathers" is not given, but it probably points to the ancestors of the sages who passed on to their children the wisdom they had received from earlier generations from time immemorial.

The importance of gaining knowledge from past generations (→ 15:17-18; 20:4) is due to the brevity of the present generation. One person's lifetime is not long enough to gain an adequate understanding of life. Therefore, the wisdom of many people out of the past is needed to supplement our present knowledge. Our time on earth is so short that it seems like only **yesterday** (v 9) that we began our existence. Bildad compares the human life span to that of **a *fleeting* shadow** (*ṣēl*). This is a common motif in the OT for the shortness of human life (1 Chr 29:15; Pss 102:11 [12 HB]; 109:23; 144:4; Eccl 6:12).

This truism is even more pertinent today than in biblical times. The modern tools of astronomy have given us an even greater sense of the brevity of a human life when compared to the age of the universe.

Bildad also underscores the lack of knowledge possessed by any one human being: **we . . . know nothing**. The point is not that we know nothing at all but that our knowledge is so minute when compared to the collective human wisdom of all previous generations. If we are ever going to understand the meaning of life, we must learn to trust the lessons that past generations have discovered and passed down to the present.

By using the first plural pronoun **we**, Bildad includes all his listeners (even modern ones). They all should acknowledge this truth; and they all do. Even Job was in complete agreement with Bildad on this point, for he had already spoken of the brevity of his own life, comparing it to a "breath" of air (7:7, 16). He will also use the metaphor of **a shadow** in a later speech (14:2). The place where Job parts company with Bildad is at the point of his own experiences, which did not fit into the wisdom of former generations. But Bildad would not accept Job's life experiences as valid. They were limited and subjective, whereas the collective wisdom of the sages is broad and objective. Bildad was right that the wisdom traditions have much to teach us, but he was ignorant of the real reason for Job's sufferings. Therefore, his counsel was worthless.

■ **10** Bildad now challenges Job to accept the teachings of past generations: *Will they not teach you, will they not speak to you, will they not bring forth important words* [GKC, §125c] *from their collective wisdom?* The antecedent of **they** is "the former generation" in 8:8. The word is emphasized in Hebrew to point out the significance of these ancient teachers. The NIV phrase **from their understanding** is literally "from their heart." In the OT the word "heart" refers frequently to a person's inner thoughts and emotions, but here the word is almost a synonym for "the collective wisdom" produced by the great thinkers and sages out of the past. "If Job is to find restoration, he must cease challenging honored doctrines on the basis of his own experience and develop a listening attitude to the honored teachings of the fathers" (Hartley 1988, 159).

The Wisdom Traditions

The wisdom traditions are the body of knowledge collected by the sages and passed down from generation to generation both orally and in written form from as far back as 2700 BC. Solomon gave official support to this tradition through his interests and skills, but the tradition existed in Israel over a long period of time. It was also prevalent in many other countries. Both Egypt and Mesopotamia produced large literary collections of this wisdom (see *ANET*, 405-52, 589-607). So when Bildad directed Job's attention to the wisdom of former generations, he was building a solid foundation for his position. One does not easily refute a principle, such as the law of retribution, that has stood the test of time. Just as Eliphaz's trump card was his divine vision, Bildad's was the wisdom that had proven true over centuries of time and in many cultures.

3. There Is No Hope for the Godless (8:11-19)

In this section Bildad turns to the topic of the godless. Their lives are tenuous and hopeless. He compares their pathway to that of a papyrus plant without water (vv 11-13), a spider's web trying to withstand the pressure of a large object (vv 14-15), and a garden plant that is destroyed (vv 16-19). None will survive for very long. No doubt, he hoped that Job would see himself in these illustrations from nature. Job, too, had had a sudden reversal of fortune.

■ **11-13** Bildad begins this section with a proverb about the need of reeds, such as **papyrus**, for water (v 11). Papyrus is a green plant with a long triangular stem and a bushy top. It is an aquatic plant that grows only in swampy areas containing standing water, such as along riverbanks and around lakes. In ancient times the plant was plentiful along the Nile River in Egypt and in the Huleh Valley north of the Sea of Galilee. Both places were quite marshy (also 40:21). In their native habitat in northern Africa these plants may grow up to fifteen feet tall.

The plant was very light and buoyant and thus useful in making baskets and boats (Exod 2:3; Isa 18:2). It was also quite valuable for making a paperlike product called "papyrus." The stem of the plant was cut into thin strips and glued together to make pages for writing.

Aquatic plants such as papyrus cannot **thrive** (lit. "become great"; same verb in Job 8:7) without water. They will **wither** and die very quickly. The literal translation of v 12a is "while yet in its freshness" (BDB, 1). Some take this as a description of the "greenness" (KJV) of the plants; others as a reference to their being "in flower" (NRSV) or "tender" (NJPS). The NIV encompasses all of these: **while still growing**.

Verse 13 provides the interpretation for the illustration. Just as papyrus plants cannot survive without adequate water, so **the godless** cannot survive long without God. They will perish prematurely. **All who forget God** (*El*; in the sense of rejecting him) and **the godless** are synonyms for "the wicked" (*rĕšā'îm*) in Job (20:5; Ps 50:16-22).

The word **godless** (*ḥānēp*) appears eight times in Job, but only five times in the rest of the OT. It refers to "those whose lives are a 'perversion' or a 'distortion' of what God intends" (Balentine 2006, 153). Forgetting God and perishing are two parts of a cause-and-effect relationship that is deeply embedded in Israel's theology. In Deut 8:11-20 the Israelites are commanded to remember God, his mighty acts, and his covenant with them, for if they forget him they will surely perish. Bildad's point is that those who forget God have no **hope** (*tiqwâ*) of a better life. Their pathway will be dismal and shortened.

The NIV **destiny** is based on an emendation following the LXX. The MT has *'orḥōt*, which means "ways, paths," but a number of versions prefer the emended form *'aḥărît*, meaning "end, future, destiny." The MT makes sense, but the emended form is supported by two other passages (Prov 23:18; Jer 29:11) that connect "hope" with "future." Following the rules of textual criticism, the harder and preferable reading is "paths" (*'orḥōt*). Thus, a better rendering is: **such are the pathways of all who forget God**.

■ **14-15** Using the illustration of **a spider's web** (v 14; lit. "house of a spider"), Bildad describes the life of the godless as unstable. Their "confidence" (*kislô*; v 14a NRSV) and "trust" (*mibṭaḥô*; v 14b NRSV) are not based on a solid foundation.

The Hebrew for **fragile** (*yāqôṭ*) appears only here in the OT, so its meaning is uncertain. Numerous suggestions and emendations have been proposed, but there is no consensus (Clines 1989, 199-200). Some versions treat the word as a noun or adjective and try to find a parallel with **spider's web** in the second clause. Thus, the NIV has **fragile** and the NRSV uses "gossamer." Others regard the word as a verb form from *qwṭ*, meaning "cut off," and see a parallel with **perishes** in v 13 (Hartley

1988, 159, n. 2). Because of the uncertainty, it is best to treat the verse as simply a further statement about the unstable, flimsy life of the godless.

In v 15 Bildad provides further comment on the spider web illustration by noting that a person cannot **lean *against*** it nor **grasp** it, for it **gives way** very quickly. Spider webs are designed to trap light insects, not support great physical weight. Thus, the godless have no source of stability in life—nothing to provide them "hope," "confidence," or "trust" (vv 13-14 NRSV).

■ **16-19** Bildad now speaks of a second type of a plant, one that grows in a **garden** (v 16) rather than in a "marsh" (v 11). At first, the garden plant appears to be quite healthy, ***full of sap*** (*rāṭōb*; HALOT) and growing vigorously **in the sunshine**. It sends **its shoots** out across the top of the ground, seeking nourishment from the soil. Even **rocks** (v 17) are not a hindrance to this plant, for **its roots** seek out every crack and crevice.

The opening description of this plant is very positive, and this has led some scholars to create "a parable of two opposite plants" (vv 11-15 = the **godless** person, and vv 16-19 = "the righteous person") similar to Ps 1:3-4 and Jer 17:5-8 (Gordis 1978, 521; Seow 2013, 522-24). However, the more traditional interpretation sees the second plant as just another illustration of the **godless** person, and this interpretation fits the context best.

In the beginning everything is going well for this garden plant, but suddenly it is "destroyed" (Job 8:18 NRSV; lit. "one swallows it"), and other plants take its place (v 19). Its demise is so complete that no one remembers that it ever existed. It disappears without a trace or remembrance. The identification of the destroyer and the method of destruction are not mentioned, but God is probably implied.

In v 19*a* the word *měśôś* is very problematic. One interpretation derives the word from *śwś/śyś* and renders it: "this is the joy of his way" (RSV). But this translation makes no sense in this context unless it is intended to be satirical. An alternative interpretation relates the word to the verb *mśś*, meaning "dissolve, melt" yielding: ***this is the dissolution of its way***. The latter interpretation fits the context of the preceding verses much better and allows v 19 to function as a summary verse in parallel with v 13. The NIV rendering is a paraphrased version of this interpretation.

Thus, the illustration of the garden plant comes to the same conclusion as that of the papyrus plant (vv 11-13) and the spider web (vv 14-15). In each case there is a tragic end. By analogy, there is no hope for the godless person (v 13).

4. God's Ways Are Always Just (8:20-22)

Bildad's final words (vv 20-22) are similar in thought to his earlier comments in vv 5-7. Both passages offer hope to Job that his miserable life will soon improve. In vv 5-7 Bildad emphasized the conditional nature of restoration and urged Job to submit to God's will. In vv 20-22 he grounds his argument for restoration on the character of God as a just God.

■ 20 Bildad's concluding comments are meant to drive home the point that **God** (*El*) always operates in predictable ways that reveal his just character. On every occasion he will support the **blameless** (*tām*; 1:1) and reject **evildoers** (*mĕrē'îm*). This is a permanent principle embedded in the moral structure of the universe. **Strengthen the hands** (lit. "seize the hand") is used in Isa 42:6 and 51:18 to describe God's desire to "guide" his people.

■ 21 Based on the principle in v 20, Bildad now offers a word of hope. The second singular pronouns make it clear that these comments are directed toward Job. **He will yet fill your mouth with laughter** is a metaphorical expression for the joy that God will bring into Job's life if he is proved blameless (v 20). The same wording is used in Ps 126:2 to describe the joy of the returning exiles. **Shouts of joy** (*tĕrû'â*) appears later in Job with the meaning of "war cry" (39:25), but here the word refers to the jubilation that one experiences at a great event, such as bringing the ark into Jerusalem (1 Sam 4:6), laying the foundation of the new temple (Ezra 3:11), or coming into God's presence (Job 33:26).

■ 22 Anticipating that Job needs more encouragement, Bildad describes the fate of the wicked (v 20). They **will be clothed in shame**—a poetic expression for "being publicly disgraced" (Ps 35:26). In Bildad's mind, those who oppose God and the righteous will be judged in this life, so as to leave a public example for later generations. Little did he know that one day he would be one of those **clothed in shame** (→ Job 42:7-9; Alden 1993, 122). **Your enemies** is literally "the ones who hate you" (*śn'*). In the Psalms, the poets frequently refer to unnamed persons who hate them or hate God. These individuals cause suffering to others by engaging in violence, spreading false accusations, and whispering behind people's backs. They are opposed to God and his ways.

As in the Psalms, Bildad does not specify who these haters are. Most likely, he is referring to people in general who knew about Job's situation. They had already made up their minds about his guilt and were spreading rumors about his imminent death. Both Bildad and the psalmist were convinced that these haters would one day receive their just reward from God and be destroyed. They **will be no more**. Bildad uses the same particle of nonexistence (*'ênennû*) that Job used of himself in 7:8, 21. **The tents of the wicked** will not exist because the wicked themselves will no longer exist.

FROM THE TEXT

Summary of Bildad's First Speech. Even more than Eliphaz, Bildad was locked into a rigid interpretation of the wisdom theology. Whereas Eliphaz allowed for the possibility of God's discipline as a cause of suffering, Bildad never mentions it. He believed that all the events of life can be perfectly explained by the law of divine retribution. God always rewards the righteous and punishes the wicked, case closed. He knew this was true because of the observations of the sages over centuries of time. They had proved that God is always just in his treatment of human beings.

Bildad's message to Job can be summarized as follows:
- Justice is the universal principle by which God governs the world morally. There are no exceptions. Every calamity, whether caused by nature or other people, is the direct result of the sinful behavior of its victims.
- Job, if you want relief from your suffering, you must earnestly pray to God and live an upright life. God is sure to reward you shortly and fill your life again with laughter and good things.
- On the other hand, if you choose to follow the lifestyle of the godless, there is no hope for your restoration. You will suffer the consequences for your sins. You will die an early death, and no one will remember that you ever lived.
- In the case of your children, there is a strong likelihood that they suffered the consequences of their own sins.

Bildad has many religious friends in the world today. Their pronouncements that the victims of the World Trade Center collapse, the Haitian earthquake, hurricanes Katrina and Sandy, and the Indonesian and Japanese tsunamis were all to blame sound very much like Bildad's rantings. It all sounds so logical, so common sense, so black-and-white. But Bildad was wrong on four accounts: (1) He had no supporting evidence to prove his theory in relation to Job. As the prologue makes clear, Job was not suffering for any sin he had committed. (2) As with Eliphaz (→ "Cause-and-Effect Reasoning" sidebar at 4:10-11), he refused to allow for the possibility of exceptions to the rule. Real life provides plenty of examples that "the good sometimes die young. The wicked sometimes get away with murder" (Alden 1993, 122). (3) He was lacking even the most basic level of compassion for other human beings. His mention of Job's children was a blow below the belt. Jesus strongly condemned this attitude wherever he saw it in his ministry. (4) In the epilogue God is so angry at Bildad's views that he commands him and his friends to offer a huge burnt offering to atone for their erroneous beliefs and unkindness to Job.

There is a small measure of truth to Bildad's advice. The wisdom of the ages is needed to undergird and expand the limited knowledge of one person's lifetime. Otherwise society would have to reinvent the wheel every generation and be doomed to repeat the mistakes of the past. We all acknowledge that we stand on the shoulders of those who came before. But tragically his words had no relevance to Job's situation.

Job's character before the calamities was already established as blameless and upright (1:1), and he prayed and sacrificed to God on a regular basis (1:4-5). So Job was already doing everything that Bildad suggested. Without some knowledge of the heavenly scenes in the prologue, Bildad was incapable of counseling Job in a meaningful way. Thus, his assumption that Job was a sinner and needed to straighten out his ways was totally off base. On a positive note, at least Bildad still held out hope that Job could someday be restored into God's favor. Unfortunately, Job was not interested in restoration. He was so miserable he wanted to die (6:8-9).

D. Job's Response to Bildad (9:1—10:22)

BEHIND THE TEXT

Job's prior speeches (chs 3, 6—7) were loaded with emotional outbursts concerning his sufferings and the unfaithfulness of his friends to support him. In ch 9 he finally gets down to addressing the serious issues that Eliphaz and Bildad raised in their two speeches (chs 4—5, 8). The most prominent of these are God's justice and power. For Job, God's power is awesome and beyond human understanding. God does whatever he wants to do. Thus, humans are at a major disadvantage in trying to "prove their innocence before God" (9:2). God simply overpowers the blameless, crushing the life out of them and refusing to respond to their pleas for help. Justice gets lost in the process.

So Job turns to another possibility. If only there were someone who could mediate his grievances with God, a neutral party who would listen to both sides and work to achieve reconciliation. Then he could speak freely and without fear, and hopefully be vindicated. Job goes on to criticize God for turning against him and acting unjustly. He concludes by repeating his request that God leave him alone so he can die in peace (7:11-21).

Scholars have noted the large number of legal terms Job uses in ch 9 (Seow 2013, 541). He is probably not thinking of taking God to court here, for what good would it do if God is also the judge? But he does think he has a legitimate case to present to God about his innocence. Later, he will declare that he is prepared to make such a presentation (13:18-23; 23:3-7; 31:35-37). He is ready for a debate.

Job takes up six topics in this speech:
1. God's Wisdom and Power Are Overwhelming (9:1-13)
2. It Is Futile to Argue with God (9:14-21)
3. God Is Not Just (9:22-24)
4. Oh, for a Mediator! (9:25-35)
5. God, Why Have You Turned against Me? (10:1-17)
6. God, Leave Me Alone (10:18-22)

IN THE TEXT

1. God's Wisdom and Power Are Overwhelming (9:1-13)

In this section Job considers his plight hopeless for the following reasons: (1) God sets the standard of justice according to his own terms (v 2), (2) human wisdom and power are greatly inferior to God's (vv 3-10), (3) God's elusiveness discourages our communicating with him (v 11), (4) God does what he pleases (v 12), and (5) no creature in the universe can stand up to God when he is angry (v 13).

■ 1 For comments on the introductory formula → 3:2.

■ **2** What Job is agreeing with in v 2a is complicated. One would think he is referring to Bildad's statement in 8:20 that God does not reject the blameless or strengthen evildoers. In other words, God treats everyone justly. And yet he paraphrases Eliphaz (4:17) in 9:2b: ***But how can a human being be in the right*** [ṣdq] ***with God?*** Perhaps he means to combine the two into something like this: "Bildad, you are correct that God has established a standard of justice (8:3, 20) by which all human moral activities are judged. This is a point on which all of us can agree (Job himself will appeal to this standard in his next speech [13:18-19, 23]). But how can a person achieve God's standard of justice and receive divine confirmation of that? As Eliphaz said, 'No one is completely in the right with God,' because God operates on a much higher level than humanity (9:4, 10). And further, no one understands how God administers justice in the world (Andersen 1976, 144). He seems to violate his own standard of justice whenever he chooses (vv 12, 20)."

■ **3** The meaning of v 3 is confusing because the subject of the verb in each clause is missing in Hebrew. This has led to three different interpretations: (1) "If God desired to present a complaint against a human being, that person could not respond to even one of God's accusations out of a thousand" (vv 14-15; 10:2; 23:6). (2) "If a human desired to present a complaint against God, God would refuse to answer even one of that person's accusations out of a thousand" (vv 16, 19; 33:13; NEB, NJPS). (3) "If a human desired to present a complaint against God, that person could not answer even one out of a thousand of God's counterarguments" (chs 38—41; NASB, NIV, NRSV).

The last option seems most likely, but the evidence is not decisive for any of them. All options have supporting evidence in other passages in the book. In reality, there may be some truth in each of them, for there are actually two disputes occurring simultaneously in Job's mind. On the one hand, he was sure God had some grievance against him and therefore had punished him severely. On the other hand, Job strongly believed he was being punished unjustly, and therefore he raised his own grievance against God. He asked for an explanation, but he was pessimistic God would answer him.

"If one wished to contend with him" (NRSV). The Hebrew for "contend" (ryb) appears frequently in Job (7x as a verb and 5x in the nominal form rîb). The word is sometimes found in legal contexts that refer to lawsuits and legal claims against people (Exod 23:2; Ps 103:9; Isa 57:16). But it can also denote disputes and quarrels of a nonlegal nature (Prov 3:30; 17:1, 14).

In this verse Job is probably not contemplating bringing a formal lawsuit against God, but he certainly believes he has a legitimate complaint. And he desires that God would give him an adequate explanation. Of course, he knew he faced impossible odds (**one time out of a thousand**) in being able to defend himself against the overwhelming power of God. But that does not deter his desire to register his complaint against the one who is the cause of his suffering. "One out of a thousand" is used in other passages to indicate an impossible situation (Deut 32:30; Josh 23:10).

■ **4** The reason Job is pessimistic about receiving justice from God is because he is "wise of heart and mighty in power" (NJPS; also 12:13). Evidence for this appears in 9:5-10. Job's point is the futility of challenging God with these characteristics. **Who has done so and been successful** (lit. "remained whole")? The answer is, "No one." Therefore, Job has no hope of ever being vindicated.

■ **5** Job was apparently listening intently to Eliphaz's first speech (chs 4—5), even though his response (chs 6—7) never mentioned its topics. Now he finally takes up Eliphaz's theme of God's omnipotence, using a series of participles (9:5, 6, 7, 8*a*, 8*b*, 9, 10) just as Eliphaz did (5:9-13). Of course, Job's purpose is different. Whereas Eliphaz enumerated God's powers as a way of encouraging Job to seek someone greater than his problems, Job's list of powers is meant to emphasize the difficulty of presenting a grievance against someone who is much mightier than himself. God's awesomeness has left Job without any possibility of ever gaining a hearing with him. Job's list includes both destructive and creative activities of God. The literary beauty of this series of participles has led some scholars to describe them as a "soaring lyric" (Andersen 1976, 145) or a "hymnic doxology" (Clines 1989, 229).

Job 9:5 may refer to God's power through volcanos or massive landslides. Before the discoveries of modern geology, the cause of these events was unknown. Job describes them poetically as under the complete control of God and the result of his anger.

The meaning of the phrase **without their knowing it** is unclear. One suggestion is that it refers to the suddenness of these events—without warning. Another is that the mountains are unaware that God is transforming them out of his anger (see Ps 96:10 for a description of the world when God is not angry). A third possibility is a general comment on the lack of human understanding about the operation of the natural world. As if to emphasize God's destructive powers when he is angry, Job uses the same verb that appears in Gen 19:21, 25, 29 to describe the destruction of Sodom and Gomorrah (**overturns**; *hpk*).

■ **6** God's power is also seen through earthquakes. Ancient cosmology viewed the flat surface of the earth as supported by mighty subterranean pillars (1 Sam 2:8; Ps 75:3 [4 HB]). An earthquake resulted when God shook these pillars. **Pillars** (*'ammûd*) also appears in reference to the two pillars in front of the temple (1 Kgs 7:15-22, 41-42) and the pillars of cloud and of fire in the wilderness (Exod 13:21-22). It is mentioned again in Job 26:11 in connection with the pillars that support the heavens. **Tremble** (*plṣ*) appears only here in the OT.

■ **7** The heavens are another place where God exercises his power. He is able to prevent **the sun** and **the stars** from shining. **Seals off** (*ḥtm*) denotes enclosing something securely and marking its ownership. Writings, royal pronouncements, and business products were often enclosed in a container and then secured with a few wraps of twine and a piece of clay or wax. The clay or wax was then pressed with an individual's seal (mark of identification). The process of sealing an item usually shut it off from public view. Verse 7 refers to any activity by God to cause the obstruction of one's view of the sun and the stars, such as eclipses and storms.

■ **8** Verse 8a is a familiar biblical idiom related to creation (Ps 104:2; Isa 40:22; 42:5; 44:24; 51:13; Jer 10:12; 51:15; Zech 12:1). God is pictured as "spreading out" (*nṭh*) the great expanse of the sky, just as one would lay out a tent or canopy in the process of setting it up. The word **alone** (lit. "for his part") indicates the unique power and capability of God to do this. Only he could perform such a mighty act.

The NIV follows the traditional interpretation of Job 9:8b by translating *bāmâ* as **waves**. The word *bāmâ* also appears frequently in the OT in reference to the high places of worship in Canaanite religion. In connection with the sea, it could refer to the heights or waves of the sea. However, since the discovery of the Ugaritic literature, this clause has generally been translated: ***he who treads on the backs of the Sea*** (*yām*; → "Mythological Characters in Job" sidebar at 7:12). "Treading (*drk*) on a person's back" is a metaphor for conquest (Deut 33:29). In this case, the conquest of the sea-god in ancient Canaanite mythology is intended.

■ **9** The author's knowledge of astronomy is revealed in Job 9:9. He mentions at least three star constellations as objects of God's creation (→ 38:31-32). Their exact identification is disputed, but the traditional interpretation is **the Bear** (*'āš*), **Orion** (*kĕsîl*), and **the Pleiades** (*kîmâ*) (see Clines 1989, 231, for a discussion of the various other proposals).

The fourth item in the list is "the chambers of the south" (NRSV; *ḥadrê tēmān*). The meaning of the phrase is uncertain. Some connect it with constellations in the southern sky that may have only been visible in the southern hemisphere (Clines 1989, 232). Others relate it to the place where the southern winds were thought to originate (Pope 1973, 71; following Ps 78:26 and Song 4:16); and still others to an unknown constellation (Whybray 1998, 63).

■ **10** This verse is worded almost exactly the same as Job 5:9. The meaning is that the quality and quantity of God's deeds are beyond human comprehension and description. The fact that Job repeated these words of Eliphaz almost verbatim confirms he was in basic agreement with Eliphaz concerning God's awesome omnipotence. No one even comes close to God's power over the natural world.

■ **11** God's power through natural phenomena such as earthquakes and eclipses is displayed in public so that all human beings may marvel and worship him. However, another side of God's nature is his mysterious elusiveness. As Job says, "He may be right beside me, yet **I cannot see** [*r'h*] **him** or **perceive** [*byn*] **him**." Israel's God was invisible. Only the effects of his actions in the world could be seen. This further compounded Job's difficulty in making contact with God and presenting his grievance directly to him.

■ **12** God also does what he pleases without accountability to any other person. Job knew of this divine characteristic from personal experience. God had already **snatched away** (*ḥtp*) his wealth, children, reputation, and health (chs 1—2). If Job could have **stopped** [*šwb*] **him**, he would have. But human attempts to prevent

God from acting or to make him justify his actions are unsuccessful. "Who would even dare to say to God, What are you doing?" (*IBHS*, 321).

Job may also have had been hinting at his own tenuous situation. For all he knew, God might have been preparing to snatch away his life at that very moment. If he did so, Job was fully aware that no one would call God to account, for he does exactly as he pleases. This verse is further confirmation that any attempt to question God about the unjust nature of Job's suffering would be futile.

■ 13 **Rahab** (*rahab*) is another of the mythological sea monsters in the book of Job (→ "Mythological Characters in Job" sidebar at 7:12). The name appears again in 26:12 as a defeated foe of God. In 9:13 it is the **cohorts** or ***assistants*** of Rahab who cower before God in reaction to his anger.

In the Mesopotamian and Canaanite myths the sea-god and sea monsters represented the forces of chaos that had to be defeated before the land and human beings could appear. Each myth had its own divine hero (usually the native national god) who triumphed over the sea. The author of Job mentions these frightening mythological creatures to illustrate again the tremendous omnipotence of God. Even the most fearsome creatures or chaotic situations that a person can imagine are no match for **God** (*Eloah*). When he is angry, he does not rest until all his enemies are defeated.

2. It Is Futile to Argue with God (9:14-21)

In this section Job bemoans his inability to dialogue with God. The fault lies not with himself, but with God who refuses to meet with him. But even if such a meeting were arranged, the odds of Job being vindicated were not good. God's power would overwhelm him, thus denying him the justice he earnestly desired.

■ 14-15 In light of God's overwhelming power and wisdom (vv 4-13), what chance did Job have of entering into a meaningful debate with him? He knew that it would be an unequal contest, for God would ask him questions he could not answer (v 3). Job was absolutely convinced he was **innocent** (*ṣdq*; v 15) of any wrongdoing (1:1) and undeserving of the suffering he had received. He believed that the truth was on his side. Yet he is terribly aware of his weakness in comparison to the power of God. In a hypothetical debate with God, he is fearful that God would either intimidate him into silence (9:14-15) or turn his words back against him (v 20), twisting his innocence into guilt. His only recourse would be to **plead . . . for mercy** (*ḥnn*; v 15), but even that would be interpreted as coming from guilt. Thus, Job has no way to vindicate himself.

At first read, it seems that Job is inching toward Bildad's suggestion of pleading for mercy (8:5-6). But whereas Bildad called God "the Almighty" (*Shaddai*), an ancient patriarchal title of reverence, Job's title for God is **my Judge** (some translate as "my Adversary," as if in a hypothetical debate). The very title he gives to God reflects his fear of the consequences that God (as judge) would impose on him.

■ 16 Job now imagines he has the power to "summon" (*qr'*) God to a legal hearing and force him to explain the reason for his suffering. Even if this were a possibility and God agreed to such a summons, Job does not believe God would "listen" (*'zn*; NRSV) to him or acknowledge his complaint. Why would the majestic God of vv 3-13 be concerned with a grievance from one miserable human being?

Job's reasoning seems logical. Up to this point in the book, God has not said a word to him. So why should he expect any different response in the future? Further, God's power over all creation is of such magnitude that he is not obligated to answer any human being. He does what he pleases.

■ **17-18** The NIV regards v 17 as a hypothetical future torment God would impose on Job as a result of Job's summons (v 16). Other translations (NASB, NJPS, NRSV) treat this verse as Job's testimony to the calamities God has already caused in his life (chs 1—2): "he crushes me . . . and multiplies my wounds" (NRSV). Both interpretations are possible, for Job had already experienced great suffering in the past and he had no reason to doubt that God would treat him any different in the future.

Some scholars emend the word **storm** (*śĕʿārâ*) to "hair" (*śaʿărâ*) yielding the translation: "for he crushes me for a hair." In other words, God harms Job over very small matters that amount to nothing (Clines 1989, 218). This interpretation increases the parallelism in the two clauses and therefore is the easier reading. But **storm** makes good sense in light of the windstorm that took the lives of Job's ten children (1:19) and the storm from which God later will speak (38:1; 40:6).

The multiple calamities Job experienced in chs 1—2 are reflected in the second clause: "[he] multiplies my wounds without cause" (NRSV). **Wounds** (*peṣaʿ*) can refer either to physical injuries to the skin (Exod 21:25) or to nonphysical hurts suffered by one's spirit (Prov 27:6). In Job's case, he received both.

For no reason (*ḥinnām*) sums up the main cause of Job's anguish. If God would meet him and explain the reason for his suffering, then Job could accept the cause as justified. Maybe there was a good reason, but so far God had refused to speak. Thus, Job lived in darkness, enduring great pain without an adequate explanation. This phrase was used in two earlier passages by the Examiner (1:9) and by God (2:3) and thus helps support the unity of the book.

Verse 18 of ch 9 reflects Job's earlier complaints about God's oppressive torment that targeted him with continual surveillance and terrified him with nightmares every night (7:14-20). These experiences had sucked all the air out of him and left him bitter at God (*he satiates me with bitterness*; also 3:20).

■ **19** Job now summarizes his thoughts about God's power and justice. God is truly omnipotent. He is **mighty** (*ʾammîṣ*; 9:4-13)! Like a fly on the back of an elephant, Job was minuscule in comparison to God. This would be immediately obvious if he and God ever faced each other in debate. God also controls the world of morality. He established **justice** (*mišpāṭ*) and he defined it on his own terms. He now measures all human activity by his standard. How would it be possible for humans to **challenge** God's standard in relation to their own conduct? One could not even force God to debate the issue.

The last phrase in v 19b reads literally "who will summon me?" But most commentators follow the LXX and emend the translation to "who can summon him?" (NRSV).

■ 20 Here Job repeats his claim of innocence (v 15) with two parallel phrases: "though I am innocent" (ṣdq) and "though I am blameless" (tām; NRSV). Both have appeared separately heretofore (ṣdq—4:17; 9:2, 15; tām—1:1, 8; 2:3; 8:20). But they are clearly synonyms that are brought together in this verse to emphasize Job's belief about his own spiritual condition. As far as he knew, he was in the right before God. No one had produced any evidence to the contrary. Nevertheless, Job was not able to clear his own name. Only God can pronounce a person "not guilty."

Whether Job tried to debate with God (9:3), appeal for mercy (v 15), or summon God (v 16), his own mouth would undermine his innocence. The causative stem (Hiphil) of both main verbs (ršʿ—**would condemn me**; ʿqš—**would pronounce me guilty**) is used here to indicate that any attempt by Job to vindicate himself would only cause him more harm.

■ 21 Job now delivers three terse statements: **I am blameless**; *I do not know myself*; *I reject my life*. The poetic structure is designed "to suggest the intensity of Job's emotion" (Pope 1973, 73). There are multiple interpretations of the middle statement. Some regard it as a lack of concern for himself (NASB, NIV). Others, as a comment about his anguish (NJPS), or an expression of "self-doubt" (Seow 2013, 548). But it is also possible that it reflects a lack of understanding concerning his situation (as in 42:3): "I am blameless, yet I am suffering. I do not understand why. Therefore, I reject my present life as worth living" (→ From the Text for ch 3).

3. God Is Not Just (9:22-24)

In the third section of his speech Job brings several charges against certain aspects of God's behavior that call into question his justice. The first is his equal treatment of the righteous and the wicked (9:22). The second is his attitude toward the righteous when they suffer (v 23). And the third is his contribution to societal injustice by blinding community officials (v 24). Many commentators regard this section as "the strongest indictment of God to be found in the book" (Gordis 1978, 108). Job's remarks here are probably intended as a rebuttal to Bildad's comment in the previous speech supporting God's justice (8:3).

■ 22 Job has harsh criticism for God's treatment of the righteous and the wicked. The wisdom traditions taught that God rewarded the former and punished the latter. But for Job, life did not always work out according to this principle. There are exceptions to the rule. For example, everyone knows that God **destroys ... the wicked** (rāšāʿ). Eliphaz emphasized this point in his first speech (4:8-9). What is not so well-known is that God **destroys ... the blameless** (tām) as well. Job's own experiences in chs 1—2 are Exhibit A. He was clearly a blameless man, yet he suffered terrible losses, leading him even so far as to seek death rather than life. For Job, then, God's treatment of humanity is **all the same** (ʾaḥat hîʾ; lit. "it is one").

There are two implications to this charge. The first is that it is pointless for individuals to lead a blameless life. One gains no advantage by doing so. The second is that God is not really a just God (in direct disagreement with Bildad [8:3, 20]). His equal treatment of both the blameless and the wicked is good evidence that either God is unjust or he has a much different definition of justice than humans do. In Ecclesiastes, Qoheleth is just as distressed over this concept as is Job (Eccl 9:1-3). His label for it is "vanity."

At first glance, Job 9:22 seems to support Job's earlier statement to his wife that God sends both good and bad on everyone (2:10), and also Jesus' statement in the Sermon on the Mount that God blesses everyone with both the sun and the rain (Matt 5:45). But those passages are dealing with different issues (Andersen 1976, 149). Job's emphasis in Job 9:22 is clearly on God's desire to destroy both the righteous and the wicked. He is hostile toward all humanity. Such a concept is foreign to OT theology.

■ **23** According to Job, when a disaster falls upon **innocent** people (*nĕqiyyim*; 4:7) bringing **death** to them and their families, God **mocks** (*l'g*) the recipients of these awful events. Such a view not only undermines the wisdom traditions as expressed by Eliphaz and Bildad but also casts a dark cloud over the character of God. How can God be called just if he engages in this type of activity?

In the OT God sometimes directed mockery and ridicule at his enemies—those who rebelled against his rule, whether Israelites (Ps 79:4; Ezek 23:32), foreign nations (Ps 2:4), or fools in general (Prov 1:26-27). But God never treated the righteous in this way. For them he was "gracious and merciful, slow to anger and abounding in steadfast love" (Ps 145:8 and Neh 9:17 NRSV; see Ps 103:8).

If Job is correct in his criticism, then certainly God is guilty of the cruelest attitude toward the righteous. However, Job presents no evidence to support his charge. It is true that Job lost his ten children suddenly in a disaster, but he had no proof God ever mocked him. He stepped outside the bounds of fairness in charging God with such cruelty. But perhaps we can forgive him and blame this outburst on his desire to counteract the earlier blanket statements by Eliphaz (4:7-9) and Bildad (8:20) to the effect that God never rejects a blameless person or causes the innocent to perish. His response may also have been an emotional reaction to his intense suffering, which God had not commented on so far.

The Hebrew for **scourge** (*šôṭ*) means "whip." Eliphaz used this term earlier in reference to verbal abuse ("the lash of the tongue" [5:21]). The word also can refer metaphorically to natural disasters such as hail and floods (Isa 28:15, 17-18) that bring great destruction. Such is the usage here, and Job may have in mind the "fire of God" that consumed his sheep and servants (1:16) and the "mighty wind" that killed his children (1:18-19). The meaning of the Hebrew for **despair** (*massâ*) is disputed because the root is uncertain (Gordis 1978, 108), but most translations adopt the meaning **despair**, deriving it from *mss*, meaning "to melt."

■ **24** Job's third criticism of God's behavior concerns injustice in the social realm. He believes God contributes to social injustice by allowing the wicked to rule and by blinding the community leaders who are responsible for maintaining justice. Some have suggested Job is referring to a particular time in Israel's history when the land was under the control of a foreign nation. The time of the exile immediately comes to mind. But Job was not an Israelite, and his comment makes more sense when viewed as a general observation.

Every land experiences wicked rulers and judges from time to time, even up to the present. When such events occur, the innocent invariably suffer. But God, instead of answering the cry of the innocent for help, **blindfolds** (lit. "covers the faces of") the **judges** of the land, thus producing more injustice in society and more suffering by the innocent. In Exod 23:8 the blinding of community leaders is specifically related to the practice of bribery. But other evils such as monetary greed, lust for power, apathy, and incompetency may also contribute to this wickedness.

Whether Job had experienced personal suffering from such a leader is not known. His comments may simply be the result of observing life over many years.

What is significant about Job's observation is that he attributes the blindness of judges to God. This is another example in Job's mind of the unjust ways of God. The final clause in this verse is a rhetorical question used to drive home Job's point: **If it is not he, then who is it?** In other words, can anyone give me a better cause for these injustices than God himself? As mentioned earlier, Job provides little or no evidence to support his contention that God is unjust. Thus, he was just as guilty as the three friends of jumping to quick generalizations from partial evidence.

4. Oh, for a Mediator! (9:25-35)

The tone of the speech changes. Job now addresses God directly as seen in the second singular verbs (vv 28, 31). He suggests three possibilities for vindicating himself and relieving his suffering: (1) positive thinking (vv 27-28), (2) a cleansing ritual (vv 30-31), and (3) a mediator (vv 33-35). The first would only paint over his problems with whitewash. The second would be ineffective because God would respond with more calamities. And the third is impossible because no such person exists. Deep down inside, Job knew that all such attempts to resolve his dispute with God would be "in vain" (v 29). For this reason he remained bitter toward God and disgusted with his life (10:1).

■ **25-26** In earlier comments Job mentioned the rapidly approaching end of his life. He compared the swiftness of his days to "a weaver's shuttle" (7:6) and "a breath" of air (7:7). In 9:25-26 he adds three more similes: **a runner, boats of papyrus**, and **eagles**. Each represents one of the swiftest objects on land, on water, and in the air. Runners were used mainly by kings and government officials to send messages quickly to people in other parts of their kingdom (2 Chr 30:6). They were also part of a king's entourage when he traveled by chariot. Absalom (2 Sam 15:1) and Adonijah (1 Kgs 1:5) hired fifty runners to run before their chariots as a body guard and to flaunt their importance. These runners would have been young men in excellent physical condition who could run with great speed for long distances.

Boats of papyrus probably refers to light Egyptian reed skiffs that **skim**med across the water (Isa 18:1-2). **Eagles** are known for their powerful and lightning swift dives that enable them to catch small animals. Like the swiftness of the runner, the skiff, and the eagle, Job's days now **fly away** so quickly that there is no opportunity to enjoy them (lit. "they do not see good"), even if he felt like it. Job knew that earlier in his life he enjoyed the good life (Job 29), but he would never experience that again (7:7). The second clause of 9:25 reemphasizes this thought.

■ **27-28** Positive thinking is one way people pull themselves out of despair. Job suggests three ways he might do this. The first is to put his problems out of his mind: **I will forget my complaint** (v 27). The second reads literally "I will abandon my face," meaning "I will loosen, relax, my face" (BDB, 737). This is probably an idiomatic expression that needs to be rendered something like the NIV: **I will change my expression**. The third is: *I will become cheerful*.

Since Job's earlier comments have indicated that he is a very troubled individual with deep emotional pain, it is obvious that his suggestions are nothing more than an attempt to repress his pain and act as if nothing had happened. Such a course of action would take great effort on his part, but it would not solve his problems or make them go away. It would only whitewash them temporarily.

Almost as soon as the words are out of his mouth, Job recognizes the futility of carrying through with his suggestions. His mind returns to the dreadful fears he described in his introductory lament (3:25-26; → From the Text for ch 3). He even repeats the same verb he used in 3:25 (**I . . . dread** [*ygr*; 9:28]). Unless the cause of these fears was removed, Job would never find peace. To simply put a smile on his face when his heart was aching would be hypocritical.

The last clause in v 28 is the key to understanding these two verses. The words are addressed directly to God. No matter what changes Job made in his disposition, unless God changed his stance toward Job, the suffering and pain would continue. Up to this point, Job had received not even one ray of hope from God that the future would be different. Instead, he had been treated as if he were the worst of sinners. As long as he continued to experience pain, he would assume that God still regarded him as guilty of some great offense, even though he believed he was innocent.

Norman Vincent Peale attracted a great deal of attention with his book *The Power of Positive Thinking* (1952, Simon and Schuster). Many people were helped by it and believed it changed their lives. There is certainly much to be said for maintaining a positive attitude in life. Our world would be a much more pleasant place to live if everyone had a good disposition. But positive thinking is not what Job needed. He was in great physical pain and wrestling with some of the deepest questions that a human being has ever faced.

What he really needed was for God to meet him and explain the cause of his suffering. Unfortunately, God was not willing to do that at this time. Job quickly recognized he had spoken too hastily. He withdrew his suggestions and slid back into his tormented existence.

■ **29** Verse 29*a* is a restatement of v 28*b*. Based on his assumption that God would continue to treat him as a guilty person, Job asks rhetorically, **Why should I struggle in vain? Struggle** (*yg'*; sometimes translated "labor, toil") refers to Job's attempts to vindicate himself. The word is usually applied to people who are enduring physical or emotional exhaustion due to hard physical labor, long periods of sickness, or intense emotional experiences (Pss 6:6 [7 HB]; 69:3 [4 HB]; Isa 40:28, 30-31). Such struggles are worthwhile if they produce the desired results. But Job knew that his struggle was **in vain** (*hebel*; 7:16), for God had refused to help him or answer his questions.

■ **30-31** Another suggestion from Job is that he might perform a self-cleansing ritual that would signify his innocence. But **even if** he **washed** (Pss 26:6; 73:13; Deut 21:6) himself **with soap** and "cleanse[d] [his] hands with lye" (NRSV), God would immediately counter his actions by plunging him into a **slime pit**. The end result would leave him in even worse shape than before. Either he would be so filthy that even his clothes would reject him (Clines 1989, 242), or his filthy clothes would make him an abomination (Seow 2013, 570-71). In either case, Job dismisses his suggestion as worthless as soon as he utters it. Both the washing and the cleansing are hypothetical actions that Job would willingly undertake if they had any hope of success. But as in Job 9:27-28, Job knew they would accomplish nothing.

The Hebrew for **soap** (*šeleg*) is usually translated as "snow." But in this one passage many modern versions find cognates in Mishnaic Hebrew and Akkadian that render the translation **soap** preferable. The parallel term in v 30*b* is "lye" (*bōr*; NRSV), an alkaline cleaning substance produced from burnt wood or plant material. The word for **pit** (*šaḥat*) is the same one Job and Elihu later use in speaking of Sheol (17:14; 33:18, 22, 24, 28, 30), but here it refers to any kind of muddy pit that would render Job filthy.

Earlier Job had accused God of attacking him with poisonous arrows (6:4) and terrifying nightmares (7:14). Thus, his description of God as an uncontrollable tyrant ready to pounce again is not surprising. Job's view of God will have to change before his soul can find the peace it so desperately seeks.

■ **32** The crux of Job's problem, which he has complained about throughout his speech, is that there is a major difference between himself and God that prevents the establishment of his innocence. God's wisdom and power place him in a dimension totally different from the human. Thus the playing field is not level. By this, Job is implying that if they were on equal terms, he could get his grievance settled quickly. But that is an impossibility when one's opponent is God. The last clause may be a request from Job: "Let us come together into arbitration" (*mišpāṭ*). However, most versions treat it like the NRSV as a consecutive dependent clause: "that we should come to trial together." Job has in mind here the kind of arbitration that produces a just settlement.

■ **33** If only there were *a mediator* between us (this requires an emendation of the particle *lō'* to *lû*). Because of the tremendous gulf between God and humanity, there needs to be *a mediator* (*môkîaḥ*) who understands both parties to the dispute and who is able to help them engage in conversation as well as resolve their differences. Such mediators are well-known in the modern world, and they have been extremely useful in negotiating nasty labor disputes, settling boundaries between countries, and even sorting out marital conflict. Such a mediator could "lay his hand" (NRSV) on each of them, thus bringing them together in proximity, as Job suggested in v 32. Pope notes the possibility that this request by Job may reflect the ancient Mesopotamian practice of appealing to one's personal god to mediate a grievance between a human being and one of the great gods of the pantheon (1973, 76).

In modern labor negotiations, the two opposing parties may never see each other face to face. The mediator acts as the go-between, relaying and interpreting messages for each side. Perhaps Job wished for something similar in his case. He has already voiced his inability to explain his grievance to God (v 20) and to respond to God's rebuttal (vv 3, 14-15). A mediator could help him out by explaining to God what he was trying to say and eliminate the need for him to actually confront God face to face.

Verse 33 is the third of Job's suggestions for resolving the impasse between himself and God (→ vv 27-28 and 30-31). As with his previous suggestions, Job knew this one would not work, but it was worth mentioning to show that he was putting forth a good effort to resolve his dilemma. Gibson calls this verse, along with 16:19 and 19:25, the three most important contributions Job makes to his "quest for God" (1985, 86-87). The passages are all surrounded by multiple words of anguish and despair, but for three brief moments we see Job reaching out to God for a way out of his awful suffering. Some commentators think the request for a mediator is pointless because it assumes that the mediator would have authority over God (Pope 1973, 76). But Job was not asking for the appearance of a person greater than God. He simply desired a neutral party, skilled in mediation, who would treat each side fairly, answer all their questions, resolve their differences, and facilitate reconciliation.

Is Jesus the Answer to Job's Request for a Mediator?

Unfortunately, no. In Christian theology Jesus is the Mediator who provided the means, by way of the cross, for sinful humanity to be reconciled with a holy God. All humanity is desperately in need of such a mediator. Job's situation is different. He was not seeking forgiveness, for he was already "blameless and upright" before God (1:1). Rather, he was seeking an explanation for why he was suffering. He did need a mediator for that, because God had remained silent.

We are led to believe from the entire book that God has never provided an adequate explanation for many types of human suffering. Humanity has always been in the dark and probably always will be. Thus, even if Job had lived after Jesus' death, his request for a mediator would not have received a satisfactory answer.

While Jesus did talk about some aspects of suffering and did experience suffering himself as part of God's plan of salvation, he left many questions unanswered. Thus, the mournful *Why* that arose out of Job's terrible calamities remains with us still.

■ **34-35** Job identifies the source of his **terror** as **God's rod** (v 34). The word **rod** (*šēbeṭ*) is well-known from its usage in Ps 23:4 (KJV) where it symbolizes God's protection of his people. But the word is used more frequently in reference to the rod of authority (Gen 49:10; Ps 45:6 [7 HB]; Ezek 19:11, 14), the rod of discipline (Prov 10:13; 13:24; 22:15; 23:13, 14; 26:3; 29:15), or the rod of punishment (Pss 2:9; 89:32 [33 HB]; Isa 10:5, 24).

In Job 9:34 and 21:9 **God's rod** is a metaphor for his wrath that continued to torment Job both day and night so that he preferred death over life (6:4; 7:13-15). One of the tasks of the mediator Job requested in 9:33 would be to bring the two parties together on an equal level so one side would not have an innate advantage over the other. Job wishes that a mediator could be found who would **remove God's wrath** so Job would no longer be terrified of meeting him. Then he could speak freely and present the proof of his innocence.

The literal translation of v 35*b* is: "For I am not so in myself." The interpretation of this clause is problematic, and most versions opt for a paraphrase. One option relates the clause to Job's inability to speak to God: **but as it now stands with me, I cannot.** Another reflects Job's conviction that he is not guilty of sin: "For I know myself not to be so" (NJPS). A third suggestion is: "I am not right with myself," meaning "he feels at odds with himself" (Hartley 1988, 182). Hence, his following statement in 10:1*a*: "My soul feels disgust with my life." The issue is not resolved.

5. God, Why Have You Turned against Me? (10:1-17)

Job continues to challenge God on several points: (1) God acts like a human being instead of like God (10:3-6). (2) God is two-faced and undependable. At first, God showed kindness and compassion by carefully creating Job and watching over his life, but now God has turned against him and is seeking to destroy him (vv 8-14). (3) God has no meaningful reward system. He treats the righteous the same as the wicked (vv 7, 15). (4) God hunts Job down like a lion and employs the three friends as his agents of attack (vv 16-17).

■ **1** This is the third time Job has expressed loathing for himself (7:16; 9:21). In his two previous remarks, he used the verb *m's*. Here he turns to a synonym (*qwṭ*) that means "to feel great disgust and aversion toward something to the point of rejection" (Ps 95:10; Ezek 6:9; 20:43; 36:31). Job's wish in Job 3 was that his life had never started (3:3, 11, 16). Now he simply wishes his life would quickly end (6:9; 7:15). He is sick of living and ready for a quick death to end his misery. The second and third clauses restate his comments in 7:11. His revulsion against his own life has freed him to speak his mind. He has nothing to lose by complaining about his suffering or questioning God, for if God becomes angry and kills him, so much the better. He is ready to die. For comments on the phrase **the bitterness of my soul** → 3:20; 7:11.

■ **2** Job is convinced that **God** (*Eloah*) has already condemned him and found him guilty of some offense. God is now punishing him to the extreme limit of his endurance. Therefore, Job demands that God give him a reason for his actions: *Inform me upon what grounds you contend with me.* Job's request is legitimate. Accused persons want to know the charges against them. Of course, the reader knows that God had not condemned Job at all. In fact, the very opposite was true. God had already praised him twice in the prologue (1:8; 2:3). Unfortunately Job was not aware of this praise. From his perspective it felt like he was being punished. For comments on the verb *contend* → 9:3.

■ **3** In 10:3-7 Job asks God several pointed questions. The first probes into God's motive for bringing so much misery into Job's life: "Does it seem good to you to oppress?" (NRSV). The word "good" (*ṭôb*) has been interpreted in several different ways: (1) "Does it bring you pleasure?" (2) "Does it bring you profit?" (3) "Is there some divine benefit that contributes to your plan for this world?" In essence, Job is asking a simple question: "Why are you doing this to me?" The answer to this question is especially important to Job because he desperately desires to know why he is suffering.

In the last two clauses Job gives an example of God's inconsistency in dealing with human beings. God **reject**s those whom he has toiled over and influenced to obey him. At the same time he **smiles** upon **the wicked**. In Job's mind, this type of behavior was more characteristic of humans than of God. Therefore, God must have some hidden motive for acting this way. If Job knew what this motive was, he might better understand his own suffering. The word for **work/toil** (*yĕgîa'*) appears in other OT passages only in association with *human* labor and the goods that hard work produces (e.g., Gen 31:42; Pss 78:46; 109:11). Here Job attributes this labor to God when he created human beings. God invested a great deal of effort into each individual person. So why would he turn against someone like Job while at the same time rewarding the wicked? Surely God intended a better life for Job than this. Job repeats this thought in Job 10:8.

■ **4** The second question raises the issue of God's ability to understand Job's situation: **Do you see as a mortal sees?** This question is rhetorical and the expected answer is no. Two interpretations are possible. The first is: "No, you do not have human eyes, but you are acting like you do." Job knew (31:4; 34:21) and other OT passages confirm (1 Sam 16:7; Prov 16:2; 21:2) that God sees far more than humans do. Human sight is clouded due to partial information, superficial observations, prejudice, and error. But God's vision is supposed to be perfect. "So why are you behaving like you have the limitations of a human being?" Job asks. "Are you not able to see that I am a righteous person?"

The second possible interpretation is: "No, you do not have human eyes, and therefore it is impossible for you to understand my suffering." In other words, God is so superior to humanity that he is not able to stoop to the level where Job lives and share his sorrow and pain. The context of Job 10:3-7 is Job's charge in v 2 that

God is contending with him. Therefore, the first interpretation is preferable and was probably delivered in a sarcastic tone.

■ **5-6** Job's third question is based on another limitation of human existence—its length. God's eternal nature (Pss 90:2; 102:25-27 [26-28 HB]) should enable him to see the entire length of Job's life. Such a perspective should confirm that Job is blameless and without sin. Instead, God was acting as if he had the limited experience of a human being with a short life span. He was doggedly seeking to find in Job's life some evidence of sin—a sin that he ought to know is not there—in a limited amount of time.

Job 10:6 uses two verbal synonyms to describe God's actions against Job—**search** (*bqš*) and **seek** (*drš*; 3:4; 5:8). Both verbs imply that God's scrutiny is diligent and relentless. This same thought appeared in Job's earlier speech where he described God as "the watcher of humanity" and himself as God's "target" (7:20 NRSV). Job is not admitting that he has committed some sin. He still believes he is blameless. But the continual pressure he felt had convinced him that God was not going to let up his search until he found what he was looking for—sin. Two of the three main OT words for **sin** are used here in parallel: ***iniquity*** (*'āwōn*) and **sin** (*ḥaṭṭā't*) (→ 3:20-21).

■ **7** As mentioned earlier (9:15, 20-21), Job is convinced of his own sinlessness. Throughout the entire book, he professes his innocence. Here in 10:7 he claims that God also knows he is innocent. Thus, Job is caught on the horns of a dilemma that has left him confused and bitter. If God knew he was not guilty, why was he punishing him and relentlessly searching for sin in his life (v 6)? Job had no satisfactory answer to this dilemma.

The interpretation of the second clause is divided. The NIV follows most translations in making this a dependent clause: **that no one can rescue me from your hand**. However, it is better regarded as an independent statement (Clines 1989, 246-47; Gordis 1978, 98; Hartley 1988, 183, n. 5; Pope 1973, 78). The sense of the verse is as follows: "Although you know I am not guilty, you refuse to admit it; and I have no one to prove it to you. There is no one to deliver me from your power." No doubt, Job was still wishing for the appearance of a mediator (9:33), for he knew he was powerless to help himself.

■ **8** In 10:3 Job briefly mentioned the creative activity of God using the phrase ***the toil of your hands***. Human beings exist only because God toiled over the dust of the earth and formed it into a human shape. In v 8 Job returns to this theme using the verbs **shaped** (*'ṣb*) and **made** (*'śh*). The same imagery is found in the Genesis creation story (Gen 1:26, 31; 2:4, 7) and other passages (such as Job 4:17; Pss 95:6; 100:3; 119:73). Job's word picture borrows from the activity of the potter who shapes a piece of clay into a useful vessel matching the mental image of what the finished product should look like.

However, from Job's perspective God had changed his mind. Whereas once God's **hands** carefully formed Job into a human being (also v 3), now they seem intent on destroying him. Such a divine reversal seems incomprehensible, just as it would be in the human sphere. A potter would not destroy a newly formed vessel unless a major flaw was discovered. The word Job uses for **destroy** (*bl'*) is the same one used by God in the prologue when he complained about the Examiner's enticement to destroy Job (2:3). **Will you now turn** (*yaḥad sābîb*) is literally "altogether round about." Scholars have proposed a number of emendations to deal with its ambiguity (see Clines 1989, 221). Most versions render the phrase similar to the NIV, meaning that God has now turned from his benevolent shaping of Job to destroying him. The NIV and NASB render the second clause as a question although it is not indicated in the Hebrew. The NRSV and NJPS regard it as a statement.

■ **9** Job now repeats the theme of v 8 but adds two additional words—**remember** and **clay**—that change the meaning slightly. The imperative of **remember** (*zkr*) is a form Job used earlier to call God's attention to his frailty. His life was nothing more than a "breath" of air (7:7). In 10:9 the image is **clay** (*ḥōmer*), and the emphasis is on the special treatment Job received from God when he was created. He was made like a potter forms clay.

Anyone who has watched a potter knows that a great deal of effort and time goes into making pottery. Each pot formed on a wheel is unique, as opposed to pottery made in molds. Job wishes God would continue to give him the same degree of attention and care he received earlier in life. Instead, God now seems intent on turning him back to dust as quickly as possible. Other passages in the Bible that portray God as a potter molding clay or soil include: Gen 2:7, 19; Job 33:6; Isa 45:9; 64:8 [7 HB]; Jer 18:2-11; Rom 9:20-21.

■ **10-11** Here Job gives a poetic description of the conception and development of a fetus. Just as **milk** is **poured** into a bag and left to **curdle** into **cheese**, so liquid semen is poured into a woman's womb where it solidifies into a solid embryo (→ Job 3:10; Ps 139:13-16). Of course, God is involved in the process, determining when conception takes place and when it does not (→ Job 3:10). That is why Job addresses his words to God as a rhetorical question: "Did you not do this, God, in order to make me?"

Verse 11 of ch 10 continues the description of the formation of the human body. **Skin** and **flesh** soon enclose the small embryo like clothing, while **bones** and **tendons** add structure within. The whole body is **knit . . . together** (*skk*; lit. "interwoven"). The only other place where this verb is used in the OT is the well-known passage in Ps 139:13.

■ **12** **Life** (*ḥayyîm*), ***faithful love*** (*ḥesed*), and ***watchful care*** (*pĕquddâ*) are generally not linked together in the OT. But in Job 10:12 they seem appropriate as the final stage in Job's description of the development of a human being. From conception (v 10), to the formation of a physical body (v 11), to life outside the womb (v 12), God watches over his creation. One cannot help but connect this passage with Gen 2:7 where God breathes into the newly created human creature the "breath of life" (*nišmat ḥayyîm*). Job probably had in mind more than just filling a person's lungs with air. God also provided abundant life for Job prior to his period of suffering.

The word *ḥesed* is translated in many different ways ("loyalty," "kindness," "steadfast love," "loving-kindness," "mercy," etc.) depending on the context. In most instances in the OT, the word refers to God's faithful, covenantal love for his chosen people. But since Job was a non-Israelite he was probably using it as a general term for God's faithful love to all his creatures.

■ **13** Job now turns abruptly from a positive view of God's care in creating and sustaining him to some negative comments about God's secret intentions. Job had naively assumed that God cared about him, for his life had been blessed for many years (v 12). But the calamities had forced him to make a reevaluation. He came to realize that God's benevolence was only a smokescreen that masked his real desire to find Job guilty of sin.

When God could not find sin in Job's life, he brought intense suffering against him, hoping Job would eventually crack under the extreme pressure. All of this God **concealed** (*ṣpn*) in his **heart**, so that Job was completely fooled until the calamities began. Now Job has a more accurate understanding of the true purposes of God. He goes on in the following verses (vv 14-17) to explain what God really has in mind.

If Job is correct in his reevaluation, then God must be viewed as some kind of divine monster who blesses people into a false sense of trust and security, all the while secretly predestining them to later lives of misery. Job's view of God in this verse is very troubling, but not surprising, considering his numerous accusations. God had made him a target (6:4; 7:20), terrified him with nightmares (7:14), watched his every move (7:17-19), and even mocked him (9:23). Job never said such things about God in his earlier years. But his sufferings had forced him to blame God for all his misery and had left him bitter in soul (10:1).

■ **14** As an example of God's deceptive ways, Job introduces a hypothetical situation—**If I sinned**. Since God knows everything that happens (7:20), he would be aware of any moral failure on Job's part. However, instead of leading Job to a point of confession and forgiveness, as most people would expect God to do, God turns against the sinner. **If I sinned**, he would not "acquit me of my iniquity" (NRSV).

■ **15** Job finds himself in an impossible situation. Whether **guilty** (*ršʿ*) or **innocent** (*ṣdq*), he knows he will suffer. Everyone agreed that God would punish him if he turned to wickedness. That is a fixed moral law inherent in the universe. The only appropriate response is: **woe to me!** "I will get what I deserve."

What is not so well-known, according to Job, is that the innocent also suffer just like the guilty. They experience the same calamities in spite of the fact they are innocent of wrongdoing. Job describes his humiliation over his predicament as so great he **cannot** even **lift** up his **head**. He is **full of shame** (*qālôn*) and **misery** (*ŏnî*).

Misery describes the plight of a person who is greatly distressed—physically, mentally, and/or emotionally. The word is used of three women in the OT who were emotionally distraught over personal problems—Hagar (Gen 16:11), Leah (Gen 29:32), and Hannah (1 Sam 1:11). It also describes the condition of the Israelites while in bondage in Egypt (Exod 3:7).

The phrase **lift my head** is a metaphor for a feeling of confidence, strength, and self-worth. It appears in the OT with either the verb *ns'* (Ps 83:2 [3 HB]) or *rwm* (Ps 27:6). People like Job whose heads are bowed feel defeated, humiliated, cast down, and degraded. They are fearful of the present and pessimistic about the future.

■ **16** The first Hebrew word in v 16 (*g'h*) has been the object of much discussion. It is the same verb used to describe the growth of papyrus to a great height in 8:11. Most scholars suggest some type of emendation that yields a meaning related to "lifting up one's head" (see v 15). The sense of the verse is probably something like this: "If I try to raise my confidence out of the depths of despair, you hunt me down like a lion hunts its prey and continually manifest your power against me." Thus, even if Job could regain some of his former confidence, he believes God would quickly begin to attack him again (much like 9:30-31). **Display your awesome power** (*pl'*) is the same verb used in 5:9 and 9:10 in a much more positive sense.

■ **17** Job concludes this section of his speech by charging God with additional attacks against him, using **witnesses, anger,** and ***reinforcement troops***. Job may be partly referring to the calamities that inaugurated his time of suffering (chs 1—2). However, those calamities took place many chapters earlier, and 10:17 speaks of **renewed** (*ḥdš*) and **increasing** (*rbh*) attacks. By this time in the story, Job probably suspected that God was using the three friends to increase his discouragement. Two of the friends have already spoken (chs 4—5, 8) and brought more grief to his life. The third will have his opportunity very shortly (ch 11). The Hebrew for **witnesses** (*'ēd*) indicates a person or object that testifies to the truth (1 Sam 12:5; Ps 89:37 [38 HB]; Isa 8:2). Thus, it could refer to either the three friends or the sufferings Job had experienced or to both. Some scholars emend **witnesses** to "hostility" (Clines 1989, 250; Pope 1973, 81), but **witnesses** makes good sense here. The Hebrew for **anger** (*ka'aś*) has already appeared in two earlier passages with a slightly different meaning (Job 5:2; 6:2).

In the third clause, the phrase *ḥălîpôt wěṣābā'* is difficult. The literal rendering of the clause is "changes and hard service [7:1] are with me." Clines follows this interpretation, suggesting that Job is referring to the ups and downs of his tortured existence—first hard service, then a change to relief, then back to hard service again (1989, 222). But in light of earlier comments where Job describes God's attacks as so powerful and relentless that he cannot even catch a breath of air (7:17-18; 9:17-18), one has to assume that Job is not speaking of relief here, but of renewed attacks. The only change Job had experienced so far was a deeper level of suffering. Thus, most versions follow the alternate meaning of *ṣābā'* ("troops" [Gen 26:26]) and treat the phrase as a hendiadys meaning "changing/reinforcement troops." Job believed that God was continually reinforcing his attack using whatever means were available to him.

6. God, Leave Me Alone (10:18-22)

In the final section of his speech, Job returns to several earlier comments. But his main point is a request for God to turn away from him so that his last days will be peaceful.

■ **18-19** If Job had been stillborn, he would have gone straight from his mother's **womb** (v 18) to the **grave** (v 19) and thus would have avoided all of his suffering. When Job expressed this wish earlier (3:11-19), it was directed at no one in particular. Now in 10:18-19 he lays the responsibility for his birth directly on God. In essence, he says to God: "If *you* knew when you brought me into the world that I would suffer all these calamities, why did you not prevent my birth? You had the power to do so and failed to act. Therefore, you bear direct responsibility for my suffering." Just as he did in 3:11-12, Job uses two synonyms here for **womb**—*reḥem* (v 18) and *beṭen* (v 19).

■ **20** This verse has two Qere readings, indicating that the ancient scribes had trouble with its translation. The following rendering incorporates both Qere readings and fits the context best: ***Are not my days few? Cease, and leave me alone,*** "that I may find a little comfort" (NRSV; 9:27).

This is actually the third time in the book Job has mentioned the small amount of time he has left to live (7:6-7; 9:25-26). As in 7:16 he couples this thought with a plea for God to leave him alone. If he has to suffer at the end of life, he would rather do so in solitude than receive God's continual harassment.

■ **21-22** Job concludes his speech by describing the conditions he will experience shortly when he arrives in Sheol. Sheol is a permanent place from which no one returns (→ 7:9-10). It is also a place ***without order*** (10:22; *lōʾ sĕdārîm*; only once in the OT). This phrase could refer to a pre-creation type of formlessness such as described in Gen 1:2 ("formless and empty"). Or it may indicate the unordered social classifications of humanity Job already alluded to in 3:13-19. In Sheol "kings," **counselors**, and **rulers**, as well as "captives" and "slaves," are all on the same level as the "stillborn child." In Job's thinking, the afterlife has not been ordered by God because God is the God of the living, not the dead.

Finally, Sheol is a land of **utter darkness**, darker than any darkness a person can experience here on earth. Job drives home his point about the misery that still awaits him after death by using a series of synonyms for **darkness**: *ḥōšek, ṣalmāwet, ʿêpātâ, ʾōpel* (three of these appeared earlier in 3:4-6). Although translators make a valiant effort to define these words, it is impossible to make clear distinctions between them in English. Job is simply saying that Sheol is so dark that **even the light is like darkness**.

This seems like a rather gloomy way to end his speech, but Job wanted everyone to know that death was not something he sought lightly. He already knew what awaited him in Sheol. But even the all-encompassing darkness of Sheol looked better to him than the tormented existence in this life that God had inflicted on him.

FROM THE TEXT

1. Summary of Job's Response to Bildad. Job found himself in an awful dilemma. On the one hand, his heart testified that he was sinless. On the other hand, his suffering was of such magnitude that he thought God must regard him as the worst of sinners. Job desperately wanted to know why this was happening to him, but so far God had refrained from speaking. Even if God did agree to a dialogue, it would be futile on Job's part to argue his case, for God would overwhelm him with his power. So Job was left without an answer.

There is another part to Job's dilemma that is even more troubling. His understanding of God had been challenged. He really did not want to accuse God of being unjust, but logically he could find no other explanation for his suffering. Only an unjust God would punish both the righteous and the wicked.

Job's suggestion of a neutral mediator to resolve the conflict between himself and God is brilliant. A mediator would enable him to get his case before God without having to face God's awesome power directly. But deep in his heart he knew such a mediator did not exist. Therefore, he saw death as the only way out of his dilemma. A future in the darkness of Sheol seemed better than his present misery. His request to be left alone in the last few days of his life arose out of his deep despair over ever resolving this dilemma.

Job's main points are as follows:
- God is so powerful. How could I ever debate my case with him? He would probably overwhelm me and skillfully twist my words against me. On the other hand, he might just choose to ignore me.
- I have thought about trying to lift myself up by my own bootstraps by thinking positively and repressing my agony, but I know God would just inflict more suffering on me.
- If only there were a mediator to bring God and me together, someone who would arbitrate our differences and bring about reconciliation.
- God, you know I am innocent of sin. Why then do you keep straining to find some iniquity in me? And you put such care into creating me. Why do you now want to destroy me?
- Sheol is not a place to look forward to. It is so dark. But right now it looks a whole lot better than life.
- God, please leave me alone, so I can have a brief moment of rest before I die.

2. Our Dilemma. Both Job and the three friends were trapped in patterns of thinking that prevented them from understanding the true nature of Job's situation. The friends believed Job was suffering because he was guilty of sin, but he would not admit it. Job agreed with them that sin causes suffering, but he knew he was not guilty of sin (10:7). However, he could not explain why, then, he had experienced so much trouble. Both were prevented from understanding the cause of Job's suffering because they had not read the prologue.

The reader of the prologue has an immense advantage over Job and his friends. However, our confusion and pain with regard to suffering today can be just as real as it was for Job. None of us are ever privileged to read *the prologue* to our own lives. When trouble comes our way, we often complain and thrash about just as Job did. Some even become "bitter in soul" (3:20; 7:11; 10:1) and wish to die (6:8-9; 10:18-19). Our dilemma is sometimes no different from Job's.

E. Zophar's First Speech (11:1-20)

BEHIND THE TEXT

Zophar is the last of the friends to speak. He has listened to Eliphaz's cautious, opening comments about God's discipline and Bildad's emphasis on the ancient wisdom theology. He has also heard Job's emotional responses. He is especially angered by two comments in Job's last speech (chs 9—10). Job had claimed that: (1) he was innocent of sin (9:15, 20-21), and (2) God was unjust (9:22-24). To disprove these assertions, Zophar attacks Job's lack of knowledge in comparison to God's omniscience.

Zophar also seems baffled by Job's lack of interest in the speeches of his friends. How can Job reject such sound advice? Not unsurprisingly, he expresses a wish that God himself would speak to Job and set him straight. God's wisdom is far greater than that of any human being. If Job would turn to God and heed his advice, his suffering would go away and his blessed life would return.

Zophar was the dogmatist of the friends. He held fast to a set of principles guided by the wisdom theology. The truth of these principles was established by their "sheer logic" (Crenshaw 2011, 79). Thus, Zophar does not need a divine revelation (Eliphaz) or the support of ancient traditions (Bildad). For him, one can arrive at the truth simply by using common sense and good deductive reasoning.

Zophar's speech divides into three sections:
1. I Wish That God Would Speak to You (11:1-6)
2. God's Wisdom and Power Are Much Greater than Ours (11:7-12)
3. Turn to God and He Will Restore You (11:13-20)

IN THE TEXT

1. I Wish That God Would Speak to You (11:1-6)

Zophar's wish for God to speak to Job is really a plea for help. The friends have gotten nowhere in their attempts to straighten out Job's thinking. If Job will not listen to their arguments, which are supported by centuries of human wisdom and good reasoning, there is only one resource left. Only God can penetrate Job's defenses and convince him to change his mind. Ironically, Job also wished that God would speak. But whereas Zophar wants God to put Job in his place, Job desired divine vindication of his innocence.

■ 1 For comments on the introductory formula → 3:2. Zophar's name and homeland (Naamah) are not found elsewhere in the OT (→ 2:11).

■ 2 Just as Bildad did in his first speech, Zophar begins by attacking Job's wordiness. He does not want Job to think he can prove his case simply by outtalking the others. Zophar has a point, for throughout the book Job's speeches are significantly longer than the others. He probably suspects that Job's "multitude of words" (NRSV) is a smokescreen for the sin that lies at the heart of his suffering. Thus, he dismisses Job's previous speeches as foolishness and moves quickly to try to silence him.

Verse 2b is literally "Is the man of lips in the right?" "Man of lips" is probably an idiomatic expression for "one who talks a lot." Here Zophar borrows from one of the most common themes in ancient wisdom literature, namely the fool. Fools are people who babble on and on about whatever pops into their minds. They love to talk and are only interested in expressing their own opinions. The antithesis to the fool is the wise person who knows when to keep silent and when to talk. Even fools could pass themselves off as wise persons if they would keep their mouths shut.

Although Zophar does not directly accuse Job of being a fool, he does imply that Job fits that description (→ 2:10 for further comments on the meaning of "fool"). The book of Proverbs contains many references to the wordiness of fools (Prov 10:8, 14, 19; 12:15; 13:3; 14:23; 15:2; 17:27-28; 18:2; 28:26; 29:20; see also Kidner 1964, 39-42, 46-49).

The Hebrew for *in the right* ($ṣdq$) has already appeared four times in Job (4:17; 9:2, 15, 20) with various shades of meaning: "be righteous, be innocent, be in the right." In 11:2 Zophar is referring to the correctness of Job's position. If Job is correct, then he is truly a righteous and just person, innocent of any sin and vindicated before both God and humanity. However, Zophar is not about to affirm that Job is in the right. To do so would be admitting his own ignorance, denying the correctness of the whole wisdom theology, and accusing God of injustice. Such an admission is impossible in Zophar's thinking, and so he rushes to attack Job with blunt and callous force. God and the wisdom tradition must be defended at all costs.

■ 3 Zophar continues to focus on Job's verbosity by describing it as *empty babbling* (*bad*). The Hebrew *bad* appears in Isa 16:6 and Jer 48:30 with the meaning of "boasting." This has led some scholars to suggest the same meaning here, which is then illustrated in Job 11:4. However, the word is parallel with "a multitude of words" (NRSV) in v 2 and may simply refer to Job's excessive wordiness, which Zophar finds irritating.

Some versions, such as the NIV and NRSV, treat this verse as an implied question that continues on from v 2. But there is no interrogative particle at the beginning, and the verse makes good sense as a hypothetical statement leading toward Zophar's wish in vv 5-6 (NJPS). In either case, the meaning is basically the same.

Zophar wishes that Job would just shut his mouth for a while and listen to the advice of the three friends. Throughout the book there are continual attempts by most of the characters to **silence** another person. This seems to be one method used to score points in the dialogue (→ 6:24 for further discussion). In Zophar's thinking, Job's wordiness, at times, even progressed to the point of mocking. There is ambiguity as to whether the object of this mocking is God or the three friends. But most likely Zophar is referring to mocking God. Job's claim of divine injustice (9:22-24) would probably qualify as mocking in Zophar's mind.

■ **4** Next, Zophar accuses Job of making this statement: **My teaching is morally right and I am pure in your eyes**. In his previous speech Job certainly claimed "innocence" (*ṣdq*; 9:15, 20) and "blamelessness" (*tām*; 9:20-21), and he believed that God knew he was correct (10:7). But he had never claimed purity. These words are exaggerations that Zophar puts in Job's mouth—a straw man he can knock down in 11:5-6.

■ **5-6** Zophar's answer to Job's claims is a deep longing that **God** (*Eloah*) would appear and reveal to Job a greater understanding of his situation (v 5). This would put Job in his place and quiet his babbling. If he could see his life as God sees it, he would never claim moral rightness and purity (v 4).

The secrets of wisdom (v 6) are "the principles of order by which God creates and sustains the universe" (Balentine 2006, 185). These secrets are known only by God and include the moral universe as well as the physical, as Zophar makes clear in vv 6c, 10-11. Zophar does not claim that he himself knew the nature of these hidden secrets. He is simply pointing out that God's ways are often mysterious and far beyond human comprehension (Eccl 8:16-17).

Job 11:6*b* reads literally "For there is a double side to wisdom." By this, Zophar means: "There is another way of looking at your life of which you are completely unaware." The word for **wisdom** (*tušiyyâ*) in this clause is different from the first clause (→ 5:12).

The translation of 11:6*c* is difficult, but one possibility is the following: **Know that God [*Eloah*] has caused some of your iniquity to be forgotten against you**. The implication is that Job had sinned much more than he was willing to admit, but God had mercifully withheld punishment for some of these sins. Thus, God had already treated Job better than he deserved.

2. God's Wisdom and Power Are Much Greater than Ours (11:7-12)

Zophar's second point is to enlarge on the ways in which God is greater than human beings. He agrees with Job here (9:1-13), but he uses this argument to encourage Job to turn to God for help with his problems. Only a witless fool would reject the wisdom God offers to suffering humanity.

■ **7** Zophar presents Job with several rhetorical questions that emphasize the inability of humans to understand the ways of God. The areas of our knowledge that are deficient are **the mysteries** [*ḥēqer*] **of God** (*Eloah*) and **the limits** [*taklît*] **of the Almighty** (*Shaddai*). The Hebrew *ḥēqer* refers to that part of God's nature and knowledge that cannot be discovered through searching and investigation (→ 5:9; 8:8; 9:10). It is beyond what humans are capable of discerning.

The parallel word *taklît* appears in other passages in Job in reference to the "boundary between light and darkness" (26:10) or the extreme underground distances to which miners will go in search of precious metals (28:3). Here it refers to the breadth of God's knowledge that is limitless by human standards.

■ 8-9 Drawing upon the ancient conception of cosmology, Zophar further defines the limitless boundaries of God's knowledge. The world consists of four parts: **the heavens** (*šāmayim*), the domain of sun, moon, stars, and clouds; **Sheol** (*šĕ'ôl*), the underworld where all humanity descends after death; **the earth** (*'ereṣ*), where people live; and the salty **sea** (*yām*), at the outer edges of the land. God's knowledge is not confined by the boundaries of any of these. It is **higher, deeper, longer,** and **wider** than all parts of creation. Therefore, what can Job **do** or **know** that in any way compares to God's immeasurable knowledge? The rhetorical nature of the questions implies that human knowledge is far inferior to God's.

■ 10-11 Zophar now moves from God's infinite knowledge to his unlimited power. If while passing through the midst of life, God notices a person's "iniquity" (v 11 NRSV) and decides to imprison him and assemble a court to pronounce a judgment, who can oppose God's power to act? No one can resist. Such a depiction of God as "investigator, prosecutor, legal assembly and judge" is, of course, metaphorical (Clines 1989, 265). But it illustrates the point Zophar is trying to make, that God is all-powerful and will punish those who are sinful.

God has no problem in identifying these worthless people (lit. "men of worthlessness"). And when he sees them, he **takes note**. By implication, he does something about them as well. Thus, Zophar defends the integrity and justice of God who is totally aware of all human activity and who judges each person by his divine standard of justice. Job's calamities were clear evidence that God had observed something wrong in Job's life and brought justice to bear.

■ 12 This verse is a proverb Zophar delivers with biting sarcasm. He uses it to reemphasize his point in vv 7-9 that human knowledge about God's ways is lacking. The original meaning of the proverb is lost, but its usage by Zophar is intended to point out the unlikelihood, if not impossibility, of a fool gaining "understanding" (NRSV).

The **witless** person in v 12*a* is literally "a hollowed-out person/an empty-headed person." In this context the word is a synonym for "a fool." The parallel thought in v 12*b* has received much comment. One interpretation compares the unlikelihood of a fool gaining understanding to **a wild donkey** giving birth to **a human** (NIV, NJPS, NRSV; → 6:5). Another compares it to **a wild donkey** giving birth to a tame donkey (Clines 1989, 253; Pope 1973, 86). The correct interpretation is uncertain, but the meaning is plain: Job has little likelihood of ever gaining a correct knowledge of his situation.

3. Turn to God and He Will Restore You (11:13-20)

In the third section of his speech Zophar lays out a course of action for Job to follow. In his mind there is still hope for restoration if Job will turn to God and acknowledge his sinfulness. Then God will bless him with confidence (v 15), light (v 17), security (v 18), and hope (v 18). His troubles and fears will disappear (vv 15-16, 19), and his influence in the community will be restored (v 19).

■ **13-14** The **if** at the beginning of v 13 introduces four conditions that Job must meet in order to turn his life around. The pronoun **you** is added for the purpose of contrasting the possibilities that lie open before Job with the lot of the fool in v 12 who is locked into an impossible situation with no hope. The first condition is to "direct [*kwn*] your heart" (NRSV) toward God (v 13*a*). Zophar is referring to an internal ordering of one's life and priorities that focuses one's attention on God (1 Sam 7:3; 2 Chr 27:6; Ezra 7:10). The road back to God always begins with a decision to change one's focus from self to God.

The second condition is to **stretch out your hands to him** (Job 11:13*b*). This expression is used eighteen times in the OT as a synonym for "pray" (e.g., 1 Kgs 8:22, 54; Ezra 9:5; Ps 44:20 [21 HB]; Isa 1:15). Generally in the ANE, pictures of worshippers at prayer show their arms raised with palms directed outward at face level (Clines 1989, 267-68). The Israelite physical position is not described in the OT but was probably similar.

The third condition is to remove all wrongdoing from his life (Job 11:14*a*). Zophar assumed that Job still had some type of sin in his life that had never been confessed and forgiven. If such were true, then Zophar would certainly be correct in his admonition. However, the reader knows from the prologue that Job is blameless and has nothing to confess.

The fourth condition is to avoid "injustice" (v 14*b* NJPS). "Injustice" (*'awlâ*) is defined in 5:16 as an evil social action against the lowly. However, the word appears frequently in parallel with other words for wickedness and thus may be translated in more of a generic sense (e.g., **evil** or "wickedness" [NRSV]). Job and his household must commit themselves to a life of righteous behavior and relationships.

■ **15** If Job will follow Zophar's advice, then life will radically change for him. God will shower him with blessing after blessing (11:15-19). Zophar's intent here is to entice Job with enough rewards so that he will seriously consider the possibility of admitting he has sinned. The first two Hebrew words in v 15 are *kî 'āz* ("surely then" [NRSV]), which indicate Zophar's absolute certainty that he speaks the truth (GKC, §159*ee*).

The rest of v 15*a* is probably his answer to Job's complaint in 10:15 that he could not lift up his head because of his humiliation over his awful predicament. Zophar counters with words of confidence that Job's humiliation will come to an end. **You will stand firm** translates a verb (*yṣq*) used in the process of casting molten metal into a mold where it solidifies (Exod 25:12; 1 Kgs 7:46). "You will not fear" (NRSV) is Zophar's answer to the anguish and fears Job has described in every previous speech (Job 3:20-26; 6:1-13; 7:11-21; 9:17-18, 25-28, 34-35; 10:1).

■ **16** Zophar also confidently predicts that Job **will . . . forget** his **trouble** (*'āmāl*; → 3:10) if he turns to God. He will not have to repress his bad memories into his subconscious and then go on living as if nothing had happened (9:27-28). Rather, his troubles will be "as waters that have passed away" (NRSV). They will no longer be able to control his life and produce fear in him. Water in the form of floods and rushing torrents appears frequently in the Psalms and the Prophets as a metaphor for devastating calamities and judgments (e.g., Pss 69:15 [16 HB]; 124:4-5; Isa 8:7-8; Jer 47:2; Ezek 26:19; Amos 5:24). Zophar uses it here in the same sense.

■ **17** At the end of his last speech, Job had bemoaned his final destiny in Sheol (Job 10:21-22). He was going to a place that was so dark that "even the light is like darkness" (10:22). Zophar's answer is that whatever **darkness** (*tě'ûpâ*) Job may be experiencing now will soon turn to **morning**. In fact, it will be brighter than the light at **noonday** (see Pss 37:6; 139:12; Isa 58:10 for a similar concept).

Light and Darkness in Job

The author of Job repeatedly places in juxtaposition the concepts of light and darkness. The word for "light" (*'ōr*) plus its synonyms appears over thirty-five times, while the word for "darkness" (*hōšek*) along with its synonyms appears over forty times. God is the source of light and he shines his light on everyone and everything (Job 25:3). "Seeing the light" is associated with living a good life (30:26; 33:27-30). In his early years, God's light helped Job walk in the midst of darkness (29:3), but now that he is suffering he wishes he had never seen the light (3:4-6, 16, 20-23).

In contrast to the light, darkness is associated with wickedness, death, and Sheol. The wicked desire to live in darkness where they can work their evil deeds (24:13-17). Their fate is to have their light put out (18:5-6, 18). God controls both the light and the darkness as seen in his power to turn one into the other and vice versa (12:22-25; Amos 4:13; 5:8).

The NT continues this same contrast between light and darkness, especially in the Gospel of John and 1 John. There God is light and totally without darkness (1 John 1:5), Jesus is the light of the world (John 1:4-5; 8:12), and Jesus' followers are people who walk in the light rather than in the darkness (John 8:12; 1 John 1:7).

■ **18-19** When Job turns to God he will experience security in two ways. First, he will be able to sleep securely through the night without fear or nightmares. And second, his social connections will revive. In fact, many people will once again seek him out for help and advice. Job has already mentioned his sleeping problems (7:13-15), so Zophar's word should be an encouragement. Job has not yet commented on the lack of respect he now receives from others. But no doubt he is deeply troubled over the social antagonism that surrounds him, for he mentions it in his next speech (12:4) and later on in more detail (19:13-22).

■ **20** In contrast to the many blessings received by the righteous (11:15-18), the wicked experience a life of turmoil. Zophar points out three types of trouble that await **the wicked**. First, their **eyes . . . will fail** (*klh*). When this verb is used with **eyes** it refers to the loss of hope that comes after a period of time when one finally realizes that relief or rescue is not going to happen (Deut 28:65; Ps 69:3 [4 HB]; Lam 4:17). The wicked find themselves in a situation where they know life is not going to get any better.

Second, there will be no way to escape the consequences of their sin. And third, any **hope** (*tiqwâ*) the wicked may have experienced in the past will disappear quickly like an exhaled breath of air (lit. "the breathing out of breath"). Some interpret this third consequence as one's last **dying gasp**. But more likely it refers to the fragile state of one's confidence in the future.

Thus, Zophar concludes his first speech with the doctrine of the two ways, a topic that appears frequently in the wisdom literature as well as in some of Jesus' parables (e.g., Matt 7:24-27). Job can now weigh the lifestyle and fate of the two ways and compare them to his own life. Since Zophar had already heard Job confess to experiencing some of the characteristics of the wicked, he was, in effect, subtly warning Job of the pathway he was on. But he waits for Job to come to this conclusion himself.

FROM THE TEXT

1. Summary of Zophar's First Speech. Zophar was a good listener. He knew exactly what Job had said and where he was wrong. His speech addresses what he believed were ten errors in Job's arguments (see Balentine 2006, 190, for the entire list). Basically, he regarded Job as a naive fool who loudly passed the blame for his suffering onto God in order to hide the truth concerning his sin. While Zophar was definitely harsher than Eliphaz or Bildad, he did hold out hope that Job's life could turn around. But Job would have to make major adjustments in his thinking and acknowledge that he was a sinner.

Zophar's major points are as follows:
- Job, your claims about your moral purity are false. If God would appear and speak to you out of his great wisdom, you would realize how wrong you are.
- You think God is punishing you harshly, but God has already been far more lenient with you than your sins deserve.
- God's wisdom and power are far beyond what any human can imagine or understand. This creates a mystery about God that needs to be considered before making bold statements about the nature of God. Zophar was particularly thinking here of Job's claim that God was unjust.
- Job, there is still hope for a better life. You need to turn to God and repent of all your sins. If you do so, you will experience God's wonderful blessings again.

2. Job's Lack of Hope. One of the reasons for Job's despair was his lack of hope (17:15; 19:10; perhaps 7:6). He saw no future for himself, no possibility that life could get better. His health was deteriorating and he could die at any moment.

His wealth and his reputation were gone and would never return as long as he was ill. His children were all dead and could not be restored to life. So what did he have to hope for?

All of the friends tried to address this attitude in some way. Eliphaz encouraged Job to base his hope on his former godly life (4:6) and the character of God who does marvelous things for the needy (5:9, 15-16). He further offered hope that, after this period of discipline was over, God would restore Job's health and give him a long life and many descendants (5:17-26).

Bildad approached the topic of hope from a traditional viewpoint. The godless never have hope (8:13). That is a timeless principle. But another timeless principle is that God never rejects a blameless person. Therefore, if Job was truly blameless he would see good times again (8:20-22).

Zophar's approach was to hold out in front of Job the benefits of living a righteous life (11:15-19). His intent was to create a picture of the godly life that was so attractive that Job would confess his wrong to God, put the past behind him, and seek to live a righteous life again. However, Zophar's comments only increased Job's pain by reminding him of better times that lay in the past. For Job, the topic of hope was worthless to talk about. He answers Zophar in his next speech by noting that a tree that has been cut off at the stump has more hope of reviving than a human being (14:7-9).

F. Job's Response to Zophar (12:1—14:22)

BEHIND THE TEXT

At the beginning of the book, Job's reputation as a person of superior wisdom was known throughout the East (1:3). Yet all three of his friends, who certainly knew of his reputation, have treated him as inferior. It is not surprising, then, that he lashes out at them in a lengthy speech (seventy-five verses) intended to justify his integrity and knowledge.

Job begins by attacking the haughty attitude of his friends. They have acted as if they spoke for God, but they are mistaken. They agreed with Job on some points, such as God's omnipotence, but basically their words were only rehashed wisdom theology that was common knowledge. It had no relevance to Job's situation. Thus, they were of no help to him.

So Job then turns his attention to God. He is ready to debate God regarding his innocence. He knows this is a dangerous course of action because of God's omnipotence, but he sees no relief from suffering until God explains to him its cause. In the final verses Job briefly imagines what it would be like to be restored into God's fellowship. But he knows this will never happen. God treats him like an enemy and is determined to destroy him.

Job's speech divides into seven parts:
1. I Am as Wise as You Are (12:1-6)
2. Nature Teaches Us That God Controls Everything (12:7-10)

3. God's Power Is Overwhelming (12:11-25)
4. You Friends Are Worthless Counselors (13:1-12)
5. I Have Prepared My Case (13:13-19)
6. God, What Have I Done Wrong? (13:20-28)
7. Human Beings Are Destined for Trouble (14:1-22)

IN THE TEXT

1. I Am as Wise as You Are (12:1-6)

Job was becoming weary of the friends' claims to wisdom. So he begins his response to Zophar with a sarcastic comment about the supposed superiority of their wisdom. They are not as wise as they think they are. Their successful lives have blinded them to the inequities in life that other people experience.

■ **1** For comments on the standard introductory formula → 3:2.

■ **2-3** Verse 2 is difficult to interpret because the word for **people** (*'ām*) has no modifiers. The best solution is to follow a suggestion from J. A. Davies (quoted in Clines 1989, 278) and treat the second line as a relative clause. This yields the sarcastic comment: *Truly you are the people with whom wisdom will die!*

Job's friends have acted as if they are the only ones who possess true wisdom about life. Their haughty attitude allowed for no alternative viewpoints. How can he engage them in serious dialogue when they regard him as **inferior** in understanding? He believes his **mind** (*lēbāb*) is as sharp as theirs. So far, they have only repeated old clichés that do not apply to his situation. No doubt, Job's spirited defense of his own integrity is in response to Zophar's insult in 11:12.

■ **4** Job goes on to describe the irony, if not absurdity, of his situation—something the friends have failed to recognize and that calls into question their "wisdom" (12:2). On the one hand, he is **righteous** (*ṣaddîq*) and **blameless** (*tāmîm*). This description points back to 1:1 and is identical to the characterization of Noah in Gen 6:9. Earlier in his life, there was continual communication between himself and God. When he prayed, **God** [*Eloah*] . . . **answered** him directly.

On the other hand, even though his integrity and righteousness have not changed, his relationship with other people is radically different now. He has become a **laughingstock** (*śeḥôq*; → Job 8:21 for a more positive usage of this Hebrew word) to his friends—an object of ridicule. Most likely, Job's complaint is directed at the three friends in front of him, but there are others from among his family and acquaintances who have also lost respect for him (19:13-22).

■ **5** From Job's point of view, people who are doing well in life, like the friends, sometimes fall into the trap of believing that their righteous deeds have earned them a secure life. They also assume that people who experience **misfortune** (*pîd*) must not be living a righteous life. Therefore, their troubles are deserved, and **contempt** (*bûz*) is the accepted way to treat them. Instead of lending a helping hand, people who are well-off resort to a *blow* (*nākôn*) for **those whose feet are slipping**. Most likely, Job is describing the treatment he has received from the three friends, although it is possible he is simply stating a general observation about life. No wonder he feels like a "laughingstock" (12:4).

■ 6 What is even more disturbing to Job is that some of the most evil people in the world who delight in harming others dwell in peace (3:26). God does nothing to punish them. Even **those who provoke God** [*El*] **are secure**. How can this be considered justice? Job's observation here parallels other passages that also call into question God's treatment of the wicked (Ps 73:3-12; Eccl 7:15; 8:14). The reference to **marauders** may be Job's term for the Sabeans (Job 1:15) and the Chaldeans (1:17) who carried off his oxen, donkeys, and camels. Or it may be simply a term for evil plunderers in general.

The translation and interpretation of the last clause is problematic (see Gordis 1978, 137, for five different possibilities). Either **God** [*Eloah*] is the object (yielding "the one who brings God in his hand") or **God** is the subject (yielding "the one whom God brings in his hand"). Clines' support for the latter reading based on the singular verb and the pronoun **his** (**his hand**; 1989, 291-92) seems most reasonable, but the issue is unresolved. The interpretation of the latter reading is that God controls every human being (v 10), even the most wicked people, yet he does nothing to prevent their evil practices.

2. Nature Teaches Us That God Controls Everything (12:7-10)

Job now turns to the subject of nature—a very popular topic in the wisdom literature (see the book of Proverbs and Job 38—41). All of nature teaches us that God is in control of everything and everyone in his creation.

■ 7-8 **Ask** or **speak to** nature, and you will get a response. It will **teach** you significant lessons about life and its order. Job does not reveal the content of this teaching until 12:9, but he insists on the value of using nature for instruction. Some are bothered by the use of the word **earth** (*'ereṣ*) here and suggest that a word has dropped out, such as "swarming things" of the earth (as in Gen 7:21; Lev 11:29, 41). However, as God's later speeches clearly indicate (Job 38:4-38), the earth has as much to teach humans as the animal kingdom. The seasons, the weather patterns, the sea, and the sky all contribute to humanity's understanding.

The main issue in interpreting 12:7-8 is dealing with the singular pronouns for **you** and the singular verbs **ask** and **speak to**. Why would Job now address his words specifically to Zophar instead of to all three friends, as he does in vv 2-3? This evidence has prompted some to attribute vv 7-12 to the three friends. They are like a straw man or a "parody" that Job is setting up for verbal attack (Newsom 1996, 427; Clines 1989, 292-93). They should be introduced with the words "You say . . ."

Such an interpretation is possible in light of the fact that authors in the OT do not always indicate changes in voice (e.g., see Ps 118, which has many voice changes). These changes have to be determined from the context. However, many times differentiations in voice are based solely upon perceptions of what a person might have said and thus are speculative. In the verses under consideration, only Job 12:12 seems to represent specifically the views of the friends as opposed to Job. And even that verse could be a point of agreement between both Job and the friends that Job does not want to deny but rather to expand upon (Gordis 1978, 138). Further, other than the problem with the singular forms in vv 7-8, the content of vv 7-11 does not contradict other passages in the book that are clearly attributed to Job. Thus, it is best to regard these verses as belonging to him.

■ **9-10** The interpretation of v 9 is dependent on identifying the antecedent of the word **this**. If it refers to the main points in Zophar's speech (ch 11), then 12:9 is an attempt by Job to belittle Zophar for saying nothing new. All his ideas were common knowledge that nature had known and taught since the beginning of time. Another possible antecedent is v 6, which refers to God's unjust system of governance.

A third possible antecedent is v 10. What nature knows and teaches is that God is in control over all of life—both animal ("every living thing" [NRSV]) and human ("every human being" [NRSV]). Paul's allusion to this verse in Rom 1:20 supports this interpretation: "Ever since the creation of the world his eternal power and divine nature, invisible though they are, have been understood and seen through the things he has made" (NRSV). Isaiah 41:20 also supports the third possibility.

Both Job and his friends agreed that God was all-powerful. Where they parted company was with regard to *how* God uses his power. Is God's hand "an open palm or a clenched fist" (Clines 1989, 295)? Job's experiences have led him to a "clenched fist" understanding of God, and he will expound on this concept in Job 12:14-25.

One point of controversy in v 9 is the appearance of the word *Yahweh* (**the LORD**). This is the only usage of this word in the dialogue section of Job. A few Hebrew manuscripts have *Eloah*, which is the more common term for God in the dialogues. Clines suggests that *Yahweh* is possibly just a "scribal slip" due to the fact that "the hand of Yahweh" occurs over thirty times in the OT whereas "the hand of God" is quite rare (1989, 294-95). However, *Yahweh* is clearly the harder reading and therefore the more likely. It is possible that **the hand of *Yahweh* has done this** is a familiar saying the author felt obligated to retain in its original form (see Isa 41:20). Also, Job did use the word *Yahweh* in Job 1:21.

3. God's Power Is Overwhelming (12:11-25)

Job introduces the third section of his speech with general comments on God's wisdom and power in comparison to humanity's. He then illustrates this concept with examples of God's power to overthrow and destroy. Job agrees with Zophar (11:10) that God does whatever he wishes. But whereas Zophar believed God's destructive power was directed primarily at the wicked, Job believes it affects *all* humanity. The highest positions in human society—those charged with leadership, such as **counselors** (12:17), "judges" (v 17), "kings" (v 18), "priests" (v

19), "elders" (v 20), and "nobles" (v 21)—are no match for the power of God. Even great nations (v 23) are destroyed by him.

In this way, Job effectively addresses the friends' contention that all suffering is the result of sin, and that those sufferers who refuse to admit their sinfulness are stupid fools (11:12). Job knew from his own experiences that such was not the case. As Hartley aptly notes, "Whoever experiences God's destructive power is not necessarily stupid or worthless. People become victims of catastrophes regardless of their social status or moral standing" (1988, 212). In a previous speech (9:1-13) Job already pointed out God's destructive power, but there he also gave God credit for numerous constructive acts, such as creation and miraculous deeds (9:8-10). Here in ch 12 the constructive deeds are absent, and the emphasis is totally on God's power to destroy.

Scholars have noted a number of connections between this section and Ps 107 (see Driver-Gray 1921, 117). But whereas the psalmist praises God for using his power to deliver his people from calamity and enemies, Job describes God's power as a means of destroying people and nations.

■ **11** Job begins with a proverb that he uses to refute Zophar's insult in 11:12 that he is stupid and incapable of understanding the ways of life. Just as the "palate" (12:11 NRSV; 29:10) is able to distinguish between good and bad food, so the mind (**ear**) can **test** good and bad ideas. The **ear** is used in other passages in Job (13:1; 33:16; 36:10; 42:5) and in the rest of the OT (2 Sam 22:7; Prov 2:2; 18:15; 22:17; 23:12; Isa 6:10; 22:14; Jer 5:21) as a synonym for the heart or mind.

Job's point is that he is perfectly capable of evaluating their **words** and determining their worth. While the conventional wisdom of the past has much valuable information to teach, it is not flawless. It must be examined critically using all the available evidence. Job's own situation was one piece of evidence the friends were not willing to consider. Later in the book (Job 34:3) this proverb appears in the mouth of Elihu as a statement rather than a question.

■ **12-13** These two verses definitely go together, but the nature of the relationship is disputed. Here are four different interpretations. (1) Some take 12:12 as a simple statement: "Among the aged is wisdom, and (in) length of days is understanding" (see NASB, NEB, NLT). But this translation does not fit Job's viewpoint. Thus, proponents usually attribute this verse to the three friends and place the words "You say . . ." ahead of it to indicate that Job is repeating earlier comments of theirs (5:27; 8:8-10; also 15:10) before offering a counter view in 12:13.

(2) A second interpretation is based on an emendation. The Hebrew *lô* at the end of v 11 is moved to the beginning of v 12 where it is emended to *lō'* (**not**). This rendering appears in the NIV: **Is not wisdom found among the aged? Does not long life bring understanding?** This interpretation suggests that Job agreed with the friends concerning the greater wisdom of the aged.

(3) Others, such as the NRSV and NJPS, interpret v 12 as a question, carrying over the interrogative particle at the beginning of v 11 into 12: "Is wisdom

with the aged, and understanding in length of days?" The rhetorical nature of the question indicates that Job did not agree with this position held by the friends.

(4) A fourth interpretation treats the terms **aged** and "length of days" as titles for God, yielding: "With the Aged One is wisdom and with the Long-lived One is understanding" (Hartley 1988, 210). This interpretation has received little support.

Lacking any indication of tone of voice or facial expressions that might help to clarify the correct interpretation, it would be wise to maintain caution in translating this verse. But the interpretation that seems most likely in the context of the passage is (3). Job might agree that older people are generally more knowledgeable by virtue of the fact they have more experiences to draw upon. However, this is no reason to ascribe greater wisdom to the friends simply because they are older than he (15:10).

On the contrary, in 12:13 he emphasizes that only God possesses true **wisdom** (ḥokmâ), **power** (gĕbûrâ), **counsel** ('ēṣâ), and **understanding** (tĕbûnâ). Only he knows what to do and has the power to do it. All human beings, no matter what their age or status, are decidedly inferior in these areas. Significantly, Job does not mention justice and righteousness in this list (also v 16) of God's qualities. They are "noticeably lacking" (Balentine 2006, 206). For Job, God seems more interested in tearing down than building up (vv 14-25), a clear indication in his mind that God is unjust.

■ **14** God's destructive acts are permanent. What humans destroy can usually be rebuilt (e.g., Hiroshima, the World Trade Center in New York City). But what God **tears down** is dismantled forever. While Job does not mention the object of God's destructive power, his use of *bnh* (**rebuilt**) suggests he has in mind something humans have constructed, such as a city or house (1 Kgs 22:39).

Job 12:14b refers to people whom God **imprisons** (lit. "shuts ... in" [NRSV]). The doors for such persons are closed forever. John incorporates this same concept in his letter to the church at Philadelphia (Rev 3:7). Of course, imprisonment can include more than just the physical aspect of a person's life.

■ **15** Earlier, Job commented on God's awesome power over nature as seen in volcanoes, earthquakes, and eclipses (9:5-7). In 12:15 he notes God's control of the rain. If he sends too little rain, the land ***dries up*** and there is famine. If he sends too much, the land is ***overwhelmed*** with floods (9:5). Job's point is to emphasize God's complete control over the destructive forces of nature.

The implication of this concept is very significant to his overall argument. Because everyone is affected by these acts of nature, Job has proved his point that both the righteous and the wicked experience God's destructive power. Floods destroy everyone in their path. They do not distinguish between the house of the righteous person and the house of the wicked. Therefore, by implication, the righteous are not immune from suffering. Humans suffer for reasons other than sin.

■ **16** Verse 16a is similar to v 13, but Job uses different descriptors: **strength** ('ōz) and ***wisdom*** (tûšiyyâ). **Strength** is an attribute that is frequently applied to God (e.g., Ps 62:11 [12 HB]). As noted earlier (5:12), *tûšiyyâ* can refer to either wisdom or the effects of wisdom. The first is more probable here.

Job 12:16b speaks of two categories of people who are under God's control: "the one who goes astray" and "the one who causes someone else to stray" (both are from the same root—*šgh*). The verb *šgh* generally refers to unintentional moral errors that people commit against God, but the causative (Hiphil) form of the second occurrence indicates a purposeful action.

Job has already admitted the possibility that he himself could have committed such a moral error, and he has asked the friends to show him where he has gone astray (6:24). So far, however, the friends have produced no evidence. Whether Job intended for these two categories to include all humanity (i.e., the two extremes and everyone in between) is questionable. Certainly he did not include himself in either category, but he probably would place his friends in one of them.

■ **17-21** Job now turns to God's power over the leaders of society. God deals with each category of people in a way that strips them of their authority and leaves them powerless. The **counselors** (v 17) are the professional advisers whom the king consults when he needs to make an important decision. God **leads** them **away stripped** (from the verb *šll*, meaning "plundered" of their capacity to advise). An alternative reading, based on the usage of this word in Mic 1:8 is "barefoot." In biblical times prisoners of war were sometimes roped together and led away barefoot by the conquering nation. In like manner, God **makes . . . judges *look foolish***.

God also controls the **kings** of the world (Job 12:18; see Luke 1:52). Clines' translation ("he loosens the belt of kings") is similar to many who emend *mûsār* ("discipline") to *môsēr*, meaning "an object that binds, such as a belt or fetter" (1989, 275). This verse describes God's power to strip kings of the royal garments of their authority and leave them humiliated, wearing only a meager **loincloth**.

The language of Job 12:19a is exactly the same as v 17 with the substitution of **priests** for **counselors**. God has the power to strip religious leaders of their authority to lead the community in worship (for comments on the alternate reading "barefoot" → above). In v 19b the Hebrew word *'ētānîm* is probably derived from the verb *ytn*, meaning "be constant, enduring." Hence, the NIV rendering **officials long established** refers to people whose authority is considered permanent. This may be a synonym for the **priests** in the first clause whose position was hereditary and lasted for a lifetime, or it may indicate some other long-established position in the community. God also **overthrows** these individuals.

Every community needs its **trusted advisers** and **elders** (v 20) to provide sound advice and direction for the future. But God's power destroys their effectiveness when he **takes away** their ability to speak (lit. their **lips**) and to discern. The Hebrew for **discernment** (*ṭa'am*) is normally used in reference to "taste" (6:6 and the verbal form in 12:11), but it may also denote the mind's ability to make good decisions (e.g., Ps 119:66).

The final group of leaders who must experience God's power are **nobles** and **the mighty** (Job 12:21). **Nobles** were highly respected, upper-class people who gave generously to their community (Exod 35:5, 22). God humiliates them in ways that make their generosity look contemptible. The Hebrew for **the mighty** (*'ăpîqîm*) appears only here in the OT. It probably denotes military leaders. When God **loosens** (*rph*) their **belt** (*māzîaḥ*) that tucks in their robe and holds their weapon, he renders them unprepared for battle and thus inoperative.

■ **22** The next example of God's power is his disclosure of **deep things** (*'ămuqôt*) that have been hidden in **darkness** (*ḥōšek*). The question is: What are these mysteries, hidden in **the deepest darkness** (*ṣalmāvet*; → Job 3:5), that God brings forth into the **light**? Are they the depths of Sheol that Zophar mentioned in 11:8? Are they the schemes of the leaders Job has just mentioned in 12:17-21? Are they the hidden secrets of humanity in general? Or are they God's own hidden plans that Job is just starting to realize? There are supporters for each of these interpretations, but perhaps the answer lies in the context.

This verse sits in the midst of a passage focusing on God's awesome power over everything in creation. He does whatever he wishes to both nature and humanity. In v 22 Job is pointing out that God even controls the **darkness**—*the deepest darkness* imaginable. He is able to change it into **light** if he so wishes, for he has done it before (as in Gen 1:3; Alden 1993, 155).

■ **23** The translation of Job 12:23 is problematic. Some scholars interpret all four verbal forms as indicating God's negative impact on the nations of the world: "He leads some nations astray and destroys them; Others he scatters and leads away" (Habel 1985, 212). Others believe the first verb in each clause is positive and the second negative: "He makes nations great, then destroys them; he enlarges a people, then disperses them" (Hartley 1988, 211). And still others treat the verbs in the second clause as negative first and then positive: "He makes nations great, and he destroys them; he disperses nations, and he leads them" (Clines 1989, 276).

The correct translation is unclear, but the overall meaning is that God controls the destiny of the nations of the world, causing them to rise and fall. This is a view of history strongly supported by the prophets in the OT (e.g., Amos 1—2; Isa 13—23; Jer 46—51).

■ **24-25** God's power over the nations applies to their leaders as well. He ***removes*** (*swr*) their ability to make good decisions (lit. their "heart" [*lēb*]) and **makes them wander** in a ***wasteland*** (i.e., in confusion). The word for ***wasteland*** is *tōhû*, the same word used in Gen 1:2 to describe the watery, formless nothingness before creation. Here in Job 12:24 it refers to a deserted place on land without markers or trails. This word has already appeared in 6:18 with the same meaning.

Verse 25 of Job 12 adds to the description of the leaders' confusion with two word pictures. **They grope** (see 5:14) about in the dark trying to find their way, and God **makes them stagger** [the same verb (*t'h*) is used in 12:24 for **wander**] **like drunkards**.

4. You Friends Are Worthless Counselors (13:1-12)

Job has complained about his friends before (6:14-30). In this section he criticizes them again for taking God's side instead of supporting him. If they would just keep their mouths shut and listen to his complaints, maybe they would understand his position. As it is, their advice is worthless. Job now sees that only God can explain his suffering.

■ **1-2** Job's comments in 13:1-2 support his earlier viewpoint (12:3) that *his* understanding of suffering and the issues associated with it is as great as, if not greater than, the three friends'. His **eyes** and **ears** have served him well in gathering pertinent information through personal experience rather than through the wisdom of the ancients. And his mind has processed this information giving him both knowledge and understanding. Job's claim to understanding is not an egotistical boast that places him on a par with God. He has already acknowledged that God is far superior in wisdom (9:4; 12:13) and that God's ways are sometimes unknown to humanity (9:10-13; 10:13). His claim is simply an attempt to defend himself against the haughty attitude of his friends. He repeats his statement—**I am not inferior to you** (12:3*b*)—in 13:2*b* just to make his point again.

■ **3** By this point in the dialogue Job has heard enough to know that his friends are not able to help him. Their ideas are trapped in the wisdom traditions of the past. What he really wants is a dialogue with **the Almighty** (*Shaddai*), an opportunity to talk *to* God rather than only *about* him. Because of God's superior wisdom (9:4; 12:13) and destructive power (12:14-25), such a dialogue would be frightening, to say the least. God's presence terrifies him (7:13-14, 20; 9:17-19, 34; 10:16-17). Certainly a mediator would be helpful in arbitrating their differences (9:32-33). But Job is willing to take a risk. In his mind this is the only course of action that has any possibility for success. If God has caused his suffering, then only God can explain it. Thus, God must somehow be engaged in conversation.

Job uses a verb here (**argue**; *ykḥ*) that has a variety of meanings. In some contexts it refers to God's "reproof" or "rebuke" of individuals in order to correct them (5:17; 13:10). In others, it can mean "lay a charge against someone, as in a lawsuit" (see Ps 50:21). Here in Job 13:3 Job seeks to engage **God** (*El*) in a "rational discussion" (Andersen 1976, 164) in which he is allowed to debate his side of the issue. More than anything else, Job wishes that God would just begin to talk to him. His goal is the restoration of a relationship that he believes can only be achieved through dialogue.

■ **4** In vv 4-12 Job attacks his friends again with serious criticisms, much like he did in 6:14-30. He begins by accusing them of being **plasterers of deception** and **worthless physicians** (lit. "healers of worthlessness"). The exact meaning of the first phrase is problematic because of the rarity of the root for **plasterers** (*ṭpl*; only here, 14:17, and Ps 119:69). Some derive the meaning in Job 13:4 from one of the other passages, but the best context for this verse is probably v 7, where Job questions his friends about their deceptiveness. Since the very beginning of the dialogue (ch 4), they had been deceitful rather than helpful. They had accused

Job of hiding his sinfulness, and they claimed to speak for God. They also believed that their words had been proven true over many centuries of time. Job regards them as frauds who plaster over the truth with "clichés" and "simplistic language" (Newsom 1996, 430-32).

He also characterizes them as incompetent. The quality of physicians in the ancient world was a far cry from that of physicians today. There was no scientific understanding of the causes of disease, and there were no educational and licensing standards to be met. Just about anyone could claim to be a physician. Many of them were **worthless**. While the three friends never claimed that they possessed medical powers of healing, they did advise Job to confess his sins, which they believed would lead to his physical healing (5:8-27; 8:5-7; 11:13-20). Thus Job's criticism is a valid one. These **physicians** were incompetent. Nothing the friends have said thus far has enlightened him on the reasons for *his* suffering.

■ **5-6** In an earlier passage (6:24) Job offered to quit talking if his friends could show him where he was wrong. Now he asks them to **keep silent** (13:5a) and **listen attentively** to his words (v 6). That would be the best thing they could do to help him, and it would be a sign of their **wisdom** (v 5b; Prov 17:28). Perhaps Job was wishing for the earlier seven-day period of silence when they first arrived (2:13).

Job is putting his friends on notice that he is getting ready to lay out his case before God. He has thoroughly prepared his line of reasoning, just as if he were headed into a court of law. And he believes he is in the right (13:18). He uses two parallel terms in v 6 to describe the points he will make. The first is **argument** (v 6a; *tôkaḥat*). The word is derived from the verb *ykḥ* that Job used in v 3 to indicate his desire to engage God in a debate. The parallel term in v 6b is **pleas** (*ribôt*). In some passages the word refers to conflicts in general (Prov 17:14); in others to specific disputes between two parties that may end up in a lawsuit (Deut 19:17). In Job 13:6 the word simply indicates the evidence Job will present as he argues his case with God.

■ **7-8** Here Job directs a series of questions at the three friends that reveals his distrust of their ability to help him. As he said in v 3, his issue is really with God, not with the friends. He was hoping the friends would support him, but if not, at least that they would not take sides in the debate. Instead they were already prejudiced against him. They had spoken **injustice** (*'awlâ*; v 7a) and **deception** (*rĕmiyyâ*; v 7b) and shown **partiality** (v 8a) toward God (lit. "will you lift up his face?"). They thought they were arguing God's side of the debate. But they are false witnesses (Exod 20:16; Deut 19:16-19) whom God will reject.

■ **9-11** Job presses the friends further by asking them how they would fare if God **examined** them (v 9a). Would they still continue their charade of deception against God (v 9b)? Job's questions are meant to warn the friends that their practices are headed toward failure. Even if the friends' **partiality** for God occurs only "in secret" (v 10b NRSV), it cannot be hidden from God who will search out the guilty persons and "rebuke" (v 10a NRSV) them. God cannot be deceived like humans can. Neither does God need false witnesses to testify in his behalf. Those who claim to speak for God are only deceiving themselves. For the third time in this section Job uses a form of the verb *ykḥ* (vv 3, 6). This time it means "rebuke" (NRSV).

Job continues to warn his friends in v 11. Not only will God rebuke them, but he will **terrify** them as well. **Terrify** (*b't*) is not a new word to the friends, for Job has already used it twice (7:14; 9:34) to describe how God has directed his power against him. In effect, Job is saying, "My experience of suffering will become yours if you continue to speak falsely and deceptively for God." Ironically, Job is convinced that God will bring justice against the friends for their false arguments, even though God had not treated him with justice (Terrien 1954, 1003).

■ 12 Job concludes, for the time being, his criticism of the friends by pointing out how flimsy their arguments are. He compares them to **proverbs of ashes** and **defenses of clay**. The translation of the Hebrew *gab* as **defenses** is uncertain. Many commentators prefer a rendering that is more parallel to **proverbs** in v 12*a* and connect *gab* with a cognate word in several Semitic languages meaning "answers, responses, replies." In either case, the basic meaning is preserved. There is no substance to the arguments of the friends. They would not be able to withstand the rigors of a thorough examination by God. How appropriate for Job to speak of **ashes** and **clay** while sitting on an ash heap containing thousands of broken pottery sherds.

5. I Have Prepared My Case (13:13-19)

Job believes he has an airtight case to present to God, if and when God ever shows up. He is worried that God will simply overwhelm him and may even kill him. Nevertheless, he wants to speak to God. He knows he would be vindicated.

■ 13 Job has already asked for silence once in this speech (v 5). The first occasion was a wish. Here it is a command. Since no one is ever interrupted anywhere in the book, this seems like a meaningless request. But Job is striving for a rhetorical effect here. Asking for silence is his way of preparing his friends for the important points that follow.

■ 14 This verse can be interpreted in two ways. One is to disregard the *'al mâ* at the beginning as an example of dittography carried over from v 13. The rest of the verse is then treated as a statement by Job: "I will take my flesh in my teeth, and put my life in my hand" (NRSV). The second interpretation retains the *'al mâ* as an interrogative introducing an indirect question from the friends: *[Maybe you are asking] why I take my flesh in my teeth and place my life in my hand?* (see NIV). Either interpretation is possible, and the meaning is essentially the same in both. Job is aware of the danger he is putting himself in by confronting God.

Both clauses in v 14 contain idiomatic expressions dealing with risky behavior. The first appears only here. The second has parallels in other passages (Judg 12:3; 1 Sam 19:5; 28:21; Ps 119:109). A modern idiom similar to both is: "I am putting my life on the line."

■ **15** There is a long Jewish and Christian tradition of treating Job 13:15a as a statement of trust in God (e.g., KJV—"Though he slay me, yet will I trust in him"; and ACCS, 6:76). But this interpretation is no longer accepted by a number of modern scholars and translators. The first clause begins literally **Behold, he may kill me** (*qtl*). Job is aware, as he stated in v 14, that the bold tactics he is about to undertake may cost him his life. God may choose to get rid of him rather than engage him in debate.

The rest of the clause is more difficult. The Kethib reading with *lō'* ("not") is, "I will not hope/wait" (see NRSV). The Qere with *lô* ("for him") is, "I will hope in/wait for him" (see NIV). Both readings appeared in Jewish manuscripts as early as the second century AD (Clines 1989, 312), so the problem of interpretation has been around for a long time. This writer prefers the Kethib based on the context, yielding: ***I will not wait (silently), but I will defend my ways to his face.***

Job is extremely doubtful that God will ever speak to him. But he plans to defend himself, even though he has no hope that God will listen. This supports an earlier comment where he complained that God would not speak to him. God was only interested in crushing him (9:16-17). The sense of the verse, then, is probably something like this: "God may kill me if I try to challenge him in a debate. I know I am taking a great risk. As I have mentioned already, I have no hope that he will pay any attention to me. However, I will not remain silent. I will vigorously defend my innocence to his face."

■ **16** In spite of his doubts that God will listen to him, Job takes comfort in the thought that his boldness in coming to God may work to his advantage. **Godless people** (*ḥānēp*; 8:13) hide from God rather than approach him. Adam's and Eve's actions in the garden (Gen 3:8) were typical of all people who sin. Job is hoping his willingness to meet with God will attract God's attention and prod him to consider Job's innocence. Even this little bit of success will seem like **deliverance** (*yĕšû'â*) to Job. That in turn may give him the opportunity to defend his integrity and righteousness. Paul echoes the thought of a difficult situation working out to one's advantage when speaking of his own possible deliverance from prison (Phil 1:19).

■ **17** Job's earlier request for silence (Job 13:13) is followed here by a call to **listen carefully**. He adds an infinitive absolute to the imperative form to intensify his demand (GKC, §113r). He wants his friends to be well informed about the main points in his argument with God. Perhaps they will come to his side when they see how thoroughly he has prepared his case (v 18). In v 17b most translations add an implied verb to create two parallel clauses ("and let my declaration be in your ears" [NRSV]). But the first verb can do double duty for both direct objects. The meaning is the same in either case.

■ **18** In an earlier speech Job used the verb '*rk* ("prepare") to describe how God had prepared his terrors against him (6:4). Here Job uses the same word to emphasize that he, too, has made a thorough preparation in arranging his arguments prior to confronting God. When the verb is used with *mišpāṭ*, it means "prepare a (legal) case" (also in 23:4).

In 13:18b Job utters a brief word of confidence: **I know *I am in the right*.** The arguments he presents in his defense will demonstrate conclusively the correctness of his position, which is that he is innocent of sin and has been wrongly punished (also 23:7). Of course, all is dependent on whether God will give him a hearing. If God refuses to meet with him, as Job surmises, then Job's rightness will never by proven.

■ **19** Job's confidence (13:18) expands into a boastful challenge in v 19: "Who is there that will contend [*ryb*] with me?" (NRSV). In other words, who is able to answer my arguments and prove me wrong? The answer in Job's mind is: "No one—neither God nor human being!" He believes his case is strong enough to deflect any charge that may be hurled at him. However, if perchance he has miscalculated and God is able to answer his arguments successfully, then Job will cease his arguing and accept the consequences. He is sure it will mean his death.

Job is correct on this point: No one can prove he is guilty of wrongdoing, for God confirmed in the prologue that Job was blameless and upright (1:8; 2:3). Thus, when God does finally speak near the end of the book, he never even mentions this topic. The issue of Job's guilt or innocence that is so prominent in the dialogues will finally be seen as insignificant when God begins to speak (chs 38—41).

6. God, What Have I Done Wrong? (13:20-28)

The object of Job's attention now shifts from the friends to God. In previous speeches Job voiced complaints about how God had treated him and requested for God to leave him alone (7:11-21; 10:1-22). But in this section he gathers his courage and directs two pointed questions at God that get at the heart of his distress: (1) In what ways have I sinned against you (13:23)? (2) Why do you treat me like your enemy (v 24)? Job is clearly ready to begin a debate on these topics.

■ **20-21** Job needs God to do two things before the debate can begin. The request is actually worded very strangely in the negative (lit. "Only two things do not do to me"). What Job means is for God to discontinue doing two negative things against him. The first is: **Withdraw your hand far from me.** The Hebrew for **hand** (either *kap*, as in v 21, or *yād*) when applied to God in the book of Job refers to his power or control over something. God may exercise his power either positively (5:18; 10:8; 14:15) or negatively (1:11; 2:5; 6:9; 19:21; 30:21). Job definitely regarded his losses and physical suffering as caused by God's hand (2:10), so his request is that God restrain his power and quit harassing him.

Job's second request—"Do not let dread of you terrify me" (NRSV)—is a repetition of what he said in 9:34. He has already commented on how God frightens him continually so he cannot sleep at night (7:13-15). God had crushed him so severely he could not even get his breath (9:17-19). Further, he was terrified at the thought of coming into God's presence (9:34-35) and knew this would prevent him from speaking clearly and forcefully. So relief from God's hand and terror is a logical request in 13:21 that needs to be met before Job will feel free to argue his case.

Job's statement in v 20*b* about not hiding from God seems strange following his boastfulness in vv 18-19. Job had never considered hiding from God, as the first couple did in the Garden of Eden (Gen 3:8). He had no reason to hide from God's view, for he believed he was right (Job 13:18). But he knew that God's awesome presence makes human beings very uncomfortable. His natural inclination would be to back away from such an encounter. Therefore, he asks God to remove his hand and quit terrorizing him so the debate can proceed.

■ **22** Job's next word to God is an invitation to start the debate. He politely and respectfully gives God the privilege of speaking first. Whether there was a pause at this point to allow God to speak is not indicated in the text. But this is not really an issue, for Job certainly knew that God could break in at any time he desired. Job was the one who asked for a debate in the first place, so he probably sees himself as the plaintiff. His questions to God begin immediately in v 23.

■ **23** "How many are my iniquities and my sins? Make me know my transgression and my sin" (NRSV). Job's first question goes straight to the heart of the controversy between him and his friends: "Am I a sinner or not?" Both Job and his friends believed that God had caused Job's suffering. The crucial question is, "Why?" Was it due to sin in his life, as the friends have said? Or is there some other explanation? The right to know what one is charged with is an essential part of any fair judicial system. Job staunchly believed in his own righteousness, and he was well prepared to defend that position if God should challenge him. Since God is the only one who can give a definitive answer to this question, Job wishes to hear directly from God himself. And he wants the friends to hear the answer too.

As he did in 7:20-21, Job brings together the three standard words for "sin" in the OT: "iniquity" (*ʿāwôn*), "sin" (*ḥaṭṭāʾt*), and "transgression" (*pešaʿ*). There are slight differences of meaning in each, but here they are used as synonyms (→ 7:21 for a more detailed discussion). As Hartley notes, "The combination of these words for sin encompasses all the possible ways of breaking God's law" (1988, 227).

If God had stepped in at this point and answered Job's question, the book could have ended with ch 13. But God's silence continues until ch 38. The reason for God's delay in answering human prayers is one of the intriguing mysteries of the book.

■ **24** The second significant question Job asks God is, **Why do you hide your face . . . ?** The hiddenness of God is a topic that appears on a regular basis in the OT, usually in one of two forms. Some passages emphasize God's hiddenness as a sign of his supernatural mysteriousness (34:29; Prov 25:2; Isa 45:15). Job has already drawn upon this image in Job 9:11, complaining that it hinders divine-human communication. "God may be very near," Job says, "but I cannot see him." The implication is, "Therefore I cannot talk to him about my suffering." A second group of passages speaks of God's hiddenness as a sign of his anger (Deut 32:16-20; Ps 89:46 [47 HB]; Mic 3:4). God "hides his face" from individuals or nations because of their sinfulness. Job 13:24*b* confirms that God's anger is the reason intended here.

In previous passages Job has implied that God treated him like an **enemy** (6:4; 7:12-20; 9:17-19; 10:2-17). But this is the first time he actually uses that word. There is a great similarity in Hebrew between the word for **enemy** (*'ôyēb*) and Job's own name (*'iyyôb*). Some suggest that the author has created a play on words here to enliven Job's speech in a way that will cause God to consider whether he has confused the two (Reyburn 1992, 262).

■ **25** This verse contains two metaphors that enlarge upon the question raised in 13:24. Why does God desire to **terrify** (*'rṣ*) and **pursue after** (*rdp*) something so insignificant as a **leaf** or **chaff**? There is no logic to God's actions. In treating Job as an enemy, God has brought all his divine powers to bear against a helpless individual who is now close to death. The contest is very one-sided and unfair.

■ **26** Job now begins a series of accusations against God. The first portrays God as a judge who has sentenced (**you write down**) Job to a life of suffering. The judgment was designed to be **bitter** and it had certainly achieved its goal, for Job has already described himself as bitter in soul three times (3:20; 7:11; 10:1).

The second accusation connects Job's suffering with unnamed sins during his youth (Ps 25:7). Apparently, youthful indiscretions (lit. "the iniquities of my youth" [NRSV]) were a part of Job's earlier life. Job may have long forgotten the details of these distant events, but God has not, for he has caused Job to **inherit** the consequences for his earlier actions.

The fact that Job mentions these iniquities indicates he was aware of wrongdoing in his life at an early age. However, he would probably say in his own defense, either: (1) these were trivial indiscretions committed before adulthood and are therefore not significant enough to cause his immense suffering; or more likely, (2) these youthful sins had all been forgiven by God at some point in the past. Thus, he is now blameless as described in the prologue (1:1).

This is the first time Job has even come close to hinting that he himself may be the cause of his suffering. But he is only raising a possibility here that no one has mentioned before. In essence, he is saying to God, "I am accusing you of punishing me for the sins of my youth. Please respond and tell me whether or not this is true." By doing so, he hoped God would speak and identify the real cause of his suffering.

■ **27** Job hurls three more accusations against God for restricting his movement. These should be taken as metaphors describing how God's judgment has impacted Job's ability to function in life. First, he cannot go anywhere to escape from God because God has "put my feet in the stocks" (NRSV). The word for "stocks" (*sad*) appears only here and in 33:11. Cognates in Syriac and Aramaic point to some type of wooden restraint with holes in it for the feet (Gordis 1978, 146).

Second, God **watches** his every movement (**my paths**). Even if he could wriggle out of the stocks, God's surveillance of him would prevent his escape.

The third accusation is the most difficult to interpret. The literal rendering is: "you inscribe for yourself on the roots of my feet." "Roots" (*šōreš*) is usually taken to mean **soles** of the feet. Some have proposed that this refers to making some kind of mark on the soles of slaves' feet so they can be followed and captured if they escape (NIV). But there are no examples in the ANE of marking slaves on their feet. Another suggestion is to treat the verb "inscribe" (*ḥqh*, related to *ḥqq*) as meaning "draw a boundary around" (Prov 8:27). This yields: "you set a bound to the soles of my feet" that limits my movement (NRSV). This interpretation is more likely, but the third accusation remains unclear.

All these accusations are parallel with earlier complaints by Job about being God's target (6:4; 7:20), God's prey (10:16), and God's enemy (13:24). As Job describes it, God will not quit harassing him.

■ **28** The pronoun "he" (*hû'*) at the beginning of this verse has caused much discussion. One interpretation is that Job has switched to speaking about himself in the third person: "That one [meaning 'myself'] is worn out" (*blh*) (Clines 1989, 323). Another is to treat v 28 as beginning a new section with the antecedent of "he" being "humanity as a whole" ("mortals") in 14:1 (Gordis 1978, 146). The former is preferable based on the literary structure of the passage (Clines 1989, 323).

Because of the things God has done to him (13:26-27), his life has now disintegrated **like something rotten**. The LXX emends the word for **rotten** (*rāqāb*) to "wine skin" (*rōqeb*). This is a possibility (see Josh 9:4 where *blh* is used with another word for "wineskin"). But *rōqeb* does not appear anywhere else in the OT and *rāqāb* makes good sense. Job knew that his physical condition was not getting any better. His body was gradually wasting away **like a garment eaten by moths**.

7. Human Beings Are Destined for Trouble (14:1-22)

In 7:1-6 Job connected his own misfortunes with those of all humanity in a few brief statements. In ch 14 he returns to the same topic in much greater depth. For Job, all human beings are faced with multiple troubles throughout their lifetime. In vv 13-17 he briefly imagines exiting this world until God's anger subsides. Thus he could avoid any further suffering. But he quickly comes back to reality, recognizing the impossibility of what he has just imagined. The rest of the chapter is composed of mournful observations on the human condition, directed at God.

■ **1-2** Three times previously Job has mentioned that his time on earth is short-lived (7:6-7; 9:25-26; 10:20). He has also repeatedly complained about the **turmoil** (*rōgez*; 3:17, 26) in his life. In 14:1 he expands on this thought to include all humanity. We all live relatively short lives and experience times of suffering. Eliphaz and Bildad have already agreed with him on this point (5:6-7; 8:9), and the psalmist adds support as well (Ps 90:9-10).

The phrase **born of woman** (*yĕlûd 'iššâ*) appears two other times in Job (15:14; 25:4) and nowhere else in the OT. Some have suggested the phrase implies human weakness or ritual uncleanness at the time of birth. But more likely, in all these passages it is simply a Hebrew idiom for a "human being," similar to the phrase "son of man" (*ben 'ādām*) used throughout the book of Ezekiel (e.g., Ezek 2:1).

In Job 14:2 Job adds two illustrations to support his observation on the shortness of life. First, he compares it to **flowers** of the field that blossom beautifully during the rainy season but **wither away** when the rain stops. His second example is **fleeting shadows** that disappear whenever light is present. Both metaphors appear in other OT passages: "flowers" (Ps 103:15-16; Isa 28:1, 4; 40:6-8); "shadows" (Job 8:9; 1 Chr 29:15; Pss 102:11 [12 HB]; 109:23; 144:4; Eccl 6:12; 8:13).

■ **3** In light of the brevity and turmoil of human life, Job wonders why God pays human beings any attention at all. Why bother with a creature so insignificant? Job has complained several times already that God was watching him too closely (7:16-20; 10:16; 13:27). He wished that God would leave him alone. In 14:3 he accuses God of treating other human beings in the same way. He fixes his eagle eye on everyone, looking for wrongdoing. Further, God brings each one into **judgment** (*mišpāṭ*) with him, whether or not a sinner.

In v 3*b*, instead of **them**, the MT has the pronoun "me" (*'ōtî*) whereas the LXX has "him" (*'ōtô*). "Me," being the harder reading, is most likely the original. One can easily understand why a scribe would change "me" to "him" since the principal topic throughout this section is human beings in general. However, Job moves freely back and forth throughout ch 14 between his own experiences and those of all humanity. He tends to project his own troubles onto everyone else. So the meaning of the verse is basically the same no matter which pronoun is used. Other examples of this practice occur in 3:20-26 and 7:1-6.

■ **4** This verse begins with the idiomatic expression *mî yittēn*, which indicates an unfulfilled desire: "if only . . ." / "would that . . ." The form has appeared several times already (6:8; 11:5; 13:5). The literal translation of v 4*a* is: "If only a clean thing from an unclean thing." The words for "clean" (*ṭāhôr*) and "unclean" (*ṭāmē'*) in both their verbal and nominative forms occur repeatedly in Leviticus, Numbers, and Deuteronomy in reference to various regulations regarding ritual purity, but Job is not talking about ritual purity here. His concern is the kind of moral cleanness/uncleanness that is subject to God's judgment (v 3).

The main problem in interpreting this verse is related to a missing main verb. Some insert a verb such as "produce," yielding the following: "If only a clean thing could be produced from an unclean thing" (see NIV, NJPS, NRSV). By this, Job wishes that humans could be made morally clean. His emphatic answer, **No one!**, indicates this is impossible because all human beings are naturally unclean and remain so.

However, this view sounds more like something Eliphaz would say (4:17-21; 15:14-16). Certainly Job regarded *himself* as righteous, so not everyone was unclean. And further, Job is speaking to God here. He would not likely describe God as being unable to make someone clean (Lev 16:30; Ps 51:2, 7, 10 [4, 9, 12 HB]; Jer 31:31-34; 33:8; Ezek 36:25-27, 29, 33).

Some early church fathers used this verse in support of the doctrine of original sin ("Clement of Rome, Clement of Alexandria, Cyprian of Carthage, Ambrose of Milan, Augustine, Jerome" [Seow 2013, 670]). But this is pushing the meaning too far.

Other scholars prefer a verb such as "distinguish," rendering: "If only a clean thing could be distinguished from an unclean thing" (Gordis 1978, 147). God, when he judges people, should be able to distinguish between the righteous and the wicked. But apparently God cannot make this distinction, for he treats them all the same. Job has already accused God twice of this fault (9:20-23; 10:14-15), so this is the more likely interpretation. But the verse remains difficult.

■ **5-6** Job's thoughts in 14:5 are on the span of time that God allows for human life in general, not for each individual person. Whether Job had in mind a set number of years, such as the biblical ideal of seventy years (Ps 90:10), is unknown. The important point is that God has set **limits** (Job 14:5*c*; *ḥōq*) on human existence that are very short (v 1). The same word is used in other parts of Job in reference to God's limits on the dividing line between light and darkness (26:10), the boundary of the sea (38:8-11), the times for rain (28:26), and the courses of the stars (38:33). All of these contribute to one of the principal concepts in the wisdom literature, namely that God has established his order in the universe.

Since life spans on earth are limited, Job implores God to **look away** (v 6*a*) from humanity and **let him alone**. Job's plea in behalf of all humanity is the same that he voiced for himself in two previous speeches (7:16, 19; 10:20). If God would turn his attention somewhere else, then maybe humans could "enjoy, like laborers, their days" (14:6*b* NRSV) (meaning "their brief time on earth"). In a previous passage (7:1), Job described the work of a day laborer as "hard labor," certainly nothing to "enjoy" (*rṣh*). Sensing a problem here, some versions find another meaning for *rṣh*: "fulfills" (NASB), "finishes" (NJPS), **put in his time** (NIV). But as Seow notes, the word "enjoy" may be used ironically here (2013, 686).

■ **7-9** Job now moves from commenting on the human condition to observations about trees. He uses these trees as an illustration for his next main point in 14:10-12.

The kind of tree Job has in mind is of a type such as the olive tree that is very hardy and difficult to kill. Some in Palestine are hundreds of years old. After these trees are **cut down** (v 7), and from all appearances look dead, often **new shoots** will appear out of the old **stump** (v 8). Even trees that seem to die from old age or drought can be brought back to life with additional watering. As Job describes it, they are so eager to live again that if water is even in the vicinity (**at the scent of water** [v 9]), these trees **will bud** and begin to grow *like a new seedling* (*neṭa'*). Thus, **there is hope** [*tiqwâ*] **for a tree** (v 7). In other words, parts of God's creation live with a constant hope that life can get better; it can be rejuvenated. This helps them survive through even the worst of times.

■ **10-12** But whereas trees have every hope that they will be rejuvenated after they are cut down, human beings experience the exact opposite. They "do not rise again" (v 12 NRSV). Their removal from this life is permanent. It will last **till the heavens are no more**, that is, forever.

Job adds a further illustration to support his point. Just as the water in a **lake** (*yām*) or **river** (*nāhār*) can dry up and disappear, so a *strong man* (*geber*; → 4:17) loses his power and strength in death and vanishes from sight. People ask, *"Where is he?"* (14:10*b*), but they will never see him again.

■ **13** "An impossible dream" (Clines 1989, 330) is Job's next topic. He wishes for a place to **hide** from the anger of God. The verse begins with the interrogative phrase, **If only**, that has appeared twice in this speech already (13:5; 14:4 [translated as "who"]). It indicates a hypothetical scenario that he knows will never happen. Job was aware that there was no spot on earth exempt from the presence of God, for he had already spoken of God's knowledge of and power over every human being (7:17-18; 12:10). His only option of escape, then, was to exit this world temporarily into **Sheol** (3:19) until God's **anger** dissipated.

Of course, Job knew that Sheol was the land of no return (7:9; 14:14). "To go to Sheol" meant to die and be removed from life on earth forever. So he wants God to establish first **an appointed time** ($ḥōq$) for his release, lest he be forgotten. In effect, he is asking God to make a mark on his calendar or tie a string around his finger as a reminder. Then at the appointed time, God would **remember** him and bring him back to life on earth again. This verse confirms that Job believed God's anger was responsible for his suffering (12:9; 13:24-27).

■ **14** The rhetorical question in 14:14a acknowledges that Job's wish in v 13 was a pipe dream. When someone dies, their time on earth is finished. There is no possibility of ever returning to life in this world.

The LXX renders the question into a statement: "He will live!" This translation probably is the result of a shift in theological thinking during the intertestamental period when Judaism began to develop the concept of a resurrection and a meaningful afterlife. Job's comment as recorded in the MT would have been regarded by many as heresy at the time the LXX was being translated.

One interpretation of Job's **hard service** is the time he would spend in Sheol waiting for God to call and release him (v 15). But in 7:1 Job referred to "hard service" as the difficult lot of day laborers. Thus, 14:14bc is probably a reference to his present tortured existence from which he desires relief in Sheol (v 13). "I would wait" (NRSV) indicates Job's desperation to be released from suffering. The statement is similar to our modern idiom: "I would give my right arm to make this happen."

■ **15** Here Job describes what his new life on earth would be like once he returns from Sheol. No longer would God hide his face and regard Job as his enemy (13:24). Instead, God would seek him out and **call** his name. God would even **long for** fellowship with "the work of your hands" (NRSV). In Job's imagination of the future, God's treatment of him would be totally different from what he is experiencing at the present moment (10:3-17).

For his part, Job would immediately **answer** God. Unlike Adam and Eve who hid from God because of guilt over their sin (Gen 3:8-9), Job had nothing to hide (13:18). He would welcome the opportunity for communication with God. No doubt, Job was thinking back to the time before his suffering began. He knew exactly how God treated righteous people because he had already experienced it in prior days. Significantly, the life of fellowship with God that Job desires here is the norm for any follower of God. Both Testaments confirm this (Ps 23; John 10:14-15; 1 Cor 1:9; 1 John 1:3).

Job 14:15 is crucial for understanding Job's heart. His previous speeches created the impression that death was his only interest now (ch 3; 6:8-9; 10:18-22). But 14:15 reveals a tiny, tiny flicker of hope buried deep within. In spite of all his whining and complaining, Job really does desire fellowship again with his Creator. "If only . . ." is his heart's deepest cry.

Unfortunately, Job sees no way to make this happen. In spite of repeated requests for God to talk to him, God has avoided any contact. So Job's hope has basically disintegrated into wishful thinking, overwhelmed by his pain and suffering. As he says in v 19, God has destroyed his "hope."

■ **16-17** These two verses are capable of two different interpretations. One carries on Job's "impossible dream" from vv 13-15 (NIV, NJPS, NRSV). The other returns to the harsh reality of Job's present anguish (13:24-27 NEB). Here are the problems scholars wrestle with: (1) The Hebrew adverb *'attâ* (14:16a) can be translated as "now," indicating a present condition, or **then**, implying a future possibility (e.g., Amos 6:7; Mic 5:3 [4 HB]; 7:10). The context calls for **then**. (2) **You would count my steps** (Job 14:16a) can refer to God's close examination of Job's life in a hostile or a benevolent way. (3) Sealing up Job's transgressions in a bag (v 17a) and plastering over his iniquities (v 17b; 13:4) can be interpreted as arising from a desire to preserve evidence for later accountability, or as compassionate measures to remove any barriers to fellowship between God and Job.

The "impossible dream" interpretation seems best in this context, meaning God would no longer be looking for every possible **sin** (*ḥaṭṭā't*), "transgression" (*pešaʻ*; NRSV), or "iniquity" (*ʻāwôn*; NRSV) that he could uncover (these words are all synonyms; → 7:20-21; 13:23). If any existed, he would seal them up **in a bag** or **plaster over** (→ 13:4) them, thus removing them from his sight. Job is not admitting that any sins are a part of his life. But he believes that God is determined, for whatever reason, to find some fault in him that he can use against him. Job has even suggested that God may be using some obscure indiscretion out of his youthful past (13:26) as a pretext for punishing him. However, all that close examination of his life would disappear when God released him from Sheol.

■ **18-19** Before finishing this speech, Job returns to his mournful comments on the human condition (14:1-12). In this present life, human beings have no **hope** for the future (v 19). They are not like the tree (vv 7-9) that is capable of rejuvenation even after it is cut down. They are more like the **mountain** that **crumbles** away, the **rock** that tumbles to a different place, the **stones** that are worn smooth by the waters of a stream, and the **soil** that is washed away by a sudden downpour (the word imagery moves from the greater to the lesser [Seow 2013, 679]). Just as the forces of nature—water, sun, wind, and earthquakes—are constantly wearing away and reshaping the appearance of the earth, so God relentlessly **destroy**s any **hope** (*tiqwâ*; 11:18) that humans may have for a better life without suffering.

In 14:19*b* many emend the Hebrew *sĕpîḥeyhā* ("second growth") to *sĕḥîpâ* ("rainstorm," "downpour") (following *HALOT*, 749, 764). Others relate the word to an alternate meaning of *sph* ("pour out," *CDCH*, 301). In either case the context calls for a translation such as **torrents** or ***downpours***.

■ **20** Life ends at God's discretion. As Job describes it, after God has harassed individuals sufficiently, he finally **overpowers** them and **sends them away** to Sheol. Before death, though, God adds one last insult. He imposes a change on the doomed person's appearance (lit. "[you] change his face"). No doubt, Job is thinking of his own appearance at this point, knowing he is in the final chapter of his life, and wondering how long it will be until God sends him away.

■ **21-22** In Sheol social interaction ceases (3:17-19) and parents lose contact with their children. The dead are unaware whether their children succeed (**are honored**) or fail (**are brought low**).

Some regard 14:22 as also descriptive of Sheol, but such a view is not likely. While the description of hell in the NT is that of a place of constant torment (Matt 8:12; 13:42, 50; 22:13; 24:51; 25:30; Luke 13:28; Rev 20:10, 14-15), in the OT torment is generally not attributed to Sheol (Job 26:5 may be an exception). Thus, 14:22 concerns people at death's door. These individuals become preoccupied with their own rapidly crumbling existence. The physical pain and emotional suffering experienced by their **bodies** and souls consume whatever energies they have left.

FROM THE TEXT

Summary of Job's Response to Zophar. Throughout this speech Job emphasizes God's overwhelming power to do whatever he desires. He controls all levels of human society. Even great nations are no match for him. Thus, Job knew that God could avoid speaking with him if he so chose. Nevertheless, he challenges God to listen to his side of the story. He has his case all prepared and is ready to deliver it if God shows up.

One of the remarkable characteristics of this speech is that Job says so little in his own defense. We are led to believe in 13:13-19 that he is ready to deliver a masterful oration that will challenge God's evaluation of him and demonstrate his personal integrity. In these verses Job utters brave words of challenge, acknowledges the risks he is taking that may cost him his life, points out the thoroughness of his preparation, and confidently predicts that he will be vindicated. This seems to be a high point in his enthusiasm.

Yet when he finally begins to argue his case, there is nothing noteworthy about his presentation (13:23-27). His case boils down to these two issues: (1) a request for a list of the sins he has committed; and (2) a question about why God treats him so cruelly without any explanation. He presents no evidence concerning his own righteousness or of God's vindictiveness toward him. All his bravado vanishes very quickly by the end of ch 13, and he slips back into depression in ch 14. Further, he says very little directly to God in the remainder of the book. This may mean, as Clines notes, that he has said "all he wants to" (1989, 316). On the other hand, it may indicate that Job had promised more than he could deliver. We are left wondering what happened to his bold enthusiasm. His claims ring hollow.

Job's speech ends on a very dismal note. His challenge to God (13:20-28) that was presented with such vigor went unanswered, leaving him deeply depressed. Further, Job saw the rest of humanity as no better off than himself. God just gradually destroys us, like lakes that dry up or mountains that erode away (14:11, 18-19). We all are without hope of a good life.

Job's response to Zophar contains the following points:

- My friends, you treat me as inferior, yet your claims to speak for God are inaccurate and deceptive. Ask nature if you want to know the truth. Someday God will rebuke you for your false counsel.
- Only God has perfect wisdom. Therefore, I will seek his counsel rather than my friends'.
- God is more powerful than any person or nation. He can destroy them whenever he pleases. He may destroy me when I claim my innocence to him, but I am determined to defend my integrity.
- God, I deserve to know what sins you are punishing me for. I also would like to know why you treat me like your enemy. You act as if I am the worst of sinners, yet I know differently.
- Life for human beings is so hopeless. Even a tree stump has more hope for a better future.
- I deeply wish there were some way I could disappear for a period of time until God ceases to hate me. Perhaps I could hide in Sheol, but before I go I would want God to set a time for my release.
- I remember fondly the good old days when God and I enjoyed fellowship. How I wish that could be repeated. But I know God will never allow it. He just mercilessly wears me down to nothing. It won't be long until I descend to Sheol.

IV. SECOND CYCLE OF SPEECHES: JOB 15—21

15:1—
21:34

BEHIND THE TEXT

The second cycle of speeches follows the same order as the first. Each of the friends speaks without interruption followed by a response from Job. This time around the tone is considerably harsher. Job "has touched a nerve" in the first cycle that needs their immediate response and condemnation (Chase 2013, 96). There also seems to be a common theme from all of them. Each friend is intent on describing the punishments that God inflicts on the wicked (15:17-35; 18:5-21; 20:4-29).

The purpose of such a united attack is probably twofold. First, they want to make Job fully aware of the troubles that await him if he refuses to heed their advice. There is no escape from the consequences of sin. In the friends' way of thinking, Job already had one foot in the camp of the wicked, and he was close to putting the other foot in as well. He needed to be warned before it was too late.

The second purpose is to suggest very subtly that Job may already be experiencing God's judgment for sins committed in the past. His present sufferings sound exactly like what the wicked endure. This has to be more than just coincidence. Job looked like a sinner, talked like a sinner, acted like a sinner, and was being punished like a sinner. Therefore, he must be one. The comparison was so obvious. One can almost hear them mutter under their breath, "Oh by the way, do you know anyone around here who is experiencing these afflictions right now?" Significantly, not one of the friends encourages Job with words of hope about a better future (in contrast to the first cycle of speeches).

Job responds by calling his friends worthless again. They are just plain wrong in their evaluation of his situation. He pointedly blames God for all his suffering, noting that God treats other people unjustly as well. He also reveals the toll he has had to pay in his social relationships. They have disintegrated completely. He still believes he is innocent of sin and makes a bold pronouncement about his future. He has a witness in heaven who will testify to his innocence (16:19) and a redeemer who will someday vindicate him (19:25).

Finally, in his last speech to Zophar (ch 21) he addresses the main topic the friends have raised—God's punishment of the wicked. His observations are completely different from theirs. The wicked are rewarded, not punished. God does not seem to judge them at all.

IN THE TEXT

A. Eliphaz's Second Speech (15:1-35)

Eliphaz has had some time now to listen to his colleagues' arguments and think about Job's responses. He senses that Job is not listening to them at all. When they presented what they believed was the correct way to view his problems, Job seemed to go off in another direction. So for his second speech, Eliphaz turns up the volume. Probably most parents are guilty of doing the same when they sense their children are not listening.

Eliphaz has three main points:
1. Do You Know More than We Do? (15:1-13)
2. All Human Beings Are Sinful (15:14-16)
3. The Wicked Suffer Terribly (15:17-35)

1. Do You Know More than We Do? (15:1-13)

In contrast to his first speech, there is no complimentary beginning. Eliphaz immediately goes on the attack, accusing Job of being a windbag and talking like he is the only one with wisdom. But Job has more problems than just wordiness. His speeches reveal a lack of reverence for God and major deficiencies in his knowledge. Job needs to listen more carefully to the three friends, for they speak the truth passed down by the sages over centuries of time.

■ 1 The character of **Eliphaz** is discussed in 2:11 (→). For comments on the standard introductory formula → 3:2.

■ 2-3 In Job's preceding speech (chs 12—14) he claimed twice that his wisdom was as great as that of the friends (12:3; 13:1-2). He also accused the friends of misrepresenting God's position and speaking falsely and deceptively (13:7). Eliphaz is not about to let this charge go unanswered, for he is convinced Job does not know what he is talking about.

Using a series of rhetorical questions in 15:2-3, Eliphaz challenges Job's claim to wisdom: "**Would a wise person** speak like you have been speaking?" The implication is that Job does not speak with the depth of thought and discipline for which the sages were known (Prov 17:27). Instead, his words are nothing more than "windy knowledge" (Job 15:2a NRSV), and his passionate outbursts sound as if his **belly** (v 2b) is filled with the **east wind**. The **east wind** was known for being hot and destructive and may have been the source of the windstorm that killed Job's children (1:19). In addition, Job's arguments are **useless** (15:3) and **have no value**. There is no point in addressing rebellious questions to God because God will never answer them. He expects devotion, not complaints. In short, Job's arguments and style of speaking are clearly unlike those of the true sages.

■ 4 Eliphaz's next accusation is a religious one. Job has **undermined** (*prr*) **reverence** (lit. "fear") for God and **hindered/*diminished*** (*gr'*) "serious thought" (Gray 2010, 238-39; the NRSV renders *śîḥâ* as "meditation" following Ps 119:97, 99) about **God** (*El*). Job's view of the world is one of disorder. His questioning of God's justice upsets the traditional way the sages looked at the world. Job is not only wrong in his theology but also "dangerous" (Andersen 1976, 175). His criticisms of God threaten the principles of the wisdom theology and raise doubts in the minds of others about God's goodness. In Eliphaz's mind, Job is a one-person wrecking ball to all religious faith.

■ 5-6 According to Eliphaz, Job's attitude is sinful, causing him to say things he never said before. "Iniquity" (*'āwôn*; NRSV) has captured his heart and now "teaches" (NRSV) his **mouth** to speak words that are **crafty** (→ 5:12). Probably Eliphaz had in mind Job's repeated attempts to deflect criticism away from himself and onto God and the three friends. Job had claimed that God had caused his suffering and now refuses to tell him why (10:2; 12:9-10; 13:23-27). He also believed that the friends were ignorant of the ways of God (13:7, 12). But Job's words were nothing more than a smokescreen designed to disguise his own failures by talking about others.

In Eliphaz's thinking, the only person Job is deceiving with this craftiness is himself. The proof of Eliphaz's judgment is found in Job's own **mouth** (15:6), for he says things that are not true. Eliphaz does not have to prove him wrong, for Job's words are evidence enough that he is guilty of sin and ignorant of God's ways.

■ 7-9 In his previous speech (chs 12—14) Job insisted that his knowledge was as great as the friends, if not greater (12:3; 13:1-2). He further pointed out that their advice was absolutely worthless (13:4, 12). Therefore, he sought to hear directly from God rather than the friends (13:3, 22).

Eliphaz's response in 15:7-9 indicates that he is greatly disturbed by Job's quick dismissal of their advice. He seeks to counter Job's arrogant attitude with a series of rhetorical questions. In essence, Eliphaz is questioning Job's credentials. What makes him think he is the only one with **wisdom** (v 8*b*)? Is he older than everyone else? Has he obtained some additional knowledge from God that no other human being possesses?

Verse 7 questions his level of experience; v 8, his access to God. Both questions are worded in a sarcastic way that emphasizes the impossibility of Job having more wisdom than anyone else. In Rom 11:34 Paul alludes to Job 15:8 by praising God's superior knowledge over all human beings. No person has ever "listened in the council of God [*Eloah*]" (NRSV).

Some scholars connect v 7*a* with Adam before the fall (Gordis 1978, 160). Others, with an ancient myth about a primeval man who existed in the heavenly realm before Adam (Hartley 1988, 245-46). This man had extraordinary wisdom because he could eavesdrop on God's council of divine beings (1:6; 2:1). This myth, which appears in the intertestamental literature, may also be alluded to in Ezek 28:12-15. "Adapa" (*ANET*, 101-3), an Akkadian myth from the fourteenth century BC, has also been cited as a possible source for the imagery of a primeval man (Seow 2013, 700-701). Whether there is an allusion here to any of these is unclear. What is certain is that Eliphaz is totally convinced of the folly of Job's claim to wisdom.

In 15:7*b* Eliphaz connects Job's claim with Lady Wisdom's statement that she was the first of God's creative acts, appearing before the rest of the world and assisting God in the acts of creation (Prov 8:22-31). The author of Job has borrowed this concept from Proverbs to show how ridiculous Job's arguments appear to the friends.

■ **10** The literal translation of Job 15:10*a* is: **The gray-haired** [sg.] **and the aged** [sg.] **are** "with us" or "among us." Does the phrase "with us" refer to the intellectual support the aged provide for the position of the friends (NIV, NRSV), or to the actual physical presence of an elderly person in their midst (NASB, NJPS)? Scholars are divided on the correct interpretation. If the former is correct, then Eliphaz is mustering support for his position by connecting it with the well-established wisdom theology of the ancient world (i.e., the sages are **on our side**). Both he (5:27; 15:17-18) and Bildad (8:8-10) have already advocated for this view. And Job has acknowledged that the concept is supported by the friends, although he does not agree with it (12:12-13).

If the latter interpretation is accurate, Eliphaz is claiming superior wisdom for himself due to his greater age. Job is too young to understand the nature of his troubles. He needs to consult the expertise of the aged—people **even older than your father**. Either interpretation is possible, but this writer leans toward the latter view. If correct, then this is the only passage in the book that hints at the relative ages of the participants. Eliphaz would have been the oldest, maybe even as old as Job's father, and the other friends would have been around the same age as Job or a little older. However, one needs to be cautious in speaking of their ages without additional evidence.

■ **11-13** Eliphaz now questions Job's failure to accept **God's** [*El*] **consolations** as a source of encouragement (v 11). Although God had not yet talked to Job directly, Eliphaz believed that God had used the words of the friends to comfort Job until such time as his suffering ceased. In fact, Eliphaz stated earlier that one of his messages came directly from God in a vision (4:12-21).

In his first speech Eliphaz was very careful to speak **gently** to Job. He complimented Job, pointing out his fear of God and his kindness to others who were experiencing hardships (4:3-6). He also held out hope that Job would soon be experiencing God's blessings after a brief time of discipline (5:17-27). He really expected Job to accept their counsel as coming from God himself. However, Eliphaz's gentle approach has hardened by the time of his second speech. He is alarmed that Job has changed from a model of righteousness into a raging firebrand, venting angry emotional outbursts (15:12-13).

2. All Human Beings Are Sinful (15:14-16)

If the angels are morally inferior to God, then logically human beings must be even more inferior. Thus, Job has no grounds to stand on when he claims he is innocent of sin. The implication here, as in 4:17-19, is that all humanity including Job should expect some amount of discipline from God or punishment for sin, because God's level of perfection is impossible to attain. This thought is repeated for a third time by Bildad in 25:4-6, so this is a concept that is deeply ingrained in the friends' theology.

■ **14-16** Eliphaz returns to his earlier vision about the tremendous moral gulf between God and humanity (4:17-19). God's moral perfection is far superior to that of any other creature whether on earth or in heaven. No human being (for one **born of woman** [15:14*b*], → 14:1) is **pure** (*zkh*; 15:14*a*) or **righteous** (*ṣdq*; v 14*b*). All are sinful in their natural state. As a point of comparison, Eliphaz turns to the **holy ones** (v 15*a*; another term for "angels" [4:18; 5:1]) and **the heavens** (15:15*b*) for examples.

The heavenly beings and the place where they lived were usually regarded as pure because of their closeness to God himself. But even they fall far short of the moral perfection of God. Therefore, how much less in God's eyes are human beings? To God, human creatures are **vile** (v 16) and morally **corrupt**. They quench their thirst on "wrongdoing" (*'awlâ*; NJPS; → 11:14) as if it were nourishing water. The word for **vile** (*t'b*) refers to something that is detestable to God (e.g., Canaanite religious practices [Lev 18:26-30]).

3. The Wicked Suffer Terribly (15:17-35)

The three friends have already briefly mentioned God's punishment of the wicked (4:8-9; 8:13; 11:11, 20). But in the second cycle of speeches this topic will become a major theme. Using a variety of illustrations and metaphors, the friends expound on the terrible life the wicked must endure. Many calamities will befall them, affecting them in multiple ways—physically, mentally, emotionally, and socially.

On the surface Eliphaz seems to be delivering a straightforward description about the consequences of wickedness, but his list of woes sounds very familiar. He knows that Job has already experienced many of these same troubles, and Job has also been aggressive toward God (15:25-26). So his speech is designed as a wake-up call. In Eliphaz's thinking, Job needs to reexamine his life and submit to God's evaluation (5:8) before his sufferings increase even further.

■ **17-19** Eliphaz begins the third section by calling on Job to listen to him, just as Job had earlier demanded the friends' attention (13:13). He is about to present to Job a long list of woes experienced by the wicked. These unfortunate people live miserable lives. They are continually beset with trouble, and they are tormented both internally and externally.

What I have seen (*hzh*; 15:17*b*) may hint at some type of divine revelation such as described in 4:12-21 (Isa 1:1; Amos 1:1; Mic 1:1). But his words are based primarily on the teachings of the sages. Thus, if Job wishes to disagree with him, he will have to refute many generations of time-honored traditions that **their ancestors** (Job 15:18*b*; lit. "their fathers") have passed down to the present. Eliphaz regards these traditions as true and reliable. The NRSV has the correct reading for v 18*b*: "and their ancestors have not hidden."

The meaning of **the land** (v 19*a*) is uncertain. Some have tried to connect it with Joel 3:17 [4:17 HB], a verse that speaks of an ideal, holy Jerusalem devoid of foreigners. But Eliphaz, a non-Israelite, would certainly not be referring to the land of Israel. If anything, he had in mind his own land of Teman. The reference, then, would be to an ancient Temanite tradition that regarded their land as one of the original sources of wisdom. He believed that the wisdom of the Temanite sages was unadulterated in its earliest form, before **foreigners** began to modify it (Job 15:19*b*).

A better interpretation that fits the context is that of Seow (2013, 703). God gave to the sages at the beginning of time the wisdom needed to govern **the earth** (v 19*a*) according to his order. Unfortunately, **strangers** (v 19*b*) to this tradition had sometimes garnered attention and distracted from the truth. But the sages continued to hold up the wisdom theology as God's true plan for the earth.

■ **20** Eliphaz's list of woes that befall **the wicked** and **the ruthless** ("the godless" [v 34] is another synonym) begins here. These people are in inner turmoil throughout their lifetime. They "writhe in pain" (NRSV). The kind of pain Eliphaz has in mind is that associated with childbirth (e.g., Isa 26:17-18; Jer 4:31; Mic 4:10). As long as they live, the wicked will experience intense suffering.

■ **21** The wicked are also tormented by **terrifying sounds** and the fear of a surprise attack by "the one who destroys" (*šdd*; lit.). At the very moment when the wicked are relaxing **in peace**, "the destroyer will come upon them" (NRSV). Clines identifies this destroyer as "a demonic power" (1989, 357). However, in Jeremiah the same Qal participle (*šôdēd*) appears twelve times in reference to Yahweh or an agent of Yahweh who brings destruction upon people. A similar meaning is appropriate here—either God or evil plunderers in general (→ Job 12:6) who act as God's agent. This entire section (15:20-35) implies that the sufferings of the wicked are a judgment from God (v 25) against those who reject him.

■ **22** Like miners trapped underground by a cave-in, the wicked have no hope they will ever escape from (lit. "return from"; *šwb*) the **darkness** that surrounds them. Further, there is an even greater darkness awaiting them in Sheol. Job has already acknowledged that he will be in Sheol, the land of darkness, very shortly (10:20-22). Eliphaz may have been trying to connect this earlier comment of Job's with his description of the sufferings of the wicked and thus force him to admit that his troubles were very similar (i.e., guilt by association).

In any case, darkness is a recurring theme in the book of Job (3:4-6; 5:14; 12:25; → "Light and Darkness in Job" sidebar at 11:17). Eliphaz will mention it two more times in this speech (15:23, 30). In v 22*b* Eliphaz points out that the wicked live with the constant fear they will die a violent death (**marked for the sword**). This clause echoes v 21*b*.

■ **23** Scholars have proposed a number of emendations for this verse based on the reading in the LXX translation. There *'ayyēh* (**where?**) is replaced by *'ayyâ* (**vulture**) as a parallel to **sword** in v 22. This yields: "He is cast out as food for vultures" (Clines 1989, 341; the NIV is similar). However, the MT also provides an acceptable meaning: **He wanders about for food. Where (is it)?** (NASB, NJPS, NRSV). The wicked will have a hard time finding the food they need to survive because it is not readily available. Either interpretation is possible. The second clause repeats the thought of v 22*a*. The wicked know that the **darkness** of Sheol will soon encompass them.

■ **24** Job has already admitted that he is terrified by God (7:14; 9:34; 13:21). So Eliphaz seizes the opportunity to connect Job's fears with the fears experienced by the wicked. He uses the terms **distress** and **anguish** to characterize the intense emotional feelings of the wicked. Their pain and despair is extreme and unbearable (15:20-23).

He then adds a simile in the second clause, likening the fears of the wicked to those of a person who must face **a king *ready for battle*** (v 24). Distress and anguish ***overpower*** the wicked, just like a superior military force crushes an opponent. The word for ***battle*** (*kîdôr*) appears only here in the OT. Scholars usually derive its meaning from either an Arabic or Syriac cognate.

■ **25-27** In spite of their inner turmoil, the wicked are outwardly defiant of **God** (*El*; v 25). Their rebellion against **the Almighty** (*Shaddai*) is the real reason for their troubles. God will not tolerate their raised fists and ***arrogant*** attitudes. Eliphaz illustrates this haughtiness by using the metaphor of a young, **strong-necked** (v 26) warrior ***running*** against God with a **thick, *ornamented*** shield to protect himself. Eliphaz's point is that the wicked attempt to challenge the power that rightfully belongs to God by flaunting their own power.

Verse 25a reads literally "Because they stretched out their hands against God" (NRSV). The idiom "stretch out the hand" is used frequently in the OT with God, Moses, or Aaron as the subject. A number of these references appear in the plague stories in Exodus (Exod 7:5, 19; 8:5-6 [1-2 HB], 17 [13 HB]; 9:15, 22; 10:12, 21-22) and in the narrative of the Red Sea crossing (Exod 14:16, 21, 26-27; 15:12). They all point to God's power over nature. Other passages with God as the subject refer to his judgment against nations with whom he is angry (Isa 5:25; Ezek 6:14; 25:7, 13, 16; Zeph 1:4; 2:13). Only in Job 15:25 is the idiom used with rebellious human beings as the subject.

Verse 27 reads: **although he covers his face with his fat, and adds fat on his loins**. The word **although** (*kî*) connects this verse with vv 25-26. Even though the wicked rail at God and charge at him in a display of bravado, their indulgent lifestyle has left them ill-prepared to take on the Almighty. Their faces and midsections are covered with excess fat. They are "nothing more than a fat fool clumsily attempting to play the warrior" (Habel 1985, 259).

The word for fat (*hēleb*) in v 27a appears mostly in passages that refer to the fatty part of a sacrificial animal, but it is used in two places in connection with the excessive lifestyles of the wicked and the arrogant (Pss 73:7; 119:70). The word for *fat* (*pîmâ*) in Job 15:27b occurs only in this passage in the OT. Its meaning as *fat* is usually derived from the parallel word in v 27a.

■ **28-30** The wicked have a bleak future ahead of them. They will be forced to live in the ruins of **destroyed cities** (v 28). They may gather **wealth** for a period of time (v 29), but it **will not endure**. It *will no longer extend* over the land. They will be enveloped in **darkness** (v 30), both in this life and the next. And their physical vitality "will dry up" (NRSV) like plant **shoots** burned by a **flame** (this could refer to a forest fire, as in Ezek 20:47 [21:3 HB], or more likely, the sun). The word for **shoots** (*yôneqet*) generally refers to the new sprouts that develop on a plant or tree that is trying to revive after dormancy or after parts have been cut off (8:16; 14:7). But Eliphaz may be alluding to the offspring of the wicked who will die at an early age.

The translation of 15:30c is uncertain, and many emendations have been proposed (see Clines 1989, 344). The literal translation of the MT is: "he will turn (him) away by the wind of his mouth," meaning that God will drive back the charging wicked person (v 26) using a blast of wind from his mouth. The LXX provides a much different text: "his blossom will fall off." This is similar to v 33b and may have been influenced by it. While the exact translation is not clear, the meaning of v 30 seems to be that the wicked will face the destructive forces of both fire and wind.

■ **31** This verse is sometimes interpreted as being out of context. Some scholars emend the text to conform to the verses on either side that speak of plants, but the MT is understandable and connects with vv 32-33. The NRSV translation is probably the best rendering: "Let them not trust in emptiness, deceiving themselves; for emptiness will be their recompense." Eliphaz here admonishes the wicked to consider the consequences of their actions. If they sow the seeds of "emptiness/worthlessness" (*šāw'*; 7:3; 11:11), they will reap the same. The word for "recompense" (*těmûrâ*; **in return**) appears also in 20:18 and 28:17 with a slightly different meaning.

■ **32-33** The NIV follows the LXX in the first clause of 15:32, emending the verb to one that continues the plant theme from v 30: **Before his time he will wither**. However, the verb in the MT calls for a feminine singular subject, which is supplied by "recompense" in v 31. The NRSV makes the connection between the two verses: "It [i.e., the recompense of the wicked] will be paid in full before their time." In other words, the wicked—those who invest their lives in emptiness—will receive in exchange the "wages of sin" (Rom 6:23), which is an early death. In Job 15:32*b* the illustration of a ***palm branch*** (*kippâ*; Isa 9:14 [13 HB]; 19:15) that ***will not leaf out*** points to a diseased life that will not last long.

The same theme continues in Job 15:33 with two similes. The first is a grape vine that ***violently shakes off*** its fruit before ripening, and the second is **an olive tree** that ***throws off*** its blossoms before they can develop into fruit. In each case, this premature loss of fruit signals that the plant is not healthy and will likely die. So it will be with the wicked.

■ **34** Eliphaz describes the wicked with two more synonyms. The first is **the community of the godless**. **Community** (*'ēdâ*) refers to a group of people who have a common purpose or a common way of living (also 16:7). The word for **godless** (*ḥānēp*) appears eight times in Job (→ 8:13).

The second synonym is "the tents of bribery" (NRSV). This is a metaphor for those who try to secure favors by offering gifts. Bribery is condemned multiple times in the OT because it perverts justice (Exod 23:8; Deut 16:19; Prov 17:23). Job has already denied his own participation in this practice (Job 6:22). God's punishment against the wicked will be severe. These people will be **barren** (3:7) (i.e., without children), and **fire will consume** them and all who live with them.

■ **35** Eliphaz concludes his speech by enlarging on the activities of the wicked, without reference to their punishment as in previous verses. Their desire to do evil is compared to the process of reproduction. They **conceive**, **give birth**, and **their wombs *produce***, not normal children, for they are barren (v 34), but rather the fruits of wickedness—**trouble** (*'āmāl*), **evil** (*'āwen*), and **deceit** (*mirmâ*; acts of fraud and deception). The description of the wicked here is very similar to that in Ps 7:14 [15 HB].

FROM THE TEXT

Summary of Eliphaz's Second Speech. In this chapter Eliphaz is insistent that the wicked are punished for their sins, but he never directly connects Job's suffering with that of the wicked. His speech is more like a general essay on the fate of those who turn against God, using observations gathered by the sages over centuries of time (15:18). But Job could not fail to notice that Eliphaz was subtly speaking about him, for he had already confessed to experiencing many of the same calamities—turmoil (v 20), plunderers (v 21), darkness and the sword (v 22), approaching death (v 23), destroyed house (v 28), loss of wealth (v 29), and fire (v 34). Job disagrees completely with Eliphaz's assessment, and he will eventually fashion a response (ch 21) that presents different evidence and turns Eliphaz's theory on its head. But first he returns to attacking the friends and complaining to God (chs 16—17).

Eliphaz's speech may be summarized as follows:
- Job, you do not speak like a wise person. You sound like a sinner—arrogant, disrespectful of your elders, and critical of God.
- God regards all his creatures, both human and divine, as morally inferior to himself. Thus, you, Job, will undoubtedly receive some amount of suffering for your sins, just like everyone else.
- People who choose a life of wickedness are troubled throughout their life. Outwardly, they may seem to do well, but inwardly they are terrified by threats of attack, darkness, and an early death.

IN THE TEXT

B. Job's Response to Eliphaz (16:1—17:16)

In Job's response to Eliphaz, he repeats several themes he has mentioned before: his friends' ineffective advice, God's hostility toward him, and his own innocence. He also introduces one new concept. He believes there is a witness in heaven who will someday testify in his behalf. But he has no hope this will happen before he dies. Without any possibility of ever enjoying a good life again, Job believes he would be better off in Sheol. And that is where he is headed very shortly.

There are four parts to Job's speech:
1. My Friends, You Are Miserable Comforters (16:1-6)
2. God Has Made Me His Target (16:7-17)
3. I Have a Witness (16:18-22)
4. I Have No Hope for a Better Life (17:1-16)

1. My Friends, You Are Miserable Comforters (16:1-6)

In Job's earlier criticism of his friends (6:14-30), he had only heard from Eliphaz at that time. He was disappointed in Eliphaz's comments, but he was willing to listen to all of them enlighten him from their vast knowledge of the wisdom theology. He needed sound advice that would relieve him of his suffering. But they let him down. They said nothing that applied to his situation. Now that he has heard from all three of them, he recognizes that their advice is worthless. They are unable to understand his plight because they have never experienced troubles like his before. They need to walk in his shoes for a while before handing out advice.

■ **1** For comments on the standard introductory formula → 3:2.

■ **2** Job was not impressed by Eliphaz's second speech. He had heard these things before from both Bildad and Zophar. In his mind, all three friends were worthless to him. Back in 2:11 the author described the purpose of the visit by the friends as seeking to comfort (*nḥm*) Job. But thus far, they have been **miserable comforters** (lit. "comforters of trouble"; → 3:10). Their continual accusations and false remedies have only served to increase his pain and misery. This is the second contemptuous phrase Job has applied to his friends to express his displeasure with their attempts to help him (→ 13:4, "worthless physicians").

■ **3** Job and his friends have already traded barbs over the windiness of each other's speeches (6:26; 8:2; 15:2), so this verse should come as no surprise in the overall scheme of the narrative. Job had tried to shut off the conversation several times (6:14-30; 12:1-6; 13:1-12), but the friends just kept talking. Job's two questions in 16:3 are pointedly directed at Eliphaz in one more attempt to quiet him. He calls Eliphaz's speech nothing more than "windy words" (NRSV), that is, words without any meaningful content.

Job also wants to know *why* Eliphaz continues to argue against him. Is there something bothering him that provokes him to continue talking this way? The Hebrew for **ails** (*mrṣ*) is used in 6:25 in reference to the pain speech can bring. This suggests that Job is asking about a possible painful experience or physical ailment that may be the cause of Eliphaz's windiness.

Clines and Seow take a slightly different approach to this verse. They find it unusual for Job to be addressing only one of the three friends rather than all of them as a group. So they regard 16:3 as a satirical summary of what the friends have said about Job (1989, 378-79; 2013, 732). The speech is generic enough that either interpretation is possible. The NIV, NRSV, and NJPS follow the traditional interpretation.

■ **4-5** To quiet their criticisms of him, Job suggests they consider the possibility of the shoe being on the other foot. How would they want Job to react to them if their roles were reversed and they were the ones who were suffering (→ Eliphaz's role reversal in 5:8)? In such a situation Job **could make fine speeches** (lit. "join words together") that sounded logical and impressive, and he could **shake** his **head** in disagreement with them as they have been doing. Such is the privilege of those who are not suffering. They have all the answers but no experience to support their ideas. **Shake** (*nwʿ*) refers to a back-and-forth movement of the head that signals disagreement and sometimes even ridicule (Pss 22:7 [8 HB]; 109:25).

However, Job might take a much different approach. He could **strengthen** them with his **mouth** (Job 16:5*a*) or remain respectfully silent (v 5*b*; lit. "Sympathy could hold back my lips" [Seow 2013, 742-43]). In his earlier life Job had gained a reputation for providing both encouragement and resources to those in need (4:3-4; 29:7-25). Here he indicates that he could continue that same practice in the future if his friends should fall on hard times.

Verse 5*b* of ch 16 is difficult to interpret. Because the verb lacks a direct object, some supply "your pain" from the context of the same verb in v 6 (i.e., "the consolations of my lips would soothe your pain" [Clines 1989, 367, 369]). Others follow the LXX ("the sympathetic movement of my lips would not be held back"; Hartley 1988, 256), emphasizing the continuous words of encouragement that would pour from Job's mouth. But Seow's interpretation (also Gordis 1978, 175; Newsom 1996, 458) above is best.

■ **6** At the end of the day, all these comments about speaking mean nothing, for Job's experiences tell him that neither wordiness nor silence have helped him understand his suffering. He has tried them both to no avail. God refuses to answer him, and his suffering continues unabated. As if to emphasize that his level of suffering has not diminished since it first began, Job uses the same word for **pain** (*kĕ'ēb*) that the author used in the prologue (2:13). **Is not relieved** (lit. "is not held back"; *ḥśk*) is the same verb as in 16:5*b*.

2. God Has Made Me His Target (16:7-17)

Job turns from criticizing his friends to complaining about God. He has nothing good to say about how God has treated him since the calamities struck. He now considers God his enemy. Seow draws a number of parallels between this section and the complaints against God in the book of Lamentations (2013, 737).

■ **7** No word for **God** appears in this verse, but he is clearly the subject. Job bemoans that God has **worn** him **out** and **devastated** his **entire household** (lit. "all my community"). The word for **household** (*'ēdâ*) is normally applied to large groups of people such as the community of Israel (Exod 12:3; Num 14:1). In this context it refers to all of Job's extended family and his servants. The word also appeared in Job 15:34 in reference to "the ***community*** of the godless." Job slips briefly into addressing God directly in 16:7*b* and 8*a*, but in the remainder of this section he talks about God in the third person.

■ **8** Job's skin disease, which he believes was caused by God, has so disfigured his appearance that his own body now **testifies against** his claims of moral innocence. He looked like he was experiencing the consequences of sin, and thus his appearance supported the position of the friends. In the last chapter Eliphaz pointed this out to Job with a long list of the characteristics of the wicked (15:17-35). Job's problems matched exactly.

In general, Job agrees with Eliphaz's assessment that sin does have consequences, and he has admitted that his appearance looks like that of a sinner. But in his heart he knows he is innocent. If only he could convince everyone else that his suffering was not related to sin. Until God appears and testifies in his behalf, he will have to live with the condemnation of the community.

The verb **shriveled** (*qmṭ*) appears twice in the OT (here and 22:16), so there is little context to provide a good translation. Some opt for a meaning such as "seize/bind" (BDB, 888). But others relate it to a Syriac root meaning "wrinkle" (NIV, NJPS, NRSV). The latter makes sense in light of the parallel with **gauntness** in the second clause.

■ **9** The hostility Job has received from God is very painful. God "has torn" him, "gnashed his teeth" at him, and "sharpens his eyes" at him (NRSV). The verb for "torn" (*ṭrp*) usually expresses an action by wild animals such as wolves and lions that tear apart their prey (Ezek 22:25, 27). "Gnashing one's teeth" (*ḥrq*) is an outward sign of an inner hatred against someone. There is a slight allusion to this clause in the description of the Sanhedrin who "gnashed their teeth at" Stephen when they heard his powerful message about Jesus (Acts 7:54).

The verb for "sharpens" (*lṭš*) appears in three other passages in reference to sharpening tools (1 Sam 13:20), swords (Ps 7:12 [13 HB]), and razors (Ps 52:2 [4 HB]). But in the context of Job 16:9, this verb probably means "to fix one's eyes firmly on a subject so as not to let it get away."

God's hostility was of such magnitude that Job calls him his **enemy** (**opponent**). By this he means that God is actively trying to harm him. Job 16:7-14 provides the evidence Job uses to prove his point. Apparently, the feeling was mutual, for God also treats Job as his enemy, at least as Job sees it (19:11 [*ṣar*]; also 13:24; 33:10 ['*ôyēb*]). The word for **enemy** (*ṣar*) is applied most frequently to nations that attacked Israel (e.g., Num 10:9; Ps 44:5 [6 HB]). But in a few instances God himself is called an enemy of the Israelites because of their disobedience to him (Isa 1:24-25; Lam 2:4).

■ **10** No specific subject is indicated in Job 16:10, so the generic **they** could refer to the three friends. But more likely, Job is speaking of the community in general who know of his plight. They have **opened their mouths** against him. The verb for **opened** (*p'r*) appears one other time in Job (29:23) in reference to the people who opened their mouths to drink from Job's wisdom. In 16:10 the opening of the mouth is for the purpose of mocking and humiliating him. The humiliation of great public figures is a favorite pastime of some people still today.

Verse 10*b* is probably a metaphor for the insults Job has experienced from passersby. It is hard to imagine anyone actually wanting to touch Job and infect themselves with his skin disease. Their mocking had hurt him just as much as a physical slap on the side of the face.

Later in the book, Job will summarize the changes that came into his life after the disasters struck (29:2—30:31). Before he lost everything, people respected him and sought out his advice. He was not lacking for friends, and his influence reached his entire community. But now he is humiliated and reviled by all who pass by his dwelling place at the town garbage dump. No one in his community has befriended him, not even his family and former friends (19:13-22). Even God has turned against him (16:11). As he says in v 10*c*, he feels like the whole world has risen up against him.

■ **11 God** (*El*) is solely responsible for Job's misery. He could have healed Job or at least protected him from the insults of others, but instead he delivered Job into the hands of wicked people who were continually mistreating him.

In v 11*a* the MT has '*ăwîl*, which means "a child" (19:18; 21:11). But this word is not parallel with **the wicked** in 16:11*b* and hence not likely. Most versions emend this to '*awwāl*, meaning "evildoer"—a much more common word in Job (18:21; 27:7; 29:17; 31:3).

■ **12** Earlier in his life Job was *at ease* (*šālēw*); nothing threatened his well-being. But God put an end to his comfortable existence. God **broke** him **in pieces** (*prr*).

This verb is used frequently in reference to breaking the covenant (Deut 31:16; Isa 24:5).

Further, like a predator animal downing its prey, God **seized** him **by the neck** and **mauled** (*pṣṣ*) him. This verb is rare. In the two other occurrences in the OT it refers to the shattering of rocks and mountains by God (Jer 23:29; Hab 3:6). Job is now convinced God has made him **his target** (Job 16:12c). The **target** motif has appeared twice already with different vocabulary (6:4; 7:20). Here the word is *maṭṭārâ* (also in 1 Sam 20:20; Lam 3:12), which seems to mean "a mark" at which archers aim.

■ **13** Metaphorically, God's onslaught is like an attack by **archers**. The word for **archers** is plural, indicating that God has employed multiple means of assault. Job feels helpless in the face of arrows coming from so many directions. The arrows find their mark in his **kidneys**. In the OT the kidneys are often used as a metaphor for one's innermost being—one's heart or the emotions that spring from the heart (Pss 7:9 [10 HB]; 16:7; 26:2; Prov 23:16)—but here Job is referring to his physical kidneys. In warfare an arrow that pierced one's midsection would likely cause the secretion of various fluids out of the wound. The word for **gall** (*mĕrērâ*, from *mrr*, meaning "be bitter") likely refers to these liquids, one of which is the bitter gall produced by the liver.

Without pity describes God's lack of compassion. The Divine Archer relentlessly targets Job with attack after attack. The calamities of the prologue are now well behind Job. But his three friends, whom Job thinks are being used by God, continue to harass him verbally. Later in the book (Job 19:13-22), Job also mentions the social antagonism he has experienced from his family and community. No wonder he feels **surround**ed by all types of enemies. God's lack of compassion is probably the most troubling and bitter aspect of Job's suffering, for it calls into question the goodness of God's character.

■ **14** The next word picture is that of a fortified city under attack. God opens up multiple breaches in the wall as the siege progresses. This leaves Job weak and vulnerable. "To make a breach in a wall" (*prṣ*) was a common method of attack in ancient warfare. The word appears in several accounts of Israel's wars (e.g., 2 Sam 5:20; 2 Kgs 14:13; 2 Chr 26:6). It is also used in some of Israel's communal laments to describe God's actions against Israel (Pss 60:1 [3 HB]; 80:12 [13 HB]; 89:40 [41 HB]).

The final assault against Job occurs when God ***runs*** through the breaches **like a *mighty*** warrior (*gibbôr*). The verb for ***runs*** (*rwṣ*) is the same one Eliphaz used in the previous chapter to speak of the wicked running defiantly against God (Job 15:26). Job's experience is exactly the opposite. God has rushed at him seeking to destroy him.

■ **15** God's attacks (vv 7-9, 11-14) have had a severe impact on Job. He now wears **sackcloth** for clothing. **Sackcloth** was a dark-colored material (Isa 50:3) probably made out of goats' hair. It may have looked something like a gunnysack, but its size and shape are unknown.

The purpose for wearing sackcloth was to declare publicly a state of mourning either for someone who had died (2 Sam 3:31) or in anticipation of someone's death (Esth 4:1-4; Ps 35:13). Job may have had both purposes in mind. Certainly, sackcloth was appropriate attire to mourn for his ten children. But he may also have worn it in anticipation of his own death (Job 7:7-8, 21; 10:20-22).

Job 16:15*b* reads literally "I have thrust my horn in the dust." The word for "horn" (*qeren*) normally refers to the horn of an animal (such as a ram or ox), an object made from an animal horn, or a protrusion that looks like an animal horn. Several additional passages in the Psalms speak of people or nations as having horns (Pss 75:10 [11 HB]; 89:17, 24 [18, 25 HB]; 112:9; 148:14). This figure is a metaphor for their status and dignity in life. God exalts or lifts up the horns of the righteous and cuts off the horns of the wicked. In Job 16:15 Job uses this metaphor as a symbol of his humiliation and defeat. He has thrust his horn in the ground signifying his helplessness before the **mighty warrior** of v 14.

■ **16** Here is the first acknowledgment by Job of **weeping**. His tears have been so profuse that there is now "deep darkness" (*ṣalmāwet*; → 3:4-6) on his "eyelids" (NRSV). He does not go into detail as to the time of his weeping, but some type of emotional outcry is not surprising considering the extent of his suffering. His darkened eyelids may also indicate the sunken facial features of a sick person approaching death.

■ **17** In Job's thinking, all of God's actions in 16:7-16 were totally unreasonable and unjust. God had attacked him in spite of his faithfulness (1:1). He mentions two examples of his total devotion to God. They illustrate both the outward and inward manifestations of his spiritual condition in the manner of Ps 24:4 ("clean hands and a pure heart"). Outwardly, he has avoided **violent wrong** (*ḥāmās*) toward others. No one has ever accused Job of this extreme form of evil behavior, but Eliphaz did come close in 15:25-26. Inwardly, his prayers to God have been **pure** (*zakkâ*).

Not all prayers are pure. Some are prayed for selfish reasons. But Job's motive in seeking God was not for personal gain. He simply wants to know the truth about the reason for his suffering. If he is innocent, why has God punished him so severely? There is no justifiable reason. In Job's thinking, his faithfulness means nothing to God.

3. I Have a Witness (16:18-22)

The third section focuses on a heavenly witness who will testify to Job's innocence and righteous life. Job may not live long enough to receive the benefit of his witness's testimony, but he is convinced that someday his witness will plead with God on his behalf and secure his vindication. As in two other passages (9:33; 19:25), Job reaches out to someone outside his present earthly existence who may be able to help him. In 9:33 it was a **mediator**, here it is a "witness," and in 19:25 it will be a "redeemer."

■ **18** Job knew that his death was imminent. He was also aware of the ancient belief that the unnatural death of an innocent person called for justice to be meted out (Gen 4:10; Isa 26:21; Ezek 24:7-8). Figuratively, the blood of the innocent person cried out for justice against the murderer. It was the responsibility of the kinsman-redeemer (Job 19:25-27)/blood avenger (Josh 20:3, 9) to see that the guilty party was identified and punished.

As regards his own situation, Job believes that the guilty party is God. He is here asking that his **blood** (and his body) not be covered up in the grave when he dies but that it remain exposed so it can continue to cry out for vindication. Job wants the truth about his innocence to be made known publicly, even if it occurs after his death. So he calls on the **earth** to support him in his plea because he knows the earth will last longer than he will.

In the OT the earth and the sky were seen as silent witnesses to all the events of humankind. Sometimes they were called upon to bear witness to the truth or render a verdict against a sinner (Deut 4:26; 30:19; 31:28; 32:1; Jer 6:19; Mic 1:2).

■ **19** Job believes he has a **witness** (*'ēd*) to support his claim of innocence. Just as the earth was called upon in the previous verse, so now **heaven** will take up Job's cause. The word **witness** indicates much more than the term "mediator" (→ Job 9:33). There Job was hoping for a neutral party who could bring God and himself together in reconciliation. A witness is not neutral. This is a person who is firmly on one's side. This person would know Job's life history from beginning to end and thus would be able to advocate for him factually, passionately, and effectively.

The synonym for **witness** in 16:19*b* is *śāhēd* (**advocate**), which is Aramaic in origin. A variant of this word appears in Gen 31:47 where Laban names the pile of stones *yĕgar-śāhădûtā'* ("the heap of witness").

There have been a number of suggestions as to the identity of this witness. (1) Job could be speaking of **heaven** in general as was the case with the "earth" in Job 16:18, that is, all creation will support Job's cause. The mention of **heaven** immediately after his appeal to the earth makes this a strong possibility.

(2) Another suggestion is one of the heavenly beings (like the Examiner in the prologue) who is responsible for advocating for innocent people (see Zech 3:1) (Pope 1973, 125; Newsom 1996, 460; Balentine 2006, 258-59). Job has already noted the need for a mediator who would bring reconciliation between God and himself, but he was not confident that such a person existed (Job 9:33). This was mainly a wish on his part. Verse 19 of ch 16 expresses a much bolder assertion that Job's witness does exist. But why would Job appeal to a third party in heaven when he knows that God is already aware of everything about him (10:7)? God does not need others to fill him in on the details of Job's righteousness (1:8; 2:3).

(3) A third possible witness is the permanent record of Job's life and his cry for vindication that is on file in heaven (Clines 1989, 390; Seow 2013, 739-40). This cry would remain alive and vigilant until Job received justice. This is a valid suggestion.

(4) A fourth possibility is that the witness is God himself, who will finally speak and set the matter straight (Gordis 1978, 526-28; Andersen 1976, 182-83; Hartley 1988, 264). The main problem with this interpretation is that it sets up a tension between the God who caused Job's trouble and the God who will relieve it. How can God testify in Job's behalf against himself? But perhaps there is a subtlety here that has not been recognized. By naming God as his witness, Job is calling on God to step out of his self-imposed silence and testify to the truth. In effect, he is attempting to issue a subpoena. He cannot force God to appear (9:4, 11-12), but he is hoping that God will respond because God would be the best witness he could call in his defense. As Hartley notes, Job still maintains "genuine confidence in God regardless of the way it appears that God is treating him" (1988, 264).

A number of scholars have noted the similarities between Job's description of a heavenly witness (16:19-20) and Jesus' comments in the Gospel of John about the Holy Spirit/Paraclete/Spirit of truth (John 15:26—16:15). In NT theology the Holy Spirit is given the role of heavenly witness. His primary responsibilities are to advocate for Jesus (15:26; 16:14), to teach all things concerning spiritual truth (14:26; 16:13), and to prove wrong the world's views on sin, righteousness, and judgment (16:8-11). If Job had known of the doctrine of the Trinity, he probably would have called on the Holy Spirit to be his witness/advocate. However, Jesus makes it clear that the work of the Holy Spirit is focused primarily on glorifying Jesus (John 16:14). Thus, Job's concept of a witness was somewhat different from that of the Holy Spirit. Job wanted someone who would advocate to God for him concerning his innocence and who would prove the three friends wrong.

God's Paradoxical Nature

The tension between God as "judge" and God as "witness" (16:19-21) is similar to other tensions about God's nature that theologians have discussed for centuries. For example, is God's nature "love/mercy/compassion" or is it "holiness/justice/wrath" (19:11)? Actually, God is both. This is a paradox that cannot be resolved with logical lines of reasoning, for there are biblical passages that support both sides. Sometimes our well-reasoned theologies get in the way of acknowledging the paradoxical truths of Scripture.

In Job's case, he is convinced of two things about God. First, God has caused his suffering for some unknown reason. Second, God knows that Job is innocent of sin. He cannot explain this paradox. But even though he is angry that God has afflicted him, he has no other place to go for help than to this same God who knows him intimately and would be his best witness. As Gordis notes, "Job is affirming his faith that behind the God of violence, so tragically manifest in the world, stands the God of righteousness and love—and they are not two but one" (1978, 527)! As we will see very shortly (19:25), Job also believes that God is his "redeemer/vindicator."

■ **20** The translation of v 20 is problematic. The first clause has traditionally been translated as: "My scoffers are my friends" (see NRSV). However, the word for "scoffer" (*mēlîṣ*) carries a completely different meaning in its other occurrences: "interpreter" (Gen 42:23; Isa 43:27), "envoy" (2 Chr 32:31), "mediator" (Job 33:23). The NIV follows this interpretation, although it emends the MT to the singular: **My intercessor is my friend**. This is probably correct, for Job is certainly not calling the three friends his intermediaries with God. Rather, he is referring to the possibility of an advocate in heaven who would testify on his behalf (16:19) and plead with God for reconciliation (v 21). Such a person would be worthy of being called **my friend**.

The meaning of the verb *dlp* in v 20*b* is also difficult. Some relate it to an Akkadian root meaning "be exhausted, sleepless" (Clines 1989, 372). But the versions favor the meaning "drip, leak" (see Eccl 10:18): **My eyes pour out tears to God** (*Eloah*). The context also seems to support this interpretation, for Job has just commented on his weeping (Job 16:16).

■ **21** Here Job enlarges on the role of the intermediary in v 20. Job has not been able to convince God to speak with him, but perhaps God would be more open to speaking with an intermediary—a person who would plead with **God** (*Eloah*) just as earnestly **as one pleads for a friend**. The participial form of the verb **pleads** (*ykḥ*) is the word Job used for "mediator" in 9:33.

■ **22** Job knows that he has little time left to settle his dispute with God and clear his name with his friends. Strangely, he speaks here of **a few years** that still remain to him. Yet both before and after this verse he talks as if his death is imminent (16:18; "days" in 17:1). And earlier passages hinted that his time was limited (7:6-8; 10:20). He even put on sackcloth in anticipation (16:15). Perhaps this is another evidence that disease was not well understood in the ancient world. People gauged the time they had left by the amount of pain they had at the moment (→ "Disease in the Ancient World" sidebar at 2:7-8).

The end of the verse returns to a concept that Job has already mentioned several times (7:9; 10:21; 14:12). Sheol, the place where he is headed, is the land of **no return**.

4. I Have No Hope for a Better Life (17:1-16)

A comparison of several versions of ch 17 reveals a wide variety of translations because of some difficult Hebrew constructions whose meaning can only be guessed at. Nevertheless, the overall message is clear. Job's life is without hope due to hostility from God, mocking from his friends, and the deterioration of his health. He is headed for Sheol where he will make his home very shortly.

■ **1** Job begins the final section of his speech by acknowledging the reality of his approaching death. His destination is Sheol, and he is simply waiting for his transportation to arrive and whisk him off to the land of "no return" (16:22). His **spirit** (*rûaḥ*) has no hope of anything different (17:15-16). His **days have come to an end**, and **the graveyard is waiting** for him. **Graveyard** (*qĕbārîm*) is probably a "plural of extension" meaning literally "place of many graves" (GKC, §124*c*). Whether the actual moment of death occurs tomorrow or within a few years (16:22) is immaterial. Death will claim him whenever God decides the time is right.

■ **2** Job is not only dealing with physical pain and inner turmoil but also contending with the hostility of his community. The **mockers** (lit. "mockery") probably include the three friends, but Job also has the larger community of Uz in mind (16:10-11). He will provide more details about specific members of this community in his next speech (19:13-22). Job confesses that he cannot get his attention off those who are mocking him. His mind dwells on these people and their animosity. He is not only shocked but also hurt by their behavior.

■ **3** Scholars are divided on the meaning of this verse. God is the obvious object of address, although his name is not mentioned in the MT, but what is Job asking here? Is he asking God to make a pledge that vouches for his innocence until such time as his case is resolved (NIV, NRSV)? Or is Job asking God to accept his own pledge of innocence as valid (Clines 1989, 393-94)? The latter meaning seems to fit the context best, yielding this translation: *Accept now for yourself my pledge*. The phrase *my pledge* ('*ērbōnî* in place of '*orbēnî*) is an emended form most scholars accept. Giving a pledge was like making an oath that guaranteed the accuracy of one's statement (Gen 38:17-20).

Job continues with this same thought in Job 17:3b. He uses an idiomatic expression ("strike the hand"; *tq' yād*) that means "to make a legal agreement that guarantees the payment or fulfillment of an obligation by another party." It is like cosigning a loan so your son or daughter can buy their first car. This expression also appears three times in Proverbs with *kap* ("palm") substituted for *yād* (Prov 6:1; 17:18; 22:26). Job is asking God, *Who (except you) will accept my guarantee?* Job knew the friends would not accept either his pledge or his guarantee. They only mocked him (Job 17:2; 16:10-11). But he hopes that God will look favorably on his pledge of truthfulness.

■ **4** The reason no one would accept Job's testimony as true was because God had **closed their minds to understanding**. He had prevented them from seeing the truth about Job's innocence. The pronoun **their** could refer to just the three friends. But more likely he is including his entire community, as he does several times in this speech (17:2, 6; 16:10-11). Job has no proof that God is responsible for other people's ignorance. But the fact that not even one person has stepped forward to support him is pretty good evidence in Job's mind that God is orchestrating this hostility behind the scenes.

However, God will regret this action against Job: **therefore you will not *be exalted***. The verb in 17:4b is active in the MT (*tĕrōmēm*, from *rwm*, meaning "you will not exalt them"). But Gordis's suggestion of emending to the passive stem (Polal; *tĕrōmām*, as in Ps 75:10 [11 HB]; Neh 9:5) makes better sense (1978, 181).

Job is subtly attacking God's justice here by accusing him of purposely withholding the truth from Job's community and thus increasing his suffering. When God's actions are made known, people will no longer exalt him.

■ **5** Scholars generally agree that Job 17:5 is an older proverb, but they disagree on its interpretation. The traditional understanding will be followed here. The original proverb was probably directed against people who harm others for personal gain. They will reap the consequences in the lives of their family. Job uses the saying against his "mockers" (v 2) who have **denounced** him and made his life miserable. Their insults derive from minds that have been "closed" by God (v 4). They seek a **reward** (i.e., some benefit) for turning against a friend (specifically, Job). The word for **reward** (*ḥēleq*) refers to a portion of goods received from a distribution (20:29; 27:13; 31:2). The **children** of the mockers will suffer for their parents' act of betrayal. The failing of their **eyes** is probably a metaphor for their loss of hope (11:20; 31:16). Life will not go well for them.

■ **6** The description of Job's mockery (17:2) continues. He has now become a **byword** (*mšl*). This word is usually translated as "proverb," but in a few instances the meaning is clearly **byword** (Deut 28:37; 1 Kgs 9:7; 2 Chr 7:20; Pss 44:14 [15 HB]; 69:11 [12 HB]; Jer 24:9; Ezek 14:8; Joel 2:17). What Job means is that he has become the prime example of what happens to people when God is angry at them. Just as "Abraham" was a **byword** for the life of faith, so "just like Job" is now a phrase people use to describe a person who has grieved God extremely and suffered terrible consequences as a result.

"I have become spittle to the face" is further evidence of the mockery against Job (Job 17:6*b* lit.). The word for "spittle" (*tōpet*) is used only once in the OT, but Job expresses the same thought again in 30:10 with a different word. Job's earlier comments included examples of how people had been unkind to him since his troubles started (6:14-21; 12:4; 16:10-11; 17:2), but spitting in his face was certainly one of the worst insults he could receive (also Deut 25:9; Isa 50:6).

■ **7** Job's troubles had affected him not only socially (Job 17:2, 6) but also physically (v 7). In particular, his eyesight had **grown dim** (*khh*). This verb and its adjective *kēheh* are used in three other passages in reference to eyes that have become dim due to old age (Gen 27:1; Deut 34:7; 1 Sam 3:2). Job's eyes are not necessarily old, but his eyesight has faded as a result of his **grief** and weeping (Job 16:16). The psalmist expresses a similar thought in Ps 6:7 [8 HB] due to his poor health. There have also been changes to Job's body: ***All of my limbs are like*** a **shadow**. His limbs have shriveled due to loss of weight. They are no thicker than a shadow.

■ **8-10** These verses are a major problem for all commentators. Some move them to other locations, and others eliminate them altogether. Even those who keep these verses in place have trouble making them fit the context of Job's speech. The comments that follow are indebted to Clines (1989, 396-98) and seem to present the best interpretation.

In Job 17:8 **the upright** (*yĕšārîm*) and **the innocent** (*nāqî*) and in v 9 **the righteous** (*ṣaddîq*) and **those with clean hands** (*ṭŏhor yādayim*) are parallel synonyms, even though the first is plural and the others are singular. These terms normally refer to people who are in a right relationship with God. However, Job is using them in a satirical way to condemn their persecutions of him. The friends, and the wider community, may see themselves as upright, innocent, and so forth, and they may think they are speaking for God, but they do not understand Job's situation. Not one of them is **wise** (v 10). Here is the essence of what Job is saying against them:

> You (who claim to be upright, innocent, etc.) are horrified at my suffering because you think my condition is God's punishment for some terrible sin I have committed. You attack the **ungodly** (which you think I am) condemning their sins, making them a byword, and even spitting on them (v 6) because you want them to repent. Dogmatically you **hold** onto your black-and-white principles and do not waver from them. And the longer you talk, the louder, the harsher, and the more arrogant you become because you think you are right. But every one of you is a fool; you are ignorant of my situation.

■ **11** In vv 11-16 Job descends from the attack mode of v 10 to doleful despair that climaxes in vv 15-16. The meaning of v 11 is similar in form and content to v 1. The end of his life is near, leaving him no hope for the future. Whatever **plans** or **desires** he may have had in earlier years will not come to pass. They have been **shattered** because of his troubles.

■ **12** There are two main interpretations of v 12. The first is as a response to 11:17 where Zophar promised that Job's darkness would turn to light if he turned away from sin. Job's satirical reaction is: "They make night into day; 'The light,' they say, 'is near to the darkness'" (NRSV). In other words, the friends make "night" sound like "day," and they talk like it is a simple matter to move from one to the other. The second interpretation is to make 17:11c the subject of v 12, yielding: **Yet the desires of my heart turn night into day; in the face of the darkness light is near.** Here turning darkness into light is the deepest desire of Job's heart. Either interpretation is possible, but the first has the advantage of connecting Job's speech with a previous statement by the friends.

■ **13-16** Verses 13-14 are a series of conditional clauses that identify Job's new family members in Sheol and reiterate his desire to die (3:20-26; 6:8-9; 10:18-19). The clauses skillfully interweave language borrowed from family life (**home, bed, father, mother, sister**) with synonyms for death (***Sheol**, darkness, *pit*, *maggot***) producing a poetic delight. A paraphrase of these clauses would read something like this: "If I desire Sheol for my home, if I choose to sleep in Sheol, if I accept the grave pit and the maggot as my closest family members, then . . ."

The apodosis for these clauses is the four rhetorical questions in 17:15-16 where Job makes satirical jabs at the friends' earlier comments about **hope** (*tiqwâ*; 4:6; 5:17-26; 8:20-22; 11:13-19). **Hope** is a word that is easy to throw out to people who are being battered by life's troubles. It is like tossing a life preserver to one who is drowning. But when that person is struggling against the current at the edge of Niagara Falls, a life preserver seems too little, too late.

Such was Job's situation. His family was destroyed. His wealth and health were gone. He had lost his reputation. And he was very close to death. When he dies, hope will die with him, for hope does not exist in Sheol (→ "Sheol" sidebar at 3:17-19).

In 17:16a, the Hebrew for "bars" (NRSV) or **gates** is *bad*, which has a number of different meanings. The word appears numerous times in Exodus and Numbers for the "poles" used to carry various pieces of furniture in the tabernacle (e.g., Exod 35:12-13, 15-16). From this usage comes the suggestion that Job 17:16 may refer to the "bars" on the **gates** of Sheol. Gordis follows another meaning of *bad* that yields "chambers of Sheol" (1978, 172, 185). A third possibility is the LXX reading "with me" based on an emended form. None of these proposals are conclusive. **The dust** (v 16b) is another synonym for Sheol.

FROM THE TEXT

1. Summary of Job's Response to Eliphaz. One would think that Job's identification of his heavenly witness (16:19-21) would cheer him up, for this witness would enable him to receive the vindication he was due. But it does not lift Job's spirit. Except for these few verses, the rest of the speech is filled with gloom, criticisms of God, and longing for death.

In this speech Job calls God his enemy. He believed God had orchestrated a campaign of hostility that included the death of his family members, social mocking, and severe sickness. This relentless onslaught had completely worn Job out and crushed any hope of a better future. He now wears sackcloth, a sign of his impending death. Job's accusations against God as being "harsh and cruel" (16:7-14) are some of the strongest in Scripture (van Wolde 1997, 76). They reveal the depths of his anguish.

Job's main points are as follows:
- You, my friends, are worthless to me. You mock me instead of trying to help me.
- God has become my enemy. He has destroyed my health, turned my community against me, and robbed me of hope. In short, he treats me like his punching bag.
- I have a witness in heaven who knows my life from beginning to end. He will verify that I am not a sinner. Even if I die, my witness will continue to press my case and seek my vindication.
- My home will shortly be in Sheol.

2. Job's Moods. Commentators have noted the great fluctuation in Job's mood throughout the book. He goes from the deepest depths of despair to the heights of hope and confidence and back to despair again, sometimes within the same chapter. Such is the case in this speech. Job moves from calling God his enemy (16:9), to identifying a heavenly witness who will support him (16:19), to restating his wish to die (17:13-16).

Robinson has created a graph of Job's moods that clearly shows this tremendous oscillation (1955, 14). He identifies ch 17 as the lowest point of Job's depression and 19:25-27 as the point of his highest confidence. Other chapters that reflect his depression according to Robinson are 6—7, 9, 16, 21, and 23—24.

Chapters that show his confidence are 10, 12—14, 26—28, and 31. Such oscillation is not unexpected in a person whose whole life has collapsed around him.

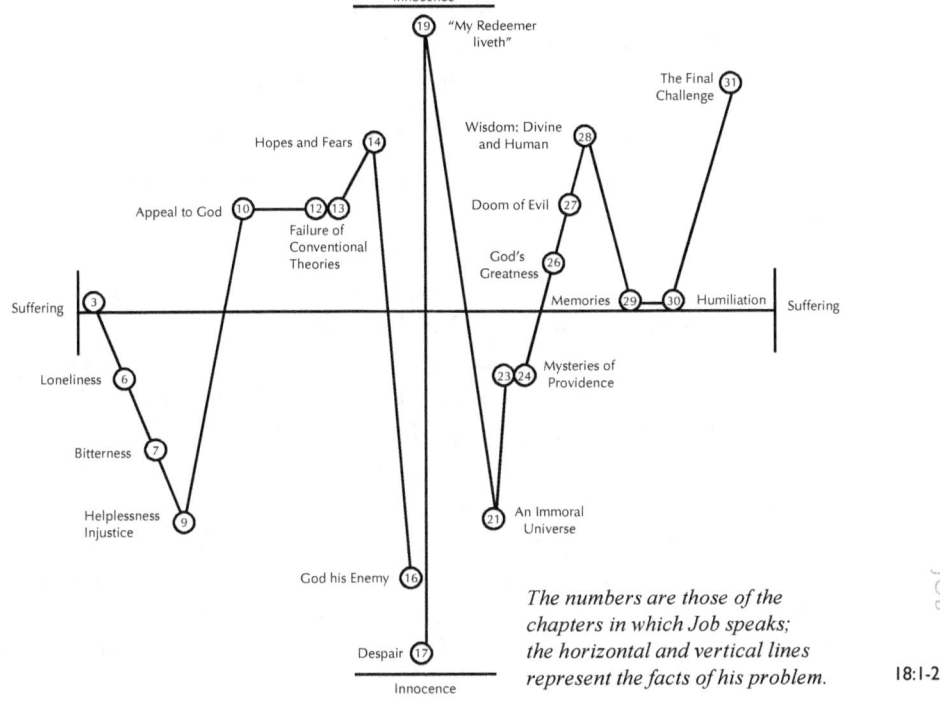

The numbers are those of the chapters in which Job speaks; the horizontal and vertical lines represent the facts of his problem.

Reproduced by permission from Robinson (1955, 14).

IN THE TEXT

C. Bildad's Second Speech (18:1-21)

Bildad's first speech (ch 8) focused on God's justice. God measures the righteousness or wickedness of each person and treats them accordingly. There are no exceptions. This is a truism supported by multiple past generations of sages. By way of example, he pointed to the death of Job's children as possibly being the result of their sin. But Bildad also offered hope to Job that his suffering was only temporary. If he would seek God and live an upright life, God would restore his well-being.

In Bildad's second speech (ch 18), he holds out no hope for Job. He sees that Job will not even consider the friends' advice, so there is no point in offering him a way out of his troubles. Instead, Bildad speaks only of the punishments God inflicts on the wicked. They are frightening, and Job should be alarmed. He was experiencing some of them already, and they will only get worse. The most significant punishment is the extinction of any memory of the wicked after their death. No one will remember they ever lived. By using this blunt approach, Bildad hopes to shock Job into reconsidering his position. Perhaps he can still persuade Job to drop his belligerent attitude and accept the truth of the friends' arguments.

There are two sections to Bildad's speech:
1. Why Do You Treat Us as Stupid? (18:1-4)
2. The Wicked Die Suddenly and Are Not Remembered (18:5-21)

1. Why Do You Treat Us as Stupid? (18:1-4)

Bildad's second speech begins with angry words about how Job has acted toward him and his friends. Why does he treat them like stupid animals?

■ **1** For comments on the introductory formula → 3:2.

■ **2** Bildad's first words are more comments on Job's wordiness. As in his previous speech (8:2), he uses the words "how long" (NRSV)—a typical Hebrew way to express one's frustration with another person's actions. Bildad wishes that Job would quit talking and acknowledge the truth of what the friends are saying.

Throughout the dialogues, there are continual charges between Job and his friends over who is the worst windbag and who is the least willing to be quiet and listen (6:24; 8:2; 11:2-3; 15:2-3; 16:3). Neither side will give ground on this issue, for both are convinced that their own position is correct and the other side is in error. The more one side speaks in defense of its own point of view, the more the other side regards it as foolish "babble" (11:3 NRSV). Real dialogue will not occur until both sides set some ground rules for debate and commit themselves to really listening to the other side.

Both 18:2 and 3 contain second plural verb forms and pronouns that imply Bildad is addressing more than one person. Yet the content of his speech is directed solely at Job. There is no good answer to this problem, although many scholars have tried to come up with one (see Clines 1989, 409-10, for a discussion of the various proposals). Some retain the plurals of the MT and propose that Bildad is treating Job as exemplifying a class of people: "How long until people like you put an end to words?" Most versions, however, simply follow the LXX, which uses only singular forms.

■ **3** In an earlier speech Job had claimed that all of nature supported him in his belief that God controlled everything. Therefore, it was clear that God had caused his suffering (12:7-9). Apparently, Bildad interpreted Job's comments as implying that the three friends possessed less knowledge than the animals, birds, plants, and fish (12:7-8). Job had further attacked their lack of wisdom in 17:10. Bildad felt offended by this criticism of their intelligence. How dare Job regard them as **stupid** and treat them like **animals**! The Hebrew for cattle (*běhēmâ*) is really a collective noun that refers to animals in general, either domestic or wild (Gen 1:24-26). Thus, the translation **animals** is probably more appropriate here in response to Job's remarks in Job 12:7-8. Unfortunately, both sides engaged in this derogatory name-calling, which only increased the tension between them.

■ **4** In 16:9 Job had accused God of tearing him like a wild animal tears into its prey. Bildad's response is that God is not at fault. Job has torn himself by working himself into an emotional frenzy. He has only himself to blame for his deep distress. Bildad would agree that Job has experienced severe and multiple troubles, but he has only compounded his predicament by railing against God and his friends. His arrogance betrayed a self-centered attitude that expected God and the world to bend to his wishes.

Bildad's comments about **the earth** being **abandoned** and **the rocks** being **moved** probably refer to disasters such as earthquakes that devastate and depopulate inhabited lands. Since only God can cause such disasters, does Job expect God to do these things just to meet his demands?

2. The Wicked Die Suddenly and Are Not Remembered (18:5-21)

As mentioned at the beginning of the second cycle of speeches (ch 15), each of the speeches by the three friends in this cycle contains a list of afflictions experienced by the wicked. No wicked person will escape God's judgment. Some of God's punishments are physical; others are mental or social. Bildad is particularly interested in the consequences that occur after the wicked die. Their children will not survive to carry on the family name, and even the memory of the parents and children will disappear. It will be as if they never lived.

■ **5-6** *Light* and *darkness* are two major themes in the book of Job, with **light** and its synonyms appearing over thirty-five times and darkness and its synonyms over forty times (→ "Light and Darkness in Job" sidebar at 11:17). These words are metaphors for life and well-being versus death and suffering. The four clauses of 18:5-6 all speak of the transition from life to death using the metaphor of a **light** going out. Death comes early and abruptly for the **wicked**. There are no dimmer switches that gradually lead them into the darkness of Sheol. Bildad does not give a reason for the sudden transition to death. But clearly the cause of this calamity, as well as all the others in vv 5-21, is God's judgment against the **wicked** (v 21; → Job's disagreement in 21:17).

The setting for 18:5, whether indoors or outdoors, is not specified, whereas v 6 is definitely in a **tent**. Tents are also mentioned in vv 14-15, but this does not prove Job lived in a tent, for these verses contain many metaphors. **Tent** is simply a figurative term for "a home, a place of residence."

Verse 6*b* reads: "And the lamp above them is put out" (NRSV). Many ancient oil lamps were rounded on the bottom. They needed to be balanced on a ledge or in a recess in the wall to prevent them from being knocked over accidentally by a child or pet. The word *above* (**beside**) may indicate that lamps in a tent were somehow hung from the top of the tent by cords or placed on a high pedestal. An alternative reading for *above* is "on account of" (Seow 2013, 781-82, following the Targum).

■ **7** The wicked also experience travel restrictions. Their once vigorous steps that took them wherever they wanted to go are restrained from further activity. Whether their restraint is the result of premature aging, injury, or social barriers is not stated. The point is that their lack of movement from place to place will diminish their ability to accomplish things and influence other people.

The word for **schemes** (*'ēṣâ*; v 7*b*) can refer to either good (12:13) or evil (10:3) **plans**. Here Bildad uses the word in the sense of plans that are self-generated for personal gain rather than derived from God's will. Such plans come back to harm the wicked and are thus doomed to failure. The verb in the MT of this clause is *šlk*, which means **throw . . . down/cast off** (→ 15:33). The LXX translation is taken from another verb (*kšl*) meaning "cause to stumble." This is likely the result of a handwriting error known as metathesis.

■ **8-10** Next, Bildad uses a series of images from the equipment of hunters to describe another peril of the wicked. Their journey through life is constantly beset by traps that are hidden from their view. At any moment one of these traps may be sprung. The emphasis is on the terror experienced by the wicked when they are suddenly and unexpectedly captured by God and removed from this life, just like animal prey.

Bildad mentions six different kinds of traps, indicating the author's great familiarity with the language of hunting. In 18:8*a* the *rešet* is a **net** that was dropped on top of prey, such as a bird (Hos 7:12), a lion (Ezek 19:8), or a crocodile (Ezek 32:3). Or it could be placed on the ground to entangle their feet (Pss 9:15 [16 HB]; 25:15). The word *šĕbākâ* (**mesh**) in Job 18:8*b* appears several times in Kings and Chronicles in reference to the lattice design on the capitals of the temple columns (e.g., 1 Kgs 7:17-18). The usage in Job 18:8 is the only connection with an animal trap and is thought to mean a lattice-type arrangement of branches that concealed a pit beneath.

The word *paḥ* (**trap**) in v 9*a* clearly pertains to a bird trap in six passages (Pss 91:3; 124:7; Prov 7:23; Eccl 9:12; Hos 9:8; Amos 3:5). In order to catch a bird by the **heel**, the trap was possibly a type of noose attached to a bent tree branch that snapped back when the bird stepped into the noose.

The nature of the *ṣammîm* (**snare**) in Job 18:9*b* and the *malkōdet* (**trap**) in v 10*b* is unknown, as these words occur only here in the OT. The *ḥebel* (**noose**) in v 10*a* is a rope/cord probably used like the *paḥ*.

■ **11** Bildad continues to stress the sudden **terrors** that engulf the wicked. Now there is not just the threat of a net or a pit in the pathway, but "terrors frighten them on every side" (NRSV), and, Bildad would probably add, at any time—24/7. The second clause **and they harass him at his feet** connects this verse with the traps that ensnare one's feet in vv 8-10.

■ **12** There are two different interpretations of v 12*a*. One approach is to take the Hebrew *'ōnô* as "strength" or "power," yielding: "Their strength is consumed by hunger" (NRSV). A second approach is to emend the Hebrew to *'āwen*, rendering: **Calamity is hungry for him**. The first option makes good sense and follows the MT, but the latter has the advantage of providing a better parallel with v 12*b*: **Disaster is ready for *his stumbling*.** The meaning of the verse, then, is that **calamity** and **disaster** are two of the "terrors" mentioned in v 11 that hound the wicked. Bildad heightens their frightful nature by personifying them as ferocious beasts just ready to pounce.

■ **13** The image of calamity being "hungry" (v 12) is carried forward into v 13 with the verb *'kl* (**eats, devours**) appearing twice. The wicked are devoured by physical diseases, specifically those that affect the **skin** and **limbs**. These diseases are visible to onlookers and provide an outward sign of a wicked heart. Not by coincidence, Job just happened to have such a disease. The subject of v 13*a* is not clear. It could refer to "calamity" and "disaster" in v 12 or **death's firstborn** in v 13*b*. The sense of the passage is basically the same either way.

Death's firstborn devours his limbs is a metaphor that personifies death and attributes to him a child who attacks humans like a ravenous beast. Some have noted the similarity here between personified **death** (*māwet*) and the god Mot, ruler of the underworld in Canaanite mythology. While the author has probably borrowed some of the mythological language of the Canaanites, there is no biblical evidence that Israel believed in the existence of a deity who ruled the underworld separate from Yahweh. **Death's firstborn** is a figurative phrase for disease, the primary agent of death. Darkness (vv 5-6), "traps" (vv 8-10), "terrors" (v 11), and "calamity" and "disaster" (v 12) could all be classified as lesser agents of personified death. But "disease" (v 13 NRSV) ranks first as the primary destroyer of human life.

■ **14** As in v 6, Bildad uses the word **tent** as a figurative term for a wicked person's dwelling. One's home is usually the most secure place a person has in life. To be forcefully removed from one's home, never to return again, is a major tragedy for the wicked. Further, the wicked are **marched off to the king of terrors**. **The king of terrors** (*melek ballāhôt*) is a metaphor for "death" that appears nowhere else in the OT. Personified "death" has sent his agents ahead of him to terrorize and trap the wicked (vv 5-12). He then has sent his "firstborn" to destroy their bodies (v 13). Finally, he demands that the wicked be removed from the land of the living and brought to Sheol. This is their final end.

■ **15** After the wicked are taken from their homes, nothing remains of their families and possessions. In the first clause the MT reads literally "Nothing belonging to him" [*mibbĕlî lô*] **resides in his tent**. However, there is a great temptation to find a more appropriate parallel for ***brimstone*** (**burning sulfur** [v 15*b*]) by emending *mibbĕlî* to *mabbēl* (**fire**), yielding: **Fire resides in his tent**. Fire and ***brimstone*** are connected in several other well-known passages (Gen 19:24; Ps 11:6; Ezek 38:22), so this is a possibility. However, sometimes emendations are a little too convenient for the translator, and this is one of those cases. The MT is preferred as the harder reading.

Brimstone **is scattered over his *house and lands*** indicates that the entire property of the wicked is destroyed by fire. ***Brimstone*** (*goprît*) is the English name given to **burning sulfur**. Sulfur occurs naturally as a yellow, nonmetallic element that is highly flammable. Every appearance of this word in the OT is associated with God's punishment against the wicked. The translation **dwelling** (*nāweh*) is too limited. In Job *nāweh* seems to encompass all a person's property, including **house and lands** (→ 5:3, 24).

■ **16** Here Bildad uses the metaphor of a tree to emphasize the annihilation of the wicked. Both **above** and **below** ground—what is seen and what is hidden—the tree dries up. The pairing of **roots** and **branches** (possibly "fruit, shoots, blossoms") to describe the total destruction of people appears in other passages as well (Isa 5:24; Ezek 17:9; Hos 9:16; Amos 2:9; Mal 4:1 [3:19 HB]). There is the additional possibility that Bildad may be hinting at the destruction of the children of the wicked, for **branches** and fruit are what a tree produces (→ Job 18:17, 19).

■ **17** Preservation of one's **memory** is a desire of all human beings. Examples of people who go to extremes to make this happen are abundant in both the ancient and modern world (e.g., the pyramids in Egypt). Thus, the loss of the remembrance of a person's **name** after death is another blow to the wicked that is hard to bear. It is even more difficult when one learns of this dreadful situation *before* death. Some passages in the Psalms attribute the eradication of one's name after death to God's punishment for sin (Pss 34:16 [17 HB]; 109:13-15). The people most likely to preserve the memory of the deceased are their children. Their survival and faithfulness to their parents' desires are vital to keeping alive the family name. In Job's case, his children were already gone. No doubt, Bildad's comment here only increased Job's anxiety that his own family name would end with his death.

■ **18** The theme of Job 18:18 is the same as vv 5-6—the transition of the wicked from life to death using the metaphors of **light** and **darkness**. The main difference in v 18 is the use of active verbs with third plural subjects: ***They drive him from light into . . . darkness, and they chase him*** from the world. The antecedent of ***they*** is the agents of death—all the traps, terrors, and disease mentioned in vv 8-13. Their combined power overcomes the wicked driving them into the **darkness** of Sheol. The verb for ***drive*** (*hdp*) refers to physically moving or pushing someone to another location (e.g., driving the Canaanites out of the land of Canaan [Josh 23:5]).

■ **19** This verse repeats the thought of Job 18:17: No one remembers the wicked after their death because none of their descendants survive. The world goes on as if they never lived because their names are obliterated from human memory. The words for **offspring** (*nîn*) and **descendants** (*neked*) are always used together when they appear in the OT (Gen 21:23; Isa 14:22; and here). They are synonyms, but *nîn* may refer primarily to one's children, while *neked* more to later generations.

Where once he lived is literally "where he sojourned." A sojourner is an immigrant living temporarily in a land as a foreigner. This verse seems to imply that the agents of death (Job 18:8-13) even blot out the memory of the wicked in other communities where they had once lived. The word for **survivor** (*śārîd*) is used in other passages for a person who survives a military battle (e.g., Josh 8:22), but here it indicates someone who remains alive after a calamity.

■ 20 People of the west are *horrified* at his *day;* those of the east are seized with *shuddering*. With another metaphor Bildad enlarges the number of those who are impacted by the terrible news of the downfall of the wicked. Everyone—from west to east—is *horrified*. The terms west (*'aḥărōnîm*) and east (*qadmōnîm*) literally mean "behind" and "before." In a few passages they appear together with "sea" (*yām*) to mean "the sea behind" (i.e., the western sea or Mediterranean Sea) and "the sea before" (i.e., the eastern sea or Dead Sea) (Joel 2:20; Zech 14:8). The direction of orientation is facing east.

His fate (lit. "his day") appeared earlier in reference to the birthdays of Job and his children (1:4; 3:1). But here something different is intended: the day of the death of the wicked and the calamities leading up to it. This news is devastating to all who hear it, not because the wicked do not deserve it, but because it occurs so early in life and with such merciless agony. Such a death could easily have been avoided. This is a tragedy of extreme proportion.

■ 21 The final verse of Bildad's speech sums up the life of the wicked. Their "tent" is now a nameless place—dark and in ruins (vv 6, 15). It no longer serves as a home. Bildad calls it by the generic terms, a **dwelling** or simply a **place**. He believes that its destruction is a sure sign they did not **know God** (meaning, "they did not live in a right relationship with him"). When you see one, you should know it is caused by the other. The OT contains many examples of *evildoer*s who for one reason or another—rebellion, turning to other gods, self-centered interests, forgetfulness, and so forth—chose to break off their relationship with God (e.g., many of Israel's kings). The consequences of such a decision were always devastating. Bildad has pointed this out throughout ch 18.

FROM THE TEXT

1. **Summary of Bildad's Second Speech.** After a brief angry reaction to Job's belligerent attitude, Bildad got right to the point. The wicked experience one calamity after another—darkness, failure, traps, terror, disease, sudden death, destruction of their property, and loss of remembrance of their family name. Clines holds that Bildad was not speaking of Job in particular in this speech, but only of the wicked in general while attempting to defend God's justice and "the stable moral order" of the universe (1989, 409, 423-24).

However, most scholars believe that Bildad was attacking Job. While he never mentioned Job's name, it is no coincidence that Job's suffering matched exactly with Bildad's list of calamities. The conclusion was obvious. Job had sinned against God and was now receiving God's judgment for his sin. Job's response in the next chapter (19:2-6) indicates he knew full well what Bildad was up to.

Like a skilled prosecutor, Bildad presented every shred of evidence known to him to arrive at a guilty verdict. Unfortunately for him, he was unaware of the conversations in heaven described in the prologue. This is the one piece of evidence he really needed to solve the mystery of Job's sufferings.

Readers of this chapter should recognize the importance of exercising caution when forming opinions about other people. Hasty conclusions, without all the evidence, inevitably lead to errors and strife. Only God is aware of the total picture.

Bildad's main points are as follows:
- Job, you are self-centered and arrogant. You treat even your friends as stupid.
- The wicked experience a variety of awful calamities. They are forced to live in darkness. They are in constant dread of disease and sudden death. And their children die early, thus obliterating any memory of their family.
- Job, you have already experienced all these calamities. Thus, your guilt is obvious.

2. Bildad's Cruelty. Most people are very careful to be positive when speaking of other people's children. But Bildad cruelly drags Job's children into the conversation (18:19). Previously he mentioned the *possibility* that Job's children had died because of their own personal sins (8:4). Now, however, he connects their death with Job's sins. He is absolutely certain that the early death of one's children is one of the consequences of living a wicked life. Because Job had lost all ten of his children, he must be guilty of some immense sin.

This was a very mean-spirited attack—probably one of the cruelest statements in the book. Bildad was so caught up in trying to maintain his black-and-white, cause-and-effect theory of God's justice that he forgot that his primary reason for coming was to comfort Job (2:11). He believed that universal principles of retribution must be upheld at all costs, even if it means "kicking people when they are down" (Andersen 1976, 188).

IN THE TEXT

D. Job's Response to Bildad (19:1-29)

By this point in the book, Job feels isolated and alone. His three friends continue to attack him, and God refuses to answer his cries for help. Even his family and household staff now avoid him. No one, either in heaven or on earth, supports Job in his hour of greatest need. The reader knows differently, for God is still his number one supporter (1:8; 2:3), but this is how Job feels.

Job still possesses a deep conviction that he is innocent of any sin. And he believes that God is a just God in his overall governance of the world. Therefore, he is totally convinced God will someday vindicate him. His words concerning a "redeemer/vindicator" (19:25-27) are his most hopeful comments in the entire book. He desperately wishes he could receive God's vindication before he dies, but inwardly he senses this is not going to happen. His death is too close. So his mind imagines creating a permanent record of his life and his plea for justice that will survive beyond his death. Thus, God would always have available the evidence of Job's innocence.

Job's speech has four sections:
1. My Friends, Why Do You Persist in Tormenting Me? (19:1-6)
2. God Is the One Who Has Caused My Misery (19:7-12)
3. My Social Relationships Have Disintegrated (19:13-22)
4. I Will Be Vindicated Someday (19:23-29)

1. My Friends, Why Do You Persist in Tormenting Me? (19:1-6)

Job is bothered by his friends' repeated attacks. They will not stop tormenting him. This is especially aggravating when they present no proof to support their arguments. Job cannot understand why they are so intent on correcting him. Even if he is wrong about what has caused his suffering, what does it matter to them? God is the only one who should be offended, not them.

■ **1** For comments on the introductory formula → 3:2.

■ **2** Job begins his response to Bildad with the same words Bildad used at the beginning of his two speeches (8:2; 18:2 NRSV)—**How long?** In other words, two can play this game of complaining. By this time in the dialogue, it is obvious that both Job and his three friends are very angry at each other. Job believes his friends are trying to **torment** and **crush** him with their words. Even though he requested that God crush him (6:9), he is not about to let the friends succeed in their endeavors.

■ **3** Job accuses the friends of **ten** attacks against him, even though there have only been five speeches from the friends thus far. He is not trying to be exact here. **Ten** is simply a large, exaggerated number indicating their relentless persistence. It is also the number of completeness (Job 1:2-3; Gen 31:7, 41; Num 14:22; 1 Sam 1:8). It reinforces his point that the friends will not stop their fusillade of criticism until he agrees with their arguments.

The verb for **attack** (*hkr*) appears only here in the OT. Scholars have sought for cognates in other Semitic languages, but none are conclusive; so its exact meaning is unknown. The translation **attack** is acceptable as a parallel to **reproached** in the first clause.

■ **4** In Job 7:20 Job questioned God concerning the impact of his sin on the Almighty. If perchance he had committed a sin against God, how would that hurt God? Would it cause God so much agony that he would be forced to inflict severe suffering upon Job? Now in 19:4, Job places the same issue before the three friends. Hypothetically, if he had strayed away from God and mistakenly claimed innocence, how would that hurt the friends? In Job's thinking, it should not hurt them at all, for the matter would be between him and God: **my error *resides with me***. So why, then, are the friends being so antagonistic to him? Why are they repeatedly attacking him and making his life miserable?

The verb **gone astray** (*šgh*) and the noun **error** (*mĕšûgâ*) are related. They refer to inadvertent errors or unintentional mistakes that are later discovered to have offended God and to be in need of atonement (also 6:24; 12:16). The sin offering was designated to deal specifically with this situation (Lev 4:1-35). Clearly, Job is not speaking here of gross sins such as rebellion or apostasy. But he is willing to admit to unintentional errors if God will show him what they are (Job 13:23). He has even admitted to the possibility of youthful sins in the distant past (v 26). In any case, even if he was guilty of such hypothetical wrongs, this should not call for the kind of ruthless criticism thrown at him by the friends.

■ **5-6** These two verses are usually taken as a single conditional sentence. The condition (19:5) is already taking place. The GNT has captured its sense in this way: "You think you are better than I am, and regard my troubles as proof of my guilt." This characterization of Job's friends is correct. They have continually presented themselves as superior to him, and they have attacked his beliefs as ignorant and even stupid (Eliphaz [15:2-18]; Bildad [8:2-3; 18:2-4]; Zophar [11:2-6, 12]). They were trapped in a legalistic mindset that regarded all suffering as caused by sin. Thus, Job's troubles were self-caused and proof of his sinfulness. This was in spite of Job's righteous reputation in the prologue, which God confirmed (1:1, 8; 2:3).

Job, on the other hand, believes **God** (*Eloah*) has caused his troubles and for no good reason. Therefore, God has **wronged** (*'wt*) him ("acted perversely with" him [Seow 2013, 814]) by treating him as if he were a sinner, even though he is blameless. The verb *'wt* means "to bend or distort something from its normal state." Ecclesiastes uses the same verb to describe how God sometimes distorts the world from the way humans think it should function (Eccl 1:15; 7:13). Both Bildad (Job 8:3) and Elihu (34:12) believed that God never wrongs anyone. He never "pervert[s] justice" (8:3; 34:12). But Job is convinced differently. His own life is exhibit number one of God's unjust treatment of human beings. And he has many more examples to share in his next speech (21:7-21).

In 19:6*b* the Hebrew *māṣôd* can mean either **net** (here and Ezek 12:13) or "siege works" (Isa 29:3). The NIV and NRSV prefer **net**, connecting the verse with the traps of Bildad's previous speech (Job 18:8-10). The NJPS uses "siege works," thus providing a bridge to the military imagery a few verses later (19:12). Although different images are used, the meaning is the same in either case. God has surrounded Job with restrictive barriers (this reiterates Job's comments about the hedge in 3:23).

2. God Is the One Who Has Caused My Misery (19:7-12)

In 19:6 Job made a transition from criticizing his friends to complaining about God's mistreatment of him. Now in vv 7-12 he continues this thought using a series of metaphorical images.

■ **7** Job's first complaint is that there is no response to his cries for help. ***Violent wrong!*** (*ḥāmās*) was apparently a loud scream for help that a person uttered when attacked by someone intending to do them harm (Jer 20:8; Hab 1:2). Whether Job had actually shouted out this specific word is not stated. But there are definite indications in the book of tremendous emotional distress when he could have done so (Job 3:3-26; 6:2-3, 8-9; 7:11-21; 10:1-22; 14:13).

His point is that no matter how often or how loudly he cries out, no one has yet come to offer assistance. This complaint is directed particularly at God, but Job would gladly accept help from any sympathetic ear. The request for **justice** (*mišpāṭ*) in 19:7*b* lays his complaint squarely at God's feet. Job has complained about God's justice before (7:20-21; 9:13-24; 10:5-7, 14-15; 16:7-14). He was especially critical that God treats the righteous the same as the wicked (9:22). But until God breaks his silence, Job will have to endure his suffering without justice.

■ **8** A second complaint is that God has restricted his journey in life by placing obstacles in his **way** and by obscuring his path with **darkness**. This reiterates an earlier complaint about being hedged in (3:23 [for comments on the words for **way** in Job → 3:23]).

■ **9** Job's third complaint is that God has **stripped** him of his **honor** (lit. "glory") and **crown**. He is speaking here of the respect and honor he formerly received as a wealthy leader of his community. He was once an honorable patriarch of a large family and an outstanding example of righteousness (1:1-3; 29:2-25). He had a sterling reputation that he wore like a robe and turban (29:14). Now God has **stripped** him of that **honor** and left him sickly (7:5; 30:30) and attired in "sackcloth" (16:15). There may be an allusion here to the "glory" and "honor" God crowns every human being with because they are his creatures (Ps 8:5 [6 HB]). In Job's thinking, God no longer wanted him as his creature.

■ **10** Job uses two additional metaphors in this verse to complain of God's total destruction of his life. They contrast downward and upward motion. First, he is like a building that God **tears . . . down** from all sides. Then he is like a tree that God **uproots** from the ground. A tree that is cut off leaving its stump intact is still capable of coming back to life (14:7-9). But when the stump also is removed, the death of the tree is inevitable.

The word for **hope** (*tiqwâ*) has been used numerous times already by both Job and his friends. Job believes that God has destroyed any possibility of a better future for him. His only hope now is that God will destroy him quickly and thus end his suffering (6:8-9; 7:6; 14:7, 19; 17:15).

■ **11** Job's fifth complaint is directed at God's **anger** toward him. A number of people in the OT are described as being angry (e.g., Cain, Jacob, Moses, Samuel, Saul, David, etc.), but the person displaying this characteristic most frequently is God. In the book of Job alone, anger is associated with God eleven times (4:9; 9:5, 13; 14:13; 16:9; 19:11; 20:23, 28; 21:17; 35:15; 42:7). This is not surprising considering that the book is the story of a man who regards God ***as his enemy*** (*ṣar*; 16:9) and believes God thinks of him in the same way.

By this time in the story, the relationship between Job and God has deteriorated significantly. Job has not cursed God as the Examiner predicted (1:11; 2:5), but he regards God as a silent enemy whose anger has stripped him of his family, possessions, health, and reputation.

In the OT the picture of God as angry occurs frequently because of the numerous times individuals and nations turned away from him to serve other gods. However, this picture must be set alongside other depictions of God that characterize him much differently. For example: "The LORD is compassionate and gracious, slow to anger, abounding in love. He will not always accuse, nor will he harbor his anger forever" (Ps 103:8-9). "For his anger lasts only a moment, but his favor lasts a lifetime" (Ps 30:5 [6 HB]). (→ "God's Paradoxical Nature" sidebar at Job 16:19 for further discussion on God's nature in the book of Job.)

■ 12 Job's final complaint uses the metaphor of an attacking army to symbolize the hopelessness of his defenses against the power of God. God's **troops** have massed together, built a road or **siege ramp** against him, and set up their camp around him, thus cutting off any escape. The irony of 19:12 is that all this military activity is directed against Job's **tent** (→ 5:24). Job was helpless against such an onslaught.

3. My Social Relationships Have Disintegrated (19:13-22)

In vv 13-22 Job reveals for the first time how significantly his social relationships have deteriorated. There have been hints of this in earlier speeches (12:4; 16:10-11; 17:2, 6), but here Job provides more details about the reaction to his suffering by those in his household and community. This is a heart-wrenching passage from a person who feels totally isolated. He no longer has a social network of family and friends to support him. All the people whom he cared about and with whom he spent the most time have deserted him in his time of need. This may be the key reason why he decided to live at the town garbage dump rather than in his own home (2:8).

■ 13 The first groups to abandon Job were his "brothers" and **acquaintances**. The Hebrew for "brother" (*'āḥ*) carries a wide range of meanings from blood brother (Exod 7:1) to tribal members (Josh 1:14-15) to people in neighboring countries (Amos 1:9, 11). Here the word probably means his extended family including siblings and their families. These individuals show up again at the end of the book, this time bringing kind words and gifts after Job's fortunes change for the better (Job 42:11).

Job blames God for "removing" (see NASB and NKJV) these family members from him. He does not mean they have moved to a new community. He is referring to the social barriers such as fear and disgust that have shut off communication between them.

In the LXX the "brothers" are the subject, and the verb is plural in 19:13*a*. This provides a parallel with v 13*b*. In contrast, the MT has a singular causative verb making God the subject. Either interpretation is possible, but the MT provides a solid bridge between this section and Job's complaints against God in vv 7-12.

■ 14 Job's **relatives** (lit. "closest ones") and "those who have known me" (v 14*a*) were the second group that wanted nothing to do with him (they "have failed me" [NRSV]). In Lev 21:2-3 a person's "closest ones" (*qārôb*) are defined as "mother, father, son, daughter, brother, and unmarried sister." The book of Ruth (2:20; 3:12) expands this relationship even further to include more distant clan members.

In Job 19:14*b* many scholars support moving the first two Hebrew words of v 15 to the end of v 14 as the subject of that clause. This provides a more normal line length and meter pattern for both vv 14 and 15, yielding "the sojourners of my house" **(my guests) have forgotten me**. "Sojourners" were people who immigrated to another land and were considered foreigners by the native population (18:19; Gen 23:4; Exod 2:22). "The sojourners of my house" probably refers to foreigners who were living on Job's property or at least in proximity and were benefiting from their association with him. If Job was as wealthy as indicated in Job 1:3, he may have had many sojourners who rented some of his property and/or wanted to be near him.

■ 15 *My female servants regard me as a stranger; I am a foreigner in their eyes.* The role of a servant or slave was to help with the household tasks and business interests of the family that owned them. The prologue indicated that Job had many male servants who took care of his animals before the calamities struck (1:15-17). In 19:15 he mentions **female servants** under his control as well. Even though respect and obedience were expected from servants, these women no longer respected Job as their master. His appearance and mannerisms had disgraced him in their eyes. They treated him as a **stranger** (*zār*) and **foreigner** (*nokrî*). These parallel synonyms sometimes refer to despised foreign ethnic groups (Lam 5:2; Obad 11).

■ 16 Even when Job pleads with his servants for help, they do not respond. They know he has no power over them in his present condition, and they probably assume he will die shortly anyway. In all likelihood, Job is speaking broadly of his changed relationship with his family's servants, but he could also be referring to a specific servant who was still bringing food and other necessities to him at the dump. Perhaps this individual was being especially obnoxious to him.

The Hebrew for **beg/plead** (*ḥnn*) usually appears in passages where the speaker is pleading to *God* for mercy or favor (Job 8:5; 9:15). The word is used frequently by the psalmist in the laments (e.g., Ps 51:1 [3 HB]). Job 19:16 and 21 are a couple of rare instances where the speaker is imploring another human being.

■ 17 Next Job focuses on the reaction by his **wife** and brothers. In v 17*a* the Hebrew *rûaḥ* can mean either **spirit** or breath, leading some scholars to take this as a reference to halitosis—one of the side effects of Job's skin disease. However, it is hard to see how his breath would be noticeable over his other odors, considering he lived at a garbage dump and had probably not bathed in weeks. If **breath** is the intended meaning, then it must be part of an idiomatic expression, for *rûaḥ* is never used for the smell of one's breath (Clines 1989, 448).

More likely, Job's breath was not the problem, but everything else about him had become "repulsive" (NRSV) to his wife—his looks, attitude, emotional outbursts, depressed spirit, and so forth. Thus, ***my spirit*** (meaning "I") is a better translation. Job is alluding to his wife's distance from him. She was close enough to know he was still living but far enough away that she did not have to interact with him. The sense of the clause, then, is: "Being in my presence is repulsive to my wife."

Verse 17b is literally **I am loathsome to** *the children of my womb*. *Children of my womb* (*běnê beṭen*) sounds like a reference to Job's children, but they were all dead. The best interpretation is that Job is speaking of his siblings and the womb that bore them—the womb of his mother. The translation of *ḥnn* as **I am loathsome** (this verb appeared in v 16 from a different root) is based on cognates in Arabic and Syriac, for the word is found only here in the OT (Hartley 1988, 287, n. 5).

■ **18** Young children have no status in society, so their rejection of Job would have little social significance. However, they were probably taught by their parents to respect their elders. Job was especially deserving of respect because of his great wealth and standing in the community. The fact that these children have now "turned their backs" (NLT) on Job indicates the total rejection of him by his community, even down to the least significant.

The "young children" (NRSV) of this verse (*'ăwîl* appears only here and 21:11 in the OT) are not Job's, but probably those of his relatives, servants, and community (19:13-17). Some of the younger ones may have rejected Job simply out of fear of his physical appearance. Others were reflecting prejudices they had heard from their parents or older siblings. Job's mention of this slight is just another example of the humiliating, emotional pain he was experiencing.

■ **19** *All the men of my council* (v 19a) and **those I love** conclude Job's list of individuals who have turned against him. The word ***council*** (*sôd*) was used earlier by Eliphaz in reference to God's council of divine beings (15:8). Here it means "the company of men in the community who were Job's intimate friends" (see Ps 55:13-14 [14-15 HB]).

■ **20** There is no consensus on the meaning of Job 19:20. Clines has over five pages of comments on possible interpretations from both ancient and modern scholars (1989, 430-32, 450-52). The literal translation of v 20a is: ***My bones cling to my skin and my flesh*** (see Ps 102:5b [6b HB]). One would expect the statement to be reversed ("My skin clings to my bones") since the bones provide the solid framework for the body. Therefore, Job is probably creating a different word picture. Here he means that his body is so weak and worn down that only his **skin** and ***flesh*** keep his **bones** connected together. His skeleton is in danger of coming apart.

The traditional interpretation is that this is a comment on Job's emaciated physical condition, and v 20b is a statement that he has just barely escaped death (the source of the English idiom "by the skin of my teeth"). The LXX translation is based on a different Hebrew text and interprets both clauses as references to his physical condition. The main problem with both the LXX and the traditional interpretation is that they fail to explain why Job would insert a remark about the status of his health into a passage on his deteriorating social relationships.

This is not a problem for some, but others look for an alternative meaning. For example, Seow and Clines hold that Job's poor health is only a metaphor for his "shattered state" of mind (Seow 2013, 801) and "psychic sense of isolation" (Clines 1989, 452). His sickly body symbolizes the utter despair and alienation in which he finds himself. This may be the best way to connect this clause with the preceding verses.

Verse 20b is just as troublesome. The verb *mlṭ* means "escape from something" (1:15-19), which has been interpreted as "escape from death." But Job has already mentioned several times that he is not interested in escaping death. In fact, he looks forward to it to put him out of his misery (3:3-26; 6:8-9). So this clause is not about any narrow escape from Sheol. Most likely, Job is speaking of what is now left to him, following the calamities and his rejection by family and friends. Thus, **I have escaped *with (nothing but)* the skin of my teeth**. Or ("Since my relatives and former friends have deserted me"), ***I now survive with only* the skin of my teeth**. Teeth do not have skin, so scholars have suggested several meanings, such as "gums," "cheeks," or "lips." None are conclusive. The phrase is probably an idiomatic expression whose meaning has been lost.

■ **21** After listing all the people in his community who have repudiated him, Job turns to his three friends and asks cynically if they will help him. There is probably some bitterness in his calling them **my friends**, for they have not acted like friends up to this point. The repetition of his plaintive cry for help—***Be merciful to me! Be merciful to me!***—is a rhetorical technique to press upon them his desperation (see the same in Ps 123:3). As with Job 19:16, this is a rare usage of the verb *ḥnn* as a plea to another human being rather than to God. In v 21b and continuing into v 22, Job returns to his earlier claims that **God** (*Eloah*) is to blame for turning all these people against him (vv 6-12).

■ **22** Job now asks a double question of the three friends. First, he asks why they have taken God's side against him. The Hebrew for **pursue** (*rdp*) can mean either "persecute" or **pursue**. Job probably means both. **God** (*El*) was responsible for the original calamities in the prologue (1:21; 2:10; 12:9-10), and he is also continuing to pursue Job with attacks, nightmares, and emotional distress up to the present moment (19:8-19; 7:14; 10:16-17).

While Job's friends have not harmed him physically as God had, they have hounded him with false accusations, specifically trying to force him to admit his sinfulness. They may not see themselves as working for God, but Job regards them as another component of the same divinely organized conspiracy to destroy him.

Second, Job asks why they have acted like predatory animals. He made a similar accusation against God in 10:16. Why will they not ***be merciful to*** him (19:21a)? They may not understand his situation, but they are not naive. They are purposely united in attacking him with never-ending cruel and vicious barbs. Like predators, they have torn at the **flesh** of their prey. In a later passage (vv 28-29) Job warns that they will receive divine judgment if they continue this persecution.

4. I Will Be Vindicated Someday (19:23-29)

There is no question that vv 25-27 are the most positive remarks to be found in all of Job's speeches (→ From the Text for ch 17). And they are also some of the most well-known verses due to the influence of Handel's *Messiah*. Unfortunately, this section contains numerous grammatical problems that have led to multiple interpretations. What we can say for sure is that Job expected to be vindicated someday, but he did not know when this would occur. He was also confident that the friends would experience God's punishment if they continued to persecute him.

■ **23-24** Job turns abruptly to a different topic in 19:23. He knows his death is imminent (7:7-8; 9:25-26; 10:20-22). He welcomes it, for death will bring an end to his suffering, but he is afraid he will die before God takes up his case. Therefore, he wishes that a permanent record be made of his words so his side of the story can be told, even if he is gone. He has no one on earth to defend him because everyone has turned against him (19:13-22). A written record is his only means of ensuring his vindication.

Job does not identify what **words** he has in mind (v 23), but most likely he was thinking of the evidence he collected earlier for his case against God (13:17-18). This would include: (1) all the events in his life that attest to his righteousness as described in 1:1, (2) carefully worded arguments that challenge God's motives for causing his suffering, and (3) a plea for God to restore his good name even if he is not alive.

The nature of the writing materials is not clear. The NIV supports the possibility of three different surfaces: **on a scroll** (v 23), **on lead** (tablets; 19:24a), or **in rock**. But the more common interpretation is that only one surface is intended: ***on a stone*** (v 24b). The verb in v 23b (*ḥqq*) is generally used with engraving on a hard material such as a stone (Isa 22:16) or a brick (Ezek 4:1). So Job 19:23b would be: ***Oh that they were inscribed on an inscription*** (*sēper*)*!*

(Oh that) with an iron stylus and lead they were engraved on a stone forever! There has been much discussion concerning the ***stylus*** (*'ēṭ*) in v 24. Iron tools were definitely needed to engrave on stone, but **lead**, being a softer metal, was useless. Some have suggested that the tool was an alloy of iron and lead. Others that the lead was poured into the incised letters to make them more durable and readable (as in Darius I's [522-486 BC] Behistun Inscription). And still others that Job's words were recorded on lead tablets. None of these suggestions is conclusive. Perhaps there was some usage of lead by ancient stone carvers that has been lost to modern interpreters.

In any case, Job's wish is for the creation of a permanent stele (of which there are many examples from the ancient world, such as the Code of Hammurabi and the Mesha Stele) that would last **forever** (in answer to Bildad's characterization of the wicked as forgotten [18:17]). He would much rather speak to God in person while he is still alive. But failing that, a stele would at least preserve his arguments in a permanent form so that at some point in the future God would have to declare him innocent.

■ **25** With absolute certainty Job suddenly leaps from his valley of despair and proclaims from the mountaintop of faith that he has a **redeemer** (*gō'ēl*). He is confident of this truth (**I know**; with emphatic I [*'ănî*]) and that his redeemer is living. Other passages that have used this same verb to indicate certainty include: 9:2, 28; 10:13; 13:18.

The concept of a redeemer derives from an ancient practice in Israelite society. A redeemer was a person's relative who came to the rescue when a family member was in trouble (much like the concept of a "rich uncle" in American society). Sometimes because of difficult financial circumstances people were forced to sell themselves, their family, or their property to someone else to pay off a debt. The kinsman-redeemer was obligated to buy back the people or property in order to keep them within the clan and maintain the honor of the family.

The kinsman-redeemer had other responsibilities as well, such as going to court to defend the rights of a clan member (Prov 23:10-11), marrying a widow within the clan and having children by this widow in order to preserve the family name of a deceased man (Ruth 4:14), and capturing the murderer of a family member and putting that person to death according to the *lex talionis* ("an eye for an eye" [see Num 35:19]). All the instructions regarding these practices are found in Lev 25:25-55; 27:1-33; Num 35:16-34; Deut 19:4-6, 11-13.

Strictly speaking, the only part of a typical redeemer's role Job is interested in is his vindication in a court setting. He wishes for someone of authority to stand up on his behalf and declare him "blameless and upright" (Job 1:1). Both the NIV and the NRSV acknowledge this understanding in the marginal reading "vindicator," which is probably a more accurate translation in this context.

The concept of a redeemer is also applied to God in many passages, particularly in Isaiah and the Psalms. As one would expect, most of these passages emphasize God's greatest acts of redemption when Israel was in the most trouble—in Egypt (Ps 106:10) and in Babylonia (Isa 48:20). God was the Redeemer of Israel on those occasions as well as many others.

So who is Job's redeemer/vindicator? This person is certainly not a member of his family or a close friend, for they have all turned against him (Job 19:13-22). Neither is his redeemer a divine go-between such as an angel (5:1) or a mediator (9:33). Both of these passages questioned whether Job would find any help from them, even if these individuals existed.

Most likely, his redeemer is God himself. God is the only one who knows all the facts about Job's case and can restore his honor. Thus, he will make an excellent "witness" on Job's behalf (16:19). But to an even greater extent, he is the only one who can declare Job innocent of sin. A third party (intermediary) could not do this. Further, God is obligated to help Job because of Job's complete devotion to him (1:1). Even though God is punishing him now for some unknown reason, Job believes this same God will one day end the punishment and become his Redeemer/Vindicator.

Of course, this creates a tension between the God who caused his suffering and the God who can and will relieve it, between the God who is Judge of all and the God who is also Redeemer. But such is the complex nature of this God whom the author is trying to describe (→ "God's Paradoxical Nature" sidebar at 16:19 for further discussion of this difficult problem). Both the Psalms and Isaiah portray God as both Judge and Redeemer (Pss 9:4, 8 [5, 9 HB]; 19:14 [15 HB]; 50:6; 58:11 [12 HB]; 78:35; 103:4; Isa 11:3-4; 33:22; 41:14; 43:14; 44:6; etc.).

There is an additional reason why God is Job's Redeemer. If God is truly a God of justice, he must stand up for Job at some point in time. He cannot allow Job's sterling character, which readers are aware of from the prologue, to be blackened forever. Otherwise his claims to be a just God (Pss 9:8 [9 HB]; 33:5; 37:28; 89:14 [15 HB]; 99:4; 103:6; etc.) are for naught.

Job believes that someday his Redeemer **will stand on the earth**. The verb **stand** (*qwm*) can be taken as a legal term meaning "stand up and witness in a courtroom" (Job 16:8; 31:14). The courtroom in this case will be **on the earth** (lit. "on the dust"). This could be a reference to God's appearance at the dusty ash heap where Job now resides. But "dust" (*'āpār*) can also be used as a synonym for "earth" (28:2; 41:33 [25 HB]), and this is the meaning here. Job's use of this phrase signifies a public setting where God will declare to all humanity that Job is innocent. This is the vindication he has been seeking.

Job cannot predict exactly when his vindication will occur, for God has remained silent. His use of the word *'aḥărôn* here indicates his uncertainty. Some interpret *'aḥărôn* as a title for God: "the Last One," as in "the First and the Last" (Isa 41:4; 44:6; 48:12; Seow 2013, 823-24). Others see an eschatological reference to the end of time: **in the end**, "at the last" (NRSV). But more likely, Job is using the word adverbially, meaning "later, in coming days, at some point in the future." The word is used this way in the Psalter when speaking of the coming generation (Pss 48:13 [14 HB]; 78:4; 102:18 [19 HB]).

Job is fully aware that his own death is not far off, so God's pronouncement will probably not come until after his death. He would prefer that God act sooner. But whether he is alive or in Sheol, he knows his Redeemer will come through for him in the end, for his Redeemer is a *living* Redeemer who will outlive him. This living Redeemer is worth even more to Job than the stone stele of Job 19:24.

■ **26-27** The literal translation of v 26a makes no sense at all: "And after they have stripped off my skin this." The subject "they" and the antecedent of "this" are unspecified. Also, the verb in the clause (*nqp*) is used in only one other OT passage (Isa 10:34) in reference to cutting down trees with an axe. Among the many proposals to smooth out the translation, the best is to treat the third plural verb as a singular passive (GKC, §144g) and take the antecedent of "this" as the entire second clause of Job 19:25. Connecting the two verses together yields: ***And at some point in the future he will stand upon the earth, and this, after my skin is stripped off.*** The "stripping off of Job's skin" is a metaphor for his death. He believes he will die before his vindication is secured.

However, Job really wishes that **God** (*Eloah*) would make an appearance on earth before his death. Verses 26b and 27ab are three parallel lines emphasizing Job's desire to see God up close, **not (as) a stranger** (*zār*). Since the calamities, Job and God have treated each other as "strangers" (the same word was used to describe the relationship between Job and his female servants in v 15). Job even pointed out how their relationship had deteriorated to the status of "enemies" (v 11; see 16:9). He wants this barrier between them broken down. "Seeing God" is a metaphor for reconciliation and being in fellowship with God (Pss 17:15; 27:4; 46:8 [9 HB]). This desire to **see God** lies at the very heart of all Job's speeches. He would do anything to renew his fellowship with God, even descending into Sheol for a period of time if need be (Job 14:13-17). The author carries this theme of "seeing God" to the very end of the book, for in Job's final comments he acknowledges that his wish has been granted: "now my eye sees you" (42:5 NRSV).

Opinion is divided as to when Job thinks he will get to see God. One view is that Job will behold God and be reconciled to him after his death and at the time of his resurrection. This interpretation is supported by the translations in the Latin Vulgate and the KJV, and it has been the predominant interpretation throughout most of Christian history (ACCS, 6:105-6; Wesley 1765, 1566). However, the doctrine of the resurrection of the dead belongs in the NT. Further, Job has already described his death as a one-way trip to Sheol from which he will not return (7:9-10; 10:21; 14:14; 16:22; 17:13-16). Thus, this view is not likely (although Janzen has tried to revive it [1985, 135-50]).

A second view is that Job will see God restore his honor *after* he gets to Sheol (lit. "away from/without my flesh" [19:26]). He will not be brought back to life, as would happen in a resurrection, but he will somehow be made aware that God has vindicated him on earth. This approach is a strong possibility based on Job's earlier comments. He knew his time on earth was short, so there was little opportunity to see God now. But he believed he had a good case to present to God and he knew he would be vindicated when his Redeemer considered his permanent inscription (vv 23-24; 13:18). However, Job earlier noted the unlikelihood of people in Sheol knowing what is taking place on earth (14:21).

A third view is that Job knows he will see God very shortly and be vindicated *before* he dies ("from"/**in my flesh**). The existence of his Redeemer (v 25) is the reason for his confidence. Thus, the imperfect form of the verbs of vv 26-27 would be translated in the future tense: "In my flesh I shall see God, whom I shall see on my side, and my eyes shall behold [him]" (NRSV). This approach has much to commend it, but it fails to account for the general sense of hopelessness that pervades all of Job's speeches both before and after this statement.

If Job knew for certain that his Redeemer would restore his honor before his death, why would he be so critical of God now (16:7-17)? Why would he ask God to leave him alone so he can die by himself in peace (7:11-21; 10:18-22)? And why would he desire to create an engraved stone to preserve his memory after death (19:23-24)? Further, how could he possibly know that he would be vindicated before death if God will not talk to him?

In contrast to these theories, Clines proposes that there should be a major distinction between what Job knows for certain (v 25) and what he desires (vv 26-27; 1989, 461-62). He knows he has a Redeemer (v 25), but he does not know when his Redeemer will come to his rescue. Therefore, he can only hope to see God while he is alive (**in my flesh** [v 26]). In this interpretation the verbs in vv 26-27 are translated as modals ("In my flesh I would see God . . ."). The passage is thus rendered: ***In my flesh I desire to see*** [*hzh*] ***God*** [*Eloah*]***, whom I desire to see*** [*hzh*] ***for myself, and my eyes desire to see*** [*r'h*] ***(him), not (as) a stranger.*** To see God before he dies is Job's fervent desire, but realistically he knows it will probably not happen.

Verse 27c is literally "my kidneys fail in my chest." The word "kidneys" is sometimes used as a metaphor for the heart or inner being of a person (Pss 7:9 [10 HB]; 16:7; 26:2; 73:21; 139:13). Thus, this clause is usually interpreted as a deep longing to see Job's desires in Job 19:25-27 come to pass: **How my heart yearns within me!** But others see here a sudden return to the reality of Job's present situation. He is exhausted and weak: "My heart pines within me" (NJPS). The normal usage of the verb *klh* ("fail"; Pss 69:3 [4 HB]; 71:9 [NJPS]; 73:26) favors the latter interpretation.

■ **28-29** Job concludes this speech with one long sentence that criticizes his friends for things they have said and then warns them of the consequences that lie ahead. The sentence begins with a *kî* that some versions (NIV, NRSV) take as a conditional particle, meaning **If you say** . . . But in light of the fact that the friends have already tormented Job severely, the particle should be interpreted as concessive: **Although you say** . . . (Ps 21:11 [12 HB]; Isa 54:10; Hos 13:15). Job accuses them of conspiring to persecute him ("How we will persecute him" [Job 19:28*a* NRSV]). The friends have never explicitly said this, but their harsh verbal attacks have hurt Job as deeply as the loss of his family and health. As he said in v 22, he feels like he is being torn apart by a predatory animal.

"The root of the matter is found in him" (v 28*b* NRSV) is the comment that hurts Job the most. All three of his friends have accused him of causing his own troubles by sinning against God (Eliphaz [15:5-6, 12-16]; Bildad [8:5-6]; Zophar [11:4-6, 14]). No matter what he says in his own defense, he has been unable to convince them that God is the real culprit. The MT has "in me" at the end of 19:28, but the LXX reading **in him** is preferred.

Verse 29 is a word of warning to the friends lest they think they are above reproach. They have used their tongues as swords against Job (Pss 57:4 [5 HB]; 59:7 [8 HB]; 64:3 [4 HB]). Their **wrath/*anger*** was obvious in these attacks (Eliphaz [Job 15:2-6]; Bildad [8:2-3; 18:2-4]; Zophar [11:2-6, 12; 20:2-3]). However, God's **sword** will strike them down if they continue their persecution of Job. The word **sword** (*hereb*) is often used in the OT as a symbol of God's punishment against the wicked (Pss 7:12 [13 HB]; 17:13; Isa 34:6; Jer 12:12; Ezek 32:10).

The last clause in Job 19:29 emphasizes God's **judgment** against the friends if they continue to torment Job with false accusations. This thought echoes his earlier charge that the friends were misrepresenting God's position (13:7-12). He warned them at that time that their words of deceitfulness (v 7) would not go unnoticed by God, and his judgment would terrify them (v 11). As we discover later,

Job's warning to the friends proves to be prophetic, for God severely rebukes them at the end of the story (42:7-8).

FROM THE TEXT

Summary of Job's Response to Bildad. There is no question that ch 19 is Job's most important speech in the book. He addresses three concerns. First, he castigates the friends again for their unkindness to him. They acted like violent predators intent on destroying him. Second, he blames God for driving his family and friends away from him. God, too, was out to destroy him. And third, he proclaims his certainty that God will eventually vindicate him. His comments about his "Redeemer/Vindicator" are one of the high points in the book.

Job's main points are as follows:
- My friends, why do you continue to attack me so severely? I have not harmed you in the least. If I have sinned, the matter is between me and God.
- God has wronged me. Even though I cry out for his help, he refuses to bring justice. He continues to treat me as his enemy.
- I feel totally isolated. All my social relationships are gone. I do not have even one single friend left in the world.
- I wish I could leave a permanent written engraving on stone that would verify the truth about my life. Then, even after I die, God will still have the evidence needed to vindicate me.
- I am absolutely certain that God will one day vindicate me of any moral wrongdoing.
- You, my friends, have placed yourselves in great danger of being severely punished by God.

IN THE TEXT

E. Zophar's Second Speech (20:1-29)

After a brief comment about his need to speak again, Zophar launches into a long description of the tribulations that are experienced by the wicked. He includes the same type of afflictions mentioned by Eliphaz and Bildad in their second speeches (15:17-35; 18:5-21). One of his key ideas is that the wicked will suffer a divine reversal in their lives. They may be joyful, prosperous, and successful for the moment, but someday God will pour out his anger against them and remove all the good things in their lives. They will find themselves in Sheol at an early age. Zophar is convinced that this is the fate of every wicked person for two reasons—first, because the wisdom of the ages has proven this true since the beginning of time (20:4-5), and second, because God has decreed it (v 29).

Like the other friends Zophar does not accuse Job directly of being wicked, but some of the items in his list of afflictions are things Job has already endured.

So Zophar's intention is obvious. He is trying to convince Job to admit his sinfulness and warn him that God's punishment will only get worse if he refuses to repent. Ironically, Zophar's hard-hitting speech follows directly after Job's most positive comments so far (19:25-27). He could have picked up on that theme and encouraged Job to continue to hold onto his faith in his Redeemer. Instead, he reverts back to the same arguments the other friends have presented. This indicates that he really was not listening to Job. His mind was already made up, and his response is on an emotional level only. Nothing he says helps Job in the least.

There are two main sections to Zophar's speech:
1. I Have to Speak Again (20:1-3)
2. The Wicked Suffer a Sudden Divine Reversal (20:4-29)

1. I Have to Speak Again (20:1-3)

Job has just pleaded for mercy from his friends (19:21) and testified to having a Redeemer who will vindicate his name (v 25). These are certainly topics that merit a response from the friends. But the only statement that caught Zophar's attention was Job's concluding remark about God's judgment on the friends (v 29). This was an offense against his dignity that compelled him to reply.

■ 1 For comments on the introductory formula → 3:2.

■ 2 Earlier Eliphaz spoke of his **troubled thoughts** when he was awakened in the middle of the night by a divine spirit that scared him to death (4:13). Zophar has not had any such nighttime visitors, but his speech reveals a person who is deeply disturbed by Job's remarks. He simply cannot understand how a person like Job who had experienced so much suffering could continue to deny any responsibility for causing it. He feels he must make one more attempt to lay out the consequences that Job should expect from God in the days ahead.

Job 20:2b reads literally "because of my feelings within me." The word for "feelings" (*ḥûšî*) is disputed. Some take it from the root *ḥwš*, meaning "hurry," and others from another meaning of this root denoting "feel." The latter is followed here, although this root occurs with this interpretation in only one other passage (Eccl 2:25).

■ 3 Zophar takes Job's words in 19:29 as **a reproof that insults** him. The word **reproof** (*mûsār*) was used earlier by Eliphaz for God's "discipline" (5:17). As Eliphaz saw it, God was attempting to discipline Job by bringing suffering into his life. Zophar means something much more severe—a reproof or a reproach. How dare Job, a sinner, question his words of wisdom! This is an insult that calls for a strong rebuttal. His "discerning spirit" causes him **to reply**. "Discerning spirit" (lit. "my spirit of understanding") is a translation suggested by Habel that conveys Zophar's sense of his own superior wisdom (1985, 310). He is not about to admit that Job's wisdom is greater than his, so he feels compelled to go on the attack, just as he did in his first speech (ch 11).

2. The Wicked Suffer a Sudden Divine Reversal (20:4-29)

This section contains a long list of afflictions that descend upon the wicked. They are all horrible experiences no one would want to endure. On the surface, the wicked may appear to be well-off, enjoying the pleasures of life for a season. But suddenly their lives take an unexpected, downward turn that is no accident or coincidence. Zophar believes this is God's judgment on their sins (→ 5:9-16 where Eliphaz spoke of a possible, *positive*, divine reversal in the life of Job).

■ **4-5** Before beginning his list of afflictions, Zophar makes a connection between his views and the ancient wisdom traditions. The things he is about to mention are not new. They have been known since the beginning of time. Zophar attempts to accomplish two things by speaking in this way. The first is to ground his arguments in an authority that stretches back many generations. People have known since the very first couple was placed in the Garden of Eden that the wicked are punished for their sins. Both Eliphaz (15:17-18) and Bildad (8:8-9) used this same argument to support their views. Thus, all three friends have fallen back on the wisdom theology as something of a trump card that cannot be overturned—a universal principle that has been proven true over centuries of time. Therefore, if Job wishes to disagree with Zophar, he will have to find a way to disprove the collected wisdom of humanity.

The second purpose Zophar hopes to accomplish is to force Job to see how stupid he is. He does this by formulating his argument as a question: "Do you not know this from of old?" (20:4a NRSV). By this he means: "Why don't you know this? Everyone else knows this except you!" Job needs to recognize how out of touch he is from the rest of humanity. He stands isolated from the prevailing views of his time.

Zophar concludes his question with the first item in his list of afflictions. Job should already be aware of the brevity of good times in the life of the wicked. They may briefly experience ***rejoicing*** and **joy**, but suffering will come quickly (v 5). In v 4a the word "not" is missing in the MT. But the LXX adds it and so do most modern translations, for it is clearly implied in the question.

■ **6-7** The wicked sometimes rise to towering heights of power and influence that seem to reach the heavens. Their exalted stature is noticed by all. The psalmist admits that even the righteous are sometimes envious of the prosperity and success of the wicked (Ps 73:3-12). Nevertheless, their greatness is as short-lived as their "joy" (Job 20:5). They **will perish forever** like **dung** (v 7). So thorough will be their fall and disappearance that no one will remember they ever existed. Here Zophar is echoing a thought presented earlier by Bildad (18:17-19).

Some have attempted to relate this imagery to a tall tree that raises its top into the sky (Ps 37:35-36) or to ancient mythological deities that rebelled against the high gods and tried to usurp their place (Clines 1989, 485). But the connection is ambiguous.

■ **8-9** The wicked will fly away into nothingness just like a **dream** or **vision** vanishes upon waking from sleep (v 8). **Flies away** is a metaphor for dying, as in Ps

90:10. People who know the wicked will find that their relationship has suddenly ended. They will not even catch a glimpse of their former acquaintances. Even the **place** where they live will lose sight of them because they have disappeared into Sheol (v 9).

■ **10** This verse has generated many questions, but generally it speaks of the sudden loss of **wealth** by the wicked. Their prosperity will disappear quickly, just as their "joy" (v 5) and their exalted status (vv 6-7). This will leave their family even worse off than **the poor**, whom they will have to beg for assistance.

■ **11** One moment the wicked are full of limitless energy, the kind that is only found in children and young people, but in the blink of an eye they lie motionless in the grave.

■ **12-14** If wickedness were always viewed in connection with its outcome, very few people would be attracted by its appeal. However, wickedness is good at disguising its consequences behind its claims of sweetness, secrecy, instant gratification, and wealth (Prov 1:10-19; 7:6-27; 9:13-18; 20:17; 23:31-32).

At first, wickedness is **sweet** like a jawbreaker that lasts for hours. Children learn how to roll this candy around in their **mouth** both under their **tongue** and against their *palate* while enjoying the sugary taste. But unlike the jawbreaker that is sweet to the very end, wickedness has a surprise ending. Upon reaching one's **stomach**, it quickly turns into the **venom** of a poisonous snake (→ Job 20:16), bringing intense pain and the likelihood of death.

This is another metaphor for the sudden reversal in the fortunes of the wicked. Their sins that seemed so enjoyable at first will come back to destroy them in the end. The writer of Proverbs came to the same conclusion. The back door to the house of Lady Foolishness leads straight to Sheol (Prov 7:27; 9:18). The word for **venom** (*mĕrōrâ*) refers to the bitter bile produced by the liver (Job 20:25; 16:13). Apparently ancient people thought that the **venom** of snakes originated in the liver.

■ **15** Great wealth is another attractive enticement for the wicked (Prov 1:13), but any wealth gained through wickedness is enjoyed only temporarily. Like a forceful discharge of **vomit**, the wealth of the wicked will depart quickly and turbulently. This is the first time in this chapter that Zophar has mentioned **God** (*El*) as the cause of these sudden reversals in the life of the wicked. But the implication throughout the passage is that all their troubles are due to God's punishment for sin (Job 20:23, 26, 28-29). Thus, these tragedies are viewed as *divine* reversals.

■ **16** The pursuit of wickedness is like a child nursing at its mother's breast. The main difference is that the liquid received through "suckling" is not nourishment at all, but **the poison of serpents**. The wicked will surely die from this. ***The tongue of a snake*** will kill him (v 16b) indicates an ancient belief that the ***tongue*** (*lāšôn*) of a poisonous snake had something to do with the killing of its prey, even though snakes deliver their venom through their fangs.

The author of Job uses three different words for **snake** or **serpent**. The more general term *nāḥāš* appears in 26:13 in reference to the mythological sea monster

Rahab. In ch 20 two more words are used: *peten* (vv 14, 16) and *'ep'eh* (v 16). Both of these words refer to poisonous snakes such as the viper or cobra, but it is impossible to determine exactly which kind of snake is intended.

■ **17** A further deprivation the wicked experience is that they will not benefit from the well-watered land and its rich agricultural products. They will be sucking the poison of snakes (v 16) instead of feasting on **honey and cream**. Even though the meaning of v 17 is plain, the wording is quite awkward in Hebrew. Some scholars are uncomfortable with three repetitive words referring to streams—***water channels*** (*pĕlaggôt*), ***rivers*** (*nahărê*), and ***streams*** (*naḥălê*). They emend the word for ***rivers*** to *yiṣhār* or *šemen*, meaning "oil" (Clines 1989, 475). This yields a translation similar to 29:6 and Mic 6:7: "streams of olive oil" in parallel to ***streams of honey and cream***. This is a possibility, but a simpler emendation is to change the word ***rivers*** from the construct to the absolute state yielding the following: ***They will not benefit from the water channels and the rivers, or the streams of honey and cream***. In any case, the exact translation remains problematic.

Honey (*dĕbaš*), produced from either bees or date palms, is the same word used in Exod 3:8, 17 to describe the agricultural richness of the land of Canaan—"a land flowing with milk and honey." The Hebrew *ḥem'â* (**cream**) refers to some type of milk product. Some equate it with a thick, coagulated form of milk in the form of curds such as cottage cheese; others associate it with a product that flows, such as butter, cream, or yogurt. The connection with ***rivers*** and ***streams*** in v 17*a* favors the latter. Also, in Judg 5:25 Sisera asked Jael for water to drink and she gave him *ḥem'â*. This would indicate a product that is somewhat liquid.

■ **18** Zophar continues with the imagery of food by noting that the wicked will not get to eat the produce they have grown. They will be forced to give it away. Some have suggested that the verb **give back** (*šwb*) refers to vomiting (v 15), but more likely v 18*a* connects with v 19. The wicked will have to give their goods to the poor whom they have exploited. Their impoverished children will then have to beg the poor for food (v 10). In v 18*b* the emphasis is on wealth gained through **trading** rather than through labor. The wicked **will not enjoy the profit** from this as well.

■ **19** The reason why the wicked will experience a sudden reversal in their fortune is because they have severely harmed **the poor**. They have "crushed and abandoned" (NRSV) them, and they have **seized** their **houses** as well. Mistreatment of the poor and needy is a sin condemned repeatedly in the book of Proverbs (14:31; 19:17; 21:13; 22:9, 16, 22-23; 29:7). Job was aware of this, and he later testifies that he has never mistreated them (Job 31:16-23). What is most interesting here is that Zophar raises this sin above all others (Clines 1989, 491), whereas other parts of the OT emphasize different sins as the most significant (e.g., Gen 2:16-17; Exod 20:3-17; Deut 30:15-20). Zophar seems focused too narrowly on only one kind of sin. Social sins are also prominent in Eliphaz's thinking, as seen in his next speech (Job 22:6-9).

■ **20-22** These verses concentrate on the self-destructive greed of the wicked. There is a churning in the pit of their stomach that is fed by their craving for new conquests and more wealth and power. Something within agitates them to devour every possible good thing in life, but their success is fleeting. At the height of their achievements, numerous calamities (lit. "all the power of trouble" [v 22*b*]) will afflict them. The wicked are like the wind-blown fire that races across the forest consuming everything in its path, until it dies a sudden death for lack of more fuel.

■ **23** The translation of v 23*a* is difficult because no subject is expressed. The NIV relates the clause to the previous verses that speak of the wicked as feeding themselves on all the riches and power they can devour. The second and third clauses then describe God's **anger** as the consequence of their sinfulness. The NRSV makes God the one who forces his anger into the bellies of the wicked. Either option makes sense, but the first fits better in the overall context of Zophar's speech.

The Hebrew for **burning anger** (lit. "the heat of anger") is frequent in the OT. It is always used in reference to God's anger against sinful human beings (Pss 69:24 [25 HB]; 78:49; 85:3 [4 HB]). Thus, in Zophar's mind, the wicked will not escape the severe consequences of their sins. God's wrath will consume them (Job 20:26). Verse 23*c* reads literally "(he will) cause his warfare to rain on him." The word for "warfare" (*lĕḥûm*) is rare. It can mean either "flesh" or "warfare." Neither one provides a satisfactory translation in this context. Scholars have proposed numerous emendations (see Clines 1989, 477-78). The best is *laḥmô*, which yields: "and cause it to rain on him as his food." But this does not provide a meaningful parallel with **burning anger**. The closest parallel is "warfare," which some interpret as a metaphor for "weapons" (NJPS), "anger" (Gordis 1978, 219), or "hostility" (Seow 2013, 857-58), but the interpretation remains problematic.

■ **24** In this verse and the next Zophar draws on earlier comments by Job that God has used him as a target and shot poison-tipped arrows into his body (6:4; 7:20; 16:12-13). Zophar continues this metaphor with a humorous illustration that points out the impossibility of escaping from God's wrath.

When God sends his "burning anger" against the wicked (20:23), they try to flee. They may escape from the first calamity and think they are safe, but they will be confronted by another disaster very shortly, for the wicked cannot escape the judgment of God. Two other passages in the Prophets use this same imagery in speaking of the attempt by the wicked to avoid God's wrath against sin (Isa 24:18; Amos 5:19).

The type of **iron weapon** mentioned in Job 20:24*a* is unclear. Many think it refers to a sword, but it could also be an iron-tipped arrow, javelin, or spear in parallel with the second clause. The literal "bow of bronze" in v 24*b* is probably a figurative expression for **a bronze-tipped arrow** (see 2 Sam 22:35 for a literal usage). Iron is a much stronger metal than bronze, and so an iron weapon would be preferable in warfare. But either type of metal can kill a person, and that is the crux of the humor in the verse.

■ **25** When God's "arrow" (v 24) penetrates the **back** of the wicked person who is trying to flee, the wounded individual or someone else may pull the arrow out. But the **gleaming point** has struck the **liver**, causing a fatal blow. The sight of the bloody arrowhead brings **terrors** to the wicked, for death is inevitable. The word for **gleaming** (*bārāq*) usually refers to lightning (38:35), but several passages denote the light reflected from a metal sword or spear (Deut 32:41; Ezek 21:10, 15, 28 [15, 20, 33 HB]; Nah 3:3; Hab 3:11).

■ **26** The terrors of Job 20:25 are specified in v 26 with two metaphors—**total darkness** and **a fire unfanned**. These will destroy the wicked as well as every person in their family and every possession of value to them. The **total darkness** that lies in wait for them is Sheol (10:21-22). The fire that will devour them is not one ignited by humans, but rather a fire created by God that destroys everything (→ 1:16 for other OT references to the "fire of God"). This fire will **devour** (lit. "graze on") any "survivor" (lit.; *śārîd*) that **is left in his tent**.

■ **27** The wicked have no possibility of escaping the consequences of their sins, for both **the heavens** and **the earth** will testify against them. No doubt, Zophar is subtly criticizing Job's previous comment where he called on heaven and earth to defend him because they knew the truth about his innocence (16:18-19). Zophar believes Job is mistaken to think that heaven and earth will speak in his favor. Rather, they will **uncover his iniquity** and **rise up against him**. In Zophar's mind, Job's calamities were proof enough that God had already pronounced him guilty of sin.

■ **28** Zophar now switches to **waters** as a metaphor for God's wrath. **A flood** [lit. "a stream of water"] **will wash away** the **house** of the wicked, leaving nothing behind. This is another depiction of the sudden divine reversal in the life of the wicked. In v 28*a*, the subject *yĕbûl* (lit. "agricultural produce") is usually emended to *yûbal* (Jer 17:8) or *yābāl* (Isa 30:25; 44:4), meaning "a stream of water." This provides a coherent parallelism with the second clause. Likewise, the verb *yigel* is emended to *yāgōl* (*gll*) with the meaning "roll away" (or in this case, **wash away**).

■ **29** Zophar's conclusion is that the sudden downfall and punishment of **the wicked** is inevitable because **God** (*Elohim* in v 29*a*; *El* in v 29*b*) has determined it will happen. The word for **heritage/inheritance** (*naḥălâ*) appears most frequently in the OT in reference to the land of Israel. God gave the land as a whole to the nation (Deut 4:21, 38), and in sections to the tribes (Num 26:53-56) and individual families (Num 27:7-11). In Job 20:29 the word is a metaphor for the consequences of sin. The ***inheritance*** of the wicked is one calamity after another leading straight to Sheol.

FROM THE TEXT

1. **Summary of Zophar's Second Speech.** In his first speech Zophar pointed out how God sometimes treats us better than we deserve (11:6). But in this speech there is no sense of God's mercy. The wicked receive due punishment for all their sins. There are no exceptions. However, sometimes God delays his judg-

ment. Thus, the wicked may appear to be successful for a period of time, but their eventual punishment is assured.

Zophar's main points are as follows:
- Job, I am deeply disturbed by your comments in your last speech. You are obviously not listening to what we are saying.
- Ever since the beginning of time, the wisdom theology has taught us that the wicked experience an early death. They may prosper for a period of time, but at some point in the future their fortunes suddenly change. They experience a *divine reversal*.
- God has decreed that sin will always be punished.

2. God's Punishment of the Wicked. In the second cycle of speeches all three friends support the concept that God punishes the wicked. In the words of Paul, "God will repay each person according to what they have done" (Rom 2:6). But some argue that God does not actually punish people for sin. Rather, sin contains within it the seeds of its own consequences. Human beings create their own destruction. They build a pit and then fall into it, hurting themselves.

Actually, the OT contains passages that support both sides of the argument (the former—Gen 3:14-19; 6:5-7, 13; Pss 11:6; 145:20; Prov 21:12; Isa 11:4; 13:11; Jer 25:31; the latter—Pss 7:15 [16 HB]; 9:16 [17 HB]; 141:10; Prov 11:5). It is important to keep in mind that the ancient world did not distinguish between primary and secondary causes. The three friends believed, as did most Israelites, that God was the primary cause of all events in life, both good and bad.

IN THE TEXT

F. Job's Response to Zophar (21:1-34)

Job begins again with some brief comments on the lack of respect he has received from his friends. But then he quickly moves to answer the arguments that all three friends have made about the fate of the wicked. In contrast to their belief that the wicked experience horrible suffering as a consequence of their sins (15:17-35; 18:5-21; 20:4-29), Job's observations have been much different. For him, the wicked seem to have an easy lifestyle. They live long lives (21:7). Their children do well (vv 8, 11). Their houses are secure (v 9). Their farm animals thrive (v 10). They reject God but receive no punishment in return (vv 14-15). They enjoy festive occasions with musical entertainment (v 12). And they die a peaceful death (v 13). Even after death there is a grand funeral for them (vv 32-33). "How is this right?" asks Job. "How can God allow this to happen? Someone needs to teach God how to judge."

Job's speech divides into the following sections:
1. My Friends, Please Listen to Me (21:1-5)
2. The Wicked Do Well in Life (21:6-16)
3. God Does Not Judge Correctly (21:17-26)
4. My Friends, You Are Wrong (21:27-34)

1. My Friends, Please Listen to Me (21:1-5)

Once again, Job pleads for a hearing from his friends. They should be horrified over his appearance and suffering, instead of attacking him with their theories and explanations.

■ **1** For comments on the introductory formula → 3:2.

■ **2-3** Job asks his friends to **listen carefully** to what he has to say (13:5-6, 13, 17). Then they will better understand his suffering and be able to help him. If they do this, it will be the best **consolation** they could give him, much more so than all the speeches they have rendered heretofore. To this point, Job has had no success in getting them to really listen to him or back off from their positions. They have been "miserable comforters" (16:2) and "worthless physicians" (13:4). So Job encourages them to refrain from judging him while he speaks one more time. Then if they want to continue to **mock** him, they can do so.

■ **4** Having a **complaint** is not unexpected considering all that Job has endured. He has used this word several times before (7:11, 13; 9:27; 10:1). What is similar about these passages is that they all are directed against God. Job's friends keep pestering him with useless words of advice, but Job regards his friends as mainly an annoyance. God, on the other hand, who caused Job's suffering and has refused to speak to him thus far, has created an agitation in Job's spirit that has left him frustrated and exhausted.

He is **impatient** to hear from God, who is the only one who can provide a legitimate answer to his complaint. Job's attention is clearly focused in the right direction (42:7-8). The verb **be impatient** (*qṣr*) appears in two other passages that speak of one's irritation over a situation that does not work out as it should (Num 21:4; Mic 2:7).

■ **5** Job pleads with his friends to take his side of the argument and *be horrified* at his undeserved suffering. The verb form here is the causative *hāšammû* (Hiphil), but many versions (NIV, NJPS, NRSV) emend it to the passive *hiššammû* (Niphal). The context supports this reading.

The act of placing one's **hand** over one's **mouth** denotes the inability to say anything. The phrase occurs two other times in Job. In 29:9 it is an act of respect that people showed Job before his calamities began. He was an outstanding person, and people were in awe of him. In 40:4 Job places his own hand over his mouth indicating his humility and lack of words in the presence of Almighty God. In v 5 the act is an outward sign of horror over Job's condition.

2. The Wicked Do Well in Life (21:6-16)

Listening to the friends, one gains the impression that life is pretty gruesome for the wicked. They must endure pain, terror, emptiness, calamity, disease, and the loss of their children (15:20-21, 24, 31; 18:11-13, 17, 19; 20:22, 24-26, 28). However, Job has a much different perspective. In spite of long-standing and popular theories that God always punishes the wicked, Job is aware of many wicked who have never been punished (Qoheleth is also aware of this [Eccl 7:15; 8:14]). They are living the good life and acting as if God did not exist.

■ **6** Scholars are divided over whether Job 21:6 concludes the previous section (vv 1-5) or begins a new section (vv 7-16) dealing with how the wicked get away with their sinfulness. The latter is preferable. Job is **terrified** by what he is about to say concerning the wicked because it upsets the whole moral order of the universe and calls into question the nature of God. Every time he recalls how God fails to punish the wicked, he is extremely troubled. But someone has to call God to account.

■ **7** The first item in Job's list of the benefits that come to the wicked is their longevity. They live to an advanced age and become stronger and more powerful in their community as they grow older. Job frames his observation in the form of a question, as if this should not happen. Job's view contrasts with the friends' assertion that wicked people die early (15:20; 18:5; 20:5).

■ **8** The second item Job refers to is the **children** (lit. "seed") and **descendants** of the wicked. Whereas Job has lost his family, the children of the wicked are **established** (*kwn*), meaning they are well-off and free from danger. Job's comments again refute the claims of the friends that the children of the wicked are impoverished and cut off at an early age (15:30, 34; 18:16-17, 19; 20:10, 26). The end of 21:8*a* contains two prepositional phrases—literally "before their face" and "with them." Most versions omit one or combine both into one thought, such as the NIV's **around them.**

■ **9** The friends have contended that the houses (or tents) of the wicked are utterly destroyed by God as punishment for their sins (15:28, 34; 18:15; 20:26, 28). Both their possessions and the family members who live with them are consumed by fire. Job believes the opposite. **Their homes are safe *from trembling*** (*paḥad* refers to trembling caused by fear; → 3:25). **The rod of God** (*Eloah*; → 9:34; 37:13), a metaphor for God's judgment, is never used against the wicked.

■ **10** Job extends the well-being of the wicked to include their farm animals. **Their bulls** breed successfully, producing a steady succession of new calves. The friends have not commented specifically on what happens to the animals of the wicked, but surely they are part of the possessions God destroys (v 9).

■ **11** Job returns to the children of the wicked (v 8), comparing their behavior to sheep that **leap about** in youthful play. This verb is the same one used to describe David when he leaped about before the ark of the covenant as it was brought into Jerusalem (1 Chr 15:29).

■ **12** Job now turns to the many festive occasions enjoyed by the wicked. Their celebrations are enhanced by music from three types of musical instruments. The *tōp* was a shallow **drum** with an animal skin stretched over a small wooden frame. It was held in one hand and struck with the palm of the other. It probably looked like a modern tambourine without the metal discs around the sides (Jones 1992, 936).

The *kinnôr* (**lyre**) consisted of a horizontal wooden sound box for the base that supported two vertical wooden arms on each end. Strings ran from the sound box to a stick stretched between the arms. The number of strings is unknown. It could be played with the fingers or a pick (Jones 1992, 937). David was skilled in playing the lyre (1 Sam 16:16, 23).

The nature of the *'ûgāb* (**reed-pipe**) is uncertain. Some regard it as a vertical flute or reed-pipe. Others, following the LXX, believe it was some type of stringed instrument (Jones 1992, 937-38).

■ **13** In Job 21:13a Job notes the **good** (*ṭôb*) that the wicked experience, in contrast with the lack of good in his own life (7:7; 9:25). Many versions translate *ṭôb* as **prosperity**, but the word refers to more than economic well-being. Job is commenting on the overall success of the wicked in all areas of their lives.

The wicked **descend to Sheol in peace**. The friends have already stated their belief that the wicked die horrible deaths brought about by violence, disease, and fire (15:21-22, 34; 18:13; 20:24-26). In contrast, Job is convinced that the wicked die peacefully. Their deaths are just as serene as their lives. The Hebrew *bĕrega'* (**in peace**) is usually translated **in an instant** (NIV mg.), meaning they die quickly without a painful death. But in this passage some (like the NIV) derive its interpretation from a second meaning of the verbal root *rg'*—(lit.) "be at rest."

■ **14-15** Here Job places words in the mouths of the wicked. He claims that they say four things to and against **God** (*El*). First, **Leave us alone!** (v 14a). The imperative form indicates a strong desire to avoid any relationship with their Creator and rightful Lord. Such a statement as this indicates a knowledge of God's prevenient grace. As the *hound of heaven* he seeks out every human being with his unconditional love, but the wicked are uncomfortable in his presence because of their self-centeredness. Thus, they call on God to turn away from them.

Second, **We have no desire to know your ways** (v 14b). The word for **ways** (*derek*) appears dozens of times in the OT in reference to the pathway of life that one is pursuing. A person is either on the way of the righteous or the way of the wicked (→ 3:23). The books of Psalms and Proverbs make repeated use of this concept enumerating the characteristics, lifestyle, and fate of the people on each way (e.g., Ps 1). The ways of God are the best ways in life; in fact they are perfect (Ps 18:30 [31 HB]). The psalmist repeatedly asks to be taught God's ways (25:4; 27:11; etc.). But the wicked seek to avoid all knowledge of them. They are confident that their own plans for life are better than God's.

Third, **Who is the Almighty [***Shaddai***], that we should serve him?** (v 15a). The wicked are not impressed by God. They believe he has no authority over them. He has not punished them for their evil deeds (v 9), so why should they fear him? Why should they serve someone who is powerless?

Fourth, **What would we gain by praying** [lit. "pleading"] **to him?** (v 15b). According to the wicked there is nothing to be gained by pleading with God for help. He does not reward his followers, so prayer is a pointless endeavor. Job's point in these two verses is that the wicked reject any relationship with God because they are doing well and they believe God is not a factor in their well-being. This view is the opposite of the friends' argument that the wicked experience extreme suffering because God has rejected them for their evil deeds (chs 15, 18, 20).

■ **16** The interpretation of v 16*a* is disputed. The NRSV (also Clines 2006, 509-10) adds an interrogative particle at the beginning, yielding: "Is not their prosperity indeed their own achievement?" In other words, the wicked believe they have arrived at success through their own efforts, not with God's help. Seow supports this interpretation but with a statement rather than a question: "Indeed prosperity is in their hands" (2013, 864; see Deut 8:17).

The more likely interpretation is that of the NIV and NJPS. They render the MT literally as a strongly negative reaction to the statements by the wicked in Job 21:14-15: **Behold their prosperity is not in their own hands**. The wicked may think that they cause their own success, but they are mistaken. In reality, God is the one who allows them to prosper. This is the same position Job took in an earlier speech, only there he was questioning why God did this: "Why do you bestow your favor on the plans of the wicked and reject me, the work of your hands?" (10:3, 8).

In 21:16*b* Job distances himself from **the plans of the wicked**. Even though God may smile on these plans, they are not the way of life Job has chosen for himself.

3. God Does Not Judge Correctly (21:17-26)

Job now turns to questioning the nature of God's justice in all of this. How can he be called just if he allows the wicked to live long, successful lives? God needs some instruction in judging, but no one is capable of doing so.

■ **17-18** This section begins with a series of rhetorical questions that cast doubt on the punishment of the wicked for their sins. How often have the friends actually seen wicked people being punished? Job is pressing them for hard evidence attached to people's names, not just theories or traditional beliefs they have received from previous generations.

The first question (v 17*a*) borrows Bildad's image of a lamp (also Prov 24:19-20) being extinguished as a metaphor for an early death (Job 18:5-6). In the second and third (21:17*bc*) he challenges Bildad's assertion that the wicked always experience disaster (18:12). Do the wicked ever provoke God's **anger** enough that he brings destruction on them?

The fourth and fifth (21:18*ab*) ask how often the wicked are blown about like **straw** and **chaff** in a severe windstorm. The answer Job is looking for in all these questions is, "Rarely, if ever." In his mind, the wicked seldom receive the punishment they deserve. If the friends have evidence to the contrary, they should present it for him to consider.

■ **19-21** How the sins of the wicked affect their children is a topic that has appeared several times already. The view of the friends is that the wicked are always punished for their sins. But if perchance they manage to avoid any punishment, God will certainly impose his judgment on their children. Eliphaz noted how the children of the wicked are "far from safety" and "crushed *at the gate*" after their sinner-father is taken from them (5:4). Bildad argued that even the memory of the wicked ends with their death because none of their children survive (18:19).

Zophar reemphasized Eliphaz's point by drawing attention to the extreme poverty that falls on the children of the wicked (20:10).

Other biblical passages support this concept noting that God's punishment affects one's children even to the third and fourth generations (Exod 20:5; 34:6-7; Deut 5:9). However, some passages support the opposite position—that people are punished only for their own sins, not the sins of their parents (Deut 24:16; 2 Kgs 14:6; see also Jesus' comments in John 9:1-3). This became a crucial argument in the ministry of Jeremiah and Ezekiel, who were trying to help people at the time of the exile to accept responsibility for their own sins rather than blame their parents (Jer 31:29-30; Ezek 18:2-4).

Job's comments here address the matter of fairness in justice. If **God** (*Eloah*) is truly just, why would he punish the children of the wicked (Job 21:19)? Why not punish the wrongdoers themselves? Let them **experience** (also **see** and **drink** [v 20]) the suffering that sin produces so they will know the foolishness of their sinful choices.

Job believes that if the wicked knew they could avoid **the wrath of the Almighty** (*Shaddai*) and pass it on to their children, they would likely continue to sin, for after they die they have no knowledge of what happens to their children (v 21; 14:21-22). The word for **punishment** (*'āwen*; 21:19a) refers to *the trouble/ adversity* inflicted by God as a punishment for sin.

■ **22** **Can anyone teach knowledge to God?** is a rhetorical question expecting a negative answer. **God's** (*El*) **knowledge** (and power) is vastly superior to humanity's. He is judge over everyone, even *the exalted ones* (probably a reference to angels). This is a view that Job has expressed before (12:13-25) and with which the three friends all agree (4:17-21; 11:5-9; 15:8-16). Job's point is that God needs some lessons on how to judge, but unfortunately no one is capable of instructing him. If it is true that God punishes the children of the wicked (21:19-21), or that he causes all to die without any consideration of their success or lack thereof (vv 23-26), then God's system of justice is flawed (also 19:7). Terrien sees here a subtle tone of "defiance" (1954, 1070). Job wishes he could be that person who is allowed to instruct God in the proper administration of justice. He would tell God a thing or two if given the opportunity.

■ **23-26** The next four verses illustrate the kind of mixed-up world that God administers. On the one hand, some people experience well-being and security all their lives. They are well-fed and in excellent health. When they finally die, they are still **in full vigor** (21:23; lit. "with his bone[s] of perfection"). On the other hand, other people never enjoy the good things of life. They become embittered and no doubt welcome their death. The point is that both die, and their dead bodies become covered with **maggots**. They both descend to Sheol, which Job has already described as a place that treats all classes of people the same. Job regards this as unfair. A God who is truly just should provide a better reward system that blesses the righteous and punishes the wicked, both in this life and the next.

Verse 24a is difficult. The literal translation is: **his '*ăṭîn* are full of milk**. The word *'ăṭîn* occurs only here in the OT, so there is much speculation about its meaning. One suggestion is a part of the body that produces **milk** such as the breasts or the male sex organ (NRSV). Others have proposed a container for carrying milk, such as a pail or bucket (Clines 2006, 513-14). Still others have emended **milk** (*ḥālāb*) to "fat" (lit.; *ḥēleb*) and then treated *'ăṭîn* as "sides of the body" (lit.) or "intestines" (LXX). Whatever the exact meaning, Job's intent is to describe a lifestyle that is well-off. **His bones are moist with marrow** (v 24b) is probably an idiomatic expression further signifying the excellent health of some people.

4. My Friends, You Are Wrong (21:27-34)

The friends are clearly on a different wavelength than Job. Their belief that God always administers retribution to the wicked is simply not true. Job has conversed with people from other cultures and lands who agree with him, so he is not about to back down. His evaluation of the friends' point of view is that it is empty of meaning and worthless in application to his own situation.

■ **27** Job was not clairvoyant, but he had heard enough from his friends after two cycles of speeches to have a good understanding of their position. He knows how they think and what their next response to his speech will likely be. Also, as Clines notes insightfully, Job knows exactly what they are thinking because he once thought the same way himself before he experienced so much suffering (2006, 532).

Interestingly, Job characterizes their attacks against him as **schemes** meant to do him harm. The friends would probably disagree with Job on this point. Their intent has mainly been to restore his health and wealth by correcting his erroneous thinking and leading him back to a right relationship with God. But the emotional tone of their speeches has gone over the top at times giving Job the sense they are more interested in proving their points than in helping him recover. Some of their illustrations of how God punishes the wicked have been nothing more than thinly disguised attempts to force him to admit that he has some hidden sin in his life. Further, they have never showed him one bit of compassion, so he is justified in accusing them of scheming against him.

■ **28** One of the points each of the friends made in the second cycle of speeches was that God destroys the houses/tents of the wicked (15:28, 34; 18:6, 14-15, 21; 20:9, 26, 28). This is one of the ways God punishes them for their evil deeds. For the sake of argument, Job repeats this view of theirs before attacking it in 21:29-30. In most passages the word for **the great/the nobleman** (*nādîb*) refers to a person of high standing with a generous spirit (→ 12:21). But in 21:28 the word is parallel with **the wicked**, indicating that the high position of these nobles was probably gained through corruption.

■ **29-30** Job's friends have repeatedly appealed to the wisdom of previous generations in their attempts to reinforce their position (8:8-10; 15:10, 17-18; 20:4-5). To counter their arguments, Job now directs their attention to the testimony of travelers who have visited faraway places and observed people in other cultures. No doubt, he talked to many traveling merchants in his earlier business dealings, especially those involved with camel caravans (1:3). Certainly, his servants traveled widely and brought back many stories, and perhaps even Job himself made a few extended trips. Job claims that people who have a wide range of experiences because they interact with foreigners on a regular basis support his position that **the wicked** are not punished by God (21:30). Their houses remain intact, and their families are safe (vv 8-13). They are **spared** God's judgment.

The day of calamity (Deut 32:35; Jer 18:17; 46:21; Obad 13) and **the day of wrath** (Ezek 7:15-19; Zeph 1:15, 18) are usually associated with times when God vents his fury against wicked people or nations. These days are terribly frightening because there is nowhere to hide from the wars, natural disasters, disease, and famine that God has at his disposal. But Job believes that calamity and wrath do not affect the wicked. They are spared these disasters and live to a ripe old age in prosperity and peace (Job 21:7-13).

■ **31** So far in ch 21 Job has spoken disparagingly of God's easy treatment of the wicked. God simply refuses to punish them. So who is going to hold the wicked accountable for their evil deeds? Unfortunately, no one. The two rhetorical questions in v 31 expect a negative answer. No one either in heaven or on earth is willing to confront the wicked or bring justice to bear. They get away with their evil deeds.

■ **32-33** To add insult to injury, the wicked are rewarded at the end of life with the grandest of funerals. They are buried in an impressive tomb, and servants are assigned to keep watch over it, both to honor the deceased and protect against grave robbers. Job does not reveal what type of grave he has in mind, but apparently it is topped with a mound composed of *clods from a wadi* (a dry streambed; v 33*a*). These clods are described as **sweet** (the same word is used in 20:12 in speaking of food) to the deceased. In other words, not only in life but also even in death the wicked are surrounded by pleasant things. Job's description of the death of the wicked is in sharp contrast to the friends' view that death is a terrifying experience for evildoers (15:20-22, 30-34; 18:13-21; 20:5-9, 22-29).

Verse 33*bc* of ch 21 describes a huge **throng** of people following **after** the wicked and going **before them**. Scholars differ over whether Job is speaking of the death of other human beings before and after the wicked, or whether this is a description of the great number of people in the funeral procession. The latter seems to fit the context best.

■ **34** Job's final words in this speech are a rebuke to everything the friends have tried to tell him. He uses two parallel words to describe their efforts: *hebel* (v 34*a*; "empty nothings" [NRSV]) and *ma'al* (v 34*b*; ***disloyalty/unfaithfulness***). The word *hebel* is translated as "vanity" (NRSV) over thirty times in Ecclesiastes. It can refer to something lacking in substance, fleeting in existence, or worthless in value (→ 7:16). A combination of the first and third meanings applies to the usage here. From Job's point of view the friends' speeches have amounted to nothing more than babbling, without any content that applies to his situation. They are ***worthless nothings***.

The word *ma'al* is normally used in passages that refer to the breaking of covenantal obligations. Here Job could be accusing his friends of ***disloyalty*** to the covenant of friendship with himself or of ***disloyalty*** to God by claiming to represent him while at the same time arguing that God always punishes the wicked. Job probably has both in mind.

FROM THE TEXT

Summary of Job's Response to Zophar. All three friends have now vigorously defended the traditional understanding of divine retribution against sin. Their speeches have been emotional and pointedly directed at Job, whom they believe is a sinner. But Job will have none of this. His observations of life have driven him to a much different conclusion. It is the innocent who suffer, not the wicked. In fact, God seems to reward the wicked rather than punish them.

With this speech Job has effectively undermined the principle of divine retribution. It does not ring true in real life. But Job has also raised significant questions about the traditional understanding of God. The answers to these questions will have to wait until God speaks (chs 38—41).

Job's speech emphasizes these points:
- My friends, you seem to think that God always punishes the wicked, but I know differently. And so do those who have traveled widely in the world and observed more people than you have.
- The wicked live long lives of prosperity, security, and happiness. Even their funerals are grand affairs. They have no use for God and act as if he does not exist, yet God fails to punish them.
- If you think that God's punishment of the wicked sometimes falls on their children instead of them, your concept of justice is distorted. This is not real justice.

V. THIRD CYCLE OF SPEECHES: JOB 22—27

BEHIND THE TEXT

The third cycle of speeches is shorter than the previous two. This may indicate that exhaustion has set in. The friends now see that Job is a hopeless case. He refuses to consider their advice, so there is not much else they can say. But it may also indicate that there has been damage to the text in the process of transmission. Based on content, the sections in this cycle most likely belong to the following individuals.

22:1-30	Eliphaz
23:1-17	Job
24:1-17	Job
24:18-24	one of the friends
24:25	Job
25:1-6	Bildad
26:1-4	Job
26:5-14	Job
27:1-6	Job
27:7-10	probably Job
27:11-12	Job
27:13-23	one of the friends

The reader notices immediately that there is not the same symmetry as found in the first two cycles. The third cycle looks very scrambled in chs 24—27. In addition, Bildad has a very short speech with an abrupt beginning, and Zophar's speech is missing altogether. Two passages (24:18-24 and 27:13-23) are located in speeches by Job, but they support arguments made by the friends. Almost unanimously, scholars are puzzled by what to do with them. The question that all scholars have to wrestle with is: Why would a skilled, meticulous writer such as the author of Job break the beautiful symmetry of the book and leave the third cycle in such disarray? As yet, there is no consensus, only a bewildering number of possibilities. Snaith lists over twenty-four different attempted solutions to the problem (1968, 100-103).

The resolution to this problem usually occurs in one of three ways. Some leave the order of the text intact and maneuver the questionable passages into Job's speeches by adding the words, "You say . . ." at the beginning of each. Thus, Job is mocking the friends by throwing their words back at them. This interpretation still leaves Bildad with few words and Zophar with none at all. It also places the blame for the confusion in chs 24—27 on the author. Apparently, he disrupted the text on purpose to show that communication between Job and his friends had now disintegrated completely.

Another theory is that the author never completed the third cycle. What we have are bits and pieces that he hoped to develop later into a full cycle like the first two (Snaith 1968, 61-62). This also places the blame on the author.

A third theory is that the book must have experienced slight damage during transmission that caused the loss of some verses. In the attempt to reconstruct the book, the editors did the best they could with the text that was left, but they misplaced a few passages. These scholars attempt to correct the damage by moving some passages that seem to be spoken by the friends to other locations, giving Bildad a longer speech and providing some words for Zophar. This creates a much more symmetrical third cycle. This interpretation places the blame for the confusion, not on the author who was something of a literary genius, but on the circumstances of transmission.

The third method of interpretation yields a more reasonable text than the other two. Unfortunately, there is no agreement on which passages should be moved where, for these decisions are inevitably speculative. Even good literary critics have problems with chs 24—27. The fact that there are so many different opinions about these chapters is good evidence that some type of disruption has taken place. And the damage will never be totally corrected if some verses are still missing. This does not mean that chs 24—27 are so confused that they are unintelligible. It simply means that the reader has to work harder and more cautiously at exegesis and interpretation.

This commentary supports the movement and/or reidentification of only two passages—24:18-24 and 27:13-23 (→ Behind the Text for chs 23, 25, 26, and 27 for more comments). The order of the entire third cycle, then, is as follows:

22:1-30	Eliphaz's Third Speech
23:1-17; 24:1-17, 25	Job's Response to Eliphaz
25:1-6; 24:18-24	Bildad's Third Speech
26:1-14; 27:1-12	Job's Response to Bildad
27:13-23	Zophar's Third Speech

There are many biblical books that have undergone redaction at the hands of ancient copyists, so it should come as no surprise that the book of Job has experienced something similar. What is unique about Job in chs 24—27 is that the editors were not trying to press home a theological point, make the book more applicable to a later audience, or clear up unfamiliar words or confusing syntax. They were simply trying to put back together a scroll that had been damaged. Unfortunately, we will never know the details of the extent of the damage or the process of restoration. Thus, this section of the book remains problematic. All we can do is use our best judgment to try to re-create the original order and thus restore the author's intent. We are always hesitant to rearrange a biblical text, but this seems to be the best recourse to explain a very confusing section of the book.

IN THE TEXT

A. Eliphaz's Third Speech (22:1-30)

Job's criticism of how God treats the wicked (ch 21) brings a swift and sharp rebuttal from Eliphaz in ch 22. He is no longer the gentle, mystical person that appeared in chs 4—5. He now believes Job is completely wrong in his understanding of how God governs the world. Thus, he goes on the attack, making one last attempt to break Job's resistance. After accusing Job directly of great wickedness and listing some of his supposed sins, Eliphaz addresses Job's charge from ch 21 that God does not know how to judge. Perhaps Job's belief is based on a false understanding of God's transcendence. Perhaps he thinks God is so far away that he cannot see what is happening on earth. If such is the case, then Job is completely misinformed. Eliphaz concludes with another call for Job to repent. If he will confess his sins and submit to God, he will experience once again the blessed life he enjoyed in the prologue.

22:1-11

There are three sections to Eliphaz's speech:
1. Job, You Are a Sinner (22:1-11)
2. God's Transcendence Is Not a Hindrance to His Ability to Judge (22:12-20)
3. Repent, and You Will Be Restored (22:21-30)

1. Job, You Are a Sinner (22:1-11)

According to Eliphaz, Job is guilty of numerous sins. He has especially been cruel and merciless to the needy—the naked, the thirsty, the hungry, the widows, and the orphans. Are any of Eliphaz's accusations true? The answer is no, and Eliphaz knows it. He presents no evidence to support his charges. And further, he actually contradicts himself, for he earlier commended Job for his treatment of the poor and weak (4:3-4).

So why does Eliphaz change his tune here? Perhaps he is exhausted by this time in the dialogue and exasperated by Job's attacks against God (21:7-26). Perhaps he is alarmed at Job's powerful assault against the wisdom theology. Job's whole worldview is terribly distorted. Or perhaps he believes his list of possible sins will jog Job's memory and force him to acknowledge an earlier transgression he forgot. He grasps at whatever straws he can, whether or not true, to try once again to change Job's way of thinking.

■ **1** The character of **Eliphaz the Temanite** is discussed in 2:11. For comments on the standard introductory formula → 3:2.

■ **2 Can a *strong man* [*geber*] be of benefit to God [*El*]?** The word *geber* normally refers to a man as opposed to a woman, but its derivation from the verb *gbr* (lit. "be strong") suggests the nuance of **strong man** in some contexts such as here (→ also 4:17).

Of all the outstanding human qualities that might bring benefit to God, neither strength nor wisdom (22:2), neither righteousness nor blamelessness (v 3) add anything to God he does not already possess. Eliphaz's point is that God is perfect in all possible attributes and sufficient in himself. He receives neither gain nor loss from human behavior.

In v 2*b* the pronoun **him** is ambiguous. Some believe it refers to God (NIV, NJPS, NRSV). Others interpret it as the reflexive "himself," meaning that the wise only benefit themselves, not God (NASB, RSV). The first interpretation is more likely in that it supports the parallelism of all four clauses in vv 2-3.

■ **3** Eliphaz applies the principle in v 2 directly to Job in v 3. **The Almighty** (*Shaddai*) is not indebted to Job in any way. He is not obligated to treat Job differently simply because Job claims to be **righteous** and **blameless**. Otherwise, people could buy their way into God's favor through their good behavior.

Eliphaz is not implying that God is indifferent to human choices and actions. He firmly believes that God wants people to live righteous lives, and this is why he rewards the righteous and punishes the wicked (4:7-9; 15:20-35). Rather, Eliphaz is trying to emphasize God's objectivity in his governance of the world. God treats all people according to his own impartial principles of justice, and he will not be swayed by human requests for special favors. Job's assertion that God rewards the wicked (21:7-26) is false, and to claim that God does not know how to judge (21:22) is simply nonsense.

■ **4-5** The fact that Job is suffering does not prove he is guilty of sin. Eliphaz has already stated that some suffering may be due to God's discipline and may actually work to one's benefit (5:17-26). However, Job's criticism of the way God judges the world casts a different light on Job's case. If God has been trying to discipline Job, it obviously has not worked, for Job's speeches have belligerently attacked God and proclaimed his own innocence. Therefore, Eliphaz has concluded that Job must indeed have some hidden sins in his life that he refuses to acknowledge. Certainly,

God is not punishing him for being righteous. The real reason for Job's suffering is his sin, which Eliphaz now exaggerates to include multiple offenses against God (**your wickedness great . . . your *iniquities* endless** [22:5]).

This is the first time in the dialogues that anyone has accused Job directly to his face of being a sinner. The reader, of course, sees the irony in Eliphaz's question in v 4. Why would God cause anyone who is righteous to suffer? This is unthinkable. Yet the prologue has already made it clear that Job's suffering is indeed the result of his righteousness. It is entirely due to a disagreement in heaven over Job's motives for living a righteous life. Thus, the author challenges us to think more deeply about the real cause(s) of suffering recognizing we are not privy to all the evidence, just as Eliphaz and Job were not.

■ **6** In vv 6-9 Eliphaz presents a list of sins that he attributes to Job. These are all social sins involving actions against the poor and needy by someone with wealth and power. Eliphaz offers no proof that Job is guilty of any of these sins. They are only imaginary sins that a person of high standing might commit. The sense of these verses is that Job "must have done" something like this to cause God to punish him so severely (Clines 2006, 555).

Job's first sin deals with "pledges/***securities***" "exacted" (NRSV) from family members. People in debt were allowed to give a personal object to their lender as a security that they would repay their debt in full in the future. When the debt was repaid, the object was returned to the owner. There are a number of regulations in Israelite law regarding debts and the type of securities that were allowed (Exod 22:25-27 [24-26 HB]; Deut 24:6, 10-13).

Job's supposed sin is threefold: he has taken securities from his own kin rather than trusting them, he has done this **for no reason** (Job 22:6*a*; 1:9; 2:3; 9:17) that could be considered reasonable or legitimate, and he has **stripped** off **clothing** as security from debtors who really needed it to be presentable in public (22:6*b*).

■ **7** Job's second sin is withholding **water** and **food** from those who are starving. This is a criticism of his lack of compassion for the poor by refusing to help them secure their basic needs for survival.

■ **8** There is much disagreement as to the interpretation of v 8. The verse has two third-person verbs, so it is not another item in the list of Job's sins. Some regard it as a proverbial statement that reflects the typical arrogance of people who are powerful and believe all the resources of society belong to them: "The powerful possess the land, and the favored live in it" (NRSV). By implication Job is one of these members of the upper class who owns lots of land and treats the poor with disdain. Others introduce the verse with "you say" or "you believe" as if Eliphaz had heard Job say this before (Gordis 1978, 245-46). Still others take the verse as a description of Job's former position as **a powerful man** who owned large plots of land. Either of the first two interpretations is preferred.

■ **9** Eliphaz continues to add to Job's sins with the mention of his mistreatment of **widows** and **the fatherless/*orphans***. In the OT an orphan is generally defined as a child without a father, although both parents could be missing. In addition to being without immediate family support, **widows** and ***orphans*** likely lacked an extended family to care for them as well. They are usually paired together as representing the most vulnerable and needy members of society. The Pentateuch lays out specific regulations for their care (Exod 22:22-24 [21-23 HB]; Deut 10:17-18; 14:28-29; 24:17-22; 26:12-13; 27:19). Job is accused of sending widows away who have requested his help for their basic needs. This in turn leaves the children of these widows without food and without **strength**. This sin is more than just a lack of compassion. It is an intentional rejection of the vulnerable who have requested his help.

■ **10-11** Eliphaz concludes his list of sins with four types of punishment that Job will receive from God: ***traps***, "terror" (NRSV), "darkness" (NRSV), and ***a torrent of water***. Eliphaz is borrowing imagery from earlier speeches by the friends (Job 15:22-24; 18:5-6, 8-11, 18; 20:26, 28). Job has already admitted to experiencing these calamities (7:14; 9:17-18; 13:21; 16:8-9, 12-14; 19:6, 8-12), so Eliphaz is not telling him anything new. Eliphaz is simply trying to connect the punishments with their cause and answer Job's criticisms in the previous chapter that God does not know how to judge (21:7-26, especially v 22).

So far, however, Job has refused to acknowledge that he has sin in his life. In his mind these calamities are entirely undeserved and come from a God who is intent on destroying him for no reason at all.

2. God's Transcendence Is Not a Hindrance to His Ability to Judge (22:12-20)

Eliphaz turns now to what he thinks are Job's beliefs about the transcendence of God. God is out there somewhere, but he is so far removed from humanity and his vision is so clouded that he cannot possibly know all that humans are doing. Therefore, it is impossible for him to judge correctly. Eliphaz equates this belief with the typical way wicked people think about God because it enables them to mentally escape responsibility for their sins. But this view is incorrect. For Eliphaz, God always punishes the wicked as evidenced by their early demise, and the righteous rejoice when they see God's justice displayed.

■ **12** Eliphaz begins this section by locating God's home in **the heights of heaven**, far removed from the earth. Up there where **the highest stars** (lit. "top of the stars") are found is the place from which **God** (*Eloah*) directs his divine activities. Job has not commented on this topic, but he would probably agree with Eliphaz, since this was a common view in the ancient world.

■ **13-14** Eliphaz then interprets what he thinks is Job's position on God's transcendence and how this interferes with his role as judge. Because **God** (*El*) is so far away from earthly activities, he is limited in his knowledge of people's lives. Further, he is enveloped in **thick clouds** that obscure his vision, even though he ***walks about*** daily ***on the vault of the heavens***. Thus, God is unable to **judge** properly. This is why Job thinks God has misjudged him. God is treating him as if he were wicked because God does not have a clear view of his innocence.

The word for **vault** (*ḥûg*) refers to the ancient view of a dome in the heavens. God existed above this dome, but the clouds and the sun, moon, and stars were located below it. The word translated "firmament" (KJV, NKJV) in the creation account of Gen 1:6-8 refers to this dome (although it is not the same Hebrew word). There the dome served to separate the waters above the heavens from the waters below the earth.

■ **15-16** Immediately after describing what he thinks is Job's view concerning why God is not a good judge, Eliphaz dismisses it as out of date. The use of a rhetorical question implies that no one still holds such a belief. Maybe some people believed like Job in earlier times, but they are now gone. They experienced a calamity, and their early death is proof that their views were incorrect. Eliphaz cleverly connects the destruction of the wicked with the suffering of Job by using the image of **a flood/river** (*nāhār*) that washes away the **foundations** of the wicked in parallel with the **torrent of water** that covers Job (Job 22:11).

■ **17-18** Eliphaz now repeats the statements made by Job in his previous speech regarding the rejection of God by the wicked (21:14-16). **They *say* to God** [*El*], "Leave us alone! What can the Almighty do *for* us?" (22:17). The wicked believe that God provides them no help whatsoever; therefore, he is not needed by them. Eliphaz agrees that the wicked treat God this way. The end of v 17 reads "for them" (lit.) in Hebrew, but most versions emend the phrase to *for us* following the LXX and reflecting the original context in 21:15.

Eliphaz is also willing to grant Job that God gives the wicked a measure of success: he fills **their houses with good things** (22:18). Job had said in 21:16*a*: "their prosperity is not in their own hands," meaning that whatever good fortune the wicked have is the result of God's enablement, not their own skills. However, Eliphaz parts company with Job in regard to the time element. Whereas Job believes that God gives the wicked long, successful lives (21:7-13), in Eliphaz's thinking, God only allows the wicked to succeed for a brief time before he cuts them off (22:16, 20).

Job's reaction to the success of the wicked was to separate himself as far as he could from the way they lived their lives: **the plans of the wicked *are far from me*** (22:18*b*). While these words were originally Job's (21:16*b*), they resonate with Eliphaz as well. He, too, rejects the plans of the wicked but for a different reason. He believes their plans result in God's judgment (22:19-20) rather than success.

■ **19-20** The final downfall of the wicked brings rejoicing and even mocking from the righteous, for they regard the destruction of the wicked and their possessions as confirmation of God's justice. Earlier in ch 22 Eliphaz used the image of water as the means of destruction (vv 11, 16), but here it is **fire** that God sends upon the wicked (v 20).

Verse 20 has significant problems with regard to the translations **our foes** and **their wealth** (see Clines 2006, 543). There is no overall consensus on the correct reading, but scholars are generally agreed that this verse refers to God's destruction of the wicked and all they possess.

The concept of laughing at the afflictions of the wicked is quite foreign to Christianity, but it appears in several passages in the Psalms (Pss 52:6-7 [8-9 HB]; 58:10 [11 HB]; 107:42). Even God (Pss 2:4; 37:13; 59:8 [9 HB]) and Lady Wisdom (Prov 1:26-27) are known to laugh at the wicked on occasion. The meaning of these passages is found in the American proverb, "The one who laughs last, laughs best."

The OT normally portrays wicked people as cocky, arrogant, self-centered, and opposed to God. They seek to destroy God's people and mock at them when they suffer hardship (Pss 10:2-11; 22:6-8 [7-9 HB]; 36:1-4 [2-5 HB]; 37:12, 14, 32, 35; 80:6 [7 HB]). The righteous are often forced to cry out to God for protection from the wicked (Pss 3, 7, 10, 12, 17, etc.). But God and his people have the last laugh. When the wicked finally receive their much-deserved punishment from God, after they have been warned repeatedly of the consequences of their folly (Prov 1:20-25, 29-30), God's people rejoice. They do so, first, because God has demonstrated that he is a just God as he promised, and second, because God's side has triumphed over evil.

3. Repent, and You Will Be Restored (22:21-30)

Eliphaz concludes his third speech with a final call to repentance. If Job will just acknowledge his sin before God and follow God's instructions, his life will be completely changed. Eliphaz's speech is loaded with enticing rewards—such as "prosperity" (v 21), restoration (v 23), "gold" (v 25), "delight" (v 26), and "light" (v 28)—that will come to Job if he submits his life to God. Thus, Eliphaz returns to an appeal he made in his very first speech (5:8, 17-27). Committing one's life to God is the best and only way to live.

■ 21 Eliphaz challenges Job one more time to quit denying his sinfulness and to humble himself before Almighty God. There must be some major, hidden sin in Job's life that is forcing God to punish him (22:4-5). Job's denial of this sin is clearly a sign of rebellion in Eliphaz's thinking. The only viable route back to a life of well-being is through repentance and reconciliation. Job needs to "Agree with God" (v 21a NRSV; *HALOT* has "be reconciled with God") instead of fighting him. "In this way good will come to you" (v 21b NRSV).

Ironically, at the end of the book Job does acquiesce to Eliphaz's advice (42:5-6). He does finally "agree" with God, and in so doing, gain an inner peace. But he never confesses to **wickedness** and ***iniquities*** (22:5) as Eliphaz and the other friends have demanded. He discovers in the end that he can agree with God while at the same time upholding the integrity of his conscience that he is not guilty of sin.

■ 22 Eliphaz takes the opportunity again to parade his knowledge of the wisdom theology (5:27; 15:10, 17-18) by using a wisdom saying. He exhorts Job to receive the oral instructions that were passed from God to the sages of old. The word for **instruction** (*tôrâ*) occurs only here in Job, but twelve times in Proverbs, usually in reference to the wisdom traditions—the wise and ancient moral teachings passed down from parent to child for generations.

Eliphaz's advice to Job is to receive these teachings and internalize them, making them a permanent part of his life and using them to guide his future decisions. The language here is very similar to admonitions in the book of Proverbs (1:8-9; 2:1-8; 3:13; 4:1-6, 10-13, 20-22; 5:7; 6:20-21; 7:1-3, 24; 8:10-11; 22:17-21; 23:12). What Eliphaz does not mention is that thus far in the book of Job God has been silent. Job would love nothing more than to receive God's teachings directly (Job 10:2; 13:18-24). But Eliphaz was not thinking of God speaking in the present moment. His attention was focused solely on the wisdom traditions out of the past.

■ **23** The next several verses are difficult to interpret. Verse 23 of ch 22 begins with the conditional particle **if** (*'im*), but translators disagree over how far the condition extends. Some include through v 26 (NJPS), some through v 25 (NRSV), some through v 24 (NASB, NIV), and others all or part of v 23 (NKJV). This commentary will follow the NKJV.

Verse 23 repeats the thought of v 21. Job must make a conscious decision to **return to the Almighty** (*Shaddai*). Then he will **be restored** into God's fellowship, and **wrongdoing** will be removed from his **house** (lit. **tent**). In order to facilitate this outcome, Job must accept God's instructions (v 22) and agree with him (v 21).

■ **24-25** Scholars have proposed two main interpretations of these verses. Some see here an admonition to trust in **the Almighty** rather than in material things such as **gold** and **silver**. At this point Job had no wealth left; he lost it all in ch 1. But perhaps he still had an emotional attachment to it that was preventing him from turning to God. Eliphaz exhorts Job to "regard" (NJPS; imperative of *šyt*) his former wealth as water under the bridge. He should think of it as returned to **the dust** and **the rocks** *of the wadis* (dry streambeds), that is, restored to its "former original state" (Habel 1985, 342). He should make God his most valuable treasure instead.

Others interpret the verses as a promise of future wealth if Job returns to God. "The Almighty would then have 'become' his gold and silver in the sense of having been the provider of it" (Clines 2006, 565). This interpretation connects vv 24-25 with vv 21*b*, 23*a*, and with the list of rewards in vv 26-30. Either interpretation is plausible. However, Job's response to this passage in 31:24-25 clearly indicates that he understood the first interpretation as Eliphaz's intent.

The location of **Ophir** (also in 28:16) is still unknown, but it is generally placed in southern Saudi Arabia or Yemen. The word is used in seven other passages in the OT in connection with gold (1 Kgs 9:28; 10:11; 22:48 [49 HB]; 1 Chr 29:4; 2 Chr 9:10; Ps 45:9 [10 HB]; Isa 13:12). Apparently, **gold** from **Ophir** was regarded as of the highest quality.

In Job 22:25 (**then the Almighty will be . . .** *your heaps of* **silver**), the translation *heaps* for *tô'āpôt* is only a guess. The word appears in Num 23:22 and 24:8 in reference to the "horns" (NRSV) of a wild ox and in Ps 95:4 to the "heights" (NRSV) of the mountains, but its precise meaning in Job 22:25 is unknown. Some think it refers to the amount of silver and others to its value. Clines notes that the author has created some wordplays in these two verses between **dust** (*'āpār*) and **Ophir** (*'ôpîr*) and between **gold** (*bāṣer*) and *in the rocks* (*běṣûr*) (2006, 566). This may indicate a proverbial origin for these verses and lie at the root of the difficulty in translating.

■ **26-28** The remainder of Eliphaz's speech deals with the rewards that Job will receive if he turns to God. The particles *kî 'āz* at the beginning of v 26 indicate absolute certainty by the speaker (also in 11:15) that Job's life will get better once he has mended his relationship with God. First, Job "will delight" (NRSV) greatly **in the Almighty** (*Shaddai*), rather than regarding God as his *enemy* ("opponent"; 16:9). He **will lift up** his **face to God** (*Eloah*) in confidence and trust, instead of fearing further divine attacks (6:4; 7:14; 10:16-17; 16:7-9, 11-14; 19:8-12).

Then, he will renew his normal religious activities (22:27). His prayer life will be reestablished with full assurance that God hears his prayers. And he will once again be able to worship God by paying his **vows**. Finally, his influence and authority will return (v 28). The decisions he makes in the future will work out well because they are guided by God. His pathway that was once dark (19:8) will be illuminated by God's **light**.

■ **29-30** These two verses contain numerous translation difficulties that are still not resolved (see Clines 2006, 546-47 for a discussion of multiple emendations and interpretations). This commentary will follow the NIV translation that interprets 22:29-30 as continuing with the topic of Job's influence and authority in v 28 (see also Gordis 1978, 251-52). This interpretation has problems, but no more so than the other proposals.

According to Eliphaz, when Job finally turns to God, he will rise to the level of one who is able to intercede with God for the benefit of others. When people fall prey to hard times, Job will say to them, "Rise up!" (Gordis 1978, 242, 252). His prayers (v 27), his good decisions (v 28), and his clean hands (i.e., his morally good deeds; v 30) will attract God's attention and be the reason why God **will save the downcast** (*in eyes*) (v 29). At Job's request, God will go so far as to **deliver even one who is not innocent** (v 30).

Some have suggested that these verses provide the context for Job's intercession for his friends at the end of the book (42:7-9; Habel 1985, 344). With these final words Eliphaz returns to the point from where he started in 4:3-4. Job's actions in helping the downtrodden will blossom again once he has reestablished his relationship with God.

FROM THE TEXT

Summary of Eliphaz's Third Speech. Job and the three friends have uttered some pretty heated words against each other. But amazingly, Eliphaz still holds out hope to Job this far into the dialogues. This must indicate he still wanted to be Job's friend. He had been prodded into saying some nasty things against Job (such as 22:4-11) due to Job's belligerent and stinging attacks against them. But deep within he still saw himself as an evangelist for the wisdom theology. Maybe one more altar call would bring Job to repentance and restoration.

Eliphaz's main points are as follows:

- Job, you are guilty of great wickedness. Your treatment of the needy is detestable.
- You may think that God is wrongly punishing you because he cannot adequately evaluate your life from his heights in the heavens. But this is a typical excuse from the wicked, and it is not valid.
- There is still time to repent. If you will turn to God and follow his instructions, he will restore you to the blessed life you enjoyed before.

B. Job's Response to Eliphaz (23:1—24:17, 25)

BEHIND THE TEXT

Job's response to Eliphaz's emotional speech in ch 22 reveals a change in his focus of attention. Eliphaz had accused Job of being a sinner and had urged him to repent, but Job knows Eliphaz's accusations are false and do not even deserve an answer. Much more important to Job is *God's view* of his suffering. So Job turns away from his friends' arguments and back to a topic he mentioned much earlier in the first cycle of speeches (13:18-22). He wants to meet God and have the opportunity to defend himself. He is still very confident, as he was in ch 13, that he will be vindicated if such a meeting can be arranged. But he is also very fearful of encountering God, for God does whatever he pleases.

Job also changes his outlook from expecting exoneration after his death (19:23-27) to calling for God to vindicate him right now. Perhaps his hopes have been revived by Eliphaz's positive words in 22:23-30. As Job remembers the blessings God bestowed on him before the calamities, his heart yearns to get his case settled as quickly as possible. His only hang-up is his inability to find God. God seems to be hiding from him.

In the latter part of the speech Job presents a long list of examples of wicked people who were never punished for their wrongdoing. Why does God not do anything about this? He should set regular times to administer justice if he wants to be known as a just God.

Job's speech divides into three sections:
1. I Wish I Could Talk to God (23:1-7)
2. I Am Confident but Terrified (23:8-17)
3. Why Does God Not Punish the Wicked? (24:1-17, 25)

As mentioned in Behind the Text for chs 22—27, 24:18-24 is extremely difficult to interpret. These verses are located in a speech by Job, but they support arguments made by the three friends. Here are five different ways of interpreting them.

(1) Some retain this passage in its traditional location, but because the concepts are so different from Job's speeches, they interpret them as statements from the friends that Job is quoting or mimicking in order to show how far removed

they are from his own position. These scholars introduce 24:18 with the words "You say . . ." in order to indicate that this section is not supported by Job (RSV; Gordis 1978, 531-34, 669).

(2) Other scholars translate these sections as a wish on Job's part that God would act in this way (NKJV), or as a curse by Job against the wicked (NJPS). This proposal requires the emendation of a number of verbs and their treatment as optatives (e.g., v 18: "They should be swift on the face of the waters, their portion should be cursed in the earth, so that no one would turn into the way of their vineyards" [NKJV]; or "May they be flotsam on the face of the water; may their portion in the land be cursed; may none turn aside by way of their vineyards" [NJPS]). Several ancient versions (LXX, Vulgate, Syriac) as well as modern commentaries have accepted this solution to the problem (Andersen 1976, 214; Hartley 1988, 353-54; Balentine 2006, 371-74).

(3) Still others accept the canonical order of the verses as valid and attribute the contrasting views in this speech to the painful "cognitive dissonance" in Job's mind between the way the world is and the way it should be (Newsom 2003, 164-68; Seow 2013, 29-30). Along the same line, Childs thinks the author is trying to present Job as a wise sage who thoroughly understands the wisdom theology and can state its principles verbatim. In 24:18-24 Job defends the overall scope of the moral order even as he rejects its application to himself (1979, 542-43; Seitz 1989, 12-13).

(4) Some think this section of the book was damaged during its early transmission. Parts of the scroll became dislodged from their original location and some were lost. The copyists were confused about the proper order because some verses were missing. Thus, their restoration left the text in some disarray. Because Bildad has such a short third speech (25:1-6) and Zophar has none at all, there is a strong likelihood that this passage belongs to Bildad or Zophar rather than Job (Pope 1973, 195; Rowley 1976, 167; Clines 2006, 667-69).

(5) Finally, some versions simply include the verses as statements, as if Job agrees with them, even though the reader knows he does not (NASB, NIV, NRSV).

In trying to resolve this difficult problem, the key is v 25, which provides an important interpretive clue. In this verse Job expresses his absolute confidence in a position he knows the friends do not support. This means that vv 18-24 cannot immediately precede v 25 without a major reinterpretation of their meaning, along the lines of proposal 2 above. It is impossible to imagine Job closing his speech with such a strong challenge in v 25 immediately after quoting the view of his friends or the traditional wisdom theology. Thus, proposals 1, 3, and 5 are ruled out. The only proposals that merit any attention are 2 and 4. If one wishes to maintain the canonical order of verses, then vv 18-24 must be reinterpreted along the lines of proposal 2, although this requires extensive internal emendations.

The simplest and most likely solution is proposal 4. The text was damaged at some point in its transmission, and vv 18-24 were originally somewhere else.

This allows a more natural placement for v 25 immediately following vv 1-17. Those who accept this proposal have different theories about where vv 18-24 were originally located. Probably the most likely location is in Bildad's third speech following 25:6, although other scenarios are possible (→ Behind the Text for ch 25).

IN THE TEXT

1. I Wish I Could Talk to God (23:1-7)

In the first section of his speech Job presses home his desire for a meeting with God. He knows others will probably interpret his pursuit of God as rebellious, but this does not bother him in the least. If he can just find God and present his case, he believes God will acknowledge his righteousness and deliver him from further suffering.

■ **1** For comments on the introductory formula → 3:2.

■ **2** Today *again* **my complaint is** *rebellious* is Job's admission that his complaining has now grown to the level of rebellion. The persistent attacks by his friends, as exemplified in Eliphaz's last speech, have made him openly defiant against any suggestions that the friends might propose at this late date. His attention now turns back to God and what he would say to God if they could meet (23:3-17). He would be defiant against God, as well.

The word for *rebellious* (*měrî*) is the same one used by Samuel in his well-known condemnation of Saul's disobedience (1 Sam 15:23). In this context it introduces some of Job's strongest complaints against God. He will not shut up until God answers him or takes his life. Some scholars have suggested that the word **today** (*hayyôm*) indicates that the dialogues lasted over several days. An extended period of time is possible, but this one word is not proof. The author never tells us the length of time that Job and his friends engaged in conversation.

[Even though] **my hand is heavy** *upon* **my groaning** has received much comment (see Clines 2006, 575). There is a great temptation to emend *yādî* (**my hand**) to *yādô* (**his hand**), because the concept of God's hand being powerful and oppressive appears throughout the book (1:11; 2:5; 5:18; 6:9; 8:4; 10:7; 12:9-10; 13:21; 19:21; 27:11; 30:21). This reading is also supported by the LXX. But perhaps the more difficult reading is correct here. Job could be referring to his inability to suppress his groaning by placing his hand over his mouth. Even a heavy hand cannot stifle his outbursts of anger and pain.

■ **3** In earlier speeches (9:14-16; 13:3, 14-22; 19:7) Job expressed a strong desire for a meeting with God so he could defend his innocence, but so far, God has not spoken. Job refuses, though, to let the matter die. In 23:3 he makes it known that he is willing to go to God if God will not come to him. His only problem is he does not know where to find God. The word for **dwelling** (*těkûnâ*) is literally "established place." In this context it refers to God's place of residence.

■ **4-5** Job has in mind that he would do two things if he could gain an audience with God. First, he would lay out his **case** *to his face* with good arguments supporting his innocence and integrity (v 4). Second, he would listen carefully to God's response in order to learn the reasons for his suffering. Deep in his heart Job knows he is right (v 7; 13:18), but perhaps he has missed something that God wants to bring to his attention. Therefore, his imaginary meeting with God would allow time for God to instruct him concerning the divine plan for his life.

The Hebrew words for **I would *lay out* my case** (*'rk mišpāṭ*) and **arguments** (*tôkāḥôt*) are exactly the same as Job used previously in asking for a meeting with God (13:6, 18). These words are legal terms associated with lawsuits and legal evidence, but Job is not expecting to challenge God in court. His main concern is to present directly to God an impassioned and well-reasoned defense of his spiritual uprightness, thereby prodding God to declare him innocent and relieve his suffering.

■ **6-7** The language of the law courts continues in 23:6*a* with this question: "Would he contend with me?" (NRSV). Job has used the verb ***contend*** (*ryb*) several times already (9:3; 10:2; 13:8, 19). It can refer to disputes of either a legal or nonlegal nature. Job is thinking of a nonlegal dispute here, but one critical to his well-being. He questions how God would react to him if he ever were allowed to present his case. Would God crush him with overwhelming arguments?

This is a legitimate question when confronting the Almighty. One would naturally be apprehensive if God could not be trusted to treat people fairly. In earlier requests to meet God, Job was rather fearful of the outcome. He was afraid that God would simply destroy him and walk away (9:3-4, 16-19, 32, 34-35; 13:21). However, Job's attitude here is much different. He is now confident that God will listen to his case ("he [emphatic 'he'] would give heed to me" [23:6 NRSV]) and be moved to acknowledge that Job is **upright** (v 7; *yāšār*), which the reader has known from the beginning (1:1, 8; 2:3). This would free him from any further harassment from God.

2. I Am Confident but Terrified (23:8-17)

In the second part of his speech Job speaks of his inability to find God. God has simply disappeared. Therefore, he has not been able to present his case to God. But if such a meeting would occur, Job knows that God would declare him innocent, for his past life has been exemplary in regard to his obedience to God's commands. God would evaluate his character as of the same quality as gold.

In spite of his confidence in his own innocence, Job remains terrified that God will continue to punish him rather than meet with him. God's sovereignty and freedom allow him to do whatever he pleases, so Job has no hope that the future will be any better than the past.

■ **8-9** Job is frustrated over not being able to find God (also 9:11). No matter where he turns, God **is not there**. In 23:3 he stated that he would go to God if he only "knew where to find him." Verses 8-9 reinforce that idea by noting the places where Job has looked. In his search for God he has traveled to the **east** (*qedem*), **west** (*'āḥôr*), **north** (*śĕmō'l*), and **south** (*yāmîn*). These same words are also used in

Hebrew to indicate the directions of movement from where a person is standing—"forward," "behind," "to the left," and "to the right." Some versions choose the former meanings (NIV, NJPS) and some use the latter (NASB, NRSV). In either case, the meaning is the same: Job cannot find God in any direction.

The interpretation of v 9 is complicated by the third singular verbal forms. Is Job speaking of God who is active **in the north** and in **the south**, or is he describing himself as looking for God in these areas? The former retains the MT reading and makes reasonable sense (NIV), but not all scholars agree on the meaning of the two verbs (see Clines 2006, 577-78). The latter parallels the thought of v 8 much better, but this requires emendations of both verbs. The matter is not resolved, but Job's dissatisfaction in not being able to speak to God is clear.

■ **10** *For* he knows *my pathway.* Even though Job cannot find God, he is confident that God knows where he is. And further, God is aware of the quality of his life. The phrase *my pathway* is literally "the way with me," meaning "the righteous way that I conduct myself." This phrase is awkward in Hebrew but understandable, and it does not need to be emended as many try to do (see Clines 2006, 578).

When he *examines* me, I will come forth as gold. The verb for *examines* (*bḥn*) means "to test something for its quality or value." In other contexts the word is used in reference to testing "gold" (Zech 13:9), people's hearts (Ps 17:3), or words and ideas (Job 12:11). Earlier Job accused God of testing him so severely that he preferred death rather than life (7:14-18). The testing that Job is referring to in 23:10 could be the suffering he has already endured. But more likely, he means the examination that will come when he lays out his case before God (vv 2-7). He is certain that if God will grant him an audience and carefully examine his life and his arguments, he will be exonerated. God will plainly see that the quality of Job's life is of the same value as **gold**, the most precious of metals.

Job is absolutely correct in this evaluation of himself, for God has already spoken to the Examiner about Job's superb righteousness ("There is no one on earth like him" [1:8; 2:3]). If Job had been privy to these words in the prologue, he would not be so frustrated with God now. Peter makes a slight allusion to this verse in speaking of the Christian faith as "being more precious than gold." It retains its value even when "tested by fire" (1 Pet 1:7 NRSV).

■ **11-12** Job now explains why he "will come forth as gold" (v 10) when God *examines* him (also 9:21). He has followed God's guidance and obeyed his commands. He has done everything God has asked him to do. **I have treasured the words of his mouth *in my heart*** is Job's answer to Eliphaz's admonition in 22:22. He has already been doing what Eliphaz said he needed to do.

■ **13-14** Nevertheless, in spite of Job's righteousness and faithfulness to God's commands (vv 11-12), God has chosen to punish him for reasons known only to God. In Job's mind, there should be a cause-and-effect relationship between the actions of human beings and the consequences of these actions. But they are not related at all in real life. God **does whatever he pleases** (v 13*b*). Job has already spelled out the inequity in God's judgment of the wicked (21:7-26). He does not punish them for their sins. Yet Job, who is righteous, endures hideous forms of suffering that should be reserved for the most wicked of human beings. Job is also worried that God still has in mind to impose more suffering on him (23:14*b*).

Scholars are divided over the interpretation of v 13*a* (lit. "he is in one"). Some hold that it refers to God's authority to make a decision. The NEB supports this position with its translation: "He decides, and who can turn him from his purpose?" (also Habel 1985, 350-51). Others think Job is referring to God's uniqueness as one (**he stands alone**). Still others relate it to God's unchangeableness ("he is unchangeable" [RSV]). Most likely Job is speaking of God's sovereignty, based on the context of vv 13*b*, 14.

■ **15-16** In the course of listening to Job throughout the dialogues, Eliphaz mentioned twice that Job was terrified of God (4:5; 22:10). Job does not deny this at all. They both agree on this point. Job's terror arises out of his uncertainty about the future based on **God**'s (*El*) treatment of him in the past. What other forms of suffering does God have up his sleeve in addition to the loss of his possessions, his children, and his health? Hartley summarizes his dilemma in this way: "Job's struggle for faith reaches its severest test when his confidence in God collides with his fear of God" (1988, 342).

■ **17** In 23:17*b* Job notes that the terror that surrounds him (vv 15-16) is like a thick cloud of **darkness that covers** his **face**. He does not know where he is or how to get out of his troubles. But the relation of this to v 17*a* is unclear, and multiple renderings appear in modern versions. The NIV has **I am not silenced by the darkness**, meaning that Job plans to continue rebelling (v 2) against God until God considers his case. The NJPS emphasizes that God is still keeping him alive for some unknown reason: "I am not cut off [destroyed] by the darkness." The NRSV emends the negative *lō'* to *lu'* to express a wish: "If only I could vanish in darkness." The NJPS interpretation seems to fit the context best, but the issue remains unresolved.

3. Why Does God Not Punish the Wicked? (24:1-17, 25)

In ch 22 Eliphaz accused Job of mistreating the needy in society—the naked, the hungry, the thirsty, the widows, and the orphans. Job now takes up this topic in ch 24, but he refuses to admit his participation in such practices. Rather, the wicked are the ones who are guilty of these acts of social injustice. People such as murderers, adulterers, and thieves are the ones who should be blamed (vv 14-15).

However, Job's real point of contention is not Eliphaz's accusations. He is much more disturbed over God's failure to punish the wicked for their evil deeds. Even when the needy cry out to God for relief from this oppression by the wicked, God pays no attention to their prayers (v 12). Job has complained about this injustice before (21:6-26). If God is truly just, the righteous should always be rewarded and the wicked punished. But Job knows from his own experience and from observing others that God does not do this on a regular basis. Throughout ch 24 Job gives multiple examples of incidences where the wicked have received no punishment. The implication is that God does not act in a just manner. Job concludes this speech with a challenge for anyone to prove him wrong on this matter (v 25).

■ **1** The translation of v 1*a* is problematic, as the verb *ṣpn* can mean "hide" or "store up." But the point of the verse is to question God's lack of justice in the world. Since a just God would certainly punish the wicked for their evil deeds, why do **those who know him** "never see" (v 1*b* NRSV) these judgment days? "Why are times not kept by the Almighty?" (v 1*a* NRSV). Job would like for God to give him a reasonable explanation to this troubling question, but so far God has refused (→ 34:23 for Elihu's answer to this question).

■ **2-3** The list of evil deeds now begins. Those who engage in these acts are not specifically named, but Job is clearly speaking of the wicked throughout this chapter (as indicated in the LXX). The first item in the list is the moving or removal of **boundary** markers on the borders of a person's property. Farmers would often mark their property lines by taking stones out of their fields and piling them up along the edges.

Israelite law regarded property as a gift from God—offered to them through the covenant with Abraham (Gen 12:7; 13:14-15; 15:18-21) and received in the time of the conquest (Josh 13:7—19:51; 24:13). The land was passed down from generation to generation, being subdivided multiple times to accommodate increases in the population but always remaining in the same family. People who moved the ancient boundary markers were considered thieves because they were stealing the farmland that belonged to another family who needed it to survive. They could be prosecuted in a court of law (Deut 19:14; Prov 22:28; 23:10-11), and their status with God was regarded as cursed (Deut 27:17; Hos 5:10).

The wicked person's thievery also included the stealing of farm animals. Sheep and goats are intended in Job 24:2, while donkeys and oxen are mentioned in v 3. Verse 3 also implies that some forms of stealing may be within the law but are nevertheless outside of God's will for the needy. **Orphan**s or **widow**s could become destitute in hard times and be forced to give up their only **donkey** or **ox** as collateral for a debt, but Israelite law sought to protect these needy members of society from such heartless practices. They deserved special protections due to their vulnerable position and also as a reminder of Israel's former status as slaves in Egypt before God redeemed them (Deut 24:17-22; → Job 22:9 for further references in the Pentateuch regarding the protection of orphans and widows).

■ **4** The continual harassment by the wicked of **the needy** and **the poor** forces them to avoid traveling on public roads. They must "hide themselves" (NRSV) from contact with the wicked lest they become the target of further insults and injustices.

■ **5-6** In the next four verses Job emphasizes the wretched conditions that the needy must endure because of the way they are treated by the wicked. His description is very similar to the plight of the homeless in modern society. He compares their circumstances to that of **wild donkeys** who must forage in desert regions for their food (24:5). Away from civilized areas where the wicked are in control, they must eke out their survival on land that is not very productive. No doubt their farms have been taken from them by the wicked, so they must scavenge for food wherever they can find it.

Their miserable situation is further illustrated in v 6. Having lost their family farms and their means of producing their own food, they must now **gather grain** "in a field not their own" (NRSV) and **glean [grapes] in the vineyards of the wicked**. Like Ruth, their survival is dependent on finding sufficient leftover grain and grapes in the fields of others that have already been harvested (Ruth 2:2-23).

■ **7-8** Lacking a home and property, the needy have no **shelter** from the elements. Just like the "wild donkeys" in Job 24:5, they seek out whatever protection they can find in caves and among the **rocks** in desert and mountainous regions. They have no means to purchase clothing that is adequate for living outdoors, and so they must endure the **cold** and the **mountain rains** as if they were **naked**.

■ **9** The subject of v 9 is again the wicked. This time their crime concerns the merciless breakup of families by demanding the children of **the poor** as security for **a debt**. In v 3 Job criticized the taking of donkeys or oxen as securities from orphans and widows, because these were important animals that the poor needed to farm their land. Here the issue is even more serious—the taking of children. When poor people had no material things left to secure a debt, they were allowed to use family members or even themselves as guarantees (Exod 21:7-9; Lev 25:39-43; 2 Kgs 4:1; Neh 5:5).

The passage in Lev 25 spells out the protections provided in the law in regard to this practice. Israelites who were given to a creditor for the payment of a debt were supposed to be treated better than slaves, and they were to be given back their freedom when the debt was paid or in the seventh year of their slavery (Exod 21:2; Deut 15:12; Jer 34:14). Job's mention of this practice sounds very cruel—as if nursing infants were **snatched from** their mother's **breast**, but he is overly exaggerating to get his point across. Realistically, creditors preferred children who had economic value, that is, who were of sufficient age to be used as farm laborers (Clines 2006, 608).

■ **10-11** The subject now reverts back to "the needy" and "the poor" (Job 24:4). When they can find work, they gladly accept it; but Job's keen mind notes the irony of their predicament. While working for wealthy landholders, they are surrounded by the produce they need to survive—grain, **olives**, and grapes. But they cannot partake of it themselves because the landholders are not compassionate enough to pay them adequate wages or to share their bounty. The needy are only cogs in the machinery of production that contribute to getting these products to market. Thus, they personally remain **hungry** and **thirsty**, all the while holding the staples of life in their hands. They also are too poor to afford adequate clothing for working outdoors. Job poetically describes them as **naked**.

The three agricultural products mentioned in this verse—grain, olive oil, and wine—appear together frequently in the OT as symbols of God's provisions for his people when they obey him (Deut 7:13; 11:14; 28:51; Jer 31:12; Hos 2:22 [24 HB];

Joel 2:19; Hag 1:11). In response to God's goodness Israel was required to pay tithes of these products back to him (Num 18:12; Deut 12:17-19; 14:22-23; 18:4).

■ **12** Job finally gets to his punch line in v 12. His long list of examples of how the wicked mistreat the needy (vv 2-11) is stated for one purpose only—to criticize God for allowing this to happen. **God** [*Eloah*] **charges no one with wrongdoing**. It is bad enough that the wicked oppress the downtrodden of society, but it is unthinkable that God would allow this situation to continue without administering justice. Surely he is aware of this wrong, for the needy are constantly groaning and **crying out for help**. God's refusal to punish the wicked for these evil deeds is convincing proof that he is unjust.

The word for **the dying** (*mētîm*; v 12*a*) is an emended form of *mĕtîm* (lit. "men") that many scholars accept as a parallel to **the wounded** in v 12*b*. The word is used as a synonym for the needy who have nothing to look forward to except death. **Wrongdoing** (*tiplâ*; → 1:22) is sometimes emended to *tĕpillâ* (lit. "prayer") yielding: "God pays no attention to their prayer" (NRSV). This thought is certainly implied by Job, and it resonates with his own pleas for God to speak to him (13:22-24; 19:7-12; 23:3-7). But the NIV reading is probably correct, for it supports Job's earlier contention that God fails to punish wickedness and wrongdoing (21:7-26).

■ **13** In 24:13-17 Job mentions three specific types of lawbreakers who survive in the dark underbelly of society—"the murderer" (v 14), "the adulterer" (v 15), and "thieves" (v 16). He begins with a general comment about the nature of these individuals. They are examples of people who purposely **rebel against the light**. The word **light** has a double meaning here. The first meaning is "the light of day" that is contrasted in the next four verses with the darkness of nighttime when lawbreakers prefer to operate.

The second meaning is "the moral light" God shines upon humanity through the revelation of himself by general and special means. In the Psalms and wisdom literature light is associated with God's instructions that are handed down from generation to generation (Ps 119:105; Prov 4:10-19; 6:20-23; Eccl 2:13). The wise and the righteous choose to walk in this pathway of light because it provides life, guidance, and wisdom (Job 3:20; 12:25; 22:28; 29:3; 33:28, 30). God's light is also expressed in the ways societies organize themselves through codes of law such as the law of Moses (Ps 119:105) and the Code of Hammurabi (*ANET*, 164-65, "The Prologue," i and v). Hence, lawbreakers are people who **rebel against the light**.

The opposite of light is darkness, where the wicked carry out their evil deeds and try to hide (34:22). They stumble around in deep darkness because they cannot see the pathway of life (Prov 4:19). And the most extreme form of darkness is found in Sheol, the place of the dead (Job 10:21-22; 17:13; 18:18; 20:26; 38:17). In the book of Job light and darkness are frequently mentioned as opposites (→ "Light and Darkness in Job" sidebar at 11:17). The contrast between spiritual light and darkness is further amplified in the NT, especially in the Johannine literature (John 3:19-21; 1 John 1:5-7; 2:8-11).

■ **14** The first lawbreaker is **the murderer**. This person rises at daybreak (lit. "at the light") to prey upon **the poor and needy**. This time the intent is not just to make life miserable for the downtrodden (Job 24:2-4, 9). Rather, it is to take their lives. Killing people in the lower classes seems strange since they are a threat to no one and they have few if any belongings to steal from, but this detestable crime is also mentioned in Ps 94:6. Perhaps these murderers kill simply for the thrill of flaunting their power over another human being. If so, they are truly evil.

Job 24:14c is literally "and in the night [he] is like a thief" (NRSV). The topic of thieves appears later in v 16, and so some scholars move this clause to the beginning of that verse. But its location in v 14 is acceptable if the meaning is intended to indicate that the murderer prowls around both day and night.

■ **15-16** The second lawbreaker is **the adulterer** who seeks sexual encounters with the wife of another man. This person, for obvious reasons, takes great precautions to keep his identity **concealed** by covering **his face** and not going out until **dusk**.

The third lawbreaker is the thief. He, too, operates only at night. The Hebrew for **thieves** is not found in v 16, but the word is implied from their actions. These are individuals who **break into houses** for the purpose of stealing people's belongings. This would apply primarily to houses made of mud bricks. The same method of burglary is described in the Code of Hammurabi (*ANET*, 167, #21).

■ **17** Job notes the attraction of these lawbreakers to the "deep darkness" (*ṣalmāwet*; NRSV; → 3:5) of nighttime. This is the period when they feel free to prowl about looking for easy targets to kill, molest, and burglarize. They know this time well, for they are night shift workers who begin their workday when the sun goes down.

■ **18-24** For comments on 24:18-24 → section C, 2, and Behind the Text for ch 23.

■ **25** Verse 25 of ch 24 naturally follows v 17 as an appropriate conclusion (→ Behind the Text for ch 23). Job has been insistent throughout this speech that the wicked do terrible things to other people. Their crimes against the poor and needy are especially heinous. And yet God fails to regard these atrocities as wrongdoing, as evidenced by his lack of judgment against the wicked (24:12). One can almost visualize Job gesturing wildly and shouting these words at his friends: "If it is not so, who will prove me a liar?" (NRSV). Job utters these words without expecting a rebuttal from the friends, for he is fully confident that he is correct in his own understanding of these issues. This verse is very similar to Job's statement in 9:24c.

FROM THE TEXT

Summary of Job's Response to Eliphaz. The heart of Job's complaint is found in 24:1, 12. God fails to judge according to the principles of justice laid out in the wisdom theology—whether applied to the wicked or the righteous. How can God be called just if he operates this way? For Job, he cannot. For reasons known only to God, he allows the wicked to continue their evil deeds and fails to help the needy who are oppressed. His sovereignty allows him to do whatever he pleases, even if unjust (23:13). Therefore, humans are terrified about what may lie in the future, because the universe seems to lack a moral structure. God's freedom to act as he chooses whenever he chooses creates a fearful uncertainty about life. Job's anguish is driven by this uncertainty.

Job emphasizes these points in chs 23—24:
- I wish I could speak with God and present my case. I believe he would vindicate me. In fact, he would evaluate my character as *golden*, for I have lived righteously all my life.
- But I cannot find God, no matter where I look.
- Unfortunately, God is sovereign. He does whatever he pleases.
- Therefore, I am terrified because my future is so uncertain. God does not kill me, but neither does he heal me. What other troubles does he still have in store for me?
- There are many people in this world who are wicked. They do horrible things to other people, especially to the lower classes of whom they can take advantage. But God never punishes them. Why does God not do so?
- I am absolutely convinced that the way God governs his world is unjust. Can anyone prove me wrong?

C. Bildad's Third Speech (25:1-6; 24:18-24)

BEHIND THE TEXT

Chapter 25 is only six verses long. Some have suggested that this is evidence of a loss of fervor by this time. The speakers are simply too exhausted to continue their vigorous dialogue. However, this seems rather strange in light of the length of all the earlier speeches and the carefulness by which the author has structured his book with balanced remarks on either side of the debate. More likely, the original text was damaged at some point in the past and the other part of Bildad's speech was either lost or got separated (for further comments on the arrangement of chs 22—27, → Behind the Text for ch 22).

When the book was damaged, the copyist was faced with the dilemma of how to restore a damaged scroll. He probably placed 24:18-24 in Job's speech (chs 23—24) because there is a point of agreement between 24:21 and 24:3, 9. All three verses speak of the mistreatment of widows by the wicked. However, the context around 24:21 (vv 18-24) reflects the view of the three friends, not Job.

The words in 24:18-24 could come from any of the three friends, but most likely they belong to Bildad or Zophar since Eliphaz already has a long third speech. Some scholars place them at the end of Zophar's third speech (following 27:13-23) because Zophar has been leading up to the death of the wicked by describing their sufferings. But a better location is at the end of Bildad's third speech (25:1-6) as a direct rebuttal to Job's anger over God's failure to punish the wicked (24:1-12). Bildad agrees with Job that the wicked cause harm to widows, but he strongly disagrees that they are left unpunished. As he says, "God drags away the mighty by his power" (v 22) and they "wither like the heads of grain" (v 24 NJPS). The transition from 25:6 to 24:18 is a little awkward, but additional verses may have been lost when the text was damaged.

There are two sections to Bildad's speech:
1. God's Power and Purity Far Surpass That of Humanity (25:1-6)
2. The Wicked Are Destroyed Because of Their Evil Deeds (24:18-24)

IN THE TEXT

1. God's Power and Purity Far Surpass That of Humanity (25:1-6)

In this section Bildad directs Job's attention to God's omnipotence and purity. These divine attributes are reason enough for humans to respect God's governance of the world. Bildad is probably trying to counter Job's confidence that he will win his case against God if a meeting can be arranged (23:4-7). As Bildad sees it, Job is badly mistaken. God is so powerful that Job has no chance whatsoever of defeating him in a debate.

■ **1** The character of **Bildad** is discussed in 2:11. For comments on the introductory formula → 3:2.

■ **2-3** Without the typical introductory remarks (which may have been lost), Bildad plunges directly into the dialogue. Job's complaint about God's failure to punish the wicked (24:1-12) is based on his ignorance of God's omnipotence. God is all-powerful, and he knows how to govern both this world and the heavenly realms. God has at his command ***troops*** that are too numerous to be counted (Job mentioned these troops in 19:12 as being arrayed against him). And he shines his **light** on every person in the world. No one can avoid it. In other words, Almighty God controls every aspect of this world. He does so through forceful means, creating *fear* (awe; 25:2a) in the hearts of his subjects. No one can challenge God's power. Even other divine beings in heaven must submit to him.

■ **4** God's (*El*) moral purity also proves he knows how to govern the world. The two rhetorical questions in v 4 imply that it is impossible for human beings to achieve God's level of purity. This argument is not new. Eliphaz has already stated this position three times (4:17-21; 5:7; 15:14-16), and Job has agreed with it twice (9:2; 14:4), although for different reasons. Bildad is thus rehashing old arguments.

■ **5-6** Here Bildad compares humanity to **the moon** and **the stars**. These very bright objects in the night sky have the appearance of something clean and spotless, yet God regards them as unclean in comparison to his purity (Eliphaz made a similar comparison in 4:18-19; 15:15-16). How much lower down the scale of moral purity are human beings? Their rank is no higher than that of **a maggot** or **a worm**. Since maggots and worms are associated with decaying bodies, humans must be considered as very unclean. Bildad's point is to deny Job's claim that God does not punish the wicked and therefore he is unjust (24:1-12). In Bildad's thinking, humanity is so far below God's level of purity that any criticism of God's justice is absurd.

2. The Wicked Are Destroyed Because of Their Evil Deeds (24:18-24)

The swift demise of the wicked is the topic of 24:18-24. This is one of the two misplaced passages in Job (→ Behind the Text for chs 23 and 25). Throughout this section the subject alternates between singular and plural (Clines 2006, 654), but most versions disregard this and translate them all as plurals.

■ **18-20** These three verses bring together several different metaphors that portray the short life span of the wicked—a concept supported by the three friends in the past (15:20-35; 18:5-21; 20:4-29; 22:16). Verse 18a of ch 24 compares the wicked to light objects that are caught in the current of a rapidly flowing stream. One sees them for only a few brief moments before they float out of sight, for "swift are they on the **surface** of the waters" (NRSV). The second and third clauses consider the nonproductiveness of their land. It is **cursed**, and therefore people avoid it.

In v 19 Bildad compares the life span of the wicked to rapidly melting **snow**. ***Sheol*** snatches away those who ***sin*** just as quickly as ***dryness and heat*** rid the land of **snow**. In v 20 the focus is on how quickly the wicked are forgotten after their death. Even their own mothers lose the memory of them once the ***maggot*** starts to feed on their body. And finally, just like **a tree** is suddenly snapped in a strong wind, so God brings to an end the ***injustice*** caused by the wicked.

■ **21** The wicked see nothing wrong in harming women who are **childless** or **widows**. This is another example of the great evil they inflict on others. This injustice is most detestable when imposed on some of the weakest members of society—those who should be receiving compassion and protection rather than abuse.

■ **22-24** These three verses deal with God's punishment of the wicked. No subjects are specified in v 22, but **God** is most likely the subject in v 22a and **the mighty** (the wicked) in v 22b. God's power is greater than that of the wicked, which enables him to punish them for their evil deeds. Even though they may ***rise up*** in prominence for a period of time, **they have no assurance of life**. God can cut their lives short at any moment.

The same concept is repeated in v 23. God may provide **security** and support to the wicked for the time being, but he continually keeps **his eyes** on them, ready to punish them when the time is right. Verse 24 summarizes the fate of the wicked. Their exaltation is only temporary. Then they are **brought low** and ***snatched away. They wither*** like heads of grain.

FROM THE TEXT

Summary of Bildad's Third Speech. Bildad's main points are as follows:
- God is all-powerful and pure. Nothing else in all creation even comes close to his level of perfection.

- God does not allow the wicked to escape the consequences of their sins. They may flourish for a brief time, but God is constantly watching them. When God is ready, he brings them to an untimely death. And after death, they are forgotten by those who knew them.

D. Job's Response to Bildad (26:1-14; 27:1-12)

BEHIND THE TEXT

In almost all the dialogue speeches to this point there has been a short introduction in which the speaker complains about the remarks of the previous speaker or defends his own wisdom before moving on to his main topic. The first verses in this section (26:1-4) fit this type of introduction perfectly, but the matter of who actually spoke these words is disputed. The second singular verbs and pronouns suggest that these words were directed at Job by one of the friends, yet the section is introduced with Job's name as the speaker (v 1). Job has been very consistent to this point in using second plural verbs and pronouns when addressing the friends so as to include all three of them in his remarks (with the possible exception of 12:7-8; 16:3); whereas the friends, who are speaking to only one person (Job), have regularly adhered to the second singular. Thus, the singular forms suggest that these words (26:2-4) are from one of the friends. However, many scholars regard them as from Job, based on their content, and this commentary accepts that conclusion. So these are some of the few words in the book where Job's words are directed only at one friend, in this case, Bildad. Job uses these verses to criticize Bildad's failure to help him.

The subject of the remaining verses in the chapter (vv 5-14) is the power of God, especially as revealed through creation, but the speaker is not specified. Many hold that these words are Bildad's and should be moved to the end of his third speech following 25:6 (Gordis 1978, 534-35; Clines 2006, 628-30). They carry on the topic of God's power that Bildad mentioned in 25:2-6. Further support is provided by the abnormally short length of Bildad's speech, which is very awkward. The addition of 26:5-14 would make his third speech more comparable in length to the previous speeches.

Others think these words come from Job and should remain in their present position. Job has talked about God's power before (9:1-13; 12:7-25). In these earlier passages his words were in the context of his fear of having to defend himself before such a mighty God. Here in 26:5-14 there is nothing about his fear of God. Instead, we find an elegant poem on God's incredible power as displayed throughout creation. This writer takes the position that these words are indeed from Job.

Two pieces of evidence support this scenario. First, Job is the only person who has mentioned "the Sea" (NRSV) and "Rahab" (vv 12-13) in earlier speeches (7:12; 9:13). Second, when the friends have spoken of God's power in the past, their words have been used to emphasize either humanity's weakness and unrighteousness (4:17-21; 15:14-16; 25:2-6) or God's punishment of the wicked (4:9-11;

5:9-14; 11:10-11; 15:17-35; 18:5-21; 20:4-29; 22:12-20). Neither of these contexts is found in this passage. Thus, these verses relate more naturally to Job. The transition from 26:4 to v 5 is a little awkward, but it is possible that 27:11-12 originally stood between them, providing a segue between Bildad's advice (26:3) and Job's teaching (27:11). This would yield for this speech: 26:1-4; 27:11-12; 26:5-14; 27:1-10.

This section uses a number of images from the creation story in Gen 1. For example, the ***void/emptiness*** in Job 26:7 is the same word used in Gen 1:2, the ***waters bound up in the clouds*** in Job 26:8 are like the waters above the dome/firmament in Gen 1:7, and the ***circle on the waters*** in Job 26:10 is similar to Gen 1:4, 9. The author also borrows terminology found in ancient creation myths such as the Babylonian *Enuma Elish* and the Ugaritic myths about Baal. The references to "the Sea" (NRSV), "Rahab" (Job 26:12), and "the fleeing serpent" (v 13 NRSV) come from these earlier sources (→ "Mythological Characters in Job" sidebar at 7:12).

Job's speech has four sections:
1. You, Bildad, Have Not Helped Me a Bit (26:1-4)
2. God's Power Is Evident in All Areas of the Cosmos (26:5-14)
3. I Swear That I Am Innocent (27:1-6)
4. May God Punish My Enemy (27:7-12)

IN THE TEXT

1. You, Bildad, Have Not Helped Me a Bit (26:1-4)

26:1-4

Verses 2-4 are Job's rebuttal to Bildad's comments in the previous speech. Sarcastically, he asks how Bildad's words have helped him deal with his suffering or understand its cause. In Job's thinking, Bildad is only interested in showing how great God is in comparison to humanity, and therefore no human being should question God's ways or accuse him of being unjust. Instead of helping Job, Bildad has only made him feel worse.

■ **I** For comments on the introductory formula → 3:2.

■ **2-3** *How have you helped the one who has no power? How have you saved the arm that has no strength? How have you advised the one who has no wisdom? And (what) wisdom have you fully made known?* In this series of questions addressed to Bildad alone, Job takes the position, for argument's sake, that he is powerless before God and ignorant of God's ways. If this is true, then how has Bildad helped him? What new knowledge or power has Bildad provided to make up for the deficiencies in Job's understanding? These are all rhetorical questions that challenge Bildad's effectiveness as a counselor. So far he has said nothing that has encouraged Job or shown him the way out of his suffering.

■ **4** Next Job criticizes the source of Bildad's words. Where did his ideas come from? The implication of the rhetorical questions is that Bildad is certainly not speaking for God. He is only expressing his own opinion or ideas he borrowed from the other friends.

2. God's Power Is Evident in All Areas of the Cosmos (26:5-14)

Since the beginning of time, God has controlled the entire cosmos—the heavens, the earth, and the underworld. In these verses Job provides a sampling of examples to illustrate this truth. These samples are only a tiny fraction of all God's stupendous activities.

■ **5-6** God's power extends even to the underworld. According to the ancient understanding of the cosmos, there is an ocean of water underneath the flat earth, and then Sheol is beneath that (→ "Sheol" sidebar at 3:19). God is not in Sheol because it is an unclean place, but he definitely controls it and is aware of everything that goes on there. Verse 6 speaks figuratively of **Sheol** as being **naked** before him. The **spirits of the dead** who inhabit it **writhe in terror** (v 5a). They cannot communicate with God or experience his steadfast love, and they fear what he may do to them in the future. The word *rĕpā'îm* in v 5 is usually translated "shades" (NRSV), **spirits of the dead**, or just **the dead**. It refers to the inhabitants of Sheol (Ps 88:10 [11 HB]; Prov 2:18; 9:18; 21:16; Isa 14:9; 26:14, 19).

In Job 26:6 **Abaddon** is paired with **Sheol** as a synonym. In 28:22 it is paired with "Death" (*māwet*). The word is derived from the root *'bd* (meaning "perish") and, if translated, is usually rendered as **Destruction**. The word appears elsewhere only in 28:22; 31:12; Ps 88:11 [12 HB]; and Prov 15:11; 27:20.

■ **7** *He stretched out Zaphon over the emptiness* describes God's power in creating the heavens and the earth. **Zaphon** (*ṣāpôn*) is the normal Hebrew word for the direction "north" (a different word is used in 23:9). There is also a mythological mountain by this name that appears in Ugaritic literature as the place where the Canaanite god Baal resided and the gods of the pantheon assembled (Isa 14:13). But neither of these meanings is intended here. Most likely this is a metaphor for the highest heaven from where God rules, in contrast to the depths of Sheol and Abaddon (Job 26:6; Hartley 1988, 365-66). In support of this are the numerous references where "the heavens" are the object of the verb "stretched out" (*nṭh*) (e.g., Job 9:8; Ps 104:2; Isa 40:22).

Job is comparing the creation of the heavens to spreading out a tent covering over poles. The pillars at the edges of the heavens (Job 26:11) acted as poles. God then stretched his heavens over them and over the **emptiness** (*tōhû*) in the middle. The same word for **emptiness** is used in Gen 1:2 to describe the formless void that existed before God began to create. In Job 26:7b **the earth**, also supported by pillars, was suspended over **nothingness**—a metaphor for the great subterranean ocean.

■ **8-9** Job now turns to God's use of the clouds. Metaphorically, he *wrapped up* the rain he needed to water the earth within the **clouds** as if they were great waterskins. **Their weight** was very heavy, but God prevented them from bursting open to flood the earth. God also used the clouds to conceal his throne from human view: *He covered the face of (his) throne* (v 9a). In the Psalms God is frequently pictured as sitting on a throne in the heavens (Pss 9:4, 7 [5, 8 HB]; 11:4; 45:6 [7 HB]; 47:8 [9 HB]; 93:2; 97:2; 103:19). The word for **throne** in Job 26:9 (*kissēh*) is an alternate spelling of the more normal form *kissē'*. Some emend the word to *kese'* (**full moon** [NIV, NRSV]), but **throne** makes better sense when referring to the acts of creation.

■ **10** This verse is based on an ancient belief concerning the farthest limits of the cosmos. At the time of creation God established a permanent boundary line on the face of the oceans that surrounded the created world (Prov 8:27). This line was what we know as **the horizon** today and thus was circular (Isa 40:22). Outside of this boundary line was perpetual darkness and chaos, so it marked the separation **between light and darkness**.

■ **11-13** In ancient cosmology **the pillars of the heavens** (v 11) supported the great dome/firmament that overarched the sky. They were probably thought of as high mountains near the outer boundary line of the cosmos (v 10). These pillars **trembled** and **were horrified** when God's power was displayed at the beginning of creation in his defeat of "the Sea" (v 12 NRSV) and the sea monsters **Rahab** and "the fleeing serpent" (v 13 NRSV; either a synonym for **Rahab** or the sea dragon Leviathan [3:8; Isa 27:1]). The translation of *bārîaḥ* as "fleeing" is the traditional conjecture. Others have suggested: **gliding**, "twisting" (NEB), "straight," and "evil."

These mythological characters were borrowed by the author from Mesopotamian and Canaanite myths in the ANE (→ Job 7:12; 9:13). They represent chaos. Their usage enhances even further God's omnipotence, which is the theme of this section. He "stilled the Sea" (NRSV), **smote Rahab**, **made the heavens beautiful**, and **pierced** "the fleeing serpent" (NRSV).

God drew upon four resources to accomplish these conquests—**his power** (*kōaḥ*), "his understanding" (NRSV; *tĕbûnâ*), **his breath** (*rûaḥ*), and **his hand** (*yād*). Three of these manifest themselves in physical ways, whereas "understanding" refers to the use of God's wisdom and knowledge. God was able to outsmart these mythological creatures as well as deal them a physical deathblow.

■ **14** Job closes this speech by calling God's powerful acts at the beginning of creation only **the edges of his ways**, that is, a small sampling of the things God has done and is capable of doing. The implication is that God's ways are far beyond human understanding.

When God acted at the beginning of time to bring the cosmos into existence, it was awesome and frightening. God's power was like a loud clap of nearby **thunder**. But that sound has diminished over time. Humanity is now far removed from these primordial events and is only aware of them as a **faint . . . whisper** passed down through the generations. So who can understand the ways of God? Job's answer is: "No one."

3. I Swear That I Am Innocent (27:1-6)

BEHIND THE TEXT

Scholars disagree significantly on the interpretation of ch 27. Verses 1-12 are definitely from Job as indicated by the second plural verbs and pronouns in vv 5, 11, and 12. But vv 13-23 are very similar in style and content to the friends' comments on the sufferings of the wicked in their second cycle of speeches (15:17-35; 18:5-21; 20:4-29). These words cannot be from Job unless one takes the position that Job is mimicking their earlier speeches, but that would be a strange way to end the dialogues. Further, Job would not likely talk about the death of his own children as in 27:14-15.

An alternative proposal is that these words are directed by Job at the friends whom he now considers to be wicked (v 13). This is the lesson that Job wants to teach them (v 11) about their future. They are headed for the death of their children, the sudden loss of their health and wealth, and a terror-plagued life. However, the content sounds very much like the typical wisdom theology that Job has previously rejected. Also, Job has called his friends "worthless physicians" (13:4) and "miserable comforters" (16:1), but he has never accused them of being "wicked" (27:13).

More likely, vv 13-23 are a part of Zophar's missing third speech. Originally, they may have been placed either here or between chs 26—27. If located here, the dialogue section (chs 4—27) ends with these rather dismal words by Zophar. Job only responds (chs 29—31) after the interlude (ch 28). If located between chs 26—27, the dialogues maintain their regular pattern of presenting a speech from Job after each of the friends' speeches (→ Behind the Text for ch 22).

IN THE TEXT

In these verses Job's concern is to reaffirm his integrity by swearing an oath of innocence.

■ **1** "Job again took up his discourse [*māšāl*] and said" (NRSV). This introductory verse as well as 29:1 are conspicuous because they deviate from the normal standard formula that has introduced each of the speeches up to this point (→ 3:2). Coming as it does in the middle of Job's speech, some have suggested that it indicates a pause while Job waited for Zophar to speak. Others think it was created by a later copyist who was trying to make sense out of the damaged parts of the book (chs 24—27). He credited all the verses in chs 26—31 to Job, but he knew that parts of them were separate speeches. The two unique introductory statements (27:1 and 29:1) are the copyist's way of dividing up this long section into three subsections (chs 26, 27—28, 29—31).

■ **2-4** Job now utters an oath declaring his honesty in all he has previously said and will say in the future. **By the life of God** (*ḥay 'ēl*) is a typical phrase at the beginning of an oath formula that is often translated, "As God/Yahweh lives" (Ruth

3:13; 1 Kgs 1:29; 2 Kgs 3:14; 4:30; 5:16; etc.). Sometimes in the Prophets, God himself used this formula in swearing an oath concerning Israel: "As I live . . ." (Isa 49:18; Jer 22:24; Ezek 16:48; Zeph 2:9; etc.). Bringing God into the oath was one way oath-takers vouched for the absolute truthfulness of their testimony. Job may also have in mind "to force God to act" (Habel 1985, 380) by swearing in his name. In Job 31 Job will expand his oath-making to include even curses against himself if he has not been totally honest and righteous in all his dealings.

In the remainder of 27:2 Job criticizes God for causing him great agony. God has **denied me justice** and **made my life bitter**. No doubt, Job is mainly referring to God's refusal to speak to him. As long as God remains silent, the issue of Job's innocence cannot be resolved, and hence justice is prevented from occurring. This has been an increasing source of bitterness for Job since the beginning of the book (3:20; 7:11; 10:1; 21:25), but he will not back down from his claim of innocence as long as he lives (27:3). He will never compromise his standard of truthfulness by speaking false and deceptive words (v 4; 6:28-30). The irony here is unmistakable. Job swears by the God who is punishing him. His claim to be truthful and innocent can only be verified by the one who has **denied** him **justice**.

■ **5-6** The point of 27:5-6 is basically the same as vv 2-4. Job knows he is right in his heart, and he will continue to maintain his innocence as long as he lives. However, he adds some words of criticism specifically directed against his friends: "Far be it from me to say that you are right" (v 5 NRSV). Several times in earlier speeches the friends have argued that no person is ever completely right with God, because humanity can never rise to the level of God's purity. Even the angels are impure when compared to God (4:17-21; 15:14-16; 25:4-6). But Job begs to differ ("My heart does not reproach me" [27:6*b* NRSV]). As far as he knows at that moment, there is no sin in his life. He is morally right with God.

Every reader of the book knows he is telling the truth, for both the author and God have confirmed that Job is correct (1:1, 8; 2:3). Therefore, Job remains committed to what his heart tells him is true. He cannot accept his friends' evaluation of his life because "if he were to agree with them, he would be denying what he knows to be true about himself. That would be to lie; that would be to abandon his integrity" (Clines 2006, 647).

4. May God Punish My Enemy (27:7-12)

These verses contain words of imprecation against Job's friends and conclude with Job's offer to teach them the truth.

■ **7** May my enemy be *(treated)* like the wicked, *and may the one who rises up against me be (treated) like the evildoer.* This verse is a word of imprecation against an unnamed **enemy** (*'ōyēb*) that God's judgment would fall on this person(s) in the same way he punishes the wicked. The speaker of the verse is disputed. Clines thinks these words are the beginning of Zophar's missing third speech (2006, 663). However, none of the friends have ever spoken about an enemy. Certainly, they have disagreed with Job about many things. They have told him he was full of wind (8:2; 11:2-3; 15:2-3), mistaken in his claim of purity (11:4-6), lacking in wisdom (11:12), turning away from God (15:4-6), arrogant and insulting (18:3-4; 20:3), and even a sinner (22:5). But they have never called him an **enemy**. They see Job primarily as a long-time friend whom they want to help, but he refuses to listen to their advice.

More likely, 27:7 is a continuation of Job's speech in vv 2-6 because Job has spoken about enemies in previous speeches. But who does Job have in mind, if these words are from him? There are plenty of candidates. One of them is God. Job called God an enemy (*ṣar*) in 16:9 and stated that God regards him as his enemy (*'ōyēb*) in 13:24. He also has complained numerous times about God's hostilities against him (3:23; 6:4; 7:11-21; 9:13-24; 10:2-7, 16-20; 16:7-14; 19:6-12). But God cannot be the enemy Job has in mind here, for he speaks of God in 27:8 as the one who will punish his enemy.

A second possibility is Job's family and acquaintances. He is aware that many in his community have turned against him (19:13-22). Job has never called them his enemy, but he has certainly complained about their treatment of him. The third and most probable candidate for Job's enemy is the three friends whom he has engaged in intense debate for many chapters. Some combination of them and his family and community associates may be the persons he has in mind here. Job may have purposely not named his enemy because he knows he has more than one opponent. As Hartley says, it may be that "the identification of the enemy is left intentionally vague in order to emphasize that Job is requesting complete deliverance from all hostility" (1988, 371). One important point of interpretation is that the verse does not say that Job's enemies are wicked. Rather, Job requests that his enemies be punished by God *in the same manner* that he punishes the wicked.

■ **8-10** The rhetorical questions in 27:8-10 emphasize the breakup in fellowship between God and the wicked. The **godless** (*ḥānēp*; → 8:13) no longer **take pleasure** in the Almighty (27:10*a*), and he no longer responds to their cries for help (v 9). Further, **God** [*Eloah*] **cuts them off** at an early age, and thus they have no **hope** (*tiqwâ*) for the future (v 8). Job wishes that God would treat his enemies (v 7) exactly like this.

■ **11-12** Job now offers to teach his friends a proper understanding of **God** (v 11; *El*) without holding anything back. He knows they have seen the same things he has seen, so they should be familiar with the nature of God. But for some reason their eyes in regard to this matter are blind. All they have spoken is **meaningless talk** (v 12; *hebel*), that is, babble without substance. This is the same word that appears over thirty times in Ecclesiastes with the meaning of "vanity" (→ 7:16).

The ending of Job's speech with these words seems somewhat strange. We would expect them to be followed by a significant essay on the nature of God. Perhaps this is more evidence of damage to the text in this section of the book. Or better, perhaps these two verses originally preceded Job's speech on the power of God (26:5-14).

FROM THE TEXT

Summary of Job's Response to Bildad. The dialogue section is almost finished. The speakers now see that their arguments have not changed any minds, so any further discussion is useless. But before moving into the next section Job makes one final pronouncement. He swears in the name of God that he is innocent of any sin. He will never change his mind about that.

Job's main points are these:
- Bildad, I wish you had offered some advice that could help me, but unfortunately, your advice is worthless.
- If you really want to know what God's power is like, I will give you some examples. At the time of creation God ordered the entire cosmos—heavens, earth, underworld—as he saw fit. It all still remains under his control.
- I swear I am innocent of any sin against God. I will continue to affirm that until I die.
- May God treat all those who are harassing me in the same way he treats the wicked.

E. Zophar's Third Speech (27:13-23)

BEHIND THE TEXT

There is much confusion and speculation about these verses. This writer attributes them to Zophar (→ Behind the Text for 27:1-6). The reason this passage belongs to Zophar and not Bildad is v 13, which is almost exactly the same as the final verse in Zophar's second speech (20:29). In other words, for his third speech Zophar picks up exactly where he left off in ch 20 and proceeds with the same line of argument without ever acknowledging the material that has been covered in the speeches in between. He just dogmatically continues to play the same string on his banjo, no matter what song the other musicians are playing. The only item that is missing here is the standard introductory formula: "Then Zophar answered and said" (→ 3:2). Apparently, it disappeared when the text was damaged. The copyist, not knowing where this section belonged, attached it to the end of the dialogues.

IN THE TEXT

1. God Will Surely Punish the Wicked (27:13-23)

There is only one topic in this section—God's punishment of the wicked.
■ **13** *This is the wicked person's allotment with God* [*El*], *the inheritance of the ruthless that they receive* **from the Almighty** (*Shaddai*). The topic of vv 14-23 is the sufferings of the wicked. Verse 13 ties these sufferings directly to God. The words are almost exactly the same as 20:29 (→). **Ruthless** refers to those who bring terror into other people's lives (6:23).

■ **14-15** Some parts of the OT state that the sins of a wicked person affect that person's entire family, even to the third and fourth generation (Exod 20:5; 34:7; Num 14:18; Deut 5:9). Zophar's view is similar (for an alternative view on individual responsibility see Jer 31:29-30; Ezek 18:2-4). The children of the wicked will receive the punishment due their parents. They will be buried early in life by the "familiar sinister trio of death—war, famine and plague" (Clines 2006, 665). In other words, one of the consequences of wickedness is having to bury your own children (Bildad expressed a similar idea in Job 18:16-19). Zophar's insensitivity here is grossly offensive, for Job has already experienced this calamity in his own family and does not need Zophar to remind him of it again.

Their widows refers to the spouses of the evildoers and the wives of their children. It may also be a subtle reference to Job's spouse and the wives of his children (following LXX). The reason for their not weeping is not given. Perhaps their own survival is in doubt. Or perhaps the fear of a contagious disease prevents the family from having a normal burial. A further possibility is that the family has been so overwhelmed by so many deaths that they have no tears left. In any case, the family of the wicked person is not able to provide the proper mourning rituals that usually accompany death. This is another consequence of their sins.

■ **16-17** Hoarding is one of the characteristics of the wicked, as it provides them a sense of security (like a high city wall around them according to Prov 10:15; 18:11). But whether measured in precious metals like **silver** or in abundant **clothes**, the heaping up of life's possessions yields only a false sense of security, for the hoarders will not live long enough to enjoy their wealth. Their riches will be taken away in a moment of time (Job 27:18-21; on God's "day of wrath" according to Prov 11:4) to be enjoyed by **the righteous** and **the innocent**. How this transfer of wealth takes place is not explained. The friends have all talked about the calamities that will befall evildoers, but this is the first time that any of them have suggested that the righteous will benefit from the downfall of the wicked.

■ **18-19** Whatever wealth the wicked accumulate is only temporary. It may disappear at any time. Their wealth is compared to the **cocoon** from which a moth emerges. The word for "moth" (*'āš*) is disputed on the grounds that it is not parallel to **hut** in the second clause. Some suggest a "bird's nest" (Clines 2006, 659) and others a "spider's web" (Hartley 1988, 358, n. 8) as a better translation, but the metaphor using "moth" is understandable and should be retained. In any case, the temporary nature of the object is clear.

Job 27:18*b* speaks of a small **hut** where **a watchman** lives for a short period of time. The building is constructed at harvesttime to provide shelter for the watchman who guards the fields until the crops are harvested and stored away. It is disassembled as soon as the harvest is over.

Verse 19 reinforces the suddenness of the loss of wealth that the wicked experience. They go to bed one night confident they have enough riches to provide them a life of security and ease, but in the morning **all** their wealth **is gone**.

■ **20-23** Using a number of metaphors, Zophar describes additional calamities that will strike the wicked, leading to their ultimate death. God will use the forces of nature to batter them **without mercy** (v 22). The **flood** (v 20), the **tempest**, and the powerful **east wind** (v 21) off the Arabian desert will drive them from their homes. Their final days will be filled with **terrors** (v 20). Zophar's personification of the forces of nature is enhanced by the use of several strong verbs to describe the actions of the wind against the wicked. It "carries them off" (NRSV), **hurls itself at them without mercy** (v 22), **claps its hands** (v 23) at their misery, and **hisses** at them in contempt and **derision**.

FROM THE TEXT

Summary of Zophar's Third Speech. The dialogue section is now officially ended. The original manuscript may have included a final speech from Job in response to Zophar's speech in 27:13-23. If so, it has been lost. On the other hand, the author may have left the dialogues without closure on purpose. After a brief interlude (ch 28) that lessens the tension, Job delivers his final summary in chs 29—31.

Zophar has one main point:
- The punishment of the wicked is a sure thing. They lose their children and their wealth; they are terrified with fear; and they die an early death—all at the hand of God.

EXCURSUS I: PROGRESS IN THE NARRATIVE

Before moving on to the remainder of the book, it would be helpful to pause briefly and reflect on the progress in the narrative. Job and his friends have gone round and round over various issues. The tone has become more heated, and the substance has sometimes been repetitious. Often readers reach this stage in a state of confusion over what has actually transpired. Hopefully, the following will clear up the confusion and establish a foundation for the rest of the story.

A. The Failure of Job's Friends

Eliphaz, Bildad, and Zophar traveled to Uz for the purpose of comforting Job. Their initial reaction upon seeing his physical condition was one of shock and horror. They were dumbfounded and could not utter a word for a whole week. They were shocked again when Job began to speak. They had never heard anyone utter such distraught, angry curses against his own life.

Nevertheless, they saw an opportunity to help an old friend overcome his sorrow and pain. As older, wiser sages, they had a wealth of personal experiences to draw upon, as well as the ancient teachings of the wisdom traditions. They felt confident they could redirect Job's attention away from his suffering and point him toward God.

And so they began to use different methods to teach Job in the ways of wisdom. They were cautious at first, but then more intense as Job became more obstinate. All three spoke highly of the wisdom theology, compiled from centuries of observations about human experience, as having the answers to Job's questions. Eliphaz added a message he had personally received from a supernatural spirit. They all believed Job should respect their maturity and great knowledge as wise counselors. They even looked around for someone else to blame, fastening their attention on Job's children, whose tragic deaths must have been deserved. They threw everything at Job they could think of. And when none of these methods showed any sign of cracking Job's resistance, they resorted to direct attack against Job's character, telling him outright that he was a sinner. They finally shut up only after recognizing they had failed. There was nothing more they could say.

Up to this point, the friends have presented eight basic arguments to Job.

(1) Things do not happen without a reason. Our world operates by divine cause-and-effect principles. Therefore, there must be some reason for Job's suffering. It could be a secret sin that he refused to admit. Or he may have grieved God in ignorance or by omission. Or God may have penalized Job for his children's sins. But there has to be a reason, for nothing ever occurs by chance or coincidence. People reap what they sow.

(2) God has created an ordered world in which justice always prevails. In God's world the righteous are always blessed. The wicked are the ones who are punished, and their punishment is sometimes horrendous. At first, the friends insist on immediate, divine retribution for every sin, no exceptions. But as the dialogues proceed, they begin to modify their position. Sometimes what seems like punishment is actually God's discipline to correct us. Sometimes retribution is delayed. The wicked may be successful for a while, but at some point God will cause a divine reversal in their lives. And sometimes God punishes the children of the wicked rather than the wicked themselves (but Job says this is not really retribution [21:19-20]).

(3) God is a mysterious and transcendent being whose knowledge and power are far greater than ours. Thus, his ways may seem incomprehensible and even contradictory at times. But he knows what he is doing. His plans make sense to him.

(4) All humanity is imperfect. Only God is perfect. So everyone should expect some suffering in life as a consequence of the times when they mess up. Trouble is a part of our human existence.

(5) God is not the cause of humanity's troubles. We are. Sin, suffering, and evil come from us. Therefore, again, we should all expect to suffer sometimes.

(6) The best course of action in times of trouble is: commit your life to God and be patient. God will eventually turn things around for you. While waiting for God to act, examine your life. If confession is needed, do it.

(7) There can be value in suffering. God sometimes sends trials to discipline us. He reveals his concern for our spiritual health by chastening us.

(8) If you have done something wrong, repent! Humans can never enjoy fellowship with God and experience a blessed life if they have unconfessed sin in their lives.

Are any of these arguments completely false? No. Some need further clarification and refinement, but they all contain at least some measure of truth. This is the heart of the wisdom theology that the book of Proverbs teaches over and over again. And many people today still think about suffering in these terms.

So why can't Job's friends solve his problems? Why don't they have the right solution? The answer is very simple. They have not read the prologue. They are not privy to all the evidence pertaining to Job's case. Job's suffering is for another reason that is known only in the courts of heaven. Thus, all the friends' pleading, posturing, and railing have been for naught. In addition, the wisdom theology they have tried to defend is shown to be a total failure in explaining Job's suffering. The three friends illustrate how people "with good intentions and hallowed ideas can fall into gross error" if they fail to maintain an open mind and a humble attitude before God (Eaton 1985, 43).

At this point in the book, what can we learn from these arguments by the three friends? We should learn that we may never know the real reason why some suffering takes place. There are mysteries about life and about God that human beings cannot penetrate. Our suffering may never have a satisfactory reason in this world because some of the evidence is known only in heaven.

B. Job's State of Mind

2:11— 27:23

Job's speeches reveal a very troubled person. And he has multiple, good reasons to be so. No human being could suffer the loss of family, possessions, health, and reputation in a short period of time without experiencing intense, emotional pain, anger, and depression.

The appearance of Job's friends was probably a welcome relief to his aching soul. He had someone he could talk to. But he soon discovered they were not there to comfort him. They only wanted to teach him their misguided beliefs. So Job turned his attention more and more to God. His failure to hear from God only increased his agony.

The author presents Job as a character with whom it is easy to sympathize. We all have experienced loss and heartache, but our loss has been small in comparison to his. The great magnitude of Job's losses only increases our admiration for him. But Job also raises questions for us about the proper way to react to loss and suffering.

On the one hand, his calm voice in the prologue makes us question his sanity. Who could say, "The LORD gave and the LORD has taken away" (1:21), after losing ten children? On the other hand, his awful cursing against his birth date (ch 3) and his angry railings against God seem to be excessively emotional and out of control. Who is the real Job, and what can we learn from him about facing loss in our own lives? The answer to this latter question may not be apparent until the end of the book.

Job's understanding of his situation is summarized below in three categories.

1. Job's Thoughts about Himself

- I am absolutely convinced that I am innocent of sin. My conscience is clear about this.
- I am a victim of God's unjust treatment.
- I may have committed some sins in my youth that have caused me some suffering, but I know of nothing in my life right now that would bring me such terrible loss.
- I have no hope of ever experiencing a good life again.
- I believe God will take my life very shortly, and I would welcome death as an alternative to life. I am in such agony that I wish God would take my life right now.
- I feel all alone. My whole social world of family and friends is shattered.

2. Job's Thoughts about His Friends

- My friends are worthless counselors. Instead of bringing comfort, they attack and mock me.
- They do not understand my situation and are not even attempting to try.
- They think I am guilty of sin, but I refuse to admit it.
- Their explanations of suffering may work in some circumstances, but they do not apply to my situation at all.
- They think life is always just and fair, that the wicked are always punished and the righteous always blessed. But I know differently.

3. Job's Thoughts about God

- God has caused my suffering, but he will not tell me why.
- God has been unjust and even cruel to me. He continually torments me and treats me like an enemy. He acts like he does not care about what happens to me.
- I would like to have a face-to-face meeting with God where I could present my case to him. But I fear he would overpower me. What I need is a mediator who can bring God and me together and arbitrate our differences.
- I believe I have a witness in heaven who knows my life and will testify on my behalf.
- I wish I could engrave the story of my life on a stone monument to be preserved for when God is finally willing to listen to my case.
- Even better, I believe I have a living Redeemer in heaven who will vindicate me someday. But it will likely be after my death.

VI. INTERLUDE: THE SOURCE OF WISDOM: JOB 28

BEHIND THE TEXT

28:1-28

Chapter 28 is a separate discourse on the analogy between mining and wisdom. It is divided into three sections based on the refrain in vv 12 and 20. The first section (vv 1-11) is simply a beautiful poem on ancient mining practices that reveals the author's extensive knowledge of mining technology. The second (vv 12-19) compares the value of wisdom to that of costly minerals and gems. The third (vv 20-28) focuses on God as the source of wisdom. He alone knows how to find wisdom, and therefore humans can only acquire wisdom through him. This reflects the distinguishing feature of the wisdom tradition in Israel—that the fear of Yahweh is the beginning of wisdom (Ps 111:10; Prov 1:7; 9:10; 15:33; Eccl 12:13; Isa 33:6; Mic 6:9).

The relationship of this chapter to the rest of the book is a matter of dispute. There is no introductory formula, so in its present position it seems to be a part of a long speech by Job stretching from Job 26 to 31. However, the calmly worded, didactic nature of the piece and its focus on the main tenet of the wisdom theology, that is the *fear of the Lord*, are completely different from any of Job's speeches on either side of it. It is hard to conceive how Job could have switched the content and style of his speaking so abruptly and then switched back to his earlier style again.

Many scholars today do not accept Job as the speaker in ch 28. A few attach this chapter to Zophar's third speech in 27:13-23, but this does not sound like Zophar either. Others believe ch 28 should follow ch 37 as the conclusion to Elihu's speech (Clines 2006, 908-9; Greenstein 2003, 269-70). But again, the tone of ch 28 does not match the angry style of Elihu (→ ch 32). Nor is it likely that a young man like Elihu would have so much knowledge of the mining industry.

A further point of contention is the authorship of ch 28. Many hold that this chapter is so different from the rest of the book that another author must have composed it and inserted it here at a later date. Two pieces of evidence argue against this. (1) It is highly unlikely that a later author would insert ch 28 near the middle of the book. More likely, it would have been added at the end (after ch 42) so as not to interrupt the narrative. This would provide a fitting conclusion that summed up the sages' concept of wisdom and tied the book to the wider world of the wisdom literature. Only a creative author would consider placing ch 28 as an interlude to break the tension of the dialogues before continuing on with the rest of the story.

(2) Terrien has pointed out a number of phrases that are common in both chs 28 and 38—41, for example, "the deep" and "the sea" (28:14; 38:16); "the sons of pride" (lit.; 28:8; 41:34 [26 HB]); and so forth. This indicates a common theme by the same author (1954, 1100). Likewise, Ticciati (although coming to a different conclusion) has noted the similarities between the vocabulary of ch 28 and ch 3, for example, three words for "darkness" (*ḥōšek* [3:4, 5; 28:3]; *'ōpel* [3:6; 28:3]; and *ṣalmāwet* [3:5; 28:3]) (2005, 188). These connections indicate that the same author wrote all three passages.

The most logical interpretation is that ch 28 is a poetic interlude placed here by the author to relieve the tension that has been building throughout the dialogues. The passage is not spoken by any of the characters and should be understood as solely reflecting the views of the author. As such, it provides insight into the author's background as a sage and reveals his definition of "wisdom." The proof of the independent nature of ch 28 is the introductory formula in 29:1: "Job again took up his discourse and said" (NRSV). Obviously, some type of interruption preceded 29:1, and that interruption is ch 28 (Newsom 1996, 516, 528). Further, this chapter is not a speech that interacts with the other speakers on the cause of Job's suffering. It is more like a self-contained essay on humanity's search for wisdom.

Chapter 28 not only has an important literary function but also contributes significantly to the message of the book. It states clearly that human beings will never find wisdom in the same manner as they search for minerals and gems. Rather, they can only obtain wisdom through *a type of living* that honors the one who created the cosmos and ordered everything within it.

The chapter divisions are as follows:

A. Humans Are Skilled in Finding Hidden Minerals and Gems (28:1-11)
B. Where Can One Find Wisdom? (28:12-19)
C. Only God Knows How to Find Wisdom (28:20-28)

IN THE TEXT

A. Humans Are Skilled in Finding Hidden Minerals and Gems (28:1-11)

The first section describes the human skill of extracting minerals and gems from beneath the surface of the ground. These valuable commodities were not just lying around for the picking. They had to be mined, sometimes by way of deep underground shafts. Every ancient nation needed these materials for tools, weapons, jewelry, religious objects, and displays of wealth. Those countries that had naturally occurring deposits within their boundaries were clearly more fortunate than their neighbors who had to buy or trade for them. Israel was one of the latter. Minerals and gems were sometimes the prize of wars. The losing country had to surrender its supply to the victor (e.g., Rehoboam gave up his treasury to Shishak [1 Kgs 14:25-26], and Hezekiah to Sennacherib [*ANET*, 288, col. 1]).

■ **1-2** The four most sought-after minerals in the ancient world were **silver**, **gold**, **iron**, and **copper**. The origin of the mining of silver, gold, and copper dates to the Chalcolithic period (4300-3300 BC). Iron was known for many centuries, but the technology to smelt it was only developed around 1200 BC.

The first clause in each verse speaks of the mining of these mineral ores. The second describes the refining process. See van Wolde (2003, 11-22) for an excellent discussion of ancient mining practices.

■ **3-4** Ancient mines were usually in places far removed from civilization, such as the Negev and Sinai deserts and the Arabah region south of the Dead Sea. The labor crew typically consisted of slaves or prisoners of war who lived on-site. Workers chiseled out horizontal tunnels into the sides of mountains or vertical **shaft**s into the ground. At the bottom of the shafts, additional horizontal tunnels branched out in different directions. Miners followed veins of **ore** into **the blackest darkness** until the deposits came to an end.

In vertical mines, miners were lowered into the shafts using ropes that **dangle**d and **sway**ed. The ore was raised to the surface in baskets. The work was extremely dangerous. There were no ventilation systems. Miners' oil lamps consumed much of the oxygen, but the lamps were an absolute necessity to **put an end to the darkness**. No doubt, many workers were killed or injured from cave-ins and underground accidents, but the high demand for minerals and gems forced countries to maintain active mines regardless.

■ **5-6** Verse 5 contrasts the normal food-producing activities that occur above ground with the hidden actions of miners below the surface. No one sees the work that miners do, but they transform the underground regions as if a **fire** had swept through the ground creating a myriad of blackened tunnels and debris.

Some think the mention of **fire** refers to the process of splitting rocks by heating them and then pouring water on them (although it is hard to visualize how miners could have survived in smoke-filled tunnels). Others think it is a comment on the black basalt rocks produced underground by volcanoes. Perhaps the simplest explanation is that this is a reference to the blackened walls and ceilings of the tunnels caused by oil lamps.

Lapis lazuli (*sappîr*; "sapphires" [NRSV]) was one of the most highly prized gems of the ancient world. It is a beautiful royal blue color, and some varieties contain pyrites that resemble **flecks** (not **nuggets**) **of gold**. The main source of this gem was Afghanistan. Jewelry and other objects made of **lapis** have been found in Mesopotamia and Egypt indicating extensive trade networks in ancient times.

■ **7-8** The concealed nature of mining activities is stressed in vv 7-8. The tunnels and shafts (**path**) that miners create underground are unknown to the animal kingdom. Even those birds and animals with the keenest eyesight, sharpest sense of smell, and greatest strength—**birds of prey, falcons, proud beasts** (lit. "sons of pride"), and **lions**—are unaware of what takes place beneath the surface of the earth in mining regions.

■ **9-11** These verses return to the extraordinary efforts miners undertake to find valuable minerals and gems (vv 3-4). They **tunnel through** solid **rock** cutting **channels** deep into the heart of the earth (v 10). Van Wolde believes **flinty rock** (v 9a) refers to the miners' tools, which were made of this material. Thus, a better translation of v 9a is: ***They stretch out their hands with flint tools*** (2003, 19-20).

Their labors undermine the very ***foundations***/**roots of the mountains**. There in the bowels of the earth they discover all types of hidden **treasures** (v 10; → 3:21) that are hauled to the surface. The verb in 28:11a is usually now emended from *ḥbš* (lit. "dam up, seal off") to *ḥpś* (lit. "seek, search") based on evidence from Ugaritic literature (Clines 2006, 900). **The sources of the rivers** are sometimes springs that bubble out of the ground. This phrase is a metaphor for the underground regions miners **search**.

B. Where Can One Find Wisdom? (28:12-19)

Here the author turns to the main topic of his essay. Where can one find wisdom and understanding about life? Humanity seems to have no problem finding the costliest minerals and gems buried deep in the earth (vv 1-11). But wisdom, which is worth far more than these valuable objects, cannot be acquired through human efforts or purchased with costly goods.

■ **12-14** **Wisdom** (*hokmâ*; → 4:21) and **understanding** (*bînâ*) are key terms in the wisdom literature (28:12). They appear in parallel three times in this chapter (vv 12, 20, 28) as well as in two other passages (38:36; 39:17). The book of Proverbs has six other examples (1:2; 4:5, 7; 9:10; 16:16; 23:23). There may be slight differences of meaning in some passages, but in Job the two words are basically synonyms.

People eagerly seek **wisdom** and **understanding**. Who does not want to know the nature of the universe or how to live a good life? The questions in Job 28:12 are key to understanding the meaning of ch 28 (they are repeated in v 20). They are asked as if there were a geographical place where one could go to gain insight into the ways of life. But, alas, there is no such place. **Humanity does not know its way** (v 13a; → 3:23)—that is, the pathway to find wisdom—because **it cannot be found in the land of the living** (28:13b). The source of wisdom is located outside of this world. The translation "way" (NRSV) follows the LXX translation that is based on the emended form *darkāh* instead of *'erkāh*. **The land of the living** is a phrase that appears frequently in Psalms, Isaiah, Jeremiah, and Ezekiel in reference to the world that humans inhabit.

The terms **the deep** (*tĕhōm*) and **the sea** (*yām*; → 7:12) are associated with the creation story (Gen 1:2, 10). Thus, their origin goes back to the beginning of time. These ancient parts of the cosmos, which hide many things from human view, should surely know where to find **wisdom** and **understanding**. But even they are at a loss to explain the way to wisdom. As personified entities, they speak the words: **It is not in/with me** (Job 28:14).

■ **15-19** The remainder of the second section is devoted to comparing the value of wisdom to the most costly minerals and gems in the ancient world: **the finest gold and silver** (v 15); **the gold of Ophir** (→ 22:24), **onyx**, and **lapis lazuli** (28:16; → v 6); *glass* (**crystal**) and **ornaments/vessels of gold** (v 17); **coral**, *rock crystal* (jasper), and *pearls* (**rubies**) (v 18); and **the topaz of Cush** (the area south of Egypt) and **pure gold** (v 19).

The brilliant array of colors of these gems and precious metals would have dazzled even the richest and most powerful kings of antiquity. Their origins, spanning the entire ANE from Spain and Egypt in the west, to Arabia and the coast of Africa in the south, to Afghanistan in the east, would have required a huge trading network to secure them. The exact identification of some of these items is still unsettled (see Clines 2006, 902-3 and 918-19), but the overall meaning of the passage is clear. Wisdom and understanding are worth far more than any other object known to humankind. Their value is so high that they cannot be purchased in exchange for even the costliest of commodities.

C. Only God Knows How to Find Wisdom (28:20-28)

The beginning of the third section (vv 20-22) parallels the beginning of the second (vv 12-14). Here, however, the author focuses on God's unique knowledge concerning the pathway to wisdom. He is the only one who knows how to find it. So, humanity must turn to him to obtain wisdom, which means fearing him and turning away from evil.

■ **20-22** Verse 20 essentially repeats the question found in v 12, and v 21 notes again wisdom's inaccessibility (→ v 13). **Wisdom** is unknown to human beings because **it is hidden from the eyes of every living thing**. Even **the birds** that observe everything on earth from high in the sky have no knowledge of where wisdom is located (→ vv 7-8).

Verse 22 (→ v 14) states that even outside "the land of the living" (v 13) wisdom is not known. The place of the dead (normally "Sheol," but here **Abaddon [Destruction] and Death**; → 26:6; see Rev 9:11) has heard only a report of it. That is, the dead know no more than a rumor that wisdom may exist. Thus, they have no direct knowledge of how to find it.

■ **23-24** The author has finally arrived at the main point of his essay. **God** [*Elohim*] **... alone** knows how to find wisdom. This conviction is at the heart of all the biblical wisdom literature (Job 9:4; Pss 19:7; 90:12; 104:24; 136:5; Prov 1:7; 2:1-6; 8:22-36; 9:10; 30:5; Eccl 2:26; see also Gen 41:15-16; Dan 2:27-28, 47). It clearly places the author of Job among those individuals known as sages. God alone views all of life, seeing **everything under the heavens** (Job 28:24). His gaze extends as far as **the ends of the earth**. Nothing escapes his attention. He knows the location and interrelation of everything. And he should, for he created it.

Some scholars interpret the verbs in v 24 as preterites rather than imperfects, thus limiting God's activity to the past—to the creation event (Clines 2006, 920-21). They appeal to the subsequent context (vv 25-27) for support, as well as Prov 8:22-31 where God created wisdom before proceeding with the rest of the created order. More likely, the author intended Job 28:24 to refer to all of time, beginning at creation but also extending into the future. God sees, has seen, and will see everything under the heavens. His view is unlimited. Verses 25-27 remind the reader that God has ordered life since the beginning of time. Therefore, his knowledge of how to find wisdom is unique.

■ **25-27** Here the author provides several examples of God's use of wisdom to organize the natural world. They are representative of the entire extent of God's activity in the cosmos. These will suffice for the moment until a much fuller description of God's wisdom and power is given in chs 38—41.

Verse 25*a* of ch 28 speaks of God allocating to the **wind** a specific *weight* or **force** to push against objects. Verse 25*b* refers to the boundaries that God established for the **waters** of the sea (7:12; 38:8-11). The focus in 28:26 is on God's instructions (**decree** [*ḥōq*]) to the **rain** and the ***thunderbolt*** (lit. "lightning of thunder"). God designed these natural phenomena at the time of creation, and he has kept them in check ever since.

In v 27 the author uses four verbs to describe God's initial encounter with wisdom. **Then he <u>saw</u> it** and *he* <u>appraised</u> it; he <u>established</u> it and <u>scrutinized</u> it (emphasis added). The exact nuance of each verb is debated, but the meaning of the verse is obvious. God liked **wisdom** from the very beginning, and he appropriated it to his purposes in creating and organizing the natural world (Prov 8:22-31). The Hebrew word for **wisdom** is not in Job 28:27, but it is the most logical antecedent of the direct object *it* (→ vv 20, 28).

■ **28** Up to this point in the chapter, the author has stressed the inability of human beings to find or purchase **wisdom** and **understanding**. God is the only one with access to wisdom. But in v 28 the author reverses course and offers to the entire **human race** the ability to be wise. The formula for achievement is very simple: **fear the Lord** and *turn away from* evil. The author frames this message as an authoritative utterance from God (**and he said to the human race** [*'ādām*]). But it is also the author's own implicit advice (in answer to the questions in vv 12 and 20) to all who seek wisdom. This is, after all, his essay, and it is a major theme that lies at the heart of the wisdom theology (see Ps 111:10; Prov 1:7; 9:10; 15:33).

This terminology recalls Job 1:1. Two of Job's characteristics in the prologue were that "he feared God and *turned away from* evil." Clearly, the author considered Job a wise person, for he was already performing God's admonitions in 28:28. Unfortunately, this was not the message that Job had been seeking. He had plenty of wisdom and understanding already, but that did not prevent his suffering. What he really wanted was a face-to-face meeting with God that would settle the matter of his innocence once and for all.

The phrase **the fear of the Lord** (*yir'at Adonai*) is unique in the book of Job. Only here does the word *Adonai* appear. Perhaps the author wished to use the more common wisdom phrase "the fear of Yahweh" (found numerous times in Proverbs [e.g., 1:7; 2:5; 9:10; 10:27, etc.]) but substituted *Adonai* for "Yahweh" because of the Gentile setting of the story.

FROM THE TEXT

1. **Summary of the Interlude**. There are three main points in the interlude:
- Undaunted by obstacles, human beings have developed skillful technologies for mining precious minerals and gems from within the earth. But their skills are ineffective in obtaining wisdom.
- Some people possess great wealth, but the cost of wisdom is far greater than the richest person can afford.
- Human beings can only gain access to wisdom by submitting their lives to God and turning away from evil, for only God knows how to access wisdom.

2. **The Importance of the Interlude**. Chapter 28 has something of a *hinge* quality to it that connects God with human beings by means of wisdom. Newsom calls it a "speculative wisdom poem" on "the place of wisdom in the cosmos and its relation to God on the one hand and humanity or Israel on the other" (2003, 171-72). Its content is similar to Prov 8, Sir 1 and 24, Bar 3:9—4:4, and *1 En.* 42. Humanity's lack of wisdom, in spite of intense efforts, is compared to God's awesome wisdom about everything in creation. But humans can gain some small part of God's wisdom by establishing a relationship with him.

The key position of ch 28 in the book also makes it a hinge looking both backward and forward. Job and his friends have been passionate and determined in their speeches thus far, like miners searching for hidden minerals and gems. But they have failed to find the reason for Job's suffering, because they lack the evidence needed to make them wise. The author notes that their searching, and that of all human beings, for wisdom about life is doomed to failure because the source of wisdom is not found in "the land of the living" (vv 13, 21). Wisdom can only be found through God, and he has yet to speak in the book. His impressive wisdom about all matters is only touched on briefly in the interlude. Thus, the reader is given a hint of things to come in chs 38—41.

Two central tenets of the wisdom tradition appear prominently in ch 28: (1) God knows everything under the heavens, and (2) humans must fear God and turn away from evil to gain wisdom. However, the author has not forgotten the primary question Job raised throughout the dialogues: "If God knows everything, he must know that I am suffering even though I fear him. So why does he not do something about my suffering?"

Job agrees with the author that God knows everything, including how to find wisdom. So common sense would suggest that God should want to relieve suffering whenever it affects his people—the righteous. But God does not do that, at least in Job's case. Job has repeatedly pointed out that God allows the wicked to live long, fruitful lives. He blesses them with riches and large families. But the righteous (represented by Job) must suffer extreme pain and poverty. The logical conclusion to all of this is that God is not just. We must wait until the end of the book to see if Job ever receives a satisfactory answer to this most perplexing question.

VII. JOB'S MANIFESTO: JOB 29—31

BEHIND THE TEXT

After the beautiful interlude on wisdom's relationship to God (ch 28), Job brings the reader's attention back to the problem at hand by way of a lengthy summary of his situation, what Wharton calls: "three . . . self-portraits" (1999, 118). In ch 29 he reminds everyone of the blessed life he lived before the calamities struck. He was cared for by God and highly respected in his community.

Chapter 30 recounts how his fortunes changed suddenly and he found himself the object of scorn. He cried out for help, but his community turned against him and God refused to answer his prayers. Thus, he now suffers alone, his only companions the wild animals.

Job's speech concludes in ch 31 with a personal testimony about his innocence. He presents a list of possible sins that someone might accuse him of, and then swears he is not guilty of any of them. He even pronounces a series of curses against himself if anyone can prove he is lying.

Job's intended audience for this long speech is first of all the friends. The list of possible sins in ch 31 provides an opening for the friends to respond if they wish. But they are now exhausted emotionally. And they really had no proof that Job was a sinner in spite of Eliphaz's brief accusations in 22:5-9. Thus, they listen in silence.

The other person in Job's audience is God, whom Job addresses briefly in the second person (30:20-23). He hopes that God will not only listen but respond as well. He even offers to carry around a big signboard inscribed with God's written accusations against him if God will make Job's sins known. However, he has no confidence that God will speak to him. He believes that God's only desire is to hasten his entrance into Sheol (30:23).

Some have criticized Job for being very egotistical in this section because his remarks highlight only his own character and accomplishments (Good 1990, 299; van Wolde 1997, 93-94). But they are no more self-centered than Paul in 2 Cor 11:21-28, who was trying to defend himself against his critics. Some situations, such as when one is under attack, call for an honest presentation of the evidence, even if it concerns oneself. Such is the nature of this passage.

Job's speech here probably includes material he would use in his defense against God if that ever occurred (13:18; 23:4). Proving that he was blameless and upright as described in the prologue (1:1, 8; 2:3) would be very important in making his case that God had no justifiable reason to punish him in this way. There is probably some embellishment here, but no more so than that of typical defendants who want to prove their innocence in a court of law.

IN THE TEXT

A. My Former Life (29:1-25)

In ch 29 Job recounts his former reputation as: (1) a righteous person who was pleasing to God (vv 2-5, 14); (2) an extremely wealthy person who drew from his riches to help the needy (vv 6, 11-13); (3) a champion of social justice for the handicapped and weak (vv 15-17); (4) a wise counselor (vv 21-24); and (5) a leader of his community by virtue of the respect he had earned (vv 7-11, 25). He was truly a remarkable individual—a supersaint, as the prologue described earlier.

The first section of his speech divides as follows:
1. God Was Blessing Me (29:1-6)
2. My Community Respected Me (29:7-17)
3. I Was Enjoying the Good Life (29:18-20)
4. People Sought My Advice (29:21-25)

I. God Was Blessing Me (29:1-6)

Job's former life was remarkably different from his present circumstances. God carefully watched over him and guided his footsteps, blessing him and his family on a regular basis.

■ **I** After the interruption of ch 28, we find the same unusual introductory formula as in 27:1 (→ Behind the Text for ch 28).

■ **2-6** Verses 2-6 of ch 29 are one long sentence in Hebrew that expresses Job's deep longing for his former life: "Oh, that . . ." (NRSV). He would give anything to turn back the clock to those earlier days when **God** [*Eloah*] **watched over** him (v 2) and provided **light** for his pathway (v 3). God's care and guidance were a normal, daily part of his life. Even when he **walked through (*places of*) darkness**, God guided him with light from above.

The time period Job is referring to in v 4 cannot be pinpointed exactly, as some translate *bîmê ḥorpî* as "in the days of my youth" and others "in the days of my prime" (lit. "winter"). But v 5 clearly indicates that Job is thinking of his adult years when he enjoyed a large, happy family of ten children (some being adults). Then **God's** [*Eloah's*] ***protection was over my tent*** (v 4b) and **the Almighty** [*Shaddai*] **was still with me** (v 5a). The word for ***protection*** (*sôk*) is an emended form for the MT *sôd* and is accepted by the LXX and a number of scholars (Clines 2006, 934-35). God's protection and presence are repeatedly mentioned in the Psalms as key evidence of God's compassion and blessing on his people (Pss 3:3, 6 [4, 7 HB]; 4:3, 8 [4, 9 HB]; 23:1, 4; 121:5-8, etc.).

God's blessing on Job in his earlier years is further described with two extravagant metaphors in Job 29:6: ***My steps were washed* with cream, and the rock poured out for me streams of olive oil**. As mentioned in the prologue (1:3, 14), Job had extensive land holdings that he farmed for various agricultural products such as **cream** and **olive oil**. **Cream** was some type of liquid milk product (→ 20:17) produced from goats, cattle, or camels. Its usage here is a hyperbole for an extravagant lifestyle where ordinary water for washing was bypassed in favor of a much more expensive milk product.

Olive trees were usually planted in rocky soil, often on terraced hills in Palestine. **The rock** probably refers to the large stone olive presses where olives were crushed between two large stones. The oil from the crushed olives could be directed to a collecting basin by means of ***channels*/streams** (*peleg*; the same word is used for the artificial water channel in Ps 1:3). For Job, the oil figuratively **poured out** in a steady stream. The abundance of these products was not an indication of his business or farming skills, but a sign of God's blessing on his life.

2. My Community Respected Me (29:7-17)

Job's righteous life had impacted his community so much that when he went to the gate of his city everyone stopped what they were doing to show how much they respected him.

■ **7-10** In this long sentence Job describes the profound respect he received from the citizens of his town when he went out in public. In most ancient towns **the gate of the city** (v 7) was a normal gathering place for people. Usually there was an open plaza just inside the gate where people socialized and conducted commercial and legal activities. In the book of Ruth, Boaz knew to head directly to the city gate in

Bethlehem to settle an issue regarding his marriage to Ruth and the purchase of Naomi's property (Ruth 4:1). The leaders and prominent men of each town may even have had their own specific seats in the gate area.

When Job went to take his seat, there was a remarkable display of admiration. From the bottom of society to the top (**the young men**, **the old men** [Job 29:8], ***the city leaders*** [v 9], and **the nobles** [v 10]), everyone felt obligated to show their respect. Some withdrew themselves, some stood up, some placed a hand over their mouth (→ 21:5), and some immediately **hushed** their conversation (also 29:21-23). His appearance at a gathering was almost like that of a king/queen, president, or pope. People became speechless. However, there is no tone of boastfulness on Job's part. This is simply the way things were. Job had earned the highest respect from his community through the many good deeds he lists in the verses that follow.

■ **11-13** Verse 11 describes the reaction to Job's good deeds by those who had either heard of them from someone else or actually seen them. Clearly, everyone in Job's community praised him for his benevolence to the needy. Two groups who were the recipients of Job's kindheartedness are mentioned in v 12—**the poor** (*'ānî*) and **the fatherless** (*yātôm*) (→ 22:9 for the translation **fatherless** in lieu of **orphan**). Job never failed to answer their cries for help.

Two additional groups are identified in v 13—***the person who was perishing*** (*'ōbēd*) and **the widow** (*'almānâ*) (more groups are named in vv 15-16). This time Job mentions the reaction to his kindness by those who were receiving it. They **blessed** him and rejoiced over the one who had delivered them from their difficult circumstances.

Job does not mention the specific things he did to help the needy, but from his great wealth he was likely able to provide resources such as food, clothing, and housing (→ also 31:16-22). And for those in 29:15-16 he probably provided additional help as a legal advocate or intermediary of some type. No doubt, his gifts, friendship, and encouragement relieved the despair in the lives of many who were suffering.

■ **14** Metaphorically, Job speaks of wearing **righteousness** (*ṣedeq*) and **justice** (*mišpāṭ*) like articles of clothing. What he means is that these godlike qualities became identified with him just like a garment he wore on a regular basis. He desired to be a godly person, and his good deeds were proof that his very nature exemplified **righteousness** and **justice**. In the same way that Christians speak of becoming Christlike (i.e., embodying the spirit of Christ) Job claims that his life was *righteous-like* and *justice-like*.

The items of clothing he mentions—a **robe** (*mĕ'îl*) and **turban** (*ṣānîp*)—were nicer than the normal Israelite garments for everyday dress. They were typically worn by prominent people such as kings and priests (Exod 28:4; 1 Sam 24:4 [5 HB]; 1 Chr 15:27; Isa 3:23). Job and his friends all wore this type of robe (Job 1:20; 2:12), indicating they belonged to the upper class.

■ **15-16** Job lists four more groups in 29:15-16 that he looked out for—**the blind, the lame, the needy** (→ 5:15), and **the stranger** (lit. "the one I did not know"). Here Job's kindness involved helping people who were physically handicapped or low in status, that is, the type of people who were looked down on. He was even willing to examine **the *legal* case** (*rîb*) of a person he had never met before. Such was his passion for justice that anyone with a need could count on Job to provide some kind of support by means of becoming what they were lacking—**eyes, feet, father,** advocate.

■ **17** *I smashed the jaws of the evildoer, and cast the prey from his teeth.* In v 17 Job's support for the needy changes from benevolent acts of kindness to aggressive attacks against their oppressors. The wicked are metaphorically portrayed as ferocious animals (like lions in 4:10-11) that prey on the needy, but Job would not allow this to happen in his community. He took away their power to do harm by figuratively "smashing their jaws." The word for *jaws* (*mětallĕ'ôt*) always appears in parallel with the word for **teeth** (Ps 58:6 [7 HB]; Prov 30:14; Joel 1:6), and thus some translate it as **fangs**. Goldingay comments perceptively: If God or people intend to be just, there are times when they must also be "violent" or "associated with violence" (2013, 139).

3. I Was Enjoying the Good Life (29:18-20)

Job was living a happy life that he thought would continue for many years into the future.

■ **18** Before the calamities struck, Job fully expected that he would have a very long life span, enjoying the blessedness and tranquility God bestows on the righteous. He thought he would ***pass away*** peacefully at a very old age surrounded by his beloved family (lit. "within my nest").

There is some disagreement over the interpretation of *kaḥôl* in v 18*b*. Some translate it "as the sand" (NASB), drawing on the image of an infinite number of objects like the sand on the seashore (Gen 22:17; 32:12 [13 HB], etc.). Others find an alternative reading of *kaḥûl*, meaning "like the phoenix" (NRSV; see NJPS), a mythological bird that lived for hundreds of years before dying and coming back to life. Either metaphor supports Job's expectation that his days would be numerous.

■ **19** Like a well-watered tree (see Ps 1:3 for a similar image), Job had experienced a healthy life in his earlier years, and he had every reason to expect that his well-being would continue into the future. In the Middle East trees receive their nourishment from **dew** as well as from streams and rain.

■ **20** In his earlier years there was a sense of freshness/youthfulness that he relished. He was not a tired old senior citizen rapidly approaching Sheol. Instead, he was constantly receiving new ***honor/glory***. His **bow**, a military or hunting weapon used here to symbolize his power and strength, also remained powerful as if it were newly made.

4. People Sought My Advice (29:21-25)

Job had gained such a renowned reputation for his wise counsel that his community eagerly listened to him for advice.

■ **21-23** These verses are similar in concept to vv 7-10. Although Job does not mention the city gate as the place where he counseled the people in his community, no doubt this is where the majority of his speaking occurred. Job remembers the **silence** that preceded and followed his words (v 21). People waited quietly and respectfully even before he opened his mouth (also vv 9-10), for they knew they were in the presence of a very wise person. His wisdom was greatly valued and much anticipated.

In v 23 he likens their expectancy to people with their mouths wide open hoping to catch some drops of gently falling rain. Further, when Job was finished speaking, the people's silence continued as they reflected on the truth of his wisdom. No one was willing to present an alternative idea or challenge his remarks. **The spring rain** (*malqôš*), sometimes called "the latter rain," was an extension of the normal winter rainy season for a few weeks into late March and April. Since it did not occur every year, it was regarded as a blessing from God (Deut 11:13-15; Jer 3:3; 5:24; Hos 6:3; Joel 2:23; Zech 10:1).

■ **24** Even Job's facial expressions were a part of his influence on people. They treasured his kindhearted countenance (lit. **the light of my face**). His smile brightened their day. Their worries seemed to vanish in his presence. People were astonished that he was actually interested in their individual welfare.

■ **25** Job compares his status in his community to that of a **chief** or **king**. This was not a position he inherited or to which he was elected. Nevertheless, everyone accepted him as their de facto leader, probably because of his wealth and wise counsel. This gave him the opportunity to guide the community in the direction they should go. Like **a king among his troops** or a comforter to those *in mourning*, Job was able to lead his community through good times and bad.

B. My Present Humiliation and Suffering (30:1-31)

Chapter 30 describes Job's present circumstances. His blessed life (ch 29) changed radically when calamity struck. He lost his impeccable reputation. He no longer had the means to help the needy or champion social justice. And people no longer turned to him for advice. Instead, his community now mocks him. He has repeatedly sought God's help, but God refuses to answer. His deteriorating health is a sign that God is trying to destroy him.

This section of Job's speech has three divisions:

1. I Am Mocked by My Community (30:1-15)
2. God Continues to Make Me Suffer (30:16-23)
3. My Condition Worsens Even Though I Plead for Help (30:24-31)

1. I Am Mocked by My Community (30:1-15)

Job now turns to the mockery he has received from people in his community. He is especially distressed that even the scum of society and their children make fun of him. For all practical purposes he has no friends. His entire community has turned against him (very similar to 19:13-22). He has been reduced from a place of honor to an object of derision. His name is now only a byword.

■ **1** In biblical times young people treated their elders with great respect. Job knew he deserved such treatment, not only because of his age but also because he had provided abundant resources for his community for many, many years. In earlier times everyone who knew him appreciated his generosity and wisdom (29:7-17, 21-25). Thus, Job is completely baffled and greatly upset by the antagonism he now receives. People seem to enjoy humiliating him. Even the children of parents who are at the bottom of society ridicule him. These parents are so worthless and despicable that Job would not have hired them to work alongside his **dogs** in tending his sheep, yet their children dare to **mock** him. To call a person a dog in Israelite society was an insult (1 Sam 17:43; 2 Sam 3:8; 16:9), so there is a tone of disdain in Job's voice as he characterizes these people as of less value than dogs.

■ **2-8** Job now delineates some of the characteristics of those who have mocked him. Verse 2 describes their lack of **vigor**. Whether this was due to a lack of food or laziness is not spelled out, but the end result is the loss of their ability to provide useful labor.

Their dwelling places are in desert regions on the outskirts of society (vv 5-8). They live among the rocks and bushes along the slopes of wadis (**dry stream beds** [v 6]) and in caves. They are forced to live in these regions because their communities have rejected them as worthless. They are treated like **thieves** (v 5), probably because they are viewed by the community as only taking from society rather than contributing to it. Their food is neither raised on a farm nor purchased. It is scavenged from the meager plants in desert regions. No doubt they are hungry all the time (vv 3-4). In v 4b many scholars emend *laḥmām* (**their food**) to *lĕḥammām* or *lĕḥummām* ("to warm themselves" [NRSV]) because **the root of the broom bush** is inedible, but it can be made into charcoal (Clines 2006, 946).

Job's evaluation of these mockers is that they are *foolish*/**base** and **nameless** (v 8a). *Foolish* (lit. "children of a fool") has a moral connotation equivalent to "wicked" in some passages, but in this context it refers to people who are "low class," people with no recognized standing or respectability in society (→ 2:10). **Nameless** (lit. "children of one without a name") refers to something or someone without identity. In Gen 2:19-20 the first human being gave identity and order to the animals by naming them. Job's mockers are nondescript people with a status so low they are not worthy of being named.

Job's point in all this is not to ridicule the homeless outcasts of society. Rather, it is to hold them up as examples of a society that from top to bottom has acted cruelly toward him. Even the lowest classes of people, who have no right to condemn anyone since they are not contributing to their communities, participate in the mocking of Job.

Mockers

Verses 1-8 seem to portray a much harsher side to Job than the kindhearted philanthropist of 29:12-13, 15-16. Why would Job regard mockers as less worthy of his generosity than the poor, the orphans, and the widows? The answer is found in the book of Proverbs where numerous verses characterize mockers as people who are sinful, arrogant, self-centered troublemakers (Prov 21:24; 22:10; 24:9; 29:8). Even God has no use for mockers (Prov 3:34; 19:29) because they refuse to accept correction (Prov 9:8; 13:1; 15:12).

Job was not guilty of favoring one class of the needy over another. He was simply agreeing with Proverbs that the people known as mockers cannot be helped. They are too proud and self-centered to think they need assistance from either Job or God. As long as they make light of God and his people, they are beyond help. Job would gladly share his resources with them if they would gratefully accept his gifts, but they are only interested in biting the hand that comes to their aid.

■ **9-10** After describing the characteristics and lifestyle of his mockers from the lower classes (vv 1-8), Job takes up the topic of how these people treat him. They "abhor" (v 10 NRSV) him and **keep their distance** from him, but yet they sometimes venture close enough to **spit** on him. In their conversations with each other, they have made Job's name a **byword** (*millâ*) for "a sinner who is being punished by God." This thought echoes 17:6, although with a different Hebrew word for **byword**. They have even created ***mocking songs***—musical ditties to humiliate him (as in Lam 3:14). In their minds, since God was angry at Job, Job was fair game for their insults and mockery.

■ **11** Job's mockers show no **restraint** in their attacks on him. They know he is sick and helpless to defend himself. He looks horrible and is close to death. His weakness has emboldened them even more. Job blames God for allowing this to happen: ***because he*** [God] ***has loosened my tent cord and oppressed me***. The Hebrew for God's name does not appear as the subject of the first clause, but the context calls for it (see Job 30:11*a* NIV). Just as the loosening of a tent cord brings down the entire tent, so God's calamities against Job have weakened his ability to survive the verbal attacks of his mockers. His life, symbolized as a tent, is close to collapse. The word for ***tent cord*** (*yeter*) can also mean "bowstring" (a possible relationship with 29:20), and some versions accept this translation (NIV, NRSV). But since the word has already been used in Job with the meaning of ***tent cord*** (4:21), that image is retained here.

■ **12-14** Using military imagery, Job describes how his mockers further attack him. He is like a city under siege, trying to defend himself against their coordinated efforts. They ***rise up on my right hand*** (30:12) building **siege ramps** up to the wall. They **break up my *pathway*** (v 13) so there is no possibility of escape.

They tear open a "wide breach" (v 14 NRSV) in the wall and pour (lit. "roll on") through the opening, knocking his feet out from under him. *(There is) no one restraining* (emending *'ōzēr* to *'ōṣēr* in v 13c makes better sense) the unruly mob from destroying Job's life.

■ **15** Terror and fear have been gnawing at Job's soul ever since his first monologue (3:25-26; 6:4; 7:14-15; 9:28, 33-35; 13:21; 23:15-17). He places the blame for this squarely on God (30:11) whom he believes has attacked him and crushed him without mercy and without a reason. The mockery by the lower classes (vv 1-14) is only one more example of God's dislike of him. God could easily intervene in his situation and prevent people from harassing him, but God has done nothing so far. Thus, the **honorable respect** (v 15b) he once received from his entire community (29:2-25) is now gone, and his **security** (30:15c) from the troubles of life has vanished.

2. God Continues to Make Me Suffer (30:16-23)

In this section Job focuses on the cause of his misery. God is the one who has brought him so much pain, assaulting him without mercy. In vv 20-23 Job briefly addresses God directly, accusing him of cruel treatment and of refusing to answer his cries for help. God is obviously through with him in this life and is directing him toward death.

■ **16-17** God's attacks on Job have brought **suffering** (v 16b) both to his soul and his body. The vitality for life he once knew as a younger person "is poured out" (v 16a NRSV), leaving him weak and emotionally exhausted; and pain continually racks his body. He feels like someone is **gnawing** on him while he is trying to sleep (v 17b; → 7:13-15). The translation of 30:17a could be one of two possibilities: **Night pierces my bones** (personifying **night** as in 3:3-10), or *at* **night** *he* [God] **pierces my bones**. Since God is the object of Job's complaints in the following verses (30:18-23), the latter alternative is better.

■ **18-19** *With great power he* [God] *seizes my clothing.* Verse 18 is very difficult, but Job seems to be depicting God as a person of violence. Like a professional wrestler he has seized Job by his **clothing** and thrown him to the ground. God's grip is like a powerful bear hug, squeezing Job into a restricted space **like the opening of my tunic** (v 18b). The verb for *seizes* (*tpś*) is an emended form of the MT *ḥpś* that is supported by the LXX and many scholars. *I have become like* **dust and ashes** is Job's description of his insignificance after being worked over by God. He has been diminished to the value of the dirt on the ground and the **ashes** on his town's ash heap.

■ **20** In the first cycle of speeches (chs 4—14) each of the three friends encouraged Job to seek God. Job's response is, "I have already done that repeatedly, but God refuses to speak to me." Neither his cries for help nor his standing up to gain God's attention have succeeded in making God respond. For some reason, God has hidden his face from Job (13:24) so that Job does not even know where to find him (9:11; 23:3, 8-9). And now he seeks to destroy Job through violent actions (30:21-

23). The word **merely** is not found in the Hebrew of v 20*b*, but most versions add a similar word or the negative "not" (RSV).

■ **21-22** *You have become cruel towards me.* From Job's perspective, God has treated him cruelly and persecuted him with the full **might** of his **hand**. This is not a new charge, for Job has complained about God's attacks in earlier speeches and even called God his enemy (6:4; 7:20; 9:17-18; 13:24; 16:7-9, 11-14; 19:8-12). Certainly, there is justification for this accusation considering all the suffering Job has had to endure.

The impact of God's persecution is illustrated in 30:22. Job feels as if God has jerked him up off the ground and flung him about in the winds of a **storm** (lit. "roar of a storm"). The final Hebrew word in v 22 (*těšuwwâ*) is emended by most scholars to *těšu'â*, meaning "a roar or sound of thunder produced by a storm" (36:29; 39:7).

■ **23** In 29:18-20 Job described his earlier belief that he would live a long life and receive God's abundant blessings, but the reality of the present situation is much different. Job is now headed for Sheol—*the meeting house* **for all the living**. And God is responsible for this turn of events.

3. My Condition Worsens Even Though I Plead for Help (30:24-31)

If God truly cares about his creatures, one would assume he answers their cries for help by relieving them of their distress. And if human beings truly care about their friends and neighbors, one would also assume that they provide support for them in their times of calamity. However, Job believes he is the exception to the rule. Instead of support, he has received cruelty from God (vv 18-23) and mocking from his community (vv 1, 9-15). As a result, his emotional stability, his social relationships, and his physical health are worsening rapidly.

■ **24-26** In earlier days Job had been an optimist by nature. He **hoped for good** and *waited* **for light** (v 26). According to the wisdom theology, he had good reason to expect a bright future, for he lived a righteous life (1:1; 29:2-6, 14), and he helped others in their times of need (4:3-4; 29:12-13, 15-16). He had even been emotionally distraught over the poor, identifying with their plight (30:25). So when Job's turn came to experience calamity, he naturally assumed that both God and his community would rally around him with compassion and support.

The wisdom traditions taught that God always responds to the cries of his people and that good people always seek to help the needy around them. If these principles were true, why then did Job experience the opposite? Why did he not receive help from God and his community? Instead of **good** (v 26), he was subjected to **evil** (i.e., calamities and suffering), and instead of **light** he was surrounded by **darkness**.

Verse 24 is very difficult, but the following translation provides a reasonable rendering based on the context: **Surely no one** *stretches out* **a hand** *against a ruined person* **when he cries** *out to them in his misfortune*. In other words, no decent person ever kicks other people when they are down or rejects their pleas for help. Job not only believed that but practiced it.

■ **27** In the remainder of this section Job recounts how God's persecution has affected him emotionally, socially, and physically. As a result, his present condition is drastically different from the blessed life of the past (ch 29), and it is getting worse all the time. Emotionally, his *inner parts are in turmoil*. There is a constant **churning** in the pit of his stomach as he tries to comprehend the cause and meaning of his suffering.

■ **28-29** Socially, Job is now isolated from his family and community (19:13-19). He has become **a brother of jackals** (30:29) and **a companion of** *ostriches* (lit. "daughters of the desert"). Like these desert animals, he must fend for himself without the support of others. He describes himself as *one who has become dark*, **but not by the sun** (v 28*a*). Some scholars see this as a reference to his darkened skin due to disease (v 30), while others believe it describes his black clothing, as one in mourning (v 31). Either interpretation is possible since both appear in the immediate context.

Clines believes that v 28*b* indicates Job is still living in his house and regularly going to the city gate as before the calamities (2006, 1010), but this is unlikely. It is hard to imagine that someone who complained so strongly about the way his family and community treated him (19:13-19) would be spending much time in public where he would receive mocking and spitting (30:1, 9-15). If he did go to the gate, it was probably only briefly, and then only to defend his integrity and **cry for help** (v 28*b*).

■ **30** Physically, his **skin *has become* black**, as if severely bruised. Perhaps the constant scraping of his sores with a potsherd (2:8) produced numerous dark blotches that altered his appearance. The sooty ashes of the ash heap where he resided may also have contributed to his darkened skin. Additionally, a constant **fever** grips him. His ***bones*** seem to be on fire (Ps 102:3 [4 HB]).

■ **31** The drastic change in Job's condition is now summarized using a metaphor involving musical instruments. His **lyre** and ***reed*-pipe**, which once made joyful music (→ Job 21:12), are reduced to playing only the lamentations of funeral mourners.

C. My Innocence and Personal Integrity (31:1-40)

Job's summary concludes with a personal testimony concerning his avoidance of wrongdoing. These words are intended to establish his innocence and personal integrity, thus proving that his suffering is not a divine judgment against any personal sins. By denying he has committed a variety of sins, Job is challenging God either to speak up and prove him incorrect or to agree with him and then reveal the true cause of his suffering.

The form in this chapter is very similar to an Egyptian mortuary text called the Book of the Dead where the speaker lists possible sins that have been avoided

(*ANET*, "The Protestation of Guiltlessness," 34-36). This form was quite popular in Israelite writings. Oftentimes speakers stated a sin they had not committed and then called down a curse on themselves if proven false (Ruth 1:17; 1 Sam 3:17; 12:1-5; 14:44; 1 Kgs 19:2; 20:10; Pss 7:3-5 [4-6 HB]; 15:2-5; 24:3-4; 26:4-7).

Gordis finds fourteen sins in Job's list (1978, 542), but other scholars arrive at different totals. This commentary lists ten. Some of these sins are outward sins that would easily be recognized by the people around Job, for example, the mistreatment of his servants (Job 31:13-15) or a lack of compassion for the needy (vv 16-23). But others such as lust (vv 1-4) or greed (vv 24-25) are secret sins of the heart that would only be known by God, what Janzen calls "the prick of conscience" (1985, 210-12).

Job is so confident he has avoided these sins that he pronounces four curses against himself (vv 8, 10, 22, 40) in case anyone can prove him wrong. Wharton calls these curses Job's "'cross my heart and hope to die' declaration of innocence" (1999, 131). Thus far in the book only Eliphaz has directly accused Job of being a sinner (22:5-9), but his charges lacked any proof. Job's righteousness has already been established in the prologue (1:1, 8; 2:3), and he will further disprove Eliphaz's charges in this chapter.

Several scholars suggest that there has been damage to the text of ch 31. They rearrange the verses to fit a preconceived notion of what topics should go together. But the only real possibility of damage might be in vv 35-37 (→ vv 35-37 for an explanation of what might have happened there).

There are eleven divisions to this section of Job's speech:
1. I Have Not Looked Lustfully at Young Women (31:1-4)
2. I Have Not Been Dishonest or Strayed from God's Way (31:5-8)
3. I Have Not Committed Adultery (31:9-12)
4. I Have Not Mistreated My Servants (31:13-15)
5. I Have Not Withheld Compassion from the Needy (31:16-23)
6. I Have Not Substituted Wealth or Pagan Worship for My Worship of God (31:24-28)
7. I Have Not Been Vindictive against My Enemy (31:29-30)
8. I Have Not Withheld Hospitality from the Passing Traveler (31:31-32)
9. I Have Not Hidden My Transgressions from Public View (31:33-34)
10. I Am Prepared to Defend Myself, if God Will Just Tell Me What I Have Done Wrong (31:35-37)
11. I Have Not Exploited My Land or Laborers (31:38-40)

1. I Have Not Looked Lustfully at Young Women (31:1-4)

■ **1-4** Job begins by noting how he has protected himself from temptation. He knows that the mind/heart is influenced by the "eyes" (v 7*b*), so he has **made a covenant with** his **eyes** (v 1*a*) to avoid looking at any source of temptation that might lead him away from God. Covenants were typically sealed with an oath; so at some point in the past, Job may have sworn such an oath. One example of the type of temptation Job has in mind is lust. *How could I* look . . . *at a young woman?* is his way of saying that he has scrupulously disciplined himself to avoid looking **lustfully** at any **young woman** (*bĕtûlâ*).

Lustfully does not appear in the Hebrew text, so an alternative view is that Job is referring to his refusal to look for other wives, which he might reasonably be interested in if wanting to start another family. But vv 2-3 assume that Job is thinking of something sinful, such as lust.

There is no specific commandment in the OT regarding lust, but Job's mention of it in the context of vv 1-4 implies that it was considered morally wrong. Job calls those who lust **evildoers** (*'awwāl*) and **workers of iniquity** (*pō'ălê 'āwen*) (v 3). Even though a person can lust without anyone else knowing it, Job knows that the secret sins of the mind/heart cannot be hidden from God (v 4). And **God** (*Eloah*) brings punishment against these sinners in the form of **disaster** (*'êd*) and **misfortune** (*nēker*) (v 3). Therefore, Job has disciplined himself to avoid thinking about women in lustful ways.

Verses 2-3 seem to contradict Job's earlier comments that the wicked do well in life (21:6-21, 30-33). But there he was speaking about his observations of others. Here he is talking about how God treats *him*. If he ever were to abandon his righteous life and turn to a life of sin, he knows God would see it and punish him severely.

Lust

Lust is always viewed negatively in the Bible, but Scripture does speak with a dual message on the topic of human physical attraction. On the one hand, it praises the beauty of the human body using sensuous language in the Song of Songs between young lovers who are madly in love with each other and soon to be married (Song 4:1-15; 5:10-16; 7:1-13 [2-14 HB]). By speaking of the virtues and differences of maleness and femaleness, the Song reveals the basis for mutual attraction between the genders. This is one of the reasons why a man and a woman make the decision to leave the security of mother and father and cleave to each other in a marriage relationship (Gen 2:24). The Song of Songs also makes an important theological statement about the value and beauty of human love. It is something God has created and blessed.

In contrast, passages such as Gen 34:1-4, 8 (Shechem and Dinah); 2 Sam 11:2 (David and Bathsheba); 13:1-2, 15 (Amnon and Tamar); and Prov 7:10-21 (the woman who seduces a naive and foolish young man) point out the harmful consequences of lustful attitudes and seductive attempts by people to engage in sexual activity outside of marriage. Job 31:1-4 takes the same position as these latter passages.

In the NT Jesus took the matter of lust a step further by declaring it to be as sinful as adultery (Matt 5:27-30). His point was that an inward attitude can be just as harmful to other people and as sinful to God as an outward action. He thus countered the claims of self-righteous people that they had committed no sins, meaning no *visible* sins. For Jesus, sin originates in the heart and mind long before it displays itself in outward manifestations. Jesus continually stressed this higher principle in his attempts to establish moral standards for life in the kingdom of God.

2. I Have Not Been Dishonest or Strayed from God's Way (31:5-8)

■ **5-6** In Job's second claim he disavows having **walked with falsehood** (v 5*a*) or **hurried after deceit** (v 5*b*). People who live this way do so for selfish/sinful reasons. Today's scam artists and identity thieves are a modern-day version of this type of behavior. Eliphaz already connected these dishonest practices with the wicked (15:31, 35), and the psalmist makes the avoidance of them a prerequisite for the worship of God (Ps 24:4).

Job fully agrees that these practices are evil, and so his desire to distance himself from them is no surprise. He is so confident of his integrity in this matter that he is willing for **God** (*Eloah*) to weigh his soul on an accurate balance scales to prove his **blamelessness** (i.e., "wholeness with God," *tummâ*; → Job 2:3, 9). The concept of God weighing a person's heart/spirit/deeds is found in other OT passages as well (Ps 62:9 [10 HB]; Prov 16:2; 21:2; 24:12; Dan 5:27).

In a different context Job requested that his anguish be weighed in order to verify that he was experiencing extreme suffering (Job 6:2-3). In Egyptian theology, after death a person's heart was weighed on a balance scales against a feather (the symbol of *maat*, "truth") before they could be ushered into the afterlife.

■ **7-8** Job continues to claim his integrity by noting that he has never **turned aside** from God's way nor pursued any selfish desires. And further, there is no evil **stain** left on his **hands** to contradict his claims of righteousness. He uses four parts of the body (*foot* [lit. "step"]; **heart**; **eyes**; **hands**) in 31:7 to illustrate his devotion to God in a more tangible way.

Job concludes his second claim by pronouncing a curse against himself if he is proven wrong on God's balance scales (v 6). The curse calls for the theft or destruction of the produce on his farm. He is willing to wager the loss of his food and eventual starvation as his penalty for dishonesty, because he is confident that no one will be able to produce evidence to contradict him.

3. I Have Not Committed Adultery (31:9-12)

■ **9-12** The third sin Job has avoided is adultery. This sexual sin was forbidden by Israelite law (Exod 20:14; Lev 20:10; Deut 22:22; Prov 6:23-29, 32-35), and it was also a major crime in other ancient cultures (see the law codes of Sumer ["The Laws of Ur-Nammu," *ANET*, 524, #4]; Eshnunna ["The Laws of Eshnunna," *ANET*, 162, #28]; Babylonia ["The Code of Hammurabi," *ANET*, 171, #129-130]; Assyria ["The Middle Assyrian Laws," *ANET*, 181, #13-16, 23]; and the Hittites ["The Hittite Laws," *ANET*, 196, #195]). Usually the penalty was death for one or both participants.

Job states that he had never been **enticed *unto*** (Job 31:9*a*; *'al*; BDB, 834*b*) a woman or ***lain in wait*** outside his neighbor's house looking for an opportunity to seduce his neighbor's wife (v 9b). In other words, whether the primary instigator of the adultery is the man or the woman is not crucial in Job's mind. It is still *a shameful act, a punishable offense* (v 11; lit. "an iniquity of the judges," meaning "an iniquity requiring judgment") that Job has avoided.

Metaphorically, Job compares the consequences of adultery to a scorching fire (v 12a) that pursues a person all the way to **Abaddon** (i.e., Sheol; → 26:6). The fire completely devours one's crops down to the roots, resulting in starvation. The metaphor here is borrowed from the imagery of God's judgment in Deut 32:22 (Clines 2006, 1019) and is similar to the connection of fire with adultery in Prov 6:27-29.

Again Job pronounces a curse against himself in the event he is wrong. The punishment of the curse seems to fall most heavily on his wife rather than on himself or his female partner in adultery. His wife is the one who will become the slave of another man, and she will be forced into sexual encounters with numerous other men. Whether this is the result of a gang rape or a life of prostitution is not made clear.

Here Job is not thinking of the stipulations of Israelite law that demanded the stoning of individuals guilty of adultery (Lev 20:10; Deut 22:22), for his wife was not guilty of the hypothesized sexual affair and should not be punished at all. Rather, the focus is on Job's being forced to surrender his own wife to another man and seeing her cruelly humiliated and debased in the event he has committed adultery. The stakes here are extremely high for Job, but his conscience is clear on this matter. He knows his wife is safe from such cruel punishment.

4. I Have Not Mistreated My Servants (31:13-15)

■ **13-15** Job's fourth claim concerns his actions and attitudes toward his **servants, male** and **female** (v 13). He has never rejected their complaints against him. By this he means he has never failed to listen to their grievances or failed to make some attempt to alleviate their problems. He does not mean he has granted all their requests. He bases his actions on two principles. First, **God** (*El*) listens to the cries of all his people—both masters and servants; so certainly God would know if a servant was praying about abuses by Job. How could Job defend his integrity and righteousness before God if he had failed even to listen to his servants' complaints? Second, the same God created both masters and servants in the same way (10:8-11; Prov 22:2). Therefore, he must care about both of them and expect each to treat the other with respect.

One should not read into this passage a modern manifesto on the equality of all human beings. In OT times slaves and servants were a common occurrence in most nations of the world, including Israel. Israel had a few stipulations in the covenant requiring the humane treatment of slaves (Exod 21:2-11, 20-21, 26-27; Lev 25:39-55; Deut 15:12-18) and even the possibility of their freedom in the seventh year or the fiftieth year (Year of Jubilee) of their slavery (Lev 25:40, 50, 54; Deut 15:12). This treatment was based on God's reminder to them that they had once been slaves themselves in Egypt (Lev 25:42, 55; Deut 15:15). However, in reality all slaves (both Israelite and non-Israelite in origin) were considered the property of their owners (Lev 25:45), and the masters could pretty much do with them as they pleased.

Job's comments in Job 31:13-15 reveal that he was a step ahead of his society. He was not ready to abolish slavery or proclaim equal rights for all human beings, but he did recognize that God held him accountable for how he treated those who worked for him. He believed that all persons have worth and deserve certain basic human rights. This belief is somewhat amazing in light of the way Job was being treated by his own servants at this time (19:15-16). Nevertheless, he did not abandon his belief. His willingness to respect the worth of both his male and female servants was another sign of his integrity.

5. I Have Not Withheld Compassion from the Needy (31:16-23)

■ **16-23** The fifth sin that Job has avoided is the lack of compassion for the **poor** (v 16a), the **widow** (v 16b), and the **fatherless** (v 17b; or ***orphan***). Here Job goes into greater detail than he did in 29:12-13, 15-16 in order to reemphasize his heartfelt concern for the plight of those in great need. The principal resources that he provided were food (31:17) and **clothing** (vv 19-20), but he also mentions that he looked out after their general welfare, helping to raise the orphan and guide **the widow** (v 18). The words in v 18 and in 29:15-16 could imply that he actually took some of the needy into his home and raised them. The phrases **from my youth** (31:18a) and ***from my mother's womb*** (v 18b) are usually regarded as hyperboles meaning "all my life."

Verse 20a is literally ***if his loins*** did not bless me. The word ***loins*** refers to the sides of a person between the rib cage and the hips. Job was able to warm the needy in this area of their bodies by providing wool blankets that wrapped around them.

Verse 21 speaks of the temptation to turn against the needy if there was the possibility of gaining a personal advantage that others in the community would support. Job specifically mentions **the fatherless** in this verse, but no doubt he would include widows and the poor as well. He makes it very clear that his conscience would not allow him to treat the needy in this way. His fear of what **God** (*El*) would do to him if he failed to help the unfortunate compelled him to give of his means. God desires compassion for the less fortunate, and Job wanted to please God. He was confident he had done this many times in the past.

His curse against himself in v 22 is one involving tremendous physical pain and the loss of mobility in his **arm** and **shoulder**. If he is proven wrong in regard to helping the needy, he is willing to have his **arm** separated from his **shoulder**, thus rendering him incapable of using that **arm**. Job is not afraid to make this curse because he knows it will never happen to him.

Social Activism

Some scholars criticize Job in this section for not addressing the systemic problems in society that lead to poverty and mistreatment of the needy (e.g., Clines 2006, 1021-22), but that is not generally the approach of the wisdom literature. The biblical prophets certainly spoke up against the systemic evils of Israelite society that were thrust upon the poor by the government and the upper classes. They condemned the rich and urged the Israelites to look after the poor, citing the covenant as proof of God's requirements in this regard.

However, the sages took a different approach. They were not social activists. When the wisdom literature speaks about the poor and the injustices of life, it usually does so by simply noting that life is harsh for some people and this is the way it is (e.g., Prov 14:20; 19:7). The authors seem to be more interested in observing life than trying to reform it. So we should not expect Job to put on the prophet's mantle and take society to task for neglecting the poor. His speech is intended to be a testimony of his own personal actions with regard to the needy.

This may seem rather strange to modern societies that are used to dealing with social problems from the prophetic point of view. But the wisdom literature provides another set of eyes that looks at life quite differently. It attempts to reveal the order of life with all its social tensions and contradictions. Once we know what the order of life is like, then we can arrange our lives to deal with it in ways that are pleasing to God.

6. I Have Not Substituted Wealth or Pagan Worship for My Worship of God (31:24-28)

■ **24-28** **Wealth** is one of the things that attracts people's attention away from the worship of God. Job was once extremely wealthy (1:2-3), but then he lost all his children, all his animals, and many of his servants in a series of calamities (1:13-19). Verse 24 of ch 31 may be an indication that he still retained some of his wealth in the form of **gold**. Sometimes those who are wealthy are tempted to trust in their wealth for security and to credit their success to their own skill and ingenuity. Job denies that he has ever fallen for this temptation. God is the one who blessed him with wealth. And further, he knew from experience that one's riches can suddenly disappear. Wealth is not the security that some people think it is.

In the NT Jesus warned the wealthy of his day about the same temptation (Matt 6:19-21, 24; 19:16-26). He urged people to put their trust in God and their treasures in heaven.

Likewise, the worship of other deities can draw people away from God (Job 31:26-27). The worship of **the sun, the moon,** and the stars was widely practiced in the religions outside of Israel. The Israelites were strictly forbidden to worship these deities (Deut 4:19; 17:2-7), but many did it anyway (2 Kgs 23:5; Jer 8:1-2; Ezek 8:16; Zeph 1:5), usually conducting their services on rooftops or in open air sanctuaries.

Job testifies that he was never enticed to turn away from God and worship these deities, even in secret. He knows he could have secretly blown them **a kiss of homage** (Job 31:27; lit. "my hand kissed my mouth") to acknowledge their importance in his life. But this would be a ***punishable offense*** (v 28; just like adultery [v 11]). It would also be **unfaithful to God** (*El*).

7. I Have Not Been Vindictive against My Enemy (31:29-30)

■ **29-30** Verse 29 introduces a series of three claims (vv 29-34) that have no main verb in Hebrew. The best explanation is that Job's thinking was interrupted by another thought (vv 35-37) before he could finish.

Verses 29-30 address the human desire to seek the downfall of one's enemies. When one hears that **misfortune** or ***evil*** have overtaken ***the one who hates me***, the tendency is to rejoice because justice has been served. Even those who are righteous may experience a feeling of satisfaction upon hearing of an enemy's downfall (→ Eliphaz's comments in 22:19-20). However, Job claims that he has never **gloated** upon hearing of his enemies' troubles and never asked God to punish them by pronouncing a **curse** against them (in contrast to numerous passages in the Psalms, e.g., Pss 35:1-8, 26; 69:22-28 [23-29 HB]; 109:6-20, 27-29; 137:7-9). Job does not go as far as Jesus (Matt 5:43-48; Luke 6:27-36; 23:34) or Stephen (Acts 7:60) in praying for the welfare of his enemies, but he does abide by the OT admonitions to love one's neighbor, to treat one's enemies kindly, and to avoid rejoicing over an enemy's misfortune (Exod 23:4-5; Lev 19:18, 34; Prov 17:5; 24:17-18; 25:21-22).

8. I Have Not Withheld Hospitality from the Passing Traveler (31:31-32)

■ **31-32** Hospitality was considered a social obligation in biblical times. The scarcity of decent inns required that people put up passing travelers in their homes for the night (Gen 19:1-3; Judg 19:15-21). Job not only did so, but he entertained his guests with a full-course meal that even included **meat**, usually reserved for festive occasions and religious feasts. All the members of Job's clan (lit. "all the men of my tent") knew of his kindness in this matter, and they had often joked, ***Who has taken from his (Job's) meat and not been satisfied?*** The Hebrew *gēr* usually means "a sojourner, resident alien," but in Job 31:32*a* it appears in parallel with *'ōrēaḥ*, **traveler** (an emendation from *'ōraḥ*; lit. "way") and thus refers to ***a person who is passing through***.

9. I Have Not Hidden My Transgressions from Public View (31:33-34)

■ **33-34** If I have concealed my ***transgressions like Adam***. Job's next claim is that he has never sinned and then tried to cover up his evil deeds because of his fear of what others would think. He uses ***Adam*** (NASB, NJPS; some versions, such as the NIV and NRSV, take this as a reference to humanity in general) as an example of what people usually do when they sin. Their guilt and fear of being found out led them to withdraw from situations where their sin might be exposed. **Like Adam**, they hide and then blame others when confronted with the evidence.

Eliphaz confronted Job earlier with the accusation that he was a sinner (22:4-5). He mentioned several possible sins that Job might have committed (22:6-11) and then encouraged him to repent (22:21-26). The point was that Job must have done something evil to bring God's wrath on him, for God would not punish an innocent man. If Job had not sinned openly, then he must have done something in secret that aroused God's anger; and he must now be hiding it from public view. Job's claim in this passage effectively refutes Eliphaz's argument. He has no need to hide anything from anyone because he has been sinless throughout the book (→ 1:1 on the meaning of "sinlessness").

The Interior Dimension of Holiness

The list of Job's claims in ch 31 reveals that God's requirements for holy living include both inner and outer cleanness. A holy God desires the whole person—not only the things we do with our hands and our mouth but also the thoughts, attitudes, and motives concealed in our minds and hearts. God is even interested in shaping our conscience in ways that help us fulfill his commands to love him with our heart, soul, and might (Deut 6:4-5) and to love our neighbor as ourself (Lev 19:18; quoted in Matt 22:37-40; Mark 12:29-33; Luke 10:27; Rom 13:9; Gal 5:14).

Job knew, and we should too, that people cannot claim to be blameless and righteous before God unless both their outer actions and their inner thoughts are pure, and there is no object of worship other than God himself. Because of this strong emphasis on the interior dimension of holiness, Gammie calls ch 31 "a high-water mark in Old Testament ethics" (1989, 146). And so it is, but it is not unique. Other OT passages include: 1 Sam 15:22-23; Pss 24:3-4; 51:10, 16-17 [12, 18-19 HB]; 86:11; 139:1-4, 23-24; Jer 31:31-34; Ezek 36:25-27.

10. I Am Prepared to Defend Myself, if God Will Just Tell Me What I Have Done Wrong (31:35-37)

■ **35-37** For one last time, Job pleads with God to speak to him about the reason for his suffering. On many previous occasions he has challenged God on this issue, but with no response. He even prepared a case, in the sense of a legal defense, to prove that he was righteous and undeserving of such intense suffering (Job 13:18-28; 23:2-7). Job never formally composed a written document, but in his mind he knew exactly what he would say to defend himself (probably most of chs 29—31). And now he even figuratively signs this hypothetical document in another effort to convince God to meet with him. **Here is my mark** (31:35*b*; lit. "my *tāw*"). The last letter of the Hebrew alphabet, *tāw* (which looked something like an X or a +), was sometimes used by people as a signature on business and legal documents. Job's signature certifies that he stands behind his defense 100 percent.

Job's final plea comes with an offer to display publicly a copy of God's **indictment** against him (v 35c), either on his **shoulder** or on his head **like a crown** (v 36; lit. "crowns"). He is willing to advertise his sins, much like wearing an old-fashioned sandwich board, if God will just tell him what they are. But God never does, so Job is still left wondering.

In v 37 Job reveals his utmost reverence for God, even if God refuses to speak to him. He would approach him with the respect that one *noble* shows toward another, recounting the entire story of his life for God to evaluate.

Many scholars have wondered about the placement of vv 35-37. This section interrupts the series of Job's claims and seems more appropriate as the conclusion to the entire list. As the text stands, these verses present Job as losing his train of thought and digressing briefly on his desire for God to tell him why he is suffering. He then returns to his list with a final claim in vv 38-40. If this order is correct, it would help explain the lack of a concluding oath to v 34.

Another possibility is that vv 38-40*b* became detached somehow from the original list. A scribe, not knowing where they belonged, simply attached them at the end. The former seems more likely, but there is not enough evidence to settle the matter one way or the other. So the text will be left in its canonical order in the commentary.

11. I Have Not Exploited My Land or Laborers (31:38-40)

■ **38-40** Job's final claim of innocence concerns his relationship with his **land** (v 38). The **land** here is personified as a living being capable of crying out against him over abuses and mistreatment. The type of exploitation is not specified, but it could have included: the failure to follow good farming practices such as rotating crops, resting the land every seven years (Exod 23:10-11; Lev 25:2-7; 26:34-35), maintaining the land's fences and irrigation ditches, pulling up the weeds and thornbushes, and keeping out the birds and wild animals. In the Song of the Vineyard (Isa 5:1-10) God's failure to do these things for the land of Israel and Judah is a symbol of his wrath. But in this passage, the failure to be a good farmer is a sin against God and creation. The land has a right to cry out against its owner if it is neglected or overworked.

In Job 31:39*a* Job claims he has not exploited the people who work on his land by withholding their pay. In v 39*b* he denies causing the *owners* of the land *to groan*. Since Job is the actual owner of the land, he is speaking either of the original owners whom he forced off their land or of tenant farmers who live on the land and are not being treated properly. Both practices are forbidden in the OT (Lev 19:13; Deut 24:14-15; Isa 5:8; Mic 2:2; Mal 3:5), but the latter is more likely in this context as it provides a better parallel with Job 31:39*a*.

In v 40*ab* Job closes his series of claims by pronouncing a curse on his land if anyone can provide evidence that he has exploited his land or his laborers. He is willing to accept a harvest of **thornbushes** and **stinkweed**s as the penalty for this transgression. As with the earlier curses in this chapter, Job knows he is in no danger of experiencing the effects of this curse, for he is a righteous person (29:14) and God has no reason to punish him.

The author ends Job's speech with the following comment: **The words of Job are *completed***. Actually, Job will speak on two more occasions (40:3-5; 42:1-6), but these are only brief responses to God's long speech in chs 38—41. There will be no more extensive and detailed arguments from Job defending his innocence, bewailing his suffering, pleading to be left alone to die, and calling on God for a personal meeting or at least an explanation. Multiple times Job has poured out his heart with words of passion, anguish, frustration, and even anger, but now he falls silent. He has said all he knows to say up to this point.

The final words in ch 31 are like the closing of a curtain on this act in Job's life. One expects the curtain to remain closed until God is ready to respond to Job's oath of innocence. However, the author has a surprise up his sleeve. A brand-new character by the name of Elihu takes the stage in ch 32. His entrance is totally unexpected, and his long speech is not conventional by any means. This literary technique livens up the story and creates more tension before God finally appears.

FROM THE TEXT

1. Summary of Job's Manifesto. The point of Job's final speech is that he has lived an exemplary moral life, just as described in the prologue. No matter what the circumstances, he has stayed true to his personal moral code. Not only has he scrupulously avoided all possible outward sins, but he has even guarded his thought life. Others may look on the loss of his family, wealth, and health as God's punishment for sin. But Job knows differently. Sin is not the reason for his suffering. The fact that not one of his friends steps forward to dispute his testimony is the author's confirmation that Job is still sinless at this point in the story.

Job's main points are these:
- Before God struck me with terrible calamities, my life was unbelievably blessed. God's presence was continually with me, providing guidance and protection. My family life was a great joy to me. My community respected me for my leadership and wise counsel. My personal resources were quite extensive, allowing me to help whoever had a need. This was a ministry that I enjoyed thoroughly. I could not have asked for a better life.
- Now my life situation has drastically changed. My community no longer respects me. They mock and even spit at me because they think I am the worst of sinners. Even more frightening, God has turned against me. He has taken away my health and filled me with terror. I have repeatedly pleaded with him for help and tried to hope for better days. But he responds by treating me more cruelly. I know I have little time left to live. I am headed for Sheol.

- In spite of what others think of me, I refuse to accept their evaluations and remedies. My conscience is clear. I know I am innocent of sinning against God. Neither my outward deeds nor my inward thoughts have given God any reason to punish me. I am so convinced of this that I have pronounced curses against myself if I am wrong, but I know they will never come to pass. If perchance God finds even the tiniest sin in my life, let him write it down on a big signboard. I would gladly display it so that all could see how God has unjustly punished me for such a small grievance.

One has to admire Job for his dogged determination to maintain his personal integrity and protect his righteous reputation. His willingness to pronounce curses against himself is good evidence that he is confident of his innocence. People do not tell God to curse them if there is even the slightest hint of sin or hypocrisy in their lives. None of Job's curses ever happened, so we know he is speaking the truth.

2. Job's Former Life. As people grow older, they tend to forget their earlier struggles and to focus on their successes and accomplishments. The past is sometimes portrayed as much better than it really was. In ch 29 Job may have fallen prey to this tendency, for he paints a picture of himself that is almost utopian. He did everything right, and he never seemed to have a problem before calamity struck. However, it would be wrong for anyone to expect that God provides his followers with a trouble-free life, no matter how righteous they are. Such a hypothesis is a major error in the thinking of those who believe in the gospel of success.

Of course, Job had problems in his earlier life. He even mentions some in his youthful years (13:26). In ch 29 the author is not suggesting that Job never suffered or had a problem in former days. He is simply allowing Job the opportunity to provide his own evaluation of himself, for it confirms with more details what both the author (1:1-5) and God (1:8; 2:3) had said about him in generalities in the prologue.

3. Job's Loss of Ministry. In ch 29 Job reveals a part of his agony that he has not mentioned before—his present inability to help his community by means of compassionate deeds (vv 12-13, 15-16) and wise counsel (vv 21-25). These acts sprang from his heart in former days and indicated his true self. In return, they had earned him a reputation that left others in awe when they were in his presence (vv 7-11). Chase calls this "Job's deepest wound," even greater than his loss of family, possessions, health, and communion with God (2013, 223). Whether it is possible to rank Job's hurts in this way is questionable, but to hear Job describe it, he greatly missed the opportunity to minister to others.

4. He Helped Others, but He Could Not Help Himself. In spite of his numerous good deeds, miraculous healings, and helpful teachings, Jesus was taunted on the cross with words that mocked his inability to save himself (Matt 27:42-44; Mark 15:31-32; Luke 23:35). In similar fashion, Job's helping hand was extended to others, yet he was totally unable to help himself. He needed someone to stand up for him or do for him what he had done for others, but his earlier plea for an advocate or mediator (Job 9:33) had gone unanswered.

The reader knows that the real cause of Job's suffering lay outside of this world, and therefore the solution to his problems would have to come from there as well. No earthly being was able to help him as he had helped others. Only God could relieve this kind of suffering. Thus, Job would be forced to endure his pain until such time that God chose to end it.

VIII. ELIHU'S SPEECHES: JOB 32—37

BEHIND THE TEXT

The character of Elihu is something of an enigma. He is young, impatient, and brash, but yet very sharp intellectually. He knows all the arguments that have been presented thus far. Some he has accepted, and others he wants to attack. He is disturbed to the point of anger about some of the things he has heard. His basic problem is that he is overly confident in his ability to understand Job's suffering. He thinks he knows it all. He is not afraid to challenge either Job or the friends on points with which he disagrees. His exact age is unknown, but he belongs to a later generation than Job and his friends (32:6). A person of college age or in their twenties might fit the character of Elihu.

Elihu's speech is actually a series of four speeches (32:6—33:33; 34:1-37; 35:1-16; 36:1—37:24), each prefaced by the standard introductory formula (→ 3:2). These formulas are merely a literary device to break up this lengthy material into smaller sections, as there is no sense that he stopped or paused at the end of each speech. In essence, then, Elihu's contribution is a highly emotional monologue that lasts for six chapters (the longest speech in the book).

Scholars have raised a number of issues with regard to the authenticity of this section of the book:

- Elihu is the only major character in the book with a Hebrew name (two of Job's daughters also have Hebrew names [42:14]).
- He is the only character who is not mentioned in either the prologue or the epilogue. He appears suddenly after Job's last speech, delivers the longest speech in the book, and then disappears just as abruptly. No one ever responds to his speech, so the reader is left without any sense of its value.
- There are various linguistic differences between Elihu's section and the rest of the book. Gordis notes the following examples: the usage of the divine names *El*, *Eloah*, and *Shaddai* in different proportions; similar differences in the appearance of the first singular pronouns *'ănî* and *'ānōkî*; the lack of archaic forms in some prepositions; and the avoidance of some enclitics. There is also more of an Aramaic influence in this part of the book (1978, 547-48). A further difference is Elihu's frequent usage of Job's name (9x).
- The most serious challenge to Elihu's authenticity is his supposed interruption to the flow of the story. After Job's final speech (chs 29—31), the logical climax would be a message from God that resolves the tensions that developed in the dialogue section and that answers Job's question about the cause of his suffering. Instead, according to some scholars, Elihu's appearance only delays the climax for a considerable length of time. Some would even go so far as to say that he adds nothing to the story and is "irrelevant to the book of Job" (Rowley 1976, 206). Therefore, chs 32—37 must be a later addition to the book by another author.

However, most of the reasons for a second author are either insignificant or subjective. None of them effectively removes the author entirely from this section of the book. There are good reasons to retain only one author for the entire book:

- One would expect an author to vary somewhat the speech of a new character to indicate a different personality.
- If there was a second author, this person would likely have tried harder to cover his tracks. A later writer could easily have chosen a non-Hebrew name and avoided the linguistic changes to disguise any new material.
- The linguistic differences are not really as great as some claim. In fact, there are some linguistic similarities that tie Elihu's speeches to the rest of the book, for example, (1) the use of the emphatic infinitive absolute with the imperative of *šm'* in 37:2; 13:17; and 21:2 (Gordis 1978, 425); and (2) the appearance of "repetition in parallelism" throughout the book (ibid., 508-13). In addition, there are some verses in Elihu's speech that are very similar to verses in other parts of the book, for example, 34:3 is very similar to 12:11. The same author must have written both.
- The appearance of Job's name in 38:1 suggests that there was always an additional speaker between 31:40 and 38:1 (Wilson 2007, 358-59, 422).

- The appearance of God out of a "storm" (38:1) is totally unexpected and in need of explanation without Elihu's prior, extended comments on God's power through a storm (36:27—37:18). The introduction to God's speech (38:1) makes much more sense if Elihu's final speech was delivered as a storm actually approached.
- There is no good reason why Elihu's appearance should be seen as an interruption to the story. His speech heightens the drama and creates more suspense about how the story will end. This is a good literary technique (a surprise turn-of-event before the climax) that many authors use. It also adds a new freshness to a story that has started to drag. Any criticism about the flow of the story is primarily based on a subjective sense of what *should* occur in the narrative.

A much more logical explanation of this issue is that the author probably took a long time, maybe even an entire lifetime, to write a book of this length and complexity (Gordis 1978, 548-49). It is very likely that the author composed several drafts, and the section on Elihu was probably added in a later draft at a later period in his life. This would help explain the linguistic differences. The fact that Elihu is not mentioned in the prologue and the epilogue may indicate the author's desire not to rewrite parts of the book that were satisfactory. Even though Elihu's entrance is sudden, the prose introduction to his speech adequately explains why he did not appear earlier.

Some scholars view the author as a very clever writer who inserted Elihu at a critical point to provide "comic relief" from the tensions of the dialogue (Hartley 1988, 427). Others think the author used Elihu's speech to set the stage for God's appearance and to introduce some of the themes that God will take up in the following speech (chs 38—41) (Habel 1985, 37; Seow 2013, 31-37). There is a further possibility that few have recognized. The author may be using the character of Elihu to evaluate and criticize some of the arguments by Job and his friends. Since God's speech barely comments on issues raised in the dialogues, Elihu's speech gives the author the opportunity to rebut some of the more erroneous ideas presented earlier and to defend God's character against some of Job's harsh criticisms (→ From the Text for ch 37).

It is incorrect to say Elihu contributes nothing to the flow of the story. While he repeats some of the earlier arguments made by the friends, he does provide another viewpoint from the mind of an energetic young adult who is not bound by the wisdom traditions. He also develops more extensively than Eliphaz (5:17) God's use of suffering for the purpose of discipline.

There may be another, more subtle contribution. Why would the author choose this one Hebrew name when the setting for the story is outside of Israel? Could it be that in a later draft he felt a need to add the views of a typical Israelite through the character of Elihu, thus making the story more interesting and applicable to an Israelite audience? Elihu insists he has a true understanding of God (which an Israelite would certainly agree with). And he is very angry at the friends and Job (most Israelite readers would probably also be very offended at the way God has been treated in the dialogues). Elihu is not an Israelite, but he does bring Israelite ways of thinking into the story. If an Israelite connection can be shown, the total lack of a response to his speech and his nonappearance in the epilogue make more sense. Most Israelite readers would probably have said that Elihu does not need to be rebuked like the others because he has many points of agreement with God. Thus, the author avoids having to provide God's critique of Elihu.

Interestingly, the evaluation of Elihu's character has gone through several stages over the centuries. The pseudepigraphic *Testament of Job* (100 BC-AD 200) regarded Elihu as an evil character—a person inspired by Satan and not forgiven by God (*Testament of Job*, #41-43; Boss 2010, 179). But Jewish exegetes in the medieval period treated him much better. Saadiah Gaon (b. AD 862), Rashi (b. AD 1040), and Maimonides (b. AD 1135) all considered him to be God-inspired. They even regarded God's own speeches, which follow in chs 38—41, as merely confirming that Elihu was correct (Vicchio 2006b, 96, 100, 112).

Today Elihu is often demoted to secondary status due to a widespread opinion that his speeches were written by a later author. Gibson even removes Elihu's speeches to an appendix and refuses to comment on them in any detail (1985, 268-81). But not all agree. As mentioned above, there are good and satisfactory reasons for maintaining his status as an important contributor to the overall narrative.

IN THE TEXT

A. Introduction of Elihu (32:1-5)

Verses 1-5 are a brief prose section that the author inserts here as an introduction to the character of Elihu. Since his name has not appeared previously, the author provides a considerable amount of information about his family background along with reasons for the long delay in his speaking.

■ I After Job's long speech in chs 29—31, a response from the three friends is expected; but they have contributed all that the author intends for them to say. Verse 1 gives the rationale for their silence: Job was **right in his own eyes** (in the book of Proverbs, this is one of the definitions of a fool [Prov 1:7; 10:8; 12:15; 15:5]). He was convinced he was correct, and no amount of arguing from the three friends could get him to change his thinking.

They interpreted Job's reaction to their arguments as indicating both a prideful, arrogant personality who refused to consider alternative views and a sinner who was hiding his past sins. In either case, the friends saw that it was useless to argue with Job anymore. No doubt, they were emotionally exhausted as well.

■ 2-5 In v 2 the author introduces an angry, young man by the name of **Elihu**. His lineage is quite extensive (the longest in the book), perhaps to indicate he was from a prominent family and therefore was qualified to speak. **Elihu** (*'ĕlîhû'*) is a Hebrew name meaning "he is my God," but his family was probably non-Israelite. Other OT characters with the name of Elihu are men from Ephraim (1 Sam 1:1),

Manasseh (1 Chr 12:20 [21 HB]), Judah (1 Chr 27:18), and the clan of Korah (1 Chr 26:7). None can be identified with this name in Job. Newsom speculates that **Elihu** may be the name of the actual, later author of chs 32—37, "an angry reader who literally wrote himself into the book" (1996, 562). But even if there were a later author, the family lineage and homeland in Job 32:2 would rule out an Israelite and thus not be likely.

The name of Elihu's father, **Barakel** (*barak'ēl*), does not appear elsewhere in the OT. **Buz** (*bûz*) is the name of a nephew of Abraham (Gen 22:21) who lived in northern Mesopotamia. But more likely, the word is a place name in northwest Arabia that is associated with the towns of Tema and Dedan (Job 6:19; Jer 25:23). The significance of **Ram** (*rām*) is not known. Two men with this name appear in the lineage of Judah (Ruth 4:19; 1 Chr 2:9-10, 25, 27), but they are not connected with **the family of Ram** in Job 32:2.

Elihu joined the group of four men at the ash heap in Uz at some unknown point in the past (possibly at the same time as the three friends [2:11-13]). No doubt, he already knew of Job's previous reputation in the community and was curious about the cause of the terrible calamities Job had experienced. He had listened to each speaker as the debate raged back and forth and as the arguments became more heated, but he had remained silent out of respect for the age of the other men (32:4). **They were older than he**, and social customs required young people to respect the wisdom of their elders.

Then suddenly all was quiet. This infuriated Elihu. The passage speaks four times of **his anger** in vv 2-5 using a colloquial Hebrew expression *ḥrh 'ap*, meaning literally "his nose became hot." Elihu **was . . . angry at the three friends** because they quit before achieving victory (vv 3, 5). He believed they had some good arguments, but they had failed to convince Job of his errors. Their silence was an admission of defeat that Elihu could not accept. He decided he would take up their mantle and continue where they had left off.

He **was** also **angry** at Job for claiming he was right and **God** (*Elohim*) was wrong (v 2*b*). Such a claim was clearly erroneous, maybe even blasphemous, and needed to be attacked. The silence of everyone else provided him an opportunity to speak, and he grabbed it. Even though he was young, he was extremely confident he could solve the problems that had been raised in the dialogues. Unfortunately for him, **anger** is one of the characteristics of a fool (Prov 14:17; 29:11; Eccl 7:9), so it is not entirely clear if the author regards Elihu as a serious character. But most seem to think so.

Job 32:3*b* contains another of the *Tiqqune Sopherim* (→ 7:20) passages that were altered by the Jewish scribes. The original apparently read: "because they (the friends) had found no answer and thus had placed God in the wrong" (Gordis 1978, 360). The scribes believed this statement was offensive to God and so changed "God" to **Job**. This change is followed by the NIV and NRSV. But the original is more likely in light of Elihu's later admonition in 34:10-12.

B. Elihu's First Speech (32:6—33:33)

Elihu begins by addressing both Job and the friends with a very long justification as to why he waited so long to speak and why he believes he can resolve Job's problems. Some regard these verses as excessively wordy, and they are; but that seems to be Elihu's style. He was youthful, bright, talkative, energetic, and fearless.

Elihu has seven main points in his first speech:
1. True Wisdom Comes from God and May Be Acquired at Any Age (32:6-10)
2. I Will Succeed Where the Friends Have Failed (32:11-14)
3. I Will Hold Nothing Back (32:15-22)
4. Job, You Can Trust Me to Tell You the Truth (33:1-7)
5. Job, You Are Wrong to Claim You Are Pure and God Treats You like an Enemy (33:8-12)
6. Job, You Are Wrong to Complain That God Will Not Speak to You (33:13-30)
7. Job, Listen to Me! (33:31-33)

1. True Wisdom Comes from God and May Be Acquired at Any Age (32:6-10)

Elihu enters the debate with great enthusiasm. After listening for hours to the speeches by Job and his friends, he now recognizes that he has as much wisdom as they do.

■ **6-10** For comments on the introductory formula in v 6a → 3:2. After the brief prose section in vv 1-5, the book now returns to poetry. In vv 6-7 Elihu states in his own words what the author has already narrated in v 4. He explains that he refrained from speaking out of respect for the other participants who were much older than he. His anxiety about sharing his views was prompted by his supposition that each of the previous speakers was much wiser than he because they were also older. So it was not appropriate for him to enter into the conversation.

However, as he listened to their arguments, he began to realize that his supposition was wrong. **Wisdom** (v 7) is not dependent on age. True **wisdom** comes directly from **the Almighty** (v 8; *Shaddai*), and it is infused into the **spirit** of a human being by God's **breath** (*nĕšāmâ*; the same word is used in Gen 2:7 for the breath that God breathes into humans to give them life). Therefore, a person of any age can be **wise** (v 9).

Elihu, believing he has been enlightened by God (36:2-4), is confident he is now as qualified to speak as anyone else in the dialogues. He pleads with them to **listen** to him (32:10). The verb for **listen** (*šm'*) is in the singular, but he probably intended for all the group to hear him out.

2. I Will Succeed Where the Friends Have Failed (32:11-14)

Elihu is fully confident that he can prove Job wrong.

■ **11-14** Elihu now criticizes the friends for their inability to refute Job's claims. He **waited** and waited for them to press home their verbal attacks and prove Job wrong (v 11). However, their efforts failed. Not one of them was able to overturn Job's arguments. He also admonishes them to avoid turning over to **God** (*El*) their responsibility to engage Job in debate (v 13*b*). They have an obligation to continue the dialogues. However, since they have failed, Elihu promises to carry on their criticisms of Job (v 14). Job has not yet spoken to him, so he will propose new arguments and use different tactics than the friends. As it turns out, most of his arguments are no different from the friends'.

In v 13 Elihu puts words in the friends' mouths that are ambiguous. Some think they refer to a recognition that Job was smarter than them: "We have found wisdom in Job, and he is more than a match for us. Therefore, we will quit talking and let God defeat him" (Davidson 1884, 224). Others believe the wisdom they have found is the decision to end the debate: "The wisest thing for us to do is to shut up and let God deal with Job" (Tur-Sinai 1967, 460). Still others view the statement as a claim to wisdom for themselves: "We have demonstrated wisdom in the things we have said, but God will have to finish the debate."

The last position borrows from some passages in Proverbs that equate finding wisdom with gaining knowledge and understanding about the ways of life (Prov 2:5-6; 3:13; 8:17, 35; 10:13; 24:14; see also Job 28:12, 28, where the author makes it clear that human beings can only find wisdom by fearing God). This view makes the most sense in the context. Elihu is criticizing the friends for claiming to be wise when they have run away from the battlefield of debate leaving God to bring about Job's final defeat (Hartley 1988, 435). Their actions are more cowardly than wise. In defense of the friends, only God truly knows whether or not Job has sinned, so the decision by the friends to remain silent may be more prudent than Elihu is willing to acknowledge.

3. I Will Hold Nothing Back (32:15-22)

Elihu is eager to expose the errors in the speeches of both Job and the friends. He promises to give them the unbiased truth.

■ **15-17** In vv 15-16 Elihu refers to the three friends in the third person. This means he has now turned his attention to Job, whom he will mention by name in 33:1. He describes the friends as being **dismayed**. The verb *ḥtt* often means "be fearful or terrified" (7:14; 31:34), but here Elihu is speaking of them as being ***disheartened/discouraged***. However, their dismay, leading to their silence, should not prevent others from engaging Job in debate. Elihu boldly announces that he will declare his knowledge on the matter.

Verse 17 of ch 32 is a very forceful statement with the phrase I, ***even I*** appearing in both *a* and *b*. He was through waiting for the friends to have their say. He was ready to go on the attack against Job's claims.

■ **18-20** Here Elihu reveals his eagerness to speak. Even wild horses could not hold him back. He is so **full of words** he feels like he is about to explode (v 18). The only way to get relief is to start talking. He compares his situation to the fermentation of **wine** in **new wineskins** (v 19). Without proper ventilation, they can only stretch so far before they **burst** open. These words confirm the author's description of him in vv 2-5 as a person who is about to explode with anger.

■ **21-22** Elihu also makes it clear that he will hold nothing back in his efforts to speak the truth. He does this by promising to refrain from showing **partiality** (lit. "I will not lift up the face of a man") or bestowing **flattery** (lit. "I will not give honor to a human") on any of the participants. What he means is that he no longer respects their opinions simply because of their age or their claims to be wise. He has been listening to them for a very long time, and he has come to the conclusion that they do not know what they are talking about. Therefore, his presentation will expose the weaknesses in their arguments. If he offends them, then so be it. Let the chips fall where they will. In his mind it is more important to get the issue settled than to observe proper etiquette. He seems to exaggerate a little in v 22*b* saying that God (**my Maker**) will get rid of him if he is not truthful. But the statement is intended to show the seriousness with which he approaches his task.

4. Job, You Can Trust Me to Tell You the Truth (33:1-7)

Elihu's first words directed specifically at Job challenge him to be ready for a hard-hitting, serious debate.

■ **1-3** Up to this point Elihu has spoken to the group as a whole, but now he focuses his attention specifically on Job, calling him by name in v 1 and urging him to **listen** carefully to his **words**. He declares he will speak from the **uprightness** of his **heart** (v 3). The word for **uprightness** (*yōšer*) is related to "upright" (*yāšār*), which was used to describe Job's character back in 1:1. In other words, Elihu is claiming the same character trait as Job. He believes his views are objective and truthful. He promises he will go straight to the facts without any side excursions into nonessential matters. Further, he will speak *purely* (33:3*b*), that is, without a hidden agenda. His only desire is to help Job.

■ **4-7** In vv 4 and 6*b* Elihu uses various images to connect his own existence with the actions of God. **God, the Almighty** (*El*, *Shaddai*) is the one who **made** him, breathed life into him, and *formed* (lit. "pinched off") him *from* **a piece of clay** (→ 4:19; 10:9 for earlier connections of humanity's origin with clay). Elihu's purpose in speaking this way is to note that he is on an equal level with Job (33:6*a*) due to his creation by God. Therefore, his arguments should be taken seriously. The fact that he is younger than Job should not place him at a disadvantage, for it is **the breath of the Almighty** (v 4) that provides a person with wisdom (32:8-9), not the age and life experiences of that individual.

In 33:5 Elihu challenges Job to be ready to debate with him: ***Set (your words) in order before me*** (v 5*b*). He uses the same verb (*'rk*; ***set in order***) Job used earlier to describe his readiness to present his case before God (13:18; 23:4). If Job is prepared to contend with God, then certainly he should be up to the task of debating with Elihu. Elihu's challenge is further intensified with the words: ***Take your stand!***

(33:5b). This verb (*yṣb*) is often used in military contexts with regard to preparing for battle against an enemy (Deut 7:24; Josh 1:5; 1 Sam 17:16; Ps 2:2).

Perhaps sensing he has gone too far in his bold, blustery approach, Elihu encourages Job not to fear the ensuing debate (Job 33:7). No doubt, he is referring to the fear Job expressed earlier in anticipation of debating God (13:20-21; 23:15-16). But Elihu does not possess overwhelming power (**my hand**) to destroy Job, as God does. Therefore, Job has nothing to fear from him.

Some view this section as mainly an attempt by Elihu to establish rapport with Job and engage him in an honest debate on the reasons for Job's suffering. However, his tone of voice is not indicated in the passage. Other passages, such as the repeated description of him as "angry" (32:1-5), his own testimony that he will show no "partiality" to anyone (32:21-22), and his later claim to speak for God and to do so "perfectly" (see 36:2-4), lend a different tone to his speech. At the very least, he possesses an extremely overly confident attitude that he will be able to demolish Job's arguments and force Job to accept his point of view. He finds Job's views totally unacceptable. Therefore, Job better be prepared for a fierce verbal exchange.

5. Job, You Are Wrong to Claim You Are Pure and God Treats You like an Enemy (33:8-12)

Job's attempts to blame God for his troubles while claiming moral purity for himself are incorrect. God's ways are simply too great for Job to comprehend.

■ **8-9** Beginning here and continuing into ch 34, Elihu attacks several of Job's positions. These are all quotations or inferences he heard Job make earlier in the dialogues. The first is in v 9: **I am pure,** *without transgression;* **I am clean,** *without iniquity.* Bildad and Zophar have already accused Job of claiming moral purity (8:6; 11:4), even though Job has never used the exact words **pure** (*zak*) and **clean** (*ḥap*) to describe himself. The closest he has come is in reference to his "prayer" being "pure" (16:17).

However, Elihu has correctly identified the essence of Job's claim (Clines 2006, 728), for Job has previously spoken of his "innocence" (*ṣdq*; 9:15, 20; 27:6) and his being "blameless" (*tām*; 9:20-21). Job has also stated that God knows he is innocent of sin (10:7; 13:18; 23:10-12; 31:4-6). And he has even challenged God to identify his *transgressions* and *iniquities* (7:21; 10:6-7, 14; 13:23; 31:35-37) and forgive those he can find. But he knows that God will never find any, except perhaps those committed in his youth (13:26).

■ **10-11** In 33:10 Elihu recalls occasions when Job has complained that God *finds grounds for opposition against me.* No doubt, he is thinking here of many previous statements by Job that God has made him a target (6:4; 7:20), terrified him with nightmares (7:12-15; 23:15-17), caused him to gasp for breath (9:18), hunted him down like a lion stalks prey (10:16), gnashed his teeth at him (16:9), made his name a byword to other people (17:6), enclosed him in a net and hemmed him in by a wall and troops (19:6-12), turned his family and friends against him (19:13-22), and violently and cruelly crushed and wounded him (9:17; 16:7-14; 30:18-23).

Verse 11 of ch 33 is a quotation of Job's from 13:27 emphasizing that God has restricted his movement by figuratively placing his **feet in *the stocks***. God also conducts nonstop surveillance of all his activities (7:17-20; 10:13-14). God's attacks against Job have become so intense that Job believes God now regards him as an **enemy** (33:10) seeking to destroy him (10:8; 13:24; 19:11).

■ **12** Verse 12 of ch 33 is sometimes placed at the beginning of the next section, but its content goes more naturally with vv 8-11. After laying out Job's position in vv 8-11, Elihu proceeds to attack it with a very brief answer: **You are not right, for God** [*Eloah*] **is greater than any mortal**. Job is completely wrong. How can he honestly claim purity for himself and accuse God of acting like an evildoer when he is so far below God's power and knowledge? Job is playing in the minor leagues in comparison to God's level of activity.

6. Job, You Are Wrong to Complain That God Will Not Speak to You (33:13-30)

Even though Job denies it, Elihu believes that God has been trying to communicate with Job about his suffering. He gives three examples of God's methods of communication: dreams, illness, and divine messengers.

■ **13-18** A second claim by Job concerns God's lack of communication with him. On several occasions Job has stated that God will not answer him (9:16; 13:22, 24; 19:7; 23:3-5, 8-9; 30:20). Even though he has cried out for God to meet him and explain the reasons for his suffering, God has failed to appear and, in fact, seems to be hiding from Job (13:24). Nonetheless, Elihu is convinced that God will eventually appear, if he has not already, for he always does. God desires to communicate with humankind and does so in multiple ways. But people such as Job may not be aware that God is near because they are not perceptive enough.

Here Elihu is answering some of Job's earlier remarks about the difficulty in finding God (9:11; 23:3, 8-9). He particularly stresses God's communication through **a dream** or **a vision** (33:15) while individuals are sleeping. People may regard them only as nightmares, but God uses these terrifying dreams ***to divert*** (v 17*a*) them from their sinful deeds and from **pride** (v 17*b*) in those deeds that leads them to an early death (v 18).

Job testified earlier to experiencing nightmares, which he blamed on God (7:14). By reminding Job of those terrifying dreams, Elihu is saying, "God was trying to warn you about the downward progression of your life, but you failed to perceive his message. Your failure to hear God speaking to you is due to your own pride, not to any lack of communication on God's part."

Pit (33:18*a*; *šahat*) is a synonym for Sheol—the place of the dead (17:14; → "Sheol" sidebar at 3:17-19). Elihu uses this term a total of five times in this chapter (33:18, 22, 24, 28, 30). In v 18*b* the Hebrew *šālaḥ* is sometimes interpreted as coming from *šelaḥ*, meaning "a weapon"/**sword** (also in 36:12). However, there is more agreement today on an alternative meaning of ***river/channel***, as a way of providing a parallel with ***Pit*** in 33:18*a* (Clines 2006, 697, 733). In ancient Mesopotamian and Greek mythology a dead person had to cross over a river in order to descend into the underworld. Elihu is probably referring to that mythology here. Thus, v 18 should be rendered: **He (God) keeps back his soul from the Pit, his life from crossing over the river (of death)**. For comments on the number pattern in vv 14 and 29 → "Number Patterns" sidebar at 5:19.

■ **19-22** Elihu now speaks of another method that God employs to communicate with people—through disease and physical **pain** (33:19*a*). Severe ailments that result in aching **bones** (v 19*b*; lit. "the conflict of his bones"), loss of appetite (v 20), and emaciated bodies (v 21) have a way of getting people's attention. The prospects of a premature **death** (v 22) are also intended to frighten people to return to God. Elihu describes this action by God as ***chastening/reproving*** (v 19*a*; *ykḥ*). Back in 5:17 Eliphaz used this same verb to describe how God disciplines people in order to warn them of the sinful direction in which they are headed. His discipline is for their own good and should be considered a *blessing* because it has the potential to turn their lives around and rescue them from sin and its consequences. Chastening, even though painful, is one component of God's grace that shows how much he cares for humanity.

The meaning of **messengers of death** (33:22*b*; lit. "the ones who kill/cause death") is unclear. Some suggest that Elihu is referring to a belief in divine beings who usher a person from the land of the living into Sheol (Gordis 1978, 376-77). Others emend the text to provide a more suitable parallel for ***Pit*** in v 22*a* (for the meaning of **pit**, → v 18). More likely, Elihu is simply personifying the diseases that bring death, as Bildad did in 18:13.

The purpose of speaking this way is to connect Job's sickly appearance with its cause—God's chastening. God is trying to get Job's attention by afflicting him with a terrible skin disease. If Job will not listen to God and make appropriate changes in his life, he is headed for Sheol. But there is still opportunity for him to learn from his errors and heed God's warning.

■ **23** A third way God is able to communicate with humanity is through a divine **messenger**—an **angel** (*mal'āk*). Elihu begins this verse with the word **if**, as if he is not certain that such an angel exists. But **if** can indicate a probability as well as a possibility, and there is no question that he believes this divine being does exist. Elihu characterizes this angel as **an intermediary, one among a thousand**, whose purpose is **to make known to a human being what is right**. Perhaps God has appointed such an **angel** for Job as he did for the psalmist (Ps 34:7 [8 HB]).

The word for ***intermediary*** (*mēlîṣ*) refers to a "go-between/envoy" (lit.) who speaks in behalf of one person (in this case, God) to another (Job 16:20). Very interestingly, one of the Targums of Job translates this word with the Aramaic word *pĕrāqlîṭā*. "This translation connects with the Greek word *paraklētos* [*sic*], thus to the role of the Paraclete or 'Advocate' in Johannine literature" (Balentine 2006, 550). The Targum is certainly not trying to make a connection with the Third Person of the Trinity, but the role that each intermediary plays is remarkably similar.

The phrase **one *among* a thousand** was used earlier by Job in 9:3. Its interpretation in 33:23 is difficult, but perhaps Elihu was thinking of a large multitude of angels who function as God's servants. God may have assigned one such angel to explain to Job what he needed to do to be right with God and to guide him through the process of reconciliation. While a person may miss God's voice given through nightmares (vv 15-18) and illness (vv 19-22), there should be no mistaking God's direct attempt to communicate through a personal ***intermediary*** (messenger).

Here Elihu addresses Job's earlier requests for a ***mediator*** (9:33), a "witness" (16:19), or a "redeemer" (19:25). The divine being that Elihu envisions does not actually fulfill any of these roles as Job described them (→ comments on each passage), but nevertheless this person can be an invaluable resource to Job by guiding him through the necessary steps needed to end his suffering. This concept certainly provides more hope for Job than Eliphaz's earlier denial of help from the heavenly beings (5:1).

■ **24-25** The conditional clause beginning with **if** in 33:23 continues in v 24 with a description of what the angel does to rescue a person from **going down to the *Pit***. First, **he is gracious** (*ḥnn*). The verb means "show grace, mercy, favor, kindness" toward someone, and it is used of God frequently (Exod 33:19; Pss 86:15; 103:8; 111:4; 116:5; 145:8). The psalmist pleads continually for God to be gracious to him (Pss 4:1 [2 HB]; 6:2 [3 HB]; 25:16; 51:1 [3 HB]; etc.).

Up to this point, Job may have received only nightmares (Job 33:15-18), illness (vv 19-22), and silence (30:20), but Elihu is suggesting that God may now be prepared to show his grace to Job in a way that will save him from an early death. God's angel is able to request that God ***deliver*** chastened persons from their downward progression toward the ***Pit*** (Sheol, → v 18).

The angel's request is based on new evidence: **I have found a ransom**. The Hebrew for **ransom** (*kōper*) normally refers to a monetary amount or significant item of value paid to free someone from an obligation or criminal charge (Exod 21:30; 30:12; Num 35:31-32; Prov 13:8; 21:18; Isa 43:3). But the angel does not have money in mind with this statement. The value of a person's salvation cannot be calculated in monetary terms (Ps 49:7-9 [8-10 HB]). The exact nature of the **ransom** is not spelled out by the angel. Some of the possibilities are as follows:

- The angel's pledge to provide a ransom is the surety God will accept.
- Job's tremendous suffering has now been of sufficient duration to satisfy God's demands.
- Job's refusal to curse God has met with God's approval (1:22; 2:10).
- Job will offer a ritual offering to atone for his sin.
- Job's repentance with a prayer (33:26) and a confession (v 27) will deliver him from his suffering.

This last suggestion may be what Elihu had in mind, for he regards Job as a rebellious sinner (34:37). But despite the lack of clarity regarding the ransom, Elihu clearly believes that the angel will be able to find the means to satisfy God's requirements for reconciliation, thus freeing Job from his suffering. Further evidence of the angel's desire to help Job is seen in his request for Job's **flesh** not only to be healed but also to be **restored** to its appearance at the time of his **youth** (33:25).

■ **26-28** The focus in the protasis (vv 23-25) of this long conditional sentence is on the actions of an intermediary angel who is involved in the reconciliation of human beings with God. The apodosis (vv 26-28) turns our attention to the sinner who is the recipient of the angel's kindness and to God's response. The exact order of all these events is confusing to some commentators, but Elihu is more concerned with the final result than the details of the process.

The sinner **prays to God** (v 26) and **shouts for joy** upon being reconciled to him (v 26). He then *sings* to others a confession of sin and an acknowledgment of receiving God's grace—a grace that treats people better than they deserve (v 27).

For his part, God will *take pleasure* in the former sinner, reveal himself anew, give back to him his *righteousness*, and *deliver* this one from an early death (v 26). The result will be that the sinner experiences **the light of life** (vv 28, 30) rather than the darkness of Sheol.

■ **29-30** These two verses reiterate Elihu's conviction that God makes multiple attempts to communicate with human beings. God's purpose in doing so is to save people from an early death in the *Pit* (Sheol, → v 18) and to enlighten them with his light (**the light of life**). Verse 30 parallels v 28, but it is written from Elihu's viewpoint rather than the testimony of the restored sinner. The three methods of communication that Elihu listed in the previous verses (vv 13-28)—through dreams, illness, and divine messengers—all apply to Job's situation, so there should be no question that God has attempted to communicate with him. (For comments on the number pattern in v 29 → v 14 and 5:19.)

7. Job, Listen to Me! (33:31-33)

■ **31-33** Elihu concludes his first speech by inviting Job to respond to his words thus far. If Job has something to say, he should say it. If not, he should **be silent** and **listen** to Elihu (v 31). Elihu has made this appeal several times already (32:10; 33:1, 5). *Speak, for I desire to set you right* (v 32b). Elihu's real intent is to correct Job's misconceptions about God and bring him to an admission of sin. As long as Job hangs onto beliefs that are erroneous, he will never escape his suffering. Elihu sees himself as the last and best resort that Job has to free himself from his miserable condition.

While this statement reveals Elihu's overconfidence in his ability to solve Job's problems, it also indicates his belief that there is still hope for Job in the future if he will change his way of thinking. Elihu will do everything he can to teach Job the truth, but he needs a cooperative student who will listen and learn. **Wisdom** is what Elihu claims he can teach Job (v 33).

C. Elihu's Second Speech (34:1-37)

Hearing no response from Job or the friends, Elihu launches into his second speech. His words here are mainly intended to defend God's justice against Job's earlier criticisms. He is very disturbed over Job's ignorance regarding God's method of governing the world. He directs his remarks first at the three friends, attempting to rally their support to his side. Then he goes on the attack against Job. The speech concludes with a new charge. Job is not only a sinner, he is even a rebel against God.

There are five sections to this speech:

1. You Friends, Listen to Me! (34:1-4)
2. Job Is Making Preposterous Claims (34:5-9)
3. It Is Unthinkable to Accuse God of Being Unjust (34:10-15)
4. Job, if God Is All-Powerful, He Is Also Just (34:16-30)
5. Job, You Are a Rebel against God (34:31-37)

1. You Friends, Listen to Me! (34:1-4)

■ **1** For comments on the introductory formula in v 1 → 3:2.

■ **2-4** Elihu begins his second speech by calling on the friends to support him in his arguments with Job. He addresses them as **wise men** and **men of *knowledge*** (34:2; lit. "ones who know"; → vv 10, 34) because they presented themselves as such in the dialogues (chs 4—27). They claimed to speak for the ancient wisdom traditions (4:7; 5:27; 8:8-10; 15:10, 17-18; 20:4-5).

In 34:3 Elihu repeats a proverb in the form of a simile that Job mentioned earlier (12:11). The ***mind*** (lit. **ear**) is able to test **words** and ideas to determine their validity, just as the ***palate*** (**tongue**) can distinguish the tastiness of **food**. Elihu then challenges the friends to use their minds wisely to ascertain the difference between his position and Job's. As learned men, they should be able to pick out the position that is **right** (*mišpāṭ*; v 4*a*) and **good** (*ṭôb*; v 4*b*).

2. Job Is Making Preposterous Claims (34:5-9)

In Elihu's thinking, Job's speeches sound like they are spoken by a wicked person. He cannot believe that Job is so scornful of God.

■ **5-6** Elihu lays out his case against Job by first noting four claims he heard Job make in the dialogue section. These are not exact quotations, but some are very close. First, Job had claimed he was **innocent** of wrongdoing (**I am *in the right***) (v 5*a*; → 9:15, 20-21; 13:18; 27:5-6). By this Job meant he was not a sinner worthy of the kind of suffering he was experiencing.

A second claim was that God had denied him justice (lit. **God** [*El*] **has *removed my* justice**) (34:5*b*; → 27:2). God's refusal to speak to him had left his innocence unproven. As long as Job's status with God was unclear, he was deprived of justice.

The translation of Job's third claim is difficult, but perhaps something like the following is what Elihu intended: ***Concerning my judgment, (people say,)*** "I *lie*" (v 6a). Job's physical condition led people to assume that he was a sinner experiencing God's punishment. His claims of innocence, therefore, sounded phony and untruthful. People thought he was lying. But Job had steadfastly maintained that he was not a liar (6:28; 24:25).

Fourth, Job had made claims about being a target for God's arrows: **My arrow *is* incurable (*though I am*) *without transgression*** (34:6b; → 6:4; 9:17; 16:12-13). His belief that he was without transgression appears frequently throughout the book (→ 33:9).

■ **7-9** Elihu is dumbfounded that Job would speak as he does in 34:5-6. What sane person would make such outrageous claims against God? Yet Job's criticism of God has seemingly become a regular part of his life, as natural as drinking **water** (v 7). He gorges himself on mockery and **scorn**, which he then uses to lambaste God.

In Elihu's thinking, Job is not just a lone sinner with a personal complaint against God. He has now joined **company with** all the **evildoers** who actively criticize God (v 8a). He is like **the wicked** person (v 8b) in Ps 1:1 who "sits in the seat of scoffers" (RSV). To drive home his point, Elihu notes one additional statement he has heard Job make. Job had claimed that **God** (*Elohim*) does not reward the righteous. Therefore, there is no benefit in serving him (Job 34:9). No doubt, Elihu is referring to Job's comments about God being unjust and rewarding the wicked rather than the righteous (9:22-23; 21:7-26; 24:1-17; 30:26). If Elihu's characterization of Job is correct here, then the Examiner certainly was wrong about Job in the prologue (1:9). Job does serve God "for nothing" because God does not reward the righteous.

3. It Is Unthinkable to Accuse God of Being Unjust (34:10-15)

God has always upheld justice in his governance of the world.

■ **10-12** Elihu now begins a defense of the character of God. He exhorts the three friends to **listen** to him, praising their wisdom in these matters (v 10a). He insists by means of an oath (**Far be it from God** [v 10b]) that **God** (*El*) cannot possibly be accused of acting unjustly. God treats every human being according to their ways—rewarding the righteous and punishing the wicked. If he did not act in this manner, he would cease to be God, for he would be guilty of **perverting justice** (v 12b). In speaking this way, Elihu knows he has a sympathetic audience, for he has heard each of the friends make a similar point about God's judgment of the righteous and the wicked (8:3, 20; 15:20-35; 18:5-21; 20:4-29; 24:18-24).

■ **13-15** God answers to no one. The rhetorical questions in 34:13 emphasize God's sovereignty and total control over the entire world. This is not because some supervisor **appointed him** to take charge, but because he created it himself and continues to sustain it (v 14). As Creator, God has embedded his order into the world the way he likes it. This includes the way justice is meted out to the righteous and the wicked (vv 11-12). Human attempts to criticize God's order and accuse him of being unjust are off the mark. Humans simply do not understand how God operates.

Elihu emphasizes the point regarding God's control by describing how dependent humanity is on God. God breathed his very **breath** (v 14)—the "breath of life" (Gen 2:7)—into human beings when he created them. But he also has the power to destroy them. If he **withdrew** his **breath** at any time, **all *flesh* would perish together;** ***humanity*** **would return to the dust** from which it was formed (Job 34:15). Such is the awesome power that God holds over the world.

The phrase **all *flesh*** (*kol-bāśār*) in v 15*a* could be limited to just human beings because of the parallel with ***humanity*** (*'ādām*) in v 15*b*. But in some passages it refers to all created beings—animals as well as humans (e.g., Gen 7:15-16, 21; 8:17; 9:11, 15-17; Lev 17:14; etc.). Either interpretation is possible.

4. Job, if God Is All-Powerful, He Is Also Just (34:16-30)

God sees the righteousness or wickedness of all people and nations and treats them accordingly at the appropriate time. No one escapes God's power to judge, not even those in high places.

■ **16-20** Elihu now turns his attention back to Job, beginning with a rhetorical question that asks whether a person who **hates justice** can effectively **govern** (v 17*a*). If God is unjust, as Job claims, he is unqualified and unable to rule the universe. Real governing, in Elihu's thinking, can only be accomplished by one who is **just** and fair (vv 11-12), as well as righteous and powerful (v 17). Elihu knows Job agrees with him that God is all-powerful, for he has listened to his previous remarks on this topic (12:7-25; 26:5-14). So he cannot understand why Job denies God's justice. If God is omnipotent, he can do whatever he pleases. He can create or he can destroy (34:13-15). He can act justly or unjustly. The fact that he suddenly deposes **wicked** people in high places (vv 18-20) is a sure sign that he has chosen to govern his world in ways that are just.

Just like Job (ch 12), Elihu gives several examples of God's power over people of high standing. **Kings, nobles, princes,** and **high officials** (34:18-19) have no special status before God. He can take away their lives **in an instant, in the middle of the night** (v 20) if he evaluates them as ***vile*** and **wicked** (v 18). God requires of them the same moral standards that he expects of everyone else. And the reason for this is because all human beings are God's creatures—**the work of his hands** (v 19*c*). They are completely dependent on him for their existence (vv 14-15).

Thus, these rulers are obligated to obey their Creator and to rule justly as God rules. Their obedience is the criterion that God uses to judge them, not their social standing among other human beings. By ruling the world in this way, God avoids Job's charge of favoring the wicked over the righteous (21:6-26; 24:1-17) and thus being unjust.

The Hebrew *bĕliyyā'al* (v 18) means **worthless** in some passages, but in this context the parallel with **wicked** calls for a stronger meaning, such as ***vile*** (also Deut 13:13 [14 HB]; Judg 19:22; 20:13; 1 Sam 2:12; Nah 1:11).

■ **21-22** In Job 34:21-30 Elihu offers a series of examples to illustrate the tremendous might of God's power. The first is God's ability to see everything that takes place on earth. No one can **hide** from him (v 22). Even the ***darkness*** and the ***deepest darkness*** that Job longed for in 3:4-5 cannot conceal evildoers from God's penetrating gaze. Job has already stated his agreement with Elihu on this point (7:20; 14:16; 31:4).

The terms ***darkness*** (*ḥōšek*) and ***deepest darkness*** (*ṣalmāwet*) (34:22a) are sometimes used as synonyms for Sheol (10:21). But here (as in 12:22) they refer to the darkest imaginable place that humans may hide to escape God's power (such as in the depths of a mine shaft; 28:3). But alas, no such place exists, for God sees everywhere.

■ **23** Another example of God's power is his authority to establish the times for human judgment. Job had complained in 24:1 that God does not set regular times for human beings to be judged, and therefore the wicked escape the punishment they are due. Elihu's answer is: ***For it is not for human beings to set a time to go before God*** [*El*] ***in judgment***. By this he means, human beings cannot pressure God to speed up or delay judgment. God sets his own times as he sees fit. There is widespread agreement that *'ôd* (lit. "yet") should be emended to *mô'ēd* (***time***). The translation above also requires a grammatical emendation of *yāśîm* to the infinitive construct *śîm* or *lāśîm* (***to set***; Gordis 1978, 390).

■ **24-25** A third example of God's power is his treatment of **the mighty** (34:24; a reference to the wicked people in high places mentioned in vv 18-19). They may be extremely powerful over others, but they are no match for God. He **smashes** them and **overthrows** them, leaving them **crushed** (v 25). He does so even without investigating their individual cases, for he already knows everything they have done (vv 21, 25). At the same time he is destroying some, he raises up others to take their places who are more worthy (v 24). The phrase ***at night*** (v 25) indicates that God's actions against the mighty are sudden and unexpected (a repetition of v 20).

■ **26-28** When God does choose to punish the mighty, he does so publicly so that all will know that **wickedness** has terrible consequences (v 26). The primary sin Elihu mentions is the mistreatment of **the poor** and **the needy** (v 28). Elihu is echoing here a major tenet of OT teachings that is found in the Law (Lev 19:9-10; Deut 15:11), the Prophets (Isa 3:14-15; Amos 2:6-7), and the Psalms (Pss 41:1 [2 HB]; 140:12 [13 HB]). God wants **the poor** to be cared for.

Job agrees with this and has already noted his own compassion for the poor (Job 29:12-13, 15-16; 31:16-23). When the poor are mistreated, they cry out to God for help, and he comes to their rescue. Thus, the mighty who profit off the maltreatment of the poor find themselves in opposition to God, for "God always sides with the poor" (Hartley 1988, 459).

■ **29-30** Elihu acknowledges that not all God's actions are visible to human view. Sometimes God chooses to work quietly behind the scenes. This is in answer to Job's complaint in 23:3, 8-9 that he cannot find God. But whether visible or not, he is still in charge, and he is constantly working to prevent wicked people in high places from oppressing others. Elihu's point is that God's superior power over **nations** and **individuals** provides the assurance to humanity that justice will always prevail.

5. Job, You Are a Rebel against God (34:31-37)

Job, the three friends, and Elihu have all expressed their opinions about the reasons for Job's suffering. Elihu longs for God to appear and settle the debate once and for all. If God would agree to do so, Elihu is confident that God would find Job guilty of spiritual rebellion.

■ **31-32** The interpretation of vv 31-32 is very problematic. Some regard these verses as a question of a general nature that Elihu then applies to Job in v 33: "For has anyone said to God [*El*], . . . ?" (NRSV). Others emend the text to an imperative and move the interrogative *He* on *he'āmar* to the previous word: "Indeed you should say to God [*Eloah*], . . ." (Clines 2006, 745). The former could be understood as a subtle way of getting Job to make a confession of sin, but since Elihu is not prone to subtlety, the latter makes better sense. Elihu is challenging Job to admit his sin, ask God to show him where he has erred, and promise God he will not sin **again** (v 32).

■ **33** Elihu's rhetorical question in v 33*a* is difficult to translate, but it seems to be a rejection of Job's claim of innocence. He should not expect God to judge him on the basis of his claims, for God sets his own standards for judgment. Further, why should God acknowledge that Job is right **when you reject (him)**? Elihu admits that the decision about what to do in this situation is not his to make. Job will have to decide for himself. Elihu would like to know, though, if Job has additional information he has not yet shared. If so, he should speak his mind now.

■ **34-35** Elihu now draws upon the wisdom tradition to support his criticism of Job. Both Eliphaz (5:27; 15:10) and Bildad (8:8-10) have already claimed the same support for their positions. Elihu calls the spokespersons for this tradition **men of understanding** (lit. "men of heart") and **wise men** (v 34). They are the people who have a true grasp of the nature of God and the world. Their understanding is flawless. If they were present, their evaluation of Job would be as follows: **Job speaks without knowledge; his words lack insight** (v 35). In like manner, if the friends consider themselves to be *wise men*, they, too, will acknowledge the truth of this evaluation.

■ **36-37** Some scholars think that the words attributed to the sages in v 35 continue on into vv 36-37 (Clines 2006, 784), but the use of the phrase **among us** (v 37) implies that these words are Elihu's beliefs. His wish is that God would conduct such a thorough examination of Job that there would no longer be any question about Job's guilt. Many times throughout the dialogues Job claimed moral innocence, but he talked like a wicked person. Elihu desires that God would put an end to these false claims once and for all. Ironically, in the dialogues Job also requested an examination from God, but he was confident the results would be different. If and when God examined him, he would discover that Job's character was of the same quality as gold (23:10).

Elihu is agreeing here with charges already made by the three friends. Eliphaz accused Job of "wickedness" and *iniquity* (22:5), and Bildad and Zophar strongly hinted that Job was *an evildoer* (18:21) and "wicked" (20:29) by pointing out that Job was suffering the same punishment that other wicked people suffered. However, only Elihu uses the word **rebellion** (34:37; *pešaʻ*) to describe Job's relationship to God. Thus, he places his own distinctive stamp on the accusations against Job.

The meaning of v 37 is difficult. The MT reads in the second clause: **he claps [his hands] among us**, perhaps indicating that Job had gestured with his hands to emphasize certain points throughout the dialogues. But this seems rather superficial compared to the two clauses on either side. A better interpretation is to emend *yispôq* (**he claps**) to *yaspîq* (**he doubts/questions** in Aramaic) and connect **rebellion** with the second clause rather than the first (Clines 2006, 763). This yields: *For* **he adds** *unto* **his sin,** **he doubts (his)** **rebellion** *in our midst, and he* **multiplies his words against God** (*El*). The entire verse, then, is a further indictment against Job that accuses him of rebellion and verbal attacks against God.

D. Elihu's Third Speech (35:1-16)

Elihu's third speech is short and to the point. Its purpose is to correct some earlier comments made by Job regarding the nature of God.

There are three sections to this speech:
1. Job, You Are Wrong to Claim That God Is Unjust and There Is No Benefit in Serving Him (35:1-8)
2. God Does Not Answer the Prayers of the Wicked (35:9-13)
3. Neither Will He Answer Your Complaints, Job, Because They Are Meaningless (35:14-16)

1. Job, You Are Wrong to Claim That God Is Unjust and There Is No Benefit in Serving Him (35:1-8)

Job is wrong to think that his righteousness somehow benefits God so much that God is obligated to bless him. No one can force God to do anything, for he is far greater than humankind. Job should consider, instead, how his righteousness benefits others.

■ **1** For comments on the introductory formula → 3:2.

■ **2-4** To begin his third speech, Elihu returns to two points he made earlier in ch 34. The first addresses Job's claim that God is unjust in his treatment of human beings (→ 34:5): **You say, "I am** *more* **right** *than* **God** [*El*]" (35:2*b*). Such a claim is preposterous according to Elihu (34:12). Criticizing God for how he judges individuals reveals a serious flaw in Job's understanding of God's justice. Elihu's second point (35:3) echoes 34:9. Job had claimed there was no benefit in serving God because God rewarded the wicked rather than the righteous. Therefore, why should he strive to be righteous and avoid sinning? Elihu is confident he has a better answer than the **friends** (35:4).

■ **5-8** Elihu's answer to Job's question in v 3 begins with an exhortation to **look up** in the sky (v 5). The height and grandeur of **the heavens** are a reminder that God's ways are far higher than those of human beings. Many times they are beyond human comprehension. Elihu then makes his point. Because God operates at a higher level than human beings, he is neither benefited nor harmed by our actions. Thus, we cannot compel him by means of our **righteousness** or **wickedness** to conduct himself in certain ways (v 8). He is sovereign, and he decides how and when he will act, regardless of our desires or pleas (→ 22:3; Rom 11:35). Nevertheless, even though human actions do not impact God, we should choose **righteousness** over **wickedness** because of how these affect **other people**. All human actions have *social* consequences for good or for evil.

Elihu's purpose is to defend God's method of justice against Job's claims of personal mistreatment. Job believed his righteousness should be rewarded with success and well-being. Instead, God had afflicted him with extreme suffering. Thus, God is not just. Elihu's answer is that God's ways are simply beyond Job's level of understanding. Job should be more concerned with how his **righteousness** benefits **other people**, than how it impacts God or himself.

2. God Does Not Answer the Prayers of the Wicked (35:9-13)

Job has complained on more than one occasion that God does not respond to his prayers. His requests for a meeting with God and for an explanation of his sufferings have been met with only silence. Elihu's answer to these complaints is that the fault lies with Job, not with God. God only answers prayers from those who trust him. Prayers such as Job's that are arrogant and self-centered will not receive a response.

■ **9-13** Many times **people cry out** to God for relief from their troubles (v 9). Job himself had uttered such cries in his previous speeches (19:7; 30:20-23), but so far God had refused to answer him (13:24). Elihu's reason for God's silence is simple. God does not answer cries for help that are self-centered. People naturally groan with self-pity when experiencing pain and trouble, but God does not regard these outcries as legitimate prayers. They are no better than the groans of animals when in pain.

Real prayer is motivated by trust in the one true **God** (*Eloah*) who is the Creator of all (**my Maker** [35:10*a*]). It seeks to be in relationship with him rather than pleading for divine favors. **Who gives songs in the night** (v 10*b*) is ambiguous. It could refer to God's ability to uplift people's spirits in times of distress (Clines 2006, 790) or to his placement of the stars that *sing* over his creation (38:7; Gordis 1978, 401).

Elihu believes that God only answers those who truly seek him in reverence and humility. Prayers from those who are arrogant and refuse to acknowledge his sovereignty are never answered (35:12) because **God** (*El*) considers them **empty/ worthless** (v 13). Thus, the reason Job has not received an answer from God is due to the self-centered nature of his requests.

Scholars disagree over the translation of *min* in v 11*a* and v 11*b*. Some see it as the comparative (**more than** . . . **wiser than** . . . [NIV, NRSV]) indicating God's greater revelation to human beings than to the animals and birds. Others opt for the meaning "by" (***who teaches us by means of the animals . . . , and by means of the birds***; see Pope 1973, 264-65; Balentine 2006, 588-89). This recalls Job's statement about how the animal kingdom has much to teach us (12:7). Either meaning is possible. The former, which places the emphasis on humanity's greater capacity to understand its suffering, seems better in this context, although the latter is a common concept in the wisdom literature (e.g., Prov 30:24-31).

3. Neither Will He Answer Your Complaints, Job, Because They Are Meaningless (35:14-16)

Job will have to change his attitude toward God if he expects God to listen to him.

■ **14-16** There is disagreement over whether vv 14*b*-15 are a restatement of Job's position or an additional exhortation by Elihu to Job. The former seems preferable as these are all statements that Job has made previously. He has complained on several occasions that he is prepared to defend himself, but he cannot find God to speak to him (13:18-24; 23:3-9; 31:35-37). Further, he has criticized God for not punishing the wicked (12:6; 21:7-26; 24:1-17). The problem, as Elihu sees it, is that Job is speaking **without knowledge** (35:16). His **words** are "empty" (v 13; *šāw'*) of meaning, just like the words of "the wicked" (vv 12-13). Therefore, God sees no need to answer him. Job will have to change his arrogant attitude (v 12) before God will speak to him.

E. Elihu's Fourth Speech (36:1—37:24)

Elihu's final speech begins by focusing on God's use of adversity to correct human behavior. The response one makes to God's disciplinary measures determines whether one experiences life or death. The truly wicked suffer an early death. But those who accept the divine discipline and change their ways are rewarded with a blessed life. This sounds very similar to the doctrine of the two ways, emphasized repeatedly in the wisdom literature (e.g., Prov 1:32-33; 4:18-19; Ps 1) and taught frequently by Jesus (e.g., Matt 7:13-14, 24-27). Elihu then makes the application to Job, encouraging him to reject the way of the wicked and turn to God who is wooing him.

The speech then takes a major turn. God's power and wisdom in nature are highlighted with examples from the weather. God uses his great meteorological accomplishments, which humans do not understand, to either bless or punish human beings. Finally, Elihu asks Job if he understands how God does these things and if he is capable of performing the same feats.

Elihu has five main points:
1. I Will Speak on God's Behalf (36:1-4)
2. God Corrects the Righteous and Punishes the Wicked (36:5-15)

3. Job, Quit Pursuing Your Own Worthless Solutions to Your Problems (36:16-21)
  4. God Is Awesome in Power and Beyond Our Understanding (36:22—37:13)
  5. Job, Can You Do What God Can Do? (37:14-24)

1. I Will Speak on God's Behalf (36:1-4)

Elihu begins by stressing his credentials.

■ 1 Perhaps for literary variety, the introductory formula is slightly different from the normal form (→ 3:2).

■ 2-4 In the introduction (36:2-4) to Elihu's fourth and final speech, he makes three points to bolster his credentials as a legitimate participant in the discussion.

First, he is speaking **in God's behalf** (*Eloah*) (v 2). Since God has not spoken, he will defend what he believes is God's position.

Second, he is speaking for all the wise people in the world, for he has acquired a wide range of knowledge **from afar** (v 3*a*), meaning from sources in other countries. Whereas the friends have argued that their views are supported by the wisdom traditions that stretch far back in time, Elihu finds backing geographically from the wisdom traditions in other cultures. He does not explain how he, as a young man, has accessed these foreign sources, but apparently he is either widely traveled or he has talked with foreigners visiting his home country.

Third, he will prove that God (**my Maker**) is right in his governance of the world (v 3*b*). And by implication, he will show that his own views are correct since they are the same as God's. Thus, Job better listen carefully because **one who has perfect knowledge** (v 4) is standing in front of him. By **perfect** [*tĕmîm*] **knowledge**, Elihu means "complete knowledge about a subject that is free from error" (→ 12:4, where this adjective is applied to Job's moral character).

Who is this person with **perfect knowledge**? Some think Elihu is referring to *God* based on the application of the phrase to God in 37:16 (Terrien 1954, 1155). Others hold that Elihu is simply pointing out his own "honesty and integrity" (Clines 2006, 855). But the majority of commentators correctly believe that Elihu is claiming superior knowledge for himself that is of the same quality as God's. As such, it reveals an attitude that is smug, overly self-confident, and bordering on egotism. He thinks he is the only one who knows the truth about Job's situation. And he sees a need to defend the integrity of God against Job's criticisms and complaints (34:37). As it turns out, some of Elihu's comments in the latter part of his speech (36:22—37:24) are very similar to God's remarks in chs 38—41.

2. God Corrects the Righteous and Punishes the Wicked (36:5-15)

In this section Elihu draws a clear distinction between the truly wicked who have no desire to change and the once righteous who have drifted off into sin.

God seeks to bring both to repentance, but only the latter actually make a move toward God.

■ **5-6** The translation of v 5 is very problematic. Scholars have proposed numerous emendations, but none has gained a consensus (for a full discussion see Clines 2006, 810-11). The simplest translation with the least amount of emendation is the following: **Behold** God [*El*] **is mighty but *he does not reject*,** "he is mighty in strength of understanding" (lit. "heart" [NRSV]). Even though this rendering is uncertain, the point of Elihu's remark is clear from the context that follows. God is so **mighty** he can do whatever he wants to do. Witness his awesome activities throughout nature (36:26—37:24). Yet he restrains his might when appropriate so that his justice and mercy will prevail, for he is a just God who does not reject anyone who desires his help.

In 36:6 Elihu shows how God's justice operates in dealing with humanity. God distinguishes between the truly **wicked** who are opposed to him, thus deserving of harsh punishment, and **the afflicted** righteous who sometimes drift away from him and need his corrective measures. God brings an early death to the former but provides *justice* to the latter when they turn from their sin and toward him. The actual application of this principle to Job's situation will come in vv 16-21. Elihu desires to help Job determine his relationship to God so that he can take the appropriate action to free himself from his suffering.

■ **7-12** According to Elihu, God does not abandon those who desire to be **righteous** (v 7*a*). Even if they sin against him and become entangled in the consequences of their bad choices (v 8), he encourages their repentance by disciplining them. **He tells them what they have done** (v 9*a*), and **commands *that they turn away from their iniquity*** (v 10*b*).

Their future well-being, then, is dependent on their response to God's instructions. **If they obey and serve him,** he will reward them with **prosperity** and **contentment** (v 11). But if they do not listen, they will *cross the river* [*of death*; → 33:18] **and die without knowledge** (36:12). They will die an early death because they have not appropriated for themselves the knowledge God has given them. The word **correction** (*mûsār*; v 10*a*) is the same word used by Eliphaz when speaking of God's discipline (→ 5:17). God sometimes uses suffering as a disciplinary measure to wake people up and lead them to repentance.

Verse 7*bc* of ch 36 does not mean that God rewards a repentant sinner with kingship. Rather, **he *seats* them *with* kings** (emphasis mine). That is, he frees them from the **chains** (lit. "fetters") and **cords of affliction** (v 8) that bind them and raises them to an exalted position of importance and worth such as kings enjoy. Such is the nature of God's justice.

■ **13-15** The subject of these verses is **the godless in heart**, that is, the truly wicked (v 13*a*; → v 6). These people avoid interacting with God. Even when they suffer the consequences of their sins, **they do not cry** to God **for help** (v 13*b*), for that would be to admit that God exists and that he can help them. Instead, they **harbor** resentment (lit. "lay up anger"). This phrase is unusual, but it probably means to keep one's anger bottled up and festering within (→ 22:22, "lay up . . . words").

The life span of a wicked person is very short, not even surviving into adulthood (36:14a). But God makes earnest and repeated attempts to call all sinners, whether truly wicked or only currently backslidden, to turn away from their sinfulness and come back to him. Using **affliction** as his tool, he "opens their ears" (v 15b NRSV) to the fate that lies ahead of them if they continue on their present course of action (→ vv 8-10).

The meaning of v 14b is unclear. Many render qĕdēšîm as referring to **male prostitutes** and interpret the clause as a comment on the shameful condition that engulfs the wicked at the end of their lives: "they die among the prostitutes." Others follow the LXX reading of "angels" (qĕdōšîm), placing the death of the wicked "among the angels," that is, caused by the angels. There is not enough evidence to provide a definitive interpretation, but in either case, the early death of the wicked is inevitable.

3. Job, Quit Pursuing Your Own Worthless Solutions to Your Problems (36:16-21)

Most commentators struggle over the meaning of vv 16-21 because they are extremely difficult to translate. The interpretation offered below seems to fit the context, but a number of questions remain. In general, this is a passage where Elihu addresses Job directly about his present situation and warns him about the pathway he is on. He believes God is trying to teach Job by means of his suffering (→ vv 8-12). Job needs to follow God's instructions rather than pursue his own efforts.

■ **16-18** He *[God] seeks to persuade you away from the mouth* of distress (v 16a). God is trying to lead Job out of his inner turmoil into **a spacious place free from restriction** where his **table** will be **laden with choice food** (v 16bc; lit. "full of fatness"). These phrases are metaphors for the abundant, blessed life that awaits Job if he will follow God's guidance. But Job will not listen to God or anyone else. He is more interested in what he believes are flaws in God's administration of justice.

You are *full of* the judgment *of* the wicked (v 17a). The NIV translators regard this statement as a comment on the reason for Job's suffering. He has received **the judgment due the wicked** because he is wicked himself. An alternative interpretation is that Elihu is criticizing Job for being "obsessed with" (NRSV) God's treatment of **the wicked** (21:6-26; 24:1-17). His attention has been riveted on God's supposed lack of **judgment and justice** (36:17b). This has hindered him from honestly examining his own life. Either interpretation is possible, but the latter is more likely, based on v 18.

Elihu is concerned that Job is on the verge of becoming a scoffer. *Indeed beware lest it (your criticism of God's unjust treatment of the wicked) lead you away into scoffing (at God)* (v 18a). Elihu is also afraid that Job will consider the costliness of the ransom needed for his restoration (i.e., his confession of sin; → 33:24) too great for him to meet. Thus he admonishes Job, "Do not let the greatness of the ransom turn you aside" (36:18*b* NRSV). The NIV renders *sepeq* as **riches** (instead of ***scoffing***) and *kōper* as **bribe** (instead of ***ransom***), but these seem irrelevant to Job's situation and thus not likely.

■ **19-21** In v 19 Elihu raises questions about Job's ability to get himself out of **distress**. Neither his **cry for help** (the NIV emends *šûaʿ* [**cry**] to *šôaʿ* [**wealth**]) nor his **mighty efforts** will accomplish this. Elihu also urges Job not to seek death (**the night**) as a means of escape from his suffering (v 20*a*). On several occasions Job has expressed a longing for a quick death (3:20-23; 7:21; 10:20-22; 17:13-16). In these passages the words **night**, **darkness**, and ***Sheol*** are used interchangeably as metaphors for death, but death is not the answer to Job's problems. The NRSV translation of 36:20*b* ("when peoples are cut off in their place") seems to fit the context, but the Hebrew is very awkward and most scholars are cautious about settling on a good translation.

Finally, Elihu warns Job, "Beware! Do not turn to iniquity" (v 21*a* NRSV). Elihu believes Job's iniquity is why he is suffering in the first place. The message of these three verses is that God is the only one who can relieve Job's suffering, and thus he should mind God's instructions.

4. God Is Awesome in Power and Beyond Our Understanding (36:22—37:13)

At v 22 Elihu begins a transition from Job's shortcomings to God's awesomeness. He exhorts Job to consider God's power and wisdom and remember to praise him (vv 22-25). The remainder of this section (36:26—37:13) describes various aspects of God's power in nature, using the weather as his prime example. He also mentions God's interaction with humanity in a few places. In the final verse (37:13) Elihu provides a reason for God's actions.

36:19-25

■ **22-25** In 36:22 Elihu describes two attributes of **God** (*El*). The first is his omnipotence. God is extremely powerful. No one stands above him to direct his ways or to evaluate his deeds (v 23). He is over all and free to do as he pleases. Thus, Job is not qualified to criticize God concerning his justice. Instead, Job's attitude should be one of praise. **Remember to extol his work** (v 24*a*). Possibly, Elihu is thinking of the type of hymnic poetry found in many ancient religions that praises the deity. Numerous examples of praise to Yahweh appear in the Hebrew psalms (e.g., Pss 8, 19, 29, 33, 46—48, etc.).

Second, God is a master **teacher** without equal (Job 36:22*b*), and the universe is his textbook. His lessons derive precisely from his powerful deeds that people have witnessed in nature and throughout human history (v 25). God teaches by doing marvelous things, and he has done so on countless occasions so that **all humanity** (v 25*a*) is aware of his works. **From afar** (v 25*b*) refers to God's transcendence—the great gulf between the divine and the human. This great divide prevents us from understanding the full extent of his works.

■ **26** "Surely God is great" (NRSV). Verse 26 begins with a resounding, unequivocal affirmation of God's exalted status. He is awesome in power and wisdom, as the following verses demonstrate, and he is eternal with regard to time. For this reason, he is **beyond our understanding** (also 37:5). There is and will always be a mystery about God that humans cannot comprehend. Elihu is not saying anything new here, for all three friends have voiced similar comments about God's greatness and mystery (5:9; 8:8-9; 11:7). And this is one point on which Job agrees with them as well (9:10).

■ **27-28** These verses contain numerous translation problems, but the general sense is that God provides the rain that waters the earth. He does so by drawing up **drops of water** (36:27) that he then fashions into rain **clouds** that **pour down** their **showers** on humanity in abundance (v 28). Ancient people did not know the scientific explanation for how clouds form and produce rain, but they did believe that God (or "a specific god" in a polytheistic culture) was responsible for providing the water they needed to grow their crops.

■ **29-30 Who can understand** God's works in the heavens (v 29a)? No one! The constantly changing cloud formations, the loud crashes of thunder that seem to come from deep within God's heavenly **pavilion** (v 29b), and the bright *flashes of* lightning (v 30a) that reveal every hidden thing, all contribute to the awesome mystery surrounding God.

Verse 30b is literally he "covers the roots of the sea" (NRSV). Ancient people thought of "the roots of the sea" as the base of the high mountains at the edge of the earth that held up the sky dome, but Elihu does not mention what God uses to cover these roots. Perhaps Elihu means that the **lightning** is so bright that it illuminates to the **depths**/*bottom* of the sea. In that case the verb "covers" (*ksh*) is better rendered "uncovers/reveals" according to some scholars (Clines 2006, 831). The **lightning** in v 30 is probably sheet lightning, while that in v 32 is lightning that strikes the ground (Clines 2006, 872).

■ **31** *For with them* he governs *the people* (v 31a). The antecedent of *them* is God's control of the weather as described in vv 26-30. By means of sending the rain showers to water the fields, God **provides food in abundance** (v 31b). The verb for **governs** (*dyn*) is usually used in the sense of "exacting judgment," but it also carries the more general meaning of "govern, rule, administer" (Gen 49:16; Zech 3:7). Thus, God's proper governance of the world provides food for the hungry.

■ **32-33** These verses return to God's control of the **lightning** (v 32; lit. "light") and **thunder** (v 33). Even before the rain descends, the **lightning** and **thunder** announce the arrival of God's presence through an approaching storm.

Verse 33 is very difficult to translate. The Hebrew *miqneh* usually refers to one's livestock, such as **cattle** or sheep (→ 1:3), but that seems strange in this context. Many scholars now regard the word as related to the root *qn'* (lit. "envy, be jealous"; Clines 2006, 834), yielding this literal reading: "His crash (of thunder) announces concerning him, the jealousy of (his) anger (announces) concerning that which is coming." Other possibilities for 36:33b based on emendations are: "the jealousy of (his) anger (announces) the (approaching) storm" (Gordis 1978, 424), or "the jealousy of (his) anger (announces) against iniquity" (see NJPS, NRSV). The correct rendering remains uncertain.

■ **37:1-4** Just the thought of God's awesome display of power through a thunderstorm causes an emotional reaction in Elihu. His **heart . . . leaps** within him (v 1). His call to **listen** (pl. imperative, v 2) is likely doing double duty as an admonition both to heed his words and to pay attention to the distant rumblings of an approaching thunderstorm. As a storm cloud approaches, the **lightning** (lit. "light") flashes across the entire sky, seemingly stretching **to the** *edges* **of the earth** (v 3). Claps of thunder follow, rumbling and echoing across the heavens. The sound is loud and majestic. To all who will listen, this is truly the voice of God speaking through a storm (see Pss 18:13 [14 HB]; 29:3-9).

■ **5-8** Elihu repeats his belief that there is a mystery about **God's** [*El*] **. . . ways** that are **beyond our understanding** (Job 37:5; 36:26, 29). The thunderstorm is just one example, but there are many others such as **the snow** and **the rain shower** (37:6). Through these marvelous works in nature, God controls the activities of both **people** (v 7*b*) and **animals** (v 8*a*). When he is active in the heavens, his creatures must seek shelter in their houses and **dens** (v 8*b*).

Verse 7*a* is literally "he seals up the hand of every man" (RSV). Many scholars remove the word "hand" by emending *bĕyad* to the preposition *ba'ad* (as in 9:7), yielding "he seals up every human" (lit.). But this is not necessary. The meaning in either case is that God's storms cause people to refrain from working. They stay indoors, just like the animals of 37:8. The NIV uses a paraphrase, **he stops all people from their labor**, but strangely it moves the clause to v 7*b*.

■ **9-12** The list of God's marvelous deeds goes on. The **tempest** (v 9*a*), the bitter **cold** (v 9*b*), and **ice** (v 10*a*) are added to the **moisture** (v 11*a*) and **lightning** (v 11*b*) from his previous comments. Figuratively, they are like servants that **do whatever he commands them** (v 12*c*). And whenever they appear, they reveal God's mighty power and mysteriousness. In these verses Elihu draws upon some ancient conceptions about the weather. God was thought to have **chambers** (v 9*a*) in the heavens where he stored his **winds** (v 9*b*) until such time as they were needed. And his **breath** (v 10*a*), as a metaphor for the wind, could be either very hot from the east and south (4:9) or very cold from the north (37:9-10).

■ **13** Elihu closes this section with three reasons why God causes the weather to occur in a variety of ways: "Whether for correction, or for his land, or for love, he causes it to happen" (NRSV). The first reason is literally "for the rod." The rod can be a symbol of authority, discipline, or punishment (9:34; 21:9). Here Elihu probably intends some combination of all three. God sends the powerful thunderstorms and other weather-related occurrences to punish the wicked, to discipline those who need to change, and to remind all humanity of his divine authority. The phrase "for correction" (NRSV) encapsulates this well.

The second reason God acts is "for his land" (NRSV). This phrase is somewhat ambiguous, but it probably refers to the land's need of water to produce crops and vegetation. Without God's provision through rain and snow, the earth would be a barren desert.

The third reason God acts is for **love**. The word **love** (*ḥesed*) is the great covenantal term that expresses God's faithful commitment to his people and his desire to shower them with his goodness. Job experienced that kind of love from God earlier in his life (10:12; 29:2-6), but now he sees no evidence of it. However, Elihu is not thinking here of the Israelite covenant or of God's love for an individual such as Job, but rather of God's faithfulness to care for his entire creation. The weather is one example of that.

Interestingly, the first two reasons for God's actions recognize that God does some things because there is a need. But the third one emphasizes that sometimes God acts just because he wants to. Without any explanation or justification, he involves himself in the world in ways that seem appropriate to him. His freedom to love as he pleases makes sense to him but is often "beyond our understanding" (v 5).

5. Job, Can You Do What God Can Do? (37:14-24)

In the final section of Elihu's fourth speech, he chides Job for not respecting God's power and wisdom. "Can you do what God can do?" he asks. The answer is obvious in Elihu's mind because God is so much greater than any human being. Elihu's final words return to the topic of God's awesomeness and the need for all humans to fear him.

■ **14 Stop and consider** is the underlying theme of Elihu's entire speech. If Job would quit criticizing the way God (*El*) runs the world and consider carefully his awesome deeds, he would develop a proper appreciation and respect for God that is now lacking.

■ **15-18** These verses contain three rhetorical questions aimed directly at Job. Their subject matter is the works of **God** (*Eloah*) in the heavens (the same topic as in vv 2-12). Elihu asks if Job knows how God operates the various components of the weather, such as **the clouds** (v 15*a*), the **lightning** (v 15*b*), and **the skies** (v 18*a*). The implied answer is that Job does not, and neither do any other human beings.

Verse 17 is a subtle slam against Job's complaining. Like every other person, Job gets hot when the land is under the influence of a southerly breeze. If such a minor weather occurrence can bring great discomfort to Job, how can he claim to know more about the operations of the weather than God **who has perfect knowledge** (v 16*b*)? And if he has more knowledge than God, why does he not change the weather to suit his needs instead of just enduring the heat?

In v 18*b* Elihu speaks of a ***cast mirror***. Before the usage of glass in mirrors, reflections were seen by means of a round, polished piece of metal, such as **bronze** or copper. Elihu is equating the dome over the sky (Gen 1:6-7), which was thought to be a thin, hard piece of metal, to the hardness of a metal mirror.

■ **19-20** Job has spoken twice in the past of his desire to present his case before God (Job 13:18; 23:4). He is confident he could convince God of his innocence if he were given the opportunity to speak. However, Elihu is not convinced Job knows what he is talking about. How can Job be so sure of himself when he is wrong about so many other things (33:8-30; 34:5-37; 35:1-16)?

So Elihu challenges Job to "teach" (37:19a NRSV) him and the three friends what they should say to God if they wished to confront him about some issue. How can humans engage God in debate when their knowledge is so much less than his? Human beings are in **darkness** compared to the light of God's great knowledge (v 19b).

Is someone going to tell God **that I want to speak** and I have some information that he needs to hear (v 20a)? Obviously not! **Would anyone ask to be swallowed up** (v 20b)? The translation of this clause is uncertain. The NIV and NRSV accept the meaning of the verb *blʿ* as "swallow/devour" following its other appearances in the book (2:3; 7:19; 8:18; 10:8; 20:15, 18). The sense would be: "Why would people attempt to confront God, knowing that this would cause their destruction?"

Some scholars suggest a different translation based on other meanings for *blʿ* and a different understanding of the context. For example, "Can a man speak when he is confused?" (Hartley 1988, 483); or "If a man talks, will He [God] be informed?" (Gordis 1978, 431-32). These other translations are possible, and the matter remains unsettled (for a full discussion see Clines 2006, 848).

■ **21-22** Some regard 37:21-22 as a description of the change in the weather from the storm clouds of 36:27—37:12 to the sunshine after the rain (Gordis 1978, 432-33). But more likely, Elihu is drawing an analogy between the brightness of the sun and the **awesome majesty** of God (*Eloah*; 37:22b). Just as it is impossible to look directly at the sun when it is at its brightest in a clear sky, so no one can look on the deeds of God (36:27—37:18) and comprehend the full extent of his **majesty** and **golden splendor** (lit. "gold"). He is too **awesome** and we are too puny. As Elihu said earlier, humans only view him "from afar" (36:25).

God's entrance into the world **out of the north** (37:22a; *ṣāpôn*) may refer to the mythological mountain of Ugaritic literature where the gods assembled (Isa 14:13). But as in Job 26:7 this could be a metaphor for "the highest heavens" (Clines 2006, 885). It could also be simply the direction from which God is coming in a storm at that moment (38:1; see Ezek 1:4).

■ **23** Elihu continues to remark on God's (*Shaddai*) majesty in Job 37:23. He is **exalted in power *and* justice**, and **he *will* not oppress *(one who has) an abundance of* righteousness**. This rendering follows the NRSV rather than the NIV, which attributes the quality of "abundant righteousness" to God. As Gordis notes, the verb **oppress** (*ʿnh*) requires a direct object (1978, 434), which is missing in the NIV.

While Elihu agrees with Job (23:3, 8-9) that God is **beyond our reach** (lit. "we cannot find him"), he does not accept Job's claim that God is punishing him even though he is righteous. Job's claim is a logical impossibility in Elihu's thinking, for God would not be just if he oppressed the righteous. Therefore, since God is **exalted in . . . justice**, Job must not be abundant in **righteousness**.

■ **24** The final verse of Elihu's speech is another difficult one that has produced a variety of translations (see NIV, NJPS, NRSV). Following the LXX we suggest this translation: **Therefore, people *fear* him; *indeed*, all the wise in heart *fear him*.** This rendering requires a change of *lō'* (**not**) to *lū'* (***indeed***) and of *yir'eh* (lit. "he sees") to *yirā'uhu* (= *yîrā'ûhû*; ***they fear***) and is supported by Gordis (1978, 434) and Clines (2006, 850-51). This verse builds upon the list of God's attributes in the preceding verses—"majesty" (37:22) and "power" and "justice" (v 23)—and is a fitting conclusion to Elihu's description of God's awesomeness throughout his fourth speech.

The proper human response to a God of this magnitude is summed up in one word—***fear***. Elihu is not speaking of just respect or reverence here. Those are admirable attitudes toward God, but Elihu means something much more. He intends for Job to know that God desires for people to tremble before his awesomeness and mysteriousness. His transcendence should draw forth an emotional and spiritual reaction of the heart/mind. They need to bow before him in humility and fear, rather than complain and criticize, as Job has often done. The **wise in heart** are those who have already learned to fear God. All humanity needs to follow their example.

FROM THE TEXT

Summary of Elihu's Speeches. Elihu is sometimes dismissed as irrelevant to the book of Job, but he makes important contributions to the narrative by pointing out key ideas needing to be emphasized. The conclusion of the dialogues had created an intense anger in this young man. His personality was such that he could not let the matter rest until Job's problems had received a proper explanation. He was not the sort of person who could live with ambiguity. Since neither Job nor the three friends had convincingly proven their case, Elihu felt compelled to enter the debate and point out the errors he had heard.

Elihu's criticisms of the friends dealt mainly with their silence. Why had they quit speaking? They should continue to debate until Job admitted they were right. His criticisms of Job were more serious, for he had detected major flaws in Job's thinking. Job had made some preposterous statements that could not be supported with evidence. The following are some of Job's claims that Elihu believed were false.

- Job declared that he was spiritually pure and innocent of any sin that would cause the kind of intense suffering he had endured.
- Job claimed that God treated him like an enemy.
- Job claimed that God would not speak to him or answer his cries for help.
- Job claimed that he had not received justice from God. Therefore, because God was unjust, there was no benefit in serving him.
- Job declared that he was speaking the truth about himself and about God.

Elihu's answers were designed to attack Job's faulty thinking and defend the character and integrity of God. He first criticized Job's rebellious attitude. Job thought he knew more about the way justice should be administered than God. He would not even consider a viewpoint other than his own. To counter this attitude, Elihu presented Job with multiple examples of God's omnipotence and wisdom throughout nature. He then tried to shame Job by asking him whether he could do the same things as God. Further, he exhorted Job to quit trying to solve his problems himself. God knew the reason for Job's suffering, and he had already tried to communicate with him. But Job's rebellious attitude had prevented him from hearing God's voice. Job needed to humbly yield his life to God and *really* pray, not just cry out because he was in pain.

Then Elihu sought to present a correct understanding of the nature of God. His main points are as follows:

- God created the world and established its order.
- God is sovereign over all of life. No one is outside his control.
- God is omnipotent. He has the power to do whatever he wishes to do.
- God is just in his treatment of human beings—punishing the wicked and rewarding the righteous.
- God sets his own standards by which to judge humanity. He is not influenced by human claims of goodness/righteousness.
- God does not abandon anyone who may drift away into sin. He repeatedly tries to communicate with them through various means, such as dreams, physical suffering, and angels.
- There is benefit in serving God, but it does not necessarily come in the form of material rewards. Human righteousness creates a godly environment that benefits the welfare of others.
- God's ways are beyond human understanding. Thus, there will always be a certain amount of mystery about God's purposes and activities in the world.
- God sometimes uses suffering as a disciplinary measure to cause people to wake up and turn back to him. Job's suffering could be for his benefit to lead him back to God.

Elihu was definitely overconfident in his ability to understand Job's situation. His claims to have perfect knowledge and to be a spokesperson for God were clearly brash and egotistical. Nevertheless, his logic is impressive. He seems to have a good grasp of the nature of God. And he is most sincere in his desire to help Job out of his suffering.

However, the reader knows that no matter how close Elihu gets to the truth, he is still missing the same crucial piece of evidence the three friends are missing. He is not aware of the conversation between God and the Examiner in the prologue. Thus, he will never know the real cause of Job's problems. Neither will he know how much God cares about Job. Elihu argues in ch 35 that God is not affected by human righteousness or evil, but the prologue reveals something different. God was clearly delighted by Job's righteousness and praised him as more righteous than any other person on earth (1:8; 2:3).

Further, while Elihu's logic is persuasive, it is limited by its methodology. As Newsom points out, Elihu's conclusions (and they are similar to the three friends') were the result of deductive reasoning, that is, they work backward from the principle to the individual case (1996, 576). Elihu started from the premise that God is always just in his dealings with human beings. That is his nature. Thus, if Job is suffering, he is either being disciplined or being punished. In a just world, suffering only comes to those who deserve it.

On the contrary, Job's thinking was guided by inductive reasoning; that is, he used individual cases to form broad principles. He regarded his own suffering as the primary example of injustice, but other examples were plentiful (21:6-33; 24:1-17). Therefore, the only logical conclusion was that God does not govern his world in ways that are just. Both methods of reasoning are legitimate in certain situations. But again, without all the evidence, neither method is capable of solving Job's problems or describing God's nature.

IX. GOD'S SPEECHES AND JOB'S RESPONSE: JOB 38:1—42:6

BEHIND THE TEXT

Job 38:1—42:6 contain two magnificent speeches by God (38:1—40:2; 40:6—41:34 [41:26 HB]) and two short responses from Job (40:3-5; 42:1-6). Although the three friends and Elihu are still in attendance, God's attention is directed solely at Job and his criticisms and complaints.

The subject matter of these speeches is totally unexpected. One would think that God would disclose his conversation in the prologue with the Examiner and explain the relationship to Job's suffering. Or he might agree or disagree with certain parts of Job's claims of innocence (ch 31). At the very least we would expect God to provide a word of encouragement for Job. After all, he was God's prime example of saintliness, and God was bothered by his suffering (1:8; 2:3). But God never mentions his conversation with the Examiner nor acknowledges Job's losses and misery. Instead, he vigorously bombards Job with over seventy rhetorical questions that challenge Job's understanding of God and the world's order.

In the first speech God begins with the creation of the inanimate world (38:4-11), followed by the continuing operation of the world (38:12-38), and then the nature of the animal kingdom (38:39—39:30). After a brief pause for Job to respond, God's second speech focuses on the world of morality and justice (40:6-14). Then he closes with two magnificent poems on the hippopotamus and the crocodile (40:15—41:34 [41:26 HB]). Job is left stunned by this hard-hitting, verbal parade of God's awesome activities.

Job's two responses are very brief. His first indicates his unworthiness to speak to such an awesome God. His second is a confession of his ignorance. He has spoken many things about God without knowledge. But he is now willing to give God the benefit of the doubt in all of God's plans for the world, including justice and suffering. And he submits himself to God's will for his own life.

Scholars differ over how to interpret these chapters. Some believe God takes the role of a typical wisdom teacher. He uses nature as his textbook and patiently guides his pupil Job using a series of rhetorical questions as the sages were prone to do (Bergant 1982, 179-80; Hartley 1988, 487-89; Wilson 2007, 420-21). He is mainly interested in helping Job see that God's power and wisdom in creating and sustaining his creation are far beyond human understanding. Others regard God's speeches as an attempt to force Job into submission. They point to verses that show definite sarcasm and rebuke, such as 38:4, 18, 21; 40:2, 7-14 (van Selms 1985, 140; Clines 2011, 1089).

Actually, God's purpose is a combination of both of these. On the one hand, he wants to defend himself against some of Job's false accusations. His biting questions "are designed to change Job's mind and to cause him to withdraw his charges" (Newsom 1996, 596). God has listened to Job throughout the dialogues and noted Job's often arrogant and contentious attitude. Thus, he takes a rather harsh approach toward Job, just like he did with Jeremiah (→ sidebar below). On the other hand, God certainly wants to instruct Job with a correct understanding of the nature of God and the world. The universe is much bigger and more complex than Job has ever imagined before. God has carefully crafted it according to his blueprint. If Job could see the world through God's eyes, he would see not only divine power and wisdom but also divine order, beauty, involvement, compassion, and delight.

Job and Jeremiah

There are many similarities between Job and Jeremiah. Both men complained to God about his lack of justice in the world. They believed he had deceived them. "Why do the wicked prosper and the righteous suffer?" they asked. "You, God, have the power to correct all moral injustice. Why have you not done so?" Both Job and Jeremiah became extremely depressed over this issue. Both were consumed with self-pity over their own suffering. And both reacted by cursing their birth dates (Job 3:1-3; Jer 20:14-18). They wished they had never been born into God's mixed-up world.

God's answer to Jeremiah was harsh: "Your life is going to get tougher" (see Jer 12:5), and "You, Jeremiah, need to repent" (see Jer 15:19-21). In Job 38—41 God takes a slightly different approach with Job. Here the emphasis is on Job's ignorance. He does not understand God's ways. Therefore, he is not even competent to complain. His allegations and faultfinding are meaningless. Neither Job nor Jeremiah ever received the answers from God they had hoped for, but they both survived God's harsh treatment and went on to live meaningful lives.

IN THE TEXT

A. God's First Speech (38:1—40:2)

God's speeches are the climax of the book. Since God is the only one who knows what caused Job's suffering, his appearance is vitally important to understanding the meaning of the narrative. The focus of this first speech is on God's power and wisdom as seen in the natural world. God created the world and all its components and established its original design. He now continues to govern its operation—both its animate and inanimate parts—in ways that are appropriate, meaningful, and ordered. God closes this speech with an invitation for Job to respond.

There are five sections to God's first speech:
1. I Will Question You (38:1-3)
2. Could You Have Created the World the Way I Did? (38:4-11)
3. Can You Operate the World the Way I Do? (38:12-38)
4. Can You Control the Animal Kingdom the Way I Do? (38:39—39:30)
5. Would You Care to Respond? (40:1-2)

1. I Will Question You (38:1-3)

■ 1 The author introduces God with the name **the LORD** (*Yahweh*)—Israel's covenantal name for God (Exod 3:15). Even though Job and his friends are non-Israelites, the author uses this name to convey to his Israelite audience that this is not a foreign deity who spoke to Job, but rather the same God they have worshipped for generations. This is also the name of the God who praised Job in the prologue but then caused his suffering (chs 1—2).

God's appearance here in the midst of a **storm** (*sĕ'ārâ*; lit. "tempest, storm-wind" [BDB]) heightens his formidable power. He is not to be taken lightly. The NRSV "whirlwind" suggests something like a tornado, but the Hebrew word simply refers to a strong, stormy wind. It is not the same word for the wind that killed Job's children (1:19).

While God does not always communicate with people through a **storm** (e.g., Abraham [Gen 15:1-6]; Samuel [1 Sam 3:4-14]), he sometimes creates violent acts of nature as a prelude to his speaking (Exod 19:16-19; 1 Kgs 19:11-12; Ezek 1:4; Acts 9:3; see Nah 1:3). The inevitable result is an overpowering fear of God. In the preceding speech Elihu used the imagery of an approaching storm to emphasize God's awesomeness (36:27—37:12). This storm is now over them, and from within it God begins to speak. The storm-image is thus a point of connection between the two speeches (→ Behind the Text for ch 32).

Theophanies

God's speeches are what biblical scholars call a theophany—an appearance by God to a human being. Theophanies happen rarely in the Bible. When they do, they are usually to significant people in the biblical story, for example, Abraham (Gen 15:1-21; 17:1-22), Moses (Exod 3:1—4:17), Joshua (Josh 5:13-15), Samuel (1 Sam 3:4-14), Elijah (1 Kgs 19:9-18), Isaiah (Isa 6:1-13), Paul (Acts 9:3-6). Theophanies usually result in a changed relationship with God and/or different behavior.

In Job's case, he has been requesting a theophany ever since Job 13:3. If only God would meet with him, he knows they could clear things up. He knows a theophany would restore their relationship. And he is exactly right. But he never could have guessed what God wanted to talk about—the hippopotamus and the crocodile. This unforeseen topic is one of the greatest surprise climaxes in the history of literature.

■ 2 God's first words set the tone for all that follows. **Who is this . . . ?** is a rhetorical question that would apply to all of the human speakers in the book, for they have each spoken from ignorance. But the following verses indicate that God has set his sights solely on Job. The question immediately places Job on a lower level than God. It draws attention to the tremendous gulf between God and humanity. How dare Job challenge God's governance of the world! On what basis does he presume to know more about its operation than God? Is he older than God? Is he more powerful than God? Does he have more knowledge than God? The answer to all of these is *no!* So why, then, is Job criticizing (lit. "obscuring, making dark") God's **plans** (lit. "counsel") for the world? As long as he lacks **knowledge**, he is not competent to speak.

■ 3 "Gird up your loins like a man" (NRSV) is an idiomatic Hebrew expression that means: "Prepare for action!" God is warning Job that this is going to be a contest of immense proportions, and he better prepare himself well. The saying probably derives from the practice of pulling up one's clothing and binding it around the waist with a belt so as not to be restricted in movement. Long flowing robes would get in the way of vigorous activity. The word "loins" refers to the area on either side of a person's body between the rib cage and the hip bone.

Job is challenged to do this **like a man** (*geber*). The word *geber* appears numerous times in Job with the meaning of "a human being" (e.g., 3:23; 14:10). In one passage it refers to "a male" (3:3). But in 38:3, the word implies *a strong man* who is prepared to engage in a vigorous intellectual debate with God. This is quite ironic considering that Job is sickly and thinks he is about to die. God informs Job that he is going to set the terms for the debate. He will ask the questions, and Job will be expected to give an answer.

Earlier Job had asked for just such a meeting as this (10:2; 13:22). He believed he had a good case to present to God that would defend his integrity (13:18).

But at the same time he was afraid that God might simply overwhelm him in such an encounter. Just the thought of being in God's presence terrified him (9:14-20, 32-35; 13:20-21; 23:15-16). For this reason he had requested a mediator to bridge the gap between the two of them (9:33). Now Job's worst fears are about to be realized. God is about to reveal his mighty power and wisdom, and Job has no mediator to intervene between himself and God.

2. Could You Have Created the World the Way I Did? (38:4-11)

God's first topic is the creation of the world. He is the one responsible for the world's existence. Not only did he follow a plan in constructing the world, but he also established order among the various parts, even corralling the restless sea. The questions that God asks in this section are designed to force Job to recognize his ignorance and weakness: "Where were you . . . ? Tell me, if you understand" (v 4). "Who marked off . . . ? Surely you know!" (v 5). "Who shut up . . . ?" (v 8).

These are not questions seeking information. They are pointed jabs at Job that reveal a God with tremendous power and wisdom. No single human being, or even humanity collectively, could ever plan or carry out a project such as creation. Only God was there in the beginning, and only he knows how creation was accomplished. Those who lack knowledge should refrain from criticizing.

■ **4-7** God describes the creation of the world as if he were erecting a building (also Pss 102:25 [26 HB]; 104:5; Prov 3:19-20; Isa 48:13; 51:13, 16; Zech 12:1; etc.). Using the language of construction and engineering, he speaks of the earth as having a **foundation** (Job 38:4), **dimensions** (v 5), **footings** (v 6a), and a **cornerstone** (v 6b; this may refer to the final capstone [Clines 2011, 1100]). Obviously, these are figurative expressions, but they point to a major theme in God's speeches: God's order is embedded throughout creation. When God created the world, he had a blueprint that he carefully followed. Everything was designed in a purposeful way that made sense to God.

This passage clearly reflects the ancient conception of the natural world. People believed the earth was flat and was anchored at the edges by mountains. Surrounding the land and deep under the earth was a great, mysterious saltwater sea (v 8), and overhead a metal dome protected the earth from the waters above. Within the dome the sun, moon, and stars made their daily trek across the sky (see Gen 1 for a further description of God's creative activities). With that said, the concept of the earth having a **foundation**, **dimensions**, **footings**, and a **cornerstone** made a lot more sense to ancient people.

Verse 7 speaks of **morning stars** and "heavenly beings" (NRSV; lit. "sons of *Elohim*") that were present at the time of creation. These stars are not to be taken as divine beings, as in other ancient religions. God is simply using figurative language to say that everything in the heavenly realm that existed prior to the earth's creation rejoiced at his handiwork when he **laid the earth's foundation** (v 4).

■ **8-11** God now recounts how he tamed **the sea** at the time of creation (v 8*a*). The oceans were quite fearful to ancient people. They were often associated with chaos and violence. Their restless, menacing nature is highlighted here using the metaphor of an energetic, contentious infant **bursting forth from the womb** (v 8*b*) and being clothed in **clouds** (v 9*a*) and **thick darkness** (v 9*b*; perhaps a reference to the thick fog and dark clouds that sometimes lie just offshore).

However, **the sea** was no match for God's power. He set **limits** (v 10*a*; a reference to the seashore) as to how far it could encroach onto the land (vv 10-11; also Ps 104:9). Figuratively, he restricted it behind **doors** braced by strong **bars** (Job 38:10*b*). This imagery reflects the structure of a typical ancient city gate. The massive doors were reinforced by strong timbers on the inside called bars. When the doors were closed, these timbers were dropped into wall sockets on either side of the gate to prevent the doors from being battered in.

God questions Job again: "Who did all of this?" Job knows the answer, for he has already acknowledged God's control of the sea (7:12; 26:12). But the question is an important one to raise because it reminds Job of God's power even over the most fearsome forces of nature. God is omnipotent and has been so since the beginning of time. So one should be cautious before doing battle with him whether physically or verbally. This passage brings to mind the great Babylonian Creation Epic also known as *Enuma Elish* (*ANET*, 60-72). In the epic, the god Marduk kills the menacing Tiamat, goddess of the sea waters. In Job, God does not kill **the sea**, but he completely controls its movement (7:12).

3. Can You Operate the World the Way I Do? (38:12-38)

God's next topic is his daily governance of the world. His ongoing maintenance program includes the weather, the seasons, day and night, and the sun, moon, and stars. God has established order throughout his creation from the heights of heaven to the depths of the sea. Thus, humanity can depend on a stable environment characterized by orderliness and regularity, but only God knows how these operations work.

■ **12-15** The first daily activity that God mentions is the dawning of each new day. At his command the day begins. God asks Job if he has ever given such a command. The importance of authorizing the start of a new day is spelled out in two figures of speech that emphasize various changes that take place when the light first appears in the morning (vv 13-15).

First, **the wicked** lose their freedom to operate in the darkness (v 13*b*). They must cease their evil deeds and scurry off to a hiding place (see Job's earlier description of darkness as the playground of the wicked [24:13-17]). God likens this to a housewife who shakes the dust off a blanket or a rug. Similarly, when God issues his command each morning, the personified **dawn** (v 12*b*) seizes **the earth by the edges** and **shakes the wicked out of it** (v 13). The breaking of the arrogant, **upraised arm** of the wicked symbolizes their impotence during the day (v 15).

The second figure of speech compares the dawning of a new day to the changes that light brings to a **seal** impression or a **garment** (v 14). In the dark these two objects are formless, but the morning light reveals colors, shapes, and subtle shading. Thus, light brings meaning to something that is indistinct in the darkness.

A few scholars suggest an astronomical interpretation of vv 13 and 15. They render **the wicked** as the "Dog-stars" and the **upraised arm** as the "Navigator's Line" (Clines 2011, 1103-4). The meaning is that these stars disappear when the sun comes up. However, the traditional interpretation above makes adequate sense.

■ **16-18** God now calls Job's attention to the deepest place one can descend under the earth without actually dying and entering Sheol. Here at the bottom of the ocean is where the **springs of the sea** are located that bubble forth to replenish the ocean (v 16). This is also the place where the deceased enter Sheol through **the gates of death, the gates of the deepest darkness** (v 17; → 3:4-6; 10:21-22).

God asks Job whether he has ever visited this place and viewed the **vast expanses of the underworld** (v 18) that lie just beyond these gates (here *'āreṣ* should be translated **underworld** rather than **earth**, as in Jer 17:13 [NRSV]). If Job had been to this place, then he would possess knowledge comparable to God's knowledge concerning the depths of the earth. Since Job does not respond to God's directive, **Tell me** (Job 38:18*b*), the assumption is that he has no knowledge of these places.

■ **19-21** In the Genesis creation story primeval darkness originally covered the entire world (Gen 1:2). When God created light, he separated it from the darkness and gave it its own dwelling place. Darkness was confined to Sheol (Job 10:21-22; 17:13; 18:18; 33:28) and to the region beyond the horizon (26:10). At night the darkness creeps back across the earth, held in check partially by the moon and the stars (Ps 136:9). But in the morning, darkness is banished again to the outer realms, and light reestablishes its rule over the earth. The sun rises from its abode and marches majestically across the heavens along a path established by God (Pss 19:4-6 [5-7 HB]; 136:8).

God asks Job if he can find his way to the places where **light** and **darkness reside** (Job 38:19). If so, he would know how to guide and control them, just like God does. And then God follows up with a taunting reproach of Job's claim to knowledge (v 21). The meaning is something like this: "**Surely you know where light and darkness dwell!** I mean, you were there when I assigned them their abodes, were you not? So you should know how to find them and make them function properly, right?" This in-your-face remark reveals something of God's agitation at Job's criticisms of God's operation of the world. Job needs to learn humility in the presence of Almighty God.

■ **22-24** God's governance also includes the weather. **Snow** (v 22*a*), **hail** (v 22*b*), **lightning** (v 24*a*), and **the east winds** (v 24*b*) are under his command. These elements of the weather were thought to be kept by God in heavenly **storehouses** (v 22) and unleashed at appropriate times to influence human events, such as during the **days of war and battle** (v 23; Josh 10:11; Isa 30:30). God questions Job about whether he knows the way to these storehouses and has visited them. The implication is that Job could control these weather events if he knew where they were kept.

The word for **lightning** (*'ôr*) is a problem for some scholars who prefer more of a parallel to **east winds** (Job 38:24*b*). Various emendations have yielded "heat," "west wind," "air currents," and so forth (Clines 2011, 1060). These are possibilities, but the MT **lightning** is understandable in this context and should be retained.

■ **25-27** **Rain** (v 25*a*) is vitally important for the growth of vegetation. God provides it when and where he sees fit, sometimes even sending **torrents** on places **where no one lives** (v 26*a*), such as **deserts** (v 26*b*) and **wastelands** (v 27*a*). Even though this may seem like a waste of water to human beings, God's plan for his creation includes the entire earth, not just the inhabited places. God wants to impress on Job that his governance of the world includes every single part, whether humans are interested in them or not.

The phrase **cuts a channel** (v 25*a*) brings to mind the kind of heavy downpours that occur in some tropical climates. These downpours almost seem like God has opened a heavenly floodgate and released a river of water toward earth. Verse 25*b* speaks of the "thunderbolt" (NRSV; lit. "lightning of thunder" [→ 28:26]) that follows a designated **path**. God asks Job if he knows who causes the **rain** and the ***lightning***. Of course, Job knows that God is responsible for them, but he remains silent.

■ **28-30** Here God emphasizes his control of the **rain** (v 28*a*), **drops of dew** (v 28*b*), **ice** (v 29*a*), **frost** (v 29*b*), and the frozen **surface** of a body of water (v 30*b*). These are all different forms of moisture that are personified as possibly having **a father** (v 28*a*) and a mother (v 29). God asks Job if he knows who brought these *children* into existence. Knowledge of their **father** or mother would provide access and power to control them. The answer to God's question is: They have no **father** or mother. God is the one who causes these events to occur.

■ **31-33** The next question God asks is whether Job has knowledge of how the star constellations operate, and does he have the power to **set up** the same kind of order here on **earth** (v 33*b*)? If Job could control these heavenly objects (illustrated by the verbs **bind** [v 31*a*], **loosen** [v 31*b*], **bring forth** [v 32*a*], **lead out** [v 32*b*]), then he also would have power over the earth, for the stars were thought to have some effect on the weather and the seasons.

Job has already mentioned **the Pleiades**, Orion, and **the Bear** as created by God (9:9). The identification of the fourth name (*mazzārôt*; v 32*a*) is unknown (see Clines 2011, 1063-64 for a discussion of the possibilities). Some use the generic translation **constellations** without identifying which one, while others simply opt for a transliteration—"Mazzaroth" (NRSV).

■ **34-38** God returns to the topic of the rain and the lightning (vv 25-27) by asking Job whether they obey him. When he commands them, do they say, "**Here we are**" (v 35*b*), and carry out their assignments? The assumption behind these verses is that the weather does not occur by chance or from natural causes. Rather, someone tells it when to begin and when to cease. Is Job that person who causes these things to happen?

The mention of two birds—**the ibis** and **the rooster**—in v 36 seems odd. However, in ancient times these birds were thought to make sounds or movements that predicted the rising of the Nile river in Egypt and the coming of rain (Clines 2011, 1116). God asks Job if he is the one who gave these birds their **wisdom** as weather forecasters. The **ibis** is a large bird with a downward-curved bill that probes for food in the mud and water along riverbanks.

God closes this section by speaking of one who knows how and when to **spread out** the clouds and **tip over the water jars** causing rain to fall (v 37). Certainly, this person possesses great **wisdom**, far beyond Job's level of understanding. The Hebrew for **spread out** (*yĕsappēr*) is usually translated **count**, but Gordis (1978, 453) and Clines (2011, 1066) argue for a more relevant meaning based on the context and a cognate in Arabic.

Verse 38 is literally **when the dust *flows into a solid mass* and the clods *stick fast* together**. Scholars are divided over whether this refers to extremely dry ground composed of drought-produced hard clods or to the thick mud that develops after a rainstorm. The latter is preferable, as the first verb refers to something flowing, such as molten metal.

4. Can You Control the Animal Kingdom the Way I Do? (38:39—39:30)

God's questions now change from inanimate creation to animate. He describes a series of animals and birds, pointing out the unique characteristics of each and challenging Job's knowledge of them: "Do you understand how a specific animal performs this activity? Can you do what this animal does, or go where this animal goes? Did you cause this bird to fly, or give this animal its strength?"

The purpose of these questions is to open Job's mind even further to the awesomeness of God's creation. This is a world he does not understand and certainly does not control. And it is far greater than he ever imagined. Job may view these animals and birds as odd or frightening and seek to avoid them, but God likes every one of his creatures and provides for their needs.

■ **39-40** God's list of animals and birds he has created begins with the lion, or more specifically **the lioness** (v 39*a*), since it is the female who does most of the hunting (→ 4:10-11 on the different words for "lion" in the book of Job). She must find food not only for herself but also for her cubs ("young lions" [38:39*b* NRSV]). One method of securing food is to **lie in wait** (v 40) in a place where other animals are likely to pass by. God asks Job if he is the one who provides prey for the lioness and helps her catch her food. The implication is that God has created other animals as prey for the lions, and he has given the lions the skills they need to hunt down this food.

■ **41** Likewise **the raven** must find food for its chicks. **The raven** is a ritually unclean bird that sometimes scavenges on dead animal carcasses, so its appearance immediately after the lion seems logical. God asks Job who is responsible for supplying the raven's **food** and for enabling it to find that **food** and bring it to its **young**. God's provision of **food** for the animal kingdom is the theme that connects the lioness and **the raven**.

■ **39:1-4** Next God questions Job concerning his knowledge of the pregnancy and delivery practices of **mountain goats** (modern ibex; v 1). Even though people were aware of these animals, very few, if any, had ever seen **the does** give birth because they lived in remote areas (the NIV and NRSV regard **the doe** as a separate animal [a female deer], but the parallelism in the verse could indicate a female mountain goat [Clines 2011, 1120]). Obviously, Job knew nothing about how these animals delivered their offspring, other than by comparison with the birthing practices of his own sheep and goats (1:3). God is the only one who understands these animals, even to the intimate details of their birth. He is also aware of their offspring as they grow up and then **leave** to fend for themselves (39:4).

In v 3b the NIV and others translate the Hebrew *ḥēbel* as **labor pains**. But an alternative meaning is "offspring" or "fetus," which makes better sense in this context: **They crouch down and bring forth their young**; "and they deliver their offspring" (Clines 2011, 1050, 1070).

■ **5-8** God's emphasis in these verses is on the freedom enjoyed by **the wild donkey** (v 5a; also called an *onager* in v 5b: **who untied the fetters of the onager?**). This animal is related to the domesticated donkey but has never been tamed. It roams in uninhabited areas such as deserts and **salt flats** (v 6b) as well as in the **hills** (v 8a) looking for any kind of vegetation to feed on. It avoids contact with humans as much as possible.

God describes it figuratively as laughing at the domesticated animals in towns and on farms that must endure the abuse and burdens of commerce and transportation (v 7). By contrast, the wild donkey is free to go wherever and whenever it wishes. God asks Job who allowed this animal to have such a free lifestyle. This is one of two places in the list of animals where God answers his own question (also v 17). He is the one who gave this animal its freedom and provided places for it to forage (v 6).

■ **9-12** The **wild ox** (v 9a; or ***aurochs***) is now extinct, but in ancient times it was much feared due to its large size (over two thousand pounds) and long horns that pointed forward (Num 23:22; 24:8; Deut 33:17; Ps 22:21 [22 HB]). It was related to domestic cattle but was impossible to tame. This animal had great strength and, if tamed, would have been a great asset to any farmer. But its unruly temperament prevented its usage for plowing or **hauling grain** to a **threshing floor** (Job 39:12). As God notes, a farmer could not even tie it up for the night alongside a ***feeding trough*** (v 9b). It would inevitably break loose. The absurdity of God's questions about whether Job could make this dangerous animal **serve** (v 9a) him probably brought a smile to the reader's face.

■ **13-18** The **ostrich** (v 13; lit. "screechers," based on a peculiar sound they make when frightened) is a tall, strange-looking bird with a large body, tall neck, and small head. One of its unusual characteristics is its inability to fly, but it has powerful legs that enable it to run faster than 40 mph when threatened (v 18). As God says, in a race, the ostrich leaves **horse and rider** far behind.

Verse 13 speaks of its **wings** in relation to other birds, but the point of comparison is unclear due to the difficult Hebrew. No doubt, the size of the head in relation to the body contributes to its reputation as being stupid. But this passage mentions additional features that reflect a popular mythology about this bird. It is true that the female ostrich **lays her eggs** in a shallow depression in the ground where wild animals and humans might **crush them** (vv 14-15). But the shell of an ostrich egg is very thick and unlikely to be crushed except by the heaviest of animals.

These verses also state that an ostrich abandons its chicks **as if they were not hers** (v 16). This perception may have arisen from the ostrich's tendency to run off at a rapid pace when approached by predators or humans. The purpose of this action is to distract attention away from the eggs or chicks. Other birds do this as well.

In v 17 **God** (*Eloah*) explains one of the ostrich's characteristics as a lack of **wisdom** and "understanding" (NRSV), which he purposely withheld from this bird. In other words, God created the ostrich to be this way, and he is pleased with his creation. This passage is the only place where God does not ask Job a direct question. He simply describes some of the characteristics of this strange bird, leaving Job to marvel at what he has done.

■ **19-25** The passage on the horse (v 19) is divided into two sections. In the first part (vv 19-20) God questions Job's ability to provide **the horse** with **strength** and a **mane**, and cause it to ***shake*** like a locust (Clines 2011, 1078). The meaning of the last phrase is unclear. It could refer to the excited shaking of the animal in anticipation of battle (v 24), or to the noise and shaking of the ground produced by horses at a gallop (see Rev 9:7-9 for a similar comparison of horses rushing into battle with the vibration of locusts' wings).

In the second part (Job 39:21-25) God praises the horse's qualities in warfare. It is eager to charge into battle (vv 21, 25). It shows confidence in the midst of danger (v 22). And it exhibits great speed in a full gallop (v 24).

Verse 23 speaks of the "rattling" made by **the quiver** (full of arrows), **the flashing spear**, and the ***javelin*** as the horse advances into battle. This seems like a lot of weaponry for a single horseback rider to handle. So this verse may refer to a horse hitched to a chariot. The weapons would be mounted on the chariot. Chariots usually carried two riders—a driver and an archer. If the chariot became disabled, all three weapons would be useful in the resulting hand-to-hand combat. An alternative but less likely view is that the verse refers to the sound of *enemy* arrows, spears, and javelins whistling by the horse as it charges into battle (Gordis 1978, 462).

The appearance of **the horse** in this list of wild animals seems out of place. While God's description of it makes it seem wild and fiercely energetic like the other wild animals, horses do not charge into battle on their own. This horse has been trained. But there is no mention of any soldier to ride it or guide it while standing in a chariot. This is because the focus is on the characteristics of the animal kingdom, not human interaction with these animals. Thus, the imagery fits the purpose of the speech. Further, Job's possessions (1:3) did not include horses, so this animal may have been as foreign and wild to him as the others.

Horses were probably domesticated sometime in the third millennium BC. They were expensive and thus limited to royalty and the wealthy. Their usage was primarily in warfare and hunting. By 1500-1200 BC the more powerful nations such as Egypt and the Hittites maintained sizable chariot units in their military. Horses were also ridden by military scouts. A few pictures exist of mounted cavalry from the second millennium, but it was not until the first millennium that cavalry units became prominent along with chariots (Hyland 2003, 7). Horses did not become important in Israelite culture until the reign of Solomon in the tenth century BC (1 Kgs 4:26, 28 [5:6, 8 HB]; 10:26-29). (→ Introduction: Date for comments on the relevance of this passage to the dating of the book.)

■ 26-30 God's list of animals concludes with **the hawk** (Job 39:26*a*) and **the eagle** (v 27*a*; or ***vulture***). These are two different birds, but they are seen here as representing the category of birds of prey. God's remarks about **the hawk** focus on its migratory instincts. In the fall it **spreads its wings toward the south** (v 26*b*), while in the spring it returns to the north. This pattern continues still today, as the Middle East is located along one of the main migratory bird flyways between Eurasia and Africa.

God commends **the eagle** (or ***vulture***) for its wisdom in building a secure nest on high **rocky crags** or **cliffs** (v 27). From there it is able to survey the land below looking for small rodents and dead carcasses that it brings back to its **young ones** (v 30*a*). It is a scavenger, so the dead are some of its prey. Wherever the dead appear, **there it is** (see Matt 24:28; Luke 17:37). The word for **the slain** (*ḥālāl* [Job 39:30*b*]) always refers to dead humans, so there may be a connection between this verse and the dead soldiers killed in battles where the horse was involved (vv 21-25).

God's questions to Job are again directed at the cause of these actions by birds of prey. Did Job with his great **wisdom** give them these characteristics, and does he continue to control their actions? The answer to these rhetorical questions is no! God alone has endowed the animal kingdom with its characteristics, and only he continues to direct their lives.

5. Would You Care to Respond? (40:1-2)

God concludes this speech by offering Job the opportunity to respond.

■ 1 The author inserts the standard introductory speech formula at 40:1 (→ 3:2), indicating a pause in God's forceful questioning. It is time to bring Job back into the conversation. The author uses the name **the L**ORD (*Yahweh*) again as he did at 38:1 (also 40:3, 6).

■ 2 At the beginning of this speech God made it clear that he was expecting a response from Job (38:3). He is very interested in what Job is thinking. Does Job have an answer to any of God's rhetorical questions? Has anything God has said changed Job's mind, or is he still holding on to his earlier complaints and criticisms? God pauses here to allow Job the opportunity to **correct him** if he desires to do so. God gives him permission to lay out his case in a logical manner and argue it forcefully just as God has been doing.

The offer to be corrected by someone else appears infrequently in the book (6:24-30; 24:25; 33:31-33; 37:19). Most of the speakers are so overly confident in their own correctness that no response is expected. God is certainly confident that he speaks the truth, but in his mercy he is always willing to listen to a disturbed soul. Eventually God will soften his harsh rhetoric and return to calling Job his "servant" (42:7-8) as he did in the prologue (1:8; 2:3). But at this point God is holding Job somewhat at arm's length by referring to him as **the one who contends with the Almighty** (*Shaddai*) and **him who accuses God** (*Eloah*).

FROM THE TEXT

1. Summary of God's First Speech. Job's request for God to meet him is finally answered, but God only touches briefly on Job's questions and complaints. Instead, his main topic throughout his two speeches is his governance of the world. He approaches this topic with a series of hard-hitting rhetorical questions that emphasize his wisdom and power in the natural world. Job has nowhere to hide from God's relentless questioning.

God begins with his activities at the beginning of time. He then describes his continuing involvement in governing and caring for the natural world. His final topic is his delight with the animal kingdom. Undergirding all of God's activities are his unfathomable wisdom and his awesome power. Job's lack of these qualities is what hinders him from understanding God's governance of the world.

God covers the following points in his first speech:
- I had a blueprint when I created the world. I followed it step by step even to the minutest detail. Job, were you there to watch me when I did this, so that you understand what I accomplished?
- I continue to operate the world with the same careful attention to detail. The weather, the seasons, and day and night are all under my control. From the depths of the sea to the stars in the heavens, I have established my order in the entire world. Even Sheol is under my control. Do you understand how all of this operates? Surely you do, for your life span is long, right?
- Within my world there are countless animals and birds that I have created. Each has unique characteristics that I delight in. I know the details of every one of their lives. Can you say the same?
- So, Job, what do you say for yourself? How do your wisdom and power stack up against mine? Do you still think you are qualified to criticize my governance of the world?

2. God's Order and Mystery in the Animal Kingdom. In this first speech, God's tour through the animal kingdom is like a child's first visit to the zoo. It provides the same sense of fascination and amazement as experienced by children upon seeing giraffes, elephants, porcupines, and monkeys for the first time. This sense of wonder carries over into God's second speech where he draws an analogy between the mysteries in nature and the mysteries in morality and justice (40:6-14).

Why did God pick this list of animals and birds? Probably for two reasons: their wild nature (which Job could not control) and their foreignness to Job. On first glance, the horse seems to be an exception. But even though the horse was domesticated by this time, it still retained something of a brave, wild spirit that was useful in battle to frighten opposing soldiers. And Job did not own any horses (certainly not warhorses), so they were foreign to him. God purposely did not mention dogs, cats, sheep, cattle, and camels—animals that Job knew very well. He wanted to impress Job with his freedom to do whatever he wishes. One should also note that most of the book's readers were also unfamiliar with these animals, and even more so with the animals in God's second speech—the hippopotamus and the crocodile.

God designed the animal kingdom with order in mind. The animals and birds mentioned here may be odd-looking and odd-acting to human eyes, but each animal has unique characteristics that fit the lifestyle and location God intended for it. And each contributes to the overall sense that God knew what he was doing when he created the world. His wisdom is evident in every part of his creation, and his satisfaction with the results is evident in his words. He takes delight in what he has created.

In modern times with the aid of hidden cameras, telephoto lenses, and tracking devices, humanity is becoming more knowledgeable of the animal kingdom. But we will never attain God's level of knowledge and control. Our observations of God's creation will always instill in us a deep sense of wonder and amazement.

God's depiction of some of the animals in his first speech suggests that the world may be far more complex than Job realizes. In fact, it may even be paradoxical in some aspects. For example, the lion and the eagle exhibit exemplary parental care of their young, but the only way they can do so is by killing other animals. The wild donkey and the wild ox are amazing specimens of strength, yet their unruly and untamable nature makes them useless to a farmer. The ostrich has blazing speed, but it does not seem to care about its young. Could God be hinting to Job that what looks like injustice in the moral world is actually more complicated than it seems on the surface?

Job's friends and Elihu viewed the world through a simplistic *either/or* lens (Habel 1985, 562). Either Job was righteous and well-off, or he was sinful and suffering. He could not be both righteous and suffering at the same time (although Job believed differently about his own situation). And God was viewed either as just and caring by his use of the principle of retribution, or as unjust and indifferent if he punished the righteous and rewarded the wicked. But God operates in a *both/and* world. Job can be both innocent and suffering at the same time, while

God can be both just and the cause of innocent suffering. God does not explain this paradoxical mystery, but he subtly hints that Job should consider it.

IN THE TEXT

B. Job's First Response to God (40:3-5)

■ **3-5** Job's response to God is very brief (in fact, exceedingly brief considering the length of his speeches in previous chapters). He begins by acknowledging his inferior position in relation to God: "I am of small account" (v 4 NRSV), meaning *I am insignificant* (*qll*). Certainly, anyone who has been in the presence of God has experienced a similar reaction.

Earlier in the book Job had worried that if God did appear, he would overwhelm Job and leave him speechless (9:3, 14-15). This is why he had requested a mediator—a neutral party who would work with both sides, allow for a fair discussion of the issues, and be able to resolve their differences (9:32-33). Now that God has actually appeared to him, he is even more aware of the need for a mediator.

Placing one's hand over one's mouth can mean multiple things, such as horror (21:5) or great respect (29:9). Job's action in 40:4 indicates that God's magnificent speech has humbled him and reduced him to silence. He has nothing to say because his knowledge of the natural world is minute compared to God's.

At the same time, Job is not yet ready to concede that God has bested him with regard to the issue of his suffering. In fact, God has said nothing about the matter. Job is still looking for God to affirm his moral innocence and explain the cause of his troubles. And he would like to hear an explanation for the lack of justice in the world regarding the wicked. The sense of Job's remarks in v 5 is as follows: "I have spoken more than once about these issues (actually he has spoken many times), but I will not speak again or try to defend myself anymore. I am waiting for you to comment on these matters that weigh so heavily on my heart." (For comments on the number pattern in v 5, → "Number Patterns" sidebar at 5:19.)

C. God's Second Speech (40:6—41:34 [40:6—41:26 HB])

There are three sections to God's second speech:
1. Can You Administer Justice Better than I Can? (40:6-14)
2. Can You Control the Hippopotamus? (40:15-24)
3. Can You Control the Crocodile? (41:1-34 [40:25—41:26 HB])

The first section is a significant contribution to the book. It deals with the topic of divine justice, which Job and his friends have been discussing since ch 4. God avoids commenting on Job's specific questions about why Job is suffering and why the wicked are not punished. Instead, he attacks Job's critical attitude toward God's system of justice. He does so by daring Job to produce a better system if he can.

The second and third sections are magnificent poems on the hippopotamus and the crocodile. These animals are even more wild and uncontrollable than the animals in God's first speech. But they are not, as in ANE myths, chaotic monsters that God has to fight to bring peace to the world. They are monsters God created and likes. God uses them to bolster his arguments in his first speech about his power, wisdom, and order throughout all creation.

Some scholars believe God's second speech is a later addition by another author, but the evidence is flimsy. God needs to hear more from Job than his few words in 40:4-5. Job has confessed to his insignificance, but he has not yet retracted any of his criticism of God. God would like to know his state of mind, and so he proceeds with more descriptions of the animal kingdom, this time commenting on two of the most dangerous animals to humankind. But first he raises the issue of divine justice.

I. Can You Administer Justice Better than I Can? (40:6-14)

On the surface, God's first speech (chs 38—39) seems totally irrelevant. Why does he talk about creation and the operation of the world when Job's complaints are about the cause of his suffering? Has God not been listening to Job, or is he trying to avoid Job's questions? The answer is found in the nature of wisdom literature. The sages loved to create comparative statements that helped to explain puzzling phenomena. Using a variety of literary forms, such as analogies, deductions, value judgments, and cause-and-effect statements, they used the *known* to explain the *unknown*. Proverbs 25:3 is an example of a typical analogy: "As the heavens are high and the earth is deep, so the hearts of kings are unsearchable." The point of the proverb is that just as the distance between heaven and earth is unknown, so trying to predict what a king will do is useless.

In God's second speech he takes the information from his first speech and draws an analogy with Job's ignorance about divine justice. If Job is ignorant in one area of knowledge, then he most likely lacks knowledge in other areas as well. Job has just acknowledged by his brief answer in Job 40:4-5 that God knows far more about nature than he does. Now in vv 7-14 God draws a parallel with justice and morality. In essence, God says to Job: "If you cannot understand the physical universe, how can you claim to understand the moral universe? And if you are ignorant about morality, how can you accuse me of being unjust? All you are doing is trying to make me look bad in order to justify your own concept of justice."

God then challenges Job to act like God if he thinks he can. Job should identify all the wicked people in the world and send them to Sheol. If Job is able to do a good job of judging the world, God will be the first one in line to pat him on the back and congratulate him.

■ **6-7** Since Job has declined the offer to correct God or engage in further debate, God returns to his rhetorical questions spoken from **the storm** (v 6). He begins by repeating the words used in his first speech (38:3): "Gird up your loins like a man" (NRSV). These words admonish Job to listen carefully to what God says and prepare himself for a vigorous debate. God's first speech was impressive in its grand tour through the acts of creation and the continuing, orderly operation of the world, but God is not through with Job yet. He still has points to make regarding the topic of divine justice, which Job questioned on several occasions.

■ **8-9** God's first question inquires as to the reason why Job is so critical of God's method of administering **justice** (e.g., 9:22). Does he **condemn** God simply **to justify** his claim of innocence and his own understanding of how justice should operate? (40:8*b*).

Job has good reason to claim innocence. God knows that and expressed it several times in the prologue. But Job does not have a right to use that claim to accuse God of injustice. Tearing down others to build up one's own position is a common defense mechanism that people use to gratify their ego. But to utilize this tactic against God—one's Creator—is foolhardy if not ludicrous.

God's questions in v 9 press home his point. "Do you, Job, think you possess the power and wisdom to dispense justice properly in this world? **Do you have an arm** and **voice** like mine?" God's strong **arm** and thundering **voice** in the storm are symbols of his tremendous power as described in chs 38—39. If Job does not have this kind of power, how can he hope to do a better job than God in governing the world?

■ **10** Next God challenges Job to present himself publicly as a person of great authority. "Dress like a king (or a god)!" is the essence of what he says. The four nouns—"majesty" (*gāʾôn*; **glory**) and "dignity" (*gōbah*; **splendor**), "glory" (*hôd*; **honor**) and "splendor" (*hādār*; **majesty**) (NRSV)—are basically synonyms whose meanings are somewhat interchangeable. They all refer to a quality or object that is raised to an exalted level. The words are typically associated with God's character ("majesty" [Isa 2:10]; "dignity" [the Hebrew is translated "heights" in Job 22:12]; "glory" [Ps 148:13 NRSV]; "splendor" [Ps 104:1]). Thus, Job 40:10 is an exhortation to appear *godlike*.

■ **11-13** After improving his appearance by adorning himself in royal garb, Job should take up the task of judging all humanity. God instructs him to separate out **all who are proud** (v 11*b*) and **wicked** (v 12*b*) and punish them severely. **Unleash the fury of your wrath** against them (v 11*a*), **bring them low** (v 11*b*), **humble them** (v 12*a*), and **crush** them (v 12*b*). These verbs indicate the violence that Job should impose in his judgment on the wicked. And further, he should send the wicked to an early death (lit. "imprison their faces in the hidden place" [another term for "Sheol"]; v 13*b*). These are precisely the actions Job thought were missing from God's judgment in the past (21:7-33; 24:1-17).

God's words indicate a willingness to let Job try his hand at governing the world as he sees fit: "Prove to me that you can administer justice better than I can!" But while God is willing to give Job the opportunity to succeed, he knows that Job is sure to fail. And he presses this point home with the concluding part of his speech, so that Job also comes to realize he will fail.

Behemoth (40:15-24) and Leviathan (41:1-34 [40:25—41:26 HB]) are two animals that no human being can control. They are the most fearsome land and sea animals. Leviathan is especially dangerous (41:8-11 [40:32—41:3 HB]). God calls him the supreme example of those who are "haughty" and "proud" (41:34 [26 HB]). Ironically, the proud are exactly the ones God is now challenging Job to **bring . . . low** (40:11-12). Job is caught in a *no-win* situation. He does not want to admit that God is right in how he governs the world, but at the same time he does not have the power and wisdom to prove him wrong by humbling the **proud**.

By the end of God's second speech, both God and Job know that Job's desire to correct God's supposed injustice is impossible to achieve. The only feasible option left for him is to submit to the God who created him and all the other parts of creation (v 15). Job's final response in 42:1-6 will reveal how God's speech has impacted his thinking.

■ **14** God offers to congratulate Job if his plan succeeds, for then Job's **own right hand** would be as powerful as God's "arm" (40:9). Job would possess enough power not only to get rid of all the wicked but even to **save** himself from his misery and from false accusations by the friends.

The verb **save** (*yš'*) can also mean "gain victory" (see NRSV, NJPS; Gordis 1978, 475; Habel 1985, 564). Job's victory would be the triumph of *his* plan to administer justice over God's plan. If this indeed happens, God would certainly have to commend Job for creating a better plan than his own.

In vv 10-14 God is having some fun at Job's expense by challenging him to prove that his power is equal to or greater than God's. But the author knows that power is not the real issue in the book. God does not avoid punishing the wicked or rewarding the righteous (in Job's case, restoring his health, wealth, and reputation) because of a lack of power. He has more than enough power to do whatever needs to be done. The real issue is God's freedom to do as he pleases. When God acts in ways that make sense to him but seem illogical to humankind, he creates an element of mystery about himself. God will emphasize this sense of mystery in the remainder of this speech.

2. Can You Control the Hippopotamus? (40:15-24)

God's second speech now takes an interesting turn. He entertains Job with a magnificent poem about the hippopotamus (40:15-24), and then an even longer one about the crocodile (41:1-34 [40:25—41:26 HB]). These are two beasts whose characteristics and names (Behemoth and Leviathan) have been embellished to enhance the perception of their fearsome, wild nature. God knows that neither Job nor any other human being can explain them or control them. His rhetorical questions about how a person might try to capture one and make a pet out of it (40:24; 41:1-5 [40:24-29 HB]) are filled with humor, but also a little sarcasm. The amount of detail in the descriptions of both animals indicates that the author had actually seen them in their native habitat. This is good evidence that he had probably traveled to Egypt at some point in the past.

These poems are meant to illustrate even further the point God has just made in vv 7-14: "This is *my* world. I created it this way for reasons known only to me. I like all I have created, including the hippo and the crocodile, even though humanity may not comprehend what I have done. There will always be a mystery about this world, both in the natural world and in the administration of justice, that humans will not understand. But I know what I am doing. And you can trust me to do the right thing in regard to Job's welfare as well as in all other aspects of life."

■ **15** All the monsters mentioned thus far in the book have been sea monsters (7:12; 9:13; 26:12). But **Behemoth** (40:15-24) is a massive, plant-eating land animal that likes to lounge in rivers and marshes. Most scholars identify this animal with the hippopotamus. The name **Behemoth** is the plural form of *bĕhēmâ*, meaning "beast" or "animal" in general, either domestic or wild (12:7; 18:3; 35:11). It is applied to the hippopotamus in 40:15 as a proper name or title (see Ps 73:22) to characterize it as an unrivaled beast in regard to size and massiveness—the beast of all beasts.

Scholars have proposed many interpretations for Behemoth and Leviathan. Some treat these animals as a metaphor for "Satan/the powers of evil" or "death" (McKenna 1986, 306; Smick 1988, 1049; Fyall 2002, 126-37, 157-74), but there is no lesson on morality in the description of either animal. Others think that Behemoth symbolizes Job, and Leviathan represents God (Walton 2012, 408-10), but Leviathan is a creature of God, not God himself.

Some connect Leviathan with the source of chaos in Canaanite or Mesopotamian creation myths (Pope 1973, 329-31), but these myths speak of a tremendous battle between the gods and the monsters of chaos. In Job, God never fights a battle with Behemoth and Leviathan. Rather, they are his beloved creatures. The only connection with the creation myths may be that they influenced the choice of names for these beasts and perhaps some of their characteristics (→ 41:1).

A few scholars relate Behemoth to Egyptian mythological tales involving a hippopotamus god or goddess (Botterweck 1975, 2:18). And still others find a relationship with Egyptian artwork showing the pharaoh hunting a hippopotamus or lion to demonstrate his prowess over large wild animals (ibid.). The author of Job may well have known of these connections with Egypt, for the hippo and crocodile were common in some parts of Egypt, but they are definitely not gods in Job.

The most far-fetched interpretation is the view that these beasts are dinosaurs (Vicchio 2006c, 223), but how would the author and his audience have known that dinosaurs once roamed the earth or what a dinosaur looked like?

The best interpretation is the one that treats God's statements, **which I made along with you** and **which feeds on grass like an ox**, as factual. Behemoth and Leviathan are real animals in present time that God is challenging Job to understand and control. They are not metaphors or mythological creatures out of the past. Behemoth and Leviathan are used solely to illustrate God's ability and freedom to create all kinds of odd-looking animals and to maintain control of even the largest and most fearsome ones.

■ **16-18** God continues his poem on the hippopotamus by describing various aspects of its enormous **strength** (40:16). Its huge **loins** (*motnayim*, also 12:18; in

40:7 and 38:3 it is ḥălāṣayim) and **the muscles of its belly** (40:16) are particularly striking, and its massive legs are like solid bars of **bronze** or **iron** (v 18). The verb used with the **tail** of the hippopotamus (v 17) is ḥpṣ ("let hang"), which seems strange when compared to a tall **cedar** tree. No suitable cognate is available for comparison. Most scholars now render the verb as "stiffen" or "stand up" based on the context: "It makes its tail stiff like a cedar" (NRSV). Some see a euphemism here for sexual virility, but it is unlikely that the author would introduce this topic into a description of the animal's outward appearance, and even more unlikely that he had ever seen hippos mating.

■ **19** According to the wisdom tradition, personified Wisdom was the very first creation of God (Prov 8:22). Wisdom was then at God's side as he brought the rest of the world—both heaven and earth—into existence. Job 40:19 seems to challenge this concept by calling Behemoth the **first among the works of God** (*El*), which the NIV interprets as first in rank or importance. Davidson interprets as "first in magnitude and power" (1884, 280). However, the usage of the word **first** is most likely connected to Gen 1:24 where *bĕhēmâ* (Job 40:15) were the first land animals that God created.

The description of their enormous strength (vv 16-18) makes the hippo an animal to be avoided if at all possible: "only its Maker can approach it with the sword" (v 19*b* NRSV; this line is very difficult). The passage does not say that God actually engages this beast in battle. Rather, the emphasis is on the fact that *only God* has enough power to conquer this beast if a conflict should arise. Even such a mighty animal as the hippo is no match for God, its Creator.

■ **20-23** The hippo does not actually spend time in the **hills**, but it does profit from the water and nutrients that the river channels **bring it** from the hills (v 20). During the day the animal prefers hiding under the water to protect its hairless skin from drying out. It finds additional shade from the **lotus plants** (v 21*a*), **reeds** (v 21*b*), and **poplars** (v 22*b*) in marshy areas. At night it leaves the water and grazes on grass along the shores of rivers and lakes. Its presence provides security for other animals to **play nearby** (v 20*b*).

Verse 23 provides an image of the strength of the hippo against the rushing water of the **Jordan**. Whereas smaller animals would be swept away, the hippopotamus stands **secure**. "Even if the river is turbulent, it is not frightened" (v 23*a* NRSV). The hippo certainly did not live in Edom/northwest Arabia (the setting for the book), and it is questionable whether it ever lived along the **Jordan** River (although Clines seems to find evidence [2011, 1185]). The Nile would be much more appropriate. But the **Jordan** provides a more familiar context for Israelite readers, for many had seen this river **surge** in the springtime (Josh 3:15).

■ **24** In addition to being of massive size, hippopotami are also aggressive toward humans. They seem docile when submerged in the water, but they are ferocious attackers when threatened. In Africa, more people are killed by the hippo than any other wild animal. Thus, the rhetorical questions in Job 40:24 are quite humorous. Who would dare try to capture one of these monstrous beasts with the hooks or traps used against other wild animals or fish? Only a fool would make such an attempt, and then only once. God alone can control this beast (v 19). Capturing a hippo by its **eyes** or **nose** may refer to the fact that these are the only visible parts of the animal when it is submerged in the water.

3. Can You Control the Crocodile? (41:1-34 [40:25—41:26 HB])

As with the hippopotamus in the preceding section (40:15-24), the point of this poem is to enlighten Job on the characteristics of another ferocious animal that God has created—Leviathan, the crocodile. The passage provides balance to God's second speech by showing that God is able to control the most fearsome sea animal known to humankind as well as the most fearsome land animal. The first part (41:1-11 [40:25—41:3 HB]) contains a series of rhetorical questions poking fun at human attempts to capture, control, or tame a crocodile. God's questions are directed specifically at Job, but the implication is that no human being is a match for this powerful animal.

The latter part of the poem (vv 12-34 [4-26 HB]) focuses on some of the characteristics of the crocodile that should cause one to steer clear of it. It has frightful teeth and an impenetrable hide that is able to deflect all human weapons. It creates fear by exhaling fire and smoke, and when it thrashes around, it causes the sea to boil. The animal has no predators and is without fear of any other animal or human being (vv 33-34 [25-26 HB]).

God does not directly mention his creation of this animal or his control of it (as he did with Behemoth in 40:15, 19). But the statement in 41:33 [25 HB] that it is "a creature" plus the rhetorical questions in vv 1-11 [40:25—41:3 HB] clearly support the concept that God brought the crocodile into being and only he has enough power to subdue it.

The MT of ch 41 has a different numbering system than most English translations. The Hebrew continues on with 40:25-32 before changing to 41:1-26. Thus, 41:1-8 (Eng.) = 40:25-32 (HB), and 41:9-34 (Eng.) = 41:1-26 (HB). A number of commentaries follow the Hebrew, leading to some confusion for English readers.

■ **1-2 [40:25-26 HB]** Leviathan (*liwyātān*) is the Hebrew name for the great sea monster of ancient mythology. The name has appeared already at 3:8 as the personified force of chaos that Job wanted loosed on the night of his conception to prevent his birth, and it is alluded to at 7:12 where Job complained that God treated him as if he were the sea dragon of ancient myths who needed to be defeated. **Leviathan** is also mentioned by other biblical writers (Pss 74:13-14; 104:26; Isa 27:1; → "Mythological Characters in Job" sidebar at Job 7:12 for comments on all the monsters in the book).

The name refers to the largest sea monster that one can imagine. Ancient knowledge of the fish in the oceans was certainly not very advanced, but enough mariners had probably had encounters with whales, eels, squid, octopi, and so forth, to keep the belief in a monstrous sea dragon alive. In Canaanite literature, the god Baal defeated the monster of the sea named Lotan (possibly another name for Leviathan), a dragon with seven heads. This myth then became a metaphor for God's defeat of the Egyptians at the Red Sea (Ps 74:13-14) and his future victory over evil on the Day of the Lord (Isa 27:1).

However, the description of Leviathan in Job 41:1-34 [40:25—41:26 HB] is clearly that of the crocodile, albeit with a few mythological traits added for greater effect (e.g., smoke coming out of its nostrils and flames from its mouth, vv 20-21 [12-13 HB]). The animal has legs and walks on the land (vv 12, 30 [4, 22 HB]), but it also swims in the sea (vv 31-32 [23-24 HB]). Thus, it is not a serpent or a fish. It is an amphibious animal, and the crocodile is the choice of most scholars (→ 40:15 for other interpretations). In ancient times the crocodile was well-known along the Nile and in some of the small streams along the coast of Palestine that flowed into the Mediterranean Sea.

Verses 1-2 of ch 41 [40:25-26 HB] inquire about the method of capturing a crocodile. Would one need a **fishhook** or a **rope**? Would one try to latch onto its **tongue**, its **nose**, or its **jawbone**? None of these methods used to seize other animals or fish would apply to the crocodile. It is simply too powerful to be restrained by ordinary means of capture. The author may be referring to the practice of stringing fish on a line or using imagery drawn from ancient war practices. The Assyrian army was known for controlling prisoners of war by roping them together using hooks in their nose or jaw (2 Kgs 19:28; Isa 37:29; Ezek 38:4). Such practices would not work with a crocodile.

■ **3-4 [40:27-28 HB]** The next rhetorical questions ask if the crocodile is a submissive animal that yields to human authority. Would it accept a human being as its master **for life** (41:4 [40:28 HB])? Would it enter into **an agreement** (*bĕrît*) that acknowledges human superiority? And once it became a servant, would it ask its master for kind treatment, using **gentle words** (41:3 [40:27 HB])? Of course, the thought is laughable.

■ **5 [40:29 HB]** This verse questions the desirability of having a crocodile as a pet. Could a person "play with it as with a bird" (NRSV)? Would people trust it to be gentle with their daughters?

■ **6 [40:30 HB]** God now interrogates Job about what would happen to a crocodile in the event one was captured. Would it be cut up into pieces and **bartered** over in the marketplace? God is mocking the idea of selling this animal like one would sell farm animals or fish. How would the owner get such a large animal to market in the first place? And then, no one would want to buy an entire crocodile, so it would have to be **divided** into small portions. How could one cut it up when its skin is resistant to swords and spears (vv 7, 15-17, 26-29 [40:31; 41:7-9, 18-21 HB])? And who would want to buy and then eat such a scary-looking monster?

■ **7-9 [40:31—41:1 HB]** These verses warn of the danger in trying to capture a crocodile. Neither **harpoons** nor **fishing spears** will work (v 7 [40:31 HB]). The animal will put up such a tremendous struggle that a person will never attempt to catch one again. **If you lay a hand on it** may just be a figure of speech for venturing to get close to it (41:8 [40:32 HB]). Even the **sight** of this frightening animal has an **overpowering** effect on people's emotions that causes them to back away (41:9 [1 HB]).

■ **10-11 [2-3 HB]** Verses 10-11 [2-3 HB] in the MT contain several first-person suffixes that lead to confusion. They switch attention away from the crocodile to God, as if this were a short discourse on God's power over creation. If correct, God is saying, "No one has ever challenged me and won, for all of creation **belongs to me**." Paul's paraphrase of v 11 [3 HB] in Rom 11:35 follows this interpretation. However, one can see how a zealous scribe might have made an emendation to protect the power of God over Leviathan.

The context makes much better sense with third-person suffixes that connect the verses with the description of Leviathan. These emendations are followed by the NRSV, yielding: "No one is so fierce as to dare to stir it up. Who can stand before it? Who can confront it and be safe?—under the whole heaven, who?" This rendering is more reasonable, poking fun again at the foolishness of trying to capture a crocodile. No one "under the whole heaven" can conquer it.

■ **12 [4 HB]** God pauses briefly from his rhetorical questions to emphasize his fondness for the crocodile. He cannot keep silent about the **limbs**, the **strength**, and the **graceful form** of this wonderful animal he has created. He will describe these characteristics in more detail in the following verses. The language here is striking—full of praise and enthusiasm, and much like God's words of praise for his Son with whom he is well pleased (Matt 3:17; 12:18-21; 17:5; Mark 1:11; Luke 3:22; 2 Pet 1:17).

There is great irony here, for God is not speaking of a beautiful bird such as the peacock or a cuddly animal such as the panda bear. Rather, he is lavishing his praise on one of the most ugly and fearsome animals known to humankind. The point is that God evaluates his creatures differently than Job does.

■ **13-14 [5-6 HB]** God now draws attention to the skin of the crocodile by noting that what appears to be a **double coat of armor** (v 13 [5 HB]) is impenetrable (vv 7, 26-29 [40:31; 41:18-21 HB]). Also, its **mouth** (v 14 [6 HB]) is so frightening that no one would ever attempt to **open** it, thereby revealing rows of terrifying **teeth** within. These verses contain the last rhetorical questions in God's speech. The remaining verses are simply descriptive in nature.

■ **15-17 [7-9 HB]** The crocodile's skin is a leathery material, useful in belts and handbags, that looks like rows and rows of scales. Each scale appears to be **joined fast** (v 17 [9 HB]) with the next so that the entire body is **tightly sealed** (v 15 [7 HB]) against **air** (v 16 [8 HB]) and water. The underside of the animal is somewhat smooth, but down the **back** (v 15 [7 HB]) and along the tail are hard, sharp-pointed protrusions that look like **shields** lined up in a row.

■ **18-21 [10-13 HB]** The imagery in these verses is borrowed from ancient mythological stories about sea monsters (although the same imagery is attributed to God in Pss 18:8 [9 HB]; 29:7). Some have suggested that this passage proves that

God is speaking of a mythological sea dragon rather than a crocodile. But as already noted, many more verses point to a real animal.

God characterizes this animal as flashing **light** from its **eyes** (v 18 [10 HB]) and discharging **smoke** and **flames** from its **nostrils** and **mouth** (vv 20-21 [12-13 HB]). Some have tried to connect these images with real sprays of mist that issue from the crocodile's nostrils when it comes to the surface and with sunlight reflecting off its eyes. More likely, these figurative expressions are mainly embellishments used to heighten the sense of terror this animal produces in humans, but nothing more than that.

■ **22-25 [14-17 HB]** God now emphasizes the strength of the crocodile's **neck** and **chest** (lit. "heart") area (vv 22, 24 [14, 16 HB]). When a crocodile raises itself up on its short legs, one is able to view the underside with its **tightly joined** scales (v 23 [15 HB]), similar to those on its back (vv 15-17 [7-9 HB]). The hardness of the chest is compared to the surface of a **lower millstone** (v 24 [16 HB]).

The Hebrew word *'ēlîm* (v 25*a* [17*a* HB]) is usually translated as "the gods" (NRSV), which would lend itself to a mythological interpretation. "The cowering of the gods is a common mythological motif" (Pope 1973, 344). But the NIV and others support an emendation to *'êlîm*, meaning **the mighty**, which makes better sense in this context. Even the mightiest individuals **are terrified** by this animal.

■ **26-29 [18-21 HB]** God lists eight weapons (**sword, spear, dart, javelin, arrows** [lit. "the son of the bow"], **slingstones, club,** and **lance** [vv 26-29 (18-21 HB)]) and two metals used for casting weapons (**iron** and **bronze** [v 27 (19 HB)]) that human beings might wield to kill or capture Leviathan. Some are designed for close combat, and others are hurled from a distance. But none are effective when used against the impenetrable skin of a crocodile (v 13 [5 HB]). They are as potent as **chaff** or **straw** (vv 28, 29 [20, 21 HB]). Leviathan even **laughs** at them in derision. It is not afraid of any of the weapons that hunters and soldiers use to kill other animals and humans.

■ **30-32 [22-24 HB]** When a crocodile moves around, it leaves traces behind. On land, it leaves a **trail in the mud** that is like the impressions left by a **threshing sledge** when dragged across the ground (v 30 [22 HB]). Threshing sledges were heavy boards fitted on the underside with pieces of stone, metal, or potsherds. When pulled across a stone threshing floor, they separated the heads of the grain from the husks in preparation for winnowing. The underside of a crocodile is actually quite smooth, but it does leave characteristic impressions in the mud caused by its footprints, tail, and heavy weight.

In the water, the crocodile creates a **glistening wake** of bubbles as it glides effortlessly across the water (v 32 [24 HB]). God compares this to the beautiful **white hair** of an elderly person. But the crocodile also thrashes around when attacking prey or fighting (v 31 [23 HB]). God likens this **churn**ing of the water to the boiling contents of a cooking pot or the ingredients in a pot used to manufacture **ointment** and perfume.

■ **33-34 [25-26 HB]** The conclusion of God's speech summarizes the status of the crocodile in the animal kingdom. This remarkable beast is without **equal** (v 33 [25 HB]). As a fearsome predator, it lives at the top of the food chain and looks down on the other members of the animal kingdom. The phrase **king over all that are proud** refers to all the other predators, both on land and in the sea (v 34 [26 HB]). The same phrase was used in 28:8 to speak of animals such as the lion. The crocodile fears none of these mighty animals. It is more powerful than all.

FROM THE TEXT

1. Summary of God's Second Speech. The creatures God mentions in chs 39—41 are all outside of Job's experience and control. He is ignorant of their ways. The last two (the hippopotamus and the crocodile) are even animals that Job would not want to meet, for they are dangerous to human beings. But God made all creatures and ordered their lives in ways that are pleasing to him. The implication is that the world is much bigger than Job's knowledge and experiences.

To gain a proper understanding of the world's vastness, its complexity, and its beauty, one must view it through theocentric eyes. This is God's world, through and through. He created it for *his* purposes, not ours. Therefore, we cannot pass judgment on his plans for the world using human standards. Neither can we require him to explain why things happen the way they do. God's way of looking at the world is as difficult for us as it was for Job. We tend to limit God and his creation to our finite level of understanding gained through the use of scientific instruments and rational thought. But God's universe is much larger and more complex than we can imagine. We have only scratched the surface of what his wisdom and power have created. To claim otherwise is to find ourselves in company with the "haughty" and the "proud" (41:34 [26 HB]).

God has three main points in his second speech:
- Job, your criticism of my governance of the world calls into question my role as Judge. Let me make you an offer. If you can come up with a better plan than mine, I will step aside and let you rule the world. But to be successful, you will have to have as much power as I possess. Do you have such power?
- Behemoth (the hippopotamus) is the most powerful land animal on earth. Its body is massive and muscular. No one pushes it around, not even surging rivers. Yet it is a peaceful and beautiful animal. I created it just like you, and I like it just like it is. Do you have the power to capture or control this animal?
- Leviathan (the crocodile) is the most powerful and fearsome creature in the sea. It easily resists any attempt to capture or kill it. Its skin is like armor, impenetrable to swords, spears, arrows, and other hunting weapons. Its mouth is filled with frightening teeth. It stirs up the sea into froth when it thrashes about. Even fire and smoke seem to belch from its mouth

and nostrils. It is truly the most powerful predator on earth. Like Behemoth, I created Leviathan and like it very much. Can you capture or control this animal?

2. Contribution of God's Speeches to the Meaning of the Book. Since there seems to be little connection between God's speeches (chs 38—41) and the earlier parts of the book, scholars have wrestled with how to interpret them. Perdue summarizes the three approaches that are generally used (1991, 196-99).

(1) Some scholars focus on *the appearance of God* as a significant event that reveals his compassion for humanity. The simple fact that God shows up and engages Job in conversation is all that matters. What God actually says is not that important.

(2) Others look for meaning in *the content of what God says*. Perdue lists eight major interpretations that fit this category. The two most significant are the fifth and sixth.

> 5. God's wisdom and justice transcend human comprehension. Efforts to impugn divine justice are sheer folly.
> 6. God's sovereignty as Creator and Lord of history is upheld, leading to the rejection of false questioning and the proper response of confession and praise. (1991, 198)

(3) Still others think the key to interpretation is found in *Job's reaction* (42:2-6). God's speeches achieve the desired effect by producing a change in Job that leads him back to fellowship with God.

Actually, none should be regarded as the *only key* to a proper interpretation. All three contribute in some measure to the overall meaning of the book (→ Excursus 2: Interpreting the Book of Job following the commentary on Job 42:17).

3. God's Power. God's challenge to Job in 40:8-14 deals specifically with the power and wisdom needed to run the world. It takes unlimited power to punish the proud and the wicked (40:11-12). God has shown that he has this power by creating the world (38:1-11), operating the world (38:12-38), and controlling the animal kingdom (38:39—39:30). If Job has such power and can use it wisely, he should demonstrate it for God to see.

To stress this point even more, in his second speech God adds two more animals to his list of wild and uncontrollable creatures—the most powerful land and sea animals that humans have to face. Their long and elegant descriptions are enhanced with mythological embellishments to make them seem even more formidable. The comparison with Job's power (or lack thereof) is not spelled out by God, but Job clearly understands what the issue is, as seen in his final response (42:1-6). If Job can control these animals, then surely he is qualified to judge the world and punish the wicked. But if he does not have that kind of power, he has no right to criticize God's governance of the world.

4. God's Silence in Human Suffering. Throughout the book of Job none of the human characters understand why Job is suffering, because none are aware of the dialogue between God and the Examiner in the prologue. Thus, while many of their arguments correctly identify some of the reasons for human suffering, they never put their finger on the cause of Job's troubles. Only God and the Examiner know the real cause. Clearly, the author is attempting to make a point with regard to God's silence: God does not always reveal the cause of suffering to those who suffer. Human beings may flood the heavens with *why* questions, but God does not feel compelled to answer.

Since God never divulges the cause of Job's suffering, we have to assume that he intends to keep silent about the reasons for many of our sufferings as well. This is frustrating to most people, but it may work to our advantage by opening up new ways of thinking about God and ourselves. First, God's silence should never be interpreted as divine injustice or indifference. It simply means that he chooses to remain silent. Job was right to insist on his innocence, but he was wrong to charge God with injustice and unconcern.

Second, our knowledge, compared to his, is very limited. We are very ignorant of many aspects of God's order in the world. We may not be capable of understanding his plans even if he told us. God's silence should encourage an attitude of humility and submission to the one who knows far more than we ever will (28:28).

Third, God's silence should encourage us to trust him more. The entire Bible speaks over and over again of his love and goodness for all his creatures. He can be trusted to be working in our behalf even when we have no evidence of such. We can be confident that he has a good plan and knows what he is doing even when he acts in ways that seem strange or harmful to us.

Fourth, God's silence should increase our respect for his freedom and mystery. He cannot be put in a box, and we would not want him always to act in ways that make sense to us. That would bring him down to our level. It is much more satisfying to serve a God who "performs wonders that cannot be fathomed" (9:10) than a God who is predictable and easily explainable.

IN THE TEXT

D. Job's Second Response to God (42:1-6)

Job's final words are brief and somewhat ambiguous, but they are crucial for understanding the message of the book. Here Job finally speaks the words God wants to hear. He begins by acknowledging God's awesome power and wisdom. God knows what needs to be done and has the power to do it. By way of example, he brought the entire world into existence, and he continues to monitor and manage it so that every part functions as planned.

Job then confesses his own lack of knowledge regarding both the natural world and the world of morality. He never realized how much God cares about each part of his creation. His ignorance caused him to say things he now regrets. He is especially sorry he maligned God's character by accusing him of being unjust.

Finally, he runs up the white flag of surrender and ends his protests against God. He does not comment on his future plans, but we can surmise that he intends to return to his former way of life—a person who "feared God and shunned evil" (1:1).

The numbering system of the verses in ch 42 is now the same again as the MT.

■ **1** The author introduces Job's speech with the standard introductory formula (→ 3:2). He continues the usage of **the LORD** (*Yahweh*) for God's name, even though Job himself does not mention this name.

■ **2** In chs 38—41 God repeatedly stressed his awesome power in creating and governing the world. This was not new information for Job, for he had already acknowledged God's omnipotence in previous speeches (9:1-12; 12:13-25; 26:5-14; see also Jesus' allusion to this verse in Matt 19:26; Mark 10:27). Job begins his final speech by declaring again that he agrees with God on this point. **All things** refers to the multiple activities in which God is involved. God has just mentioned some of them, including the founding of the world, the control of the weather, and the creation of unique animals. They are all a part of God's plans for this world, which he began at creation and continues to administer on a daily basis.

Job also acknowledges that God always brings his plans to completion. They are never **thwarted**. No human being, whether acting individually or corporately, has the power to disrupt God's order or force him to change his will. Scripture does contain several examples of changes in God's mind, but these occasions are not the result of human coercion and they do not apply to God's overarching governance of the world. They are usually responses to specific situations where people have changed their behavior for good or for bad (→ v 6 for references). They illustrate God's freedom to act with divine judgment or mercy in response to the choices people make.

■ **3** Just as God's power is far greater than human might (v 2), so God's wisdom is far superior to human understanding. Job repeats a question that God raised at the beginning of his first speech (38:2): **Who is this that obscures my plans without knowledge?** and then answers it. The words **You asked** are not in the MT, but they are implied by the context. God's original question drew attention to Job's ignorance and incompetence to criticize God's governance of the world. Now Job identifies himself as the one who spoke **without knowledge**. He admits that his ignorance disqualifies him from challenging God's plans. This admission puts an end to Job's charge that God is unjust.

After God's magnificent speeches, Job certainly has gained a greater understanding of God, the cosmos, and his own relationship to both (v 5). But overall, God's works are still **too wonderful** for Job to comprehend. In the OT the works of God are frequently described as **wonderful** (*plʾ*), meaning they are "miraculous, extraordinary, beyond human expectation." Many of these wonderful activities were historical acts of deliverance in behalf of Israel that needed to be remembered and praised (e.g., Pss 71:17; 78:4, 11, 32; 98:1). But in the book of Job God's wonders occur in the natural world (5:9; 9:10; 37:5, 14). Human knowledge is too limited to comprehend them fully.

■ **4** At the beginning of God's two speeches he challenged Job to prepare himself for a vigorous round of questioning and to be ready to give a response (38:3; 40:7). In 42:4 Job repeats the words of God's challenge to him. By this means, he acknowledges that he has listened carefully to both of God's speeches and he is now ready to give an answer. The words **You said** are again missing in the MT but implied from the context. The admonition to **Listen now, and I will speak** is actually borrowed from Elihu's speech (33:31), but the words are clearly implied in God's earlier challenges to Job (38:3; 40:7).

■ **5** In this important verse Job describes a new insight that has opened up to him as a result of God's two speeches (chs 38—41). He now sees the world through God's eyes. God created it, ordered it, and sustains it continually. From the beginning, God had a plan for the world, and he continues to operate according to that plan.

Further, God's governance of the world makes sense to God, even though human beings do not understand it. For some unknown reason, God likes animals such as the hippopotamus and the crocodile. For other unknown reasons, even calamities are a part of God's plans. Job still does not know why a righteous person such as himself sometimes experiences intense suffering, but he is willing to accept God's plan for his life and trust that God knows best.

Most scholars agree on this interpretation of v 5*b*, but there is a major disagreement on how it relates to v 5*a*. The traditional interpretation is that Job is contrasting his new insights (v 5*b*) with his old way of thinking (v 5*a*). His old conception of God was like hearing about God from others versus actually seeing him with one's own **eyes**. Using a NT analogy, the old way was like seeing "in a mirror, dimly," but the new way is like seeing "face to face" (1 Cor 13:12 NRSV).

However, a few scholars find no contrast here at all. For example, Newsom translates the verse: "I have listened to you with my ears, and now my eye sees you" (1996, 628; similarly, Good 1990, 373-75, and Clines 2011, 1205). This reading provides two parallel clauses that connect with God's admonition to listen in v 4*a*. Job has been listening to God's speeches, and now, as a result, he sees God differently (the verb "see" here means "comprehend with one's mind," not "see face to face").

The difference between these interpretations is not crucial, for in either case Job's new perspective is emphasized. In support of the first interpretation, to speak of something new obviously implies that something old preceded it. But the latter interpretation has the advantage of connecting Job 42:4 and 5 more closely and thus may be the correct one. Significantly, Job's *seeing* of God is exactly what he had hoped would take place someday (19:25-27), and it happened before he died, rather than later as he feared.

■ **6** Job's final words in the book are an implicit request for renewed fellowship with God. He and God have been at loggerheads with each other since the calamities struck. In fact, he believes they became enemies for a period of time (10:8; 13:24; 19:11; see especially 33:10). In order to be reconciled with God, he needs to apologize for some of the things he has said.

The verb **I despise** (*m's*) is missing a direct object in Hebrew. Some scholars believe Job is referring to himself (as in 7:16 NIV, NRSV), and others to the things he has said (NJPS). The issue is not resolved, but either interpretation implies both meanings. An alternative reading, based on another meaning of *m's*, is: "I submit," meaning "I withdraw my case against God and submit to his sovereignty" (Clines 2011, 1219-20; see 1207-8 for his reasoning, as well as a discussion of other possibilities).

Whatever the correct translation, Job seems to be abandoning here his criticism of God and agreeing to God's way of looking at the world. His apology comes after recognizing that his attitude and his foolish and inaccurate rantings against God were shameful. He deeply regrets having accused God of being unjust to him and of acting like an enemy. How could he have said such terrible things to the one who performs such "wonders" (9:10; see 42:3)?

The traditional translation of the verb *nḥm* in v 6b is **repent** (NIV, NRSV), but this English translation implies that Job is confessing some type of sin for which he feels guilty. Such a meaning is highly unlikely, for Job has no sins to confess. He has been blameless and upright throughout the entire book (1:1, 8; 2:3). He may be guilty of "a fault deserving correction, but not a wickedness deserving punishment" (Andersen 1976, 292). God never accuses Job of sin, only of ignorance regarding God's method of governance, leading to a false accusation of injustice. Further, to falsely confess some nonexistent sins would be to acknowledge that the friends and Elihu have been right all along. But in the epilogue God makes it clear that the friends were wrong (42:7).

A second possible translation is: "I am comforted." The meaning would be: "I will no longer mourn over my losses. I will now return to normal life" (Clines 2011, 1220-21). This translation is supported by six other occurrences of *nḥm* in the book of Job, all with the meaning of "comfort" (2:11; 7:13; 16:2; 21:34; 29:25; 42:11). The primary problem with this interpretation is that Job is still struggling with the loss of his health and his income. He cannot just return to normal life on his own. He will not find personal comfort until God restores fellowship and blesses him again (v 10).

A third possibility is: ***I relent/change my mind***. This meaning occurs in passages outside of the book where God changes his mind (e.g., Gen 6:7; 1 Sam 15:11, 35; Jer 18:8, 10; Amos 7:3, 6; Jonah 3:10). In saying this, Job is indicating his desire to go in a new direction. He is through challenging and criticizing God. His deepest desire is the renewal of his faith and trust in God and the restoration of their fellowship. Such a meaning fits the context of Job 42:2-6 quite well. Even though he has no reassurance that he will regain his health and his income, he knows he has the power to change his attitude from criticism to trust. He is hoping God will respond to this change by accepting him back into fellowship (→ v 2).

In dust and ashes is an ambiguous phrase that has many possible interpretations. (1) The simplest explanation is that this refers to the ashes of the city dump upon which Job is sitting (2:8 NIV, NRSV). Garbage dumps were typically burned from time to time and covered with dirt to eliminate the smells emanating from them (→ 2:7-8). (2) Some translate the phrase as "with dust and ashes," indicating Job's remorse over how he has treated God. Sprinkling dust and ashes on one's head was one way a person showed great grief and inner anguish (2:12; 2 Sam 13:19; Esth 4:1; Jer 6:26; Lam 3:16). (3) Others suggest that Job is turning "away from dust and ashes" (i.e., mourning rituals) and beginning a new life (van Wolde 1997, 137). (4) Janzen thinks Job has changed his mind "concerning dust and ashes" (i.e., his understanding of what it means to be a human being) (1985, 255). (5) The NJPS treats it as a confession of his humiliation and mortality in comparison to God's power and wisdom ("Being but dust and ashes"; see also Konkel [2006, 238] who emends *'al* to *'ul* as in 24:9, yielding "a child of dust and ashes"). The wide range of interpretations indicates that the matter is not settled, but this writer leans toward option (5), as the same meaning is found in 30:19.

Although Job does not mention his suffering in this speech, he certainly still has questions about its cause. But he wisely refrains from raising this issue again. He now recognizes that he is only a novice trying to correct an expert. He has limited knowledge about God's relationship to human suffering, and therefore he was wrong to accuse God of being unjust. He had spoken too quickly without having all the evidence before him. God's speeches (chs 38—41) have convinced him that God knows what he is doing. His plans make sense to him even if they are a mystery to human beings.

X. EPILOGUE: JOB 42:7-17

BEHIND THE TEXT

The epilogue is a major clue that the author intended for the book of Job to be read as literature. It rounds out the book with an *and they lived happily ever after* conclusion. There are three parts, each having to do with restoration. First, God delivers a harsh criticism of the three friends that requires intercession from Job before God will forgive them. Then God restores fellowship with Job, blessing him twice as much as before the calamities. Finally, God removes the sickness and grants Job a long life. The epilogue is written in the same prose format that is found in the prologue. The name for God is **the Lord** (*Yahweh*) throughout this section (→ 1:6).

Any discussion of the epilogue must address the rationale for its existence. The book could easily have ended with 42:6. Why does the author feel a need to speak of Job's restoration? The climax is over. God has presented a magnificent description of the world that he created. And Job has responded with an apology for his criticism of God and an admission that he was ignorant of God's ways. Further, God has proved to the Examiner that the original question about rewards has been answered in God's favor. Human beings can remain faithful to God through all situations in life. Even when life goes topsy-turvy, saints will not turn against God and curse him. So why does the book conclude with an ending that seems to support the friends' argument that God always rewards the righteous in this life? Here are five possible answers that may all contain some truth:

- The author's readers were aware of the earlier oral story concerning a wealthy, righteous man who lost everything and then struggled to find relief from his situation and to gain understanding about why this happened to him. As mentioned in the Introduction, stories about Job-like characters go back to the early days of writing, and they are found in many ancient cultures. The author could not disregard these earlier stories, for he knew that his readers were familiar with them. They would demand an ending that provided resolution to Job's suffering.
- The author was probably from the intellectual upper class, since most sages were (→ Introduction: Author). Thus, the restoration of the exceedingly rich hero was probably very important in his mind. To leave Job in poverty and sickness might suggest that God was displeased with the wealthy. The author uses the epilogue to confirm that wealth can be one evidence of God's pleasure with an individual (Prov 10:22).
- The epilogue provides a concrete example of God's justice and grace in an age when the understanding of the afterlife (Sheol) was quite vague. In the OT, Sheol was not a place where God distributed rewards and punishments. That happened in the land of the living. The epilogue shows that justice does take place in this life and that God does reward people who are righteous (as the book of Proverbs boldly proclaims).

Job himself could go on living without the epilogue. He had experienced a personal encounter with Almighty God. He was now satisfied that God did indeed care about him. However, people looking at Job from the outside needed to receive confirmation that Job was once again in a right relationship with God. Justice needed to take place *in this life* with tangible rewards in order for Job's family and friends to know that God still approved of him. If he had remained poor and sickly, they would still have looked upon him as rejected by God.

- Once the test was over (the test was always intended to be for a limited time), there really was no reason for God to leave Job in his pitiful condition. In fact, it would tarnish God's character to do so. "Any judge who left a defendant to languish in prison after he had been declared innocent would be condemned as unjust" (Rodd 1990, 81).
- The epilogue is further evidence of God's freedom. God can take away, but he can also reward whenever he chooses to do so (1:21). He is a free being who often surprises humankind with his generosity and love. Wharton insightfully notes that God's blessings are restored to Job, not as rewards for good behavior, but "for lover's reasons" (1999, 185).

A further question that the epilogue raises concerns the disappearance of the Examiner at the end of the story. Why is he not mentioned in the epilogue? It would be so gratifying to see the Examiner cower before God and admit his errors. Then all humanity could rest easy and know that he is an eternal loser and can do nothing to harm God's people. But this does not happen. So what are we to make of the disappearance of the Examiner?

Some have suggested that the Examiner is not crucial to the final meaning of the story. If the book is only literature, then the Examiner is only a prop that fulfills the author's purpose in the prologue and then disappears. In that regard, he is similar to Elihu and Job's wife, who also are missing at the end. But the writer is much more skillful than that. His telling of the story has made it plain that the Examiner is a loser. He does not need to press home the point that the Examiner has been defeated by God and that his arguments and understanding of human beings were obviously wrong. Every reader should be able to figure that out without being told.

More likely, the author had a subtler purpose in mind. The fact that the Examiner disappears raises the possibility that he will continue his examination of other righteous people on future occasions. It is true that he had lost his contest with God concerning supersaint Job. But how will he fare with people far less righteous than Job—with you and me, for instance? Is his disappearance similar to modern films (such as Superman, Batman, etc.) where the bad guy is never completely destroyed, thus providing an opportunity for sequels? By leaving the Examiner out of the epilogue, the author forces us to consider his possible reappearance in other lives. Could it be that *our* times of suffering are the result of God's use of the Examiner again? This intriguing question has haunted every reader of the book and will continue to do so for as long as people continue to ponder its meaning.

The epilogue divides into two sections:
A. God Rebukes the Three Friends (42:7-9)
B. God Restores Job's Fortunes (42:10-17)

IN THE TEXT

A. God Rebukes the Three Friends (42:7-9)

In this first section God works to repair the relationship that has broken down between the three friends and both Job and God. In the heat of debate their friendship with Job had deteriorated. Both sides had spoken mean and disrespectful words to the other. God brings clarity concerning who is right and who is wrong by commending Job for speaking the truth and rebuking the friends for their foolish comments. He requires them to make a sacrifice for their sins and to ask Job to intercede for them with prayer. Both actions were needed if they wanted to be reconciled with Job and with God.

■ **7** The epilogue begins with God's criticism of the three friends. The author mentions only **Eliphaz the Temanite** (→ 2:11) as the recipient of God's words, but the speech makes it clear that all three friends are included. God describes his emotional reaction to the friends as one of anger because they **have not spoken the truth about me.** Since the friends did not respond to God's speeches in chs

38—41, this remark must refer to words spoken by them in the dialogues. God was obviously aware that the friends' speeches contained many truthful statements (→ Excursus 1: The Failure of Job's Friends after ch 27). But two specific claims are the probable cause of God's anger: (1) they insisted that God was punishing Job for sinful behavior (22:5), although they had no evidence to support this claim; and (2) they asserted they were speaking for God (Job noted this in 13:7-12). They were completely unaware of the conversation in the prologue between God and the Examiner, and yet they claimed to know the reason for Job's suffering. God does not need well-meaning but ignorant persons such as these to come to his defense.

On the other hand, God commends the words Job has said, although he never identifies what gratifies him about Job's speeches. Scholars have different ideas about what God may have had in mind, but most likely, God was pleased with one or more of the following. First, Job had consistently claimed that he was not guilty of sin in spite of numerous attacks from the friends and Elihu. Job knew his own heart. His conscience did not condemn him, and neither does God anywhere in the book. God was extremely pleased that Job continued to live and testify to a holy life. Even though the outward evidence was stacked against him (his losses, his sickness), he had not been swayed internally by the false accusations of others. He was a person of great integrity.

Second, Job had repeatedly requested an answer from *God*. While Job appreciated the advice of others, he knew that God was the only one who knew the real reason for his suffering, and the only one who could do something about it. He had not sought answers from the wisdom traditions of the past, nor had he accepted the rational explanations from his friends who claimed great knowledge about life. Rather, he had focused his attention on God, the Source of all knowledge. In spite of heaven's silence, he had not let up in his request for a divine meeting where he could question God about his suffering. Job was the only one in the story whose attention was focused in the right direction.

Third, in vv 2-6 Job admitted his ignorance, apologized for his critical attitude, and submitted his life to God's will. Humility before God is always a quality that God admires (Prov 15:33; 16:19; 18:12; 29:23; Mic 6:8; Luke 14:11; 18:14).

Fourth, Lo thinks that God is commending Job for "raising the question of divine justice" rather than blindly accepting the wisdom theology (2003, 95; Clines 2011, 1231). The first three reasons above seem to be much stronger than this one.

Prior to Job's remarks in Job 42:2-6, God was uncertain about what Job was thinking (40:2). But now that Job has apologized for his criticism of God and professed a new understanding of God's ways, God returns to calling Job **my servant** (→ 1:8; 2:3). In fact, he uses the word four times in 42:7-8. Here is strong evidence that reconciliation between God and Job has now occurred.

■ **8** God instructs the three friends to offer an enormous sacrifice consisting of **seven bulls and seven rams**. Sacrifices of this magnitude were offered rarely and then only by royalty in behalf of an entire nation (Num 23:1-2, 14, 29-30; 1 Chr 15:26; 2 Chr 29:21; Ezek 45:23). The size of this **burnt offering** indicates the enormity of their wrongdoing against God.

In addition, God requires the friends to confess their sins to Job, admit he is right, and ask him to intercede for them with prayer (Lev 5:17-19). This humiliation is the punishment for their earlier deceit and treachery (Job 6:15). Earlier in the book Job had desired empathy and a kind word from them, but they had inflicted great emotional pain on him instead. They had betrayed their friendship and were no longer worthy to be called friends.

The most serious charge of all was their unfaithfulness to God (6:14). Claiming to speak for God, they had never consulted him about the truth. So their words were false and lacking authority. While Job was not a priest, his interest in intercession is already well-known from the prologue (1:5). And his prayers were effective with God because of his righteousness (Jas 5:16). For the meaning of **folly** → 2:10.

■ 9 **Eliphaz**, **Bildad**, and **Zophar** carried out the instructions God demanded of them. The author does not indicate what they were thinking, but no doubt they were very grateful to be given the means of appeasing God's anger. One wonders why Job bothered to pray for them after all they had done to him. Surely Job's willingness was tied to the reestablishment of his relationship with God. Now that he and God were reconciled, he was ready to return to his earlier compassionate lifestyle (4:3-4; 29:7-17, 21-25; 31:13-23, 31-32, 38-40). Verses 7-9 of ch 42 are a good illustration of the biblical principle that reconciliation with God and reconciliation between human beings are closely tied together. Both are required to make a person whole again (Matt 5:23-24).

One of the major ironies of the book of Job is how God's relationship with the main characters is turned on its head at the very end of the story. The three friends, who have attempted to defend God, are soundly criticized in the epilogue for being untruthful. Job, on the other hand, who has repeatedly called God unjust, is commended for speaking the truth. The skillfulness of the author is again on display with this surprise ending. Jesus was also known for the same kind of surprises in his teachings and activities. He frequently ran into criticism for upsetting the conventional wisdom of his day (e.g., Luke 5:29-32; 6:1-11; 7:36-50; 9:23-25; 15:3-32; 16:19-31; 18:18-27).

B. God Restores Job's Fortunes (42:10-17)

The remaining verses summarize some of the events in the long process of Job's restoration. Some happened immediately (the gifts and the comfort received from his family and neighbors), and others occurred over a period of many years (the birth of ten children and the amassing of large herds of animals). The author makes it clear that God is the one responsible for restoring Job's fortunes. The one who caused Job's troubles resolves them in the end (just as Job noted in 1:21). This section and the book conclude with a statement about the length of Job's life and a final epitaph.

■ **10** The process of Job's restoration begins with his intercessory prayer for his **friends**. Now that his relationship with God is mended, he is more aware of the needs around him. He has also heard God's instructions to the **friends** and knows what he must do to help them regain God's favor. So he prays in behalf of his **friends**. As the author sees it, this prayer is connected with Job's own restoration in some way, for he immediately notes that God **gave him twice as much as he had before**. The implication is that God cannot proceed with his desire to restore Job until Job forgives his friends for their earlier unkindnesses and prays for their reacceptance by God.

Some have suggested that the doubling of Job's flocks indicates an admission of guilt on God's part for taking away Job's possessions (Exod 22:4 [3 HB]). But this would point to a connection with Israelite law and customs that is missing in the rest of the book. More likely, Job never regarded his increased wealth as a divine repayment for possessions unjustly taken from him. He would have been happy with any amount of restoration of his health, family, or possessions. For him the explanation was very simple, although the rationale was clouded in mystery. The Lord gives and the Lord takes away, for reasons known only to him (1:21). The restoration of Job's life illustrates God's loving grace and freedom (→ Behind the Text above) to bless one of his saints with whom he is well pleased.

In the prologue Job's outstanding righteousness, ideal family, and great wealth (1:1-3) had earned him the reputation as "the greatest man among all the people of the East" (v 3). But he had lost that reputation when the calamities struck. The doubling of his wealth and life span and the eventual birth of ten new children are now outward signs that Job's reputation has returned to the earlier level of greatness and even exceeded it. He is truly a saint again—the greatest of his generation.

In the following verses the author mentions various ways that God showed his favor on Job. Strangely he does not mention the healing of Job's skin disease. But likely this is included in the phrase **his fortunes**, as well as the note about the length of his life (v 16). Every aspect of Job's life is now made whole and raised to the highest level of preeminence.

■ **11** With this verse, the author introduces new people into the story—Job's **brothers, sisters**, and **everyone who had known him before**. Their arrival at Job's house is for the purpose of "sympathizing" (*nwd*) with him and "comforting" (*nḥm*) him. These same verbs were used in the prologue to describe the reason for the visit by the three friends (2:11). But whereas the friends presented only arguments and verbal attacks that caused Job extreme anguish, Job's family and neighbors brought gifts (**a piece of silver and a gold ring**) and fellowship (they stayed for a meal). **A piece of silver** is the NIV translation for *qĕśîṭâ*—a standard measure of weight used in buying and selling (Gen 33:19; Josh 24:32). Its value is unknown.

Job or members of his family could have worn the gold rings, or he may have used them to purchase new animals to establish his flocks again.

The NRSV translates *rāʿâ* as "evil" rather than **trouble**, but **trouble** (meaning "misfortune in general") is a much better rendering in this context (→ 2:11). This verse clearly attributes *all* of Job's troubles to the LORD (*Yahweh*), not the Examiner. This is probably the author's statement, although Job's family and friends could have believed the same, even without knowledge of the conversation between God and the Examiner in the prologue. Many people in the ancient world believed that God caused all situations in life.

This verse raises a great deal of curiosity about where Job's family and neighbors have been all this time. This is the first and only mention of his sizable extended family. Their fellowship and kindness were exactly what Job needed from the very beginning, but he had to wait until his recovery before receiving any sympathy from anyone. Why? Probably the author regarded these characters as minor and only added them in the epilogue to show that Job's relationships with other people returned to normal very quickly.

On a practical note, their earlier avoidance of Job may have indicated their great fear of Job's disease and their uncertainty about its contagiousness (→ "Disease in the Ancient World" sidebar at 2:7-8). Or they could have bought into the friends' argument that Job had committed a grievous sin and should be kept at a distance until such time as he was reconciled with God.

■ **12-13** The blessings Job now receives from God are very substantial. The four groups of animals that were a part of his original herds (**sheep, camels, oxen, donkeys** [42:12]) are doubled in size. With twice the ideal wealth, Job's status is even greater than before the calamities (1:3).

42:12-15

The number of Job's children is also restored (**seven sons and three daughters** [42:13]). This raises the question of whether his first wife (2:9) was still capable of bearing another ten children. One could reasonably assume that Job may have taken a second wife (as did Abraham when starting a second family later in life [Gen 25:1-4]). But the matter is one of curiosity only and not significant to the telling of the story.

The Hebrew for **seven** (*šibʿānâ*) is a unique form that appears only here in the OT. The Aramaic Targums regarded the form as having a dual ending meaning "fourteen." Some scholars have followed suit, suggesting that the doubling of Job's sons harmonizes better with the doubling of his animals (Gordis 1978, 498). But **seven** is the more likely and preferred reading.

■ **14-15** The naming of Job's daughters is unusual in the OT, and especially so when his wife and sons are not even named. There seems to be no reason for this other than to highlight their prominence and bring further distinction to their father. Clines suggests that Job is the only father in the OT to name his children (2011, 1238). But other examples do exist (e.g., Gen 4:26; 5:3, 29; 16:15; 21:3; 35:18).

The names of the three daughters are: **Jemimah** (lit. "turtle-dove"), **Keziah** (lit. "cassia tree," one of the sources of cinnamon, used in the production of perfume), and **Keren-Happuch** (lit. "horn of antimony," a black powder used for women's eye makeup). Interestingly, the first name is derived from Arabic while the latter two are Hebrew (Clines 2011, 1229, 1238). It is unclear if there is any meaning in this. These distinguished daughters were not only notable for being related to super wealthy, supersaint Job; they were also **beautiful** in their own right (v 15). The author uses a storytelling idiom, describing them as the most beautiful **in all the land.**

Job was so delighted with his daughters that he **granted them an inheritance along with their brothers**. Job's provision for their security is probably an indication of his exorbitant wealth and generosity. Normally inheritances were only passed on to the sons, unless no son was alive (Num 27:8), as the daughters would become part of other families through marriage. Schifferdecker notes how Job's delight in his daughters (individuals that he helped to create) imitates God's own delight in the animal kingdom that he created (38:39—39:30; 40:15—41:34 [40:14—41:26 HB]) (2008, 110).

■ **16** The final blessing Job receives from God is a long life (140 years). Righteous living does not automatically guarantee long life, but God graciously bestowed this honor on Job. It is unclear from the MT whether the author intended this as 140 additional years or a total of 140 years. Either interpretation is possible, but this writer leans toward the latter.

The point the author is trying to make is that God gave Job twice the ideal number of years that a well-blessed person normally lived—70 years (Ps 90:10). In actuality, the average life span in the ancient world was less than 35 years due to the high rate of infant mortality. But the setting for the book of Job is the patriarchal period when the principal male characters in the story lived lengthy lives (→ Introduction: Date). Thus, Job's longevity is not unusual for that time period. Eliphaz has already noted that a long, vigorous life is one of the rewards for a righteous person (5:26). And this is supported by other passages (Ps 91:16; Prov 3:2; 4:10; 9:11).

The LXX is much different. It adds 170 extra years to Job's life on top of his age at the time of his suffering (70) for a total of 240 years (Gordis 1978, 499). It is unknown how the LXX arrived at these figures or whether there is any symbolism attached to them. Likewise the pseudepigraphic *Testament of Job* places Job's age at the time of his suffering at 85 plus an additional 170 years for a total of 255 years. None of these figures support the phrase **to the fourth generation** (meaning "his great-grandchildren"). This phrase is more likely to be true if he lived a total of 140 years.

■ **17** The book of Job ends with a short epitaph: **And so Job died, an old man and full of years** (lit. "full/satiated of days"). The meaning is that he lived a blessed, joyful life in the ensuing years and died peacefully at a ripe old age. He was gratified with the way his life had worked out. Similar epitaphs are given to some of the great OT characters: Abraham (Gen 25:8), Isaac (Gen 35:29), David (1 Chr 29:28), and the priest Jehoiada (2 Chr 24:15).

Nothing is said about the suffering Job experienced in the book, or of any later suffering he may have encountered before his death. But epitaphs never go into great detail. They are designed to be short so as to fit on a tombstone. The other words on a tombstone are the dates of birth and death with a dash in between (e.g., AD 1915-2000). It has been said that the dash is very short but it stands for a myriad of activities in the life of the deceased. The phrase **full of years** is like the dash on Job's tombstone. It does not even begin to summarize all the events in the life of this great supersaint. The book of Job is our window into some of the events in Job's dash.

In a later century, the LXX (as well as the *Testament of Job*) incorporated additional material into the ending of the book. It included an originally different personal name for Job ("Jobab"), the name of his homeland ("Ausitis," on the northern border of Arabia), the name of one son ("Ennon"), and a family tree that names his father ("Zare"), mother ("Bosorra"), and ancestors Abraham and Esau. The account also states that he was the king of Edom and that his three friends were kings as well (Clines 2011, 1240). The *Testament of Job* also adds extensive material on the nature of the inheritances received by Job's three daughters (Balentine 2006, 716). The origin of this material is unknown, and it is generally considered to be of the nature of midrash or folklore.

EXCURSUS 2: INTERPRETING THE BOOK OF JOB

A. Major Theological Themes

As mentioned in the Introduction, there are several theological themes that are woven into the fabric of the book. The following is a brief summary of some of the more obvious.

1. The Nature of God

- God is the Creator and Sustainer of the universe. His wisdom and power to accomplish this are beyond human comprehension, for he operates on a far superior level than humankind.
- God embedded his order in both the physical world and the world of morality. To humanity, the world may sometimes look chaotic, haphazard, or unjust, but God knows what he is doing. He has a plan.
- God is a just Judge in his overall governance of the world. However, for reasons known only to him, he does sometimes allow the suffering of the innocent and the prosperity of the wicked (*injustice*, as humanity sees it) to happen. Whether God also sees it as injustice is unknown.
- God has the freedom to act as he wishes. He can bless or he can punish or he can choose to remain inactive. No one can put God in a box or tell him what to do. This creates mysteries and paradoxes about some aspects of the universe, especially in the moral realm.

2. The Nature of the Cosmos

- The universe was created and ordered by God, and he continues to sustain it.
- God likes the universe he has created, including the hippopotamus and the crocodile. These animals may be physically repulsive to human beings and uncontrollable, but God describes their beauty with elegant poetry. "This is my world," he says. "If you don't like these animals, tough! Get over it!"
- The universe finds its meaning in God and cannot be explained apart from him. To understand it, humankind must view it theocentrically rather than from a human-centered perspective.
- Human beings are an important part of creation with whom God desires fellowship.
- God designed the world as a moral world that requires human beings to make choices between right and wrong. These choices carry consequences both for the individual and others.
- Bad things do happen in this world. Some are the result of natural forces: two colliding air masses or two colliding plates in the earth's crust. Others result from bad moral choices: such as stealing someone's oxen and donkeys. And still others happen for unknown reasons. God knows about these bad things, allows them to happen, and sometimes even causes them.

3. The Nature of Suffering

- All people will suffer at some point in life, some more than others. Trouble is a part of human existence, just "as sparks fly upward" (Job 5:7).
- Sin is one of the causes of suffering, but not the only one.
- Like a good parent, God sometimes disciplines people to correct their bad choices or to encourage their spiritual health.
- As indicated in the prologue, God sometimes causes/allows innocent suffering as a test of a person's faith.
- Other people's actions—whether on purpose, through ignorance, or through carelessness—sometimes cause suffering. Certainly the Sabeans and Chaldeans as well as Job's friends caused him much trouble and anguish.
- God's Examiner may cause some human suffering, but this character is always under God's control, and thus, God is ultimately responsible. Neither Job nor the other characters in the book ever consider the Examiner as the reason for Job's suffering.
- Natural disasters such as lightning, windstorms, earthquakes, and floods (what insurance companies call *acts of God*) sometimes cause great suffering. One could also place in this category microscopic viruses, bacteria, and cancer-causing agents such as defective genes, causes of suffering and death that were unknown until the advent of modern science.

- In addition to the reasons outlined in the book of Job, there are other types of suffering in Scripture: the suffering caused by the devil and his demons (1 Pet 5:8-9), vicarious suffering for another person out of love (John 15:13), the suffering of a martyr as a testimony of one's faith (Acts 7:54-60), and the voluntary, redemptive suffering of Christ on the cross (John 3:16; 10:11, 17-18).

This brief list of the causes of suffering indicates that suffering occurs for a variety of reasons, many of them beyond our control and totally unrelated to divine judgment/punishment for sin. The reason the author conceals the real cause from Job is because this is so true to life. We can identify with Job's struggles because much of our suffering is also without an explanation as to its cause.

B. Interpreting the Book of Job

One of the major problems in interpreting the book of Job is that the author gives no moral to the story, but this is typical of Hebrew authors. They tell their stories through the speeches of the characters with a minor amount of narration to introduce the story and keep the action moving. They rarely insert comments about how to interpret their story. Thus, the interpretation of Hebrew stories depends heavily on judgments made by the interpreter (Balentine 2006, 628). Such is the case with the book of Job. Because the author refrained from moralizing, there are an amazing number of interpretations of this book in the scholarly world.

This writer's interpretation is that there are two universal questions that the author seeks to answer, and these answers provide the means for critiquing the traditional wisdom theology. This is the main purpose of the book.

1. Why Do People Serve God?

The first question is: "Why do people serve God?" The Examiner asked this question at the very beginning of the book (1:9), implying that people only serve God if they have some kind of motivation to do so, such as the promise of reward or the threat of punishment. In other words, self-interest lies at the heart of true religion. Specifically, the Examiner accused God of passing out rewards to entice people to serve him. Job's ideal family, wealth, and reputation were all the result of God's blessings. Anyone who received similar blessings from God would inevitably serve him.

The author's answer is that people can serve God without benefit of rewards. They do not have to be bribed into conversion and faithful devotion. They can choose to serve God *for nothing*, as Job did. Fellowship with God and divine love are much more powerful motivators than either rewards or punishments.

2. How Can Faith Be Maintained When Life Goes Topsy-Turvy?

The second question derives from Job's intense struggle to maintain his former faith in the midst of pain, loss, and unanswered questions: "Is it possible to maintain one's faith in God when life goes topsy-turvy?" Like Jacob (Gen 32:22-32), Job had to wrestle to find an answer to this question (Patrick 1977, 98). His wife, his three friends, and Elihu all suggested to him various courses of action to help him deal with his losses. But none could set his mind and heart at ease because none were aware of the real cause, which was only discussed by God and the Examiner. The only way to resolve Job's questions and doubts was through a personal encounter with God. And this was exactly what Job pleaded for again and again throughout the book. If he could just talk with God and find out the reason for his suffering, then he could trust in God again.

Graciously, God gave Job a personal interview, but it did not work out like he expected. God never revealed the reason for Job's suffering or sympathized with his pain. In fact, God acted as if Job's suffering was not at all important to him. Instead, God talked about the founding and operation of the natural world and his delight with hippopotami and crocodiles. And he emphasized that Job would never understand God's method of justice because God's ways are too great for humans to comprehend. But astoundingly, this conversation between Job and God left Job satisfied. His faith and trust in God were reenergized.

Why was Job satisfied? One reason was because God had met him as he requested. Now Job knew that God really did care enough about him to leave heaven and engage him—a sickly, distraught human being—in conversation at the Uz city dump. Another reason was because Job's understanding of God had changed. God had lifted Job's attention away from his own problems to God's wonders throughout the universe. In doing so, he had enabled Job to see that God can be trusted with running the universe because his wisdom and power are so great. With this new insight, Job admitted his ignorance, apologized for his remarks, and submitted his life to God.

Job never received an answer as to the cause of his suffering, but he learned a very important lesson. Fellowship with God is vastly more important than having all one's questions answered. As McKeating notes, now Job "can do something much more important than explain his sorrows. He can live with them" (1971, 246). So the answer to the author's question is: "Yes, a person can maintain faith in God when life goes topsy-turvy. Job did it with God's help, and so can we."

What does this insight mean for our understanding of faith? It means that faith, to be real and to continue even through suffering, must be grounded in a personal experience with God. Faith is not learned in school or in a book or in a rational explanation about how the mind reaches out in search of a Higher Being. It is worked out in the practical, everyday experiences of life, including suffering.

And this truth is found throughout the entire OT. Israel believed in God, not because she learned about him in school or read about him in a book or rationally proved his existence. The Israelites believed because God had called them through Abraham, had delivered them out of Egypt, had rescued them at the Red Sea, had provided for them in the wilderness for forty years, and had bound them to himself through covenant at Mount Sinai, etc., etc. This was a God who would not go away. They had encountered him again and again. There was no way they could deny that he existed or that he cared for them.

In similar fashion, each of us has experienced multiple examples of God's love and compassion. He has proven that he is *the hound of heaven* who will not go away. Those experiences are the foundation upon which we, too, can and must build our faith. In a Christian context, that foundation is the acceptance of what God *has already done* for us on the cross and *continues to do* for us each day. But faith in this God will not survive the storms and mysteries and paradoxes of life without being grounded in a personal encounter with him. God graciously blessed Job with such an encounter, and he deeply desires to meet with each of us as well.

3. The Wisdom Theology Is Inadequate to Explain All of Life's Troubles

The answers that the author gives to the two questions above point to an additional purpose to the book that is more theological and less practical. God's praise of Job and criticism of the three friends (42:7-9) proves the shortcomings of the wisdom theology from the author's viewpoint. Even though this theology had been passed down over many centuries (8:8-10) and proven true in countless lives, it was inadequate to explain *all* the examples of suffering in life. The happy little sayings in Proverbs do not always work out as stated.

The reason is because the world is not structured according to rigid cause-and-effect principles where the causes are always identifiable. We live in a world of God's creation that contains mystery, paradox, and exceptions to the rule (→ C. The Validity of Retributive Justice, below). God's overall governance of the world is plainly evident, and his rules for right living are well-known, but there is a hidden side to God that humanity cannot penetrate. His freedom and his grace produce unexpected surprises that do not fit the well-worn answers of the three friends.

Job's experiences could not be explained by the wisdom theology. Thus, he was right to question its application to him. Job finally learned that the proper response to an awesome God in this kind of a world is humble living rather than complaint or arrogant debate.

4. The Book of Job Has Some Major Deficiencies

In one major area the book is deficient. It forces people to think about the causes of suffering, as if understanding the cause would solve Job's problems. The prologue provides an easy answer, although Job was never aware of it. His suffering was due to a test of his faith designed by the Examiner and approved by God. However, even though people would dearly like an explanation of the cause of their suffering (primarily so they can avoid it happening again or know who to blame), a much more helpful topic would be *the proper reaction* to suffering. How can one handle intense suffering when it happens? How should one behave? How can one remain oneself in the midst of suffering (Clines 1999, 19)? And what resources are available to help survive suffering? The book of Job has little to offer, other than to seek God (5:8). But Job was already doing that.

Much more helpful are passages in both Testaments that offer substantial resources, such as God's continual presence and love (Josh 1:9; John 14:16-21), the support of the body of Christ (John 15:12, 17; Gal 6:2), and the encouragement that there is a limit to what God will allow (1 Cor 10:13). Job could have used someone to point him to these resources.

One could also add that the book of Job is deficient in its failure to provide a satisfactory understanding of judgment, which may be imposed after death (→ "Sheol" sidebar at 3:17-19). This would certainly cast a different light on the issue of justice in this life. But the author cannot be faulted for omitting concepts that developed later. He was a product of his time. However, a word of caution is needed here. The belief in a meaningful life after death with a final judgment and eternal rewards makes us feel better about the eventual judgment of bad people who are not punished before death, but it does not really solve the problem of suffering in this life. It only serves to reinforce Job's complaint that sometimes life *in this world* is unjust (Patrick 1977, 86).

5. God Is the Hero of the Book

At the end of the book Job returns to the life of a supersaint. His questions have not been answered, but he is satisfied with his new life and he lives happily ever after. The other characters also fade away. But one person still remains in the foreground. God Almighty still retains his awesome wisdom and power, going about his daily task of governing his universe in ways that are pleasing to him. The story of Job has taken some strange twists and turns, but the focus all along has been on God. His relationship with the world is still mysterious, but we now know for certain that he is the measure of all things both in heaven and on earth.

C. The Validity of Retributive Justice

One of Job's complaints was that the wicked sometimes do well while the righteous sometimes suffer. If true, and a brief glance at the history of humanity shows that it is true, then many biblical passages are called into question. A major principle in the book of Proverbs, as well as in Jesus' and Paul's teachings, is that people reap what they sow. Job's three friends and Elihu certainly believed this, and so did Job, although after his encounter with God he recognized that God's power and wisdom sometimes trump the principle of retribution.

So what are we to believe about retribution? One way of understanding it is by a comparison with the interpretation of biblical proverbs. Generally speaking, proverbs are true 99 percent of the time. If they were not, they would never have been preserved and collected into Scripture. The proverbs provide general principles about God's order in the world. They are easily memorized and extremely helpful to parents in teaching the next generation about the proper way to live from God's viewpoint.

However, proverbs are very short and so do not have the space to comment on the circumstances that produce exceptions to the rule. A good example is the well-known proverb: "Pride goes before destruction, a haughty spirit before a fall" (Prov 16:18). Generally speaking, this proverb is true. A self-centered, haughty attitude toward others does lead to one's corruption and downfall. However, everyone knows haughty people who have never experienced destruction, as well as people who have experienced destruction but have never been haughty.

As people move from childhood into adulthood and a more mature understanding of life, they begin to recognize these kinds of exceptions and sometimes begin to question the validity of the original proverb. But there is nothing wrong with the proverb. It still describes the general moral order in God's universe. However, it needs to be balanced with the reality that sometimes there are exceptions that arise due to other factors. And these exceptions create mystery and paradox that cannot be resolved by human investigation, no matter how serious the effort (→ "Cause-and-Effect Reasoning" sidebar at 4:10-11).

This is the problem Job was wrestling with. He knew that people reap what they sow. The principle of retribution was valid, for he had seen its effects in other people's lives again and again. But he also knew that it definitely did not apply to him. He was an exception, for he was totally righteous and yet he suffered. And this created tremendous doubt in his mind about God's justice.

God never resolved this paradox for Job (neither does the author for us). Instead, God emphasized Job's ignorance of the natural world. There is *order and harmony* throughout nature even though Job did not comprehend it. By analogy, there is also *order and meaning* throughout the moral world even though Job was not always aware of it (Gordis 1965, 133). Therefore, Job was incompetent to question God's justice or God's character. The implication is that all of us are as ignorant of God's ways as Job was. Because God designed his universe this way, our best course of action is the same as Job's—submission to God, obedience to his will, trust in his wisdom, and acceptance of life's mysteries that come our way.

www.ingramcontent.com/pod-product-compliance
Lightning Source LLC
Chambersburg PA
CBHW070232240426
43673CB00044B/1760